www.wadsworth.com

www.wadsworth.com is the World Wide Web site for Wadsworth and is your direct source to dozens of online resources.

At *www.wadsworth.com* you can find out about supplements, demonstration software, and student resources. You can also send email to many of our authors and preview new publications and exciting new technologies.

www.wadsworth.com

Changing the way the world learns®

Essentials of

PHYSICAL ANTHROPOLOGY

Fifth Edition

ROBERT JURMAIN
San Jose State University

LYNN KILGORE
Colorado State University

WENDA TREVATHAN
New Mexico State University

HARRY NELSON

THOMSON

WADSWORTH

Australia • Canada • Mexico • Singapore • Spain
United Kingdom • United States

THOMSON

WADSWORTH

Anthropology Editor **Lin Marshall**	*Text Designer* **Ox and Company**
Assistant Editor **Analie Barnett**	*Art Editor* **Hespenheide Design**
Editorial Assistant **Amanda Santana**	*Photo Researcher* **Hespenheide Design**
Technology Project Manager **Dee Dee Zobian**	*Copy Editor* **Janet Greenblatt**
Marketing Manager **Diane Wenckebach**	*Illustrator* **Alexander Productions, DLF Group, Hespenheide Design,**
Marketing Assistant **Michael Silverstein**	**Randy Miyake, Paragon 3, Sue Sellars, Cyndie Wooley**
Advertising Project Manager **Linda Yip**	*Cover Designer* **Hespenheide Design**
Project Manager, Editorial Production **Paul Wells**	*Cover Image* **Two red colobus monkeys, © Patricio Robles Gil**
Print/Media Buyer **Karen Hunt**	*Cover Printer* **The Lehigh Press, Inc.**
Permissions Editor **Joohee Lee**	*Compositor* **Hespenheide Design**
Production Service **Hespenheide Design**	*Printer* **Quebecor World/Taunton**

Printed in the United States of America
2 3 4 5 6 7 07 06 05 04 03

For more information about our products, contact us at:
Thomson Learning Academic Resource Center
1-800-423-0563
For permission to use material from this text, contact us by:
Phone: 1-800-730-2214   **Fax:** 1-800-730-2215
Web: http://www.thomsonrights.com

Library of Congress Control Number: **2003105186**

Student Edition: ISBN 0-534-61434-5
Instructor's Edition: ISBN 0-534-61436-1

Wadsworth/Thomson Learning
10 Davis Drive
Belmont, CA 94002-3098
USA

Asia
Thomson Learning
5 Shenton Way #01-01
UIC Building
Singapore 068808

Australia/New Zealand
Thomson Learning
102 Dodds Street
Southbank, Victoria 3006
Australia

Canada
Nelson
1120 Birchmount Road
Toronto, Ontario M1K 5G4
Canada

Europe/Middle East/Africa
Thomson Learning
High Holborn House
50/51 Bedford Row
London WC1R 4LR
United Kingdom

Latin America
Thomson Learning
Seneca, 53
Colonia Polanco
11560 Mexico D.F.
Mexico

Spain/Portugal
Paraninfo
Calle/Magallanes, 25
28015 Madrid, Spain

Brief Contents

Contents

Lynn Kilgore

Courtesy, Dept. of Library Services, American Museum of Natural History

Courtesy, Arlene Kruse/Bonnie Pedersen

Robert Jurmain

Robert Jurmain

CHAPTER 9

HOMO ERECTUS AND CONTEMPORARIES | 217

Courtesy, Denis Etler

Harry Nelson

Courtesy, David Frayer

Lynn Kilgore

Russ Mittermeier, Conservation International

CHAPTER 14

LESSONS FROM THE PAST, LESSONS FOR THE FUTURE | 357

Preface

Much has happened in the past three years since publication of the last edition of *Essentials of Physical Anthropology*. Two areas of research fundamental to human evolution have seen the greatest change: molecular biological investigations of DNA and fossil studies of early human ancestors (or close relatives).

Many of you have heard of the international research aimed at sequencing human DNA (called the "Human Genome Project") and of the progress in this field that has produced revolutionary changes throughout the biological sciences. Indeed, just as our last edition was published in the summer of 2000, widespread press coverage announced the completion of the first full map of the human DNA. Remarkably, this achievement came in less than half the time initially estimated when the program began in the early 1990s. Such is the nature of technological progress.

A more complete and more accurate depiction of DNA as the basic molecule underlying all life on earth is providing a basis for new techniques and new perspectives in understanding life, the relationships of organisms, and the genetic basis of several diseases. All of these topics are discussed in this text.

Equally spectacular in the last three years has been the second area of research: new finds of humanlike (what we call "hominid") fossils have been announced from sites in East, Central, and South Africa, the Republic of Georgia, and Portugal. The discoveries from Africa have been the most numerous and the most surprising. When the last edition of this text was published, we could reasonably and confidently estimate the age of the oldest hominid at around 4.4 million years ago. In 2002, the discovery of a remarkably well-preserved fossil skull from Chad (Central Africa) has likely pushed this date back to 7 million years (thus extending the time range of the human family by almost 60%!). And, that is not all. In 2000 and 2001 other very old fossil hominids were unearthed in East Africa (from Ethiopia and Kenya). Each of these discoveries has been given a new scientific designation—greatly expanding the number of hominid forms and, at the same time, greatly increasing the complexity of our interpretations. This text has been substantially revised to deal with both the opportunities and the challenges presented by these extraordinary new discoveries.

Organization of the Fifth Edition

As you read through this textbook, you will discover that physical anthropology in *all* its applications and perspectives deals with the understanding of human evolution. As such, it is firmly placed within the biological sciences. We thus first introduce the basic approaches relating to understanding evolutionary theory, cells, cell division, mechanisms of heredity, and, of course, DNA. We next provide an overview of the primates, the group of organisms to which humans belong (also including prosimians, monkeys, and apes). An understanding of our closest relatives informs us directly about human biology.

The next section of the text reviews the history of hominid evolutionary development, a field which, as noted above, has been dramatically impacted by a host of new discoveries.

Lastly, we take up the ongoing evolution of the human species. Here we focus on understanding human variation and adaptation as reflected in contemporary populations of our species.

What's New in the Fifth Edition?

As mentioned, we have considerably altered and updated this textbook from its last edition. We have expanded our coverage of cloning (Chapter 3), a topic which in the last few years has become highly controversial. The new and increasingly precise evidence relating to human DNA sequencing has had an impact on a variety of topics in this text. Since these developments are so crucial to all of human biology, we have discussed aspects of DNA technology and new genetically based methods for the treatment of disease (Chapter 3), genetic relationships among primates (Chapter 5), sequencing of ancient DNA found in Neandertal fossil remains (Chapter 10), the use of contemporary genetic patterning to reconstruct the origins of modern humans (Chapter 11), and advances in identifying and measuring genetic variation in human populations as well as the utility of this evidence for understanding larger patterns of human diversity (Chapter 12).

The chapters on nonhuman primates (Chapters 5 and 6) have been refocused to emphasize and clarify the contemporary approach of behavioral ecology. Moreover, we continue with our emphasis on primate conservation and provide new and disturbing data relating to a dramatic increase in the bush meat trade (Chapter 5).

Chapter 7, which concentrates on macroevolution, has been extensively reorganized and includes a new section on evolutionary interpretations (focusing on cladistics). The chapters concerning hominid evolution (Chapters 8–11) have been extensively updated. New materials are included throughout these four chapters, including discoveries from Central Africa (*Sahelanthropus*), East Africa (*Orrorin, Ardipithecus, Australopithecus*) as well as from South Africa, Western Asia, and Europe. All these discoveries are potentially highly significant, in many cases requiring serious reevaluation of the course of human evolution. Thus, not only are the "nuts and bolts" presented (what? where? how old?), but the significance of each discovery is also discussed—in so far as current analysis and publication permit.

In-Chapter Learning Aids

- **Chapter outlines** at the beginning of each chapter list all major topics covered.
- A **running glossary** in the margins provides definitions of terms immediately adjacent to the text when the term is first introduced. A **full glossary** is provided in the back of the book.

- **Figures,** most in full color, including numerous photographs, line drawings, and maps, are carefully selected to clarify text materials and are placed to directly support discussion in the text.
- **Photo Essays** introduce key topics (e.g., Primate Studies: Free Ranging and Captive Research) to stimulate student interests in applied work currently being done by physical anthropologists.
- A **Most Significant Finds** section has been added to chapter summaries in fossil chapters to highlight the most important discoveries for understanding human evolution.
- **Questions for Review** at the end of each chapter reinforce key points and encourage students to think critically about what they have read.
- **Suggested Further Readings,** also found at the end of each chapter, are carefully selected to direct interested students toward accessible and authoritative sources for further reading.
- **Multimedia Resources** at the end of each chapter guide students to the companion Web site where they will find a wide range of enrichment materials including updated Internet exercises and InfoTrac® College Edition exercises.
- **Full bibliographic citations** throughout the entire book provide sources from which the materials are drawn. This type of documentation guides students to published source materials and illustrates for students the proper use of referencing; all cited sources are listed in the comprehensive bibliography at the back of the book.
- Icons are strategically placed throughout the text to integrate text materials with those found in the **Virtual Laboratories for Physical Anthropology CD-ROM,** Third Edition, prepared by John Kappelman of the University of Texas at Austin. The icons are found in the margins adjacent to related materials in the text:

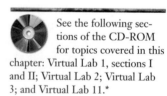 See the following sections of the CD-ROM for topics covered in this chapter: Virtual Lab 1, sections I and II; Virtual Lab 2; Virtual Lab 3; and Virtual Lab 11.*

Acknowledgments

The publication of a textbook is a task requiring the contributions of many skilled people—all of whom together have made this edition possible. For this text we are especially grateful to the reviewers who so carefully commented on the manuscript and made such helpful suggestions: Diane Everett Barbolla, San Diego Mesa College; Claire Marie Cesareo-Silva, Saddleback College; Mary E. Glenn, Humboldt State University; Sharon Gursky, Texas A&M University; Sunil K. Khanna, Oregon State University; and Mark G. Taylor, Northern Arizona University.

We also wish to thank at Wadsworth Publishing: Lin Marshall, Anthropology Editor; Analie Barnett, Assistant Editor; Amanda Santana, Editorial Assistant; Dee Dee Zobian, Technology Project Manager; Diane Wenckebach, Executive Marketing Manager; Paul Wells, Project Editor; Eve Howard, Editor-in-Chief; and Susan Badger, President and CEO. Moreover, for their unflagging expertise and patience we are grateful to our copy editor, Janet Greenblatt; our production coordinator, Gary Hespenheide; and his skilled staff at Hespenheide Design: Patti Zeman, production coordinator; and Bridget Neumayr, proofreader/editor.

To the many friends and colleagues who have generously provided photographs we are greatly appreciative: Art Aufderheide, C. K. Brain, Günter Bräuer, Desmond Clark, Raymond Dart, Jean deRousseau, Denis Etler, Diane France, David Frayer, Kathleen Galvin, David Haring, Ellen Ingmanson, Fred Jacobs, Peter Jones, Arlene Kruse, Richard Leakey, Carol Lofton, Margaret Maples, Russ Mittermeier, Lorna Moore, John Oates, Bonnie Pedersen, Lorna Pierce, David Pilbeam, William Pratt, Judith Regensteiner, Sastrohamijoyo Sartono, Eugenie Scott, Rose Sevick, Elwyn Simons, Meredith Small, Fred Smith, Judy Suchey, Li Tianyuan, Philip Tobias, Alan Walker, Milford Wolpoff, and Xinzhi Wu. We also want to express our thanks to David M. Fagerstrom, Head of the Science Library, University of Colorado, Boulder, for his assistance in researching obscure publications.

Robert Jurmain
Lynn Kilgore
Wenda Trevathan

Supplements

Supplements for Instructors

Instructor's Manual with Test Bank. This comprehensive manual offers chapter outlines, learning objectives, key terms and concepts, lecture suggestions and enrichment topics as well as 40–60 test questions per chapter. Concise user guides for InfoTrac College Edition and WebTutor are included as appendices.

ExamView® **Computerized Testing** Create, deliver, and customize tests and study guides (both print and online) in minutes with this easy-to-use assessment and tutorial system. *ExamView* offers both a Quick Test Wizard and an Online Test Wizard that guide you step-by-step through the process of creating tests, while the unique "WYSIWYG" capability allows you to see the test you are creating on the screen exactly as it will print or display online. You can build tests of up to 250 questions using up to 12 question types. Using *ExamView's* complete word processing capabilities, you can enter an unlimited number of new questions or edit existing questions.

Primate Evolution Module
This 48-page free-standing module is actually a complete text chapter featuring the same quality of pedagogy and illustrations that are contained in this book—offering you an excellent opportunity to incorporate the basics of primate evolution into your course. Jurmain examines primate evolution over the last 60 million years, helping students understand the ecological adaptations and evolutionary relationships of fossil forms to each other and to contemporary primates. Also available to view in full color online.

Anthropology Module
This 48-page free-standing module is actually a complete text chapter featuring the same quality of pedagogy and illustrations that are contained in the text—offering you an excellent opportunity to incorporate the basics of forensic anthropology into your course. The author introduces students to the essentials of forensic anthropology as it is practiced in the United States and Canada, exploring the field's myths and realities, what it is, how it is applied, and careers available within the field. Edited by Robert Jurmain, the module is consistent with chapters in the physical anthropology text. Also available to view in full color online.

Classroom Presentation Tools for Instructors

Wadsworth's Physical Anthropology Transparency Acetates 2004 This set of four-color acetates features images from Wadsworth's 2004 physical anthropology texts to help prepare lecture presentations.

Multimedia Manager for Anthropology: A Microsoft PowerPoint® **Link Tool** This *2004 CD-ROM* contains digital media and PowerPoint presentations for all of Wadsworth's 2004 introductory Anthropology texts, placing images, lectures, and video clips at instructors' fingertips. Start with our pre-assembled PowerPoint Presentations which include chapter outlines and key terms. Then easily add video and images from Wadsworth's Anthropology texts all included on the CD-ROM. Instructors can also add their own lecture notes and images to create a custom-made lecture presentation. The new Wadsworth Multimedia Manager also includes an exciting Earthwatch Institute Research Feature!

Wadsworth Anthropology Video Library Qualified adopters may select full-length videos from an extensive library of offerings drawn from excellent educational video sources such as *Films for the Humanities and Sciences*.

***CNN Today Physical Anthropology* Video Series, Volumes I–V** The *CNN Today Physical Anthropology* Video Series is an exclusive series jointly created by Wadsworth and CNN for the physical anthropology course. Each video in the series consists of approximately 45 minutes of footage originally broadcast on CNN within the last several years. The videos are broken into short two- to seven-minute segments, which are perfect for classroom use as lecture launchers, or to illustrate key anthropological concepts. An annotated table of contents accompanies each video with descriptions of the segments and suggestions for their possible use within the course.

Supplements for Students

Study Guide This useful guide enables students to fully comprehend and appreciate what the text has to offer. Each chapter of the study guide features learning objectives, chapter outlines, key terms, concept applications, and practice tests consisting of 30–40 multiple choice questions and 5–10 true/false questions with answers and page references, in addition to several short answer and essay questions.

***Virtual Laboratories for Physical Anthropology* CD-ROM, Third Edition** By John Kappelman, University of Texas at Austin. The new edition of this interactive CD-ROM provides students with a hands-on computer component for doing lab assignments at school or at home. It encourages students to participate actively in their physical anthropology lab or course through the taking of measurements and the plotting of data, as well as giving them a format for testing their knowledge of important concepts. Contains full color images, video clips, 3-D animations, sound, and more. New to this edition is a special quizzing section where students can take online tutorial quizzes based on the 12 laboratories and have their answers scored and e-mailed to their instructor!

***Lab Manual and Workbook for Physical Anthropology*, Fifth Edition** Written by Diane France, this lab manual emphasizes human osteology, forensic anthropology, anthropometry, primates, human evolution, and genetics, and provides students with hands-on lab assignments to help clarify difficult concepts in physical anthropology. The extensively revised and reorganized Fifth Edition is more problem-oriented as chapters are organized around new opening critical thinking questions and the techniques used to answer the questions. Each chapter concludes with a new "Reexamining the Issues" feature that addresses the answers to the initial chapter questions. Chapter exercises have been increased in number and offer a wider variety of question types and levels of difficulty. The Fifth Edition features increased coverage of evolution and genetics, new skeletal comparisons of quadrupeds, brachiators, and bipeds, a new fossil summary chart, and many more enhancements.

***Researching Anthropology on the Internet*, Second Edition** Written by David Carlson, this useful guide is designed to assist anthropology students in all of their needs when doing research on the Internet. Part One contains general information necessary to get started and answers questions about security, the type of material available on the Internet, the information that is reliable and the sites that are not, the best ways to find research, and the best links to take students where they want to go. Part Two looks at each main discipline in anthropology and refers students to sites where the most enlightening research can be obtained.

Web Resources and Supplements for Instructors and Students

Anthropology Online: Wadsworth's Anthropology Resource Center The Wadsworth Anthropology Resource Center contains a wealth of information and useful tools for both instructors and students. After logging on to the Wadsworth home page at http://anthropology.wadsworth.com, click on Course Materials, Physical Anthropology, and the *Jurmain* book cover. Proceed to the Student Resources section by clicking "For Students." There, students will find many exciting chapter specific resources such as CNN video clips, crossword puzzles, Internet Exercises, InfoTrac Exercises, practice quizzes that calculate results which can then be e-mailed to instructors, and much more. Instructors, too, will find a wealth of materials such as an online Instructor's Manual and PowerPoint Lecture slides.

A Virtual Tour of Applying Anthropology This special section of the Web site serves as an online resource center for the anthropology student. Students will find Applied Anthropologists at Work, Graduate Studies info, Job boards, Internships and Field Work, and an Essay on Careers with video.

InfoTrac College Edition Ignite discussions or augment lectures with the latest developments in physical anthropology. InfoTrac College Edition (available as a free option with newly purchased texts) gives instructors and students 4 months free access to an easy-to-use online database of reliable, full-length articles (not abstracts) from hundreds of top academic journals and popular sources. Among the journals which are available 24-hours a day, seven days a week, are *American Anthropologist, Current Anthropology, Journal of Contemporary Ethnography, Canadian Review of Sociology and Anthropology*, and thousands more. Contact your Wadsworth/Thomson Learning representative for more information.

WebTutor Advantage™ on WebCT and Blackboard For students, **WebTutor Advantage** offers real-time access to a full array of study tools, including chapter summaries, flashcards (with audio), practice quizzes, interactive maps and timelines, online tutorials, and Web links. Professors can use **WebTutor Advantage** to provide virtual office hours, post syllabi, set up threaded discussions, track student progress with quizzing material, and more. **WebTutor Advantage** provides rich communication tools, including a course calendar, asynchronous discussion, "real-time" chat, a whiteboard, and an integrated e-mail system. New to WebTutor Advantage is seamless access to the power of **InfoTrac College Edition.** Also new to **WebTutor Advantage** is access to *NewsEdge*, an online news service that delivers the latest news to your **WebTutor Advantage** site daily.

CHAPTER
1

INTRODUCTION

CONTENTS

See the following sections of the CD-ROM for topics covered in this chapter: Virtual Lab 1, sections I and II, and Virtual Lab 2.

Hominidae The taxonomic family to which humans belong; also includes other, now extinct, bipedal relatives.

Hominids Members of the family Hominidae.

figure 1–1 Early hominid footprints at Laetoli. The tracks to the left were made by one individual, while those to the right appear to have been formed by two individuals, the second stepping in the tracks of the first.

Introduction

One day, perhaps at the beginning of the rainy season some 3.7 million years ago, two or three individuals walked across a grassland savanna in what is now northern Tanzania in East Africa. These individuals were early members of the taxonomic family **Hominidae,** the family that also includes ourselves, modern *Homo sapiens*. Fortunately for us, a record of their passage on that long-forgotten day remains in the form of fossilized footprints, preserved in hardened volcanic deposits.

As chance would have it, shortly after heels and toes were pressed into the dampened soil and volcanic ash of the area, a volcano, some 12 miles distant, erupted. The ensuing ashfall blanketed everything on the ground surface, including the footprints of the **hominids** and those of numerous other species as well. In time, the ash layer hardened into a deposit, which preserved a quite remarkable assortment of tracks and other materials that lay beneath it (fig. 1–1).

These now-famous Laetoli prints indicate that two hominids, one smaller than the other, perhaps walked side by side, leaving parallel sets of tracks. But because the prints of the larger individual are obscured, possibly by those of a third, it is unclear how many actually made that journey so long ago. What is clear from the prints is that they were left by an animal that habitually walked

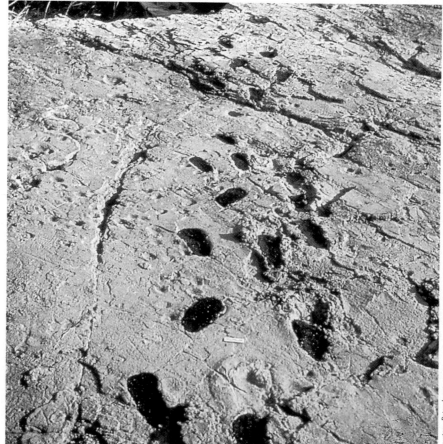

Courtesy, Peter Jones

bipedally (on two feet). It is this critical feature that has led scientists to consider these ancient passersby as hominids.

In addition to the preserved footprints, scientists at Laetoli and elsewhere in Africa have discovered numerous fossilized skeletal remains of what we now call *Australopithecus afarensis*. These fossils and prints have volumes to say about the beings they represent, provided we can learn to interpret them.

What, then, have we actually gleaned from the meager evidence we possess of those creatures who beckon to us from an incomprehensibly distant past? Where did their journey take them that far-gone day, and why were they walking in that particular place? Were they foraging for food within the boundaries of their territory, or were they going to a nearby water source? Did the two (or three) indeed travel together at all, or did they simply follow the same route within a short period of time?

We could ask myriad questions about these individuals, but we will never be able to answer them all. They walked down a path into what became their future, and their immediate journey has long since ended. It remains for us to sort out what little we can know about them and the **species** they represent. In this sense, their greater journey continues.

From the footprints and fossilized fragmentary skeletons, we know that these hominids walked upright. Thus, they were, in a great many respects, anatomically similar to ourselves, but their brains were only about one-third the size of ours. Although they may have used stones and sticks as tools, much as modern chimpanzees do, there is no current evidence to suggest they manufactured stone tools. In short, these early hominids were very much at the mercy of nature's whims. They certainly could not outrun most predators, and their lack of large canine teeth rendered them relatively defenseless.

Chimpanzees often serve as living models for our early ancestors, but in fact, the earliest hominids occupied a different habitat, exploited different resources, and probably had more to fear from predators than do chimpanzees. However much we may be tempted to compare early hominids to living species, we must remind ourselves that there is no living form that adequately represents them. Just like every other living thing, they were unique.

On July 20, 1969, a television audience numbering in the hundreds of millions watched as two human beings stepped out of a spacecraft and onto the surface of the moon. To anyone born after that date, this event is taken more or less for granted, even though it has not often been repeated. But the significance of that first moonwalk cannot be overstated, for it represents humankind's presumed mastery over the natural forces that govern our presence on earth. For the first time ever, people actually walked upon the surface of a celestial body that (as far as we know) has never given birth to life.

As the astronauts gathered geological specimens and frolicked in near weightlessness, they left traces of their fleeting presence in the form of footprints in the lunar dust (fig. 1–2). On the atmosphereless surface of the moon, where no rain falls and no wind blows, the footprints remain undisturbed to this day. They survive as mute testimony to a brief visit by a medium-sized, big-brained creature who presumed to challenge the very forces that had created it.

We humans uncovered the Laetoli footprints, and we question the nature of the animal who made them. Perhaps one day, creatures as yet unimagined will ponder the essence of the being that made the lunar footprints. What do you suppose they will think?

Bipedally On two feet. Walking habitually on two legs is the single most distinctive feature of the family Hominidae.

Species A group of organisms that can interbreed to produce fertile offspring. Members of one species are reproductively isolated from members of all other species (i.e., they cannot mate with them to produce fertile offspring).

figure 1–2 Human footprints left on the lunar surface during the *Apollo* mission.

Primate A member of the order of mammals Primates (pronounced "pry-may´-tees"), which includes prosimians, monkeys, apes, and humans.

Humans, who can barely comprehend a century, can only grasp at the enormity of 3.7 million years. We want to understand those creatures who traveled that day across the savanna. By what route did an insignificant but clever bipedal **primate** such as *Australopithecus afarensis* or perhaps a close relative, give rise to a species that would, in time, walk on the surface of a moon some 230,000 miles from earth? How did it come to be that in the relatively short (geologically speaking) span of fewer than 4 million years, a fairly inconsequential animal evolved into the species that has developed the ability to dominate much of life on the planet?

How did it happen that *Homo sapiens,* a result of the same evolutionary forces that produced all other life on this planet, gained the power to control the flow of rivers and alter the very climate in which we live? As tropical animals, how were we able to leave the tropics and disperse over most of the earth's land surfaces, and how did we adjust to local environmental conditions as we so expanded? How could our species, which numbered fewer than 1 billion individuals until the mid-nineteenth century, come to number more than 6 billion worldwide today and, as we now do, add another billion every 11 years?

These are some of the many questions that physical (biological) anthropologists attempt to answer, and these questions are largely the focus of the study of human **evolution,** variation, and adaptation. These issues, and many more, are the topics covered directly or indirectly in this textbook, because physical anthropology is, in part, human biology seen from an evolutionary perspective.

Evolution A change in the genetic structure of a population. The term is also frequently used to refer to the appearance of a new species.

As biological organisms, humans are subject to the same evolutionary forces as all other species. On hearing the term *evolution,* most people think of the appearance of new species. Certainly, new species formation is one consequence of evolution; however, biologists see evolution as an ongoing process with a precise genetic meaning. Quite simply, evolution is a change in the genetic makeup of a population from one generation to the next. It is the accumulation of such changes, over considerable periods of time, that can result in the appearance of a new species. Thus, evolution can be defined and studied at two different levels. At one level there are genetic alterations *within* populations. Although this type of change may not lead to the development of new species, it frequently results in variation between populations with regard to the frequency of certain traits. Evolution at this level is referred to as *microevolution*. At the other level is genetic change sufficient to result in the appearance of a new species, a process termed *macroevolution* or speciation. Evolution as it occurs at both these levels will be addressed in this text.

See Virtual Lab 2 for several examples of evolution and human adaptation.

But physical anthropologists are not involved solely in the study of physiological systems and biological phenomena. When such topics are placed within the broader context of human evolution, another factor must also be considered: the role of **culture.** Culture is an extremely important concept, not only as it pertains to modern human beings, but also in terms of its critical role in human evolution. It has been said that there are as many definitions of culture as there are people who attempt to define it. Quite simply, and in a very broad sense, culture can be said to be the strategy by which humans adapt to the natural environment. In this sense, culture includes technologies that range from stone tools to computers; subsistence patterns ranging from hunting and gathering to agribusiness on a global scale; housing types, from thatched huts to skyscrapers; and clothing, from animal skins to high-tech synthetic fibers (fig. 1–3). Because religion, values, social organization, language, kinship, marriage rules, gender

Culture All aspects of human adaptation, including technology, traditions, language, religion, marriage patterns, and social roles. Culture is a set of learned behaviors that is transmitted from one generation to the next by nonbiological means.

(a)

(b)

(c)

(d)

roles, inheritance of property, and so on, are all aspects of culture, each culture shapes people's perceptions of the external environment, or **world view,** in particular ways that distinguish one culture from another.

One fundamental point to remember is that culture is passed from one generation to the next independently of biological factors (i.e., genes). In other words, culture is *learned*, and the process of learning one's culture begins, quite literally, at birth. All humans are products of the culture in which they are raised, and since most of human behavior is learned, it follows that most behaviors, perceptions, and reactions are shaped by culture.

It is important to emphasize, however, that even though culture is not genetically determined, the human *predisposition to assimilate culture and function within it is influenced by biological factors*. As you will see, many nonhuman animals, especially primates, rely heavily on learned behavior, and chimpanzees, in

figure 1–3 (a) An early stone tool from East Africa. (b) Assortment of implements available today in a modern hardware store. (c) A Samburu woman building a simple, traditional dwelling of stems, plant fibers, and mud. (d) A modern high-rise apartment complex, typical of industrialized cities.

World view General cultural orientation or perspective shared by members of a society.

particular, exhibit numerous aspects of culture. The predisposition for culture is perhaps the most critical component of human evolutionary history, and it was inherited from early hominid or prehominid ancestors. It may well have even existed in the common ancestor we share with chimpanzees. But in the course of human evolution, the role of culture increasingly assumed an added importance. Over time, culture and biology interacted in such a way that humans are said to be the result of **biocultural evolution**. In this respect, humans are unique among biological organisms.

Biocultural interactions have resulted in such anatomical, biological, and behavioral changes as increased brain size, reorganization of neurological structures, decreased tooth size, and development of language in humans, to name a few, and they continue to be a critical factor in changing disease patterns as well. As a contemporary example, rapid culture change (particularly in Africa) and changing social and sexual mores may have influenced evolutionary rates of HIV, the virus that causes AIDS. Certainly, these cultural factors influenced the spread of HIV throughout populations in both the developed and developing worlds.

The study of many of the biological aspects of humankind, including **adaptation** and evolution, could certainly be the purview of human biologists, and it frequently is. However, particularly in the United States, when such research also considers the role of cultural factors, it is placed within the discipline of **anthropology.**

Biocultural evolution The mutual, interactive evolution of human biology and culture; the concept that biology makes culture possible and that developing culture further influences the direction of biological evolution; a basic concept in understanding the unique components of human evolution.

Adaptation Functional response of organisms or populations to the environment. Adaptation results from evolutionary change, specifically as a result of natural selection.

Anthropology The field of inquiry that studies human culture and evolutionary aspects of human biology; includes cultural anthropology, archaeology, linguistics, and physical (or biological) anthropology.

What Is Anthropology?

Stated ambitiously but simply, anthropology is the study of humankind. The term *anthropology* is derived from the Greek words *anthropos*, meaning "human," and *logos*, meaning "word" or "study of." Anthropologists are not the only scientists who study humans, and the goals of anthropology are shared by other disciplines within the social, behavioral, and biological sciences. The main difference between anthropology and such related fields is that anthropology integrates the findings of many disciplines, including sociology, economics, history, psychology, and biology.

In the United States, anthropology comprises three main subfields: cultural, or social, anthropology; archaeology; and physical, or biological, anthropology. Some universities also include *linguistic anthropology* as a fourth area. Each of these subdisciplines, in turn, is divided into several specialized areas of interest. Following is a brief discussion of the main subdisciplines of anthropology.

See Virtual Lab 1, section I, for a discussion of physical anthropology as a subdiscipline of anthropology.

Cultural Anthropology

Cultural anthropology is the study of all aspects of human behavior. The beginnings of cultural anthropology are found in the nineteenth century, when Europeans became increasingly aware of what they termed "primitive" societies in Africa and Asia. And, in the New World, there was much interest in the vanishing cultures of Native Americans.

The interest in traditional societies led numerous early anthropologists to study and record lifeways that unfortunately are now mostly extinct. These studies produced many descriptive **ethnographies** that became the basis for subsequent comparisons between groups. Early ethnographies emphasized various phenomena, such as religion, ritual, myth, use of symbols, subsistence strategies, technology, gender roles, child-rearing practices, dietary preferences, taboos, medical practices, and how kinship was reckoned.

Ethnographic accounts, in turn, formed the basis for comparative studies of numerous cultures. Such *cross-cultural* studies, termed *ethnologies*, broadened the context within which cultural anthropologists studied human behavior. By examining the similarities and differences between diverse cultures, anthropologists have been able to formulate many theories about certain fundamental aspects of human behavior.

The focus of cultural anthropology shifted over the course of the twentieth century. But traditional ethnographic techniques, wherein anthropologists spend months or years living in and studying various societies, are still employed, although the nature of the study groups may have changed. For example, in recent decades, ethnographic techniques have been applied to the study of diverse subcultures and their interactions with one another in contemporary metropolitan areas. The subfield of cultural anthropology that deals with issues of inner cities is appropriately called *urban anthropology*. Among the many issues addressed by urban anthropologists are the relationships between ethnic groups, those aspects of traditional cultures maintained by immigrant populations, poverty, labor relations, homelessness, access to health care, and problems facing the elderly.

Medical anthropology is the subfield of cultural anthropology that explores the relationship between various cultural attributes and health and disease. One area of interest is how different groups view disease processes and how these views affect treatment or the willingness to accept treatment. When a medical anthropologist focuses on the social dimensions of disease, physicians and physical anthropologists may also collaborate. Indeed, many medical anthropologists have received much of their training in physical anthropology.

Economic anthropologists are concerned with factors that influence the distribution of goods and resources within and between cultures. Areas of interest include such topics as division of labor (by gender and age), factors that influence who controls resources and wealth, and trade practices and regulations.

Another relevant area for cultural anthropologists today is the resettlement of refugees in many parts of the world. To develop plans that properly accommodate the needs of displaced peoples, governments may find the special talents of cultural anthropologists of considerable benefit.

Many of the subfields of cultural anthropology (e.g., medical anthropology) have practical applications and are pursued by anthropologists working outside the university setting. This approach is aptly termed *applied anthropology*. While most applied anthropologists regard themselves as cultural anthropologists, the designation is also sometimes used to describe the activities of archaeologists and physical anthropologists (see p. 12). Indeed, the various fields of anthropology, as they are practiced in the United States, overlap to a considerable degree, which, after all, was the rationale for combining them under the umbrella of anthropology in the first place.

Ethnographies Detailed descriptive studies of human societies. In cultural anthropology, an ethnography is traditionally the study of a non-Western society.

Archaeology

Archaeology is the study of earlier cultures and lifeways by anthropologists who specialize in the scientific recovery, analysis, and interpretation of the material remains of past societies. Although archaeology often deals with cultures that existed before the invention of writing (the period commonly known as *prehistory*), *historic archaeologists* examine the evidence of later, complex civilizations that produced written records.

Archaeologists are concerned with culture, but they differ from cultural anthropologists in that their sources of information are not living people but rather the **artifacts** and other **material culture** left behind by earlier societies. Obviously, no one has ever excavated such aspects of culture as religious belief, spoken language, or a political system. However, the surviving evidence of human occupation can often provide information regarding these important but less tangible features of the culture that created them. Therefore, the material remains of a given ancient society may serve to inform us about the nature of that society.

The roots of modern archaeology are found in the fascination of nineteenth-century Europeans with the classical world (particularly Greece and Egypt). This interest was primarily manifested in the excavation (sometimes controlled, sometimes not) and removal of thousands of treasures and artifacts destined for the museums and private collections of wealthy Europeans.

New World archaeology has long focused on the pre-Columbian civilizations of Mexico and Central and South America (the Aztecs, Maya, and Inka). In the United States, archaeological interest was sparked particularly by the large earthen burial mounds found throughout much of the southeast. In fact, Thomas Jefferson conducted one of the first controlled excavations of a burial mound on his Virginia plantation in 1784. Importantly, his goal was not simply the recovery of artifacts; he specifically wished to address the question of how the mound was constructed.

Today, sites are not excavated simply because they exist or for the artifacts they may yield; excavation is conducted for the explicit purpose of gaining information about human behavior. Patterns of behavior are reflected in the dispersal of human settlements across a landscape and in the distribution of cultural remains within them. Through the identification of these patterns, archaeologists can elucidate the commonalities shared by many or all populations as well as those features that differ between groups. Research questions may focus on specific localities or peoples and attempt to identify, for example, various aspects of social organization, subsistence techniques, or the factors that led to the collapse of a civilization. Alternatively, inquiry may reflect an interest in broader issues relating to human culture in general, such as the development of agriculture or the rise of cities. But the design of most archaeological projects centers around a number of questions that address a wide range of interests, some general and others more specific.

Archaeology is a discipline that requires precise measurement, description, and excavation techniques, for it must be remembered that when a site is dug, it is also destroyed. Errors in excavation or recording result in the permanent loss or misinterpretation of valuable information. Therefore, contrary to what many people think, the science of archaeology is much more than simply digging up

Artifacts Objects or materials made or modified for use by hominids. The earliest artifacts tend to be tools made of stone or, occasionally, bone.

Material culture The physical manifestations of human activities; includes tools, art, and structures. As the most durable aspects of culture, material remains make up the majority of archaeological evidence of past societies.

artifacts. Rather, archaeology is a multidisciplinary approach to the study of human behavior as evidenced by cultural remains.

In the United States, the greatest expansion in archaeology in recent years has been in the important area of *cultural resource management (CRM)*. This applied approach arose from environmental legislation requiring the archaeological evaluation and even excavation of sites that may be threatened by construction and other forms of development. Many contract archaeologists (so called because their services are contracted out to developers, government agencies, and municipalities) are affiliated with private archaeological consulting firms, state or federal agencies, or educational institutions. In fact, an estimated 40 percent of all archaeologists in the United States now fill such positions.

Archaeological techniques are used to identify and excavate not only remains of human cities and settlements, but also paleontological sites containing remains of extinct species, including everything from dinosaurs to early hominids. Together, prehistoric archaeology and physical anthropology form the core of a joint science called *paleoanthropology*, described below.

Linguistic Anthropology

Linguistic anthropology is the study of human speech and language, including the origins of language in general as well as specific languages. By examining similarities between contemporary languages, linguists have been able to trace historical ties between languages and between groups of languages, thus facilitating the identification of language families and perhaps past relationships between human populations.

There is also much interest in the relationship between language and culture: how language reflects the way members of a society perceive phenomena and how the use of language shapes perceptions in different cultures. For instance, vocabulary provides important clues as to the importance of certain items and concepts in particular cultures. The most famous example is the use of some 50 terms for snow among the Inuit (Eskimos), reflecting their need to convey specific information about the properties of this form of frozen precipitation. (For that matter, skiers also employ many more increasingly precise terms for snow than do nonskiers.)

Because the spontaneous acquisition and use of language is a uniquely human characteristic, it is a topic that holds considerable interest for linguistic anthropologists, who, along with specialists in other fields, study the process of language acquisition in infants. Since insights into the process may well have implications for the development of language skills in human evolution, as well as in growing children, it is also an important subject to physical anthropologists.

Physical Anthropology

Physical anthropology, as has already been stated, is the study of human biology within the framework of evolution, with an emphasis on the interaction between biology and culture. This subdiscipline is also referred to as *biological anthropology*, and you will find the terms used interchangeably. *Physical anthropology* is the original term, and it reflects the initial interests anthropologists had in describing human physical variation. The American Association of Physical Anthropologists, its journal, many college courses, and numerous publications retain this term. But the designation *biological anthropology* reflects the shift in emphasis to more biologically oriented topics, such as genetics, evolutionary biology, nutrition, physiological adaptation, and growth and development. This shift occurred largely as a result of advances in the field of genetics, especially since the late 1950s and early 1960s. Although we have continued to use the traditional term in the title of this textbook, you will find that all the major topics pertain to biological matters.

The origins of physical anthropology are to be found in two principal areas of interest among nineteenth-century scholars. First, there was increasing concern among many scientists (at the time called *natural historians*) regarding the mechanisms by which modern species had come to be. In other words, increasing numbers of intellectuals were beginning to doubt the literal, biblical interpretation of creation. This does not mean that all natural historians had abandoned all religious explanations of natural occurrences. But scientific explanations emphasizing natural, rather than supernatural, phenomena were becoming increasingly popular in scientific and intellectual circles. Although few scientists were actually prepared to believe that humans had evolved from earlier forms, discoveries of several Neandertal fossils in the 1800s began to raise questions regarding the origins and antiquity of the human species.

Paleoanthropology The interdisciplinary approach to the study of earlier hominids—their chronology, physical structure, archaeological remains, habitats, etc.

The sparks of interest in biological change over time were fueled into flames by the publication of Charles Darwin's *Origin of Species* in 1859. Today, **paleoanthropology,** or the study of human evolution, particularly as evidenced in the fossil record, is one of the major subfields of physical anthropology (fig. 1–4). There are now thousands of specimens of human ancestors housed in museum and research collections. Taken together, these fossils cover a span of at least 4 million years of human prehistory, and although incomplete, they provide us with significantly more knowledge than was available even 15 years ago. It is the ultimate goal of paleoanthropological research to identify the various early hominid species, establish a chronological sequence of relationships among them, and gain insights into their adaptation and behavior. Only then will there emerge a clear picture of how and when humankind came into being.

figure 1–4 Paleoanthropologists excavating at the Drimolen site, South Africa.

© Kenneth Garrett/NGS Image Collection

A second nineteenth-century interest that had direct relevance to anthropology was observable physical variation, particularly as seen in skin color. Enormous effort was aimed at describing and explaining the biological differences among various human populations. Although some endeavors were misguided, they gave birth to literally thousands of body measurements that could be used to compare people. Physical anthropologists use many of the techniques of **anthropometry** today, not only to study living groups, but also to study skeletal remains from archaeological sites (fig. 1–5). Moreover, anthropometric techniques have considerable application in the design of everything from airplane cockpits to office furniture.

Anthropologists today are concerned with human variation because of its *adaptive significance* and also because they want to elucidate the genetic and related evolutionary factors that act to produce variation. In other words, many traits that typify certain populations are seen as having evolved as biological adaptations, or adjustments, to local environmental conditions, including infectious disease. Other traits may be the results of geographical isolation or the descent of populations from small founding groups. Examining biological variation between populations of any species provides valuable information as to the mechanisms of genetic change in groups over time, which is precisely what the evolutionary process is all about.

Modern population studies also examine other important aspects of human variation, including how various groups respond physiologically to different kinds of environmentally induced stress (fig. 1–6). Such stresses may include high altitude, cold, or heat.

Other physical anthropologists conduct nutritional studies, investigating the relationships between various dietary components, cultural practices, physiology, and certain aspects of health and disease. Closely related to the topic of nutrition are investigations of human fertility, growth, and development. These fields of inquiry are fundamental to studies of adaptation in modern human populations, and they can provide insights into hominid evolution as well.

It would be impossible to study evolutionary processes, and therefore adaptation, without a knowledge of genetic principles. For this reason and others, **genetics** is a crucial field for physical anthropologists. Modern physical anthropology would not exist as an evolutionary science were it not for advances in the understanding of genetic principles.

Not only does genetics allow us to explain how evolutionary processes work, but *molecular anthropologists* use recently developed genetic technologies to investigate evolutionary relationships between living primate species (including humans). The techniques of molecular genetics are also being used to investigate the origins of modern humans, genetic relationships between contemporary populations, and human genetic variation.

Primatology, the study of nonhuman primates, has become increasingly important

figure 1–5 Anthropology student using spreading calipers to measure cranial length.

Anthropometry Measurement of human body parts. When osteologists measure skeletal elements, the term *osteometry* is often used.

figure 1–6 Researcher using a treadmill test to assess a subject's heart rate, blood pressure, and oxygen consumption.

Genetics The study of gene structure and action and the patterns of inheritance of traits from parent to offspring. Genetic mechanisms are the underlying foundation for evolutionary change.

Primatology The study of the biology and behavior of nonhuman primates (prosimians, monkeys, and apes).

figure 1–7 Yahaya Alamasi, a member of the senior field staff at Gombe National Park, Tanzania. Alamasi is recording behaviors in free-ranging chimpanzees.

Osteology The study of skeletal material. Human osteology focuses on the interpretation of the skeletal remains of past groups. Some of the same techniques are used in paleo-anthropology to study early hominids.

Paleopathology The branch of osteology that studies the evidence of disease and injury in human skeletal (or, occasionally, mummi-fied) remains.

Forensic anthropology An applied anthropological approach dealing with legal matters. Physical anthro-pologists work with coroners and others in the identification and analysis of human remains.

since the late 1950s for several reasons (fig. 1–7). Behavioral studies, especially those conducted on groups in natural environments, have implications for numerous scientific disciplines. Moreover, studies of nonhuman animal behav-ior have assumed a greater urgency in recent decades owing to concern over declining numbers of many species.

The behavioral study of any species provides a wealth of data pertaining to adaptation. Because nonhuman primates are our closest living relatives, the iden-tification of underlying factors related to social behavior, communication, infant care, reproductive behavior, and so on, aids in developing a better understanding of the natural forces that have shaped so many aspects of human behavior.

Nonhuman primates are also important to study in their own right, and this is particularly true today because the majority of species are threatened or seri-ously endangered. Only through research will scientists be able to recommend policies that can better ensure the survival of many nonhuman primates and thousands of other species as well.

Primate paleontology, the study of the primate fossil record, has implications not only for nonhuman primates but also for hominids. Virtually every year, fossil-bearing beds in North America, Africa, Asia, and Europe yield important new discoveries. By comparisons with anatomically similar living species, pri-mate paleontologists can make reasoned inferences regarding behavior in earlier groups as well. Moreover, we hope to be able to clarify what we know about evo-lutionary relationships between extinct and living species, including ourselves.

Osteology, the study of the skeleton, is central to physical anthropology. The emphasis on osteology exists in part because of the concern with the analy-sis of fossil material. Certainly, a thorough knowledge of the structure and func-tion of the skeleton is critical to the interpretation of fossil material.

Bone biology and physiology are of major importance to many other aspects of physical anthropology, in addition to paleontology. Many osteologists spe-cialize in studies that emphasize various measurements of skeletal elements. This type of research is essential, for example, to the identification of stature and growth patterns in archaeological populations.

One subdiscipline of osteology is the study of disease and trauma in archae-ologically derived skeletal populations. **Paleopathology** is a prominent subfield that investigates the incidence of trauma, certain infectious diseases (including syphilis and tuberculosis), nutritional deficiencies, and numerous other con-ditions that may leave evidence in bone (fig. 1–8). In this area of research, a pre-cise knowledge of bone physiology and response to insult is required.

A field directly related to osteology and paleopathology is **forensic anthropology.** Technically, this approach is the application of anthropological (usually osteological and sometimes archaeological) techniques to the law (fig. 1–9). Forensic anthropologists are commonly called on to help identify skeletal remains in cases of disaster or other situations where a human body has been found.

Forensic anthropologists have been involved in numerous cases having important legal and historical consequences. They were prominent in the iden-tification of the skeletons of most of the Russian imperial family, executed in 1918. They also participated in the identification of missing American soldiers in Southeast Asia. And most recently, many forensic anthropologists partici-pated in the overwhelming task of identifying the remains of victims of the September 11, 2001, terrorist attacks in the United States.

Lynn Kilgore

Courtesy, Lorna Pierce/Judy Suchey

figure 1–8 Healing fracture of a humerus (upper arm bone) in a skeleton from Nubia (Republic of the Sudan).

figure 1–9 Physical anthropologists Lorna Pierce (left) and Judy Suchey (center) working as forensic consultants. The dog has just located a concealed human cranium during a training session.

Anatomical studies constitute another important area of interest for physical anthropologists. In the living organism, bone and dental structures are intimately linked to the soft tissues that surround and act on them. Thus, a thorough knowledge of soft tissue anatomy is essential to understanding the biomechanics of movement. This relationship is important to the accurate assessment of the structure and function of limbs and other components in fossilized remains. For these reasons and others, many physical anthropologists specialize in anatomical studies. In fact, several physical anthropologists hold professorships in anatomy departments at universities and medical schools.

Applied approaches in physical anthropology are numerous. And while *applied anthropology* is aimed at the practical application of anthropological theories and methods outside the academic setting, applied and academic anthropology are not mutually exclusive approaches. In fact, applied anthropology relies on the research and theories of academic anthropologists and at the same time has much to contribute to theory and techniques. Within biological anthropology, forensic anthropologists provide a good example of the applied approach. But the practical application of the techniques of physical anthropology is not new. During World War II, for example, physical anthropologists, because of their expertise in measuring humans, were extensively involved in the design of gun turrets and airplane cockpits. Since that time, many physical anthropologists have pursued careers in genetic and biomedical research, public health, evolutionary medicine, medical anthropology, and conservation of non-human primates, and many hold positions in museums and zoos. In fact, a background in physical anthropology is excellent preparation for almost any career in the medical and biological fields.

Physical Anthropology and the Scientific Method

Science A body of knowledge gained through observation and experimentation; from the Latin *scientia,* meaning "knowledge."

Empirical Relying on experiment or observation; from the Latin *empiricus,* meaning "experienced."

Scientific method A research method whereby a problem is identified, a hypothesis (or hypothetical explanation) is stated, and that hypothesis is tested through the collection and analysis of data. If the hypothesis is verified, it becomes a theory.

Data (*sing.,* datum) Facts from which conclusions can be drawn; scientific information.

Quantitatively In a manner involving measurements of quantity and including such properties as size, number, and capacity. When data are quantified, they are expressed numerically and are capable of being tested statistically.

Hypothesis (*pl.,* hypotheses) A provisional explanation of a phenomenon. Hypotheses require verification.

Scientific testing The precise repetition of an experiment or expansion of observed data to provide verification; the procedure by which hypotheses and theories are verified, modified, or discarded.

Theory A broad statement of scientific relationships or underlying principles that has been at least partially verified.

 See Virtual Lab 3, section III, for a discussion of the scientific method.

Science is a process of understanding phenomena through observation, generalization, and verification. By this we mean that there is an **empirical** approach to gaining information through the use of systematic and explicit techniques. Because physical anthropologists are engaged in scientific pursuits, they adhere to the principles of the **scientific method,** whereby a research problem is identified and information subsequently gathered to solve it.

The gathering of information is referred to as **data** collection, and when researchers use a rigorously controlled approach, they are able to describe precisely their techniques and results in a manner that facilitates comparisons with the work of others. For example, when scientists collect data on tooth size in hominid fossils, they must specify precisely which teeth are being measured, how they are being measured, and what the results of the measurements are (expressed numerically, or **quantitatively**). Subsequently, it is up to the investigators to draw conclusions as to the meaning and significance of their measurements. This body of information then becomes the basis of future studies, perhaps by other researchers, who can compare their own results with those already obtained. The eventual outcome of this type of inquiry may be the acceptance or rejection of certain proposed facts and explanations.

Once facts have been established, scientists attempt to explain them. First, a **hypothesis,** or provisional explanation of phenomena, is developed. But before a hypothesis can be accepted, it must be tested by means of data collection and analysis. Indeed, the testing of hypotheses with the possibility of proving them false is the very basis of the scientific method.

Scientific testing of hypotheses may take several years (or longer) and may involve researchers who were not involved with the original work. In subsequent studies, other investigators may attempt to obtain the original results, but such repetition may not occur. For example, repeated failures to duplicate the results of highly publicized cold fusion experiments led most scientists to question and ultimately reject the claims made in the original research. While it is easier to duplicate original studies conducted in laboratory settings, it is equally important to verify data collected outside tightly controlled situations. In the latter circumstance, results are tested relative to other, often larger, samples. The predicted patterns will either be confirmed through such further research or be viewed as limited or even incorrect.

If a hypothesis cannot be falsified, it is accepted as a **theory.** There is a popular misconception that theories are nothing but hunches or unfounded explanations. But in scientific terms, a theory is a statement of relationships that has a firm basis as demonstrated through testing and the accumulation of evidence. As such, theories not only help organize current knowledge, but they also predict how new facts may fit into the established pattern.

Use of the scientific method not only allows for the development and testing of hypotheses, but also permits various types of *bias* to be addressed and controlled. It is important to realize that bias occurs in all studies. Sources of bias include how the investigator was trained and by whom; what particular questions interest the researcher; what specific skills and talents he or she possesses; what earlier results (if any) have been established in this realm of study and by whom (e.g., the researcher, close colleagues, or those with rival approaches or even rival personalities); and what sources of data are available (e.g., accessible countries or museums) and thus what samples can be collected (at all or at least conveniently).

Application of the scientific method thus requires constant vigilance by all those who practice it. The goal is not to establish "truth" in any absolute sense, but rather to generate ever more accurate and consistent depictions and explanations of phenomena in our universe. At its very heart, scientific methodology is an exercise in rational thought and critical thinking.

The Anthropological Perspective

Perhaps the most important benefit you will receive from this textbook—and this course—is a wider appreciation of the human experience. To understand human beings and how our species came to be, it is necessary to broaden our viewpoint, both through time and over space. All branches of anthropology fundamentally seek to do this in what we call the *anthropological perspective*.

Physical anthropologists, for example, are keenly interested in how humans differ from and are similar to other animals, especially nonhuman primates. For example, we have defined *hominids* as bipedal primates, but what are the major components of bipedal locomotion, and how do they differ from, say, those in a quadrupedal ape? To answer these questions, we would need to study human locomotion and compare it with forms of locomotion seen in various nonhuman primates.

Through this kind of broadened perspective, we can begin to grasp the contemporary diversity of the human experience and, in so doing, more fully understand both human potentialities and human constraints. And by extending our breadth of knowledge, it is easier to avoid the **ethnocentric** pitfalls inherent in a more limited view of humanity.

In addition to broadening perspectives over space (i.e., encompassing many cultures and ecological circumstances as well as nonhuman species), an anthropological perspective also extends our horizons *through time*. For example, in Chapter 13 we will discuss human nutrition. However, the vast majority of the kinds of foods currently eaten (coming from domesticated plants and animals) were unavailable prior to 10,000 years ago. Human physiological mechanisms for chewing and digesting foods nevertheless were already well established long before that date. These adaptive complexes go back millions of years. In addition to the obviously different diets prior to the development of agriculture (approximately 10,000 years ago), earlier hominids might well have differed from humans today in average body size, metabolism, and activity patterns. How, then, does the basic evolutionary "equipment" (i.e., physiology) inherited from our hominid forebears accommodate our modern diets? Clearly, the way to understand such processes is not just by looking at contemporary human responses, but also by placing them in the perspective of evolutionary development through time.

Indeed, most of the topics covered in this book are addressed by using a broad application of the anthropological perspective. For physical anthropologists, such an approach usually means extending the perspective over space as well as through considerable periods of time.

Ethnocentric Viewing other cultures from the inherently biased perspective of one's own culture. Ethnocentrism often results in cultures being seen as inferior to one's own.

We hope that the ensuing pages will help you develop an increased understanding of the similarities we share with other biological organisms and also of the processes that have shaped the traits that make us unique. We live in what may well be the most crucial period for our planet in the last 65 million years. We are members of the one species that, through the very agency of culture, has wrought such devastating changes in ecological systems that we must now alter our technologies or face potentially unspeakable consequences. In such a time, it is vital that we attempt to gain the best possible understanding of what it means to be human. We believe that the study of physical anthropology is one endeavor that aids in this attempt, and that is indeed the goal of this text.

Conclusion

Continuum A set of relationships in which all components fall along a single integrated spectrum. All life reflects a single biological continuum.

From this brief overview, it can be seen that physical anthropology is the sub-discipline of anthropology that focuses on many varied aspects of the biological and behavioral nature of *Homo sapiens*. Humans are a product of the same forces that produced all life on earth. As such, we represent one contemporary component of a vast biological **continuum** at one point in time, and in this regard, we are not particularly unique. Stating that humans are part of a continuum does not imply that we are at the peak of development on that continuum. Depending on which criteria one uses, humans can be seen to exist at one end of the continuum or the other, or somewhere in between. But humans do not necessarily occupy a position of inherent superiority over other species.

There is, however, one dimension in which human beings are truly unique, and that is intellect. After all, humans are the only species, born of earth, to stir the lunar dust. Humans are the only species to develop language and complex culture as a means of buffering the challenges posed by nature, and by so doing, to eventually gain the power to shape the very destiny of the planet.

Summary

n this chapter, we have introduced the field of physical anthropology and have placed it within the overall context of anthropological studies. As a major academic area within the social sciences, anthropology also includes archaeology, cultural anthropology, and linguistic anthropology as its major subfields.

Physical anthropology itself includes aspects of human biology (emphasizing evolutionary perspectives), the study of nonhuman primates, and the hominid fossil record. Especially as applied to the study of early hominids (incorporated within the interdisciplinary field of paleoanthropology), physical anthropologists work in close collaboration with many other scientists from the fields of archaeology, geology, chemistry, and many other disciplines.

In the next chapter, we present a brief overview of changes in scientific thought that led to the discovery of the basic principles of biological evolution. Evolution is the core of physical anthropology, and basic evolutionary processes explain the appearance of humans and our ancesters as well as human (and non-human) adaptation and variation.

Questions for Review

1. What is anthropology? What are the major subfields of anthropology?
2. How does physical anthropology differ from other disciplines interested in human biology?
3. What is meant by biocultural evolution, and why is it important in understanding human evolution?
4. What are some of the primary areas of research within physical anthropology? Give two or three examples of the types of research pursued by physical anthropologists.
5. What is meant by the term *hominid?* Be specific.
6. What fields, in addition to physical anthropology, contribute to paleoanthropology?
7. Define the term *science*.
8. What is the scientific method? How do you think it differs from other methods of explaining phenomena?
9. What is hypothesis testing?

Suggested Further Readings

Ferraro, Gary, Wenda Trevathan, and Janet Levy. 1994. *Anthropology, an Applied Perspective*. St. Paul: West.

Spencer, Frank (ed.). 1982. *A History of Physical Anthropology*. New York: Academic Press.

Stiebing, William H., Jr. 1993. *Uncovering the Past: A History of Archaeology*. New York: Oxford University Press.

Multimedia Resources

 Companion Web Site

Anthropology Online: The Wadsworth Anthropology Resource Center
Visit **http://anthropology.wadsworth.com** and click on the Companion Web Site for Jurmain/Kilgore/Trevathan/Nelson's *Essentials of Physical Anthropology*, Fifth Edition, to access a wide range of enrichment material to aid in your study of anthropology. Among the useful options for each chapter's self-study are learning objectives, flashcards, Internet exercises, Web links, InfoTrac College Edition exercises, and practice quizzes that can be scored and emailed to your instructor.

Research in Physical Anthropology

Physical anthropologists are interested in the study of people, both living and dead. Except for some unusual circumstances, such as natural mummification (where some soft tissues are preserved), what is left of earlier populations are the hard tissues (bones and teeth).

figure 1 The osteometric board is used to measure the length of long bones, such as the human femur shown here.

Robert Jurmain

Robert Jurmain

figure 2 A standard X-ray machine at a university student health center being used to radiograph two human long bones (femur and tibia).

Physical anthropologists can observe many useful characteristics using simple tools. (This approach is called gross analysis.) However, specialized equipment can also provide data for variables that cannot be observed directly. Standard X-rays are most helpful in revealing subsurface bone modifications, such as those resulting from healed fractures. The techniques for taking, as well as reading, the X-rays are analogous to those developed for living patients. Indeed, skeletal biologists often work closely with medical colleagues to analyze and interpret the evidence of disease and trauma in bone.

figure 3 Left and right forearm bones (ulnae) from an adult female chimpanzee killed by other chimpanzees at Gombe National Park. The right ulna (on the right) has a partially healed fracture. The left ulna is shown for comparison. This animal (Madam Bee) was attacked several times, and it appears that an earlier fracture (as evidenced by the thickened portion of the shaft) was rebroken, presumably during the fatal attack.

figure 4 X-ray of the same two elements shown in Figure 4. The partially healed fracture is clearly visible.

Research in Physical Anthropology (continued)

Forensic anthropologists (physical anthropologists who specialize in the identification of skeletal remains of crime victims or victims of mass fatalities) are sometimes asked to confirm the identities of historical figures. In 1992, a team of scientists led by the late Professor Bill Maples used standard osteological techniques to identify the skeletons of members of the Russian royal family, murdered in 1918. Positive identifications were made for Tsar Nicholas II, his wife, the tsarina Alexandra, and three of their daughters. A family physician and three servants were also identified. Missing were the remains of the tsarevich Alexis, heir to the throne, and his sister, Anastasia.

To further confirm these identities, mitochondrial DNA (mtDNA; see p. 75) was extracted from the skeletons of Alexandra and her daughters, amplified through PCR techniques (see p. 60) and compared with mtDNA provided by Prince Philip, a maternal relative of Alexandra and husband of Queen Elizabeth of England. Mitochondrial DNA taken from the tsar's skeleton and teeth was compared with samples donated by distant living maternal relatives and the exhumed remains of his brother, who died in 1899. In all cases, the results of the DNA analysis confirmed the initial results and clearly demonstrated the usefulness of mtDNA in skeletal identification.

Beyond these forensic applications, recently developed genetic technologies have tremendously impacted a variety of other subdisciplines within

figure 5 The Russian royal family.

figure 6 Professor Bill Maples examining the cranium of Tsar Nicholas II.

physical anthropology. Molecular anthropologists, involved in genetic research, are using cutting edge techniques to explore the evolutionary relationships between various human populations as well as those between humans and nonhuman primates. To do this they examine similarities and differences in DNA sequences between individuals, populations and even species.

In addition to providing a vast new source of information regarding the evolutionary relationships of contemporary organisms (e.g., humans as compared to other primates), increased knowledge of specific DNA segments also holds the promise of unraveling the genetic basis of response to infectious disease and cancer.

figure 7 Variation in DNA sequences can be studied using a variety of molecular genetic techniques. A graduate student at the University of Cambridge uses gradient gel electrophoresis (DGGE) to study variability in the chromosomal region involved in immune response (the area of DNA which helps provide protection against infection).

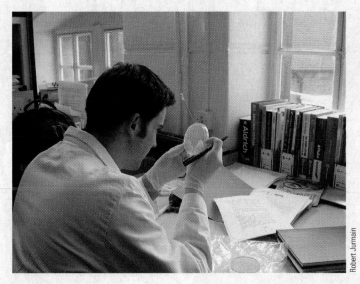

figure 8 Cloning and sequencing methods are frequently used to identify new genes in humans and nonhuman primates. This graduate student, working in the same laboratory as in the preceding figure, identifies a genetically modified bacterial clone.

*Research in Physical
Anthropology* (continued)

Physical anthropologists, working with other biomedical scientists, are also concerned with measuring health, nutrition, and physiological response to environmental stress in various populations. Treadmill tests, bicycle ergometer tests, and questionnaires are just a few of the tools used to measure functional capacity in healthy and diseased persons. In addition, these techniques can be used to assess human biological adaptation to different environments (e.g., high altitude) or to disease (e.g., coronary artery disease).

Courtesy, L. G. Moore

figure 9 Brain blood flow, volume and frequency of breathing, oxygen consumption, and carbon dioxide production are being monitored in this Tibetan subject during exercise on a bicycle ergometer. These data are used to assess physiological response to reduced oxygen availability in indigenous residents of high-altitude regions.

Courtesy, L. G. Moore

figure 10 Dr. Jianguo Zhuang (foreground) and Dr. Stacy Zamudio (rear) are separating white blood cells from whole blood samples taken from Tibetan research subjects. The white blood cells provide DNA used to investigate genetic variation in populations residing at high altitude.

figure 11 Dr. Kathleen Galvin measures upper arm circumference in a young Maasai boy in Tanzania. Note the scale she has used to record the boy's weight. To the right is an anthropometer, an instrument used to take a variety of body measurements, including, as in this example, height. These data (and others) were collected as part of a health and nutrition study of particular groups of Maasai cattle herders.

Courtesy, Kathleen Galvin

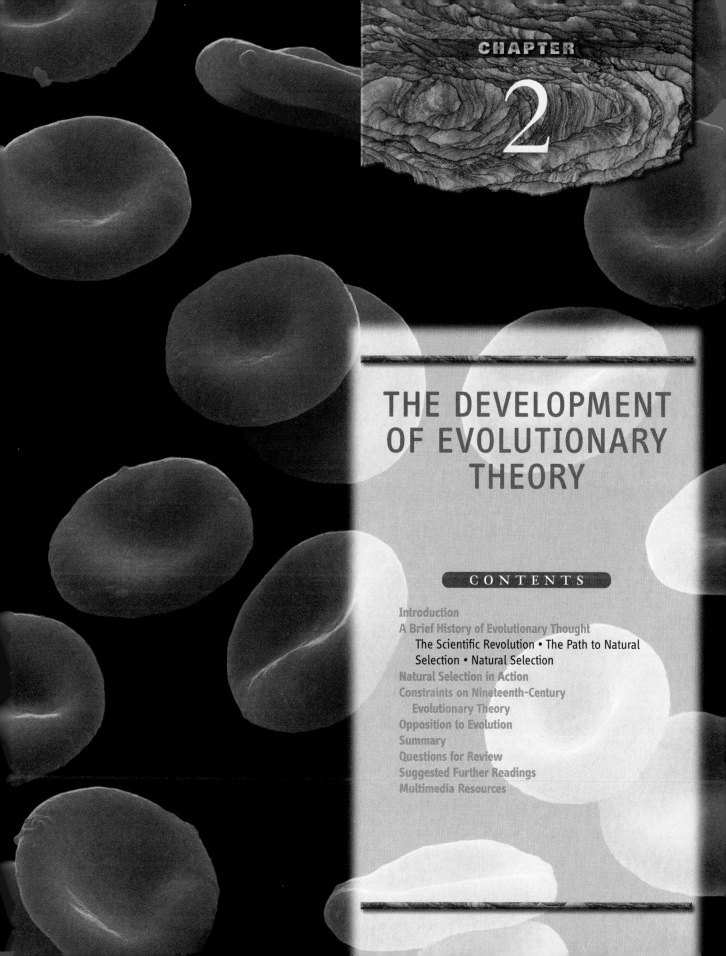

THE DEVELOPMENT OF EVOLUTIONARY THEORY

CONTENTS

Introduction

The term **evolution** is sometimes charged with emotion. The topic is often controversial, particularly in the United States, because some religious views hold that evolutionary statements run counter to biblical teachings. Indeed, as you are probably aware, there continues to be much opposition to the teaching of evolution in public schools.

Those who wish to denigrate evolution frequently insist that it is "only a theory"—an attempt to reduce its status to supposition. Actually, to refer to a concept as "theory" is to lend it support. As we noted in Chapter 1, theories are general hypotheses that have been tested and subjected to verification through accumulated evidence. Evolution *is* a theory, one that has increasingly been supported by a mounting body of genetic evidence. It is a theory that has stood the test of time, and today it stands as the most fundamental unifying force in biological science.

Because physical anthropology is concerned with all aspects of how humans came to be and how we adapt physiologically to the external environment, the details of the evolutionary process are crucial to the field. Moreover, given the central importance of evolution to physical anthropology, it is valuable to know how the mechanics of the process came to be discovered. Additionally, to appreciate the nature of the controversy that continues to surround the issue today, it is important to examine the basic evolutionary principles within the social and political context in which the theory emerged.

A Brief History of Evolutionary Thought

The individual most responsible for the elucidation of the evolutionary process was Charles Darwin. But while Darwin was formulating his theory of **natural selection,** his ideas were being duplicated by another British naturalist, Alfred Russel Wallace.

That natural selection, the single most important mechanism of evolutionary change, should be proposed at more or less the same time by two British men in the mid-nineteenth century may seen highly improbable. But actually, it is not all that surprising. Indeed, if Darwin and Wallace had not made their simultaneous discoveries, someone else would have done so in short order. That is to say, the groundwork had already been laid, and many within the scientific community were prepared to accept explanations of biological change that would have been unacceptable even 25 years earlier.

Like other human endeavors, scientific knowledge is usually gained through a series of small steps rather than giant leaps. Just as technological innovation is based on past achievements, scientific knowledge builds on previously developed theories. Given the stepwise progression of scientific discovery, it is informative to examine the development of ideas that led Darwin and Wallace independently to develop the theory of evolution by natural selection.

Throughout the Middle Ages, one predominant component of the European world view was that all aspects of nature, including all forms of life and their relationships to one another, were fixed and unchanging. This view of

Evolution A change in the genetic structure of a population. The term is also frequently used to refer to the appearance of a new species.

See the following sections of the CD-ROM for topics covered in this chapter: Virtual Lab 1, section III, and Virtual Lab 2, sections I and VII.

Natural selection The mechanism of evolutionary change first articulated by Charles Darwin; refers to genetic change or changes in the frequencies of certain traits in populations due to differential reproductive success between individuals.

natural phenomena was shaped in part by the teachings of Christianity, which were taken quite literally, and it was generally accepted that all life on earth had been created by God exactly as it existed in the present. This belief that life forms did not change eventually came to be known in European intellectual circles as **fixity of species.**

Accompanying the notion of fixity of species was the belief that all God's creations were arranged in a hierarchy that progressed from the simplest organisms to the most complex. At the top of this linear sequence were humans. This concept of a ranked order of living things is termed the *Great Chain of Being* and was first proposed in the fourth century B.C. by the Greek philosopher Aristotle. Although position within the chain was based on physical similarities between species, no evolutionary or biological relationships were implied.

It was also believed that since the creation, no new species had appeared and none had disappeared, or become extinct. Thus, to question the assumptions of fixity was seen as a challenge to God's perfection.

The plan of the entire universe was seen as the Grand Design—that is, God's design. In what is called the "argument from design," anatomical structures were viewed as planned to meet the purpose for which they were required. Wings, arms, eyes—all these structures were interpreted as neatly fitting the functions they performed, and nature was considered a deliberate plan of the Grand Designer.

The date the Grand Designer had completed his works was relatively recent—4004 B.C., according to an Irish archbishop, James Ussher (1581–1656), who worked out the date of creation by analyzing the "begat" chapter of Genesis. Archbishop Ussher was not the first person to propose a recent origin of the earth, but he was responsible for providing a precise date for it.

The prevailing notion of the earth's brief existence, together with fixity of species, provided a formidable obstacle to the development of evolutionary theory because evolution requires time. Consequently, in addition to overcoming the notion of fixity of species, scientists needed a theory of immense geological time in order to formulate evolutionary principles. In fact, until these prior concepts of fixity and time were fundamentally altered, it would have been unlikely that the idea of natural selection could even have been conceived.

fixity of species The notion that species, once created, can never change; an idea diametrically opposed to theories of biological evolution.

 See Virtual Lab 7, section I, for a discussion of several geological methods of determining the age of the earth.

The Scientific Revolution

What, then, upset the medieval belief in a rigid universe of planets, stars, plants, and animals? How did the scientific method as we know it today develop and, with the help of Newton and Galileo in the seventeenth century, demonstrate a moving, not static, universe?

The discovery of the New World and circumnavigation of the globe in the fifteenth century overturned some very fundamental ideas about the planet. For one thing, the earth could no longer be perceived as flat. Also, as Europeans began to explore the New World, their awareness of biological diversity was greatly expanded through exposure to plants and animals previously unknown to them.

There were other attacks on the complacency of traditional beliefs. In 1514, a Polish mathematician named Copernicus challenged Aristotle's long-believed assertion that the earth, circled by the sun, moon, and stars, was the center of the universe. Copernicus removed the earth as the center of all things by proposing a *heliocentric* (sun-centered) solar system.

Copernicus' theory did not attract widespread attention at the time, but in the early 1600s, it was restated and further substantiated by an Italian mathematics professor, Galileo Galilei. Galileo came into direct confrontation with the Catholic Church over his publications, to the extent that he spent the last nine years of his life under house arrest. Even so, in intellectual circles, the universe had changed from one of fixity to one of motion, although most still believed that change was impossible for living forms.

Scholars of the sixteenth and seventeenth centuries developed methods and theories that revolutionized scientific thought. The seventeenth century, in particular, was a beehive of scientific activity. The works of such individuals as Keppler, Descartes, and Newton established the laws of physics, motion, and gravity. Other achievements included the discovery of the circulation of blood and the development of numerous scientific instruments, including the telescope, barometer, and microscope. These technological advances permitted investigations of natural phenomena and opened up entire worlds for discoveries such as had never before been imagined.

Scientific achievement increasingly came to direct as well as reflect the changing views of Europeans. Investigations of stars, planets, animals, and plants came to be conducted without significant reference to the supernatural. In other words, nature was seen as a mechanism, functioning according to certain universal physical laws, and it was these laws that scientists were seeking. Yet, most scientists still insisted that a First Cause initiated the entire system. The argument from design was still defended and, indeed, it strongly persists even today.

The Path to Natural Selection

See Virtual Lab 1, section II, for a discussion of the species concept.

Before early naturalists could begin to understand the forms of organic life, it was necessary to list and describe those forms. As attempts in this direction were made, scholars became increasingly impressed with the amount of biological diversity that confronted them.

JOHN RAY   By the sixteenth century, a keen interest in nature's variation had developed, and by the mid-1500s, there were a few descriptive works on plants, birds, fish, and mammals. But it was not until the seventeenth century that the concept of species was clearly defined by Englishman John Ray (1627–1705), an ordained minister trained at Cambridge University.

Ray, who adhered to the concept of fixity, was the first to recognize that groups of plants and animals could be distinguished from other groups by their ability to reproduce with one another and produce offspring. Such groups of reproductively isolated organisms were placed into a single category he called *species* (*pl.*, species). Thus, by the late 1600s, the biological criterion of reproduction was used to define species much as it is today (Young, 1992).

Ray also recognized that species frequently shared similarities with other species, and these he grouped together in a second level of classification he called the *genus* (*pl.*, genera). In fact, he was the first to use the labels *genus* and *species* in this manner, and they are the terms still in use today.

Courtesy, Dept. of Library Services, American Museum of Natural History

figure 2–1 Linnaeus developed a classification system for plants and animals.

CAROLUS LINNAEUS   One of the leading naturalists of the eighteenth century was Carolus Linnaeus (1707–1778), of Sweden (fig. 2–1). He is best known for developing a classification of plants and animals, the *Systema Naturae* (Systems of Nature), first published in 1735.

Linnaeus standardized Ray's more sporadic use of two names (genus and species) for organisms, thus firmly establishing the use of **binomial nomenclature.** Moreover, he added two more categories: class and order. Linnaeus' four-level system of classification became the basis for **taxonomy,** the system of classification still used today.

Another of Linnaeus' innovations was to include humans in his classification of animals, placing them in the genus *Homo* and species *sapiens*. The inclusion of humans in this scheme was controversial because it defied contemporary thought that humans, made in God's image, should be considered separately and outside the animal kingdom.

Linnaeus also believed in fixity of species, although in later years, faced with mounting evidence to the contrary, he came to question this assumption. Indeed, fixity of species was being challenged on many fronts, especially in France, where voices were being raised in favor of a universe based on change and, more to the point, in favor of the relationship between similar forms based on descent from a common ancestor.

COMTE DE BUFFON   Georges-Louis Leclerc (1707–1788), who was raised to the rank of count under the name Buffon, was Keeper of the King's Gardens in Paris (fig. 2–2). He believed neither in the perfection of nature nor in the idea that nature had a purpose, as declared by the argument from design, but he did recognize the dynamic relationship between the external environment and living forms. In his *Natural History*, first published in 1749, he repeatedly stressed the importance of change in the universe, and he underlined the changing nature of species.

Buffon believed that when groups of organisms migrated to new areas of the world, each group would subsequently be influenced by local climatic conditions and would gradually change as a result of adaptation to the environment. Buffon's recognition of the external environment as an agent of change in species was an important innovation. However, he rejected the idea that one species could give rise to another.

ERASMUS DARWIN   Erasmus Darwin (1731–1802) is today best known as Charles Darwin's grandfather (fig. 2–3). However, during his life, this free-thinking, high-living physician was well known in literary circles for his poetry and other writings. More than 50 years before his grandson was to shake the world with his views on natural selection, Erasmus Darwin had expressed similar ideas and had even commented on *human* evolution. From letters and other sources, it is known that Charles Darwin had read and was fond of his grandfather's writings. But the degree to which the grandson's theories were influenced by the grandfather is not known.

JEAN-BAPTISTE LAMARCK   Neither Buffon nor Erasmus Darwin codified his beliefs into a comprehensive system that attempted to *explain* the evolutionary process. The first European scientist to do so was the French scholar Jean-Baptiste-Pierre-Antoine de Monet de Chevalier Lamarck (1744–1829). (Thankfully, most references to Lamarck use only his surname.)

But, expanding beyond the views of Buffon, Lamarck (fig. 2–4) did attempt to explain how species could change. He postulated a dynamic interaction such

Binomial nomenclature   (*binomial,* meaning "two names") In taxonomy, the convention established by Carolus Linnaeus whereby genus and species names are used to refer to species. For example, *Homo sapiens* refers to human beings.

Taxonomy   The branch of science concerned with the rules of classifying organisms on the basis of evolutionary relationships.

See Virtual Lab 1, section II, for a discussion of the Linnaean system of binomial nomenclature for classifying plants and animals.

figure 2–2 Buffon recognized the influence of the environment on life forms.

figure 2–3 Erasmus Darwin, grandfather of Charles Darwin, believed in species change.

figure 2–4 Lamarck believed that species change was influenced by environmental change. He is best known for his theory of the inheritance of acquired characteristics.

that organic forms could become altered in the face of changing environmental circumstances. Thus, as the environment changed, an animal's activity patterns would also change, resulting in increased or decreased use of certain body parts. As a result of this use or disuse, body parts became altered.

Physical alteration occurred as a function of perceived bodily "needs." If a particular part of the body felt a certain need, "fluids and forces" would be directed toward that point and the structure would be modified to satisfy the need. Because the modification would render the animal better suited to its habitat, the new trait would be passed on to offspring. This theory is known as the *inheritance of acquired characteristics*, or the *use-disuse* theory.

One of the most frequently given examples of Lamarck's theory is the giraffe, who, having stripped all the leaves from the lower branches of a tree (environmental change), strives to reach those leaves on upper branches. As vital forces progress to tissues of the neck, the neck increases slightly in length, thus enabling the giraffe to obtain more food. The longer neck is subsequently transmitted to offspring, with the eventual result that all giraffes have longer necks than did their predecessors (fig. 2–5a). Thus, according to the theory of acquired

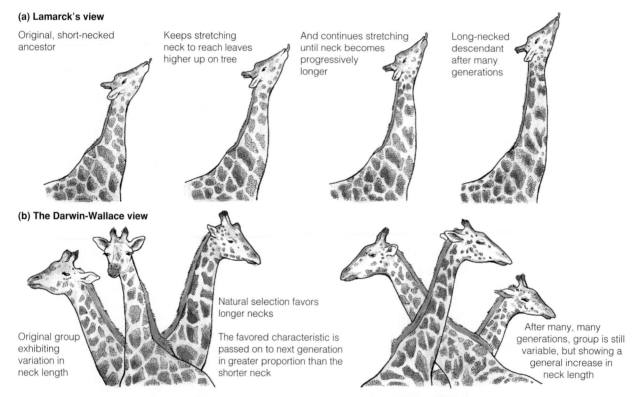

figure 2–5 Contrasting ideas about the mechanism of evolution. (a) According to Lamarck's theory, acquired characteristics can be passed to subsequent generations. Thus, short-necked giraffes stretched their necks to reach higher into trees for food, and, according to Lamarck, this acquired trait was passed on to offspring, who were born with longer necks. (b) According to the Darwin-Wallace theory of natural selection, among giraffes there is variation in neck length. If having a longer neck provides an advantage for feeding, this trait will be passed on to a greater number of offspring, leading to an overall increase in the length of giraffe necks over many generations.

characteristics, *a trait acquired by an animal during its lifetime can be passed on to offspring*. Today we know this explanation to be inaccurate, for only those traits coded for by genetic information contained within sex cells (eggs and sperm) can be inherited (see Chapters 3 and 4).

Because Lamarck's explanation of species change was not genetically correct, his theories are frequently derided. But Lamarck actually deserves much credit because he was the first to stress the importance of interactions between organisms and the environment in the evolutionary process. Moreover, Lamarck was one of the first to acknowledge the need for a distinct branch of science that dealt solely with living things (i.e., separate from geology). For this new science, Lamarck coined the term *biology*, and a central feature of this new science was the notion of evolutionary change.

GEORGES CUVIER   The most vehement opponent of Lamarck was a young colleague, Georges Cuvier (1769–1832). Cuvier (fig. 2–6) specialized in vertebrate paleontology, and it was he who introduced the concept of extinction to explain the disappearance of animals represented by fossils. Although a brilliant anatomist, Cuvier never grasped the dynamic concept of nature, and he adamantly insisted on the fixity of species. Just as the abundance of fossils in geological strata was becoming increasingly apparent, it also became more important to explain what they were. But rather than assume that similarities between certain fossil forms and living species indicated evolutionary relationships, Cuvier proposed a variation of a theory known as **catastrophism.**

Catastrophism held that the earth's geological features were the results of sudden, worldwide cataclysmic events, such as the Noah flood. Cuvier's version of catastrophism also postulated a series of regional disasters that destroyed most or all of the local plant and animal life. These areas of destruction were subsequently restocked with new forms that migrated in from neighboring, unaffected regions.

To be consistent with the fossil evidence, Cuvier also proposed that destroyed regions were repopulated by new organisms of a more modern appearance and that these forms were the results of more recent creation events. (The last of these creations is the one depicted in Genesis.) Thus, Cuvier's explanation of increased complexity over time avoided any notion of evolution while still being able to account for the evidence of change as preserved in the fossil record.

CHARLES LYELL   Charles Lyell (1797–1875), the son of Scottish landowners, is considered the founder of modern geology (fig. 2–7). He was a lawyer by training, a geologist by avocation, and for many years Charles Darwin's friend and mentor. Before he met Darwin in 1836, Lyell had earned wide popular acclaim as well as acceptance in Europe's most prestigious scientific circles, thanks to his highly praised *Principles of Geology*, first published in three volumes in 1830–1833.

In this immensely important work, Lyell argued that the geological processes observed in the present are the same as those that occurred in the past. This theory, which has come to be known as **uniformitarianism,** did not originate entirely with Lyell, but had been proposed by James Hutton in the late 1700s. Nevertheless, it was Lyell who demonstrated that such forces as wind, water erosion, local flooding, frost, the decomposition of vegetable matter, volcanoes, earthquakes, and glacial movements all had contributed in the past to

Courtesy, Dept. of Library Services, American Museum of Natural History

figure 2–6 Cuvier explained the fossil record as the result of a succession of catastrophes followed by new creation events.

Catastrophism The view that the earth's geological landscape is the result of violent cataclysmic events. This view was promoted by Cuvier, especially in opposition to Lamarck.

Uniformitarianism The theory that the earth's features are the result of long-term processes that continue to operate in the present as they did in the past. Elaborated on by Lyell, this theory opposed catastrophism and provided for immense geological time.

figure 2–7 Lyell, the father of geology, stated the theory of uniformitarianism in his *Principles of Geology*.

produce the geological landscape that exists in the present. Moreover, the fact that these processes could still be observed in operation indicated that geological change continued to occur and that the forces that drove such change were consistent, or *uniform*, over time. In other words, although various aspects of the earth's surface (e.g., climate, flora, fauna, and land surfaces) are variable through time, the *underlying processes* that influence them are constant.

The theory of uniformitarianism flew in the face of Cuvier's catastrophism and did not go unopposed. Additionally, and every bit as controversially, Lyell emphasized the obvious: namely, that for such slow-acting forces to produce momentous change, the earth must indeed be far older than anyone had previously suspected.

By providing an immense time scale and thereby altering perceptions of earth's history from a few thousand to many millions of years, Lyell changed the framework within which scientists viewed the geological past. Thus, the concept of "deep time" (Gould, 1987) remains one of Lyell's most significant contributions to the discovery of evolutionary principles. The immensity of geological time permitted the necessary time depth for the inherently slow process of evolutionary change.

THOMAS MALTHUS   In 1798, Thomas Robert Malthus (1766–1834), an English clergyman and economist, wrote *An Essay on the Principle of Population*, which inspired both Charles Darwin and Alfred Wallace in their separate discoveries of the principle of natural selection (fig. 2–8). In his essay, Malthus pointed out that if not kept in check by limited food supplies, human populations could double in size every 25 years. That is, population size increases exponentially, while food supplies remain relatively stable.

figure 2–8 Thomas Malthus' *An Essay on the Principle of Population* led both Darwin and Wallace to the principle of natural selection.

Malthus focused on humans because the ability to increase food supplies artificially reduces constraints on population growth, and he was arguing for population control. However, the same logic could be applied to nonhuman organisms. In nature, the tendency for populations to increase is continuously checked by resource availability. Thus, there is constant competition for food and other resources. In time, the extension of Malthus' principles to all organisms would be made by both Darwin and Wallace.

CHARLES DARWIN   Charles Darwin (1809–1882) was one of six children of Dr. Robert and Susanna Darwin (fig. 2–9). Being the grandson of wealthy Josiah Wedgwood (of Wedgwood pottery fame) as well as of Erasmus Darwin, he grew up enjoying the lifestyle of the landed gentry in rural England.

As a boy, Darwin displayed a keen interest in nature and spent his days fishing and collecting shells, birds' eggs, and rocks. However, this developing interest in natural history did not dispel the generally held view of family and friends that he was not in any way remarkable. In fact, his performance at school was no more than ordinary.

After the death of his mother when he was eight, Darwin's upbringing was guided by his rather stern father and his older sisters. Because he showed little interest in, or aptitude for, anything except hunting, shooting, and perhaps science, his father, fearing Charles would sink into dissipation, sent him to Edinburgh University to study medicine. It was in Edinburgh that Darwin first became acquainted with the evolutionary theories of Lamarck and others.

During this time (the 1820s), notions of evolution were becoming much feared in England and elsewhere. Certainly, anything identifiable with post-revolutionary France was viewed with grave suspicion by the established order in England. Lamarck, especially, was vilified by most English academics, the majority of whom were also members of the Anglican clergy.

This was also a time of growing political unrest in Britain. The Reform Movement, which sought to undo many of the wrongs of the class system, was under way and, as with most social movements, this one contained a radical faction. Because many of the radicals were atheists and socialists who also supported Lamarck's evolutionary theory, evolution came to be associated, in the minds of many, with atheism and political subversion. Such was the growing fear of evolutionary ideas that many believed that if it were generally accepted that nature evolved unaided by God, "the Church would crash, the moral fabric of society would be torn apart, and civilized man would return to savagery" (Desmond and Moore, 1991, p. 34). It is unfortunate that some of the most outspoken early proponents of **transmutation** were so vehemently anti-Christian, because their rhetoric helped establish the entrenched suspicion and misunderstanding of evolutionary theory that persists even today.

While at Edinburgh, the young Darwin spent endless hours studying with professors who were outspoken supporters of Lamarck. Darwin's second year in Edinburgh saw him examining museum collections and attending natural history lectures. Therefore, although he hated medicine and left Edinburgh after two years, his experience there was a formative period in his intellectual development.

Subsequently, Darwin took up residence at Christ's College, Cambridge, to study theology. (Although he was rather indifferent to religion, theology was often seen as a last resort by parents who viewed their sons as having no discernible academic leanings.) It was during his Cambridge years that Darwin seriously cultivated his interests in natural science, and he often joined the field excursions of botany classes. He also was immersed in geology and was a frequent and serious participant in geological expeditions.

It was no wonder that following his graduation in 1831 at age 22, he was recommended to accompany a scientific expedition that would circle the globe. Thus it was, after overcoming his father's objections, that Darwin set sail aboard the HMS *Beagle* on December 17, 1831 (fig. 2–10). The famous voyage of the *Beagle* was to last for almost five years and would forever change not only the course of Darwin's life, but also the history of biological science.

Darwin went aboard the *Beagle* believing in fixity of species. But during the voyage, he privately began to have doubts. As early as 1832, for example, he noted in his diary that a snake with rudimentary hind limbs marked "the passage by which Nature joins the lizards to the snakes." He came across fossils of ancient giant animals that looked, except for size, very much like living forms in the same vicinity, and he wondered whether the fossils were the ancestors of the living forms.

During the famous stopover at the Galápagos Islands (see fig. 2–10), Darwin noted that the flora and fauna of South America showed striking similarities to those of the Galápagos, as well as intriguing differences. Even more surprising, the inhabitants of the various islands differed slightly from one another.

figure 2–9 Charles Darwin as a young man.

Transmutation The change of one species to another. The term *evolution* did not assume its current meaning until the late nineteenth century.

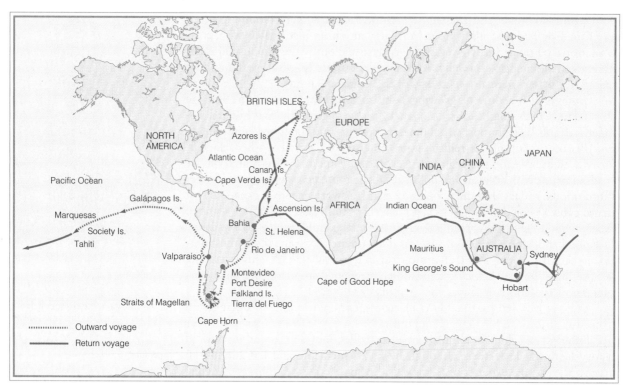

figure 2–10 The route of the HMS *Beagle*.

For example, Darwin collected 13 different varieties of Galápagos finches. These varieties shared many structural similarities, and clearly they represented a closely affiliated group. But at the same time, they differed with regard to certain physical traits, particularly in the shape and size of their beaks (fig. 2–11). Darwin also collected finches from the South American mainland, and these appeared to represent only one group, or species.

The insight that Darwin gained from the finches is legendary. He recognized that the various Galápagos finches had all descended from a common, mainland ancestor and had become modified in response to the varying island habitats and to altered dietary preferences. But actually, it was not until *after* he had returned to England that Darwin recognized the significance of the variation in beak structure. In fact, during the voyage, Darwin had paid little attention to the finches. It was only in retrospect that he considered the factors that could lead to the modification of 1 species into 13 (Gould, 1985; Desmond and Moore, 1991).

Darwin returned to England in October 1836 and almost immediately was accepted into the most eminent of scientific circles. He married his cousin Emma Wedgwood and moved to the village of Down, near London, where he spent the rest of his life writing on topics ranging from fossils to orchids. But his overriding concern was the question of species change.

At Down, Darwin began developing his views on what he termed *natural selection*. This concept was borrowed from animal breeders, who "select" as breeding stock those animals that exhibit specific traits they hope to emphasize in offspring. Animals with undesirable traits are "selected against," or prevented from breeding.

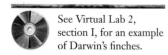

See Virtual Lab 2, section I, for an example of Darwin's finches.

Darwin was keenly interested in domestic animals, pigeons in particular, and how breeders could develop distinctive varieties in just a few generations. (The variations seen in domestic dog breeds may be the best example of the effects of selective breeding; see fig. 2–12.) He applied his knowledge of domesticated species to naturally occurring ones, recognizing that in undomesticated organisms, the selective agent was nature, not humans.

By the late 1830s, Darwin recognized that biological variation within a species was critically important. Furthermore, he acknowledged the importance of sexual reproduction in increasing variation. Then, in 1838, Darwin read Malthus' essay, and in it he found the answer to his question of how new species came to be. He accepted from Malthus that populations increase at a faster rate than do resources, and he inferred that in nonhuman animals, increase in population size is continuously checked by limited food supplies. He also accepted Lyell's observation that in nature there is a constant "struggle for existence." The idea that in each generation more offspring are born than survive to adulthood coupled with the notions of competition for resources and biological diversity were all Darwin needed to develop his theory of natural selection. He wrote: "It at once struck me that under these circumstances favourable variations would tend to be preserved, and unfavourable ones to be destroyed. The result of this would be the formation of a new species" (F. Darwin, 1950, pp. 53–54). Basically, this quotation summarizes the whole of natural selection theory.

Darwin wrote a short summary of his views on natural selection in 1842 and revised it in 1844. The 1844 sketch is similar to the argument he presented

(a) Ground finch
Main food: seeds
Beak: heavy

(b) Tree finch
Main food: leaves, buds, blossoms, fruits
Beak: thick, short

(c) Tree finch (called woodpecker finch)
Main food: insects
Beak: stout, straight

(d) Ground finch (known as warbler finch)
Main food: insects
Beak: slender

figure 2–11 **Beak variation in Darwin's Galápagos finches.**

figure 2–12 All domestic dog breeds share a common ancestor, the wolf. The extreme variation that dog breeds exhibit today has been achieved in a relatively short period of time through artificial selection. In this situation, humans allow only certain dogs to breed because they possess specific characteristics that humans want to emphasize. (We should note that not all traits deemed desirable by human breeders are advantageous to the dogs themselves.)

Wolf: John Giustina/Getty Images   Dogs surrounding wolf: Lynn Kilgore

 See Virtual Lab 2, section I, for an example of artificial selection.

15 years later in *On the Origin of Species*, but in 1844 he did not feel he had sufficient data to support his views, so he continued his research without publishing.

Darwin had another reason for not publishing what he knew would be, to say the least, a highly controversial work. As a member of the established order, he knew that many of his friends and associates were concerned with threats to the status quo, and evolutionary theory was viewed as a serious threat indeed. In addition, Darwin was a man to whom reputation was of paramount importance, and he was tormented by fears of bringing dishonor and public criticism to those he loved. So he hesitated.

ALFRED RUSSEL WALLACE   Unlike Darwin, Alfred Russel Wallace (1823–1913) was born into a family of modest means (fig. 2–13). He went to work at the age of 14 and subsequently moved from one job to the next. He became interested in collecting plants and animals, and in 1848 he joined an expedition to the Amazon, where he acquired firsthand knowledge of natural phenomena. Then, in 1854, he sailed for Southeast Asia and the Malay Peninsula to continue his study and to collect bird and insect specimens.

In 1855, Wallace published a paper suggesting that species were descended from other species and that the appearance of new species was influenced by environmental factors (Trinkaus and Shipman, 1992). The Wallace paper spurred Lyell and others to urge Darwin to publish, but still he hesitated. Wallace and Darwin even corresponded briefly.

Then, in 1858, Wallace sent Darwin another paper titled "On the Tendency of Varieties to Depart Indefinitely from the Original Type." In this paper, Wallace described evolution as a process driven by competition and natural selection. Upon receipt of Wallace's paper, Darwin despaired, fearing that Wallace might be credited for a theory (natural selection) that he himself had formulated. He quickly wrote a paper presenting his ideas, and both the paper by Darwin and the one by Wallace were read before the Linnean Society of London in 1858. Neither author was present. Wallace was not in the country, and Darwin was mourning the very recent death of his young son.

The papers received little notice at the time, but at the urging of Lyell and others, Darwin completed and published his greatest work, *On the Origin of Species*,* in December 1859. Upon publication, the storm broke, and it still has not abated. While there was much praise for the book, the gist of opinion was negative. But scientific views gradually shifted, in part because of Darwin's able friend, Thomas Huxley, who for years wrote and spoke in favor of natural selection. The riddle of species was now explained: Species were mutable, not fixed; and they evolved from other species through the mechanism of natural selection.

Natural Selection

Early in his research, Darwin had realized that selection was the key to evolution. With the help of Malthus' ideas, he saw *how* selection in nature could be explained. In the struggle for existence, those *individuals* with favorable variations would survive and reproduce; those with unfavorable variations would not.

figure 2–13 Alfred Russel Wallace independently uncovered the key to the evolutionary process.

Courtesy, Dept. of Library Services, American Museum of Natural History

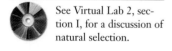

See Virtual Lab 2, section I, for a discussion of natural selection.

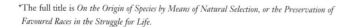

*The full title is *On the Origin of Species by Means of Natural Selection, or the Preservation of Favoured Races in the Struggle for Life.*

For Darwin, the explanation of evolution was simple. The basic processes, as he understood them, are as follows:

1. All species are capable of producing offspring at a faster rate than food supplies increase.
2. There is biological variation within all species; except for identical twins, no two individuals are exactly alike.
3. Because in each generation more individuals are produced than can survive, owing to limited resources, there is competition between individuals. (*Note:* This statement does not imply that there is constant fierce fighting.)
4. Those individuals who possess favorable variations or traits (e.g., speed, disease resistance, protective coloration) have an advantage over individuals that do not possess them. By virtue of the favorable trait, these individuals are more likely to survive to produce offspring than are others.
5. The environmental context determines whether or not a trait is beneficial. That is, what is favorable in one setting may be a liability in another. In this way, which traits become most advantageous is the result of a natural process.
6. Traits are inherited and are passed on to the next generation. Because individuals who possess favorable traits contribute more offspring to the next generation than do others, over time, such traits become more common in the population; less favorable traits are not passed on as frequently and become less common. Those individuals who produce more offspring, compared to others, are said to have greater **reproductive success.**

Reproductive success The number of offspring an individual produces and rears to reproductive age; an individual's genetic contribution to the next generation, as compared to the contributions of other individuals.

7. Over long periods of geological time, successful variations accumulate in a population, so that later generations may be distinct from ancestral ones. Thus, in time, a new species may appear.
8. Geographical isolation may also lead to the formation of new species. As populations of a species become geographically isolated from one another, for whatever reasons, they begin to adapt to different environments. Over time, as populations continue to respond to different **selective pressures** (i.e., different ecological circumstances), they may become distinct species, descended from a common ancestor. The 13 species of Galápagos finches, presumably all descended from a common ancestor on the South American mainland, provide an example of the role of geographical isolation.

Selective pressures Forces in the environment that influence reproductive success in individuals. In the example of the peppered moth, birds applied the selective pressure.

Before Darwin, scientists thought of entire species as entities that could not change. Because *individuals* within the species did not appear to be significant, they were not the object of study; therefore, it was difficult for many scientists to imagine how change could occur. Darwin, as we have pointed out, saw that variation among individuals could explain how selection occurred. Favorable variations were selected for survival by nature; unfavorable ones were eliminated.

This emphasis on the uniqueness of the individual led Darwin to natural selection as the mechanism that made evolution work. *Natural selection operates on individuals*, favorably or unfavorably, but *it is the population that evolves*. The unit of natural selection is the individual; the unit of evolution is the population.

Natural Selection in Action

A well-documented case of natural selection acting in modern populations concerns changes in pigmentation among peppered moths near Manchester, England (fig. 2–14). Before the nineteenth century, the common variety of moth was a mottled gray color. This light, mottled coloration provided extremely effective camouflage against lichen-covered tree trunks. Also present, though less common, was a dark variety of the same species. While resting on light, lichen-covered trees, the dark, uncamouflaged moths were more visible to birds and were therefore eaten more often. (In this example, birds are the *selective agent*, and they apply *selective pressures* on moth populations.) Thus, in the end, the dark moths produced fewer offspring than the light, camouflaged moths. Yet, by the end of the nineteenth century, the common gray form had been almost completely replaced by the black variety.

What had brought about this rapid change was the rapidly changing environment of industrialized nineteenth-century England. Coal dust in the area settled on trees, killing the lichen and turning the bark a dark gray. Moths continued to rest on trees, but the (light) gray variety was increasingly conspicuous as the trees became darker. Consequently, they began to be preyed on more frequently and contributed fewer genes to the next generation. In the late twentieth century, increasing control of pollutants allowed trees to return to their lighter, lichen-covered, preindustrial condition. As would be expected, the black variety of moth is now being supplanted by the gray.

The substance that produces coloration is a pigment called *melanin*, and the evolutionary shift in the peppered moth, as well as in many other moth species, is termed *industrial melanism*. Such an evolutionary shift in response to environmental change is called *adaptation*.

Another example of natural selection is provided by the medium ground finch of the Galápagos Islands. In 1977, drought conditions eliminated many of the plants that produced smaller, softer seeds, compelling a study population on the island of Daphne Major to feed on larger, harder seeds. The population already exhibited some variation in beak size, and during the drought, mortality rates were higher in birds with smaller beaks because they were less able to efficiently process the larger seeds. Consequently, although population size was dramatically reduced, average beak thickness in the survivors and their offspring

figure 2–14 Variation in the peppered moth. (a) The dark form is more visible on the light, lichen-covered tree. (b) On trees darkened by pollution, the lighter form is more visible.

(a)   (b)

was seen to increase, simply because thicker-beaked individuals were contributing more offspring to the next generation (i.e., they had greater reproductive success). But during the rains of the 1982–1983 El Niño event, smaller seeds became more plentiful and the pattern in beak size reversed itself, thus providing a beautiful illustration of how reproductive success is related to environmental conditions (Grant, 1986; Ridley, 1993).

The best illustration of natural selection, however, and certainly the one with potentially grave consequences for humans, in the increase in resistant strains of disease-causing microorganisms. When antibiotic therapy was introduced in the 1940s, it was hailed as the end of bacterial disease, but this notion did not take into account the fact that bacteria, like other organisms, possess genetic variability. Consequently, while exposure to an antibiotic will kill most bacteria in an infected individual, those pathogens with an inherited resistance to that particular therapy will survive and pass on their resistance to the next generation. Moreover, because bacteria produce new generations every few hours, antibiotic-resistant strains are continuously being produced. As a result, many types of infection no longer respond to treatment. For example, tuberculosis was once thought to be well controlled, but it has seen a resurgence in recent years because the bacterium that causes it no longer responds to antibiotic therapy.

These examples provide numerous insights into the mechanisms of evolutionary change produced by natural selection:

1. *A trait must be inherited to have importance in natural selection.* A characteristic that is not hereditary (such as a temporary change in hair pigmentation brought about by dye) will not be passed on to succeeding generations. In moths, pigmentation is a demonstrated hereditary trait.

2. *Natural selection cannot occur without variation in inherited characteristics.* If, for example, all the peppered moths had initially been gray (you will recall that some dark forms were always present) and the trees had become darker, the survival and reproduction of all moths could have been so low that the population might have become extinct. Such an event is not unusual and without variation would nearly always occur. *Selection can work only with variation that already exists.*

3. **Fitness** *is a relative measure that will change as the environment changes.* Fitness is simply differential reproductive success. In the initial stage, the lighter moths were more fit because they produced more offspring. But as the environment changed, the dark gray moths became more fit, and a further change reversed the adaptive pattern. It should be obvious that statements regarding the "most fit" life form mean nothing without reference to specific environments.

Fitness Pertaining to natural selection, a measure of relative reproductive success of individuals. Fitness can be measured by an individual's genetic contribution to the next generation compared to that of other individuals.

The examples discussed so far show how different death rates influence natural selection (e.g., moths that die early tend to leave fewer offspring). But mortality is not the entire picture. Another important aspect of natural selection is fertility, for an animal that gives birth to more young will pass its genes on at a faster rate than one that bears fewer offspring. However, fertility is not the complete picture either, for the crucial element is the number of young raised successfully to the point at which they themselves reproduce. We may state this simply as *differential net reproductive success.* The way this mechanism works can be demonstrated through another example.

In a common variety of small birds called swifts, data show that giving birth to more offspring does not necessarily guarantee that more young will be successfully raised. The number of eggs hatched in a breeding season is a measure of fertility. The number of birds that mature and are eventually able to leave the nest is a measure of net reproductive success, or offspring successfully raised. The following tabulation shows the correlation between the number of eggs hatched (fertility) and the number of young that leave the nest (reproductive success) averaged over four breeding seasons (Lack, 1966):

Number of eggs hatched (fertility)	2 eggs	3 eggs	4 eggs
Average number of young raised (reproductive success)	1.92	2.54	1.76
Sample size (number of nests)	72	20	16

As the tabulation shows, the most efficient fertility number is three eggs, since that number yields the highest reproductive success. Raising two is less beneficial to the parents, since the end result is not as successful as with three eggs. Trying to raise more than three young is actually detrimental, since the parents may not be able to provide adequate nourishment for any of the offspring. An offspring that dies before reaching reproductive age is, in evolutionary terms, equivalent to never having been born in the first place. Actually, such a result may be an evolutionary minus to the parents, for this offspring will drain their resources and may inhibit their ability to raise other offspring, thereby lowering their reproductive success even further. Selection will favor those genetic traits that yield the maximum net reproductive success. If the number of eggs laid* is a genetic trait in birds (and it seems to be), natural selection in swifts should act to favor the laying of three eggs as opposed to two or four.

Constraints on Nineteenth-Century Evolutionary Theory

Darwin argued eloquently for the notion of evolution in general and the role of natural selection in particular, but he did not entirely comprehend the exact mechanisms of evolutionary change.

As we have seen, natural selection acts on *existing variation* within species. Neither Darwin nor anyone else in the nineteenth century understood the source of all this variation. Consequently, Darwin speculated about variation arising from "use"—an idea similar to Lamarck's. Darwin, however, was not as dogmatic in his views as Lamarck and most emphatically argued against inner "needs" or "effort." Darwin had to confess that when it came to explaining variation, he simply did not know: "Our ignorance of the laws of variation is profound. Not in one case out of a hundred can we pretend to assign any reason why this or that part differs, more or less, from the same part in the parents" (Darwin, 1859, pp. 167–168).

---

*The number of eggs hatched is directly related to the number of eggs laid.

In addition to his inability to explain the origins of variation, Darwin also did not completely understand the mechanism by which parents transmitted traits to offspring. Almost without exception, nineteenth-century scholars were confused about the laws of heredity, and the popular consensus was that inheritance was *blending* by nature. In other words, offspring were expected to express intermediate traits as a result of a blending of their parents' contributions. Without any viable alternatives, Darwin accepted this popular misconception. As it turned out, a contemporary of Darwin's had systematically worked out the rules of heredity. However, the work of this Augustinian monk, Gregor Mendel (whom you will meet in Chapter 4), was not recognized until the beginning of the twentieth century.

Opposition to Evolution

As you have seen, the publication of *On the Origin of Species* fanned the flames of controversy over evolution into an inferno. Not only was the idea that species could give rise to other species offensive to many Christians but, people were horrified at the notion that humans might be biologically related to other animals and especially that they might share a common ancestor with the great apes. Even to make such a claim was degrading, for it denied humanity its unique and exalted place in the universe; in the minds of many, it denied the very existence of God.

The debate has not ended even now, almost 150 years later. For the majority of scientists today, evolution is fact. Indeed, the genetic evidence for it is indisputable, and anyone who appreciates and understands genetic mechanisms cannot avoid the conclusion that populations and species evolve. Moreover, the majority of Christians do not believe that biblical depictions are to be taken literally. But at the same time, surveys show that almost half of all Americans believe that evolution does not occur. There are a number of reasons for this.

The mechanisms of evolution are complex and do not lend themselves to simple explanations. To understand these mechanisms requires some familiarity with genetics and biology, a familiarity that most people do not possess. Moreover, people who have not been exposed to scientific training want definitive answers to complicated questions. But, as you learned in Chapter 1, science does not prove truths, and it frequently does not provide definitive answers.

Another fact to consider is that while all religions offer explanations for natural phenomena, and some even feature the transformation of individuals from one form to another, none really proposes biological change over time. Most people, regardless of their culture, are raised in belief systems that do not emphasize biological continuity between species or offer scientific explanations for natural phenomena.

The relationship between science and religion has never been easy. While both serve, in their own ways, to explain phenomena, scientific explanations are based in data analysis and interpretation. Religion, meanwhile, is a system of beliefs not amenable to scientific testing and falsification; it is based in faith. Religion and science concern different aspects of the human experience, and although they use different approaches in areas where they overlap, they are not inherently mutually exclusive. In fact, many people see them as two sides of the same coin. Moreover, evolutionary theories are not considered anathema by all religions (or even by all forms of Christianity). Some years ago, the Vatican hosted an international conference on human evolution, and in 1996, Pope John Paul II issued a statement to the Pontifical Academy of Sciences acknowledging that "fresh knowledge leads to recognition of the theory of evolution as more than just a hypothesis." Today, the official position of the Catholic Church is that evolutionary processes do occur but that the human soul is of divine creation and not subject to evolutionary processes. Likewise, mainstream Protestants do not generally see a conflict. Unfortunately, those who believe in a literal interpretation of the Bible (termed fundamentalists) do not accept any form of compromise.

Reacting to rapid cultural changes after World War I, conservative Christians in the United States sought a revival of what they considered traditional values. In their view, one way to do this was to prevent any mention of Darwinism in public schools. The Butler Act, passed in Tennessee in 1925, was one result of this effort, and it banned the teaching of evolution in public schools in that state. To test the validity of the law, the American Civil Liberties Union persuaded John Scopes, a high school teacher, to be arrested and ultimately tried for teaching evolution.

The subsequent trial was the famous Scopes Monkey Trial, in which the well-known orator William Jennings Bryan was the prosecuting attorney. The lawyer for the defense was Clarence Darrow, a nationally known labor and criminal lawyer. The trial ended with the conviction of Scopes, who was fined $100. The case was appealed to the Tennessee Supreme Court, which upheld the law, and the teaching of evolution remained illegal in Tennessee. Eventually, several other states, mostly in the South, passed similar laws, and it was not until 1967 that the last two states (Tennessee and Arkansas) ceased to prohibit the teaching of evolution.

But the story does not end there. In the more than 75 years since the Scopes trial, religious fundamentalists have persisted in their attempts to remove evolution from public school curricula. Known as creationists because they explain the existence of the universe as a result of a sudden creation, they are determined either to eliminate the teaching of evolution or to introduce antievolutionary material into public school classes. In the past 20 years, creationists have insisted that "creation science" is just as valid a scientific endeavor as is the study of evolution. They argue that in the interest of fairness, a balanced view should be offered: If evolution is taught as science, then creationism should also be taught as science. But "creation science" is, by definition, not science at all. Creationists assert that their view is absolute and infallible. Consequently, creationism is not a hypothesis that can be tested, nor is it amenable to falsification. Because such testing is the basis of all science, creationism, by its very nature, cannot be considered science. It is religion.

Still, creationists have been active in state legislatures, promoting the passage of laws mandating the inclusion of creationism in school curricula. To this effect, the Arkansas state legislature passed Act 590 in 1981. But this law was challenged and overturned in 1982. Judge William Ray Overton, in his ruling against the state, found that "a theory that is by its own terms dogmatic, absolutist and never subject to revision is not a scientific theory." And he added: "Since creation is not science, the conclusion is inescapable that the only real effect of Act 590 is the advancement of religion." In 1987, the United States Supreme Court struck down a similar law in Louisiana.

So far, these and related laws have been overturned because they violate the principle of separation of church and state provided in the First Amendment to the Constitution. But this has not stopped the creationists, who have encouraged teachers to claim "academic freedom" to teach creationism. Also, they have dropped the term *creationism* in favor of less religious sounding terms, such as *intelligent design theory*. And as recently as August 1999, the Kansas state legislature adopted a policy that, had it not been overturned, could have eliminated evolution from standardized public school curricula. Moreover, antievolution feeling remains strong among politicians. In 1999, one very prominent U.S. congressman went so far as to say that the teaching of evolution is one of the factors behind violence in America today!

Although the courts have consistently ruled against the creationists, these religious fundamentalists have nevertheless had an impact on the teaching of evolution. Many public school teachers, seeking to avoid controversy, simply do not cover evolution, or they refer to it as "just a theory" (see p. 14). Thus, students may not be exposed to evolutionary principles until they go to college—and only then if they take related courses. This consequence is ultimately to the detriment of the biological sciences (and education in general) in the United States.

Summary

ur current understanding of evolutionary processes is directly traceable to developments in intellectual thought in western Europe over the last 300 years. In particular, the contributions of Linnaeus, Lamarck, Buffon, Lyell, and Malthus all had a significant impact on Darwin. The year 1859 marks a watershed in evolutionary theory, for in that year, the publication of Darwin's *On the Origin of Species* crystallized the understanding of the evolutionary process (particularly the crucial role of natural selection) and for the first time thrust evolutionary theory into the consciousness of the general public. Debates both inside and outside the sciences continued for several decades (and in some quarters persist today), but the theory of evolution irrevocably changed the tide of intellectual thought. Gradually, Darwin's formulation of the evolutionary process became accepted almost universally by scientists as the very foundation of all the biological sciences, physical anthropology included. As we begin the twenty-first century, contributions from genetics allow us to demonstrate the mechanics of evolution in a way unknown to Darwin and his contemporaries.

Natural selection is the central determining factor influencing the long-term direction of evolutionary change. How natural selection works can best be explained as differential reproductive success—in other words, how successful individuals are in leaving offspring to succeeding generations.

Questions for Review

1. Trace the history of intellectual thought immediately leading to Darwin's theory.
2. What is fixity of species? Why did it pose a problem for the development of evolutionary thinking?
3. What was John Ray's major contribution to biology and the development of evolutionary theories?
4. In what ways did Linnaeus and Buffon differ in their approach to the concept of evolution?
5. What are the bases of Lamarck's theory of acquired characteristics? Why is this theory incorrect?
6. What was Lamarck's positive contribution to nineteenth-century evolutionary ideas?
7. Explain Cuvier's notion of catastrophism.
8. What did Malthus and Lyell contribute to Darwin's thinking on evolution?
9. Darwin approached the subject of species change by emphasizing individuals within populations. Why was this significant to the development of the concept of natural selection?
10. What evidence did Darwin use to strengthen his argument concerning evolution?
11. How did Darwin's explanation of evolution differ from Lamarck's?
12. What is meant by adaptation? Illustrate through the example of industrial melanism.
13. Define natural selection. What is a selective agent? Give an example.
14. Explain why the changes in populations of peppered moths and in some bird species serve as good examples of natural selection.
15. Explain why some people are opposed to the teaching of evolutionary principles.

Suggested Further Readings

Burke, James. 1985. *The Day the Universe Changed*. Boston: Little, Brown.

Desmond, Adrian, and James Moore. 1991. *Darwin*. New York: Warner Books.

Gould, Stephen Jay. 1987. *Time's Arrow, Time's Cycle*. Cambridge, MA: Harvard University Press.

Grant, P. R. 1991. "Natural Selection in Darwin's finches." *Scientific American* 265(4): 82–87.

Mayr, Ernst. 2000. "Darwin's Influence on Modern Thought." *Scientific American* 283(1): 78–83.

Ridley, Mark. 1993. *Evolution*. Boston: Blackwell Scientific Publications.

Scott, Eugenie C. 1997. "Antievolutionism and Creationism in the United States." *Annual Review of Anthropology* 2: 263–289.

Trinkaus, Eric, and Pat Shipman. 1993. *The Neandertals*. New York: Knopf.

Young, David. 1992. *The Discovery of Evolution*. London: Natural History Museum Publications, Cambridge University Press.

Multimedia Resources

 Companion Web Site

Anthropology Online: The Wadsworth Anthropology Resource Center
Visit **http://anthropology.wadsworth.com** and click on the Companion Web
Site for Jurmain/Kilgore/Trevathan/Nelson's *Essentials of Physical Anthropology*,
Fifth Edition, to access a wide range of enrichment material to aid in your study of
anthropology. Among the useful options for each chapter's self-study are learning
objectives, flashcards, Internet exercises, Web links, InfoTrac College Edition exercises, and practice quizzes that can be scored and emailed to your instructor.

THE BIOLOGICAL BASIS OF LIFE

CONTENTS

See the following sections of the CD-ROM for topics covered in this chapter: Virtual Lab 2, section II.

Introduction

A s you learned in the preceding two chapters, this text is about human evolution and adaptation, both of which are intimately linked to life processes that involve cells, the replication and decoding of genetic information, and the transmission of this information between generations. Thus, to present human evolution and adaptation in the broad sense, we must first examine how life is organized at the cellular and molecular levels, and this, in turn, necessitates a brief discussion of the fundamental principles of *genetics*.

Genetics is the study of the biological mechanisms that guide cellular and physiological functions; the methods by which traits are transmitted from one generation to the next; and ultimately it is genetics that links or influences many of the various subdisciplines of biological anthropology.

The discipline of genetics is largely a twentieth-century development, and much of our present knowledge has been acquired within the last 50 years. Today, insights into the numerous aspects of inheritance are increasing at an exponential rate, with new discoveries being made every day. Moreover, as genetic technologies develop and increasingly come into use, they assume an ever greater role in the lives of us all.

It is therefore more important than ever that, as people living at the beginning of the twenty-first century, we achieve a basic understanding of the factors that influence our lives. Also, from an anthropological perspective, it is only through the further elucidation of genetic principles that we can hope to understand fully the evolutionary mechanisms that have permitted humans to become the species we are today.

The Cell

To discuss genetic and evolutionary principles, we must first have a fundamental understanding of cell function. Cells are the basic units of life in all living organisms. In some forms, such as bacteria, a single cell constitutes the entire organism. However, more complex *multicellular* forms, such as plants, insects, birds, and mammals, are composed of billions of cells, all functioning in complex ways that ultimately promote the survival of the individual.

Life on earth can be traced back at least 3.7 billion years, in the form of *prokaryotic* cells. Prokaryotes are single-celled organisms, represented today by bacteria and blue-green algae. Structurally more complex cells appeared approximately 1.2 billion years ago, and these are referred to as *eukaryotic* cells. Because eukaryotic cells are found in all multicellular organisms, they are the focus of the remainder of this discussion. In spite of the numerous differences between various life forms and the cells that constitute them, it is important to understand that the cells of all living organisms share many similarities as a result of their common evolutionary past.

In general, a eukaryotic cell is a three-dimensional entity composed of *carbohydrates, lipids (fats), nucleic acids*, and *proteins*. It contains a variety of structures called *organelles* within the *cell membrane* (fig. 3–1). One of these organelles is the **nucleus** (*pl.*, nuclei), a discrete unit surrounded by a thin nuclear membrane.

Nucleus A structure (organelle) found in all eukaryotic cells. The nucleus contains chromosomes (nuclear DNA).

figure 3–1 Structure of a generalized eukaryotic cell, illustrating the cell's three-dimensional nature. Although various organelles are shown, for the sake of simplicity only those we discuss here are labeled.

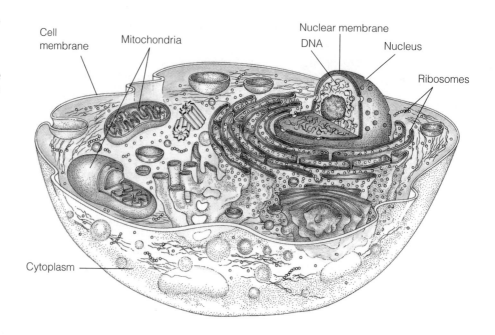

Cell membrane

Mitochondria

Nuclear membrane

DNA

Nucleus

Ribosomes

Cytoplasm

Molecules Structures made up of two or more atoms. Molecules can combine with other molecules to form more complex structures.

Deoxyribonucleic acid (DNA) The double-stranded molecule that contains the genetic code. DNA is a main component of chromosomes.

Ribonucleic acid (RNA) A single-stranded molecule, similar in structure to DNA. The three forms of RNA are essential to protein synthesis.

Cytoplasm The portion of the cell contained within the cell membrane, excluding the nucleus. The cytoplasm consists of a semifluid material and contains numerous structures involved with cell function.

Proteins Three-dimensional molecules that serve a wide variety of functions through their ability to bind to other molecules.

Protein synthesis The assembly of chains of amino acids into functional protein molecules. The process is directed by DNA.

Mitochondria (*sing.*, mitochondrion) Structures contained within the cytoplasm of eukaryotic cells that convert energy, derived from nutrients, into a form that is used by the cell.

Ribosomes Structures composed of a specialized form of RNA and protein. Ribosomes are found in the cell's cytoplasm and are essential to the manufacture of proteins.

Somatic cells Basically, all the cells in the body except those involved with reproduction.

Gametes Reproductive cells (eggs and sperm in animals) developed from precursor cells in ovaries and testes.

Zygote A cell formed by the union of an egg and a sperm cell. It contains the full complement of chromosomes (in humans, 46) and has the potential of developing into an entire organism.

Within the nucleus are two nucleic acids that contain the genetic information that controls the cell's functions. These two critically important **molecules** are **deoxyribonucleic acid (DNA)** and **ribonucleic acid (RNA).** (In prokaryotic cells, genetic information is not contained within a walled nucleus.) Surrounding the nucleus is the **cytoplasm,** which contains numerous other types of organelles involved in various activities, such as breaking down nutrients and converting them to other substances (*metabolism*), storing and releasing energy, eliminating waste, and manufacturing **proteins (protein synthesis).**

Two of these organelles—**mitochondria** and **ribosomes**—require further mention. The mitochondria (*sing.*, mitochondrion) are responsible for energy production in the cell and are thus the "engines" that drive the cell. Mitochondria are round or oval structures enclosed within a folded membrane, and they contain their own distinct DNA, called mitochondrial DNA (mtDNA), which directs mitochondrial activities. Mitochondrial DNA has the same molecular structure and function as nuclear DNA, but it is organized somewhat differently. In recent years, mtDNA has attracted much attention because of particular traits it influences and because it has significance for studies of certain evolutionary processes. See Chapters 4 and 11. Ribosomes are roughly spherical in shape and are the most common type of cytoplasmic organelle. They are made up partly of RNA and are essential to the synthesis of proteins (see p. 48).

There are basically two types of cells: **somatic cells** and **gametes.** Somatic cells are the cellular components of body tissues, such as muscle, bone, skin, nerve, heart, and brain. Gametes, or sex cells, are specifically involved in reproduction and are not important as structural components of the body. There are two types of gametes: *ova* (*sing.*, ovum), or egg cells, produced in the ovaries in females; and *sperm* cells, which develop in male testes. The sole function of a sex cell is to unite with a gamete from another individual to form a **zygote,** which has the potential of developing into a new individual. In this way, gametes transmit genetic information from parent to offspring.

DNA Structure

See Virtual Lab 2, section II, for discussions of DNA structure and replication.

As already mentioned, cellular functions are directed by DNA. If we are to understand these functions and how characteristics are inherited, we must first know something about the structure and function of DNA.

The exact physical and chemical properties of DNA were unknown until 1953, when at Cambridge University, an American researcher named James Watson and three British scientists—Francis Crick, Maurice Wilkins, and Rosalind Franklin—developed a structural and functional model of DNA (Watson and Crick, 1953a, 1953b). The importance of their achievement cannot be overstated, for it completely revolutionized the fields of biology and medicine and forever altered our understanding of biological and evolutionary mechanisms.

The DNA molecule is composed of two chains of even smaller molecules called **nucleotides.** A nucleotide, in turn, is made up of three components: a sugar molecule (deoxyribose), a phosphate unit, and one of four nitrogenous bases (fig. 3–2). In DNA, nucleotides are stacked upon one another to form a chain that is bonded along its bases to another **complementary** nucleotide chain. Together the two twist to form a spiral, or helical, shape. The resulting DNA molecule, then, is two-stranded and is described as forming a *double helix* that resembles a twisted ladder. If we follow the twisted ladder analogy, the

Nucleotides Basic units of the DNA molecule, composed of a sugar, a phosphate, and one of four DNA bases.

Complementary Referring to the fact that DNA bases form base pairs in a precise manner. For example, adenine can bond only to thymine. Thus, these two bases are said to be *complementary* because one requires the other to form a complete DNA base pair.

figure 3–2 Part of a DNA molecule. The illustration shows the two DNA strands with the sugar and phosphate backbone and the bases extending toward the center.

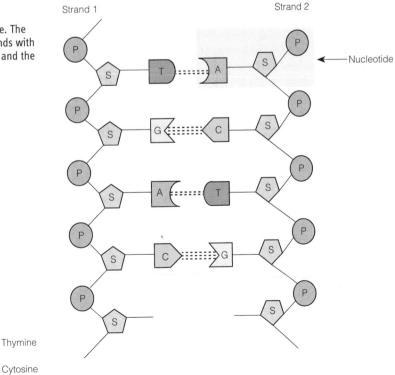

sugars and phosphates represent the two sides, while the bases and the bonds that join them form the rungs.

The secret of how DNA functions lies within the four bases. These bases are *adenine, guanine, thymine,* and *cytosine,* and they are frequently referred to by their initial letters, A, G, T, and C. In the formation of the double helix, it is possible for one type of base to pair, or bond, with only one other type: Base pairs can form *only* between adenine and thymine and between guanine and cytosine (see fig. 3–2). This specificity is essential to the DNA molecule's ability to **replicate,** or make an exact copy of itself.

Replicate To duplicate. The DNA molecule is able to make copies of itself.

DNA Replication

Growth and development of organisms and tissue repair following injury or disease are among the crucial processes made possible by cell division. Cells multiply by dividing in such a way that each new cell receives a full complement of genetic material. This is a crucial point, since a cell cannot function properly without the appropriate amount of DNA. For new cells to receive the essential amount of DNA, it is first necessary for the DNA to replicate.

Prior to cell division, specific **enzymes** break the bonds between bases simultaneously at numerous locations in the DNA molecule, leaving the two previously joined strands of nucleotides with their bases exposed (fig. 3–3). The exposed bases then attract unattached DNA nucleotides, which are already present in the cell nucleus. Because one base can be joined to only one other, the attraction between bases occurs in a complementary fashion. Thus, the two previously joined parental nucleotide chains serve as models for the formation of new strands of nucleotides. As each new strand is formed, its bases are joined to the bases of an original strand. When the process is completed, there are two double-stranded DNA molecules exactly like the original one, and each newly formed molecule consists of one original nucleotide chain joined to a newly formed chain (see fig. 3–3).

Enzymes Specialized proteins that initiate and direct chemical reactions in the body.

See Virtual Lab 2, section II, for an example of protein synthesis.

Protein Synthesis

One of the most important functions of DNA is that it directs protein synthesis within the cell. Proteins are complex, three-dimensional molecules that function through their ability to bind to other molecules. For example, the protein **hemoglobin,** found in red blood cells, is able to bind to oxygen and serves to transport oxygen to cells throughout the body.

Proteins function in myriad ways. Some are structural components of tissues. Collagen, for example, is the most common protein in the body and is a major component of all connective tissues. Enzymes are also proteins, and their function is to initiate and enhance chemical reactions. An example of a digestive enzyme is *lactase,* which breaks down *lactose,* or milk sugar, into two simpler sugars. Another class of proteins includes many types of **hormones.** Specialized cells produce and release hormones into the bloodstream to circulate to other areas of the body, where they produce specific effects in tissues and organs. A

Hemoglobin A protein molecule that occurs in red blood cells and binds to oxygen molecules.

Hormones Substances (usually proteins) that are produced by specialized cells and that travel to other parts of the body, where they influence chemical reactions and regulate various cellular functions.

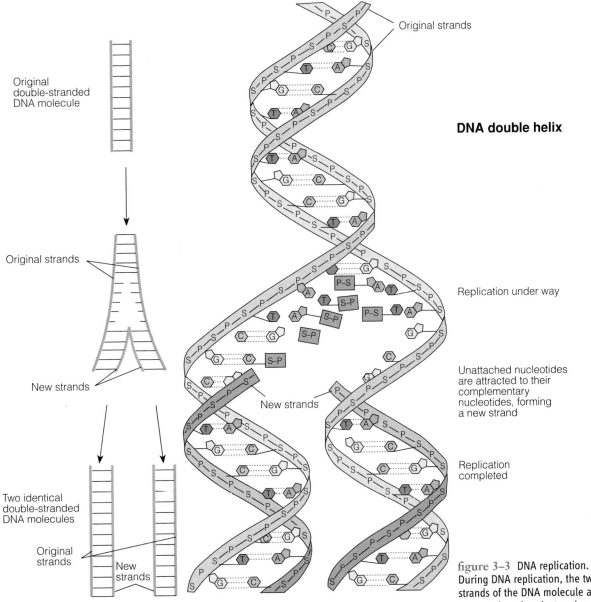

Original
double-stranded
DNA molecule

Original strands

New strands

Two identical
double-stranded
DNA molecules

Original
strands

New
strands

DNA double helix

Original strands

Replication under way

Unattached nucleotides
are attracted to their
complementary
nucleotides, forming
a new strand

New strands

Replication
completed

figure 3–3 DNA replication.
During DNA replication, the two
strands of the DNA molecule are
separated, and each strand serves
as a template for the formation
of a new strand. When replication
is complete, there are two DNA
molecules. Each molecule consists
of one new and one original
DNA strand.

Amino acids Small molecules that
are the components of proteins.

good example of this type of protein is *insulin,* produced by cells in the pancreas.
Insulin causes cells in the liver and certain types of muscle tissue to absorb essential energy-producing glucose (sugar) from the blood. (Enzymes and hormones
will be discussed in more detail in Chapter 13.) As you can see, proteins make
us what we are. Therefore, it is critical that protein synthesis occur accurately,
for if it does not, physiological processes can be disrupted or even prevented.

Proteins are composed of chains of smaller molecules called **amino acids.**
In all, there are 20 amino acids, 8 of which must be obtained from dietary
sources. The remaining 12 are produced in cells. These 20 amino acids are
combined in different amounts and sequences to produce potentially millions of
proteins. What makes proteins different from one another is the number of

amino acids involved and the *sequence* in which they are arranged. For a protein to function properly, its amino acids must be arranged in the proper sequence.

DNA serves as a recipe for making a protein, because it is the sequence of DNA bases that ultimately determines the order of amino acids in a protein molecule. In the DNA instructions, a *triplet*, or group of three bases, specifies a particular amino acid. For example, if a triplet consists of the base sequence cytosine, guanine, and adenine (CGA), it specifies the amino acid *alanine*. If the next triplet in the chain consists of the sequence guanine, thymine, and cytosine (GTC), it refers to another amino acid—*glutamine*. Therefore, a DNA recipe might look like this: AGA CGA ACA ACC TAC TTT TTC CTT AAG GTC, and so on (Table 3–1).

Protein synthesis is a little more complicated than the preceding few sentences would imply. For one thing, protein synthesis occurs outside the nucleus at specialized structures in the cytoplasm called *ribosomes* (see p. 46). A logistics problem arises because the DNA molecule is not capable of traveling outside the cell's nucleus. So the first step in protein synthesis is to copy the DNA message into a form that can pass through the nuclear membrane into the cytoplasm. This process is accomplished through the formation of a molecule similar to DNA called ribonucleic acid, or RNA. RNA is different from DNA in three important ways:

1. It is single-stranded.
2. It contains a different type of sugar.
3. It contains the base uracil as a substitute for the DNA base thymine. (Uracil is attracted to adenine, just as thymine is.)

TABLE 3-1   The Genetic Code

Amino Acid Symbol	Amino Acid	mRNA Codon	DNA Triplet
Ala	Alanine	GCU, GCC, GCA, GCG	CGA, CGG, CGT, CGC
Arg	Arginine	CGU, CGC, CGA, CGG, AGA, AGG	GCA, GCG, GCT, GCC, TCT, TCC
Asn	Asparagine	AAU, AAC	TTA, TTG
Asp	Aspartic acid	GAU, GAC	CTA, CTG
Cys	Cysteine	UGU, UGC	ACA, ACG
Gln	Glutamine	CAA, CAG	GTT, GTC
Glu	Glutamic acid	GAA, GAG	CTT, CTC
Gly	Glycine	GGU, GGC, GGA, GGG	CCA, CCG, CCT, CCC
His	Histidine	CAU, CAC	GTA, GTG
Ile	Isoleucine	AUU, AUC, AUA	TAA, TAG, TAT
Leu	Leucine	UUA, UUG, CUU, CUC, CUA, CUG	AAT, AAC, GAA, GAG, GAT, GAC
Lys	Lysine	AAA, AAG	TTT, TTC
Met	Methionine	AUG	TAC
Phe	Phenylalanine	UUU, UUC	AAA, AAG
Pro	Proline	CCU, CCC, CCA, CCG	GGA, GGG, GGT, GGC
Ser	Serine	UCU, UCC, UCA, UCG, AGU, AGC	AGA, AGG, AGT, AGC, TCA, TCG
Thr	Threonine	ACU, ACC, ACA, ACG	TGA, TGG, TGT, TGC
Trp	Tryptophan	UGG	ACC
Tyr	Tyrosine	UAU, UAC	ATA, ATG
Val	Valine	GUU, GUC, GUA, GUG	CAA, CAG, CAT, CAC
Terminating triplets		UAA, UAG, UGA	ATT, ATC, ACT

The RNA molecule forms on the DNA template in much the same manner as new DNA molecules are assembled. As in DNA replication, the two DNA strands separate, but only partially, and one of these strands attracts free-floating RNA nucleotides (also produced in the cell), which are joined together on the DNA template. This new RNA nucleotide chain is called **messenger RNA (mRNA),** and its formation is called *transcription* because, in fact, it is transcribing, or copying, the DNA code (fig. 3–4). Once the appropriate DNA segment has been copied, the mRNA strand peels away from the DNA model and a portion of it travels through the nuclear membrane to the ribosome. Meanwhile, the bonds between the DNA bases are reestablished, and the DNA molecule is once more intact.

As the mRNA strand arrives at the ribosome, the message it contains is translated. (This stage of the process is called *translation* because at this point, the genetic instructions are actually being decoded and implemented.) Just as each DNA triplet specifies one amino acid, mRNA triplets, called **codons,** also serve this function. Therefore, the mRNA strand is "read" in codons, or groups of three bases taken together (see Table 3–1).

One other form of RNA, **transfer RNA (tRNA),** is essential to the actual assembly of a protein. Each molecule of tRNA has the ability to bind to one specific amino acid. A particular tRNA molecule carrying the amino acid matching the mRNA codon being translated arrives at the ribosome and deposits its amino acid (fig. 3–5). As a second amino acid is deposited, the two are joined in the order dictated by the sequence of mRNA codons. In this way, series of amino acids are linked together to form a structure that will eventually function as a protein.

The entire sequence of DNA bases responsible for the manufacture of a protein or, in some cases a portion of a protein, is referred to as a **gene.** Or, put another way, a gene is a segment of DNA that specifies the sequence of amino acids in a particular protein. A gene may comprise only a few hundred bases, or it may be composed of thousands. If the sequence of DNA bases is altered through **mutation** (a change in the DNA), the manufacture of some proteins may not occur, and the cell (or indeed the organism) may not function properly (if it functions at all).

This definition of a gene is a functional one and is technically correct. But it is important to understand that gene action is an incredibly complex phenomenon that is only partly understood. For example, the DNA segments that are transcribed into mRNA and therefore code for specific amino acids are termed *exons.* But the vast majority of nucleotide sequences in a gene are not expressed during protein synthesis. In

Messenger RNA (mRNA) A form of RNA that is assembled on a sequence of DNA bases. It carries the DNA code to the ribosome during protein synthesis.

Codons The triplets of messenger RNA bases that correspond to specific amino acids during protein synthesis.

Transfer RNA (tRNA) The type of RNA that binds to specific amino acids and transports them to the ribosome during protein synthesis.

Gene A sequence of DNA bases that specifies the order of amino acids in an entire protein or, in some cases, a portion of a protein. A gene may be made up of hundreds or thousands of DNA bases.

Mutation A change in DNA. Technically, mutation refers to changes in DNA bases (specifically called point mutations); also refers to changes in chromosome number and/or structure.

figure 3–4 Transcription. The two DNA strands have partly separated. Free messenger RNA (mRNA) nucleotides have been drawn to the template strand, and a strand of mRNA is being made. Note that the mRNA strand will exactly complement the DNA template strand except that uracil (U) replaces thymine (T).

DNA template strand

mRNA

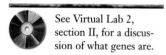

See Virtual Lab 2, section II, for a discussion of what genes are.

figure 3–5 Assembly of an amino acid chain in protein synthesis.

(a)
As the ribosome binds to the mRNA, tRNA brings a particular amino acid, specified by the mRNA codon, to the ribosome.

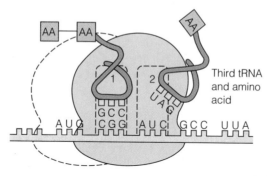

(b)
The tRNA binds to the first codon while a second tRNA–amino acid complex arrives at the ribosome.

(c)
The ribosome moves down the mRNA, allowing a third amino acid to be brought into position by another tRNA molecule. Note that the first two amino acids are now joined together.

fact, some sequences, called *introns*, are initially transcribed but subsequently eliminated before an amino acid sequence is assembled. But while introns are not instrumental in protein synthesis, they are indeed a part of the DNA molecule, and it is the combination of introns and exons, interspersed along a strand of DNA, that comprises the unit we call a gene. In addition to introns, there are other noncoding segments of DNA not included in genes. In fact only about 2 percent of human DNA is actually involved in protein synthesis! (Makalowski, 2000).

Although we usually think of genes as coding for the production of structural proteins, some genes function primarily to control the expression of other genes. Basically, these *regulatory genes* produce enzymes and other proteins that either switch on or turn off other segments of DNA. Consequently, this mechanism is critical for individual organisms and also has important evolutionary implications.

All somatic cells contain the same genetic information, but in any given cell, only a fraction of the DNA contained within exons is actually involved in protein synthesis. For example, bone cells carry the same DNA that codes for the production of digestive enzymes, as do the cells of the stomach lining. But bone cells do not produce digestive enzymes. Instead, they manufacture collagen, the major organic component of bone. Bone cells produce collagen and not digestive enzymes because of the differentiation of cell lines early in embryonic development. During this process, cells undergo changes in form, their functions become specialized, and most of their DNA is permanently deactivated through the action of regulatory genes. In other words, they become specific types of cells.

On a larger scale, alterations in the behavior of regulatory genes that influence the activities of the structural genes involved in growth and development may be responsible for some of the physical differences between closely related species. For example, some of the anatomical differences between humans and chimpanzees, who share about 98 percent of their DNA, may be the results of evolutionary changes in regulatory genes in one or both lineages.

A final point is that the genetic code is *universal;* that is, DNA is the genetic material in all forms of life (at least on earth). This means that the DNA of all organisms, from bacteria to oak trees to human beings, is composed of the same molecules using the same kinds of instructions. These similarities imply biological relationships among, and ultimately a common ancestry for, all forms of life. What makes oak trees distinct from humans is not differences in the basic DNA material, but differences in how that material is arranged.

Cell Division: Mitosis and Meiosis

Throughout much of a cell's life, its DNA exists as an uncoiled, threadlike substance. (Incredibly, there are an estimated 6 feet of DNA in the nucleus of every one of your somatic cells!) However, at various times in the life of most types of cells, normal functions are interrupted and the cell divides. Cell division is the process that results in the production of new cells, and it is during this process that the DNA becomes tightly coiled and is visible under a light microscope as a set of discrete structures called **chromosomes** (fig. 3–6).

A chromosome is composed of a DNA molecule and associated proteins (fig. 3–7). During normal cell function, if chromosomes were visible, they would appear as single-stranded structures. However, during the early stages of cell division, they are made up of two strands, or two DNA molecules, joined together at a constricted area called the **centromere.** There are two strands simply because the DNA molecules have *replicated.* Therefore, one strand of a chromosome is an exact copy of the other.

Every species is characterized by a specific number of chromosomes in somatic cells. In humans there are 46. Chimpanzees and gorillas possess 48. This difference in chromosome number does not necessarily indicate that humans possess less DNA than chimpanzees and gorillas. The DNA is simply packaged differently in the three species. Chromosomes occur in pairs. Thus, human somatic cells contain 23 pairs. One member of each pair is inherited from the father (paternal), while the other member is inherited from the mother

Chromosomes Discrete structures composed of DNA and protein found only in the nuclei of cells. Chromosomes are visible only under magnification during certain stages of cell division.

Centromere The constricted portion of a chromosome. After replication, the two strands of a double-stranded chromosome are joined at the centromere.

figure 3–6 Scanning electron micrograph of human chromosomes during cell division. Note that these chromosomes are composed of two strands, or two DNA molecules.

Centromere

Biophoto Associates/Science Source/Photo Researchers

Homologous Referring to members of chromosome pairs. Homologous chromosomes carry genes that govern the same traits. During meiosis, homologous chromosomes pair and exchange segments of DNA. They are alike with regard to size and also position of the centromere.

Autosomes All chromosomes except the sex chromosomes.

Sex chromosomes In mammals, the X and Y chromosomes.

(maternal). Members of chromosomal pairs are said to be **homologous** in that they are alike in size and position of the centromere and they carry genetic information influencing the same traits (e.g., ABO blood type). This does not imply that partner (homologous) chromosomes are genetically identical; it simply means that the traits they govern are the same. (This topic will be discussed in more detail in Chapter 4.)

There are two basic types of chromosomes: **autosomes** and **sex chromosomes.** Autosomes carry genetic information that governs all physical characteristics except primary sex determination. The two sex chromosomes are the X and Y chromosomes. The Y chromosome carries genes that are directly involved with determining maleness. The X chromosome, although termed a "sex chromosome," is larger and functions more like an autosome in that it is not actually involved in primary sex determination but does influence a number of other traits.

Among mammals, all genetically normal females have two X chromosomes (XX); they are female simply because the Y chromosome is not present. All genetically normal males have one X and one Y chromosome (XY). In other classes of animals, such as birds or insects, primary sex determination is governed by differing mechanisms.

It is extremely important to remember that *all* autosomes occur in pairs. Normal human somatic cells have 22 pairs of autosomes and one pair of sex chromosomes. It should also be noted that abnormal numbers of autosomes, with few exceptions, are fatal to the individual, usually soon after conception. Although abnormal numbers of sex chromosomes are not usually fatal, they may result in sterility and frequently have other consequences as well. Therefore, to function normally, it is essential for a human cell to possess both members of each chromosomal pair, or a total of 46 chromosomes.

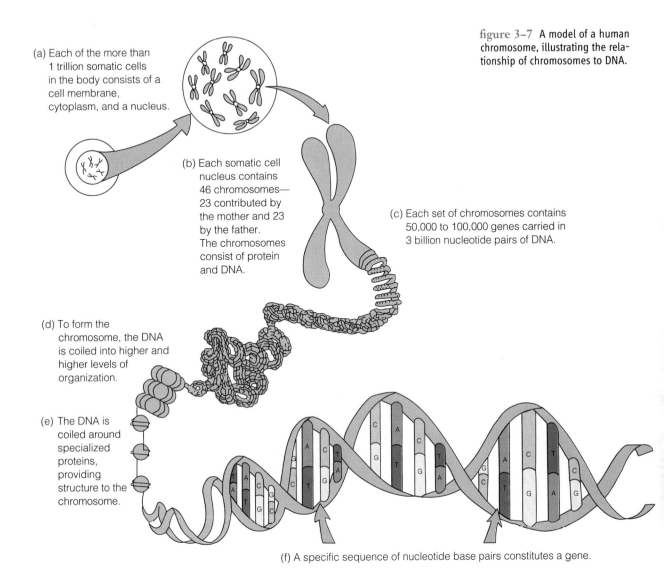

figure 3–7 A model of a human chromosome, illustrating the relationship of chromosomes to DNA.

(a) Each of the more than 1 trillion somatic cells in the body consists of a cell membrane, cytoplasm, and a nucleus.

(b) Each somatic cell nucleus contains 46 chromosomes—23 contributed by the mother and 23 by the father. The chromosomes consist of protein and DNA.

(c) Each set of chromosomes contains 50,000 to 100,000 genes carried in 3 billion nucleotide pairs of DNA.

(d) To form the chromosome, the DNA is coiled into higher and higher levels of organization.

(e) The DNA is coiled around specialized proteins, providing structure to the chromosome.

(f) A specific sequence of nucleotide base pairs constitutes a gene.

Mitosis

Cell division in somatic cells is called **mitosis.** Mitosis occurs during growth of the individual. It also acts to promote healing of injured tissues and to replace older cells with newer ones. In short, it is the way somatic cells reproduce.

In the early stages of mitosis, a human somatic cell possesses 46 double-stranded chromosomes, which line up in random order along the center of the cell (fig. 3–8). As the cell wall begins to constrict at the center, the chromosomes split apart at the centromere, so that the two strands are separated. Once the two strands are apart, they pull away from each other and move to opposite ends of the dividing cell. At this point, each strand is now a distinct chromosome, *composed of one DNA molecule.* Following the separation of chromosome strands, the cell wall pinches in and becomes sealed, so that two new cells are formed, each with a full complement of DNA, or 46 chromosomes (see fig. 3–8).

Mitosis Simple cell division; the process by which somatic cells divide to produce two identical daughter cells.

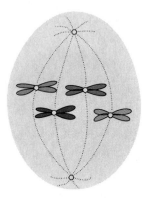

(a) The cell is involved in metabolic activities. DNA replication occurs, but chromosomes are not visible.

(b) The nuclear membrane disappears, and double-stranded chromosomes are visible.

(c) The chromosomes align themselves at the center of the cell.

(d) The chromosomes split at the centromere, and the strands separate and move to opposite ends of the dividing cell.

(e) The cell membrane pinches in as the cell continues to divide. The chromosomes begin to uncoil (not shown here).

(f) After mitosis is complete, there are two identical daughter cells. The nuclear membrane is present, and chromosomes are no longer visible.

figure 3–8 Mitosis.

Mitosis is referred to as "simple cell division" because a somatic cell divides one time to produce two daughter cells that are genetically identical to each other and to the original cell. In mitosis, the original cell possesses 46 chromosomes, and each new daughter cell inherits an exact copy of all 46 (fig. 3–9a). This precise arrangement is made possible by the ability of the DNA molecule to replicate. Thus, it is DNA replication that ensures that the quantity and quality of the genetic material remain constant from one generation of cells to the next.

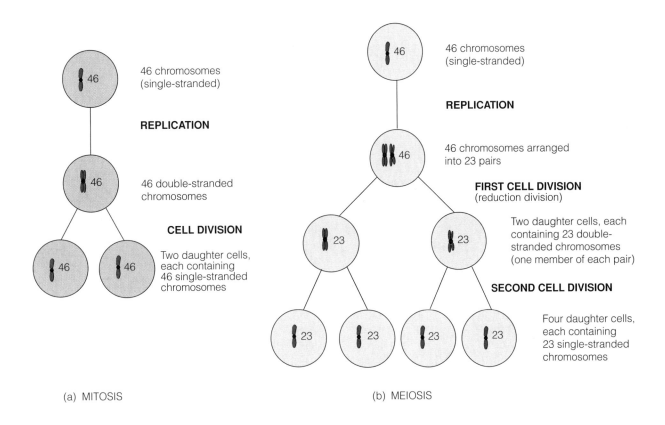

(a) MITOSIS   (b) MEIOSIS

It should be mentioned that not all somatic cells undergo mitosis. Red blood cells are produced by specialized cells in bone marrow and possess no nucleus and no nuclear DNA. Moreover, it is believed that once full growth has occurred, brain and nerve cells (neurons) do not divide, although some debate currently surrounds this issue. Liver cells also do not divide after growth has ceased unless this vital organ is damaged through injury or disease. However, with these three exceptions (red blood cells, mature neurons, and liver cells), somatic cells are regularly duplicated through the process of mitosis.

Meiosis

While mitosis produces new cells, **meiosis** may lead to the development of new individuals, since it produces reproductive cells, or gametes. Although meiosis is another form of cell division and is in some ways similar to mitosis, it is a more complicated process.

During meiosis, specialized cells in male testes and female ovaries divide and develop, eventually to produce sperm or egg cells. Meiosis is characterized by *two divisions* that result in *four daughter cells*, each of which contains only 23 chromosomes, or half the original number (fig. 3–9b).

Reduction of chromosome number is a critical feature of meiosis, for the resulting gamete, with its 23 chromosomes, may ultimately unite with another gamete that also carries 23 chromosomes. The product of this union is a *zygote*, or fertilized egg, which in humans receives a total of 46 chromosomes. In other words, the zygote inherits the full complement of DNA it needs (half from each

figure 3–9 Mitosis and meiosis compared. In mitosis, one division produces two daughter cells, each of which contains 46 chromosomes. Meiosis is characterized by two divisions. After the first, there are two cells, each containing only 23 chromosomes (one member of each original chromosome pair). Each daughter cell divides again, so that the final result is four cells, each with only half the original number of chromosomes.

Meiosis Cell division in specialized cells in ovaries and testes. Meiosis involves two divisions and results in four daughter cells, each containing only half the original number of chromosomes. These cells can develop into gametes.

figure 3–10 Meiosis.

Chromosomes are not visible as DNA replication occurs in a cell preparing to divide.

Double-stranded chromosomes become visible, and partner chromosomes exchange genetic material in a process called "recombination" or "crossing over."

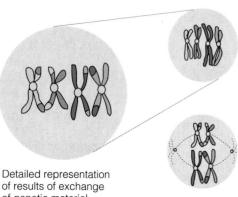

Detailed representation of results of exchange of genetic material during recombination.

Chromosome pairs migrate to the center of the cell.

FIRST DIVISION (REDUCTION DIVISION)

Partner chromosomes separate, and members of each pair move to opposite ends of the dividing cell. This results in only half the original number of chromosomes in each new daughter cell.

After the first meiotic division, there are two daughter cells, each containing only one member of each original chromosomal pair, or 23 nonpartner chromosomes.

SECOND DIVISION

In this division, the chromosomes split at the centromere, and the strands move to opposite sides of the cell.

After the second division, meiosis results in four daughter cells. These may mature to become functional gametes, containing only half the DNA in the original cell.

parent) to develop and function normally. If it were not for reduction division (the first division) in meiosis, it would not be possible to maintain the correct number of chromosomes from one generation to the next.

During the first meiotic division partner chromosomes come together, forming *pairs* of double-stranded chromosomes that line up at the center of the cell (fig. 3–10). Pairing of homologous chromosomes is highly significant, for while they are together, members of pairs exchange genetic information in a critical process called **recombination** or *crossing over*. Pairing is also important because it facilitates the accurate reduction of chromosome number by ensuring that each new daughter cell will receive only one member of each pair.

As the cell begins to divide, the chromosomes themselves remain intact (i.e., double-stranded), but *members of pairs* separate and migrate to opposite ends of the cell. After the first division, there are two new daughter cells, but they are not identical to each other or to the parental cell because each contains only one member of each chromosome pair and therefore only 23 chromosomes, each of which still has two strands (see fig. 3–10). Moreover, because of crossing over, each chromosome now contains some genetic variations it did not have previously.

The second meiotic division proceeds in much the same way as cell division in mitosis. In the two newly formed cells, the 23 double-stranded chromosomes align themselves at the cell's center, and as in mitosis, the strands of each chromosome separate at the centromere and move apart. Once this second division is completed, there are four daughter cells, each with 23 single-stranded chromosomes, or 23 DNA molecules.

THE EVOLUTIONARY SIGNIFICANCE OF MEIOSIS   Meiosis occurs in all sexually reproducing organisms, and it is a highly important evolutionary innovation, since it increases genetic variation in populations at a faster rate than mutation alone can do in asexually reproducing species. Individual members of sexually reproducing species are not genetically identical clones of other individuals. Rather, they result from the contribution of genetic information from two parents. The genetic uniqueness of individuals is further enhanced by recombination between homologous chromosomes during meiosis, because recombination ensures that chromosomes are not transmitted intact from one generation to the next. Instead, in every generation, parental contributions are reshuffled in an almost infinite number of combinations, thus altering the genetic composition of chromosomes even before they are passed on.

Genetic diversity is therefore considerably enhanced by meiosis. As was mentioned in Chapter 2, natural selection acts on genetic variation in populations. If all individuals in a population are genetically identical over time, then natural selection (and evolution) cannot occur. Although there are other sources of variation (mutation being the only source of *new* variation), sexual reproduction and meiosis are of *major* evolutionary importance because they contribute to the role of natural selection in populations.

PROBLEMS WITH MEIOSIS   For meiosis to ensure a reasonably good opportunity for the completion of normal fetal development, the process must be exact. The two-stage division must produce a viable gamete with exactly 23 chromosomes—with only one member of each chromosome pair present. If chromosomes or chromosome strands fail to separate during either of the two meiotic divisions, serious problems can arise. This failure to separate is called **nondisjunction.** The

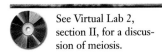

See Virtual Lab 2, section II, for a discussion of meiosis.

Recombination The exchange of DNA between homologous chromosomes during meiosis; also called "crossing over."

Nondisjunction The failure of homologous chromosomes or chromosome strands to separate during cell division.

result of nondisjunction is that one of the daughter cells receives two copies of the affected chromosome, while the other daughter cell receives none. If such an affected gamete unites with a normal gamete containing 23 chromosomes, the resulting zygote will have either 45 or 47 chromosomes.

The far-reaching effects of an abnormal number of chromosomes can be appreciated only by remembering that the zygote will reproduce itself through mitosis. Thus, every cell in the developing body will also have the abnormal chromosomal complement. Most situations of this type involving autosomes are lethal, and the embryo is spontaneously aborted, frequently before the pregnancy is even recognized.

One example of an abnormal number of autosomes is *Down syndrome*, more properly called *trisomy 21*, where there are three copies of the twenty-first chromosome. This is the only example of an abnormal number of autosomes being compatible with life beyond infancy or early childhood. Trisomy 21, which occurs in approximately 1 out of every 1,000 live births, is associated with a number of developmental and health problems. These problems include congenital heart defects (seen in about 40 percent of affected newborns), increased susceptibility to respiratory infections, and leukemia. However, the most widely recognized effect of trisomy 21 is mental retardation, which is variably expressed and ranges from mild to severe.

Nondisjunction also occurs in the X and Y chromosomes. Although these conditions do not always result in death, they frequently cause sterility and may result in other problems as well. Clearly, normal development relies on the presence of the correct number of chromosomes.

New Frontiers

Since the discovery of DNA structure and function in the 1950s, the field of genetics has revolutionized biological science and reshaped our understanding of inheritance, genetic disease, and evolutionary processes. For example, a technique developed in 1986 called **polymerase chain reaction (PCR)** now enables scientists to produce multiple copies of DNA, making it possible to analyze segments of DNA as small as one molecule. This ability is critically important because samples of DNA, such as those obtained at crime scenes or from fossils, are frequently too small to permit reliable analysis of nucleotide sequences.

In PCR, the two strands of a DNA sample are separated, and an enzyme synthesizes complementary strands on the exposed bases, as in DNA replication. Because this process can be repeated many times, it is possible to produce over a million copies of what was originally a very small sample of DNA. Thus, scientists have been able to identify nucleotide sequences in, for example, fossils (including Neandertals), Egyptian mummies, and members of the Russian royal family murdered in 1918. As you can imagine, PCR has limitless potential for many disciplines, including forensic science, medicine, and evolutionary biology.

Over the last two decades, using the techniques of **recombinant DNA technology,** scientists have been able to transfer genes from the cells of one species into those of another. The most common method has been to insert human genes that direct the production of various proteins into bacterial cells, thus causing the altered bacteria to produce human gene products. There are

Polymerase chain reaction (PCR)
A method of producing thousands of copies of a DNA segment using the enzyme DNA polymerase.

Recombinant DNA technology
A process in which genes from the cell of one species are transferred to somatic cells or gametes of another species.

numerous commercial applications for this technology, many of which are aimed at treating genetic disease in humans. For example, until the early 1980s, diabetic patients relied on insulin derived from nonhuman animals. However, this insulin was not plentiful, and some patients developed allergies to it. But since 1982, abundant supplies of human insulin, produced by bacteria, have been available; and bacteria-derived insulin does not cause allergic reactions in patients.

Human genes may also be inserted into the fertilized eggs of some nonhuman animals. The eggs are then implanted into the uteri of females who subsequently give birth to genetically altered offspring. These offspring serve as a source of various substances needed in medical practice. For example, genetically altered female sheep can carry a human gene that causes them to produce an enzyme that is present in most people and which prevents a serious form of emphysema. This enzyme is produced in the sheep's milk, and once extracted and purified, it can be administered to people who do not normally produce it.

In recent years, genetic manipulation has become increasingly controversial owing to questions related to product safety, environmental concerns, and animal welfare, among others. For example, the insertion of bacterial DNA into certain crops has made them toxic to leaf-eating insects, thus reducing the need for pesticide use. And cattle and pigs are commonly treated with genetically engineered growth hormone to increase growth rates. Although there is no current evidence that humans are susceptible to the insect-repelling bacterium or adversely affected by the consumption of meat and dairy products from animals treated with growth hormone, there are serious concerns over the unknown effects of such long-term exposure. In fact, tremendous opposition to genetically modified foods has resulted in greatly increased demand for organically grown produce and hormone-free meats, especially in Europe.

Regardless of how contentious these new techniques may be, nothing has generated as much controversy as cloning. The controversy escalated with the birth of Dolly, a **clone** of a female sheep, in 1997 (Wilmut et al., 1997). Actually, cloning is not as new as you might think. Anyone who has ever taken a cutting from a plant and rooted it to grow a new plant has produced a clone. In the early 1980s, geneticists successfully cloned mice, and since the Dolly experiment, sheep, cattle, and even a cat have been cloned.

Clone An organism that is genetically identical to another organism. The term may also be used to refer to genetically identical DNA segments and molecules.

But as exciting as these innovations are, probably the single most important advance in genetics has been the progress made by the **Human Genome Project.** The goal of this international effort, begun in 1990, has been the sequencing of the entire human **genome,** which consists of some 3 billion bases comprising approximately 30,000 genes. In February 2001, two rival teams of researchers simultaneously announced they had revealed a virtually complete sequence of human DNA. As phenomenal as this achievement is, scientists are still several years away from sorting out which DNA segments operate as functional genes and which do not. It will also be years before the identity and function of many of the proteins produced by these newly identified genes are ascertained. Put another way, it is one thing to know the chemical makeup of a gene but quite another to know what that gene does. Nevertheless, the magnitude and importance of the achievement cannot be overstated, because it will ultimately transform biomedical and pharmaceutical research and will change forever how many human diseases are diagnosed and treated.

Human Genome Project An international effort aimed at sequencing and mapping the entire human genome.

Genome The entire genetic makeup of an individual or species. In humans, it is estimated that each individual possesses approximately 3 billion DNA nucleotides.

As of September, 2000, the genomes of over 600 species (mostly microorganisms) had been either partially or completely identified. The successful sequencing of the mouse genome (Waterston et al., 2002) will assist in understanding the function of human genes. About 80 percent of mouse genes have counterparts in human genes and the functions of these genes can be studied in mice in ways not possible in humans. This research has enormous implications, not only for biomedical research, but also for studies of evolutionary relationships among species. Scientists have known for a long time that humans share many genes with other organisms, but just how many and which ones has not yet been determined. Eventually, comparative genome analysis, especially of nonhuman primates, will provide a thorough assessment of genetic similarities and differences, and thus the evolutionary relationships, between humans and other species.

Summary

 his chapter has dealt with several concepts that are fundamental to understanding human variation as well as the processes of biological evolution, topics that will be discussed in succeeding chapters.

It has been shown that cells are the fundamental units of life and that there are basically two types of cells. Somatic cells make up body tissues, while gametes (eggs and sperm) are reproductive cells that transmit genetic information from parent to offspring.

Genetic information is contained in the DNA molecule, found in the nuclei of cells. The DNA molecule is capable of replication, or making copies of itself, and it is the only molecule known to have this ability. Replication makes it possible for parent cells to retain a full complement of DNA while also transmitting a full complement to daughter cells. DNA also controls protein synthesis by directing the cell to arrange amino acids in the proper sequence for each particular type of protein. Also involved in the process of protein synthesis is another, similar molecule called RNA.

Cells multiply by dividing, and during cell division, DNA is visible under a microscope in the form of chromosomes. In humans, there are 46 chromosomes, or 23 pairs. Somatic cells divide during growth or tissue repair or to replace old or damaged cells. Somatic cell division is called mitosis. During mitosis, a cell divides one time to produce two daughter cells, each possessing a full and identical set of chromosomes. Sex cells are produced when specialized cells in the ovaries and testes divide in meiosis. Unlike mitosis, meiosis is characterized by two divisions, which produce four nonidentical daughter cells, each containing only half the amount of DNA (23 chromosomes) carried by the original cell.

Questions for Review

1. Genetics is the study of what?
2. What components of a eukaryotic cell are discussed in this chapter?
3. What are the two basic types of cells in individuals? Give an example of each.
4. What are nucleotides?
5. Name the four DNA bases. Which pairs with which?
6. What is DNA replication, and why is it important?

7. What are proteins? Give two examples.
8. What are enzymes, and what do they do?
9. What are the building blocks of protein? How many different kinds are there?
10. What is the function of DNA in protein synthesis?
11. What is the function of mRNA?
12. What is the function of tRNA?
13. Define gene.
14. Define chromosome.
15. What are homologous chromosomes?
16. How many cell divisions occur in mitosis? In humans, how many chromosomes does each new cell have?
17. How many cell divisions occur in meiosis? How many daughter cells are produced when meiosis is complete? In humans, how many chromosomes does each new cell contain?
18. Why is reduction division important?
19. What is recombination, and why is it important? When does it occur?
20. Why is the genetic code said to be universal?
21. What are the two sex chromosomes? Which two do males have? Which two do females have?
22. Why is meiosis important to the process of natural selection?
23. Why is the study of genetics important to physical anthropology?

Suggested Further Readings

Brown, Kathryn. 2001. "Genetically Modified Foods: Are They Safe?" *Scientific American*, 284(4): 51–57.

Cummings, Michael R. 2000. *Human Heredity. Principles and Issues*. 5th ed. Pacific Grove, CA: Brooks/Cole.

Ezell, Carol. 2002. "Proteins Rule." *Scientific American*, 286(4): 40–47.

Gribbin, John. 1987. *In Search of the Double Helix*. New York: Bantam Books.

Hopkin, Karen. 2001. "The Risks on the Table." *Scientific American*, 284(4): 60–61.

Ridley, Mark. 1993. *Evolution*. Cambridge, MA: Blackwell Scientific.

See entire issue of *Scientific American*, vol. 253(4), October 1985, for numerous articles pertaining to molecular genetics and evolution.

Multimedia Resources

 ### Companion Web Site

Anthropology Online: The Wadsworth Anthropology Resource Center Visit **http://anthropology.wadsworth.com** and click on the Companion Web Site for Jurmain/Kilgore/Trevathan/Nelson's *Essentials of Physical Anthropology*, Fifth Edition, to access a wide range of enrichment material to aid in your study of anthropology. Among the useful options for each chapter's self-study are learning objectives, flashcards, Internet exercises, Web links, InfoTrac College Edition exercises, and practice quizzes that can be scored and emailed to your instructor.

CHAPTER
4

HEREDITY
AND EVOLUTION

CONTENTS

Introduction

See the following sections of the CD-ROM for topics covered in this chapter: Virtual Lab 2, sections I, II, III, and IV.

I n Chapter 3, we discussed the structure and function of DNA within the cell. In this chapter, we shift to a somewhat broader perspective and focus on mechanisms that guide how characteristics are passed from parent to offspring. Then, building on this basic foundation of genetic principles, we turn our attention to the factors that contribute to evolutionary change.

For at least 10,000 years, beginning with the domestication of plants and animals, people have attempted to explain how traits are passed from parents to offspring. Although most explanations were far from accurate, farmers and herders have known for millennia that they could enhance the frequency and expression of desirable attributes through selective breeding. However, exactly why desirable traits were often seen in the offspring of carefully chosen breeding stock remained a mystery. It was equally curious when offspring did not show the traits their human owners had hoped for.

From the time ancient Greek philosophers considered the problem until well into the nineteenth century, one predominant belief was that characteristics of offspring resulted from the *blending* of parental traits. Blending was supposedly accomplished by means of particles that existed in every part of the body. These so-called *pangenes* contained miniatures of the body part (limbs, organs, etc.) from which the particles derived, and they traveled through the blood to the reproductive organs and blended with particles of another individual during reproduction. There were variations on the theme of *pangenesis*, and numerous scholars, including Charles Darwin, adhered to some aspects of the theory.

The Genetic Principles Discovered by Mendel

It was not until Gregor Mendel (1822–1884) addressed the question of heredity that it began to be resolved (fig. 4–1). Mendel was a monk living in an Augustinian abbey at Brno in what is now the Czech Republic. At the time he began his research, he had already acquired scientific expertise in botany, physics, and mathematics at the University of Vienna and had conducted various experiments in the monastery gardens. These experiments led him to explore the various ways in which physical traits, such as color or height, could be expressed in plant **hybrids.** He hoped that by making crosses between two strains of *purebred* plants and examining their progeny, he could determine (and predict) how many different forms of hybrids there were, arrange the forms according to generation, and evaluate the proportion of each type in each generation.

Mendel chose to work with common garden peas, and unlike previous researchers, he chose to consider only one trait at a time. In all, he focused on seven traits, each of which could be expressed in two different ways (Table 4–1). Because the genetic principles Mendel discovered apply to humans and all other sexually reproducing organisms, we discuss his work in some detail to illustrate the basic rules of inheritance.

figure 4–1 Gregor Mendel.

Hybrids Offspring of mixed ancestry; heterozygotes.

TABLE 4-1	The Seven Garden Pea Characteristics Studied by Mendel	
Characteristic	**Dominant Trait**	**Recessive Trait**
1. Form of ripe seed	Smooth	Wrinkled
2. Color of seed	Yellow	Green
3. Color of seed coat	Gray	White
4. Form of ripe pods	Inflated	Constricted
5. Color of unripe pods	Green	Yellow
6. Position of flowers on stem	Along stem	End of stem
7. Length of stem	Tall	Short

Segregation

The plants that Mendel used in the first cross were designated the *parental*, or *P*, generation, and all were either tall or short. The hybrid offspring of the P generation were designated the F_1 (first filial) generation. As they matured, the F_1 plants were not intermediate in height, as blending theories of inheritance would have predicted. To the contrary, they were all tall (fig. 4–2).

Next, Mendel allowed the F_1 plants to self-fertilize and produce a second generation of plants (the F_2 generation). But this time, only approximately 3/4 of the offspring plants were tall, and the remaining 1/4 were short. Regardless of the trait he examined, every time he performed the experiment, he obtained almost the same results. One expression of the trait completely disappeared in the F_1 generation and reappeared in the F_2 generation. Moreover, the expression that was present in the F_1 generation was more common in the F_2 plants, occurring in a ratio of approximately 3:1.

These results suggested that different expressions of a trait were controlled by discrete *units*, which occurred in pairs, and that offspring inherited one unit from each parent. Mendel correctly concluded that the members of a pair of units controlling a trait somehow separated into different sex cells and were again united with another member during fertilization of the egg. This phenomenon is known as the **principle of segregation.**

Today we know that meiosis explains Mendel's principle of segregation. You will remember that during meiosis, paired chromosomes (and the genes they carry) separate from each other and are distributed to different gametes. However, in the zygote, the full complement of chromosomes is restored, and both members of each chromosome pair are present in the offspring.

Dominance and Recessiveness

Mendel also recognized that the expression that was absent in the F_1 plants had actually remained present but was somehow masked and could not be expressed. To describe the trait that seemed to be lost, Mendel used the term **recessive;** the trait that was expressed was said to be **dominant.** Thus, the principles of *dominance* and *recessiveness* were formulated, and they remain today as important concepts in the field of genetics.

As you already know, a *gene* is a segment of DNA that directs the production of a specific protein or part of a protein. Furthermore, the location of a gene on a chromosome is its **locus** (*pl.*, loci). At numerous genetic loci, however, there

Principle of segregation Genes (alleles) occur in pairs (because chromosomes occur in pairs). During gamete production, the members of each gene pair separate, so that each gamete contains one member of each pair. During fertilization, the full number of chromosomes is restored, and members of gene or allele pairs are reunited.

Recessive Describing a trait that is not expressed in heterozygotes; also refers to the allele that governs the trait. For a recessive allele to be expressed, there must be two copies of the allele (i.e., the individual must be homozygous).

Dominant Describing a trait governed by an allele that can be expressed in the presence of another, different allele (i.e., in heterozygotes). Dominant alleles prevent the expression of recessive alleles in heterozygotes. (This is the definition of *complete* dominance.)

Locus (*pl.*, loci) (lo´-kus, lo-sigh´) The position on a chromosome where a given gene occurs. The term is sometimes used interchangeably with *gene,* but this usage is technically incorrect.

is more than one possible form of the gene, and these variations of genes at specific loci are called **alleles.** Therefore, alleles are alternate forms of a gene that can direct the cell to produce slightly different forms of the same protein and, ultimately, different expressions of traits.

As it turns out, plant height in garden peas is controlled by two different alleles at one genetic locus. The allele that determines that a plant will be tall is dominant to the allele for short. (It is worth mentioning that height is not governed in this manner in all plants.)

In Mendel's experiments, all the parent (P) plants had two copies of the same allele, either dominant or recessive, depending on whether they were tall or short. When two copies of the same allele are present, the individual is said to be **homozygous.** Thus, all the tall P plants were homozygous for the dominant allele, and all the short P plants were homozygous for the recessive allele. (This homozygosity explains why tall plants crossed with tall plants produced

Alleles Alternate forms of a gene. Alleles occur at the same locus on homologous chromosomes and thus govern the same trait. However, because they are different, their action may result in different expressions of that trait. The term is often used synonymously with *genes.*

Homozygous Having the same allele at the same locus on both members of a pair of chromosomes.

only tall offspring, and short plants crossed with short plants produced all short offspring; they were "pure lines" and lacked genetic variation at this locus.) However, all the F₁ plants (hybrids) had inherited one allele from each parent plant; therefore, they all possessed two different alleles at specific loci. Individuals that possess two different alleles at a locus are **heterozygous.**

Figure 4–2 illustrates the crosses that Mendel initially performed. Geneticists use standard symbols to refer to alleles. Uppercase letters refer to dominant alleles (or dominant traits), and lowercase letters refer to recessive alleles (or recessive traits). Therefore,

T = the allele for tallness
t = the allele for shortness

The same symbols are combined to describe an individual's actual genetic makeup, or **genotype.** The term *genotype* can be used to refer to an organism's entire genetic makeup or to the alleles at a specific genetic locus. Thus, the genotypes of the plants in Mendel's experiments were

TT = homozygous dominant tall plants
Tt = heterozygous tall plants
tt = homozygous recessive short plants

Figure 4–3 is a *Punnett square*. It represents the different ways the alleles can be combined when the F₁ plants are self-fertilized to produce an F₂ generation. In this way, the figure shows the *genotypes* that are possible in the F₂ generation, and it also demonstrates that approximately ¼ of the F₂ plants are homozygous dominant (TT); ½ are heterozygous (Tt); and the remaining ¼ are homozygous recessive (tt).

The Punnett square can also be used to show (and predict) the proportions of F₂ **phenotypes,** or the physical manifestations of genes. The Punnett square illustrates why Mendel observed three tall plants for every short plant in the F₂ generation. By examining the Punnett square, you can see that ¼ of the F₂ plants are tall because they have the TT genotype. Furthermore, an additional ½, (heterozygotes, Tt) will also be tall because T is dominant to t and will therefore be expressed in the phenotype. The remaining ¼ are homozygous recessive (tt), and they will be short because no dominant allele is present. It is important to note that the *only* way a recessive allele can be expressed is if it occurs with another recessive allele, that is, if the individual is homozygous recessive at the particular locus in question.

Heterozygous Having different alleles at the same locus on members of a pair of homologous chromosomes.

Genotype The genetic makeup of an individual. Genotype can refer to an organism's entire genetic makeup or to the alleles at a particular locus.

 See Virtual Lab 2, section II, for a Punnett square exercise.

Phenotypes The observable or detectable physical characteristics of an organism; the detectable expressions of genotypes.

figure 4–3 Punnett square representing possible genotypes and phenotypes and their proportions in the F₂ generation. The circles across the top and at the left of the Punnett square represent the gametes of the F₁ parents. The four squares illustrate that ¼ of the F₂ plants will be homozygous tall (TT); another ½ also will be tall but will be heterozygous (Tt); and the remaining ¼ will be short (tt). Thus, ¾ can be expected to be tall and ¼ will be short.

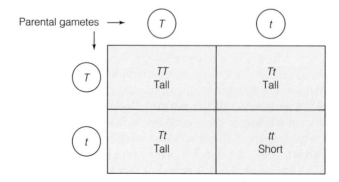

In conclusion, $^3/_4$ of the F_2 generation will express the dominant phenotype, and $^1/_4$ will show the recessive phenotype. This relationship is expressed as a **phenotypic ratio** of 3:1 and typifies all **Mendelian traits** (characteristics governed by only one genetic locus) when only two alleles are involved, one of which is dominant to the other.

Independent Assortment

Mendel also made crosses in which two characteristics were considered simultaneously to see if they were inherited together. Two such characteristics were plant height and seed (pea) color. Mendel's peas came in two colors: yellow (dominant) and green (recessive). As expected, the recessive expression of each trait was not seen in the F_1 generation; all these plants were tall and produced yellow seeds. However, in the next (F_2) generation, both recessive traits reappeared in a small proportion of plants. These results suggested that there is nothing to dictate that a tall plant must have yellow (or green) seeds. The expression of one trait is not influenced by the expression of the other trait.

Mendel stated this relationship as the **principle of independent assortment,** which says that the units (genes) that code for different traits assort independently of each other during gamete formation. Today we know this is true because the genes controlling these two characteristics are located on different (nonpartner) chromosomes, and during meiosis, chromosomes travel to newly forming cells independently of one another. But if Mendel had used just *any* two traits, his results would have been quite different. For example, if the two traits in question were influenced by genes located on the same chromosome, these genes would probably have traveled together during meiosis. Thus, the expressions of the traits would not have conformed to the ratios predicted by independent assortment. The ratios came out as Mendel predicted because the genes governing most of the traits he discussed were carried on different chromosomes.

In 1866, Mendel's results were published, but the methodology and statistical nature of the research were beyond the thinking of the time, and their significance was overlooked and unappreciated. However, by the end of the nineteenth century, several investigators had made important contributions to the understanding of chromosomes and cell division. These discoveries paved the way for the acceptance of Mendel's work by 1900, when three different groups of scientists, conducting similar experiments, came across his paper. Regrettably, Mendel had died 16 years earlier and thus never saw his work vindicated.

Phenotypic ratio The proportion of one phenotype to other phenotypes in a group of organisms. For example, Mendel observed that there were approximately three tall plants for every short plant in the F_2 generation. This is expressed as a phenotypic ratio of 3:1.

Mendelian traits Characteristics that are influenced by alleles at only one genetic locus. Examples include many blood types, such as ABO. Many genetic disorders, including sickle-cell anemia and Tay-Sachs disease, are also Mendelian traits.

Principle of independent assortment The distribution of one pair of alleles into gametes does not influence the distribution of another pair. The genes controlling different traits are inherited independently of one another.

Mendelian Inheritance in Humans

Mendelian traits (also referred to as *discrete traits* or *traits of simple inheritance*) are controlled by alleles at *one* genetic locus. The most comprehensive listing of Mendelian traits in humans is V. A. McKusick's (1998) *Mendelian Inheritance in Man,* now in its twelfth edition. This volume and its continuously updated Internet version, *Online Mendelian Inheritance in Man* (www3.ncbi.nlm.nih.gov/Omim/), currently lists over 9,600 human characteristics that are inherited according to Mendelian principles. One example is the ABO blood group system.

TABLE 4-2	ABO Genotypes and Associated Phenotypes	
Genotype	Antigens on Red Blood Cells	ABO Blood Type (Phenotype)
AA, AO	A	A
BB, BO	B	B
AB	A and B	AB
OO	None	O

Antigens Large molecules found on the surface of cells. Several different loci governing antigens on red and white blood cells are known. (Foreign antigens provoke an immune response in individuals.)

Codominance The expression of two alleles in heterozygotes. Because neither allele is dominant or recessive, both influence the phenotype.

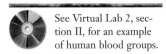

See Virtual Lab 2, section II, for an example of human blood groups.

The ABO system is governed by three alleles, *A*, *B*, and *O*, found at the ABO locus on the ninth chromosome. Although three alleles are present in populations, each individual can possess only two. These alleles determine which ABO blood type an individual has by coding for the production of substances called **antigens** on the surface of red blood cells. If only antigen A is present, the blood type (phenotype) is A; if only B is present, the blood type is B; if both are present, the blood type is AB; and when neither is present, there is no A or B antigen and the blood type is said to be O. (The *O* allele appears to have no function; i.e., it does not code for the production of any antigen.)

Dominance and recessiveness are clearly illustrated by the ABO system. The *O* allele is recessive to both *A* and *B*; therefore, if a person has type O blood, he or she must be homozygous for (have two copies of) the *O* allele. However, since both *A* and *B* are dominant to *O*, an individual with blood type A can actually have one of two genotypes: *AA* or *AO*. The same is true of type B, which results frbm the genotypes *BB* and *BO* (Table 4–2). However, type AB presents a slightly different situation and is an example of **codominance.**

Codominance is seen when two different alleles are present, but instead of one having the ability to mask the expression of the other, the products of *both* are expressed in the phenotype. Therefore, when both *A* and *B* alleles are present, both A and B antigens can be detected on the surface of red blood cells.

A number of genetic disorders are inherited as dominant traits (Table 4–3). This means that if a person inherits only one copy of a harmful, dominant allele, the condition it causes will be present, regardless of the existence of a different, recessive allele on the corresponding chromosome.

Recessive conditions are commonly associated with the lack of a substance, usually an enzyme (see Table 4–3). For a person actually to have a recessive disorder, he or she must have *two* copies of the recessive allele that causes it. Heterozygotes who have only one copy of a harmful recessive allele are unaffected. Such individuals are frequently called *carriers*. Although carriers do not actually show full-blown manifestations of the recessive allele they carry, they can pass the allele on to their children. (Remember, half their gametes will carry the recessive allele.) If their mate is also a carrier, then it is possible for them to have a child who will have two copies of the allele, and that child will be affected. In fact, in a mating between two carriers, the risk of having an affected child is 25 percent (refer back to fig. 4–3).

TABLE 4-3	Some Mendelian Traits in Humans		
Dominant Traits		**Recessive Traits**	
Condition	**Manifestations**	**Condition**	**Manifestations**
Achondroplasia	Dwarfism due to growth defects involving the long bones of the arms and legs; trunk and head size usually normal.	Cystic fibrosis	Among the most common genetic (Mendelian) disorders among European Americans; abnormal secretions of the exocrine glands, with pronounced involvement of the pancreas; most patients develop obstructive lung disease. Until the recent development of new treatments, only about half of all patients survived to early adulthood.
Brachydactyly	Shortened fingers and toes.		
Familial hyper-cholesterolemia	Elevated cholesterol levels and cholesterol plaque deposition; a leading cause of heart disease, with death frequently occurring by middle age.		
Neurofibromatosis	Symptoms range from the appearance of abnormal skin pigmentation to large tumors resulting in gross deformities; can, in extreme cases, lead to paralysis, blindness, and death.	Tay-Sachs disease	Most common among Ashkenazi Jews; degeneration of the nervous system beginning at about 6 months of age; lethal by age 2 or 3 years.
Marfan syndrome	The eyes and cardiovascular and skeletal systems are affected; symptoms include greater than average height, long arms and legs, eye problems, and enlargement of the aorta; death due to rupture of the aorta is common. (Abraham Lincoln may have had Marfan syndrome.)	Phenylketonuria (PKU)	Inability to metabolize the amino acid phenylalanine; results in mental retardation if left untreated during childhood; treatment involves strict dietary management and some supplementation.
Huntington disease	Progressive degeneration of the nervous system accompanied by dementia and seizures; age of onset variable but commonly between 30 and 40 years.	Albinism	Inability to produce normal amounts of the pigment melanin; results in very fair, untannable skin, light blond hair, and light eyes; may also be associated with vision problems. (There is more than one form of albinism.)
Camptodactyly	Malformation of the hands whereby the fingers, usually the little finger, is permanently contracted.	Sickle-cell anemia	Abnormal form of hemoglobin (Hb^S) that results in collapsed red blood cells, blockage of capillaries, reduced blood flow to organs, and, without treatment, death.
Hypodontia of upper lateral incisors	Upper lateral incisors are absent or only partially formed (peg-shaped). Pegged incisors are a partial expression of the allele.	Thalassemia	A group of disorders characterized by reduced or absent alpha or beta chains in the hemoglobin molecule; results in severe anemia and, in some forms, death.
Cleft chin	Dimple or depression in the middle of the chin; less prominent in females than males.	Absence of permanent dentition	Failure of the permanent dentition to erupt. The primary dentition is not affected.
PTC tasting	The ability to taste the bitter substance phenylthiocarbamide (PTC). Tasting thresholds vary, suggesting that alleles at another locus may also exert an influence.		

Misconceptions Regarding Mendelian Traits

Traditional methods of teaching genetics have led to some misunderstanding of Mendelian traits. Thus, virtually all introductory students (and most people in general) have the impression that these characteristics are all-or-nothing situations. This misconception especially pertains to recessive alleles, and the general view is that when these alleles occur in heterozygotes (i.e., carriers), they have absolutely no effect on the phenotype—that is, they are completely inactivated by the presence of another (dominant) allele.

However, various biochemical techniques, unavailable in the past but in wide use today, have demonstrated that recessive alleles do indeed exert some influence on the phenotype, although these effects are not usually apparent through simple observation. This influence is detectable because in heterozygotes, many recessive alleles act to reduce the amount of the gene products they control. Indeed, it is now clear that our *perception* of recessive alleles greatly depends on one important factor: whether we examine them at the directly observable phenotypic level or the biochemical level.

Scientists now know of several recessive alleles that *do* produce detectable phenotypic effects in heterozygotes. Consider Tay-Sachs disease, a lethal condition that results from the inability to produce the enzyme hexosaminidase A (see Table 4–3). This inability, seen in people who are homozygous for a recessive allele (*ts*) on chromosome 15, invariably results in death by early childhood. Carriers do not have the disease, and practically speaking, they are unaffected. However, in 1979, it was shown that Tay-Sachs carriers have only about 40 to 60 percent of the amount of the enzyme seen in normal people. In fact, there are now voluntary tests to screen carriers in populations at risk for Tay-Sachs disease.

Similar misconceptions also relate to dominant alleles. The majority of people see dominant alleles as somehow "stronger" or "better," and there is always the mistaken notion that dominant alleles are more common in populations. These misconceptions undoubtedly stem partly from the label "dominant" and the connotations the term carries. But in genetic usage, those connotations are somewhat misleading. If dominant alleles were always more common, then a majority of people would be affected by such conditions as achondroplasia and Marfan syndrome (see Table 4–3).

The relationship between recessive and dominant alleles and their functions are more complicated than they appear at first glance. For example geneticists now recognize that some traits, originally believed to be influenced by a single locus, are actually governed by two or three closely linked loci. Previously held views of dominance and recessiveness were guided by available technologies but, as genetic technologies continue to change, new theories will emerge and it is likely that one day, the concepts of Mendelian traits, as they have traditionally been taught, will be obsolete.

Polygenic Inheritance

Mendelian traits are said to be *discrete*, or *discontinuous*, because their phenotypic expressions do not overlap; instead, they fall into clearly defined categories (fig. 4–4a). For example, Mendel's pea plants were either short or tall, but none was intermediate in height. In the ABO system, the four phenotypes are completely distinct from one another; that is, there is no intermediate form between type A and type B to represent a gradation between the two. In other words, Mendelian traits do not show *continuous* variation.

However, many traits do have a wide range of phenotypic expressions that form a graded series. These are called **polygenic,** or *continuous,* traits. While Mendelian traits are governed by only one genetic locus, polygenic characteristics are influenced by alleles at two or more loci, with each locus making a contribution to the phenotype. For example, one of the most frequently cited instances of polygenic inheritance in humans is skin color, and the single most important factor influencing skin color is the amount of the pigment melanin present.

Melanin production is believed to be influenced by between three and six genetic loci, with each locus having at least two alleles, neither of which is dominant. As there are perhaps six loci and at least 12 alleles, there are numerous ways in which these alleles can combine in individuals. If an individual inherits 11 alleles coding for maximum pigmentation and only 1 for reduced melanin production, skin color will be very dark. A person who inherits a higher proportion of reduced pigmentation alleles will have lighter skin color. This is because in this system, as in some other polygenic systems, there is an *additive effect.* This means that each allele that codes for melanin production makes a contribution to increased melanization (although for some characteristics the contributions of the alleles are not all equal). Likewise, each allele coding for less melanin production contributes to reduced pigmentation. Therefore, the effect of multiple alleles at several loci is to produce continuous variation from very dark to very fair skin within the species. (Skin color is also discussed in Chapter 12.)

Polygenic traits actually account for most of the readily observable phenotypic variation seen in humans, and they have traditionally served as a basis for racial classification (see Chapter 12). In addition to skin color, polygenic inheritance in humans is seen in hair color, weight, stature, eye color (fig. 4–5), shape

See Virtual Lab 2, section IV, for a discussion of human skin color.

Polygenic Referring to traits that are influenced by genes at two or more loci. Examples of such traits are stature, skin color, and eye color. Many polygenic traits are also influenced by environmental factors.

figure 4–4 (a) This histogram shows the discontinuous distribution of a Mendelian trait (ABO blood type) in a hypothetical population. The expression of the trait is described in terms of frequencies. (b) This histogram represents the continuous expression of a polygenic trait (height) in a large group of people. Note that the percentage of extremely short or tall individuals is low, while the majority of people are closer to the mean, or average, height, represented by the vertical line at the center of the distribution.

© Corbis

Lynn Kilgore

© Corbis

Lynn Kilgore

Lynn Kilgore

Lynn Kilgore

figure 4–5 Examples of the continuous variation seen in human eye color.

of face, shape of nose, and fingerprint pattern. Because they exhibit continuous variation, most polygenic traits can be measured on a scale composed of equal increments (fig. 4–4b). For example, height (stature) is measured in feet and inches (or meters and centimeters). If one were to measure height in a large number of individuals, the distribution of measurements would continue uninterrupted from the shortest extreme to the tallest. That is what is meant by the term *continuous traits*.

Because polygenic traits usually lend themselves to metric analysis, biologists, geneticists, and physical anthropologists treat them statistically. The use of simple summary statistics, such as the *mean* (average) or *standard deviation* (a measure of within-group variation), permits basic descriptions of, and comparisons between, populations. For example, one might be interested in average height in two different populations and whether or not differences between the two are significant, and if so, why. (You should also note that *all* physical traits measured and statistically treated in fossils are polygenic in nature.)

Mendelian characteristics can be described in terms of frequency within populations, thus yielding comparisons between groups regarding incidence. Moreover, these characteristics can also be analyzed for mode of inheritance (dominant or recessive). Finally, for many Mendelian traits, the approximate or exact positions of genetic loci have been identified, thus making it possible to examine the mechanisms and patterns of inheritance at these loci. Because polygenic characters are influenced by several loci, they cannot, as yet, be traced to specific loci; therefore, such analysis is currently not possible.

Genetic and Environmental Factors

From the preceding discussion, it might appear that the phenotype is solely the expression of the genotype, but this is not true. (Here we use the terms *genotype* and *phenotype* in a broader sense to refer to an individual's entire genetic makeup and *all* observable or detectable characteristics.) The genotype sets limits and potentials for development, but it also interacts with the environment, and many aspects of phenotype are influenced by this genetic-environmental interaction. However, it is usually not possible to identify the *specific* environmental factors affecting the phenotype.

One trait, for which an environmental factor is known, is adult stature, which is strongly affected by the individual's nutritional status during growth and development (see Chapter 13). Other important environmental factors include exposure to sunlight, altitude, temperature, and, unfortunately, increasing levels of exposure to toxic waste and airborne pollutants. All these and many more contribute in complex ways to the continuous phenotypic variation seen in characteristics governed by multiple loci.

Mendelian traits are less likely to be influenced by environmental factors. For example, ABO blood type is determined at fertilization and remains fixed throughout the individual's lifetime, regardless of diet, exposure to ultraviolet radiation, temperature, and so forth.

Mendelian and polygenic inheritance produce different patterns of phenotypic variation. In the former, variation occurs in discrete categories, while in the latter, it is continuous. However, it is important to understand that even for polygenic characteristics, Mendelian principles still apply at individual loci. In other words, if a trait is influenced by seven loci, each one of those loci may have two or more alleles, with one perhaps being dominant to the other or with the alleles being codominant. It is the combined action of the alleles at all seven loci, interacting with the environment, that results in observable phenotypic expression.

Mitochondrial Inheritance

There is another component of inheritance that has gained much attention in recent years, and it involves organelles called *mitochondria* (see p. 46). All cells contain several hundred of these oval-shaped structures that convert energy (derived from the breakdown of nutrients) into a form that can be used by the cell.

Each mitochondrion contains several copies of a ring-shaped DNA molecule, or chromosome. While **mitochondrial DNA (mtDNA)** is distinct from the DNA found within cell nuclei, its molecular structure and functions are the same. The entire molecule has been sequenced and is known to contain around 40 genes that direct the conversion of energy within the cell.

Mitochondrial DNA (mtDNA) DNA found in the mitochondria that is inherited only from the mother.

Mitochondrial DNA is subject to mutations just like nuclear DNA, and such mutations can lead to certain genetic disorders, some of which have been traced to specific loci. In general, these disorders result from impaired energy conversion and can produce a wide range of symptoms. Importantly, mitochondrial DNA is transmitted to offspring only from the mother; it is thus the mother who transmits all mitochondrial traits to her offspring of both sexes.

Mitochondrial mutation rates have been used as a basis for constructing evolutionary relationships between species. They have also been used to trace ancestral relationships within the human lineage, and to study genetic variability between individuals and/or between populations. While these techniques are still being refined and remain the topic of debate, it is clear that we have much to learn from mitochondrial DNA.

Modern Evolutionary Theory

In Chapters 2 and 3, we presented an overview of natural selection and we discussed the molecular and cellular bases of heredity. So far in this chapter, we have shown how genetic information is passed from individuals in one generation to those in the next. These different levels (molecular, cellular, individual, and populational) reflect different aspects of evolution, and they are all related and highly integrated in a way that can eventually produce evolutionary change.

By the beginning of the twentieth century, the essential foundations for evolutionary theory had already been developed. Darwin and Wallace had articulated the key principle of natural selection 40 years earlier, and the rediscovery of Mendelian genetics in 1900 contributed the other major component—a mechanism for inheritance. We might expect that these two basic contributions would have been combined to establish a comprehensive theory of evolution. But instead, rival viewpoints emphasized either mutation *or* natural selection as the prime mover of evolutionary change. A *synthesis* of these two views was not achieved until the mid-1930s, and we owe much of our current view of the evolutionary process to this intellectual development.

The Modern Synthesis

Biologists working on mathematical models of evolutionary change in the late 1920s and early 1930s came to realize that mutation and natural selection were not opposing themes, but that a comprehensive explanation of organic evolution required *both*. Small new changes in the genetic material transmitted from parent to offspring are, in fact, the fuel for natural selection. The two major foundations of the biological sciences had thus been brought together in what has been termed the Modern Synthesis.

From such a "modern" (i.e., the middle of the twentieth century onward) perspective, we define evolution as a two-stage process. These two stages are:

Variation (genetic) Inherited differences between individuals; the basis of all evolutionary change.

1. The production and redistribution of **variation** (inherited differences between individuals)
2. *Natural selection* acting on this variation (whereby inherited differences, or variation, among individuals differentially affect their ability to reproduce successfully)

Definition of Evolution

As discussed in Chapter 2, Darwin saw evolution as the gradual unfolding of new varieties of life from previous forms over long periods of time, and this may indeed be the end result of the evolutionary process. But these long-term effects can come about only by the accumulation of many small genetic changes occurring every generation. To understand how the process of evolution works, we must study these short-term events. Today, we study evolutionary changes occurring between generations in various organisms (including humans) and are able to demonstrate how evolution works. From such a modern genetic perspective, we define **evolution** as *a change in **allele frequency** from one generation to the next.*

Evolution (modern genetic definition) A change in the frequency of alleles from one generation to the next.

Allele frequency In a population, the percentage of all the alleles at a locus accounted for by one specific allele.

Population Within a species, a community of individuals where mates are usually found.

Allele frequencies are indicators of the genetic makeup of an interbreeding group of individuals known as a **population.** Let us illustrate the way allele frequencies change (i.e., how evolution occurs) through a simplified example. First of all, we must look at a physical trait that is inherited—again, the ABO system.

Let us assume that your present class of students represents a population, an interbreeding group of individuals, and that we have ascertained the ABO blood type of each member. (To be considered a population, individuals must choose mates more often from *within* the group than from outside it. Of course, the individuals in your class will not meet this requirement, but for the sake of our example, we will overlook this stipulation.) The proportions of the *A*, *B*, and *O* alleles are the allele frequencies for this trait. For example, suppose we find that 50 percent of all the ABO alleles in your class are *A*, 40 percent are *B*, and 10 percent are *O*. Then the frequencies of these alleles are *A* = .50, *B* = .40, and *O* = .10.*

Since the frequencies for these genes represent only proportions of a total, it is obvious that allele frequencies can refer only to groups of individuals—that is, populations. Individuals do not have an allele frequency; they have either *A*, *B*, or *O* (or a combination of these). Therefore, an individual cannot evolve: Only a group of individuals—a population—can evolve over time.

What happens when a population evolves? Assume that 25 years from now, we calculate the frequencies of the ABO alleles for the children (offspring) of our classroom population and find the following: *A* = .30, *B* = .40, and *O* = .30. We can see that the relative proportions have changed: *A* has decreased, *O* has increased, and *B* has remained the same. Such a simple, apparently minor change is what we call evolution. Over a short span of just a few generations, such changes in inherited traits may be only very small, but if further continued and elaborated, the results can and do produce spectacular kinds of adaptation and whole new varieties of life.

Whether we are talking about the short-term effects (as in our classroom population) from one generation to the next, which is sometimes called **microevolution,** or the long-term effects through time (speciation), sometimes called **macroevolution,** the basic evolutionary mechanisms are similar. But, as we discuss in Chapter 7, they are not identical.

The question may be asked, How do allele frequencies change? Or, to put it another way, what causes evolution? The modern theory of evolution isolates general factors that can produce alterations in allele frequencies. As we have noted, evolution is a two-stage process. Genetic variation must first be produced and distributed before it can be acted on by natural selection.

Microevolution Small changes occurring within species, such as a change in allele frequencies.

Macroevolution Changes produced only after many generations, such as the appearance of a new species.

Factors That Produce and Redistribute Variation
Mutation

You have already learned that a molecular alteration in genetic material is one type of mutation. A genetic locus may take one of several alternative forms, which we have defined as alleles (*A*, *B*, or *O*, for example). If one allele changes to another—that is, if the gene itself is altered—a mutation has occurred. In fact, alleles are the results of mutation. For such changes to have evolutionary significance, they must occur in the sex cells, which are passed between generations.

---

*This is a simplified example. Because the ABO system is governed by three alleles, calculating allele frequencies is more complicated than for a two-allele system. The way allele frequencies are calculated for a simple two-allele locus is discussed in Chapter 12 and illustrated in Appendix B.

Evolution is a change in allele frequencies *between* generations. If mutations do not occur in gametes (either the egg or sperm), they will not be transmitted to the next generation, and no evolutionary change can result. If, however, a genetic change does occur in the sperm or egg of one of the individuals in our classroom (*A* mutates to *B*, for instance), the offspring's blood type will differ from that of the parents, thus causing a minute shift in allele frequencies of that generation. Examples of mutations that produce phenotypic effects (see Table 4–3) include the albinism allele, the allele producing brachydactyly, and the alteration causing Tay-Sachs disease.

Actually, it would be rare to see evolution occurring by mutation alone. Mutation rates for any given trait are quite low; thus, mutations would rarely be seen in such a small population as our class. In larger populations, mutations might be observed (1 individual in 10,000, say), but would by themselves have very little impact on shifting allele frequencies. However, when mutation is coupled with natural selection, evolutionary changes not only can occur, but can occur more rapidly.

It is important to remember that mutation is the basic creative force in evolution because it is the *only* way to produce new genetic variation either in the form of new genetic material or in new arrangements of it. Its key role in the production of variation represents the first stage of the evolutionary process.

Gene Flow

Gene flow Exchange of genes between populations.

The exchange of genes between populations is called **gene flow.** The term *migration* is frequently used instead, but strictly speaking, migration means movement of people, whereas gene flow refers to the exchange of *genes* between groups, and this can occur only if the migrants interbreed. Moreover, it should be remembered that even if individuals move temporarily and interbreed within the new population (thus leaving a genetic contribution), they need not remain as part of the population. For example, the offspring of U.S. soldiers and Vietnamese women represent gene flow, even though their fathers may have returned to their native population.

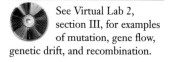

See Virtual Lab 2, section III, for examples of mutation, gene flow, genetic drift, and recombination.

In humans, social rules more than any other factor determine mating patterns, and cultural anthropologists work closely with physical anthropologists to isolate and measure this aspect of evolutionary change. Population movements (particularly in the last 500 years) have reached unprecedented proportions, and few breeding isolates remain. It should not, however, be assumed that significant population movements did not occur prior to modern times. Migration between populations has been a consistent feature of hominid evolution since the first dispersal of our genus, and this gene flow between populations (even though sometimes limited) helps explain why in the last million years speciation has been rare. Of course, migration patterns are a manifestation of human cultural behavior, once again emphasizing the essential biocultural nature of human evolution.

An interesting example of how gene flow influences microevolutionary changes in modern human populations is seen in African Americans. African Americans in the United States are largely of West African descent, but there has also been considerable genetic admixture with European Americans. By measuring allele frequencies for specific genetic loci (e.g., the Rh blood group), we can estimate the amount of migration of European alleles into the African

American gene pool. Data from northern and western U.S. cities (including New York, Detroit, and Oakland) have shown the migration rate (i.e., the proportion of *non*-African genes in the African American gene pool) at 20 to 25 percent (Cummings, 2000). However, more restricted data from the southern United States (Charleston and rural Georgia) have suggested a lower degree of gene flow (4 to 11 percent). The most consistent of these studies employ new genetic techniques, especially those involving direct DNA comparisons (discussed in Chapter 12).

It would be a misconception to think that gene flow can occur only through such large-scale movements of whole groups. In fact, significant alterations in allele frequencies can come about through long-term patterns of mate selection whereby members of a group obtain mates from one or more other groups. If exchange of mates consistently moved in one direction over a long period of time, allele frequencies would ultimately be altered.

Genetic Drift

Genetic drift is the random factor in evolution, and it is directly tied to population size. Genetic drift occurs when, because of small population size, some individuals contribute a disproportionate share of genes to succeeding generations. This situation can be a function of social status in some small societies where, for example, high-ranking males have numerous mates while others do not. This effect may also be seen in nonhuman species in which low-ranking individuals have fewer mating opportunities. In such a situation, one individual who carries a rare deleterious allele may pass it on to a high proportion of his or her descendants, and the frequency of the allele consequently increases in succeeding generations. Drift may also occur solely because the population is small; just by chance, alleles with low frequencies may simply not be passed on to offspring, eventually disappearing from the population.

The results of the particular kind of genetic drift, called **founder effect,** are seen in many modern populations. Founder effect can occur when a small migrant band of "founders" colonizes a new region away from its parent group. Over time, a new population will be established, and as long as mates are chosen only from within this population, all of its members will be descended from the founders. In effect, all of the genes in the expanding group will have been contributed by the original colonists. In such a case, an allele that was rare in the founders' parent population but that is present in even one individual in the founding group can eventually become common in that group's descendants.

Colonization is not the only way founder effect can happen. Small founding groups may also consist of a small number of survivors when famine, war, disease, or other disasters ravage large populations. The small founder population (the survivors) possesses only a sample of all the alleles that were present in the original group. Just by chance alone, some alleles may be completely removed from the **gene pool;** other alleles may become "fixed," or established, at a locus where originally there may have been two or more. The outcome is a reduction of genetic diversity, and the allele frequencies of succeeding generations may perhaps be substantially different from those of the original large population.

Genetic drift Evolutionary changes—that is, changes in allele frequencies—produced by random factors. Genetic drift is a result of small population size.

Founder effect A type of genetic drift in which allele frequencies are altered in small populations that are taken from, or are remnants of, larger populations.

Gene pool The total complement of genes shared by the reproductive members of a population.

The loss of genetic diversity in this type of situation is called a *genetic bottleneck*, and the effects can be quite detrimental to a species.

There are many known examples (both human and nonhuman) of species or populations that have passed through genetic bottlenecks. Genetically, cheetahs are an extremely uniform species, and it is believed that at some point in the past, these magnificent cats suffered a catastrophic decline in numbers. For reasons not well understood but related to the species-wide loss of numerous alleles, male cheetahs produce a high percentage of defective sperm compared to other cat species. Decreased reproductive potential, greatly reduced genetic diversity, and other factors have combined to jeopardize the continued existence of this species. Other examples include California elephant seals, sea otters, and condors. Indeed, our own species is genetically uniform, compared to chimpanzees, and it now appears that all modern human populations are the descendants of a few small groups (see Chapter 12).

Many specific examples of founder effect in human populations have been documented in small, usually isolated populations (e.g., island groups or small agricultural villages in New guinea or South America). Even larger populations that are descended from fairly small groups of founders can show the effects of genetic drift many generations later. French Canadians are one such example. While currently numbering close to 6 million, the French Canadian population of Quebec derives from only about 8,500 founders who migrated during the sixteenth and seventeenth centuries. Because the genes carried by the initial founders represented only a sample of the gene pool from which they were derived, by chance a number of alleles occurred in frequencies that differed from those in the original French population. Among these genetic disparities are the increased prevalence of several harmful alleles (a number of which are listed in Table 4–3), including those that cause cystic fibrosis, a variety of Tay-Sachs, thalassemia, and PKU (Scriver, 2001). Moreover, internal migrations within Quebec during the last 300 years have produced additional clusters of genes, again largely the result of drift acting on small populations (Heyer, 1999).

One other example of genetic drift is provided by a recently discovered fatal recessive condition called Amish microcephaly, in which a defect in DNA production results in abnormally small brains and heads in fetuses. The disorder is found only in the Old Order Amish community of Lancaster County, Pennsylvania, where it occurs in approximately one in 500 births (Kelley, R. I. et al., 2002; Rosenberg et al., 2002). Genealogical research revealed that affected families have all been traced back nine generations to a single couple. One member of this couple carried the deleterious recessive allele which, because of customs that promoted marriage within a small group, has greatly increased in frequency with very serious consequences. Indeed, much insight concerning the evolutionary factors that have acted in the past can be gained by understanding how such mechanisms continue to operate on human populations today. In small populations, drift plays a major evolutionary role because fairly sudden fluctuations in allele frequency can and do occur owing entirely to the small population size. Likewise, throughout a good deal of human evolution (at least the last 4–5 m.y.*), hominids probably lived in small groups, and drift would have had significant impact.

---

*The abbreviation m.y. stands for "million years."

While drift has been a factor producing evolutionary change in certain circumstances, the effects have been irregular and nondirectional (for drift is *random* in nature). Certainly, the pace of evolutionary change could have been accelerated if many small populations were isolated and thus subject to drift. By modifying such populations, drift can provide significantly greater opportunities for the truly directional force in evolution—natural selection.

It is important to emphasize that natural selection need not be the *only* prime mover of evolutionary change. As we have seen, both gene flow and genetic drift can produce some evolutionary changes by themselves. However, these changes are usually *microevolutionary* ones; that is, they produce changes within species over the short term. To yield the kind of evolutionary changes that ultimately result in entire new groups (e.g., the diversification of the first primates, the appearance of the hominids), natural selection most likely would play the major role. Remember, however, that natural selection does not and cannot operate independently of the other evolutionary factors—mutation, gene flow, and genetic drift. All four factors (sometimes called the "four forces of evolution") work interactively.

Additional insight concerning the relative influences of the different evolutionary factors has emerged in recent studies of the early dispersal of modern *Homo sapiens* (discussed in Chapter 11). New evidence suggests that in the last 100,000 to 200,000 years, our species experienced a genetic bottleneck, which considerably influenced the pattern of genetic variation seen in all human populations today. In this sense, modern humans can be seen as the fairly recent product of a form of genetic drift (founder effect) acting on a somewhat grand scale. Such evolutionary changes could be potentially significant over tens of thousands of years and could cause substantial genetic shifts within species.

Recombination

Since in any sexually reproducing species both parents contribute genes to offspring, the genetic information is inevitably reshuffled every generation. Such recombination does not in itself change allele frequencies (i.e., cause evolution). However, it does produce the whole array of genetic combinations, which natural selection can then act upon. In fact, we have shown how the reshuffling of chromosomes during meiosis can produce literally trillions of gene combinations, making every human being genetically unique.

Natural Selection Acts on Variation

The evolutionary factors just discussed—mutation, gene flow, genetic drift, and recombination—interact to produce variation and to distribute genes within and between populations. But there is no *directionality* to any of these factors. How, then, do populations adapt? The answer is natural selection. Natural selection provides directional change in allele frequency relative to *specific environmental factors*. If the environment changes, then the selection pressures change as well. Such a functional shift in allele frequencies is what we mean by *adaptation*. If there are long-term environmental changes in a consistent direction, then allele

See Virtual Lab 2, section I, for an example of how selection operates on variation within populations.

frequencies should also shift gradually each generation. If sustained for many generations, the results can be dramatic.

In Chapter 2, we discussed the general principles underlying natural selection and gave several nonhuman examples. Physical anthropology is, of course, centrally concerned with human evolution, and it is thus most relevant to show how natural selection operates in *human* populations. However, demonstrating clear-cut examples in our species is not an easy task. In fact, the best-documented example of natural selection in humans involves hemoglobin S, an altered form of hemoglobin that results from a point mutation in the gene that produces the hemoglobin beta chain (see p. 71). If an individual inherits this allele (Hb^S) from both parents, he or she will suffer the severe manifestations of sickle-cell anemia. Even with aggressive medical treatment, life expectancy in the United States today is less than 45 years for patients with sickle-cell anemia. Worldwide, sickle-cell anemia causes an estimated 100,000 deaths each year, and in the United States, approximately 40,000 to 50,000 individuals, mostly of African descent, suffer from this disease.

Apparently, Hb^S is a mutation that occurs occasionally in all human populations, but the allele usually remains relatively rare. In some populations, however, Hb^S is more common, and this is especially true in western and central Africa, where its frequency approaches 20 percent. The frequency of the allele is also moderately high in parts of Greece and India (fig. 4–6). Given the devastating effects of Hb^S in homozygotes, how do we explain its higher prevalence in some populations? The answer to this question lies in malaria, a serious infectious disease that has exerted enormous selective pressures in the past and continues to do so today. Malaria currently kills an estimated 1 to 3 million people worldwide annually. It is caused by one of several protozoan parasites belonging to the genus *Plasmodium*. These parasites are in turn transmitted to humans by mosquitoes.

Very briefly, after an infected mosquito bites a person, plasmodial parasites invade red blood cells, where they obtain oxygen they need for reproduction. The consequences of this infection to the human host include fever, chills, headache, nausea, vomiting, and, frequently, death. In parts of western and central Africa, where malaria is always present, the burden of the disease is borne by children, with as many as 50 to 75 percent of 2- to 9-year-olds being afflicted.

The geographical correlation between malaria and the distribution of the sickle-cell allele is indirect evidence of a biological relationship (figs. 4–6 and 4–7). Today, we know that individuals with one Hb^S allele (i.e., those with sickle-cell trait) and thus some hemoglobin S have greater resistance to malaria than the homozygous "normals." Heterozygotes resist infection because their red blood cells provide a less conducive environment for the parasite to reproduce. Thus, in environments where the prevalence of malaria is always high, individuals with sickle-cell trait have higher reproductive success than those with normal hemoglobin. Those afflicted with sickle-cell anemia, of course, have the lowest reproductive success, since without treatment, most die before reaching adulthood.

The relationship between malaria and hemoglobin S provides the best example we have of natural selection in contemporary humans. In this case, natural selection has favored the heterozygous phenotype, thus increasing the frequency of Hb^S, an allele that in homozygotes causes severe disease and early death.

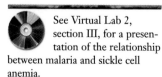

See Virtual Lab 2, section III, for a presentation of the relationship between malaria and sickle cell anemia.

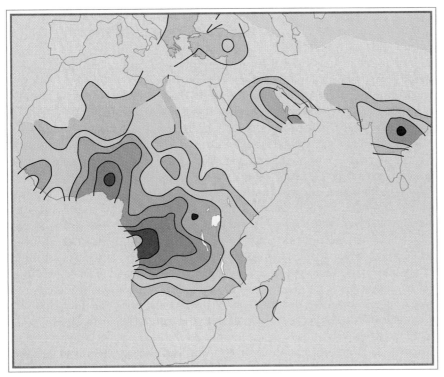

figure 4–6 A frequency map of the sickle-cell allele distribution in the Old World.

Frequencies of the sickle-cell allele:

Greater than .14	.08–.10	.02–.04
.12–.14	.06–.08	.00–.02
.10–.12	.04–.06	

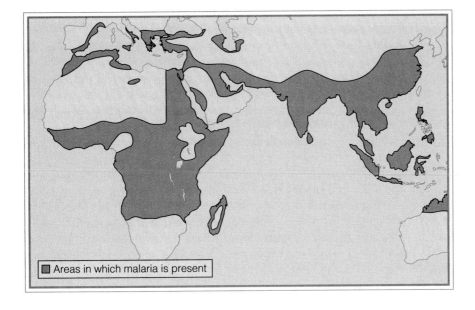

Areas in which malaria is present

figure 4–7 Malaria distribution in the Old World.

Review of Genetics and Evolutionary Factors

Beginning in Chapter 3 with a discussion of the molecular and cellular bases of heredity, we proceeded in this chapter to show how such genetic information is passed from individuals in one generation to those in the next. In this chapter, we also have reviewed evolutionary theory and its current applications, emphasizing the crucial role of natural selection. These different levels—molecular, cellular, individual, and populational—are different aspects of evolution, and they are all related and highly integrated in a way that can eventually produce evolutionary change. A step-by-step example will make this clear.

We begin with a situation in which everyone in the population has the same hemoglobin type; therefore, initially no variation for this trait exists, and without some source of new variation, evolution is not possible. How does this gene change? We have seen that a substitution of a single base in the DNA sequence can alter the code significantly enough to alter the protein product and ultimately the entire phenotype of the individual. Consider that in each generation such an incident occurs in one or a few individuals. For a mutated allele to be passed on to succeeding offspring, the gametes must carry the alteration. Any new mutation, therefore, must be transmitted during sex cell formation.

Once the mutation has occurred in the DNA, it will be packaged into chromosomes, and these chromosomes in turn will assort during meiosis to be passed to offspring. The results of this process are seen by looking at phenotypes (traits) in individuals, and the mode of inheritance is described simply by Mendel's principle of segregation. In other words, if our initial individual has a mutation in only one paired allele on a set of homologous chromosomes, there will be a 50 percent chance of passing this chromosome (with the new mutation) to an offspring.

But what does all this activity have to do with *evolution?* To repeat an earlier definition, evolution is a change in allele frequency in a *population* from one generation to the next. The key point here is that we are now looking at entire groups of individuals, or populations, and it is populations that may change over time.

We know whether allele frequencies have changed in a population where sickle-cell hemoglobin is found by ascertaining the percentage of individuals with the sickling allele (Hb^S) versus those with the normal allele (Hb^A). If the relative proportions of these alleles alter with time, evolution has occurred. In addition to discovering that evolution has occurred, it is important to know why. Several possibilities arise. First, we know that the only way the new allele Hb^S could have arisen is by mutation, and we have shown how this process can happen in a single individual. This change, however, is not an evolutionary one, because in a relatively large population, the alteration of one individual's genes will not significantly alter allele frequencies of the entire population. Somehow, this new allele must *spread* in the population.

One way this could happen is in a small population, where mutations in one or just a few individuals and their offspring may indeed alter the overall frequency quite quickly. This case would be representative of genetic drift. As discussed, drift acts in small populations, where random factors may cause significant changes in allele frequency. With a small population size, there is not likely to be a balance of factors affecting individual survival or reproduction. Consequently, some alleles may be completely removed from the population,

TABLE 4-4	Levels of Organization in the Evolutionary Process			
Evolutionary Factor	Level	Evolutionary Process		Technique of Study
Mutation	DNA	Storage of genetic information; ability to replicate; influences phenotype by production of proteins		Biochemistry, electron microscope, recombinant DNA
Mutation	Chromosomes	A vehicle for packaging and transmitting genetic material (DNA)		Light or electron microscope
Recombination (sex cells only)	Cell	The basic unit of life that contains the chromosomes and divides for growth and for production of sex cells		Light or electron microscope
Natural selection	Organism	The unit, composed of cells, that reproduces and which we observe for phenotypic traits		Visual study, biochemistry
Drift, gene flow	Population	A group of interbreeding organisms; changes in allele frequencies between generations; it is the population that evolves		Statistical analysis

while others may become established as the only allele present at that particular locus (and are said to be "fixed" in the population).

In the course of human evolution, drift may have played a significant role at times, and it is important to remember that at this microevolutionary level, drift and/or gene flow can (and will) produce evolutionary change, even in the absence of natural selection. However, directional evolutionary trends can only have been sustained by *natural selection*. The way this has worked in the past and still operates today (as in sickle-cell) is through differential reproduction. That is, individuals who carry a particular allele or combination of alleles produce more offspring. By producing more offspring than other individuals with alternative alleles, such individuals cause the frequency of the new allele in the population to increase slowly from generation to generation. When this process is compounded over hundreds of generations for numerous loci, the result is significant evolutionary change. The levels of organization in the evolutionary process are summarized in Table 4–4.

Summary

e have seen how Gregor Mendel discovered the principles of segregation, independent assortment, and dominance and recessiveness by conducting experiments on garden peas. Although the field of genetics progressed dramatically in the twentieth century, the concepts first put forth by Gregor Mendel remain the basis of our current knowledge on how traits are inherited.

Basic Mendelian principles are applied to the study of the various modes of inheritance we are familiar with today. The most important factor in all the Mendelian modes of inheritance is the role of segregation of chromosomes, and the alleles they carry, during meiosis. Although our understanding of human inheritance has virtually exploded in the last 50 years, the very foundation of our knowledge rests in the basic rules as set forth by Gregor Mendel almost 150 years ago.

Building on fundamental nineteenth-century contributions by Charles Darwin and his contemporaries and the rediscovery in 1900 of Mendel's work, further refinements later in the twentieth century added to contemporary evolutionary thought. In particular, the combination of natural selection with Mendel's principles of inheritance and experimental evidence concerning the nature of mutation have all been synthesized into a modern understanding of evolutionary change, appropriately termed the Modern Synthesis. In this, the central contemporary theory of evolution, evolutionary change is seen as a two-stage process. The first stage is the production and redistribution of variation. The second stage is the process whereby natural selection acts on the accumulated genetic variation.

Crucial to all evolutionary change is mutation, the only source of completely new genetic variation. In addition, the factors of gene flow, genetic drift, and recombination function to redistribute variation within individuals (recombination), within populations (genetic drift), and between populations (gene flow).

Natural selection is the central determining factor influencing the long-term direction of evolutionary change. How natural selection works can best be explained as differential reproductive success—in other words, how successful individuals are in leaving offspring to succeeding generations. To more fully illustrate the mechanics of evolutionary change through natural selection, comprehensive and well-understood examples from other organisms are most helpful. The detailed history of the evolutionary spread of the sickle-cell allele provides the best-documented example of natural selection among recent human populations. It must be remembered that evolution is an integrated process, and this chapter concluded with a discussion of how the various evolutionary factors can be integrated into a single, comprehensive view of evolutionary change.

Questions for Review

1. What is Mendel's principle of segregation?
2. How does meiosis explain the principle of segregation?
3. What is Mendel's principle of independent assortment?
4. Explain dominance and recessiveness.
5. Define allele.
6. What is a phenotype, and what is its relationship to a genotype?
7. Explain what is meant by a phenotypic ratio of 3:1 in the F_2 generation.
8. What is codominance? Give an example.
9. If two people who have blood type A (both with the *AO* genotype) have children, what proportion of their children would be expected to have the O blood type? Why?
10. Can the two parents in question 9 have a child with AB blood? Why or why not?
11. In a cross between two carriers for a recessive trait, why would ¾ of the offspring be expected *not* to show the recessive characteristic?

12. Explain how natural selection works. Illustrate through an example in humans.
13. What is polygenic inheritance? How does it differ from Mendelian inheritance?
14. Explain why natural selection has acted to increase the frequency of Hb^S, the allele that causes sickle-cell anemia, in heterozygotes in some populations.
15. What is the Modern Synthesis? Explain how the major components of this theory explain evolutionary change.
16. What is genetic drift? Illustrate through an example for human populations.
17. Define gene flow. Give an example in human populations.
18. What role does variation play in the evolutionary process? Where does variation come from? (*Hint:* You may wish to discuss the source of variation as completely new to a species or as it is introduced into a population *within* a species.)
19. Discuss how evolutionary change occurs as an integrated process. Illustrate through an example.

Suggested Further Readings

Cummings, Michael R. 2000. *Human Heredity. Principles and Issues*. 5th ed. Pacific Grove, CA: Brooks/Cole.

Heim, Werner G. 1991. "What is a Recessive Allele?" *The American Biology Teacher* 53(2): 94–97.

Little, Peter. 1999. "The Book of Genes." *Nature* 402: 467–468.

Ridley, Mark. 1993. *Evolution*. Cambridge, MA: Blackwell Scientific.

Wake, David B. 2001. "Evolution: Speciation in the Round." *Nature* 409: 299–300.

Multimedia Resources

 Companion Web Site

Anthropology Online: The Wadsworth Anthropology Resource Center Visit **http://anthropology.wadsworth.com** and click on the Companion Web Site for Jurmain/Kilgore/Trevathan/Nelson's *Essentials of Physical Anthropology*, Fifth Edition, to access a wide range of enrichment material to aid in your study of anthropology. Among the useful options for each chapter's self-study are learning objectives, flashcards, Internet exercises, Web links, InfoTrac College Edition exercises, and practice quizzes that can be scored and emailed to your instructor.

AN OVERVIEW OF THE LIVING PRIMATES

CONTENTS

Introduction

Thus far, we have presented the basic biological background for understanding evolutionary processes. Evolution has produced a continuum of life forms, as demonstrated genetically, anatomically, and behaviorally. To gain an understanding of any organism, it is necessary, whenever possible, to compare its anatomy and behavior with those of other, closely related forms. This statement applies to *Homo sapiens* just as surely as to any other species, and if we are to identify the components that have shaped hominid evolution, the starting point must be a systematic comparison between humans and our closest living relatives, the approximately 230 species of nonhuman primates (**prosimians,** monkeys, and apes). This chapter describes the physical characteristics that define the order Primates, gives a brief overview of the major groups of living primates, and introduces some methods of comparing living primates through genetic data. (For a detailed comparison of human and nonhuman skeletons, see Appendix A.)

Before proceeding further, we must call attention to a few common misunderstandings about evolutionary processes. Evolution is *not* a goal-directed process; thus, the fact that prosimians evolved before **anthropoids** does not mean that prosimians "progressed," or "advanced," to become anthropoids. Living primate species are in no way "superior" to their evolutionary predecessors or to one another. Consequently, in discussions of major groupings of contemporary nonhuman primates, there is no implied superiority or inferiority of any of these groups. Each grouping (lineage, or species) has come to possess unique qualities that make it better suited than others to a particular habitat and lifestyle. Given that all contemporary organisms are "successful" results of the evolutionary process, it is best to avoid altogether the use of such loaded terms as "superior" and "inferior." Finally, you should not make the mistake of thinking that contemporary primates (including humans) necessarily represent the final stage or apex of a lineage. Actually, the only species that represent final evolutionary stages of particular lineages are those that become extinct.

Primates as Mammals

The order *Primates* is a subgroup of a larger group of organisms, the mammals (technically, the class **Mammalia**). Today there are at least 4,600 species of mammals, which can be further subdivided into three major subgroups: (1) the egg-laying mammals, (2) the pouched mammals (i.e., marsupials), and (3) the placental mammals. For the moment, you should recognize that primates are members of the placental subgroup, which includes other common orders such as rodents and carnivores. Placental mammals today are distributed over most of the world in a wide variety of forms, including flying, swimming, and burrowing varieties and a host of other adaptations as well. Sizes range from the tiny dwarf shrews (just a few grams) to the whales, the largest animals ever to inhabit the earth.

See the following sections of the CD-ROM for topics covered in this chapter: Virtual Lab 1, sections II, III, and IV; Virtual Lab 3; Virtual Lab 4, sections I and II; and Virtual Lab 5.

Prosimians Members of a suborder of Primates, the *Prosimii* (pronounced "pro-sim´-ee-eye"). Traditionally, the suborder includes lemurs, lorises, and tarsiers.

Anthropoids Members of a suborder of Primates, the *Anthropoidea* (pronounced "ann-throw-poid´-ee-uh"). Traditionally, the suborder includes monkeys, apes, and humans.

Mammalia The technical term for the formal grouping (class) of mammals.

See Virtual Lab 1, section I, for a discussion of the inclusion of the primate order within the class Mammalia.

Characteristics of Primates

All primates possess numerous characteristics they share in common with other placental mammals. Such traits include body hair; a relatively long gestation period followed by live birth; mammary glands (thus the term *mammal*); different types of teeth (incisors, canines, premolars, and molars); the ability to maintain a constant internal body temperature through physiological means (*homeothermy*); increased brain size; and a considerable capacity for learning and behavioral flexibility. Therefore, to differentiate primates, as a group, from other mammals, we must describe those characteristics that, taken together, set primates apart from other mammalian groups. This is not a simple task, for among mammals, primates have remained quite *generalized*. That is, primates have retained many **primitive** mammalian traits that some other mammalian species have lost over time. In response to particular selective pressures, many mammalian groups have become increasingly **specialized.** For example, through the course of evolution, horses and cattle have undergone a reduction of the number of digits (fingers and toes) from the primitive pattern of five to one and two, respectively. Moreover, these species have developed hard, protective coverings over their feet in the form of hooves. While this type of limb structure is adaptive in prey species, whose survival depends on speed and stability, it restricts the animal to only one type of locomotion. Moreover, limb function is limited entirely to support and movement, while the ability to manipulate objects is completely lost.

Primates, precisely because they are *not* so specialized, cannot be simply defined by one or even two traits they share in common. As a result, biologists have pointed to a group of characteristics that, taken together, more or less characterize the entire order. Keep in mind that these are a set of *general* tendencies and are not all equally expressed in all primates.

The following list is intended to give an overall structural and behavioral picture of that kind of animal we call "primate," focusing on those characteristics that tend to set primates apart from other mammals. Concentrating on certain retained (ancestral) mammalian traits, along with more specific ones, has been the traditional approach of **primatologists.** Some contemporary primatologists (Fleagle, 1999) believe it is useful to enumerate all these features to better illustrate primate adaptations. Thus, a common evolutionary history with adaptations to similar environmental challenges is seen to be reflected in the limbs and locomotion, teeth and diet, senses, brain, and behaviors of those animals that make up the primate order.

A. *Limbs and Locomotion*
1. *A tendency toward erect posture (especially in the upper body).* Shown to some degree in all primates, this tendency is variously associated with sitting, leaping, standing, and, occasionally, bipedal walking.
2. *A flexible, generalized limb structure, permitting most primates to engage in a number of locomotor behaviors.* Primates have retained some bones (e.g., the clavicle, or collarbone) and certain abilities, (e.g., rotation of the forearm) that have been lost in some more specialized mammals. Various aspects of hip and shoulder **morphology** also provide primates with a wide range of limb movement and function. Thus, by maintaining a generalized locomotor anatomy, primates are not restricted to one form

Primitive Referring to a trait or combination of traits present in an ancestral form.

Specialized Evolved for a particular function; usually refers to a specific trait (e.g., incisor teeth), but may also refer to the entire way of life of an organism.

 See Virtual Lab I, section III, for a discussion of the traits typically used to define the primate order. Section IV presents mammalian and primate life history variables.

Primatologists Scientists who study the evolution, anatomy, and behavior of nonhuman primates. Those who study behavior in noncaptive animals are usually trained as physical anthropologists.

Morphology The form (shape, size) of anatomical structures; can also refer to the entire organism.

of movement, as are many other mammals. Primate limbs are also used for activities other than locomotion.

3. *Hands and feet with a high degree of **prehensility** (grasping ability).* All primates use the hands, and frequently the feet, to grasp and manipulate objects (fig. 5–1). This capability is variably expressed and is enhanced by a number of characteristics, including:

   a. *Retention of five digits on hands and feet.* This varies somewhat throughout the order, with some species showing marked reduction of the thumb or of the second digit.

   b. *An opposable thumb and, in most species, a divergent and partially opposable big toe.* Most primates are capable of moving the thumb so that it comes in contact (in some fashion) with the second digit or the palm of the hand.

   c. *Nails instead of claws.* This characteristic is seen in all primates except some New World monkeys. Some prosimians also possess a claw on one digit.

   d. *Tactile pads enriched with sensory nerve fibers at the ends of digits.* This trend serves to enhance the sense of touch.

B. *Diet and Teeth*

   1. *Lack of dietary specialization.* This is typical of most primates, who tend to eat a wide assortment of food items.

   2. *A generalized dentition.* The teeth are not specialized for processing only one type of food, a pattern correlated with the lack of dietary specialization. In general, primates are **omnivorous.**

C. *The senses and the brain.* Primates (**diurnal** ones in particular) rely heavily on the visual sense and less on the sense of smell, especially compared to many other mammals. This emphasis is reflected in evolutionary changes in the skull, eyes, and brain.

   1. *Color vision.* This is characteristic of all diurnal primates. Most **nocturnal** primates lack color vision.

   2. *Depth perception.* **Stereoscopic vision,** or the ability to perceive objects in three dimensions, is made possible through a variety of mechanisms, including:

      a. *Eyes positioned toward the front of the face (not to the sides).* This configuration provides for overlapping visual fields, or **binocular vision** (fig. 5–2).

      b. *Visual information from each eye transmitted to visual centers in both hemispheres of the brain.* In nonprimate mammals, most optic nerve fibers cross to the opposite hemisphere through a structure at the base of the brain. In primates, about 40 percent of the fibers remain on the same side (see fig. 5–2).

      c. *Visual information organized into three-dimensional images by specialized structures in the brain itself.* The capacity for stereoscopic vision is dependent on each hemisphere of the brain having received visual information from both eyes and from overlapping visual fields.

   3. *Decreased reliance on the sense of smell (olfaction).* This trend is seen in an overall reduction in the size of olfactory structures in the brain. Corresponding reduction of the entire olfactory apparatus has also resulted in decreased size of the snout (fig. 5–3). (In some species, such as baboons, the large muzzle is not related to olfaction, but to the presence of large teeth, especially the canines.)

Prehensility The ability to grasp objects, as by the hands and/or feet of primates.

figure 5–1 Primate (macaque) hand.

Omnivorous Having a diet consisting of many food types (i.e., plant materials, meat, and insects).

Diurnal Active during the day.

Nocturnal Active during the night.

Stereoscopic vision The condition whereby visual images are, to varying degrees, superimposed on one another. This provides for depth perception, or the perception of the external environment in three dimensions. Stereoscopic vision is partly a function of structures in the brain.

Binocular vision Vision characterized by overlapping visual fields provided by forward-facing eyes; essential to depth perception.

figure 5–2 Simplified diagram showing overlapping visual fields (binocular vision) in primates (and some predators) with eyes positioned at the front of the face. (The green shaded area represents the area of overlap.) Stereoscopic vision (three-dimensional vision) is provided in part by binocular vision and in part by the transmission of visual stimuli from each eye to *both* hemispheres of the brain. (In nonprimate mammals, most, if not all, visual information crosses over to the hemisphere opposite the eye in which it was initially received.)

Primary receiving area for visual information

4. *Expansion and increased complexity of the brain.* This is a general trend among placental mammals, but it is especially true of primates. In primates, this expansion is most evident in the visual and association areas of the neocortex (portions of the brain where information from different sensory modalities is integrated). Expansion in regions involved with the hand (both sensory and motor) is seen in many species, particularly humans.

D. *Maturation, learning, and behavior*

   1. *A more efficient means of fetal nourishment, longer periods of gestation, reduced numbers of offspring (with single births the norm), delayed maturation, and extension of the entire life span.*

   2. *A greater dependence on flexible, learned behavior.* This trend is correlated with delayed maturation and consequently longer periods of infant and child dependency on the parent. As a result of both these trends, parental investment in each offspring is increased, so that although fewer offspring are born, they receive more intense and efficient rearing.

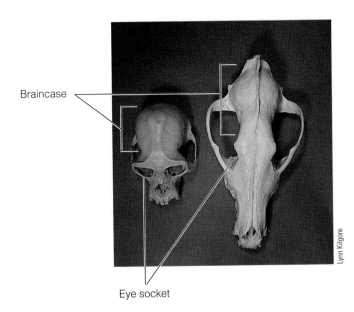

Braincase

Eye socket

figure 5–3 The skull of a gibbon, a small-bodied ape (left), compared with that of a red wolf (right). Note the forward-facing eye orbits of the gibbon and the eye orbits placed more to the side in the wolf. The absolute brain size of the gibbon is slightly larger than that of the wolf, even though the wolf, at about 60 to 80 pounds, is approximately four times the size of the gibbon (about 15 pounds).

3. *The tendency to live in social groups and the permanent association of adult males with the group.* Except for some nocturnal species, primates tend to associate with other individuals. The permanent association of adult males with the group is uncommon in mammals but widespread in primates.
4. *The tendency to diurnal activity patterns.* This is seen in most primates; only one monkey species and some prosimians are nocturnal.

Primate Adaptations

Evolutionary Factors

Traditionally, the suite of characteristics shared by primates has been explained as the result of adaptation to **arboreal** living. While other placental mammals were adapting to various ground-dwelling lifestyles and even marine environments, the primates found their **adaptive niche** in the trees. Indeed, some other mammals were also adapting to arboreal living, but while many of these species nested in trees, they continued to come to the ground to forage for food. But throughout the course of evolution, primates came increasingly to exploit foods (leaves, seeds, fruits, nuts, insects, and small mammals) found in the branches themselves. The exploitation of these varied foods enhanced the general trend toward *omnivory* in primates and toward the primate generalized dentition.

We can also see this adaptive process reflected in the primate reliance on vision. In a complex, three-dimensional environment with uncertain footholds, acute color vision with depth perception is extremely beneficial. The presence of grasping hands and feet is also an indicator of the adaptation to living in the trees. Climbing can be accomplished by either digging in with claws (as in many species, such as squirrels or raccoons) or grasping around branches with prehensile hands and feet. Primates adopted this latter strategy, which allowed a means of moving about, sometimes very rapidly, on small, unstable surfaces, and grasping abilities were further enhanced by the presence of flattened nails instead of claws.

Arboreal Tree-living; adapted to life in the trees.

Adaptive niche The entire way of life of an organism: where it lives, what it eats, how it gets food, how it avoids predators, etc.

Arboreal hypothesis The traditional view that primate characteristics can be explained as a consequence of primate diversification into arboreal habitats.

An alternative to this traditional **arboreal hypothesis,** called the *visual predation hypothesis* (Cartmill, 1972, 1992), acknowledges that forward-facing eyes are characteristic not only of primates, but also of predators, such as cats and owls, that prey on small animals. Cartmill points out that the most significant primate trends (forward-facing eyes, grasping hands and feet, and the presence of nails instead of claws) may *not* have arisen as adaptive advantages in a purely arboreal environment. According to the visual predation hypothesis, primates may first have adapted to shrubby forest undergrowth and the lowest tiers of the forest canopy, where they exploited insects and other small prey they captured primarily through stealth.

A third scenario (Sussman, 1991) proposes that the basic primate traits developed in conjunction with another major evolutionary occurrence, the rise of the *angiosperms* (flowering plants). Flowering plants provided numerous resources, including nectar, seeds, and fruits, and their appearance and diversification were accompanied by the appearance of ancestral forms of major groups of modern birds and mammals. Sussman argues that visual predation is not common among modern primates and that forward-facing eyes, grasping extremities, and omnivory may have arisen in response to the demand for fine visual and tactile discrimination, necessary when feeding on small food items such as fruits, berries, and seeds among branches and stems.

These hypotheses are not mutually exclusive. The complex of primate characteristics might well have begun in nonarboreal settings and certainly may have been stimulated by the new econiches provided by evolving angiosperms. But, at some point, the primates did take to the trees, and that is where the vast majority of nonhuman primates still live today.

Geographical Distribution and Habitats

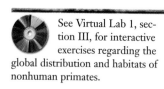

See Virtual Lab 1, section III, for interactive exercises regarding the global distribution and habitats of nonhuman primates.

With just a couple of exceptions, primates are found in tropical or semitropical areas of the New and Old Worlds. In the New World, these areas include southern Mexico, Central America, and parts of South America. Old World primates are found in Africa, India, Southeast Asia (including numerous islands), and Japan (fig. 5–5 on pp. 96–97).

The majority of primates are, as we have discussed, mostly arboreal and live in forest or woodland habitats. However, some Old World monkeys (e.g., baboons) have, to varying degrees, adapted to life on the ground in areas where trees are sparsely distributed. Moreover, among the apes, gorillas and chimpanzees spend a considerable amount of time on the ground in forested and wooded habitats. Nevertheless, no nonhuman primate is adapted to a fully terrestrial lifestyle, and all spend some time in the trees.

Diet and Teeth

See Virtual Lab 5 for an in-depth discussion of primate diets and dental adaptations.

As noted, primates are generally *omnivorous*. Indeed, the tendency toward omnivory is one example of the overall lack of specialization in primates. Although the majority of primate species tend to emphasize some food items over others, most eat a combination of fruits, leaves and other plant materials, and insects. Many obtain animal protein from birds and amphibians as well. Some (baboons, and, especially, chimpanzees) occasionally kill and eat small mammals, including other primates. Others, such as African colobus monkeys,

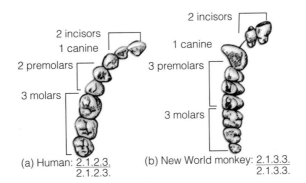

2 incisors
1 canine
2 premolars
3 molars

2 incisors
1 canine
3 premolars
3 molars

(a) Human: <u>2.1.2.3.</u>
               2.1.2.3.

(b) New World monkey: <u>2.1.3.3.</u>
                               2.1.3.3.

figure 5–4 Dental formulae. The number of each kind of tooth is given for one-quarter of the mouth.

the leaf-eating monkeys (langurs) of India and Southeast Asia, and the muriquis of Brazil have become more specialized and subsist primarily on leaves. Such an array of choices is highly adaptive even in fairly predictable environments.

Like the majority of other mammals, most primates have four kinds of teeth: incisors and canines for biting and cutting and premolars and molars for chewing. Biologists use a device called a *dental formula* to describe the number of each type of tooth that typifies a species. A dental formula indicates the number of each tooth type in each quadrant of the mouth (fig. 5–4). For example, all Old World *anthropoids* have two incisors, one canine, two premolars, and three molars on each side of the **midline** in both the upper and lower jaws, or a total of 32 teeth. This is represented as a dental formula of

<u>2.1.2.3.</u> (upper)
2.1.2.3. (lower)

The dental formula for a generalized placental mammal is 3.1.4.3. (three incisors, one canine, four premolars, and three molars). Primates have fewer teeth than this ancestral pattern because there has been a general evolutionary trend toward reduction of the number of teeth in many mammal groups. Consequently, the number of each type of tooth varies between lineages. For example, in the majority of New World monkeys, the dental formula is 2.1.3.3. (two incisors, one canine, three premolars, and three molars).

Correlated with an overall lack of dietary specialization in primates is a lack of specialization with regard to the size and shape of the teeth because tooth form is directly related to diet. For example, carnivores typically have premolars and molars with high pointed **cusps** adapted for tearing meat, while the premolars of herbivores, such as cattle and horses, have broad, flat surfaces suited to chewing tough grasses and other plant materials. Most primates possess molars that have low, rounded cusps, a morphology that enables them to process most types of foods. Thus, throughout their evolutionary history, the primates have developed a dentition adapted to a varied diet, and the capacity to exploit many foods has contributed to their overall success during the last 50 million years.

Locomotion

Almost all primates are, at least to some degree, **quadrupedal,** meaning they use all four limbs to support the body during locomotion. However, most primates use more than one form of locomotion, and they owe this important ability to their generalized structure.

Midline An anatomical term referring to a hypothetical line that divides the body into right and left halves.

Cusps The elevated portions (bumps) on the chewing surfaces of premolar and molar teeth.

Quadrupedal Using all four limbs to support the body during locomotion; the basic mammalian (and primate) form of locomotion.

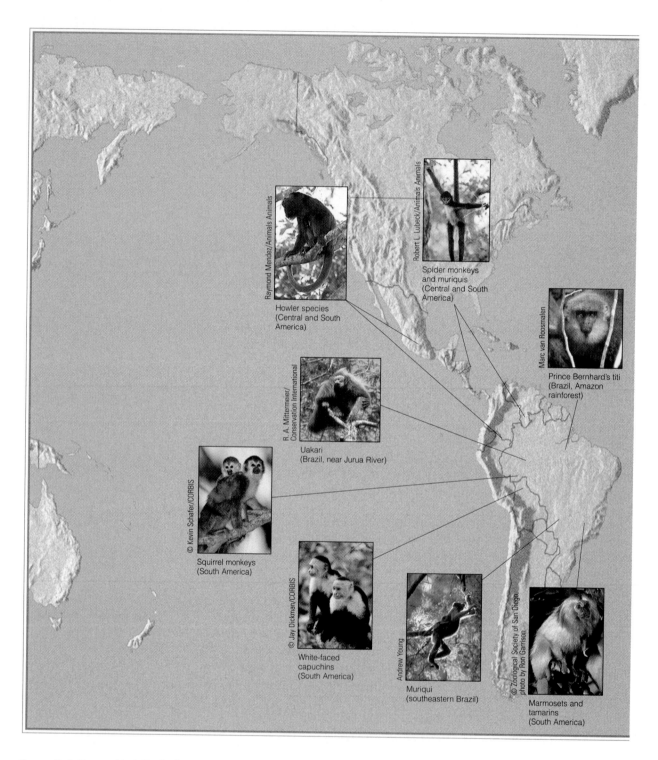

figure 5–5 Geographical distribution of living nonhuman primates. Much original habitat is now very fragmented.

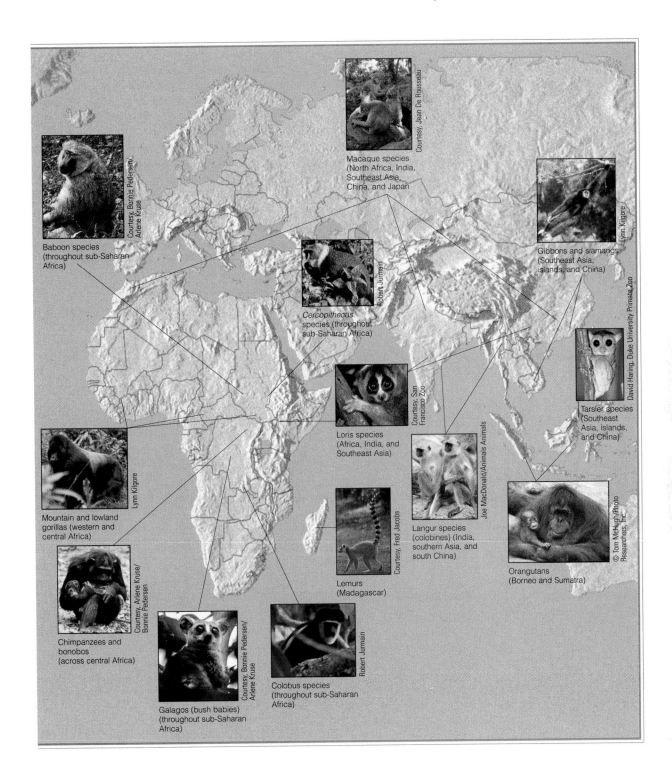

Macaque species
(North Africa, India,
Southeast Asia,
China, and Japan)

Courtesy, Jean De Rousseau

Baboon species
(throughout sub-Saharan
Africa)

Courtesy, Bonnie Pedersen/
Arlene Kruse

Gibbons and siamangs
(Southeast Asia,
islands, and China)

Lynn Kilgore

Cercopithecus
species (throughout
sub-Saharan Africa)

Robert Jurmain

Tarsier species
(Southeast
Asia, islands,
and China)

David Haring, Duke University Primate Zoo

Loris species
(Africa, India, and
Southeast Asia)

Courtesy, San
Francisco Zoo

Mountain and lowland
gorillas (western and
central Africa)

Lynn Kilgore

Langur species
(colobines) (India,
southern Asia, and
south China)

Joe MacDonald/Animals Animals

Orangutans
(Borneo and Sumatra)

© Tom McHugh/Photo
Researchers, Inc.

Lemurs
(Madagascar)

Courtesy, Fred Jacobs

Chimpanzees and
bonobos
(across central Africa)

Courtesy, Arlene Kruse/
Bonnie Pedersen

Galagos (bush babies)
(throughout sub-Saharan
Africa)

Courtesy, Bonnie Pedersen/
Arlene Kruse

Colobus species
(throughout sub-Saharan
Africa)

Robert Jurmain

Although the majority of quadrupedal primates are arboreal, terrestrial quadrupedalism is fairly common and is typical of some lemurs, baboons, and **macaques.** Typically, the limbs of terrestrial quadrupeds are approximately of equal length, with forelimbs being 90 percent (or more) as long as hind limbs (fig. 5–6a). In arboreal quadrupeds, forelimbs are shorter and may be only 70 to 80 percent as long as hind limbs (fig. 5–6b).

Quadrupeds are also characterized by a relatively long and flexible *lumbar spine* (lower back). This lumbar flexibility permits the animal to bend the body during running, thus positioning the hind limbs and feet well forward under the body and enhancing their ability to propel the animal forward. (Watch for this the next time you see slow-motion footage of cheetahs or lions on television.)

Another form of locomotion is *vertical clinging and leaping*, characteristic of many prosimians. As the term implies, vertical clingers and leapers support them-

Macaques (muh-kaks´) Group of Old World monkeys comprising several species, including rhesus monkeys.

figure 5–6a–d Differences in skeletal anatomy and limb proportions reflect differences in locomotor patterns. (Redrawn by Stephen Nash from original art in Fleagle, John G., *Primate Adaptation and Evolution*, 1988, Elsevier Science. Reprinted by permission of publisher and Stephen Nash.)

(a) Skeleton of a terrestrial quadruped (savanna baboon).

(b) Skeleton of an arboreal New World monkey (bearded saki).

(c) Skeleton of a vertical clinger and leaper (indri).

(d) Skeleton of a brachiator (gibbon).

selves vertically by grasping onto trunks of trees while their knees and ankles are tightly flexed (fig. 5–6c). Forceful extension of their long hind limbs allows them to spring powerfully away in either a forward or backward direction.

Yet another type of primate locomotion is **brachiation,** or arm swinging, where the body is alternately supported under either forelimb. Because of anatomical modifications at the shoulder joint, apes and humans are capable of true brachiation. However, only the small gibbons and siamangs of Southeast Asia use this form of locomotion almost exclusively (fig. 5–6d).

Brachiation is seen in species characterized by arms longer than legs, a short stable lumbar spine, long curved fingers, and reduced thumbs. Because these are traits seen in all the apes, it is believed that although none of the great apes (orangutans, gorillas, and chimpanzees) habitually brachiates today, they most likely inherited these characteristics from brachiating or perhaps climbing ancestors.

Some New World monkeys (e.g. muriquis and spider monkeys) are termed *semibrachiators*, as they practice a combination of leaping with some arm swinging. And in some New World species, arm swinging and other suspensory behaviors are enhanced by use of a *prehensile tail*, which in effect serves as a grasping fifth "hand." It should be noted that prehensile tails are strictly a New World phenomenon and are not seen in any Old World primate species.

Brachiation A form of locomotion in which the body is suspended beneath the hands and support is alternated from one forelimb to the other; arm swinging.

See Virtual Lab 3 for a presentation of anatomical terms. See Virtual Lab 4, sections I and II, for a discussion of the relationship between relative limb proportions and locomotion.

A Survey of the Living Primates

Primate Taxonomy

The living primates are commonly categorized into their respective subgroups as shown in figure 5–7. This taxonomy is based on the system originally established by Linnaeus. (Remember that the primate order, which includes a diverse array of approximately 230 species, belongs to a larger group, the class Mammalia.)

In any taxonomic system, organisms are organized into increasingly specific categories. For example, the order Primates includes *all* primates. However, at the next level down—the *suborder*—the primates have conventionally been divided into two large categories, Prosimii (all the prosimians: lemurs, lorises, and, customarily, the tarsiers) and Anthropoidea (all the monkeys, apes, and humans). Therefore, the suborder distinction is more specific and more precise than the order.

At the level of the suborder, the prosimians are distinct as a group from all the other primates, and this classification makes the biological and evolutionary statement that all the prosimian species are more closely related to one another than they are to any of the anthropoids. Likewise, all anthropoid species are more closely related to one another than to the prosimians.

At each succeeding level (infraorder, superfamily, family, subfamily, genus, and species), finer distinctions are made between categories until, at the species level, only those animals that can interbreed and produce viable offspring are included. In this manner, taxonomies not only organize diversity into categories, but also illustrate evolutionary and genetic relationships between species and groups of species.

The taxonomy presented in figure 5–7 is the traditional one and is based on physical similarities between species and lineages. However, this technique can

See Virtual Lab 4, section I, for video clips of primate locomotion.

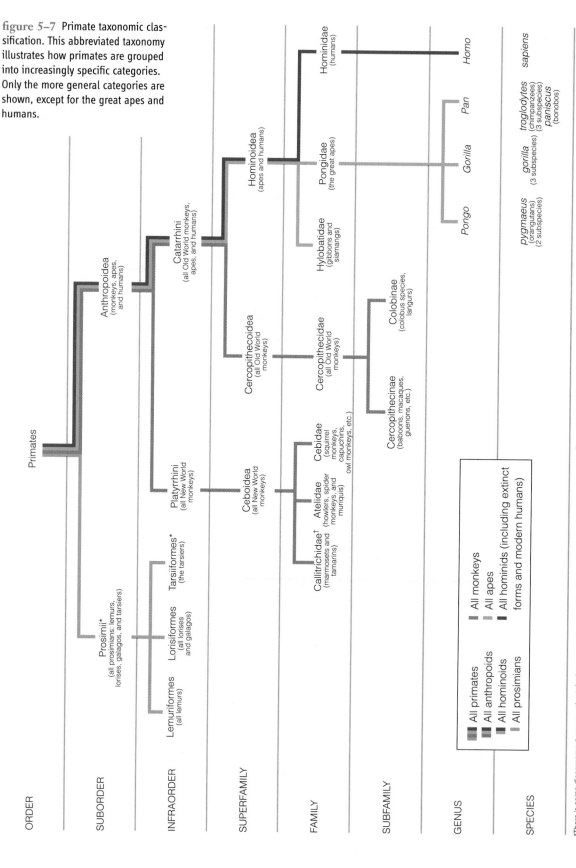

figure 5–7 Primate taxonomic classification. This abbreviated taxonomy illustrates how primates are grouped into increasingly specific categories. Only the more general categories are shown, except for the great apes and humans.

*There is some disagreement among primatologists concerning where to place tarsiers. Many researchers suggest that they more properly belong closer to the anthropoids and thus revise the primate classification to reflect this view. Here, for simplicity, we continue to use the traditional classifications.

†Fleagle (1999) and others have recently eliminated the family Callitrichidae and included marmosets and tamarins in the family Cebidae.

be problematic. For example, two primate species that superficially resemble each other (e.g., some New and Old World monkeys) may in fact not be closely related at all. Using external morphology alone overlooks the unknown effects of separate evolutionary history. But evidence such as biochemical data avoids these pitfalls and indeed shows Old and New World monkeys to be genetically and evolutionarily quite distinct.

See Virtual Lab 1, section II, for an interactive discussion of primate taxonomy and the issue of ape and human classification.

This relatively new perspective has enormous potential for clarifying taxonomic problems by making between-species comparisons of chromosomes and amino acid sequences in proteins. Direct comparisons of the amino acid sequences of various proteins (products of DNA) are excellent indicators of shared evolutionary history. If two primate species are similar with regard to protein structure, we know that their DNA sequences are also similar. Also, if two species share similar DNA, it is highly probable that both inherited their blueprint from a common ancestor.

Another technique called DNA hybridization matches DNA strands from two species to determine what percentage of bases match. The higher the percentage, the closer the genetic relationship between the two. The results of this technique indicated that 98.4 percent of the human and chimpanzee DNA base sequences examined are identical.

As useful as these techniques have been, they are *indirect* methods of examining the DNA code. But today there are procedures that make it possible to sequence the nucleotides *directly* from the DNA molecule. The technologies of *DNA sequencing* used in the Human Genome Project are currently being applied to sequence the genomes of many nonhuman species, particularly chimpanzees. Consequently, the emerging field of comparative genomics will eventually make it possible to ascertain the precise genetic and evolutionary relationships among the primates (McConkey and Vavki, 2000; O'Brien et al., 2002). In fact, more recent research suggests the difference may be as much as 5 percent (Frazer et al., 2003).

At present, amino acid sequencing and DNA hybridization, as well as other techniques, have reaffirmed the basic tenets of traditional primate classification. Moreover, they have shown how genetically close humans and the African great apes are. A systematic application of DNA hybridization (Sibley and Ahlquist, 1984) demonstrated that humans and chimpanzees are closer genetically than either is to the gorilla. For that matter, chimpanzees and humans share more genetic similarities than do zebras and horses or goats and sheep. On the basis of these results, it would be entirely consistent to classify humans and chimpanzees (perhaps gorillas as well) within the same genus. Humans would continue to be called *Homo sapiens*, whereas chimpanzees would be classed as *Homo troglodytes*. But such changes in terminology will probably have to wait for the completion of the sequencing of the chimpanzee genome.

Another area where modifications have been suggested concerns tarsiers (see p. 104). Tarsiers are highly specialized animals that display several unique physical characteristics. Because they possess a number of prosimian traits, tarsiers traditionally have been classified as prosimians (with lemurs and lorises); but they also share certain anthropoid features. Moreover, biochemically, tarsiers are more closely related to anthropoids than to prosimians (Dene et al., 1976); but with regard to chromosomes and several anatomical traits, they are distinct from both groups.

Today, most primatologists recognize tarsiers as more closely related to anthropoids than to prosimians. But instead of simply moving them into the suborder Anthropoidea, one proposed scheme places lemurs and lorises in a new figure 5–8 Revised partial classification of the primates. In this system, the terms *Prosimii* and *Anthropoidea* have been replaced by *Strepsirhini* and *Haplorhini,* respectively. The tarsier is included in the same suborder with monkeys, apes, and humans to reflect a closer relationship with these forms than with lemurs and lorises. (Compare with fig. 5–7.)

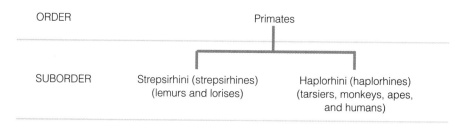

ORDER   Primates

SUBORDER   Strepsirhini (strepsirhines)   Haplorhini (haplorhines)
                (lemurs and lorises)   (tarsiers, monkeys, apes,
                                                          and humans)

suborder, Strepsirhini (instead of Prosimii), and includes tarsiers with monkeys, apes, and humans in another new suborder, Haplorhini (Szalay and Delson, 1979) (fig. 5–8). Thus, in this classification, the conventionally named suborders Prosimii and Anthropoidea are replaced by Strepsirhini and Haplorhini, respectively. As yet, this designation has not been universally accepted, but the terminology has become common, especially in technical publications.

We have presented the traditional system of primate classification here, even though we acknowledge the need for modification. At present, not all anthropologists and biologists have completely accepted the revised terminology. Until consensus is reached and new designations are formally adopted, we think it appropriate to use the standard taxonomy along with discussion of some proposed changes. It is also important to point out that while specific details and names have not yet been worked out, the vast majority of experts do accept the evolutionary implications of the revised groupings.

Prosimians (Lemurs and Lorises)

The most primitive of the primates are the lemurs and lorises. (We do not include tarsiers here, because their status is not as clear.) By "primitive" we mean that prosimians, taken as a group, are more similar anatomically to their earlier mammalian ancestors than are the other primates (monkeys, apes, and humans). Therefore, they tend to exhibit certain more ancestral characteristics, such as a more pronounced reliance on *olfaction* (sense of smell). Their greater olfactory capabilities (compared to other primates) are reflected in the presence of a moist, fleshy pad (**rhinarium**) at the end of the nose and in a relatively long snout. Moreover, prosimians mark territories with scent in a manner not seen in many other primates.

There are numerous other characteristics that distinguish lemurs and lorises from the anthropoids, including somewhat more laterally placed eyes, differences in reproductive physiology, and shorter gestation and maturation periods. Lemurs and lorises also possess a specialization known as the "dental comb." The dental comb is formed by forward-projecting lower incisors and canines, and together these modified teeth are used in both grooming and feeding (fig. 5–9). Another characteristic that sets lemurs and lorises apart from anthropoids is the retention of a claw (called a "grooming claw") on the second toe.

Rhinarium (rine-air´-ee-um) The moist, hairless pad at the end of the nose seen in most mammalian species. The rhinarium enhances an animal's ability to smell.

figure 5–9 Prosimian dental comb, formed by forward-projecting incisors and canines.

LEMURS Lemurs are found only on the island of Madagascar and adjacent islands off the east coast of Africa (fig. 5–10). As the only nonhuman primates on Madagascar, lemurs diversified into numerous and varied ecological niches without competition from monkeys and apes. Thus, the surviving species of Madagascar represent an evolutionary pattern that has vanished elsewhere.

Lemurs range in size from the small mouse lemur, with a body length (head and trunk) of only 5 inches, to the indri, with a body length of a little over 2 feet (Napier and Napier, 1985). While the larger lemurs are diurnal and exploit a wide variety of dietary items, such as leaves, fruits, buds, bark, and shoots, the smaller forms (mouse and dwarf lemurs) are nocturnal and insectivorous.

Lemurs display considerable variation regarding numerous other aspects of behavior. While many are primarily arboreal, others, such as the ring-tailed lemur (fig. 5–11), are more terrestrial. Some arboreal species are quadrupeds, and others (sifakas and indris) are vertical clingers and leapers (fig. 5–12). Socially, several species (e.g., ring-tailed lemurs and sifakas) are gregarious and live in groups of 10 to 25 animals composed of males and females of all ages. Others (the indris) live in monogamous family units, and several nocturnal forms are mostly solitary.

figure 5–10 Geographical distribution of modern lemurs.

figure 5–11 Ring-tailed lemur.

figure 5–12 Sifakas in their native habitat in Madagascar.

LORISES Lorises (fig. 5–13), which are similar in appearance to lemurs, were able to survive in mainland areas by adopting a nocturnal activity pattern at a time when most other prosimians became extinct. In this way, they were (and are) able to avoid competition with more recently evolved primates, the diurnal monkeys.

There are at least eight loris species, all of which are found in tropical forest and woodland habitats of India, Sri Lanka, Southeast Asia, and Africa. Also included in the same general category are six to nine (Bearder, 1987) galago species (fig. 5–14), which are widely distributed throughout most of the forested and woodland savanna areas of sub-Saharan Africa.

Locomotion in lorises is a slow, cautious climbing form of quadrupedalism. All galagos, however, are highly agile and active vertical clingers and leapers. Some lorises and galagos are almost entirely insectivorous; others supplement their diet with various combinations of fruits, leaves, gums, and slugs. Lorises and galagos frequently forage for food alone (females leave infants behind in nests until they are older). However, ranges overlap, and two or more females occasionally forage together or share the same sleeping nest.

Lemurs and lorises represent the same general adaptive level. Both groups exhibit good grasping and climbing abilities and a fairly well developed visual

figure 5–13 Slow loris.

figure 5–14 Galago, or "bush baby."

David Haring, Duke University Primate Zoo

figure 5–15 Tarsier.

☐ Tarsiers

figure 5–16 Geographical distribution of tarsiers.

See Virtual Lab 1, section II, for a presentation of the differences between monkeys, apes, and humans.

apparatus, although vision is not completely stereoscopic, and color vision may not be as well developed as in anthropoids. Most lemurs and lorises also have prolonged life spans as compared to most other small-bodied mammals, averaging about 14 years for lorises and 19 years for lemurs.

Tarsiers

There are five recognized species of tarsier (Nowak, 1999) (fig. 5–15), all restricted to island areas in Southeast Asia (fig. 5–16), where they inhabit a wide range of forest types, from tropical forest to backyard gardens. Tarsiers are nocturnal insectivores, leaping onto prey (which may also include small vertebrates) from lower branches and shrubs. Tarsiers are generally solitary but may form stable pair bonds (MacKinnon and MacKinnon, 1980).

As we have already mentioned, tarsiers present a complex blend of characteristics not seen in other primates. Moreover, they are unique in that their enormous eyes, which dominate much of the face, are immobile within their sockets. To compensate for this inability to move the eyes, tarsiers are able to rotate their heads more than 180° in a decidedly owl-like manner.

Anthropoids (Monkeys, Apes, and Humans)

Although there is much variation among anthropoids, there are certain features that, when taken together, distinguish them as a group from prosimians (and other placental mammals). Here is a partial list of these traits:

1. Generally larger body size
2. Larger brain (in absolute terms and relative to body weight)
3. Reduced reliance on the sense of smell, indicated by absence of rhinarium and other structures
4. Increased reliance on vision, with forward-facing eyes placed at front of face
5. Greater degree of color vision
6. Back of eye socket formed by a bony plate
7. Blood supply to brain different from that of prosimians
8. Fusion of the two sides of the mandible at the midline to form one bone (in prosimians and tarsiers they are joined by fibrous tissue)
9. Less specialized dentition, as seen in absence of dental comb and some other features
10. Differences with regard to female internal reproductive anatomy
11. Longer gestation and maturation periods
12. Increased parental care
13. More mutual grooming

Approximately 85 percent of all primates (about 195 species) are monkeys. (It is impossible to give precise numbers of species because the taxonomic status of several primates remains in doubt, and primatologists are still making new discoveries.) Monkeys are divided into two groups separated by geographical area (New World and Old World) and by several million years of separate evolutionary history.

NEW WORLD MONKEYS   The New World monkeys exhibit a wide range of size, diet, and ecological adaptation (fig. 5–17). In size, they vary from the tiny marmosets and tamarins (about 12 ounces) to the 20-pound howler monkey

Female muriqui with infant

Andrew Young

figure 5–17
New World Monkeys

Male uakari

R. A. Mittermeier/Conservation International

Prince Bernhard's titi monkey (discovered in 2002)

Marc van Roosmalen

White-faced capuchins

© Jay Dickman/CORBIS

Squirrel monkeys

© Kevin Schafer/CORBIS

figure 5–18 A pair of golden lion tamarins.

figure 5–19 Howler monkeys.

figure 5–20 Geographical distribution of modern New World monkeys.

figure 5–21 Spider monkey. Note the prehensile tail.

(figs. 5–18 and 5–19). New World monkeys are almost exclusively arboreal, and some never come to the ground. Like Old World monkeys, all except one species (the douroucouli, or owl monkey) are diurnal. Although confined to the trees, New World monkeys can be found in a wide range of arboreal environments throughout most forested areas in southern Mexico and Central and South America (fig. 5–20).

One of the characteristics distinguishing New World monkeys from those found in the Old World is shape of the nose. New World forms have broad noses with outward-facing nostrils. Conversely, Old World monkeys have narrower noses with downward-facing nostrils. This difference in nose form has given rise to the terms *platyrrhine* (flat nose) and *catarrhine* (downward-facing nose) to refer to New and Old World anthropoids, respectively.

Of the roughly 70 species of New World monkeys, the marmosets and tamarins are the smallest and most primitive. Indeed, they are the most primitive of all the monkeys, retaining claws instead of nails and usually giving birth to twins instead of one infant. They are mostly insectivorous, although marmoset diet includes gums from trees, and tamarins also rely heavily on fruits. Locomotion is quadrupedal, and their claws aid in climbing vertical tree trunks, much in the manner of squirrels. Socially, these small monkeys live in family groups composed usually of a mated pair, or a female and two adult males, and their offspring. Indeed, marmosets and tamarins, along with the douroucouli, are among the few primate species in which males are heavily involved in infant care.

Cebid and atelid (see fig. 5–7) species range in size from the squirrel monkey (body length 12 inches) to the howler (body length 24 inches). Diet varies, with most relying on a combination of fruits and leaves supplemented, to varying degrees, by insects. Most are quadrupedal, but some—for example, muriquis and spider monkeys (fig. 5–21)—are semibrachiators. Muriquis, howlers, and spider monkeys also possess powerful prehensile tails that are used not only in locomotion but also for suspension under branches while feeding on leaves and fruits. Socially, these species are found either in groups of both sexes and all age categories or in monogamous pairs with subadult offspring.

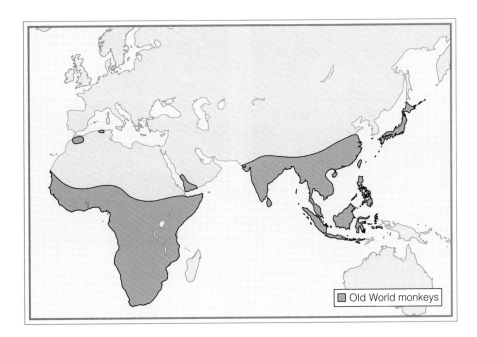

figure 5–22 Geographical distribution of modern Old World monkeys.

See Virtual Lab 4, section I, for a video of a spider monkey.

Ischial callosities Patches of tough, hard skin on the buttocks of Old World monkeys and chimpanzees.

Cercopithecidae (serk-oh-pith´-eh-sid-ee)

Cercopithecines (serk-oh-pith´-eh-seens) The subfamily of Old World monkeys that includes baboons, macaques, and guenons.

Colobines (kole´-uh-beans) The subfamily of Old World monkeys that includes the African colobus monkeys and Asian langurs.

figure 5–23 Adult male sykes monkey, one of many guenon species.

OLD WORLD MONKEYS   The monkeys of the Old World display more morphological and behavioral diversity than is seen in New World monkeys. Except for humans, Old World monkeys are the most widely distributed of all living primates. They are found throughout sub-Saharan Africa and southern Asia, ranging from tropical jungle habitats to semiarid desert and even to seasonally snow-covered areas in northern Japan (fig. 5–22).

Most Old World monkeys are quadrupedal and primarily arboreal, but some (e.g., baboons) are also adapted to life on the ground. Whether in trees or on the ground, these monkeys spend a good deal of time sleeping, feeding, and grooming while sitting with their upper bodies held erect. Usually associated with this universal sitting posture are areas of hardened skin on the buttocks (**ischial callosities**) that serve as sitting pads.

Within the entire group of Old World monkeys there is only one recognized taxonomic family: **Cercopithecidae.** This family, in turn, is divided into two subfamilies: the **cercopithecines** and **colobines.**

The cercopithecines are the more generalized of the two groups, showing a more omnivorous dietary adaptation and distinctive cheek pouches for storing food. As a group, the cercopithecines eat almost anything, including fruits, seeds, leaves, grasses, tubers, roots, nuts, insects, birds' eggs, amphibians, small reptiles, and small mammals (the last seen in baboons).

The majority of cercopithecine species, such as the mostly arboreal guenons (fig. 5–23) and the more terrestrial savanna and hamadryas baboons (fig. 5–24) are found in Africa. However, the several

Robert Jurmain

figure 5–24 Savanna baboons. (a) Male. (b) Female.

(a)   (b)

See Virtual Lab 1, section IV, for a discussion of sexual dimorphism.

Sexual dimorphism Differences in physical characteristics between males and females of the same species. For example, humans are slightly sexually dimorphic for body size, with males being taller, on average, than females of the same population.

Estrus (ess´-truss) Period of sexual receptivity in female mammals (except humans), correlated with ovulation. When used as an adjective, the word is spelled "estrous."

figure 5–25 Black-and-white colobus monkey.

species of macaque, which include the well-known rhesus monkey, are widely distributed in southern Asia and India.

Colobine species are more limited dietarily, focusing on mature leaves, a behavior that has led to their designation as "leaf-eating monkeys." The colobines are found mainly in Asia, but both the red colobus and the black-and-white colobus are exclusively African (fig. 5–25). Other colobines include several species of Asian langur and the proboscis monkey of Borneo.

Locomotor behavior among Old World monkeys includes arboreal quadrupedalism in guenons, macaques, and langurs; terrestrial quadrupedalism in baboons, patas, and macaques; and semibrachiation and acrobatic leaping in colobus monkeys.

Marked differences in body size or shape between the sexes, referred to as **sexual dimorphism,** are typical of some terrestrial species and are particularly pronounced in baboons. In these species, male body weight (up to 80 pounds in baboons) may be twice that of females.

Females of several species (especially baboons and some macaques) exhibit pronounced cyclical changes of the external genitalia. These changes, including swelling and redness, are associated with **estrus,** a hormonally initiated period of sexual receptivity in female nonhuman mammals correlated with ovulation.

Several types of social organization characterize Old World monkeys, and there are uncertainties among primatologists regarding some species. In general, colobines tend to live in small groups, with only one or two adult males. Savanna baboons and most macaque species are found in large social units comprising several adults of both sexes and offspring of all ages. Monogamous pairing is not common in Old World monkeys, but is seen in a few langurs and possibly one or two guenon species.

Hominoids (Apes and Humans)

The other large grouping of anthropoids, the hominoids, includes apes and humans. The superfamily **Hominoidea** includes the "lesser" apes in the family **Hylobatidae** (gibbons and siamangs); the great apes in the family **Pongidae** (orangutans, gorillas, bonobos, and chimpanzees); and humans in the family Hominidae.

Apes and humans differ from monkeys in numerous ways:

1. Generally larger body size, except for gibbons and siamangs
2. Absence of a tail
3. Shortened trunk (lumbar area shorter and more stable)
4. Differences in position and musculature of the shoulder joint (adapted for suspensory locomotion)
5. More complex behavior
6. More complex brain and enhanced cognitive abilities
7. Increased period of infant development and dependency

GIBBONS AND SIAMANGS   The eight gibbon species and the closely related siamang are today found in the southeastern tropical areas of Asia (fig. 5–26). These animals are the smallest of the apes, with a long, slender body weighing 13 pounds in the gibbon (fig. 5–27) and 25 pounds in the larger siamang.

The most distinctive structural feature of gibbons and siamangs is related to an adaptation for brachiation. They have extremely long arms, long,

Hominoidea The formal designation for the superfamily of anthropoids that includes apes and humans.

Hylobatidae (high-lo-baht´-id-ee)

Pongidae (ponj´-id-ee)

figure 5–26 Geographical distribution of modern Asian apes.

figure 5–27 White-handed gibbon.

permanently curved fingers, short thumbs, and powerful shoulder muscles. These highly specialized locomotor adaptations may be related to feeding behavior while hanging beneath branches. The diet of both species is largely composed of fruits. Both (especially the siamang) also eat a variety of leaves, flowers, and insects.

The basic social unit of gibbons and siamangs is the monogamous pair with dependent offspring. As in marmosets and tamarins, male gibbons and siamangs are very much involved in rearing their young. Both males and females are highly territorial and protect their territories with elaborate whoops and sirenlike "songs."

ORANGUTANS   Orangutans (*Pongo pygmaeus*) (fig. 5–28) are represented by two subspecies found today only in heavily forested areas on the Indonesian islands of Borneo and Sumatra (see fig. 5–26). Due to poaching by humans and continuing habitat loss on both islands, orangutans are seriously threatened by extinction in the wild.

Orangutans are slow, cautious climbers whose locomotor behavior can best be described as "four-handed," referring to the tendency to use all four limbs for grasping and support. Although they are almost completely arboreal, orangutans do sometimes travel quadrupedally on the ground. Orangutans are also very large animals with pronounced sexual dimorphism (males may weigh 200 pounds or more and females less than 100 pounds).

In the wild, orangutans lead largely solitary lives, although adult females are usually accompanied by one or two dependent offspring. They are primarily **frugivorous,** but bark, leaves, insects, and meat (on rare occasions) may also be eaten.

GORILLAS   The largest of all living primates, gorillas (*Gorilla gorilla*) are today confined to forested areas of western and eastern equatorial Africa (fig. 5–29). There are three generally recognized subspecies, although molecular data suggest that one of these, the western lowland gorilla (fig. 5–30), is perhaps suffi-

Frugivorous   (fru-give´-or-us)
Having a diet composed primarily of fruit.

figure 5–28 Female orangutan.

Robert Jurmain, photo by Jill Matsumoto/Jim Anderson

figure 5–29 Geographical distribution of modern African apes.

(a)

(b)

figure 5–30 Western lowland gorillas. (a) Male. (b) Female.

ciently genetically distinct to warrant designation as a separate species (Ruvolo et al., 1994; Garner and Ryder, 1996). The western lowland gorilla is found in several countries of western central Africa and, with an estimated population size of 110,000 (Doran and McNeilage, 1998), has been considered to be the most numerous of the three subspecies. However, a recently published report (Walsh et al., 2003) suggests that numbers may be far lower (see page 115). The eastern lowland gorilla is found near the eastern border of the Democratic Republic of the Congo (DRC—formerly Zaire) and numbers about 12,000. Mountain gorillas (fig. 5–31), the most extensively studied of the three subspecies, are found in the mountainous areas of central Africa in Rwanda, the DRC, and Uganda. Mountain gorillas have probably never been very numerous, and today they are among the more endangered primates, numbering only about 600.

Gorillas exhibit marked sexual dimorphism, with males weighing up to 400 pounds and females around 150 to 200 pounds. Because of their weight, adult gorillas, especially males, are primarily terrestrial and adopt a semiquadrupedal (knuckle-walking) posture on the ground.

figure 5–31 Mountain gorillas. (a) Male. (b) Female.

(a)

(b)

Mountain gorillas live in groups consisting of one (or sometimes two) large *silverback* males, a variable number of adult females, and their subadult offspring. The term *silverback* refers to the saddle of white hair across the back of fully adult (at least 12 or 13 years of age) male gorillas. Additionally, the silverback male may tolerate the presence of one or more young adult *blackback* males, probably his sons. Typically, but not always, both females and males leave their natal group as young adults. Females join other groups, and males, who appear to be less likely to emigrate, may live alone for a while, or they may join an all-male group before eventually forming their own group.

Systematic studies of free-ranging western lowland gorillas were not initiated until the mid-1980s; thus, our knowledge of their social structure and behavior is still in its infancy. In general, it appears that their social structure is similar to that of mountain gorillas, but groups are smaller and somewhat less cohesive.

All gorillas are almost exclusively vegetarian. Mountain gorillas concentrate primarily on leaves, pith, and stalks. These foods are also important for western lowland gorillas, but western lowland gorillas also eat considerably more fruit, depending on seasonal availability. Recent studies also report that western lowland gorillas, unlike mountain gorillas (which avoid water), frequently wade through swamps while foraging on aquatic plants.

Perhaps because of their large body size and enormous strength, gorillas have long been considered ferocious monsters; but in reality, they are shy and gentle. This is not to imply that gorillas are never aggressive. Indeed, male-male competition for females can be extremely violent. Moreover, males will certainly defend their group from any perceived danger, whether it be another male gorilla or a human hunter. Still, the reputation of gorillas as murderous beasts is the result of uninformed myth making and little else.

CHIMPANZEES   Chimpanzees are probably the best known of all nonhuman primates (fig. 5–32). Often misunderstood because of zoo exhibits, circus acts, television shows, and movies, the true nature of chimpanzees did not become known until years of fieldwork with wild groups provided a reliable picture. Today, chimpanzees are found in equatorial Africa, stretching in a broad belt from the Atlantic Ocean in the west to Lake Tanganyika in the east. Their range, however, is patchy within this large geographical area, and with further habitat destruction, it is becoming even more so (see fig. 5–29).

Chimpanzees are in many ways structurally similar to gorillas, with corresponding limb proportions and upper-body shape. This similarity is due to commonalities in locomotion when on the ground (quadrupedal knuckle walking). However, the ecological adaptations of chimpanzees and gorillas differ, with chimpanzees spending more time in the trees. Moreover, whereas gorillas are typically placid and quiet, chimpanzees are highly excitable, active, and noisy.

Chimpanzees are smaller than orangutans and gorillas, and although they are sexually dimorphic, sex differences are not as pronounced as in these other species. While male chimpanzees may weigh over 100 pounds, females may weigh at least 80.

In addition to quadrupedal knuckle walking, chimpanzees (particularly youngsters) may brachiate while in the trees. When on the ground, they frequently walk bipedally for short distances when carrying food or other objects. One adult male at Jane Goodall's study area in Tanzania frequently walked bipedally because one arm was paralyzed by polio (Goodall, 1986).

(a)

(b)

figure 5–32 Chimpanzees.
(a) Male. (b) Female.

Chimpanzees eat an amazing variety of items, including fruits, leaves, insects, nuts, birds' eggs, berries, caterpillars, and small mammals. Moreover, both males and females take part in group hunting efforts to kill such small mammals as red colobus, young baboons, bushpigs, and antelope. When hunts are successful, the prey is shared by the group members.

Chimpanzees live in large, fluid communities of as many as 50 individuals or more. At the core of a chimpanzee community is a group of bonded males. Although relationships between them are not always peaceful or stable, these males nevertheless act as a group to defend their territory and are highly intolerant of unfamiliar chimpanzees, especially nongroup males.

Even though chimpanzees are said to live in communities, there are few times, if any, when all members are together. Indeed, it is the nature of chimpanzees to come and go, so that the individuals they encounter vary from day to day. Moreover, adult females tend to forage either alone or in the company of their offspring. The latter foraging group could comprise several chimpanzees, as females with infants sometimes accompany their own mothers and their younger siblings. A female may also leave her community, either permanently to join another community or temporarily while she is in estrus. This behavioral pattern may reduce the risk of mating with close male relatives, because males apparently never leave the group in which they were born.

Chimpanzee social behavior is complex, and individuals form lifelong attachments with friends and relatives. Indeed, the bond between mothers and infants often remains strong until one or the other dies. This may be a considerable period, because many chimpanzees live into their late 30s and a few well into their 40s.

BONOBOS Bonobos (*Pan paniscus*) are found only in an area south of the Zaire River in the DRC (see fig. 5–28). Not officially recognized by European scientists until the 1920s, they remain among the least studied of the great apes. Although ongoing field studies have produced much information (Susman, 1984; Kano, 1992), research has been periodically hampered by political unrest. There are no accurate counts of bonobos, but their numbers are believed to be between 10,000 and 20,000 (IUCN, 1996), and these are threatened by human hunting, warfare, and habitat loss.

Because bonobos bear a strong resemblance to chimpanzees but are somewhat smaller, they have been called "pygmy chimpanzees." However, differences in body size are not striking, although bonobos have a more linear body build, longer legs relative to arms, a relatively smaller head, a dark face from birth, and tufts of hair at the side of the face (fig. 5–33).

Bonobos are more arboreal than chimpanzees, and they appear to be less excitable and aggressive. While aggression is not unknown, it appears that physical violence both within and between groups is uncommon. Like chimpanzees, bonobos live in geographically based, fluid communities,

figure 5–33 Female bonobos with young.

Courtesy, Ellen Ingmanson

and they exploit many of the same foods, including occasional meat derived from killing small mammals (Badrian and Malinky, 1984). But bonobo communities are not centered around a group of closely bonded males. Rather, male-female bonding is more important than in chimpanzees (and most other nonhuman primates), and females are not as peripheral to the group (Badrian and Badrian, 1984). This may be related to bonobo sexuality, which differs in expression from that of other nonhuman primates in that copulation is frequent and occurs throughout a female's estrous cycle.

Bonobos are relatively late to arrive on the scene of primate research. But it is crucial that studies of this intriguing species be allowed to progress. Not only do bonobos have the potential of providing information about human behavior and evolution, but they are of considerable interest in their own right and they are highly endangered. In fact, without research and protection, they, like so many other nonhuman primates, are in danger of extinction.

Humans

Humans are the only living representatives of the family Hominidae (genus *Homo*, species *sapiens*). Our primate heritage is evident in our overall anatomy and genetic makeup and in many aspects of human behavior. With the exception of reduced canine size, human teeth are typical primate teeth; indeed, in overall morphology, they very much resemble ape teeth. The human dependence on vision and decreased reliance on olfaction, as well as flexible limbs and grasping hands, are rooted in our primate, arboreal past. Humans can even brachiate, and playgrounds often accommodate this ability in children.

Humans in general are omnivorous, although all societies observe certain culturally based dietary restrictions. Nevertheless, as a species with a rather generalized digestive system, we are physiologically adapted to digest an extremely wide assortment of foods. To our detriment, we also share with our relatives a fondness for sweets that originates from the importance of high-energy fruits in the diets of many nonhuman primates.

But quite obviously, humans are unique among primates and indeed among all animals. For example, no member of any other species has the ability to write or think about issues such as how they differ from other life forms. This ability is rooted in the fact that human evolution, during the last 800,000 years or so, has been characterized by dramatic increases in brain size and other neurological changes.

Humans are also completely dependent on culture. Without cultural innovation, it would have been impossible for us to have ever left the tropics. As it is, humans inhabit every corner of the planet with the exception of Antarctica, and we have established outposts even there. And lest we forget, a fortunate few have walked on the moon. None of the technologies (indeed, none of the other aspects of culture) that humans have developed over the last several thousand years would have been possible without the highly developed cognitive abilities we alone possess. Nevertheless, the neurological basis for intelligence is something we share with other primates. Indeed, research has demonstrated that several nonhuman primate species—most notably chimpanzees, bonobos, and gorillas—display a level of problem solving and insight that most people would have considered impossible 30 years ago (see Chapter 6).

Humans are uniquely predisposed to use spoken language, and for the last 5,000 years or so, we have used written language as well. This ability exists because human evolution has modified certain neurological and anatomical structures in ways not observed in any other animal. But while nonhuman primates are not anatomically capable of producing speech, research has demonstrated that to varying degrees, the great apes are able to communicate through the use of symbols. And basically, that is a foundation for language that humans and the great apes (to a limited degree) have in common.

Aside from cognitive abilities, the one other trait that sets humans apart from other primates is our unique (among mammals) form of *habitual* bipedal locomotion. This particular trait appeared early in the evolution of our lineage, and over time, we have become more efficient at it because of related changes in the musculoskeletal anatomy of the pelvis, leg, and foot (see Chapter 8). But for whatever reasons, early hominids increasingly adopted bipedalism because they were already preadapted for it. That is, as primates, and especially as apelike primates, they were already behaviorally predisposed to, and anatomically capable of, at least short-term bipedal walking before they adopted it wholeheartedly.

Thus, while it is certainly true that human beings are unique intellectually and in some ways anatomically, we are still primates. In fact, it is quite reasonable to say that fundamentally, humans are exaggerated primates.

Endangered Primates

See Virtual Lab 1, section III, for a stark contrast between the restricted geographical ranges of nonhuman primates and humans.

In September 2000, scientists announced that a subspecies of red colobus, named Miss Waldron's red colobus, had officially been declared extinct. This announcement came after a six-year search for the 20-pound monkey that had not been seen for 20 years (Oates et al., 2000). Thus, this species, indigenous to the West African countries of Ghana and the Ivory Coast, has the distinction of being the first nonhuman primate to be declared extinct in the twenty-first century.* But it will certainly not be the last. In fact, as of this writing, over half of all nonhuman primate species are now in jeopardy, and some face almost immediate extinction in the wild.

There are three basic reasons for the worldwide depletion of nonhuman primates: habitat destruction, hunting for food, and live capture for export or local trade. Underlying these three causes is one major factor: unprecedented human population growth, which is occurring at a faster rate in developing countries than in the developed world. The developing nations of Africa, Asia, and Central and South America are home to over 90 percent of all nonhuman primate species, and these countries, aided in no small part by the industrialized countries of Europe and the United States, are cutting their forests at a rate of about 30 million acres per year. In Brazil, the Atlantic rain forest originally covered some 385,000 square miles. Today, an estimated 7 percent is all that

---

*In 2002, primatologists reported the discovery of a fresh skin of a Miss Waldron's red colobus in a West African market—gruesome evidence that a few individuals may yet remain after all.

remains of what was once home to countless New World monkeys and thousands of other species.

Much of the motivation behind the devastation of the rain forests is, of course, economic: the short-term gains from clearing forests to create immediately available (but poor) farmland or ranchland; the use of trees for lumber and paper products; and large-scale mining operations (with their necessary roads, digging, etc., all of which cause habitat destruction). And, of course, the demand for tropical hardwoods (e.g., mahogany, teak, and rosewood) in the United States, Europe, and Japan creates an enormously profitable market for rain forest products.

Primates have also been captured live for zoos, biomedical research, and the exotic pet trade. Live capture has declined dramatically since the implementation of the Convention on International Trade in Endangered Species of Wild Flora and Fauna (CITES) in 1973. Currently, 160 countries are parties to this treaty, agreeing not to allow trade in species listed by CITES as being endangered. However, even some CITES members are still occasionally involved in the illegal primate trade (Japan and Belgium, among others).

In most areas, habitat loss has been, and continues to be, the single greatest cause of declining numbers of nonhuman primates. But in parts of western and central Africa, human hunting for food now poses an even greater threat. This tragic turn of events occurred rather quickly, but during the 1990s, primatologists became increasingly aware of the immense scope of the slaughter.

Wherever they occur, nonhuman primates have traditionally been an important source of food for people. In the past, subsistence hunting by indigenous peoples, armed with snares, bows and arrows, and other traditional weapons, did not usually constitute a serious threat to nonhuman primate populations, and certainly not to entire species. But increased demand for food by ever-growing numbers of people has combined with other factors to produce disastrous consequences. The construction of logging roads, mainly by French, German, and Belgian companies, has opened up vast tracts of forest that, until recently, offered sanctuary to thousands of animals. What has emerged is an unprecedented trade in "bush meat," a trade in which logging company employees participate along with local hunters. In contrast to hunters of the past, today's hunters are armed with automatic weapons, and they can wipe out an entire group of monkeys, gorillas, or chimpanzees in minutes. Consequently, the hunting of nonhuman primates, particularly in Africa, has shifted from being a subsistence activity to a commercial practice. Indeed, it is now common to see bush meat for sale in markets, where a monkey carcass can be bought for $5 and a dead gorilla for $40 (McRae, 1997). Most disturbingly, primate meat (including that of chimpanzees and gorillas) is served in restaurants not only in West Africa, but reportedly in some Belgian and French restaurants as well (fig. 5–34).

There are no accurate numbers, but it is estimated that each year, thousands of nonhuman primates are killed and sold for meat, as well as for commercial products such as skins and body parts. And, if animals other than primates are taken into account, an estimated 1 million metric tons of meat are taken annually from the forests of Africa.

Clearly, with the low reproductive rate characteristic of most nonhuman primates, and in the face of such massive slaughter, it is impossible for populations to sustain themselves. Some observers have likened the killing in parts of Africa to the slaying of the American bison in the nineteenth century (Strier, 1999); and unless the hunting stops, many primate species, certainly gorillas, chimpanzees, and bonobos, could well be exterminated from central Africa by figure 5–34 Red-eared guenons (with red tails) and Preuss's guenons for sale in bushmeat market, Malabo, Equatorial Guinea.

Courtesy, J. Oates

the year 2010. Moreover, Walsh et al. (2003) report a fifty percent decline in ape numbers in West Africa between 1983 and 2002. In the face of hunting combined with a major ebola epidemic, these authors suggest that, without aggressive conservation efforts, gorillas and chimpanzees will be at the brink of extinction in much of West Africa by 2013.

But the problem extends well beyond Africa. As we previously mentioned, destruction of forests continues throughout the tropics at an unprecedented rate. And in South America, hunting nonhuman primates for food is also common. For example, one report documents that in less than two years, one family of Brazilian rubber tappers killed almost 500 members of various large-bodied species, including spider monkeys, woolly monkeys, and howler monkeys (Peres, 1990). Moreover, live capture and (illegal) trade in endangered primate species continues unabated in China and Southeast Asia, where nonhuman primates are eaten and also funneled into the exotic pet trade. Primate body parts also figure prominently in traditional medicines, and with increasing human population size, the demand for these products (and products from other, nonprimate species, such as tigers) has placed many species in jeopardy.

Fortunately, steps are being taken to ensure the survival of some species. Many developing countries, such as Costa Rica and the Malagasy Republic (Madagascar), are designating national parks and other reserves for the protection of natural resources, including primates. There are also several private international efforts aimed at curbing the bush meat trade. It is only through such practices and through educational programs that many primate species have a chance of escaping extinction, at least in the immediate future.

If you are in your 20s or 30s, you will live to hear of the extinction of some of our marvelously unique and clever cousins. Many more will undoubtedly slip away unnoticed. Tragically, this will occur, in most cases, before we have even had the opportunity to get to know them.

Each species on earth is the current result of a unique set of evolutionary events that, over millions of years, has produced a finely adapted component of a diverse ecosystem. When it becomes extinct, that adaptation and that part of biodiversity is lost forever. What a tragedy it will be if, through our own mis-management and greed, we awaken to a world without chimpanzees, mountain gorillas, or the tiny, exquisite lion tamarin. When this day comes, we truly will have lost a part of ourselves, and we will be the poorer for it.

Summary

n this chapter, we have briefly introduced you to the primates, the mammalian order that includes humans. As a group, the primates are generalized in terms of diet and locomotor patterns, and these behavioral generalizations are reflected in the morphology of the teeth and limbs.

We have also discussed some of the anatomical similarities and differences between the major groupings of primates: prosimians, monkeys (New and Old World), and hominoids. In the next chapter, we will turn our attention to primate social behavior and cognitive abilities. These are extremely important topics, for it is through a better understanding of nonhuman primate behavior that we can make more general statements about human behavior. Moreover, increasing our knowledge is essential if we are to prevent many of these uniquely adapted and marvelous relatives of ours from being lost forever.

Questions for Review

1. Discuss why primates are said to be "generalized mammals."
2. Summarize the major evolutionary trends that characterize the primate order.
3. How does adaptation to an arboreal environment help explain primate evolution?
4. What is the geographical distribution of the nonhuman primates?
5. What are the two major subdivisions of the order Primates?
6. Which major groups of primates are included within the anthropoids?
7. What is a dental formula? What is the dental formula of all the Old World anthropoids?
8. What are quadrupedalism, vertical clinging and leaping, and brachiation? Name at least one primate species that is characterized by each of these.
9. What are the major differences between prosimians and anthropoids?
10. What are at least three anatomical differences between monkeys and apes?
11. Name the two major categories (subfamilies) of Old World monkeys. In general, what is the geographical distribution of each?
12. Explain how a taxonomic classification scheme reflects biological relationships.
13. Where are lemurs and lorises found today?
14. In general, which primates have prehensile tails?
15. What are the two family divisions of New World monkeys? Name at least one species for each.
16. In which taxonomic family are the great apes placed?

17. Define estrus.
18. Describe the type of social organization seen in chimpanzees (*Pan troglodytes*) and gorillas.
19. How do bonobos (*Pan paniscus*) differ from "common" chimpanzees (*Pan troglodytes*)?

Suggested Further Readings

Fleagle, John. 1999. *Primate Adaptation and Evolution*. New York: Academic Press.

Kinzey, Warren G. (ed). 1997. *New World Primates: Ecology, Evolution, and Behavior*. Hawthorne, NY: Aldine de Gruyter.

Mittermeier, Russell A., Ian Tattersall, William R. Konstant, David M. Meyers, and Roderick B. Mast. 1994. *Lemurs of Madagascar*. Washington, DC: Conservation International.

Napier, J. R., and P. H. Napier. 1985. *The Natural History of the Primates*. Cambridge, MA: MIT Press.

Nowak, Ronald M. 1999. *Walker's Primates of the World*. Baltimore: The Johns Hopkins University Press.

Rowe, Noel. 1996. *The Pictorial Guide to the Living Primates*. Charlestown, RI: Pogonias Press.

Sussman, Robert W. 1991. "Primate Origins and the Evolution of the Angiosperms." *American Journal of Primatology* 23: 209–223.

Multimedia Resources

 Companion Web Site

Anthropology Online: The Wadsworth Anthropology Resource Center Visit **http://anthropology.wadsworth.com** and click on the Companion Web Site for Jurmain/Kilgore/Trevathan/Nelson's *Essentials of Physical Anthropology*, Fifth Edition, to access a wide range of enrichment material to aid in your study of anthropology. Among the useful options for each chapter's self-study are learning objectives, flashcards, Internet exercises, Web links, InfoTrac College Edition exercises, and practice quizzes that can be scored and emailed to your instructor.

Primate Studies:
Free-Ranging and Captive Research

The study of primate behavior, as a central component of *primatology* in the United States, has been largely the domain of physical anthropologists. Indeed, primatology is one of the major subdisciplines of physical anthropology.

While anthropologists occasionally have studied primate behavior in *captive* situations, their major focus has been the collection of behavioral data in natural habitats. Specialized studies in a laboratory setting (such as the language studies discussed in Chapter 6) or in zoo environments are usually undertaken by psychologists. Increasingly, in the last few years, interdisciplinary research has been conducted in which methodologies developed in free-ranging

figure 1 Dr. Jane Goodall records a chimpanzee interaction at Gombe National Park, Tanzania.

Courtesy, The Jane Goodall Institute; photographed by Penelope Breeze

figure 2 Yahaya Alamasi, a member of the senior field staff at Gombe National Park. Dr. Goodall and other primatologists rely heavily on trained observers from neighboring villages and towns. This practice not only promotes good relations with neighboring communities but also increases interest and awareness of wildlife in African localities.

Courtesy, Bonnie Pedersen/Arlene Kruse

contexts are applied to studies of captive animals. This type of research holds the promise of comparing behaviors seen in the wild with those observed in captivity in order to draw more general conclusions.

One such study, the ChimpanZoo project, was initiated by Jane Goodall and the Jane Goodall Institute in 1984. One of the initial goals of ChimpanZoo was to establish a collaborative effort between zoo personnel and university faculty and students aimed at providing much-needed information regarding the behavior and psychological and emotional needs of captive chimpanzees.

Ethologist Frans B. M. De Waal, of Emory University, has conducted another series of research projects involving zoo primates. Since the 1970s, Dr. De Waal has studied captive groups of chimpanzees, bonobos, and several monkey species in European and American zoos. This research has resulted in the publication of numerous books and journal articles that have contributed greatly to current understanding of complex social behaviors in these species.

Peter Weit,/© Bettmann/CORBIS

figure 3 The late Dian Fossey with habituated mountain gorillas.

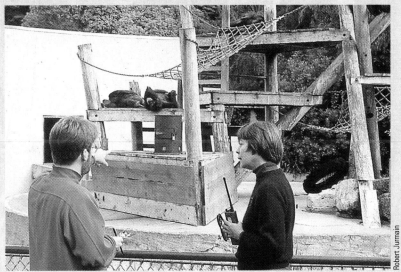

figure 4 ChimpanZoo student observer in discussion with a primate supervisor.

Robert Jurmain

There are numerous ways to study nonhuman animals. One method is to observe a group and describe (either by taking notes or speaking into a tape recorder) as completely as possible everything that occurs. Another technique is to "follow" one "focal" animal, describing everything it does. Still another frequently used method involves taking observations of a focal animal at precise intervals, usually on the minute. This last procedure is attractive, for it allows the data to be quantified, facilitating statistical analysis. When following this procedure, observers follow a focal animal, and using a series of behavior codes, they record whatever the animal does at precisely timed intervals.

To do this type of research, observers must know the animal well. Such familiarity facilitates interpreting sometimes difficult-to-assess behaviors. Moreover, this approach requires the development of an *ethogram* (a detailed list and description of behaviors). Many animal researchers devise a list of codes to refer to specific behaviors. These codes can then be written or keyed directly into a computer.

figure 5 Oakland Zoo docent records behavioral data using a specially designed software package.

figure 6 Example of a traditional, nonenriched zoo habitat. Although this mangabey has access to indoor and outdoor enclosures, his environment is sterile. Moreover, keeping such highly social animals in isolation leads to boredom, depression, and often serious behavioral disorders.

Because of increased awareness of the needs of nonhuman animals, including primates, habitat enrichment has become the goal of most zoos in recent years. Creating more attractive and interesting exhibits encourages public interest. Even more important, however, has been the changing role of zoos in the last 20 years. In the past, zoo animals were kept in bare cages designed for easy viewing by the public and easy cleaning for keepers. Today, zoos are increasingly seen as repositories for many endangered species, whose only hope for survival—at least in the short term—is captive breeding programs. As zoos become part of species survival plans, it is incumbent on them to provide naturalistic habitats in which animals will breed. This approach not only has provided the viewing public with more interesting exhibits, but also has immeasurably improved the lives of captive animals.

figure 7 An enriched indoor habitat for silver leaf-eating monkeys at the Bronx Zoo's Asian Jungle World exhibit in New York.

Habitats can be further enriched by applying knowledge of free-ranging behaviors to captive situations. Most especially, the animals can be kept engaged and stimulated by providing challenges in food searching and object manipulation (the latter is particularly important in chimpanzees).

Just as habitat enrichment is vitally important to captive primates, habitat protection has become critical for many free-ranging species. Consequently, in the last two decades, primatologists have increasingly directed their attention to understanding the complex ecological settings in which primates live.

Courtesy, Carol Lofton/Distinctive Images

figure 8 A captive chimpanzee uses a stick to obtain seeds and raisins from an artificial mound.

One example of this relatively new emphasis is the Mountain Gorilla Project, a joint collaboration of Dieter Steklis (Dian Fossey Gorilla Fund and Rutgers University) and Scott Madry (Center for Remote Sensing and Spatial Analysis, Rutgers University) aimed at producing a digitized data base of gorilla habitats in Rwanda. This project uses imaging radar from the space shuttle *Endeavor* to generate images of gorilla habitat even in cloudy and misty conditions. In addition to space shuttle technology, Rwandan trackers use global positioning systems (GPSs), which receive data from stationary satellites, to establish the precise position of, for example, gorilla groups or various types of vegetation. Ultimately, the data from these and other sources will be combined to reveal patterns of natural vegetation, gorilla ranging habits, and human use of gorilla habitat. It is hoped that this information will better enable scientists to assist local human populations in land use decisions while ensuring protection for mountain gorilla habitat.

From Harrison, C. et al., 1983. Cytogen. Cell Genet 35:21–27. S. Karger, A. G. Basel

figure 9 A three-dimensional digital image of gorilla habitat in the Virunga Mountains of central Africa.

New technologies have also been applied to genetic studies of primates. Phillip Morin, a biologist at the University of California, San Diego, and his colleagues compared DNA sequences at several genetic loci in free-ranging chimpanzees. To avoid capture of animals (for collection of blood or other tissues), researchers obtained DNA samples from chimpanzee hair collected from sleeping nests. So far, the results of this study have established paternity for some Gombe chimpanzees and have lent support to certain theories of chimpanzee behavior. Additionally, this type of DNA analysis may prove useful in determining the effects of genetic isolation in populations of chimpanzees and other species as habitat destruction continues to inhibit the migration of individuals from one group to another.

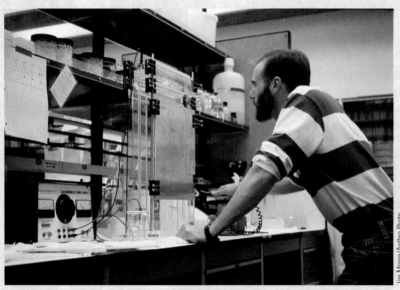

figure 10 Biologist Phillip Morin conducting analysis of chimpanzee DNA in his laboratory.

figure 11 Physical anthropologist Jim Moore collecting hair samples from a chimpanzee sleeping nest.

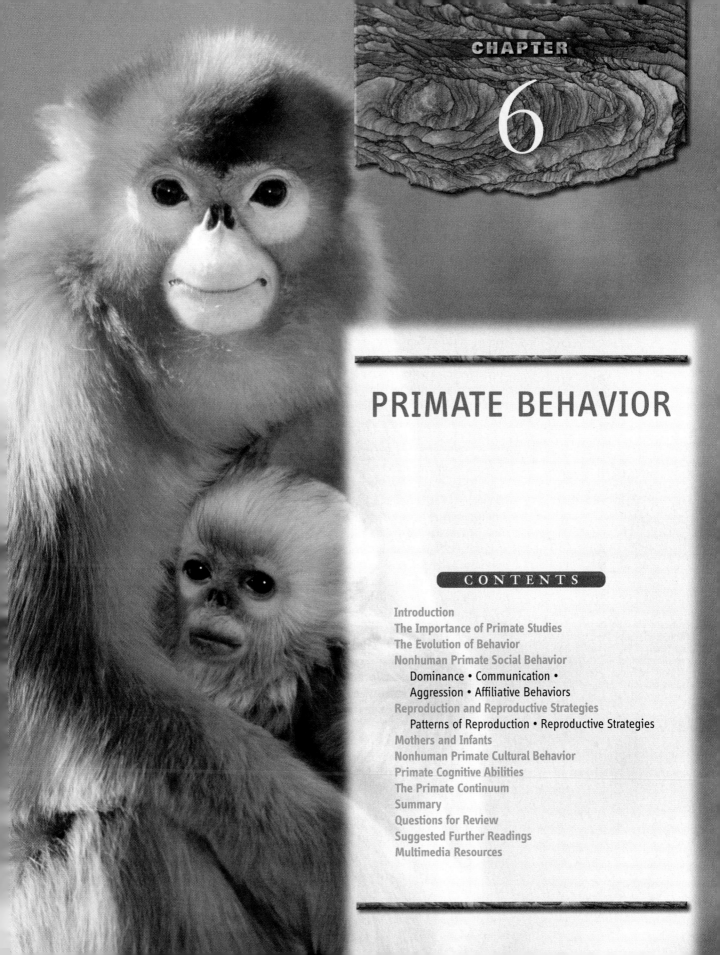

PRIMATE BEHAVIOR

CONTENTS

See the following sections of the CD-ROM for topics covered in this chapter. Virtual Lab 2, section I; Virtual Lab 5, section I; and Virtual Lab 6, sections I, II, and IV.

Introduction

In this chapter, discussion shifts from general primate characteristics to various aspects of nonhuman primate behavior and cognitive abilities. These are extremely important topics for anthropologists because one method of gaining a fuller understanding of human and early hominid behavior is to become more familiar with the behavior and intellectual capacities of living nonhuman primates. For that reason, as you read this chapter, you should be thinking of ways to apply some of the behavioral principles presented here to the early ancestors of *Homo sapiens*.

Because primates live in highly complex natural and social environments, they have evolved increasingly complex neurological structures. That is to say, there is a *feedback mechanism* between the biosocial environment and neurological complexity, so that over time, complex lifestyles have selected for increased neurological complexity, or intelligence. Intelligence, in turn, permits increasingly complex lifestyles. We know that all primates, including many prosimians, are extremely clever when compared to most other mammals. In this chapter, we will examine evidence that illustrates just how complex and intelligent are the other members of the order to which we ourselves belong.

The Importance of Primate Studies

Modern African apes and humans last shared a common ancestor between 6 and 8 million years ago. Although ape behavior has undoubtedly changed since that time, the behavior of hominids, who developed culture as an adaptive strategy, has changed much more dramatically. Accordingly, if we want to know what hominid behavior was like before culture became a factor, and if we wish to speculate as to which behaviors may have led to culture, we must look for clues in nonhuman primate behavior.

Social structure The composition, size, and sex ratio of a group of animals. Social structures, in part, are the result of natural selection in specific habitats, and they function to guide individual interactions and social relationships.

One approach is to correlate specific aspects of **social structure** with elements of primate habitats, since all living organisms must adapt behaviorally, as well as physically, to their environment. Because there are limits to the ways in which adaptation can occur, it follows that all organisms are to some degree governed by the same principles. By elucidating the various environmental pressures involved and understanding how they have influenced nonhuman primate behavior, we can better comprehend those factors that led to human emergence.

But in addition to studying nonhuman primates to learn more about ourselves, it is even more important to learn more about them in their own right. As you learned in Chapter 5, the beginning of the twenty-first century is an especially critical time for much of life on our planet, including nonhuman primates. If we hope to save even some of the many threatened and endangered species from extinction, we must understand their needs (space, diet, group organization, etc.) in the wild. Without this knowledge, we can neither preserve sufficient natural habitat for their survival in the wild nor re-create it in captivity.

The Evolution of Behavior

 See Virtual Lab 6, sections I and II, for discussion of primate behavior and field methods used by primatologists.

Scientists who study behavior in free-ranging primates do so within an **ecological** framework, focusing on the relationship between behavior, the natural environment, and numerous factors related to the biology of the species in question. This approach is called **behavioral ecology,** and it is based on the underlying assumption that the various components of ecological systems have evolved together.

Briefly, the cornerstone of this perspective is that *behavior has evolved through the operation of natural selection*. That is, natural selection acts on behavior in the same way it acts on physical characteristics. Thus, behavior constitutes a phenotype and those individuals whose genotypes influence behaviors that lead to greater reproductive success will be more fit and should pass on their genes at a faster rate than others.

Superficially, such an explanation implies the existence of genes that code for specific behaviors (e.g., a gene for aggression, another for cooperation). But explanations of behavior from an evolutionary perspective do not imply a one gene–one behavior scenario.

Much of the behavior of insects and other invertebrates, as well as that of lower vertebrates, is largely under genetic control. In other words, most behavioral patterns in these species are *innate*, not learned. However, in many vertebrates, particularly birds and mammals, the proportion of behavior that is due to *learning* is substantially increased and the proportion that is under genetic influence is reduced. This is especially true of primates; and in humans, who are so much a product of culture, most behavior results from learning. Nevertheless, it is also clear that even in higher organisms, some behaviors are partly influenced by certain gene products, such as hormones. For example, numerous studies have shown that elevated levels of testosterone increase aggressive behavior in many species.

Behavior is a complex trait, and it must be seen not only as being influenced by gene products, but also as the result of *interactions between genetic and environmental factors* that are not yet fully explained. Indeed, the ability to learn is ultimately based in the genome inherited by individuals of any species. Between species, there is considerable variation in the limits and potentials for learning, and it is important to understand that behavioral **plasticity**, or flexibility, is also a form of adaptation. But for any given species, those limits and potentials are ultimately influenced by genetic factors that have been shaped by the evolutionary history of that species. That history, in turn, has been shaped by the ecological setting, not only of that species, *but also of its ancestors*. Consequently, behaviors are viewed as adaptations to environmental circumstances, both past and present.

A problem arises when trying to establish the actual mechanics of behavioral evolution. There is a need to determine which behaviors have a genetic basis and how these behaviors influence reproductive success. To accomplish these goals, we must learn considerably more about genotype-phenotype interactions in complex traits. We also need accurate data on reproductive success in primate groups, and so far, such long-term data are almost completely lacking.

As a theoretical framework, behavioral ecology developed, in part, from the integration of two different approaches to the study of animal behavior:

Ecological Pertaining to the relationship between organisms and all aspects of their environment (temperature, predators, other animals, vegetation, availability of food and water, types of food, etc.).

Behavioral ecology The study of the evolution of behavior, emphasizing the role of ecological factors as agents of natural selection. Behaviors and behavioral patterns have been selected for because they increase reproductive fitness in individuals (i.e., they are adaptive) in specific ecological contexts.

Plasticity The capacity to change. In a physiological context, the ability of systems or organisms to make alterations in order to respond to differing conditions.

Socioecology The study of animals and all aspects of their habitats that attempts to identify relationships between components of the environment and behavior.

Sociobiology The study of the relationship between natural selection and behavior. Unlike the approach of behavioral ecology, sociobiological theory does not strongly emphasize ecological factors.

Joe MacDonald/Animals Animals

figure 6–1 Hanuman langurs.

socioecology and **sociobiology.** Socioecology, the study of animals and their habitats, attempts to establish patterns of relationships between the external environment and social behavior. Sociobiology emphasizes how natural selection shapes behavior, but its focus is narrower than that of behavioral ecology in that sociobiological theories primarily concern the relationship between genes, natural selection, and behavior without a strong emphasis on ecological factors.

One of the best and most famous examples of sociobiological theory is Sarah Blaffer Hrdy's (1977) explanation of infanticide among Hanuman langurs of India (fig. 6–1). Hanuman langurs typically live in social groups composed of one or a few adult males and several females with their offspring. Other males, usually young individuals who have left their natal group, associate in "bachelor" groups. These peripheral males occasionally attack and defeat reproductive males and oust them from their groups. Sometimes, following such takeovers, the group's infants (fathered by the previous males) are killed by the new males.

Such behavior would appear to be counterproductive, especially from the viewpoint of the species. However, individuals act to maximize their *own* reproductive success, regardless of the effects their behavior may have on the population. Ostensibly, that is exactly what infanticidal males are doing, albeit unknowingly. While a female is lactating, she does not come into estrus and thus is not sexually available. But when an infant dies, its mother ceases to lactate, and within two or three months, she resumes cycling and becomes sexually receptive. Therefore, by killing the infants, the male avoids a two- to three-year wait until they are weaned. This could be especially advantageous to him, since chances are good that his tenure in the group will not even last two or three years. Moreover, he does not expend energy and put himself at risk defending infants who do not carry his genes.

Hanuman langurs are not the only primates that engage in infanticide. Indeed, infanticide has been observed (or surmised) in many primate species, such as howlers, redtail monkeys, red colobus, blue monkeys, savanna baboons, orangutans, gorillas, chimpanzees (Struhsaker and Leyland, 1987; Strier, 2002), and humans. It also occurs in numerous nonprimate species, including rodents and cats. In the majority of nonhuman primate examples, infanticide occurs in conjunction with the transfer of a new male into a group or, as in chimpanzees, an encounter with an unfamiliar female and infant.

Numerous objections to this explanation of infanticide have been raised. Alternative explanations have included competition for resources (Rudran, 1973), aberrant behaviors related to human-induced overcrowding (Curtin and Dohlinow, 1978), and inadvertent killing during aggressive episodes, where it was not clear that the infant was actually the target animal (Bartlett et al., 1993). Sussman and colleagues (1995), as well as others, have questioned the actual prevalence of the practice, arguing that although it occurs, it is not particularly common. Yet others (Struhsaker and Leyland, 1987; Hrdy, 1995) maintain that the incidence and patterning of infanticide by males are not only significant, but consistent with the assumptions established by theories of behavioral evolution.

Hrdy's explanation of infanticide is an excellent example of the emphasis sociobiology placed on genes and individual reproductive success. But while primatologists still emphasize the importance of individual reproductive success, the focus of *behavioral ecology* has broadened to include ecological interactions that were largely ignored by sociobiology. For example, to understand the function of one particular behavioral element, such as the *social structure* of a given species, it is necessary to determine how that species is influenced by numerous factors, including:

See Virtual Lab 5, section I, for a discussion of ecological factors.

1. Diet: quantity and quality of different kinds of foods (caloric value, digestive energy required, net value to the individual)
2. Spatial distribution of food resources (e.g., dense, scattered, clumps, or seasonal availability)
3. Distribution and reliability of water sources
4. Body size and basal metabolic rate
5. Distribution and types of predators
6. Distribution of sleeping sites
7. Activity patterns (nocturnal, diurnal, **crepuscular**)
8. Relationships with other (nonpredator) species, both primate and nonprimate
9. Impact of human activities

Crepuscular Active during the evening or dawn.

Although all the relationships between ecological variables, social organization, and behavior have not yet been thoroughly elucidated, there is certainly a relationship between, for example, group size, group dynamics, and the problems of obtaining food and avoiding predators. Indeed, average group size and composition are adaptive responses to these problems (Pulliam and Caraco, 1984). For example, groups composed of several adult males and females (multimale, multifemale groups) have traditionally been viewed as advantageous in areas where predation pressure is high. This is because where members of prey species occur in larger groups, there is increased likelihood of early predator detection and avoidance.

These assumptions are supported by reports that groups of red colobus monkeys and Diana monkeys (a guenon species) form interspecific aggregations in response to predation by chimpanzees in the Tai National Forest in the Ivory Coast. Normally, these two species do not form close associations with each other. However, when chimpanzee predation increases, new groupings develop and preexisting ones remain intact for longer than normal periods of time (Noe and Bshary, 1997).

Savanna baboons (fig. 6–2) have long been cited as another example of these principles. They are found in semiarid grassland and broken woodland habitats throughout sub-Saharan Africa. To avoid nocturnal predators, savanna baboons sleep in trees; however, they spend much of the day on the ground foraging for food. In the presence of nonhuman predators, baboons flee to the safety of trees. However, if they are at some distance from safety, or if a predator is nearby, adult males (and sometimes females) may join forces to chase an intruder away. The effectiveness of male baboons in this regard should not be underestimated, for baboons have been known to kill domestic dogs and even to attack leopards and lions (Altmann and Altmann, 1970).

See Virtual Lab 6, section IV, for an in-depth presentation, including video, of savanna baboon behavior.

As you have already learned, not all primates are found in large groups. Solitary foraging is typical of many species and is probably related to diet and distribution of resources. In the case of the slow-moving, insectivorous loris, for example, solitary feeding reduces competition, which allows for less distance traveled (and thus less expenditure of energy) in the search for prey. Moreover, because insects usually do not occur in dense patches, they are more efficiently exploited by widely dispersed individuals rather than by groups. Solitary foraging is also related to predator avoidance, and it is particularly effective in species that rely chiefly on concealment rather than escape.

figure 6–2 Group of savanna baboons, which includes adult males and females as well as youngsters of various ages. Note adult male carrying infant in foreground.

Lynn Kilgore

Foraging alone or with offspring is also seen in females of some diurnal anthropoid species (e.g., orangutans, chimpanzees). These females, being relatively large-bodied, have little to fear from predators, and by feeding alone or with only one or two youngsters, they maximize their access to food, free from competition with others.

The various solutions that primate species have developed to deal with the problems of survival differ in complicated ways. Closely related species living in proximity to one another and exploiting many of the same resources can have very different types of social structure. It is only through continued research that primatologists will be able to sort out the intricate relationships between society and the natural environment.

Nonhuman Primate Social Behavior

Because primates solve their major adaptive problems in a social context, we might expect them to participate in a number of activities to reinforce the integrity of the group. The better known of these activities are described in the sections that follow.

Dominance

Many primate societies are organized into **dominance hierarchies.** Dominance hierarchies impose a certain degree of order within groups by establishing parameters of individual behavior. Although aggression is frequently a means of increasing one's status, dominance usually serves to reduce the amount of actual physical violence. Not only are lower-ranking animals unlikely to attack or even

Dominance hierarchies Systems of social organization wherein individuals within a group are ranked relative to one another. Higher-ranking individuals have greater access to preferred food items and mating partners than lower-ranking individuals. Dominance hierarchies have sometimes been referred to as "pecking orders."

threaten a higher-ranking one, but dominant animals are also frequently able to exert control simply by making a threatening gesture.

Individual rank or status may be measured by access to resources, including food items and mating partners. Dominant individuals are given priority by others, and they usually do not give way in confrontations.

Some primatologists postulate that the primary benefit of dominance is the increased reproductive success of the individual. This observation would be true if it could be demonstrated that dominant males compete more successfully for mates than do subordinate males. However, there is also good evidence that lower-ranking males of some species successfully mate; they just do so surreptitiously. Likewise, increased reproductive success can be postulated for high-ranking females, who have greater access to food than subordinate females. High-ranking females are provided with more energy for offspring production and care (Fedigan, 1983), and presumably their reproductive success is greater.

An individual's rank is not permanent and changes throughout life. It is influenced by many factors, including sex, age, level of aggression, amount of time spent in the group, intelligence, perhaps motivation, and the mother's social position (particularly true of macaques and baboons).

In species organized into groups containing a number of females associated with one or several adult males, the males are generally dominant to females. Within such groups, males and females have separate hierarchies, although very high ranking females can dominate the lowest-ranking males (particularly young males). There are exceptions to this pattern of male dominance. Among many lemur species, females are the dominant sex. Moreover, among species that form monogamous pairs (e.g., indris, gibbons), males and females are codominant.

All primates *learn* their position in the hierarchy. From birth, an infant is carried by its mother, and it observes how she responds to every member of the group. Just as importantly, it sees how others react to her. Dominance and subordination are indicated by gestures and behaviors, some of which are universal throughout the primate order (including humans), and this gestural repertoire is part of every youngster's learning experience.

Young primates also acquire social rank through play with age peers. As they spend more time with play groups, their social interactions widen. Competition and rough-and-tumble play allow them to learn the strengths and weaknesses of peers, and they carry this knowledge with them throughout their lives. Thus, through early contact with the mother and subsequent exposure to peers, young primates learn to negotiate their way through the complex web of social interactions that make up their daily lives.

Communication

Communication is universal among animals, and modes of communication include scents and unintentional, **autonomic** responses and behaviors that convey meaning. Such attributes as body posture convey information about an animal's emotional state. For example, a crouched position indicates a certain degree of insecurity or fear, while a purposeful striding gait implies confidence. Moreover, autonomic responses to threatening or novel stimuli, such as raised body hair (most species) or enhanced body odor (gorillas), indicate excitement.

Many intentional behaviors also serve as communication. In primates, these include a wide variety of gestures, facial expressions, and vocalizations,

Communication Any act that conveys information, in the form of a message, to another individual. Frequently, the result of communication is a change in the behavior of the recipient. Communication may not be deliberate but may be the result of involuntary processes or a secondary consequence of an intentional action.

Autonomic Pertaining to physiological responses not under voluntary control. An example in chimpanzees would be the erection of body hair during excitement. An example in humans is blushing. Both convey information regarding emotional states, but neither is a deliberate behavior, and communication is not intended.

Lynn Kilgore

figure 6–3 Adolescent male savanna baboon threatens photographer with a characteristic "yawn" that shows the canine teeth. Note also that the eyes are closed briefly to expose light, cream-colored eyelids. This has been termed the "eyelid flash."

some of which we humans share. Among many primates, a mild threat is indicated by an intense stare, and indeed, we humans find prolonged eye contact with strangers very uncomfortable. (For this reason, people should avoid eye contact with captive primates.) Other threat gestures are a quick yawn to expose canine teeth (baboons, macaques) (fig. 6–3); bobbing back and forth in a crouched position (patas monkeys); and branch shaking (many monkey species). High-ranking baboons *mount* the hindquarters of subordinates to express dominance (fig. 6–4). Mounting may also serve to defuse potentially tense situations by indicating something like, "It's okay, I know you didn't intend to offend me."

There are also a number of behaviors to indicate submission, reassurance, or amicable intentions. Submission is indicated by a crouched position (most primates) or presenting the hindquarters (baboons). Reassurance takes the form of touching, patting, and, in chimpanzees, hugging and holding hands. Grooming also serves in a number of situations to indicate submission or reassurance.

A wide variety of facial expressions indicating emotional states is seen in chimpanzees and bonobos (fig. 6–5). These include the well-known play face (also seen in several other primate and nonprimate species), associated with play behavior, and the fear grin (seen in *all* primates) to indicate fear and submission.

Primates also use a wide array of vocalizations for communication. Some, such as the bark of a baboon that has just spotted a leopard, are unintentional startled reactions. Others, such as the chimpanzee food grunt, are heard only in specific contexts. Nevertheless, both serve the same function: They inform others, although not necessarily deliberately, of the possible presence of predators or food.

figure 6–4 One young male savanna baboon mounts another as an expression of dominance.

Lynn Kilgore

| Relaxed | Relaxed with dropped lip | Horizontal pout face (distress) | Fear grin (fear/excitement) | Full play face |

Primates (and other animals) also communicate through **displays,** which are more complicated, frequently elaborate combinations of behaviors. For example, the exaggerated courtship dances of many male birds, often enhanced by colorful plumage, are displays. Common gorilla displays are chest slapping and the tearing of vegetation to indicate threat. Likewise, an angry chimpanzee, with hair bristling, may charge an opponent while screaming, waving its arms, and tearing vegetation.

All nonhuman animals employ various vocalizations, body postures, and, to some degree, facial expressions that transmit information. However, the array of communicative devices is much richer among nonhuman primates, even though they do not use language in the manner of humans. Communication is important, for it truly is what makes social living possible. Through submissive gestures, aggression is reduced and physical violence is less likely. Likewise, friendly intentions and relationships are reinforced through physical contact and grooming. Indeed, it is in the familiar methods of nonverbal communication that we humans can see ourselves in other primate species most clearly.

Aggression

Within primate societies, there is an interplay between **affiliative** behaviors, which promote group cohesion, and aggressive behaviors, which can lead to group disruption. Conflict within a group frequently develops out of competition for resources, including mating partners and food items. Instead of actual attacks or fighting, most intragroup aggression occurs in the form of various signals and displays, frequently within the context of a dominance hierarchy. The majority of such situations are resolved through various submissive and appeasement behaviors.

But conflict is not always resolved peacefully, and it can have serious consequences. For example, high-ranking female macaques frequently intimidate, harass, and even attack lower-ranking females, particularly to restrict their access to food. High-ranking females consistently chase subordinates away from food and have even been observed to take food from their mouths; these behaviors can result in weight loss and poorer nutrition in low-ranking females, which, in turn, can reduce their reproductive success.

Competition between males for mates frequently results in injury and occasionally in death. In species that have a distinct breeding season (e.g., squirrel monkeys), conflict between males is most common during that time. Male squirrel monkeys form coalitions to compete with other males, and when outright

figure 6–5 Chimpanzee facial expressions. (Adapted with permission of the publishers from *The Chimpanzees of Gombe* by Jane Goodall, Cambridge, Mass.: Harvard University Press, © 1986 by the President and Fellows of Harvard College.)

Displays Sequences of repetitious behaviors that serve to communicate emotional states. Nonhuman primate displays are most frequently associated with reproductive or agonistic behavior.

Affiliative Pertaining to amicable associations between individuals. Affiliative behaviors, such as grooming, reinforce social bonds and promote group cohesion.

fighting occurs, injuries can be severe. In species not restricted to a mating season, competition between males can be an ongoing process.

Aggressive encounters occur *between* groups as well as within groups. Between groups, aggression occurs in the defense of **territories.** Primate groups are associated with a **home range,** where they remain permanently. Within this home range is a portion called the **core area,** which contains the highest concentration of predictable resources and where the group is most frequently found. Although portions of the home range may overlap with the home range of one or more other groups, core areas of adjacent groups do not overlap. The core area can also be said to be a group's territory, and it is the portion of the home range that is usually defended against intrusion by others. However, in some species, such as chimpanzees, other areas of the home range may also be defended. Whatever area is defended, this portion is termed the *territory.*

Beginning in 1974, Jane Goodall and her colleagues witnessed at least five unprovoked and extremely brutal attacks by groups of chimpanzees (usually, but not always, males) on lone individuals. To explain these attacks, it is necessary to point out that by 1973, the original Gombe community had divided into two distinct groups. The larger group was located in the north of the original home range. The smaller offshoot group established itself in the southern portion, effectively denying the others access to part of their former territory.

By 1977, all seven males and one female of the splinter group were either known or suspected to have been killed. All observed incidents involved several animals who attacked lone individuals. Although it is not possible to know exactly what motivated the attackers, it was clear that they intended to incapacitate their victims (Goodall, 1986).

A situation similar to that at Gombe has been reported for a group of chimpanzees in the Mahale Mountains south of Gombe. Over a 17-year period, all the males of a small community disappeared. Although no attacks were actually observed, there was circumstantial evidence that most of these males met the same fate as the Gombe attack victims (Nishida et al., 1985; Nishida et al., 1990).

In addition to territoriality, Manson and Wrangham (1991) have proposed a number of other factors that may contribute to male chimpanzee aggression, including acquisition of females from other groups. While the precise motivation of chimpanzee intergroup violence may never be fully elucidated, it is clear that a number of interrelated factors are involved. Moreover, although chimpanzees do not meet all the criteria developed for true territorial behavior (Goodall, 1986), it appears that various aspects of resource acquisition and protection are involved.

See Virtual Lab 6,
section IV, for video
clips depicting affiliative
behaviors.

Affiliative Behaviors

Even though conflict can be destructive, a certain amount of aggression is useful in maintaining order within groups and protecting either individual or group resources. Fortunately, to minimize actual violence and to defuse potentially dangerous situations, there is an array of affiliative, or friendly, behaviors that serve to reinforce bonds between individuals and enhance group stability.

Common affiliative behaviors include reconciliation, consolation, and simple amicable interactions between friends and relatives. Most such behaviors involve various forms of physical contact, such as touching, hand holding (fig. 6–6), hugging, and, among chimpanzees, kissing. In fact, physical contact is

figure 6–6 Adolescent savanna
baboons holding hands.

one of the most important factors in primate development and is crucial in promoting peaceful relationships in many primate social groups.

Grooming is one of the most important affiliative behaviors in many primate species. Although grooming occurs in numerous species other than primates, social grooming is mostly a primate activity, and it plays an important role in day-to-day life (fig. 6–7). Because grooming involves using the fingers to pick through the fur of another individual (or one's own) to remove insects, dirt, and other materials, it serves hygienic functions. But it is also an immensely pleasurable activity that individuals of some species (especially chimpanzees) engage in for considerable periods of time.

Grooming occurs in a variety of contexts. Mothers groom infants. Males groom sexually receptive females. Subordinate animals groom dominant ones, sometimes to gain favor. Friends groom friends. In general, grooming is comforting. It restores peaceful relationships between animals who have quarreled and provides reassurance during tense situations. In short, grooming reinforces social bonds and consequently helps to maintain and strengthen the structure of the group.

Grooming Picking through fur to remove dirt, parasites, and other materials that may be present. Social grooming is common among primates and reinforces social relationships.

figure 6–7 Grooming primates. (a) Patas monkeys; female grooming male. (b) Longtail macaques. (c) Savanna baboons. (d) Chimpanzees.

(a)   (b)   (c)   (d)

Conflict resolution through reconciliation is another important aspect of primate social behavior. Following a conflict, chimpanzee opponents frequently move, within minutes, to reconcile (de Waal, 1982). Reconciliation takes many forms, including hugging, kissing, and grooming and uninvolved individuals may even take part. In addition, bonobos are unique in their use of sex to promote group cohesion, restore peace after conflicts, and relieve tension within the group (de Waal, 1987, 1989).

Social relationships are crucial to nonhuman primates, and the bonds between individuals can last a lifetime. These relationships serve a variety of functions. Individuals of many species form alliances in which one supports another against a third. Alliances, or coalitions, as they are also called, can be used to enhance the status of members. For example, at Gombe, the male chimpanzee Figan achieved alpha status because of support from his brother (Goodall, 1986, p. 424). In fact, chimpanzees so heavily rely on coalitions and are so skillful politically that an entire book, appropriately titled *Chimpanzee Politics* (de Waal, 1982), is devoted to the topic.

There are other behaviors that also illustrate the importance of social relationships, some of which can perhaps be described as examples of caregiving or compassion. When discussing nonhuman animal (or indeed, human) behavior, it is impossible to know with certainty what an individual's motivation is. Thus, the use of the term *compassion* is risky, because in humans, compassion is motivated by empathy for another. Whether nonhuman primates can empathize with the suffering or misfortune of another is not really known, but certainly there are numerous examples, mostly from chimpanzee studies, of caregiving actions that resemble compassionate behavior in humans. Examples include protection of others during attacks, helping younger siblings, and staying near ill or dying relatives or friends.

Altruism Any behavior or act that benefits another individual but poses some potential risk or cost to oneself.

Altruism, behavior that benefits another while involving some risk or sacrifice to the performer, is common in many primate species, and altruistic acts sometimes contain elements of compassion and cooperation. The most fundamental of altruistic behaviors, the protection of dependent offspring, is ubiquitous among mammals and birds, and in the majority of species, altruistic acts are confined to this context. However, among primates, recipients of altruistic acts may include individuals who are not offspring and who may not even be closely related to the performer. Stelzner and Strier (1981) witnessed a female baboon chasing a hyena that was in pursuit of a young adult male baboon. This female's unsuccessful attempt to rescue the male was intriguing because not only was she too small to engage the hyena, but she was also unrelated to the victim. Chimpanzees routinely come to the aid of relatives and friends; female langurs join forces to protect infants from males; and male baboons cooperate to chase predators. In fact, the primate literature abounds with examples of altruistic acts, whereby individuals place themselves at some risk to protect others from attacks by conspecifics or predators.

Adoption of orphans is a form of altruism that has been reported for macaques and baboons and is common in chimpanzees. When chimpanzee youngsters are orphaned, they are routinely adopted, usually by older siblings who are solicitous and highly protective. Adoption is crucial to the survival of orphans, who would certainly not survive on their own. In fact, it is extremely rare for a chimpanzee orphan less than three years of age to survive even if it is adopted.

Reproduction and Reproductive Strategies

See Virtual Lab 2, section I, for a discussion of reproductive success.

Patterns of Reproduction

In most primate species, sexual behavior is tied to the female's reproductive cycle, with females sexually receptive to males only when they are in estrus. Estrus is characterized by behavioral changes that indicate a female is receptive. In Old World monkeys and apes that live in multimale groups, estrus is also accompanied by swelling and changes in color of the skin around the genital area. These changes serve as visual cues of a female's readiness to mate (fig. 6–8).

Permanent bonding between males and females is not common among non-human primates. However, male and female savanna baboons sometimes form mating *consortships*. These temporary relationships last while the female is in estrus, and the two spend most of the time together, mating frequently. Moreover, lower-ranking baboon males often form "friendships" (Smuts, 1985) with females and occasionally may mate with them, although they may be driven away by high-ranking males when the female is most receptive.

Mating consortships are sometimes seen in chimpanzees and are particularly common among bonobos. In fact, a male and female bonobo may spend several weeks primarily in each other's company. During this time, they mate often, even when the female is not in estrus. These relationships of longer duration are not typical of chimpanzee (*Pan troglodytes*) males and females.

Such a male-female bond may result in increased reproductive success for both sexes. For the male, there is the increased likelihood that he will be the father of any infant the female conceives. At the same time, the female potentially gains protection from predators or others of her group and perhaps assistance in caring for offspring she may already have.

figure 6–8 Estrous swelling of genital tissues in a female chimpanzee.

Lynn Kilgore

Reproductive Strategies

Reproductive strategies, and especially how they differ between the sexes, have been an important focus of primate research. The goal of such strategies is to produce and successfully rear to adulthood as many offspring as possible.

Primates are among the most **K-selected** of mammal species. By this we mean that individuals produce only a few young, in whom they invest a tremendous amount of parental care. Contrast this pattern with **r-selected** species, where individuals produce large numbers of offspring but invest little or no energy in parental care. Good examples of r-selected species include insects, most fishes, and, among mammals, mice and rabbits.

When we consider the degree of care required by young, growing primates, it is clear that enormous investment by at least one parent is necessary, and it is usually the mother who carries most of the burden. Primates are totally helpless at birth. They develop slowly and are thus exposed to expanded learning opportunities within a *social* environment. This trend has been elaborated most dramatically in great apes and humans, and especially in the latter. Thus, what we see in ourselves and our close primate kin (and presumably in our more recent ancestors as well) is a strategy wherein a few "high-quality," slowly maturing offspring are produced through extraordinary investment by at least one parent, usually the mother.

Finding food and mates, avoiding predators, and caring for and protecting dependent young represent difficult challenges for nonhuman primates. Moreover, in most species, males and females employ different strategies to meet these challenges.

Female nonhuman primates spend almost all their adult lives either pregnant, lactating, and/or caring for offspring, and the resulting metabolic demands are enormous. A pregnant or lactating female, although perhaps only half the size of her male counterpart, may require about the same number of calories per day. Even if these demands are met, her physical resources may be drained. For example, analysis of chimpanzee skeletons from Gombe National Park, in Tanzania, shows significant loss of bone and bone mineral in older females (Sumner et al., 1989).

Given these physiological costs, a female's best strategy is to maximize the amount of resources available to her and her offspring. Indeed, females of many primate species (gibbons, marmosets, and macaques, to name a few) are viciously competitive with other females and aggressively protect resources and territories. In other species, as we have seen, females distance themselves from others to avoid competition.

Males, however, face a separate set of challenges. Having little investment in the rearing of offspring (except in a few species), it is to the male's advantage to secure as many mates and produce as many offspring as possible. By so doing, he is effectively increasing his genetic contribution to the next generation relative to other males.

One outcome of different mating strategies is **sexual selection,** a phenomenon first described by Charles Darwin. Sexual selection is a type of natural selection that operates on only one sex, usually males, whereby the selective agent is male competition for mates and, in some species, mate choice in females. The long-term effect of sexual selection is to increase the frequency of those traits that lead to greater success in acquiring mates.

Reproductive strategies The complex of behavioral patterns that contributes to individual reproductive success. The behaviors need not be deliberate, and they often vary considerably between males and females.

K-selected Pertaining to an adaptive strategy whereby individuals produce relatively few offspring, in whom they invest increased parental care. Although only a few infants are born, chances of survival are increased for each individual because of parental investments in time and energy. Examples of nonprimate K-selected species are birds and canids (e.g., wolves, coyotes, and dogs).

r-selected Pertaining to an adaptive strategy that emphasizes relatively large numbers of offspring and reduced parental care (compared to K-selected species). (*K-selection* and *r-selection* are relative terms; e.g., mice are r-selected compared to primates but K-selected compared to many fish species.)

Sexual selection A type of natural selection that operates on only one sex within a species. It is the result of competition for mates, and it can lead to sexual dimorphism with regard to one or more traits.

In the animal kingdom there are numerous male attributes that result from sexual selection. In some bird species, for example, males are much more brightly colored than females. For various reasons, female birds find those males with more vividly colored plumage more attractive as mates; thus, selection has increased the frequency of alleles that influence brighter coloration in males.

Sexual selection in primates is most important in species characterized by multimale social groups, but it is a factor in any species where mating is polygynous and male competition for females is prominent. In these species, sexual selection produces dimorphism with regard to a number of traits, most noticeably body size. The males of many primate species are considerably larger than females (indeed, male gorillas and orangutans can be twice as large), and males also have larger canine teeth. Conversely, in species where mating is monogamous (e.g., gibbons) or where male competition is reduced, dimorphism in canine and body size is either reduced or nonexistent. For these reasons, the presence or absence of sexually dimorphic traits in a species is a reasonably good indicator of mating structure.

See Virtual Lab 6, section II, for a video clip showing interactions between a female baboon and her infant.

Mothers and Infants

The basic social unit among all primates is the female and her infants (fig. 6–9). Except in those species in which monogamy or **polyandry** occurs, males do not participate greatly in the rearing of offspring. Observations both in the field and in captivity suggest that the mother-offspring core provides the social group with its stability.

The mother-infant bond, one of the most basic themes running throughout primate social relations, begins at birth. Although the exact nature of the bonding process is not fully known, there appear to be predisposing innate factors that strongly attract the female to her infant, so long as she herself has had sufficiently normal experiences with her own mother. This does not mean that primate mothers possess innate knowledge of how to care for an infant. Indeed, they do not. Monkeys and apes raised in captivity without contact with their own mothers not only do not know how to care for a newborn infant, but may also be afraid of it and attack and kill it. Even if they do not directly attack the infant, they may kill it indirectly through mishandling or improper nursing.

The crucial role of bonding between primate mothers and infants was clearly demonstrated by the Harlows (1959), who raised infant monkeys with surrogate mothers fashioned from wire or a combination of wire and cloth. Other monkeys were raised with no mothers at all. In one experiment, infants retained an attachment to their cloth-covered surrogate mother (fig. 6–10). But those raised with no mother were incapable of forming lasting affectional ties. These deprived monkeys sat passively in their cages and stared vacantly into space. None of the motherless males ever successfully copulated, and those females who were (somewhat artificially) impregnated either paid little attention to offspring or reacted aggressively toward them (Harlow and Harlow, 1961). The point is that monkeys reared in isolation were denied opportunities to *learn* the rules of social behavior. Moreover, and just as essential, they were denied the all-important physical contact so necessary for normal primate psychological and emotional development.

Polyandry A mating system wherein a female continuously associates with more than one male (usually two or three) with whom she mates. Among nonhuman primates, this pattern is seen only in marmosets and tamarins.

(a)

(b)

(c)

(d)

(e)

figure 6–9 Primate mothers with young. (a) Mongoose lemur. (b) Chimpanzee. (c) Patas monkey. (d) Orangutan. (e) Sykes monkey.

figure 6–10 Infant macaque clinging to cloth mother.

The importance of a normal relationship with the mother is demonstrated by field studies as well. From birth, infant primates are able to cling to their mother's fur, and they are in more or less constant physical contact with her for several months. During this critical period, the infant develops a closeness with the mother that does not always end with weaning. This closeness is often maintained throughout life (especially among some Old World monkeys). It is reflected in grooming behavior that continues between mother and offspring even after the young reach adulthood and have infants of their own.

Nonhuman Primate Cultural Behavior

One important trait that makes nonhuman primates, and especially chimpanzees and bonobos, attractive as models for behavior in early hominids may be called *cultural behavior*. Although many cultural anthropologists and others prefer to use the term *culture* to refer specifically to human activities, most biological anthropologists consider it appropriate to use the term in discussions of nonhuman primates as well (McGraw, 1992, 1998; de Waal, 1999; Whiten et al., 1999).

Undeniably, there are many aspects of culture that are uniquely human, and one must be cautious when interpreting nonhuman animal behavior. But again, since humans are products of the same evolutionary forces that have produced other species, they can be expected to exhibit some of the same *behavioral patterns* seen in other species, particularly primates. However, because of increased brain size and learning capacities, humans express many characteristics to a greater degree. We would argue that the *aptitude for culture* as a means of adapting to the natural environment is one such characteristic.

Among other things, cultural behavior is *learned*, and it is passed from generation to generation not biologically, but through learning. Whereas humans deliberately teach their young, free-ranging nonhuman primates (with the exception of a few reports) do not generally appear to do so. But human children also acquire tremendous knowledge not from instruction, but through observation in the same manner as young nonhuman primates. Nonhuman primate infants, through observing their mothers and others, learn about food items, appropriate behaviors, and how to use and modify objects to achieve certain ends. In turn, their own offspring will observe their activities. What emerges is a *cultural tradition* that may eventually come to typify an entire group or even a species.

A famous example of cultural behavior was seen in a study group of Japanese macaques on Koshima Island. In 1952, Japanese researchers began provisioning the 22-member troop with sweet potatoes. The following year, a young female named Imo began washing her potatoes in a freshwater stream prior to eating them. Within three years, several monkeys had adopted the practice, but they had switched from using the stream to taking their potatoes to the ocean nearby. Perhaps they liked the salt seasoning!

The researchers proposed that dietary habits and food preferences are learned and that potato washing was an example of nonhuman culture. Because this practice arose as an innovative solution to a problem and was imitated by others until it became a tradition, it was seen as resembling human culture.

Among chimpanzees we see more elaborate examples of cultural behavior in the form of *tool use*. This point is very important, because traditionally, tool use (along with language) was said to set humans apart from other animals.

Chimpanzees insert twigs and grass blades into termite mounds in a practice called "termite fishing" (fig. 6–11). When termites seize the twig, the chimpanzee withdraws it and eats the attached insects. Chimpanzees modify some of their stems and twigs by stripping the leaves—in effect, manufacturing a tool from the natural material. To some extent, chimpanzees even alter objects to a "regular and set pattern" and have been observed preparing objects for later use at another location (Goodall, 1986, p. 535). For example, a chimpanzee will very carefully select a piece of vine, bark, twig, or palm frond and modify it by figure 6–11 Female chimpanzee using a tool to "fish" for termites at Gombe National Park, Tanzania.

Courtesy, Jane Goodall Institute

removing leaves or other extraneous material, then break off portions until it is the proper length. Chimpanzees have also been seen making these tools even before the termite mound is in sight.

All this preparation has several implications. First, the chimpanzees are engaged in an activity that prepares them for a future (not immediate) task at a somewhat distant location, and this action implies planning and forethought. Second, attention to the shape and size of the raw material indicates that chimpanzee toolmakers have a preconceived idea of what the finished product needs to be in order to be useful. To produce a tool, even a simple tool, based on a concept is an extremely complex behavior. Scientists previously believed that such behavior was the exclusive domain of humans, but now we must question this basic assumption.

Chimpanzees also crumple and chew handfuls of leaves, which they dip into the hollow of a tree where water has accumulated. Then they suck the water from their "leaf sponges," water that otherwise would have been inaccessible to them. Leaves are also used to wipe substances from fur; twigs are sometimes used as toothpicks; stones may be used as weapons; and various objects, such as branches and stones, may be dragged or rolled to enhance displays. Lastly, sticks or leaves are used as aids in processing mammalian prey, but with one exception these practices appear to be incidental. The one exception, observed in chimpanzees in the Tai forest (Ivory Coast), is the frequent use of sticks to extract marrow from long bones (Boesch and Boesch, 1989).

Chimpanzees in numerous West African study groups use hammerstones with platform stones to crack nuts and hard-shelled fruits (Boesch et al., 1994). However, it is important to note that neither the hammerstone nor the platform stone was deliberately manufactured.* Interestingly, capuchin monkeys also use leaves to extract water from cavities in trees (Phillips, 1998) and they smash objects against stones (Izawa and Mizuno, 1977). Their use of stones in captivity (both as hammers and anvils) has also been reported (Visalberghi, 1990). (Stones serve as anvils when fruit or other objects are bashed against the rock surface.) But chimpanzees are the only nonhuman primate that consistently and habitually makes and uses tools (McGrew, 1992).

Importantly, chimpanzees exhibit regional variation regarding both the types and methods of tool use. Use of stone hammers and platforms is confined to West African groups. And at central and eastern African sites, termites are obtained by means of stems and sticks, while at some West African locations, it appears that no tools are used in this context (McGrew, 1992).

Regional dietary preferences are also noted for chimpanzees (Nishida et al., 1983; McGrew, 1992, 1998). For example, oil palms are exploited for their fruit and nuts at many locations, including Gombe, but even though they are present in the Mahale Mountains, they are not utilized by the chimpanzees there. Such regional patterns in tool use and food preferences that are not due to environmental variation are highly reminiscent of the cultural variations characteristic of humans.

Using sticks, twigs, and stones enhances the ability of chimpanzees to exploit resources. Learning these behaviors occurs during infancy and childhood, partly as a function of prolonged contact with the mother. Also important in this regard is the continued exposure to others provided by living in social groupings, and these statements also apply to early hominids. Although sticks and unmodified stones do not remain to tell tales, it is probable that our early ancestors surely used these same objects as tools in much the same manner as do chimpanzees.

While chimpanzees in the wild have not been observed modifying the stones they use, a male bonobo named Kanzi (see p. 148) has learned to strike two stones together to produce sharp-edged flakes. In a study conducted by Sue Savage-Rumbaugh and archaeologist Nicholas Toth, Kanzi was allowed to watch as Toth produced stone flakes, which were then used to open a transparent plastic food container (Savage-Rumbaugh and Lewin, 1994). Although bonobos apparently do not commonly use objects as tools in the wild, Kanzi readily appreciated the utility of the flakes in obtaining food. Moreover, he was able to master the basic technique of producing flakes without having been taught the various components of the process, even though initially his progress was slow. Eventually, Kanzi realized that he could overcome his difficulties by throwing a stone onto a hard floor, causing it to shatter, thus providing an abundance of cutting implements. Although his solution was not necessarily the one that Savage-Rumbaugh and Toth expected, it nevertheless provided an excellent example of bonobo insight and problem-solving ability. Moreover, Kanzi did eventually learn to produce flakes by striking two stones together, and these flakes were then used to obtain food. Not only is this behavior an example of tool manufacture and tool use, albeit in a captive situation; it is also a very sophisticated goal-directed activity.

---

*Observers of nonhuman primates rarely distinguish natural objects used as tools from modified objects deliberately manufactured for specific purposes. The term *tool* is usually employed in both cases.

Human culture has become the environment in which modern *Homo sapiens* lives. Quite clearly, the use of sticks in termite fishing and hammerstones to crack nuts is hardly comparable to modern human technology. However, modern human technology had its beginnings in these very types of behaviors we observe in other primates. This does not mean that nonhuman primates are "on their way" to becoming human. Remember, evolution is not goal directed, and if it were, there is nothing to dictate that modern humans necessarily constitute an evolutionary goal. Such a conclusion is a purely **anthropocentric** view, and it has no validity in discussions of evolutionary processes.

Moreover, nonhuman primates have probably been capable of certain cultural behaviors for millions of years. As we have stated, the common ancestor that humans share with chimpanzees may have used sticks and stones to exploit resources and perhaps even as weapons. These behaviors are not newly developed in our close relatives simply because we have only recently documented them. Thus, we must continue to study these capabilities in nonhuman primates in their social and ecological context so that we may eventually understand more clearly how cultural traditions emerged in our own lineage.

Anthropocentric Viewing nonhuman phenomena in terms of human experience and capabilities; emphasizing the importance of humans over everything else.

Primate Cognitive Abilities

As we have already seen, primates are extremely intelligent, as demonstrated by their complicated social interactions and problem-solving abilities. Indeed, their use of tools represents solutions to such problems as how to get termites out of their mounds or how to gain access to water in difficult places.

Although numerous studies have demonstrated the abilities of nonhuman primates, probably no research has had the impact, certainly on the general public, that the language acquisition studies have had. As previously discussed, all animals communicate through a variety of modalities, including scent, vocalizations, touch, and visual indicators (gestures, facial expressions, and body posture). However, the amount and kinds of information that nonhuman animals are able to convey are limited.

The view traditionally held by most linguists and behavioral psychologists has been that nonhuman communication consists of mostly involuntary vocalizations and actions that convey information about the emotional state of the animal (anger, fear, etc.). Nonhuman animals have not been considered capable of communicating about external events, objects, or other animals, either in close proximity or removed in space or time. For example, when a startled baboon barks, its fellow baboons know only that it is startled. What they do not know is what elicited the bark, and this they can only ascertain by looking around. In general, then, it has been assumed that nonhuman animals, including primates, use a *closed system* of communication, one in which use of vocalizations and other modalities does not include references to specific external phenomena.

In recent years, these views have been challenged (Steklis, 1985; King, 1994). Vervets (fig. 6–12) have been shown to use specific vocalizations for particular categories of predators such as snakes, eagles, and leopards (Struhsaker, 1967; Seyfarth, Cheney, and Marler, 1980a, 1980b). When researchers made tape recordings of various vervet alarm calls and played them back within hearing figure 6–12 Group of free-ranging vervets.

distance of free-ranging vervets, they observed differing responses to various calls. In response to leopard alarm calls, the monkeys climbed trees; eagle alarm calls caused them to look upward and run into bushes; and snake alarm calls elicited looking around in the nearby grass.

These results demonstrate that vervets use distinct vocalizations to refer to specific components of the external environment. These calls are not involuntary, and they do not refer solely to the emotional state of the individual animal, although this information is also conveyed. While these significant findings dispel certain long-held misconceptions about nonhuman communication (at least for some species), they also indicate certain limitations. Vervet communication is restricted to the present; as far as we know, no vervet can communicate about a predator it saw yesterday or one it might see in the future.

Other studies have now shown that numerous other nonhuman primates, including cottontop tamarins (Cleveland and Snowdon, 1982), red colobus (Struhsaker, 1975), and gibbons (Tenaza and Tilson, 1977), also produce distinct calls that have specific references. There is also growing evidence that many birds and some nonprimate mammals use distinct predator alarm calls as well (Seyfarth, 1987).

In contrast, humans use *language*, a set of written and spoken symbols that refer to concepts, other humans, objects, and so on. This set of symbols is said to be *arbitrary* in that the symbol itself has no relationship to whatever it represents. For example, the English word *flower* when written or spoken neither looks, smells, nor feels like the thing it represents. Moreover, humans can recombine their linguistic symbols in an infinite number of ways to create new meanings, and we can use language to refer to events, places, objects, and people far removed in both space and time. For these reasons, language is described as an *open system* of communication, based on the human ability to think symbolically.

Language, as distinct from other forms of communication, has been considered a uniquely human achievement, one that sets humans apart from the rest of the animal kingdom. But work with captive apes has raised some doubts about that supposition. While many people were skeptical about the capacity of nonhuman primates to use language, reports from psychologists who work with apes, especially chimpanzees, leave little doubt that these primates can learn to interpret signs and use them to communicate with their trainers and companions in their own group.

No mammal other than humans has the ability to speak. However, the fact that apes cannot speak has less to do with lack of intelligence than to differences in the anatomy of the vocal tract and *language-related structures in the brain*. Quite clearly, communication became increasingly important in hominid evolution, and natural selection increasingly favored anatomical and neurological changes that enhanced our ancestors' ability to use spoken language.

Because of failed attempts at teaching young chimpanzees to speak, psychologists Beatrice and Allen Gardner designed a study to test language capabilities in chimpanzees by teaching an infant female named Washoe to use ASL (American sign language for the deaf). Beginning in 1966, the Gardners began teaching Washoe signs in the same way parents would teach a deaf human infant. In just over three years, Washoe had acquired at least 132 signs. "She asked for goods and services, and she also asked questions about the world of objects and events around her" (Gardner et al., 1989, p. 6).

Years later, an infant chimpanzee named Loulis was placed in Washoe's care. Researchers wanted to know if Loulis would acquire signing skills from Washoe and other chimpanzees in the study group. Within just eight days, Loulis began to imitate the signs of others. Moreover, Washoe also deliberately *taught* Loulis some signs. For example, teaching him to sit, "Washoe placed a small plastic chair in front of Loulis, and then signed CHAIR/SIT to him several times in succession, watching him closely throughout" (Fouts et al., 1989, p. 290).

There have been other ape language experiments. At the Yerkes Regional Primate Research Center in Atlanta, Georgia, another chimpanzee, Lana, worked with a specially designed computer keyboard with chips attached to keys. After six months, Lana recognized symbols for 30 words and was able to ask for food and answer questions through the machine (Rumbaugh, 1977). Also at Yerkes, two male chimpanzees, Sherman and Austin, learned to communicate using a series of lexigrams, or geometric symbols, imprinted on a computer keyboard (Savage-Rumbaugh, 1986b).

Dr. Francine Patterson, who taught ASL to Koko, a female lowland gorilla, reports that Koko uses more than 500 signs. Furthermore, Michael, an adult male who was also involved in the gorilla study until his death in 2000, had a considerable sign vocabulary, and the two gorillas communicated with each other via signs.

In the late 1970s, a male orangutan, Chantek (also at Yerkes), began to use signs after one month of training when he was two years old. Chantek eventually acquired a total of approximately 140 signs, which in some situations were used to refer to objects and persons not present. Chantek also invented signs and recombined them in novel ways, and he appeared to understand that his signs were *representations* of items, actions, and people (Miles, 1990).

Questions have been raised about this type of experimental work. Do the apes really understand the signs they learn, or are they merely imitating their trainers? Do they learn that a symbol is a name for an object or simply that executing a symbol will produce a desired object? Other unanswered questions concern the apes' use of grammar, especially when they combine more than just a few "words" to communicate.

Partly in an effort to address some of these questions and criticisms, Dr. Sue Savage-Rumbaugh taught the chimpanzees Sherman and Austin to use symbols to categorize *classes* of objects, such as "food" or "tool." This was done in recognition of the fact that in previous studies, apes had been taught symbols for *specific* items. Savage-Rumbaugh reasoned that simply using a symbol as a label is not the same thing as understanding the *representational value* of the symbol.

Sherman and Austin were taught to recognize familiar food items, for which they routinely used symbols, as belonging to a broader category referred to by yet another symbol, "food." They were then introduced to unfamiliar food items, for which they had no symbols, to see if they would place them in the food category. The fact that they both had perfect or nearly perfect scores further substantiated that they could categorize unfamiliar objects. More importantly, it was clear that they were capable of assigning to unknown objects symbols that denoted membership in a broad grouping. This ability was an indication that the chimpanzees understood that the symbols were being used referentially.

However, subsequent work with Lana, who had different language experiences, did not prove as successful. Although Lana was able to sort actual objects into categories, she was unable to assign generic symbols to novel items (Savage-Rumbaugh and Lewin, 1994). Thus, it became apparent that the manner in which chimpanzees are introduced to language influences their ability to understand the representational value of symbols.

Chimpanzees learn language differently than do human children in that they must be taught. Human children learn language spontaneously, through exposure, without needing to be deliberately taught. Therefore, it is significant that Savage-Rumbaugh and her colleagues reported that the infant male bonobo Kanzi (fig. 6–13), much prior to his toolmaking days, was spontaneously acquiring and using symbols at the age of 2½ years (Savage-Rumbaugh et al., 1986a). Kanzi's younger half-sister began to use symbols spontaneously at 11 months of age. Both animals had been exposed to the use of lexigrams when they accompanied their mother to training sessions. But neither youngster had received instruction and in fact were not involved in the sessions.

The scientists involved in ape language rescarch are convinced that apes are capable, to varying degrees, of employing symbols to communicate. But this does not mean that apes acquire and use language in the same way humans do. Moreover, it appears that not all signing apes understand the referential relationship between symbol and object, person, or action. Nonetheless, there is abundant evidence that humans are not the only species capable of some degree of symbolic thought and complex communication.

From an evolutionary perspective, the ape language experiments may suggest clues to the origins of human language. Quite possibly, the last common ancestor that hominids shared with the great apes possessed communication capabilities similar to those we see now in modern great apes. If so, we need to elucidate the factors that enhanced the adaptive significance of

figure 6–13 The bonobo Kanzi, as a youngster, using lexigrams to communicate with human observers.

these characteristics in our own lineage. It is equally important to explore why these pressures did not operate to the same degree in gorillas, chimpanzees, and bonobos.

It would be difficult to overstate the significance of human cognitive abilities, as evidenced in our reliance on complex patterns of communication and our technological manipulations of the natural environment. But these capacities should not be used to set humankind apart from the rest of nature, as they almost universally are. In fact, the genetic and behavioral similarities we share with the great apes, as well as ape proficiency at symbolic communication, indicate that the very qualities we have traditionally considered unique to our species are in reality expressed in other species, too, but to a lesser degree.

The Primate Continuum

It is an unfortunate fact that humans generally view themselves as separate from the rest of the animal kingdom. This persepctive is in no small measure due to a prevailing lack of knowledge of the behavior and abilities of other species. Moreover, these notions are continuously reinforced through exposure to advertising, movies, television, and the Internet (fig. 6–14).

For decades, behavioral psychology taught that animal behavior represents nothing more than a series of conditioned responses to specific stimuli. (This perspective is very convenient for those who wish to exploit nonhuman animals, for whatever purposes, and remain free of guilt.) Fortunately, this attitude has begun to change in recent years to reflect a growing awareness that humans, although in many ways unquestionably unique, are nevertheless part of a **biological continuum.**

Where do humans fit, then, in this biological continuum? Are we at the top? The answer depends on the criteria used, and we must also bear in mind that

Biological continuum The fact that organisms are related through common ancestry and that behaviors and traits seen in one species are also seen in others to varying degrees. (When expressions of a phenomenon continuously grade into one another so that there are no discrete categories, they are said to exist on a continuum. Color is one such phenomenon.)

figure 6–14 This unfortunate advertising display is a good example of how humans misunderstand and thus misrepresent our closest relatives.

Lynn Kilgore

evolution is not a goal-directed process. Certainly, we are the most intelligent species, if we define intelligence in terms of problem-solving abilities and abstract thought. However, if we look more closely, we recognize that the differences between ourselves and our primate relatives, especially chimpanzees and bonobos, are primarily quantitative and not qualitative.

Although human brains are absolutely and relatively larger, neurological processes are functionally the same. The necessity of close bonding with at least one parent and the need for physical contact are essentially the same. Developmental stages and dependence on learning are strikingly similar. Indeed, even in the chimpanzee's capacity for cruelty and aggression combined with compassion, tenderness, and altruism, we see a close parallel to the dichotomy between "evil" and "good" so long recognized in ourselves. The main difference between how chimpanzees and humans express these qualities is one of degree. Humans are much more adept at both cruelty and compassion, and humans reflect on their behavior in ways that chimpanzees do not. While chimpanzees may not understand the suffering they inflict on others, humans do. Likewise, while an adult chimpanzee may sit next to and protect a dying relative or friend, it does not appear to feel intense grief and a sense of loss to the extent a human normally does.

To arrive at any understanding of what it is to be human, it is vastly important to recognize that many of our behaviors are but elaborate extensions of those of our hominid ancestors and close primate relatives. We share 98 percent of our DNA with chimpanzees. The fact that so many of us prefer to bask in the warmth of the "sun belt" with literally millions of others reflects our heritage as social animals adapted to life in the tropics. Likewise, it is no mistake that industry has invested millions of dollars in the development of low-calorie, artificial sweeteners. The "sweet tooth" that afflicts so many humans is a direct result of our earlier primate ancestors' predilection for high-energy sugar contained in desirably sweet, ripe fruit.

The fact that humans are part of an evolutionary continuum is the entire basis for animal research aimed at benefiting our species. Yet, even with our growing awareness of the similarities we share, we continue to cage nonhuman primates with little regard for the very needs they share with us. We would argue that nonhuman primates should be maintained in social groups and that habitat enrichment programs should be introduced. It would seem the very least we can do for our close relatives, from whom we derive so many benefits.

Summary

e have discussed many aspects of nonhuman primate behavior, such as social organization and dominance hierarchies, communication, reproduction, intra- and intergroup relationships (including mothers and infants), aggression, friendship, and culture (in the form of tool use). These behaviors have been treated, to considerable extent, from an evolutionary perspective; specifically, we have attempted to show what features of the environment are most likely to be important in shaping primate social behavior.

Group size and composition are influenced by such environmental components as diet, resource availability, and predators. Moreover, many behaviors are seen as the results of natural selection; that is, they promote increased likelihood of survival and reproduction. Therefore, individuals, ideally, should behave in ways that will maximize their own reproductive success relative to others. Although this does not imply that in mammals, and especially primates, there are genes for specific behaviors, it does suggest that genes may have mediating effects on behavior—perhaps through such products as hormones.

We have emphasized that humans are part of a biological continuum that includes all the primates. It is this evolutionary relationship, then, that accounts for many of the behaviors we have in common with prosimians, monkeys, and apes.

Questions for Review

1. What factors should be considered if one approaches the study of non-human primate behavior from an evolutionary perspective?
2. What are some of the environmental factors believed to influence group size and social organization? Give two examples.
3. How could multimale, multifemale groupings be advantageous to species living in areas where predation pressure is high?
4. How may solitary foraging be advantageous to primates? Discuss two examples.
5. How may genetic factors influence behavior?
6. Discuss a primate behavior that has traditionally been used as an example of behavioral evolution.
7. What are reproductive strategies, and what is their basic goal?
8. Primates are said to be K-selected. What is meant by this? What is r-selection? Give an example of r-selection.
9. Explain male and female differences with regard to parental investment.
10. What are dominance hierarchies? What is their function in primate groups?
11. What is believed to be the primary benefit of being a high-ranking individual? What are three factors that influence an individual's rank in a group?
12. What is grooming? Why is it so important in many primate species; that is, what functions does it serve?
13. Discuss three ways nonhuman primates can communicate information to other group members. Name at least two "threat gestures."
14. Name two ways in which nonhuman primates communicate reassurance.
15. What is meant by an open system of communication? How does it differ from a closed system?
16. What is seen as the basic social unit among all primates? Why is it so important?
17. Discuss an example of between-group aggression. What is thought to have motivated the violence between two groups of chimpanzees at Gombe?
18. Discuss two examples of nonhuman primate cultural behavior. Why is our discovery of these behaviors important to studies of early human evolution?
19. Discuss the language acquisition studies using chimpanzees, bonobos, and gorillas. What are the implications of this research?
20. What do we mean when we state that humans are a part of a biological continuum? How does the view expressed in this statement differ from traditional views expressed by most people?

Suggested Further Readings

Cartmill, Matt. 1990. "Human Uniqueness and Theoretical Content in Paleoanthropology." *International Journal of Primatology* 11(3): 173–192.

Cheney, Dorothy L., and Robert M. Seyfarth. 1990. *How Monkeys See the World.* Chicago: University of Chicago Press.

Goodall, Jane. 1986. *The Chimpanzees of Gombe.* Cambridge, MA: The Belknap Press of Harvard University Press.

King, Barbara J. 1994. *The Information Continuum: Social Information Transfer in Monkeys, Apes, and Hominids.* Santa Fe: SAR Press.

McGrew, W. C. 1992. *Chimpanzee Material Culture.* Cambridge, MA: Cambridge University Press.

_____. 1998. "Culture in Nonhuman Primates?" *Annual Review of Anthropology* 27: 301–328.

Napier, J. R., and P. H. Napier. 1985. *The Natural History of the Primates.* Cambridge, MA: The MIT Press.

Packer, C., and A. E. Pusey. 1997. "Divided We Fall: Cooperation Among Lions." *Scientific American* 276(5): 52–59.

Savage-Rumbaugh, S., and Roger Lewin. 1994. *Kanzi: The Ape at the Brink of the Human Mind.* New York: Wiley.

Smuts, Barbara B., Dorothy L. Cheney, Robert M. Seyfarth, Richard W. Wrangham, and Thomas T. Struhsaker (eds.). 1987. *Primate Societies.* Chicago: University of Chicago Press.

Strier, Karen B. 2000. *Primate Behavioral Ecology* 2nd ed. Boston: Allyn and Bacon.

Multimedia Resources

 Companion Web Site

Anthropology Online: The Wadsworth Anthropology Resource Center Visit **http://anthropology.wadsworth.com** and click on the Companion Web Site for Jurmain/Kilgore/Trevathan/Nelson's *Essentials of Physical Anthropology,* Fifth Edition, to access a wide range of enrichment material to aid in your study of anthropology. Among the useful options for each chapter's self-study are learning objectives, flashcards, Internet exercises, Web links, InfoTrac College Edition exercises, and practice quizzes that can be scored and emailed to your instructor.

PROCESSES OF MACROEVOLUTION: MAMMALIAN/PRIMATE EVOLUTIONARY HISTORY

CONTENTS

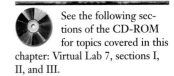

See the following sections of the CD-ROM for topics covered in this chapter: Virtual Lab 7, sections I, II, and III.

Introduction

n the two preceding chapters, we surveyed the structure, ecology, and social behavior of *living* primates. In this chapter, we shift our focus to primate evolution. To place primates, and more specifically, hominids, in their proper evolutionary context, we first give a brief summary of vertebrate and mammalian evolution.

In addition to the broad trends of evolutionary history, we also discuss some contemporary issues relating to evolutionary theory. In particular, we emphasize concepts that relate to large-scale evolutionary processes, that is, *macroevolution* (in contrast to the microevolutionary focus of Chapter 4). The fundamental perspectives reviewed here concern geological history, principles of classification, and modes of evolutionary change, and they serve as a basis for topics covered throughout much of the remainder of the text.

The Human Place in the Organic World

There are millions of species living today; if we were to include microorganisms, the total would likely exceed tens of millions. And if we then added in the vast multitudes of species that are now extinct, the total would be staggering—perhaps hundreds of millions!

How do we cope with all this diversity? Biologists, as is typical for human beings, approach complexity by attempting to simplify it. Thus, they construct a system of **classification** that organizes diversity into categories to reduce complexity and at the same time, to indicate evolutionary relationships.

Organisms that move about and ingest food (but do not photosynthesize, as do plants) are called animals. More precisely, the multicelled animals are placed within the group called the **Metazoa** (fig. 7–1). Within the Metazoa there are more than 20 major groups termed *phyla* (*sing.*, phylum). One of these phyla is the **Chordata,** animals with a nerve cord, gill slits (at some stage of development), and a stiff supporting cord along the back called a *notochord*. Most chordates today are **vertebrates,** in which the notochord has become a vertebral column (which gives its name to the group); in addition, vertebrates have a developed brain and paired sensory structures for sight, smell, and balance.

The vertebrates themselves are subdivided into six classes: bony fishes, cartilaginous fishes, amphibians, reptiles, birds, and mammals. We will discuss mammalian classification later in this chapter.

Classification In biology, the ordering of organisms into categories, such as orders, families, and genera, to show evolutionary relationships.

Metazoa Multicellular animals; a major division of the animal kingdom.

Chordata The phylum of the animal kingdom that includes vertebrates.

Vertebrates Animals with bony backbones; includes fishes, amphibians, reptiles, birds, and mammals.

Principles of Classification

Before we go any further, it would be useful to discuss the bases of animal classification. The field that specializes in delineating the rules of classification is called *taxonomy*. As mentioned in Chapter 5, organisms are classified first, and most traditionally, on the basis of physical similarities. Such was the basis of the figure 7–1 Classification chart, modified from Linnaeus. All animals are placed in certain categories based on structural similarities. Not all members of categories are shown. For example, there are up to 20 orders of placental mammals (8 are depicted). A more comprehensive classification of the primate order was presented in Chapter 5.

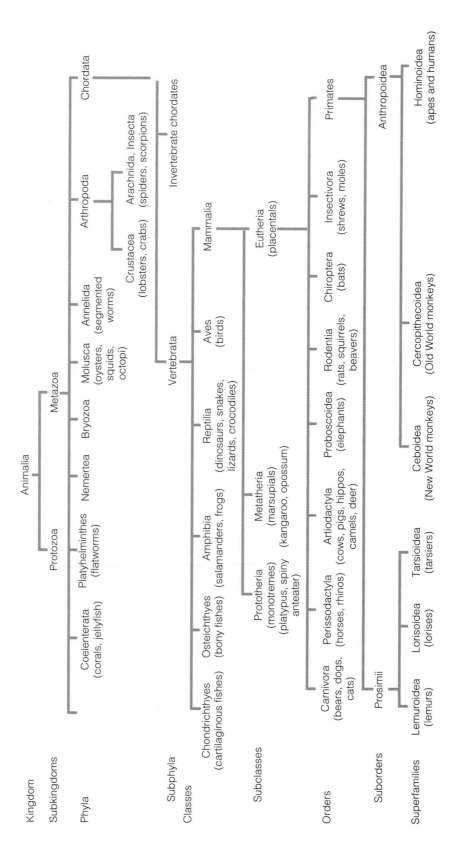

first systematic classification devised by Linnaeus in the eighteenth century (see Chapter 2).

Today, basic physical similarities are still considered a good starting point in postulating schemes of organic relationships. For similarities to be useful, however, they *must* reflect evolutionary descent. For example, the bones of the forelimb of all terrestrial air-breathing vertebrates (tetrapods) are so similar in number and form (fig. 7–2) that the obvious explanation for the striking resemblance is that all four kinds of air-breathing vertebrates ultimately derived their forelimb structure from a common ancestor.

Structures that are shared by species on the basis of descent from a common ancestor are called **homologies.** Homologies alone are reliable indicators of evolutionary relationship. But we must be careful not to draw hasty conclusions from superficial similarities.

Homologies Similarities between organisms based on descent from a common ancestor.

For example, both birds and butterflies have wings, but they should not be grouped together on the basis of this single characteristic; butterflies (as insects) differ dramatically from birds in a number of other, even more fundamental ways. (For example, birds have an internal skeleton, central nervous system, and four limbs; insects do not.).

What has happened in evolutionary history is that from quite distant ancestors, both butterflies and birds have developed wings *independently*. Thus, their (superficial) similarities are a product of separate evolutionary response to roughly similar functional demands; such similarities, based on independent functional adaptation and not on shared evolutionary descent, are called **analogies.** The process that leads to the development of analogies (also called analogous structures) such as wings in birds and butterflies is termed **homoplasy.** In the case of butterflies and birds, the homoplasy has occurred in evolutionary lines that share only very remote ancestry. Here, homoplasy has produced analogous structures separately from any homology. In some cases, however, homoplasy can occur in lineages that are more closely related (and which thus share considerable homology as well). Examples of homoplasy in closely related lineages are evident among the primates (e.g., among New and Old World monkeys and also among the great apes; see Chapter 5).

Analogies Similarities between organisms based strictly on common function, with no assumed common evolutionary descent.

Homoplasy (*homo*, meaning "same," and *plasy*, meaning "growth") The separate evolutionary development of similar characteristics in different groups of organisms.

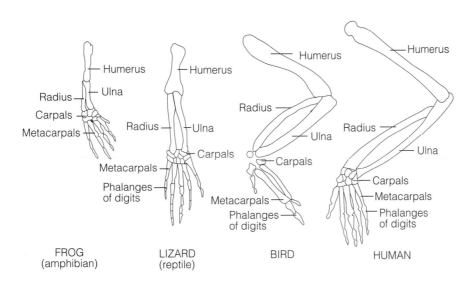

figure 7–2 Homologies. The similarities in the bones of these animals can be most easily explained by descent from a common ancestor.

FROG (amphibian)   LIZARD (reptile)   BIRD   HUMAN

Constructing Classifications and Interpreting Evolutionary Relationships

Evolutionary systematics A traditional approach to classification (and evolutionary interpretation) in which presumed ancestors and descendants are traced in time by analysis of homologous characters.

Cladistics An approach to classification that seeks to make rigorous evolutionary interpretations based solely on analysis of certain types of homologous characters (those considered derived characters).

 See Virtual Lab 7, section II, for a discussion of taxonomy and classification.

Ancestral (primitive) Referring to characters inherited by a group of organisms from a remote ancestor and thus not diagnostic of groups (lineages) branching subsequent to the time the character first appeared.

Derived (modified) Referring to characters that are modified from the ancestral condition and thus *are* diagnostic of particular evolutionary lineages.

There are two major approaches used by evolutionary biologists to interpret evolutionary relationships and thus produce classifications. The first of these, called **evolutionary systematics,** is a more traditional approach, whereas the second approach, called **cladistics,** has emerged primarily in the last two decades. While aspects of both approaches are still utilized by most evolutionary biologists, in recent years cladistic methodologies have predominated among anthropologists.

Before drawing distinctions between these two approaches, it is first helpful to note features shared by both evolutionary systematics and cladistics. First, both schools are interested in tracing evolutionary relationships and constructing classifications that reflect these relationships. Second, both schools recognize that organisms must be compared for specific features (called *characters*) and that some of these characters are more informative than others. And third (and deriving directly from the previous two points), both approaches focus exclusively on homologies.

However, there are also significant differences between these approaches in terms of how characters are chosen, which groups are compared, and how the results are interpreted and eventually incorporated into evolutionary schemes and classifications. The primary difference is that cladistics more explicitly and more rigorously defines the kinds of homologies that yield the most useful information. For example, at a very basic level, all life (except for some viruses) shares DNA as the molecule underlying all organic processes. However, beyond inferring that all life most likely derives from a single origin (a most intriguing point), the presence of DNA tells us nothing further regarding more specific relationships among different kinds of life forms. To draw further conclusions, we need to look at particular characters that are shared by certain groups as the result of more recent ancestry.

This perspective emphasizes an important point: Some homologous characters are much more informative than others. We saw earlier that all terrestrial vertebrates share homologies in the number and basic arrangement of bones in the forelimb. Thus, while these similarities are broadly useful in showing that these large evolutionary groups (amphibians, reptiles, birds, and mammals) are all related through a distant ancestor, they do not provide any usable information by which to distinguish one from another (a reptile from a mammal, for example). Such characters (also called traits) that are shared through such remote ancestry are said to be **primitive,** or **ancestral.** We prefer the term *ancestral* because it does not carry a negative connotation regarding the evolutionary value of the character in question. In physical anthropology, the term *primitive* or *ancestral* simply means that a character seen in two organisms is derived in both of them from a distant ancestor.

In most circumstances, analysis of ancestral characters does not provide enough information to make accurate evolutionary interpretations regarding relationships between different groups. In fact, misinterpretation of ancestral characters can easily lead to quite inaccurate evolutionary conclusions! The traits that cladistics focuses on, and which are far more informative, are those that distinguish particular evolutionary lineages. Such characters are said to be **derived,** or **modified.** Thus, while the general ancestral bony pattern of the forelimb in land animals with backbones does not allow us to distinguish among them, the further modification in certain groups (as hooves, flippers, or wings, for instance) does.

Among vertebrates, *only* birds have feathers and *only* mammals have fur. In comparing mammals with other vertebrates, presence of fur is a *derived* characteristic. Similarly, in describing birds, feathers are derived only in this group.

So how do we know which kind of characteristics to use? The answer is determined by which group we are describing and with what it is being compared. For the most part, it is best to use those characteristics that reflect more specific evolutionary adaptations; in other words, derived characteristics are the most informative. Moreover, we should group two forms together (say, a bat with a mouse, both as mammals), *only* when they show **shared derived** characteristics (here, both possessing fur). (See figs. 5–1 and 7–1 for examples of classifications of animals.)

One last point needs to be mentioned. Traditional phylogenetic systematics illustrates the hypothesized evolutionary relationships using a *phylogeny*, more properly called a **phylogenetic tree.** Strict cladistic analysis, however, shows relationships in a **cladogram.** A phylogenetic tree incorporates the dimension of time. (Numerous examples can be found in this and subsequent chapters.) A cladogram does not indicate time; all forms (fossil and modern) are indicated along one dimension. Phylogenetic trees usually attempt to make some hypotheses regarding ancestor-descendant relationships. Cladistic analysis (through cladograms) makes no attempt whatsoever to discern ancestor-descendant relationships. In fact, strict cladists are quite skeptical that the evidence really permits such specific evolutionary hypotheses to be scientifically confirmed (since there are many more extinct species than living ones).

In practice, most physical anthropologists (and other evolutionary biologists) utilize cladistic analysis to identify and assess the utility of traits and to make testable hypotheses regarding the relationships between groups of organisms. Moreover, they frequently extend this basic cladistic methodology to further hypothesize likely ancestor-descendant relationships shown relative to a time scale (i.e., in a phylogenetic tree). In this way, aspects of both traditional evolutionary systematics and cladistic analyses are combined to produce a more complete picture of evolutionary history.

Shared derived Relating to specific character states shared in common between two forms and considered the most useful for making evolutionary interpretations.

Phylogenetic tree A chart showing evolutionary relationships as determined by phylogenetic systematics. It contains a time component and implies ancestor-descendant relationships.

Cladogram A chart showing evolutionary relationships as determined by cladistic analysis. It is based solely on interpretation of shared derived characters. No time component is indicated, and ancestor-descendant relationships are *not* implied.

Definition of Species

Whether biologists are doing a cladistic or more traditional phylogenetic analysis, they are comparing groups of organisms—that is, different species, genera*, families, orders, and so forth. Fundamental to all these levels of classification is the most basic, the species.

It is appropriate, then, to ask, How do biologists define species? We addressed this issue briefly in Chapter 1 and there applied the most common definition, one that emphasizes interbreeding and reproductive isolation. While not the only definition of species (others will be discussed shortly), this view,

---

*Plural of *genus*.

Biological species concept A depiction of species as groups of individuals capable of fertile interbreeding but reproductively isolated from other such groups.

Speciation The process where a new species evolves from a prior species. Speciation is the most basic process in macroevolution.

called the **biological species concept** (Mayr, 1970), is the one preferred by most zoologists.

The best way to understand what species are is to consider how they come about in the first place—what Darwin called "origin of species." This most fundamental of macroevolutionary processes is today called **speciation.** According to the biological species concept, the way new species are first produced involves some form of isolation. Picture a single species (baboons, for example) composed of several populations distributed over a wide geographical area. Gene exchange between populations (gene flow) will be limited if a geographical barrier, such as an ocean or mountain range, effectively separates these populations. This extremely important form of isolating mechanism is called *geographical isolation.*

If one baboon population (A) is separated from another baboon population (B) by a mountain range, individual baboons of population A will not mate with individuals from B (fig. 7–3). As time passes (several generations), genetic differences will accumulate in both populations. If population size is small, we can predict that genetic drift will cause allele frequencies to change in both populations. Moreover, since drift is *random* in nature, we would not expect the effects to be the same. Consequently, the two populations will begin to diverge.

As long as gene exchange is limited, the populations can only become more genetically different with time. Moreover, further difference can be expected if the baboon groups are occupying slightly different habitats. These additional genetic differences would be incorporated through the process of natural selection. Certain individuals in population A would be most reproductively fit in their own environment, but would show less reproductive success in the environment occupied by population B. Thus, allele frequencies will shift further, and the results, again, will be divergent in the two groups.

With the cumulative effects of genetic drift and natural selection acting over many generations, the result will be two populations that—even if they were to come back into geographical contact—could no longer interbreed. More than just geographical isolation might now apply. There may, for instance, be behavioral differences interfering with courtship—what we call *behavioral isolation.* Using our *biological* definition of species, we now would recognize two distinct species where initially only one existed.

While the biological species concept is accepted today by most biologists as the most workable definition of species (see, for example, Wilson, 2002), there is not complete agreement on the best approach for defining species.

figure 7–3 A speciation model. This model of speciation is called branching evolution, or cladogenesis.

B ┊ A
←——→
A and B
not yet diverged

Some
isolation

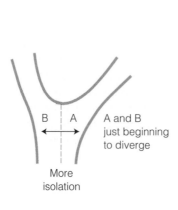

B ┊ A
←——→
A and B
just beginning
to diverge

More
isolation

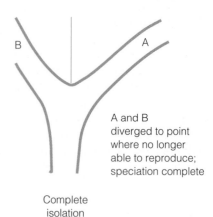

B   A

A and B
diverged to point
where no longer
able to reproduce;
speciation complete

Complete
isolation

TABLE 7-1	Biological Approaches to the Definition of Species
Concept	Definition
Biological Species Concept	The most commonly used definition of species. Here, species are defined by reproductive isolation, such that only members of the *same* species are capable of fertile interbreeding.
Recognition Species Concept	A depiction of species where the key aspect is the ability of individuals to identify members of their own species for purposes of mating (and to avoid mating with members of other species). In theory, this type of selective mating is a component of a species concept emphasizing mating and is therefore compatible with the biological species concept.
Ecological Species Concept	The concept that a species is a group of organisms exploiting a single niche. This view emphasizes the role of natural selection in separating species from one another.

Some biologists have thus proposed alternative definitions, two of which have received considerable attention: the recognition species concept and the ecological species concept (see Table 7–1 for further elaboration). It should be emphasized, however, that these varied approaches to defining species are not mutually exclusive. Indeed, aspects of all three concepts could potentially interact in the formation of new species. For example, some species isolation could *begin* the process of speciation and then be further reinforced by selective breeding (i.e., mate recognition) as well as ecological separation.

Interpretation of Species and Other Groups in the Fossil Record

Later in this chapter and throughout the next several chapters, we will be using a variety of taxonomic terms for fossil primates (including fossil hominids); you will be introduced to such terms as *Proconsul, Sivapithecus, Australopithecus,* and *Homo.* Of course, *Homo* is still a living primate, as are several others we have discussed in the previous two chapters (e.g., *Pan, Papio, Pongo,* and *Cebus*). But it is especially difficult to make these types of designations from remains of animals that are long dead (and only partially preserved as skeletal remains). In these contexts, what do such names mean in evolutionary terms?

Our goal when applying species, genus, or other taxonomic labels to groups of organisms is to make meaningful biological statements about the variation that is present. Whether looking at populations of living or long-extinct animals, we are assuredly going to see variation. The situation is true of *any* sexually reproducing organism because of the factors of genetic recombination (see Chapter 3). As a result of recombination, each individual organism is a unique combination of genetic material, and the uniqueness is usually reflected to some extent in the phenotype.

In addition to such *individual variation,* we see other kinds of systematic variation in all biological populations. *Age changes* certainly alter overall body size as well as shape in many mammals. One pertinent example for fossil hominoid studies is the change in number, size, and shape of teeth from deciduous (milk) teeth (only 20 present) to the permanent dentition (32 present). It would be an obvious error to differentiate fossil forms solely on the basis of such age-dependent criteria. If one individual were represented just by milk teeth and another (seemingly very different) individual were represented just by adult teeth, they easily could be different-aged individuals from the *same* population. Variation due to sex also plays an important role in influencing differences among individuals observed in biological populations. Differences in structural traits between males and females of the same population are called *sexual dimorphism* and can result in marked variation in body size and proportions in adults of the same species.

Keeping in mind all the types of variation present within interbreeding groups of organisms, the minimum biological category we would like to define in fossil primate samples is the *species*. As already defined (according to the biological species concept), a species is a group of interbreeding or potentially interbreeding organisms that is reproductively isolated from other such groups. In modern organisms, this concept is theoretically testable by observations of reproductive behavior. In animals long dead, such observations are obviously impossible. Therefore, to get a handle on the interpretation of variation seen in fossil groups, we must refer to living animals.

We know without doubt that variation is present. The question is, What is its biological significance? Two immediate choices occur: Either the variation is accounted for by individual, age, and sex differences seen within every biological species (it is **intraspecific**), or the variation represents differences between reproductively isolated groups (it is **interspecific**). How do we decide which alternative is at work? We clearly must refer to contemporary species.

Intraspecific Within species; refers to variation seen within the same species.

Interspecific Between species; refers to variation beyond that seen within the same species to include additional aspects seen between two different species.

If the amount of morphological variation observed in fossil samples is comparable to that seen today *within species of closely related forms*, then we should not "split" our sample into more than one species. We must, however, be careful in choosing modern analogues, for rates of morphological evolution vary widely among different groups of mammals. In interpreting past primates, we do best when comparing them with well-known species of modern primates. Nevertheless, studies of such living groups have shown that delimiting exactly where species boundaries begin and end is often difficult. In dealing with extinct species, the uncertainties are even greater. In addition to the overlapping patterns of variation *over space*, variation also occurs *through time*. In other words, even more variation will be seen in such **paleospecies,** since individuals may be separated by thousands or even millions of years.

Paleospecies Species defined from fossil evidence, often covering a long time span.

Genus A group of closely related species

The next level of formal taxonomic classification, the **genus,** presents another problem. To have more than one genus, we obviously must have at least two species (reproductively isolated groups), and the species of one genus must differ in a basic way from the species of another genus. A genus is therefore defined as a group of species composed of members more closely related to each other than they are to species from any other genus.

Grouping species together into genera is largely a subjective procedure wherein the degree of relatedness becomes a relative judgment. One possible test for contemporary animals is to check for results of hybridization between individuals of different species—rare in nature but quite common in captivity. If two normally separate species interbreed and produce live, though not necessarily fertile, offspring, they probably are not too different genetically and should therefore be grouped together in the same genus. A well-known example of such a cross is horses with donkeys (*Equus calibus* × *Equus asinus*), which normally produces live, sterile offspring (mules).

As previously mentioned, we cannot perform breeding experiments with extinct animals, but another definition of genus becomes highly relevant. Species that are members of the same genus share the same broad adaptive zone. What this represents is a general ecological lifestyle more basic than the narrower ecological niches characteristic of individual species. This ecological definition of genus can be an immense aid in interpreting fossil primates. Teeth are the most frequently preserved parts, and they often can provide excellent general ecological inferences. Moreover, cladistic analysis (see pp. 158–159) also provides assistance in making judgments about evolutionary relationships. That is, members of the *same* genus should all share derived characters not seen in members of other genera.

As a final comment, we should point out that classification by genus is not always a straightforward decision. Indeed, as mentioned earlier (see p. 101), many current researchers, pointing to the very close genetic similarities between humans and chimpanzees, would place both in the same genus (*Homo sapiens*, *Homo troglodytes*).

Vertebrate Evolutionary History: A Brief Summary

In addition to the staggering array of living and extinct life forms, biologists must also contend with the vast amount of time that life has been evolving on earth. Again, scientists have devised simplified schemes—but in this case to organize *time*, not organic diversity.

Geologists have formulated the **geological time scale** (fig. 7–4), in which very large time spans are organized into eras and periods. Periods, in turn, can be broken down into epochs (as we will do later in our discussion of primate evolution). For the time span encompassing vertebrate evolution, there are three eras: the Paleozoic, the Mesozoic, and the Cenozoic. The first vertebrates are present in the fossil record dating to early in the Paleozoic 500 million years ago (m.y.a.) and probably go back considerably further. It is the vertebrate capacity to form bone that accounts for their more complete fossil record *after* 500 m.y.a.

During the Paleozoic, several varieties of fishes (including the ancestors of modern sharks and bony fishes), amphibians, and reptiles appeared. In addition, at the end of the Paleozoic, close to 250 m.y.a., several varieties of mammal-like reptiles were also diversifying. It is widely thought that some of these forms gave rise to the mammals.

The evolutionary history of vertebrates and other organisms during the Paleozoic and Mesozoic was profoundly influenced by geographical events. We know that the positions of the earth's continents have dramatically shifted during the last several hundred million years. This process, called **continental drift,** is explained by the geological theory of *plate tectonics*, which views the earth's crust as a series of gigantic moving and colliding plates. Such massive geological movements can induce volcanic activity (as, for example, all around the Pacific rim), mountain building (e.g., the Himalayas), and earthquakes. Living on the edge of the Pacific and North American plates, residents of the Pacific coast of the United States are acutely aware of some of these consequences, as illustrated by the explosive volcanic eruption of Mt. St. Helens or the frequent earthquakes in Alaska and California.

Geological time scale The organization of earth history into eras, periods, and epochs; commonly used by geologists and paleoanthropologists.

Continental drift The movement of continents on sliding plates of the earth's surface. As a result, the positions of large landmasses have shifted dramatically during the earth's history.

figure 7–4 Geological time scale.

ERA	PERIOD	(Began m.y.a.)	EPOCH	(Began m.y.a.)
CENOZOIC	Quaternary	1.8	Holocene Pleistocene	0.01 1.8
	Tertiary	65	Pliocene Miocene Oligocene Eocene Paleocene	5 23 34 55 65
MESOZOIC	Cretaceous	136		
	Jurassic	190		
	Triassic	225		
PALEOZOIC	Permian	280		
	Carboniferous	345		
	Devonian	395		
	Silurian	430		
	Ordovician	500		
	Cambrian	570		
PRE-CAMBRIAN				

Ecological niches The positions of species within their physical and biological environments, together making up the *ecosystem*. A species' ecological niche is defined by such components as diet, terrain, vegetation, type of predators, relationships with other species, and activity patterns, and each niche is unique to a given species.

Geologists, in reconstructing the earth's physical history, have established the prior (significantly altered) positions of major continental landmasses. During the late Paleozoic, the continents came together to form a single colossal landmass called *Pangea*. In actuality, the continents had been drifting on plates, coming together and separating, long before the end of the Paleozoic (c. 225 m.y.a.), and to be more precise, the large landmass at this time should be called Pangea II. During the early Mesozoic, the southern continents (South America, Africa, Antarctica, Australia, and India) began to split off from Pangea, forming a large southern continent called *Gondwanaland* (fig. 7–5a). Similarly, the northern continents (North America, Greenland, Europe, and Asia) were consolidated into a northern landmass called *Laurasia*. During the Mesozoic, Gondwanaland and Laurasia continued to drift apart and to break up into smaller segments. By the end of the Mesozoic (c. 65 m.y.a.), the continents were beginning to assume their current positions (fig. 7–5b).

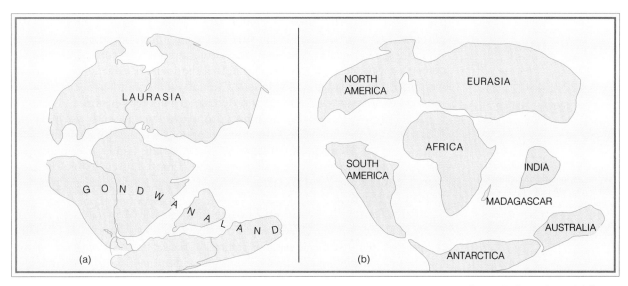

The evolutionary ramifications of this long-term continental drift were profound. Groups of land animals became effectively isolated from each other by large water boundaries, and the distribution of reptiles and mammals was significantly influenced by continental movements. Although not producing such dramatic continental realignments, the process continued into the Cenozoic. The more specific effects of continental drift on early primate evolution are discussed later in this chapter.

During most of the Mesozoic, reptiles were the dominant land vertebrates, and they exhibited a broad expansion into a variety of **ecological niches,** which included aerial and marine habitats. No doubt, the most famous of these highly successful Mesozoic reptiles were the dinosaurs, which themselves evolved into a wide array of sizes and lifestyles. Dinosaur paleontology, never a boring field, has advanced several startling notions in recent years: that many dinosaurs were

figure 7–5 Continental drift. Changes in positions of the continental plates from late Paleozoic to the early Cenozoic. (a) The positions of the continents during the Mesozoic (c. 125 m.y.a.). Pangea is breaking up into a northern landmass (Laurasia) and a southern landmass (Gondwanaland). (b) The positions of the continents at the beginning of the Cenozoic (c. 65 m.y.a.).

figure 7–6 Time line of major events in early vertebrate evolution.

PALEOZOIC						MESOZOIC		
Cambrian	Ordovician	Silurian	Devonian	Carbon-iferous	Permian	Triassic	Jurassic	Cretaceous
Trilobites abundant; also brachiopods, jellyfish, worms, and other invertebrates	First fishes; trilobites still abundant; graptolites and corals become plentiful; possible land plants	Jawed fishes appear; first air-breathing animals; definite land plants	Age of Fishes; first amphibians; first forests	First reptiles; radiation of amphibians; modern insects diversify	Reptile radiation; mammal-like reptiles	Reptiles further radiate; first dinosaurs; egg-laying mammals	Great Age of Dinosaurs; flying and swimming dinosaurs; first toothed birds	Placental and marsupial mammals appear; first modern birds

Major extinction event (between Permian and Triassic)
Major extinction event (after Cretaceous)

570 m.y.a   500 m.y.a   430 m.y.a   395 m.y.a   345 m.y.a   280 m.y.a   225 m.y.a   190 m.y.a   136 m.y.a   65 m.y.a

"warm-blooded"; that some varieties were quite social and probably also engaged in considerable parental care; that many forms became extinct as the result of major climatic changes to the earth's atmosphere from collisions with comets or asteroids; and finally, that not all dinosaurs became entirely extinct, with many descendants still living today (i.e., all modern birds). (See fig. 7–6 for a summary of major events in early vertebrate evolutionary history.)

The earliest mammals are known from fossil traces fairly early in the Mesozoic, but the first *placental* mammals cannot be positively identified until quite late in the Mesozoic, approximately 70 m.y.a. This highly successful mammalian evolutionary **adaptive radiation** is thus almost entirely within the most recent era of geological history, the Cenozoic. (See p. 174 for further discussion of adaptive radiation.)

The Cenozoic is divided into two periods, the Tertiary (about 63 million years duration) and the Quaternary, from about 1.8 m.y.a. up to and including the present. Because this division is rather imprecise, paleontologists more frequently refer to the next level of subdivision within the Cenozoic, the **epochs.** There are seven epochs within the Cenozoic: the Paleocene, Eocene, Oligocene, Miocene, Pliocene, Pleistocene, and Holocene, the last often referred to as the Recent.

Adaptive radiation The relatively rapid expansion and diversification of life forms into new ecological niches.

Epochs Categories of the geological time scale; subdivisions of periods. In the Cenozoic, epochs include the Paleocene, Eocene, Oligocene, Miocene, and Pliocene (from the Tertiary) and the Pleistocene and Holocene (from the Quaternary).

Mammalian Evolution

See Virtual Lab 7, section I, for a discussion of geological time.

Following the extinction of dinosaurs and many other Mesozoic forms (at the end of the Mesozoic), there was a wide array of ecological niches open for the rapid expansion and diversification of mammals. The Cenozoic was an opportunistic time for mammals, and it is known as the Age of Mammals. Mesozoic mammals were small animals, about the size of mice, which they resembled superficially. The wide diversification of mammals in the Cenozoic saw the rise of the major lineages of all modern mammals. Indeed, mammals, along with birds, replaced reptiles as the dominant terrestrial vertebrates.

How do we account for the rapid success of the mammals? Several characteristics relating to learning and general flexibility of behavior are of prime importance. To process more information, mammals were selected for larger brains than those typically found in reptiles. In particular, the cerebrum became generally enlarged, especially the outer covering, the neocortex, which controls higher brain functions (fig. 7–7). In some mammals, the cerebrum expanded so much that it came to comprise the majority of brain volume; moreover, the number of surface convolutions increased, creating more surface area and thus providing space for even more nerve cells (neurons). As we have already seen (in Chapter 5), this is a trend even further emphasized among the primates.

For such a large and complex organ as the mammalian brain to develop, a longer, more intense period of growth is required. Slower development can occur internally (*in utero*) as well as after birth. While internal fertilization and internal development are not unique to mammals, they are major innovations among terrestrial vertebrates. Other forms (birds, most fishes, and reptiles) incubate their young externally by laying eggs, while mammals, with very few exceptions, give birth to live young. Even among mammals, however, there is considerable variation among the major groups in how mature the young are at

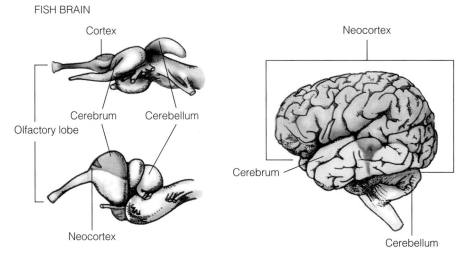

FISH BRAIN

Cortex

Cerebrum   Cerebellum

Olfactory lobe

Neocortex

REPTILE BRAIN

Neocortex

Cerebrum

Cerebellum

PRIMATE BRAIN

figure 7–7 Lateral view of the brain. The illustration shows the increase in the cerebral cortex of the brain. The cerebral cortex integrates sensory information and selects responses.

birth. As you will see, it is in mammals like ourselves, the *placental* forms, where development *in utero* goes the furthest.

Another distinctive feature of mammals is seen in the dentition. While living reptiles consistently have similarly shaped teeth (called a *homodont* dentition), mammals have differently shaped teeth (fig. 7–8). This varied pattern, termed a **heterodont** dentition, is reflected in the primitive (ancestral) mammalian array of dental elements, which includes 3 incisors, 1 canine, 4 premolars, and 3 molars for each quarter of the mouth. (See p. 95 for a more complete discussion of dental patterns as they apply to primates.) Thus, with 11 teeth per quarter segment, the primitive (i.e., ancestral) mammalian dental complement includes a total of 44 teeth. Such a heterodont arrangement allows mammals to process a wide variety of foods. Incisors can be used for cutting, canines for grasping and piercing, and premolars and molars for crushing and grinding.

A final point regarding teeth relates to their disproportionate representation in the fossil record. As the hardest, most durable portion of a vertebrate skeleton, teeth have the greatest likelihood of becoming fossilized (i.e., mineralized). As a result, the vast majority of the available fossil data for most vertebrates, including primates, consists of teeth.

Another major adaptive complex that distinguishes contemporary mammals from reptiles is the maintenance of a constant internal body temperature. Also colloquially (and incorrectly) called warm-bloodedness, this central physiological adaptation is also seen in contemporary birds (and was also perhaps characteristic of many dinosaurs as well). In fact, many contemporary reptiles are able to approximate a constant internal body temperature through behavioral means (especially by regulating activity and exposing the body to the sun). In this sense, reptiles (along with birds and mammals) could be said to be *homeothermic*. Thus, the most important distinction in contrasting mammals (and birds) with reptiles is how the energy to maintain body temperature is produced and channeled. In reptiles, this energy is obtained directly from exposure (externally) to the sun; reptiles are thus said to be *ectothermic*. In mammals and birds, however, the energy is generated *internally* through metabolic activity (by processing food or by muscle action); mammals and birds are hence referred to as **endothermic.**

REPTILIAN (alligator): homodont

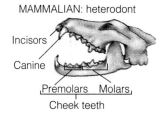

MAMMALIAN: heterodont

Incisors

Canine

Premolars   Molars

Cheek teeth

figure 7–8 Reptilian and mammalian teeth.

Heterodont Having different kinds of teeth; characteristic of mammals, whose teeth consist of incisors, canines, premolars, and molars.

Endothermic (*endo*, meaning "within" or "internal") Able to maintain internal body temperature through the production of energy by means of metabolic processes within cells; characteristic of mammals, birds, and perhaps some dinosaurs.

Major Mammalian Groups

As briefly mentioned in Chapter 5, there are three major subgroups of living mammals: the egg-laying mammals, or monotremes (fig. 7–9), the pouched mammals, or marsupials (fig. 7–10), and the placental mammals. The monotremes are extremely primitive and are considered more distinct from marsupials or placentals than these latter are from each other.

The most notable distinction differentiating the marsupials from the placentals is the type of fetal development. In marsupials, the young are born extremely immature and must complete development in an external pouch. It has been suggested (Carroll, 1988) that such a reproductive strategy is more energetically costly than retaining the young for a longer period *in utero*. In fact, the latter is exactly what placental mammals have done through a more advanced placental connection (from which the group gets its popular name). But perhaps even more basic than fetal nourishment are the means to allow the mother to *tolerate* her young internally over an extended period. Marsupial young are born so quickly after conception that there is little chance for the mother's system to recognize and have an immune rejection of the fetal "foreign" tissue. But in placental mammals, such an immune response would occur were it not for the development of a specialized tissue that isolates the fetus from the mother's immune detection, thus preventing tissue rejection. Quite possibly, this innovation is the central factor in the origin and initial rapid success of placental mammals (Carroll, 1988).

In any case, with a longer gestation period, the central nervous system is able to develop more completely in the fetus. Moreover, after birth, the "bond of milk" between mother and young also allows more time for complex neural structures to form. It should also be emphasized that from a *biosocial* perspective, this dependency period not only allows for adequate physiological development, but also provides for increased learning opportunities. That is, the young mammalian brain receives a vast amount of information channeled to it through observation of the mother's behavior and through interaction with age-mates. It is not sufficient to have evolved a brain capable of learning. Collateral evolution of mammalian social systems has ensured that young mammal brains are provided with ample learning opportunities and are thus put to good use.

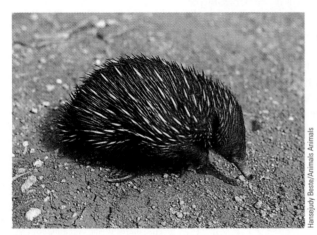

figure 7–9 The spiny anteater (a monotreme).

figure 7–10 A wallaby (marsupial) with an infant in the pouch.

Early Primate Evolution

The roots of the primate order go back to the beginnings of the placental mammal radiation circa 65 m.y.a. Thus, the earliest primates were diverging from quite early primitive placental mammals. We have seen (in Chapter 5) that strictly defining living primates using clear-cut derived features is not an easy task. The further back we go in the fossil record, the more primitive and, in many cases, the more generalized the fossil primates become. Such a situation makes classifying them all the more difficult.

As a case in point, the earliest identifiable primates were long thought to be a Paleocene group known as the plesiadapiforms. You must remember, however, that much of our understanding, especially of early primates, is based on quite fragmentary evidence, mostly jaws and teeth. In just the last few years, much more complete remains of plesiadapiforms from Wyoming have been discovered, including a nearly complete skull and elements of the hand and wrist.

As a result of this more complete information, the plesiadapiforms have been removed from the primate order altogether. From distinctive features (shared derived characteristics) of the skull and hands, these Paleocene mammals are now thought to be closely related to the colugo (fig. 7–11). The colugo is sometimes called a "flying lemur," a misnomer, really, as it is not a lemur, nor does it fly (it glides). This group of unusual mammals is probably closely linked to the roots of primates, but apparently was already diverged by Paleocene times.

figure 7–11 **Colugo.**

Given these new and major reinterpretations, we are left with extremely scarce traces of the beginnings of primates. Scholars have suggested that some other recently discovered bits and pieces from North Africa *may* be those of a very small primitive primate. Until more evidence is found, and remembering the lesson of the plesiadapiforms, we will just have to wait and see.

A large array of fossil primates from the Eocene (55–34 m.y.a.) have been discovered and now total more than 200 recognized species. Unlike the available Paleocene forms, those from the Eocene display distinctive primate features. Indeed, primatologist Elwyn Simons (1972, p. 124) has called them "the first primates of modern aspect." These animals have been found primarily in sites in North America and Europe (which were then still connected). It is important to recall that the landmasses that connect continents, as well as the water boundaries that separate them, have obvious impact on the geographical distribution of such terrestrially bound animals as primates.

Some interesting late Eocene forms have also been found in Asia, which was joined to Europe by the end of the Eocene epoch. Looking at the entire array of Eocene primates, it is certain that they were (1) primates, (2) widely distributed, and (3) mostly extinct by the end of the Eocene. What is less certain is how any of them might be related to the living primates. Some of these forms are probably ancestors of the *prosimians*—the lemurs and lorises.* Others are probably related to the tarsier. New evidence of *anthropoid* origins has also recently been discovered in several sites from North Africa, the Persian Gulf, and China. These newly discovered fossils of late Eocene anthropoids have now shown that anthropoid origins were well established by 35 m.y.a.

---

*In strict classification terms, especially from a cladistic point of view, lemurs and lorises should be referred to as strepsirhines (see p. 102).

figure 7–12 Location of the Fayum, an Oligocene primate site in Egypt.

Some new discoveries of very small primates from China are particularly interesting. These 45-million-year-old fossils have been suggested as representing early anthropoids (Gebo et al., 2000), but this hypothesis is still very tentative (there are, as yet, no cranial remains discovered, and the traits that are present are primitive rather than derived in the anthropoid direction). The most intriguing aspect of this recent discovery is the extremely small body size estimated for these primates, considerably smaller, in fact, than that of any living primate.

The Oligocene (34–23 m.y.a.) has yielded numerous additional fossil remains of several different species of early anthropoids. Most of these forms are Old World anthropoids, all discovered at a single locality in Egypt, the Fayum (fig. 7–12). In addition, from North and South America, there are a few known bits that relate only to the ancestry of New World monkeys. By the early Oligocene, continental drift had separated the New World (i.e., the Americas) from the Old World (Africa and Eurasia). Some of the earliest Fayum forms, nevertheless, *may* potentially be close to the ancestry of both Old and New World anthropoids. It has been suggested that late in the Eocene or very early in the Oligocene, the first anthropoids (primitive "monkeys") arose in Africa and later reached South America by "rafting" over the water separation on drifting chunks of vegetation. The animals we call "monkey," then, may have a common Old World origin, but the ancestry of New and Old World varieties remains separate after about 35 m.y.a. Our closest evolutionary affinities after this time are with other Old World anthropoids, that is, with Old World monkeys and apes.

The possible roots of anthropoid evolution are illustrated by different fossils from the Fayum; one is the genus *Apidium*. Well known at the Fayum, *Apidium* is represented by several dozen jaws or partial dentitions and more than 100 specimens from the limb and trunk skeleton. Because of its primitive dental arrangement, some paleontologists have suggested that *Apidium* may lie near or even before the evolutionary divergence of Old and New World anthropoids. As so much fossil material of teeth and limb bones of *Apidium* has been found, some informed speculation regarding diet and locomotor behavior is possible. It is thought that this small, squirrel-sized primate ate mostly fruits and some seeds and was most likely an arboreal quadruped, adept at leaping and springing (Table 7–2).

The other genus of importance from the Fayum is *Aegyptopithecus*. This genus, also well known, is represented by several well-preserved crania and abundant jaws and teeth. The largest of the Fayum anthropoids, *Aegyptopithecus* is roughly the size of a modern howler monkey (13 to 20 pounds) (Fleagle, 1999) and is thought to have been a short-limbed, slow-moving arboreal quadruped (see Table 7–2). *Aegyptopithecus* is important because, better than any other

TABLE 7-2	Inferred General Paleobiological Aspects of Oligocene Primates			
	Weight Range	Substratum	Locomotion	Diet
Apidium	750–1,600 g (2–3 lb)	Arboreal	Quadruped	Fruits, seeds
Aegyptopithecus	6,700 g (15 lb)	Arboreal	Quadruped	Fruits, some leaves?

Source: After Fleagle, 1999.

figure 7–13 Major events in early primate evolution.

See Virtual Lab 7 glossary, for a phylogeny and pronunciation guide of primate fossils.

known form, it bridges the gap between the Eocene fossils and the succeeding Miocene hominoids.

Nevertheless, *Aegyptopithecus* is a very primitive Old World anthropoid, with a small brain and long snout and not showing any derived features of either Old World monkeys or hominoids. Thus, it may be close to the ancestry of *both* major groups of living Old World anthropoids. Found in geological beds dating to 35–33 m.y.a., *Aegyptopithecus* further suggests that the crucial evolutionary divergence of hominoids from other Old World anthropoids occurred *after* this time (fig. 7–13).

Miocene Fossil Hominoids

During the approximately 18 million years of the Miocene (23–5 m.y.a.), a great deal of evolutionary change occurred. In Africa, Asia, and Europe, a diverse and highly successful group of hominoids emerged (fig. 7–14). Indeed, there were many more forms of hominoids from the Miocene than there are today (now represented by the highly restricted groups of apes and one species of humans). In fact, the Miocene could be called "the golden age of hominoids." Many thousands of fossils have been found from dozens of sites scattered in East Africa, southwest Africa, southwest Asia, into western and southern Europe, and extending into southern Asia and China.

During the Miocene, significant transformations relating to climate and repositioning of landmasses took place. By 23 m.y.a., *major* continental locations approximated those of today (except that North and South America were separate). Nevertheless, the movements of South America and Australia farther away from Antarctica significantly altered ocean currents. Likewise, the continued impact of the South Asian plate into Asia produced the Himalayan Plateau. Both of these paleogeographical modifications had significant impact on the climate, and the early Miocene was considerably warmer than the preceding Oligocene. Moreover, by 16 m.y.a., the Arabian Plate (which had been separate) "docked" figure 7–14 Miocene hominoid distribution, from fossils thus far discovered.

with northeastern Africa. As a result, migrations of animals from Africa directly into southwest Asia (and in the reverse direction as well) became possible. Among the earliest transcontinental migrants (soon after 16 m.y.a.) were African hominoids who colonized Asia and later Europe.

Because Miocene hominoids are so diverse, attempts to simplify their evolutionary relationships are problematic. For example, for many years paleontologists tended to think of these fossil forms as either "apelike" or "humanlike" and used modern examples as models. But as we have just noted, there are very few hominoids remaining. We should not rashly generalize from the living forms to the much more diverse fossil forms; otherwise, we obscure the evolutionary uniqueness of these animals. In addition, we should not expect all fossil forms to be directly or even particularly closely related to living species. Indeed, we should expect the opposite; that is, most lines vanish without descendants.

Over the last three decades, the Miocene hominoid assemblage has been interpreted and reinterpreted. As more fossils are found, the evolutionary picture grows more complicated. The vast array of fossil forms has not yet been completely studied, so conclusions remain tenuous. Given this uncertainty, it is probably best, for the present, to group Miocene hominoids geographically:

1. *African forms (23–14 m.y.a.)* Known especially from western Kenya, these include quite generalized, in many ways primitive, hominoids. The best-known genus is *Proconsul* (fig. 7–15). In addition to the well-known East African early Miocene hominoids, a 1992 discovery from Namibia has further extended by over 1,800 miles the known range of African Miocene hominoids (Conroy et al., 1992).

2. *European forms (13–11 m.y.a.)* Known from widely scattered localities in France, Spain, Italy, Greece, Austria, and Hungary, most of these forms are quite derived. However, this is a varied and not well understood group. The best known are placed in the genus *Dryopithecus;* the Hungarian and Greek fossils are usually assigned to other genera. The Greek fossils are called

Robert Jurmain

figure 7–15 *Proconsul africanus* skull (from early Miocene deposits on Rusinga Island, Kenya).

Ouranopithecus, and remains date to sites 9 to 10 million years of age. Evolutionary relationships are uncertain, but several researchers have suggested a link with the African ape/hominid group.

3. *Asian forms (16–7 m.y.a.)*   The largest and most varied group from the Miocene fossil hominoid assemblage, geographically dispersed from Turkey through India/Pakistan and east to the highly prolific site Lufeng, in southern China, most of these forms are *highly* derived. The best-known genus is *Sivapithecus* (known from Turkey and Pakistan). The Lufeng material (now totaling more than 1,000 specimens) is usually placed in a separate genus.

Four general points are certain concerning Miocene hominoid fossils: They are widespread geographically; they are numerous; they span a considerable portion of the Miocene, with *known* remains dated between 23 and 6 m.y.a.; and at present, they are poorly understood. However, we can reasonably draw the following conclusions:

1. These are hominoids—more closely related to the ape/human lineage than to Old World monkeys.

2. They are mostly **large-bodied hominoids,** that is, more akin to the lineages of orangutans, gorillas, chimpanzees, and humans than to smaller-bodied apes (i.e., gibbons).

3. Most of the Miocene forms thus far discovered are so derived as to be improbable ancestors of *any* living form.

4. One lineage that appears well established relates to *Sivapithecus* from Turkey and Pakistan. This form shows some highly derived facial features similar to the modern orangutan, suggesting a fairly close evolutionary link (fig. 7–16).

5. Evidence of *definite* **hominids** from the Miocene has not yet been absolutely confirmed. However, exciting new (and not fully studied) finds from Kenya, Ethiopia, and Chad (the latter dating as far back as 7 m.y.a.) strongly suggest that hominids diverged sometime in the latter Miocene (see pp. 191–194 for further discussion).

Large-bodied hominoids Those hominoids including the great apes (orangutans, chimpanzees, gorillas) and hominids, as well as all ancestral forms back to the time of divergence from small-bodied hominoids (i.e., the gibbon lineage).

Hominids Colloquial term for members of the family Hominidae, which includes all bipedal hominoids back to the divergence from African great apes.

figure 7–16 Comparison of *Sivapithecus* cranium (center) with that of modern chimpanzee (left) and orangutan (right). The *Sivapithecus* fossil is specimen GSP 15000, from the Potwar Plateau, Pakistan, c. 8 m.y.a.

Courtesy, David Pilbeam

Processes of Macroevolution

As noted earlier, evolution operates at both microevolutionary and macroevolutionary levels. We discussed evolution primarily from a microevolutionary perspective in Chapter 4; in this chapter, our focus is on macroevolution. Macroevolutionary mechanisms operate more on the entire species than on individuals or populations and take much longer than microevolutionary processes to have a noticeable impact.

Adaptive Radiation

The potential capacity of a group of organisms to multiply is practically unlimited; its ability to increase its numbers, however, is regulated largely by the available resources of food, shelter, and space. As the size of a population increases, its food supply, shelter, and space decrease, and the environment will ultimately prove inadequate. Depleted resources engender pressures that will very likely induce some members of the population to seek an environment in which competition is considerably reduced and the opportunity for survival and reproductive success increased. This evolutionary tendency to exploit unoccupied habitats may eventually produce an abundance of diverse species.

A good example of the evolutionary process known as adaptive radiation is seen in the divergence of the stem reptiles into the profusion of different forms of the late Paleozoic and especially those of the Mesozoic. It is a process that has taken place many times in evolutionary history when a life form has rapidly taken advantage, so to speak, of the many newly available ecological niches.

The principle of evolution illustrated by adaptive radiation is fairly simple, but important. It may be stated thus: *A species, or group of species, will diverge into as many variations as two factors allow: (1) its adaptive potential and (2) the adaptive opportunities of the available zones.*

In the case of reptiles, there was little divergence in the very early stages of evolution, when the ancestral form was little more than one among a variety of amphibian water dwellers. In reptiles, a more efficient egg than that of amphibians (i.e., one that could incubate out of water) had developed, but although it had great adaptive potential, there were few zones to invade. However, once reptiles became fully terrestrial, there was a sudden opening of available zones—ecological niches—accessible to them.

This new kind of egg, with a hard protective outer shell, provided the primary adaptive trait that freed reptiles from their attachment to water. The adaptive zones for reptiles were not limitless; nevertheless, continents were now open to them with no serious competition from any other animal. The reptiles moved into the many different ecological niches on land (and to some extent in the air and sea), and as they adapted to these areas, they diversified into a large number of species. This spectacular radiation burst forth with such evolutionary rapidity that it may well be termed an adaptive explosion.

The rapid expansion of placental mammals at the beginning of the Cenozoic and the diversification of lemurs in Madagascar are other good examples of adaptive radiation. This latter (primate) example is particularly instructive. As we noted in Chapter 5, the contemporary array of 61 lemur species shows considerable diversity, both in size and in lifestyle (diet, degree of arboreality, etc.). Indeed, if we also include several other species that have become extinct in the last 1,000 years (following intensive human occupation of the island), the degree of lemur biodiversity was even greater—even including a ground-living form the size of a gorilla! The diversification of so many different kinds of lemur in Madagascar is explained by their adaptive radiation from a common ancestor, beginning up to 50 m.y.a. Without competition from other types of mammals, the lemurs fairly rapidly diversified and expanded into a number of varied niches in their isolated island home.

Generalized and Specialized Characteristics

Another aspect of evolution closely related to adaptive radiation involves the transition from generalized characteristics to specialized characteristics. These two terms refer to the adaptive potential of a particular trait. A trait that is adapted for many functions is said to be generalized; a trait that is limited to a narrow set of functions is said to be specialized.

For example, a generalized mammalian limb has five fairly flexible digits adapted for many possible functions (grasping, weight support, digging). In this respect, human hands have remained quite generalized. On the other hand (or foot), there have been many structural modifications in our feet suited for the specialized function of stable weight support in an upright posture.

The terms *generalized* and *specialized* are also sometimes used when speaking of the adaptive potential of whole organisms. For example, the aye-aye of Madagascar is a highly specialized animal structurally adapted in its dentition for an ecologically narrow rodent/woodpecker-like niche—digging holes with prominent incisors and removing insect larvae with an elongated finger.

The notion of adaptive potential is a relative judgment and can estimate only crudely the likelihood of one form evolving into one or more other forms. Adaptive radiation is a related concept, for only a generalized ancestor can provide the flexible evolutionary basis for such rapid diversification. Only a generalized species with potential for adaptation into varied ecological niches can lead to all the later diversification and specialization of forms into particular ecological niches.

An issue that we have already raised also bears on this discussion: the relationship of ancestral and derived characters. While not always the case, ancestral characters *tend* to be more generalized than specialized. And specialized characteristics are almost always also derived ones.

Modes of Evolutionary Change

Until recently, the general consensus among evolutionary biologists was that microevolutionary mechanisms could be translated directly into the larger-scale macroevolutionary changes, especially the most central of all macroevolutionary processes, speciation. A smooth gradation of change was assumed to run directly from microevolution into macroevolution. But in the last two decades, this view has been seriously challenged. Many theorists now believe that macroevolution cannot be explained solely in terms of accumulated microevolutionary changes. These researchers are convinced that macroevolution is only partly understandable through microevolutionary models.

GRADUALISM VS. PUNCTUATED EQUILIBRIUM   The traditional view of evolution has emphasized that change accumulates gradually in evolving lineages—the idea of phyletic gradualism. Accordingly, the complete fossil record of an evolving group (if it could be recovered) would display a series of forms with finely graded transitional differences between each ancestor and its descendant. The fact that such transitional forms are only rarely found is attributed to the incompleteness of the fossil record, or, as Darwin called it, "a history of the world, imperfectly kept, and written in changing dialect."

Punctuated equilibrium The concept that evolutionary change proceeds through long periods of stasis punctuated by rapid periods of change.

For more than a century, this perspective dominated evolutionary biology, but in the last 25 years, some biologists have called this notion into serious question. The evolutionary mechanisms operating on species over the long run are often not continuously gradual. In some cases, species persist for thousands of generations basically unchanged. Then, rather suddenly, at least in evolutionary terms, a "spurt" of speciation occurs. This uneven, nongradual process of long stasis and quick spurts has been termed **punctuated equilibrium** (Gould and Eldredge, 1977).

What the advocates of punctuated equilibrium are disputing are the tempo (rate) and mode (manner) of evolutionary change as commonly understood since Darwin's time. Rather than a slow, steady tempo, this alternate view postulates long periods of no change punctuated only occasionally by sudden bursts. From this observation, it was concluded that the mode of evolution, too, must be different from that suggested by classical Darwinists. Rather than gradual accumulation of small changes in a single lineage, advocates of punctuated equilibrium believe that an additional evolutionary mechanism is required to push the process along. They thus postulate *speciation* as the major influence in bringing about rapid evolutionary change.

How well does the paleontological record agree with the predictions of punctuated equilibrium? Indeed, considerable fossil data show long periods of stasis punctuated by occasional quite rapid changes (on the order of 10,000 to 50,000 years). The best supporting evidence for punctuated equilibrium has come from the fossilized remains of marine invertebrates. Intermediate forms are rare, not so much because the fossil record is poor, but because the speciation events and longevity of these transitional species were so short that we should not expect to find them very often.

How well, then, does the primate fossil record fit the punctuated equilibrium model? In studies of Eocene primates, rates of evolutionary change were shown to be quite gradual (Gingerich, 1985; Brown and Rose, 1987; Rose, 1991). In another study, here of Paleocene plesiadapiforms, evolutionary changes were also quite gradual. Although no longer considered primates, these forms show a gradual tempo of change in another, closely related group of mammals. The predictions consistent with punctuated equilibrium have thus far not been substantiated in those evolving lineages of primates for which we have adequate data to test the theory.

It would, however, be a fallacy to assume that evolutionary change in primates or in any other group must therefore be of a completely gradual tempo. Such is clearly not the case. In all lineages, the pace assuredly speeds up and slows down as a result of factors that influence the size and relative isolation of populations. In addition, environmental changes that influence the pace and direction of natural selection must also be considered. Nevertheless, in general accordance with the Modern Synthesis, microevolution and macroevolution need not be "decoupled," as some evolutionary biologists have recently suggested.

Summary

his chapter has surveyed the basics of mammalian/primate evolution, emphasizing a macroevolutionary perspective. Given the huge amount of organic diversity displayed, as well as the vast time involved, two major organizing perspectives prove indispensable: schemes of formal classification to organize organic diversity and the geological time scale to organize geological time. The principles of classification were reviewed in some detail, contrasting two differing approaches: evolutionary systematics and cladistics. Because primates are vertebrates and, more specifically, mammals, these broader organic groups were briefly reviewed, emphasizing major evolutionary trends. The fossil history of primates was taken up in more detail with surveys of earliest traces from the Paleocene and Eocene epochs. The beginnings of anthropoid radiation can be traced to the end of the Eocene and to the Oligocene (the Fayum in Egypt), and the broad, complex radiation of hominoids during the Miocene is even more central to understanding human evolution.

Theoretical perspectives relating to contemporary understanding of macroevolutionary processes (especially the concepts of species and speciation) are crucial to interpreting any long-term aspect of evolutionary history, be it mammalian, primate, hominoid, or hominid. As genus and species designation is the common form of reference for both living and extinct organisms (and will be used frequently throughout the next four chapters), its biological significance was discussed in depth. From a more general theoretical perspective, evolutionary biologists have postulated two different modes of evolutionary change: gradualism and punctuated equilibrium. At present, the available primate evolutionary record does not conform to the predictions of punctuated equilibrium, but one should not conclude that evolutionary tempo was necessarily strictly gradual (which it certainly was not).

Questions for Review

1. What are the two primary goals of organic classification?
2. What are the six major groups of vertebrates?
3. What are the two main approaches to the classification of organisms? Compare them.
4. What are the major eras of geological time over which vertebrates have evolved?
5. What primary features distinguish mammals—especially placental mammals—from other vertebrates?
6. What is meant by a homology? Contrast with analogy, using examples.
7. Why do evolutionary biologists concentrate on derived features rather than primitive ones? Give an example of each.
8. What is the biological species concept? Contrast this with another definition of species.
9. Why is it difficult to identify very early primates from other primitive placental mammals?

10. How diversified and geographically widespread were hominoids in the Miocene?
11. Humans are Old World anthropoids. What other groups are also Old World anthropoids?
12. Contrast the gradualist view of evolutionary change with that of punctuated equilibrium. Give an example from primate evolution that supports one view or the other.
13. How are species and genus defined? Discuss how the definitions apply to both living and fossil groups.

Suggested Further Readings

Carroll, Robert L. 1988. *Vertebrate Paleontology and Evolution*. New York: Freeman.

Conroy, G. C. 1990. *Primate Evolution*. New York: Norton.

Fleagle, John. 1999. *Primate Adaptation and Evolution*. 2nd ed. New York: Academic Press.

Ridley, Mark. 1993. *Evolution*. Boston: Blackwell Scientific Publications.

Multimedia Resources

 Companion Web Site

Anthropology Online: The Wadsworth Anthropology Resource Center Visit **http://anthropology.wadsworth.com** and click on the Companion Web Site for Jurmain/Kilgore/Trevathan/Nelson's *Essentials of Physical Anthropology*, Fifth Edition, to access a wide range of enrichment material to aid in your study of anthropology. Among the useful options for each chapter's self-study are learning objectives, flashcards, Internet exercises, Web links, InfoTrac College Edition exercises, and practice quizzes that can be scored and emailed to your instructor.

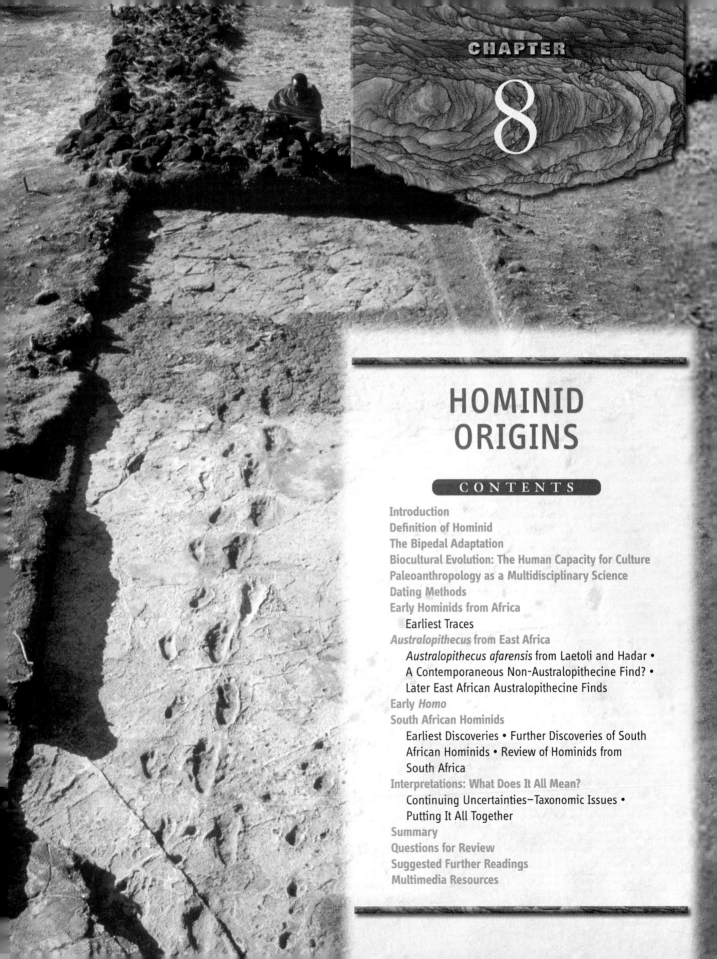

HOMINID ORIGINS

CONTENTS

See the following sections of the CD-ROM for topics covered in this chapter: Virtual Lab 8, section I; Virtual Lab 9, section I; Virtual Lab 10; and Virtual Lab 11.

Introduction

 In the last three chapters, we have seen how and why humans are grouped as primates, both structurally and behaviorally, and how our evolutionary history coincides with that of other primates. However, we are a unique kind of primate, and our ancestors have been adapted to a particular kind of lifestyle for several million years. Some primitive hominoid may have begun this process more than 10 m.y.a., but fossil evidence indicates a much more definite hominid presence beginning perhaps 5 m.y.a. The hominid nature of these remains is revealed by more than the morphological structure of teeth and bones; in many cases, we know that these animals are hominids also because of the way they behaved—emphasizing once again the **biocultural** nature of human evolution.

In this chapter, we review abundant and exciting discoveries that have come from Africa. Spanning much of the twentieth century and now into the twenty-first, these discoveries have resulted from the dedication and efforts of a number of scientists and have also frequently captured the interest of the general public. Archaeological discoveries of early cultural behavior are fascinating, as they provide information concerning the behavioral and cognitive capabilities of our more immediate ancestors. Perhaps, even more so, the remains of the hominids themselves fire the imagination, since here, in these fossils, we can more easily see the roots of human emergence. In this chapter, and in the remainder of this text, we will trace more directly the beginnings of humankind.

Biocultural Pertaining to the concept that biology makes culture possible and that culture influences biology.

Definition of Hominid

Dating to the end of the Miocene, the earliest hominid traces that have thus far been found include primarily dental and cranial pieces. Indeed, what has been preserved of the numerous hominoid fossils from throughout the Miocene (see Chapter 7) are primarily teeth and jaws. But dental features alone do not describe the special features of hominids and are certainly not the most distinctive of the later stages of human evolution. Modern humans, as well as our most immediate hominid ancestors, are distinguished from the great apes by more obvious features than tooth and jaw dimensions. For example, various scientists have pointed to such distinctive hominid characteristics as bipedal locomotion, large brain size, and toolmaking behavior as being significant (at some stage) in defining what makes a hominid a hominid.

It must be emphasized that not all these characteristics developed simultaneously or at the same pace. Indeed, over the last several million years of hominid evolution, quite a different pattern has been evident, in which each of the components (dentition, locomotion, brain size, and toolmaking) have developed at quite different rates. Such a pattern, where physiological/behavioral systems evolve at different rates, is called **mosaic evolution.** As we first pointed out in Chapter 1 and will emphasize in this chapter, the single most important defining characteristic for the full course of hominid evolution is **bipedal locomotion.** In the earliest stages of hominid emergence, skeletal evidence indicating bipedal locomotion is the only truly reliable indicator that

Mosaic evolution A pattern of evolution in which the rate of evolution in one functional system varies from that in other systems. For example, in hominid evolution, the dental system, locomotor system, and neurological system (especially the brain) all evolved at markedly different rates.

Bipedal locomotion Walking on two feet. Walking habitually on two legs is the single most distinctive feature of the hominids.

	Locomotion	Brain	Dentition	Toolmaking Behavior
(Modern *Homo sapiens*)	Bipedal: shortened pelvis; body size larger; legs longer; fingers and toes not as long	Greatly increased brain size	Small incisors; canines further reduced; molar tooth enamel caps thick	Stone tools found after 2.5 m.y.a.; increasing trend of cultural dependency apparent in later hominids
(Early hominid)	Bipedal: shortened pelvis; some differences from later hominids, showing smaller body size and long arms relative to legs; long fingers and toes; probably capable of considerable climbing	Larger than Miocene forms, but small compared to modern humans	Moderately large front teeth (incisors); canines somewhat reduced; molars quite large with very thick enamel	In earliest stages unknown; no stone tool use prior to 2.5 m.y.a.; probably somewhat more oriented toward tool manufacture and use than chimpanzees
(Miocene, generalized hominoid)	Quadrupedal: long pelvis; some forms capable of considerable arm swinging, suspensory locomotion	Small compared to hominids, but large compared to other primates	Large front teeth (including canines); molar teeth variable, depending on species; some have thin enamel caps, others thick enamel caps	Unknown—no stone tools; probably had capabilities similar to chimpanzees

Timeline markings (right side): 0.5 m.y.a., 1 m.y.a., 2 m.y.a., 3 m.y.a., 4 m.y.a., 20 m.y.a.

these fossils were indeed hominids. However, in later stages of hominid evolution, other features, especially those relating to brain development and behavior, become highly significant (fig. 8–1).

figure 8–1 Mosaic evolution of hominid characteristics: a postulated time line.

The Bipedal Adaptation

As we mentioned in Chapter 5, there is a general tendency in all primates for erect body posture. However, of all living primates, efficient bipedalism as the primary form of locomotion is seen *only* in hominids. Functionally, the human mode of locomotion is most clearly shown in our striding gait, where weight is alternately placed on a single fully extended hind limb. This specialized form of

See Virtual Lab 9, section I, for a discussion of the evolution of bipedalism.

locomotion has developed to a point where energy levels are used to near peak efficiency. Such is not the case in nonhuman primates, who move bipedally with hips and knees bent and maintain balance in a clumsy and inefficient manner.

From a survey of our close primate relatives, it is apparent that while still in the trees, our ancestors were adapted to a fair amount of upper-body erectness. Prosimians, monkeys, and apes all spend considerable time sitting erect while feeding, grooming, or sleeping. Presumably, our early ancestors also displayed similar behavior. What caused these forms to come to the ground and embark on the unique way of life that would eventually lead to humans is still a mystery. Perhaps natural selection favored some Miocene hominoids coming occasionally to the ground to forage for food on the forest floor and forest fringe. In any case, once they were on the ground and away from the immediate safety offered by trees, bipedal locomotion could become a tremendous advantage.

First of all, bipedal locomotion freed the hands for carrying objects and for making and using tools. Such early cultural developments had an even more positive effect on speeding the development of yet more efficient bipedalism—once again emphasizing the dual role of biocultural evolution. In addition, in the bipedal stance, animals have a wider view of the surrounding countryside, and in open terrain, early spotting of predators (particularly the large cats, such as lions, leopards, and saber-tooths) would be of critical importance. We know that modern ground-living primates, such as savanna baboons and vervets, occasionally adopt this posture to "look around" when out in open country. It has also been hypothesized that a bipedal stance would more effectively have aided in cooling early hominids while out in the open. In bipeds, less of the body is exposed directly to the sun than in quadrupeds. Moreover, a greater portion of the body is farther from the ground and thus more removed from heat radiating from the ground surface. It would perhaps have been most adaptive to favor such cooling mechanisms if early hominids had adopted activity patterns exposing them in the open during midday. This last supposition is not really possible to test, but if hominids had ranged more freely at midday, they would have avoided competition from more nocturnal predators and scavengers (such as large cats and hyenas).

Moreover, bipedal walking is an efficient means of covering long distances, and when large game hunting came into play (several million years after the initial adaptation to ground living), further refinements in the locomotor complex may have been favored. Exactly what initiated the process is difficult to say, but all these factors probably played a role in the adaptation of hominids to their special niche through a special form of locomotion.

Our mode of locomotion is indeed extraordinary, involving, as it does, a unique kind of activity in which "the body, step by step, teeters on the edge of catastrophe" (Napier, 1967, p. 56). The problem is to maintain balance on the "stance" leg while the "swing" leg is off the ground. In fact, during normal walking, both feet are simultaneously on the ground only about 25 percent of the time, and as speed of locomotion increases, this figure becomes even smaller.

Maintaining a stable center of balance in this complex form of locomotion necessitates many drastic structural and functional changes in the basic primate quadrupedal pattern. Functionally, the foot must be altered to act as a stable support instead of a grasping limb. When we walk, our foot is used like a prop, landing on the heel and pushing off on the toes, particularly the big toe. In addition, the leg must be elongated to increase the length of the stride. The lower limb must also be remodeled to allow full extension of the knee and to allow the legs to be kept close together during walking, thereby maintaining the center of support directly under the body. Finally, significant changes must occur in the pelvis to permit stable weight transmission from the upper body to the legs and to maintain balance through pelvic rotation and altered proportions and orientations of several key muscles.

The major structural changes that are required for bipedalism are all seen in the earliest hominids from East and South Africa. (To date, no early hominid postcranial bones have been found in central Africa.) In the pelvis, the blade (ilium—upper bone of the pelvis) is shortened top to bottom, which permits more stable weight support in the erect position by lowering the center of gravity (see figs. 8–2 and 8–3). In addition, the ilium is bent backward and downward, thus altering the position of the muscles that attach along the bone. Most important, these muscles increase in size and act to stabilize the hip. One of these muscles (the *gluteus maximus*) also becomes important as an extensor, to pull the thigh back during running, jumping, and climbing.

Other structural changes shown by even the earliest definitively hominid postcranial evidence further confirm the morphological pattern seen in the pelvis. For example, the vertebral column, known from beautifully preserved specimens from South and East Africa, shows the same forward curvature as in modern hominids, bringing the center of support forward. In addition, the lower limb is elongated and is apparently proportionately about as long as in modern humans. Fossil evidence of a knee fragment from South Africa and pieces from East Africa also shows that full extension of this joint was possible, thus allowing the leg to be completely straightened, as when a field goal kicker follows through.

Fossil evidence of early hominid foot structure has come from two sites in South Africa, and especially important are some recently announced new fossils coming from the same individual as the mostly complete skeleton currently being excavated (see p. 205) (Clarke and Tobias, 1995). These foot specimens, consisting of four articulating elements from the ankle and big toe, indicate that the heel and longitudinal arch were both well adapted for a bipedal gait.

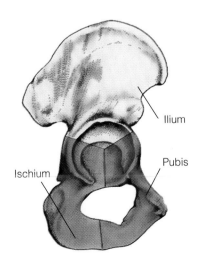

figure 8–2 The human os coxae, composed of three bones (right side shown).

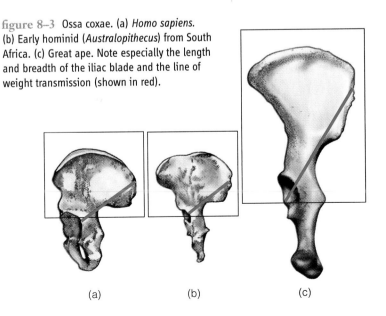

figure 8–3 Ossa coxae. (a) *Homo sapiens.* (b) Early hominid (*Australopithecus*) from South Africa. (c) Great ape. Note especially the length and breadth of the iliac blade and the line of weight transmission (shown in red).

(a)   (b)   (c)

However, the paleoanthropologists (Ron Clarke and Phillip Tobias) also suggest that the large toe was *divergent* and thus unlike the hominid pattern. If the large toe really did possess this (abducted) anatomical position, it most likely would have aided the foot in grasping. In turn, this grasping ability (as in other primates) would have enabled early hominids to more effectively exploit arboreal habitats. Finally, since anatomical remodeling is always constrained by a set of complex functional compromises, a foot highly capable of grasping and climbing is less capable as a stable platform during bipedal locomotion. Some researchers therefore see early hominids as not necessarily fully as committed to bipedal locomotion as are later hominids.

Further evidence for evolutionary changes in the foot comes from two sites in East Africa where numerous pedal elements have been recovered. As in the

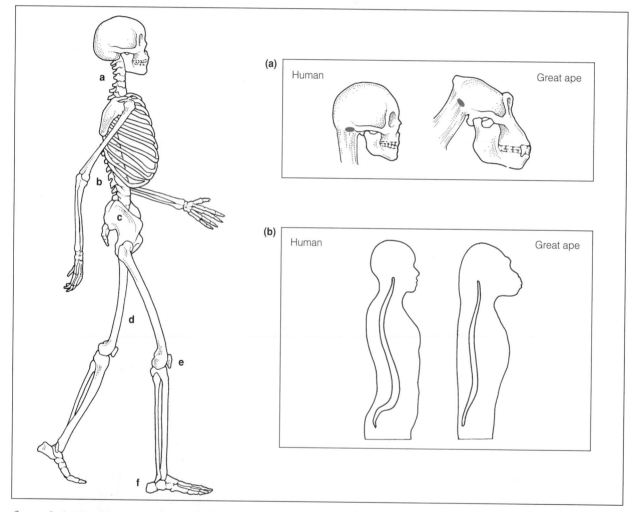

figure 8–4 Major features of hominid bipedalism. During hominid evolution, several major structural features throughout the body have been reorganized (from that seen in other primates) to facilitate efficient bipedal locomotion. These are illustrated here, beginning with the head and progressing to the foot: (a) The *foramen magnum* (shown in red) is repositioned farther underneath the skull, so that the head is more or less balanced on the spine (and thus requires less robust neck muscles to hold the head upright). (b) The spine has two distinctive curves—a backward (thoracic) one and a forward (lumbar) one—that keep the trunk (and weight) centered above the pelvis. (c) The pelvis is shaped more in the form of a basin to support

remains from South Africa, the East African fossils suggest a well-adapted bipedal gait. The arches are developed, but some differences in the ankle also imply that considerable flexibility was possible (again, suggested for continued adaptation to climbing). From this evidence, some researchers have recently concluded that many forms of early hominids spent considerable time in the trees. Nevertheless, to this point, *all* the early hominids that have been identified from Africa are thought by most investigators to have been quite well-adapted bipeds (notwithstanding the new evidence from South Africa, which will require further study), and most, if not all, early hominids probably displayed both **obligate bipedalism** and **habitual bipedalism.** For a review of the anatomical features associated with bipedal locomotion, see figure 8–4.

Obligate bipedalism Bipedalism as the *only* form of hominid terrestrial locomotion. Since major anatomical changes in the spine, pelvis, and lower limb are required for bipedal locomotion, once hominids adapted to this mode of locomotion, other forms of locomotion on the ground became impossible.

Habitual bipedalism Bipedal locomotion as the form of locomotion shown by hominids most of the time.

(c)

(d)

(e)

(f)

internal organs; moreover, the ossa coxae (specifically, iliac blades) are shorter and broader, thus stabilizing weight transmission. (d) Lower limbs are elongated, as shown by the proportional lengths of various body segments (e.g., in humans the thigh comprises 20 percent of body height, while in gorillas it comprises only 11 percent). (e) The femur is angled inward, keep-ing the legs more directly under the body; modified knee anatomy also permits full extension of this joint. (f) The big toe is enlarged and brought in line with the other toes; in addition, a distinctive longitudinal arch forms, helping absorb shock and adding propulsive spring.

Biocultural Evolution: The Human Capacity for Culture

One of the most distinctive behavioral features of humans is our species' extraordinary elaboration of and dependence on culture. Certainly, other primates, and many other animals, for that matter, modify their environments. As we saw in Chapter 6, chimpanzees especially are known for such behaviors as using termite sticks, and some even transport rocks to crush nuts. Given such observations, it becomes tenuous to draw sharp lines between early hominid toolmaking behavior and that exhibited by other animals.

Another point to remember is that human culture, at least as it is defined in contemporary contexts, involves much more than toolmaking capacity. For humans, culture integrates an entire adaptive strategy involving cognitive, political, social, and economic components. The *material culture*, the tools humans use, is but a small portion of this cultural complex.

Nevertheless, when examining the archaeological record of earlier hominids, what is available for study is almost exclusively certain remains of material culture, especially residues of stone tool manufacture. Thus, it is extremely difficult to learn anything about the earliest stages of hominid cultural development prior to the regular manufacture of stone tools. As you will see, this most crucial cultural development has been traced to approximately 2.5 m.y.a. (Semaw et al., 1997). Yet, hominids were undoubtedly using other kinds of tools (made of perishable materials) and displaying a whole array of other cultural behaviors long before this time. However, without any "hard" evidence preserved in the archaeological record, our understanding of the early development of these nonmaterial cultural components remains elusive.

The fundamental basis for human cultural elaboration relates directly to cognitive abilities. Again, we are not dealing with an absolute distinction, but a relative one. As you have already learned, other primates, as documented in chimpanzees and bonobos, possess some of the language capabilities exhibited by humans. Nevertheless, modern humans display these abilities in a complexity several orders of magnitude beyond that of any other animal. Moreover, only humans are so completely dependent on symbolic communication and its cultural by-products that contemporary *Homo sapiens* could not survive without them.

When did the unique combination of cognitive, social, and material cultural adaptations become prominent in human evolution? We must be careful to recognize the manifold nature of culture and not expect it always to contain the same elements across species (as when compared to nonhuman primates) or through time (when trying to reconstruct ancient hominid behavior). Richard Potts (1993) has critiqued this overly simplistic perspective and suggests a more dynamic approach, one that incorporates many subcomponents (including aspects of behavior, cognition, and social interaction).

We know that the earliest hominids almost certainly did *not* regularly manufacture stone tools (at least, none that have been found!). These earliest members of the hominid lineage, dating back to approximately 7–5 m.y.a., could be referred to as **protohominids.** These protohominids may have carried objects such as naturally sharp stones or stone flakes, parts of carcasses, and pieces of wood around their home ranges. At minimum, we would expect them to have displayed these behaviors to at least the same degree as living chimpanzees.

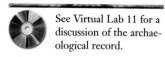

See Virtual Lab 11 for a discussion of the archaeological record.

Protohominids The earliest members of the hominid lineage, as yet only barely represented in the fossil record. Thus, their structure and, especially, behavior are reconstructed hypothetically.

Moreover, as you will see, by at least 5 m.y.a. and perhaps even 7 m.y.a., hominids had developed one crucial advantage: They were bipedal and could therefore much more easily carry all manner of objects from place to place. Ultimately, the efficient exploitation of resources widely distributed in time and space would most likely have led to using "central" locations where key components, especially stone objects, were cached (Potts, 1991).

What is certain is that over a period of several million years, during the formative stages of hominid emergence, numerous components interacted, but not all developed simultaneously. As cognitive abilities developed, more efficient means of communication and learning resulted. Largely as a result of consequent neurological reorganization, more elaborate tools and social relationships also emerged. These, in turn, selected for greater intelligence, which in turn selected for further neural elaboration. Quite clearly, then, these mutual dynamics are at the very heart of what we call hominid *biocultural* evolution.

Paleoanthropology as a Multidisciplinary Science

To understand human biocultural evolution adequately, we need a broad base of information. The task of recovering and interpreting all the clues left by early hominids is the work of paleoanthropologists. Paleoanthropology is defined as the study of early humans. As such, it is a diverse **multidisciplinary** pursuit seeking to reconstruct every bit of information possible concerning the dating, anatomy, behavior, and ecology of our hominid ancestors. In just the last few years, the study of early hominids has marshaled the specialized skills of many diverse scientific disciplines. Included primarily in this growing and exciting adventure are geologists, archaeologists, physical anthropologists, and paleoecologists (Table 8–1).

Geologists, usually working with anthropologists (often archaeologists), do the initial survey to locate potential early hominid **sites.** Many sophisticated techniques can contribute to this search, including aerial and satellite photography. Paleontologists may also be involved in this early search, for they can help find geological beds containing **faunal** remains. (Where conditions are favorable for

Multidisciplinary Pertaining to research that involves mutual contributions and cooperation of several different experts from various scientific fields (i.e., disciplines).

Sites Locations of discoveries. In paleontology and archaeology, a site may refer to a region where a number of discoveries have been made.

Faunal Referring to animal remains; in archaeology, specifically refers to the fossil remains of animals.

TABLE 8–1	Components of Paleoanthropology	
Physical Sciences	**Biological Sciences**	**Social Sciences**
Geology	Physical anthropology	Archaeology
Stratigraphy	Ecology	Ethnoarchaeology
Petrology (rocks, minerals)	Paleontology (fossil animals)	Cultural anthropology
Pedology (soils)	Palynology (fossil pollen)	Ethnography
Geomorphology	Primatology	Psychology
Geophysics		
Chemistry		
Taphonomy*		

*Taphonomy (*taphos* meaning "dead") is the study of how bones and other materials come to be buried in the earth and preserved as fossils. A taphonomist studies such phenomena as sedimentation, the action of streams, preservation properties of bone, and carnivore disturbance factors.

figure 8–5 Excavations in progress at Olduvai. This site, more than 1 million years old, was located when a hominid ulna (arm bone) was found eroding out of the side of the gorge.

Robert Jurmain

Chronometric (*chronos*, meaning "time," and *metric*, meaning "measure") Referring to a dating technique that gives an estimate in actual number of years .

Artifacts Traces of hominid behavior. Very old ones are usually made of stone.

the preservation of such specimens as ancient pigs or baboons, conditions may also be favorable for the preservation of hominid fossils.) In addition, paleontologists can—through comparison with faunal sequences elsewhere—give quick estimates of the approximate age of sites without having to wait for the expensive and time-consuming **chronometric** analyses. In this way, fossil beds of the "right" geological ages (i.e., where hominid finds are most likely) can be identified.

Once potential early hominid localities have been identified, much more extensive surveying begins. At this point, the archaeologists take over the search for hominid traces (fig. 8–5). We do not necessarily have to find the fossilized remains of early hominids (which will always be rare) to know that hominids consistently occupied an ancient land surface. Behavioral clues, or **artifacts,** also inform us directly and unambiguously about early hominid occupation. Modifying rocks according to a consistent plan or simply carrying them over fairly long distances is a behavior exhibited by no other animal but a hominid. Therefore, when we see such behavioral evidence at a site, we know that hominids were once present there.

Dating Methods

One of the essentials of paleoanthropology is placing sites and fossils into a chronological framework. In other words, we want to know how old they are. How, then, do we date sites—or, more precisely, how do we date the geological strata in which sites are found? The question is important, so let us examine some of the dating techniques used by paleontologists, geologists, and paleoanthropologists.

Scientists use two basic types of dating for this purpose: *relative dating* and *chronometric dating* (also known as *absolute dating*). Relative dating methods tell you that something is older or younger than something else, but not by how much. If, for example, a fossil cranium is found at a depth of 50 feet and another cranium at 70 feet at the same site, we usually assume that the cranium at 70 feet is older. We may not know the date (in years) of either one, but we would be able to infer a *relative* sequence. This method of dating is based on **stratigraphy** and is called *stratigraphic dating*. This was one of the first techniques used by scholars working with the vast expanses of geological time. Stratigraphic dating is based on the law of superposition, which states that a lower **stratum** (layer) is older than a higher stratum. Given the fact that much of the earth's crust has been laid down by layer after layer of sedimentary rock, stratigraphic relationships have provided a valuable tool in reconstructing the history of the earth and of life upon it.

Stratigraphic dating does, however, have a number of potential problems. Earth disturbances, such as volcanic activity, river action, and faulting, may shift the strata or materials in them, and the chronology may thus be difficult or impossible to reconstruct. Furthermore, given the widely different rates of accumulation, the elapsed time of any stratum cannot be determined with much accuracy.

Another method of relative dating is *fluorine analysis*, which applies only to bone. Bones in the earth are exposed to the seepage of groundwater, which usually contains some fluorine. The longer a bone lies buried, the more fluorine it incorporates during fossilization. Therefore, bones deposited at the same time in the same location should contain the same amount of fluorine.

The use of this technique by Professor Oakley of the British Museum in the early 1950s exposed the famous Piltdown hoax by demonstrating that the human skull was considerably older than the jaw ostensibly found with it (Weiner, 1955). Lying in the same location, the jaw and skull should have absorbed approximately the same quantity of fluorine. But the skull contained significantly more, meaning that if it came from the same site, it had been deposited considerably earlier. The discrepancy of fluorine content led Oakley and others to a much closer examination of the bones, and they found that the jaw was not that of a hominid at all, but one of a juvenile orangutan! Clearly, then, someone had planted it at Piltdown, but who was the devious forger? Until recently, there were no firm clues, but newly discovered evidence has pointed the blame at Martin Hinton, a British zoologist (Gee, 1996).

Unfortunately, fluorine is useful only for dating bones from the same location. Because of the differing concentrations in groundwater, accumulation rates will vary from place to place. Also, some groundwater may not contain any fluorine. For these reasons, comparing fossils from different localities using fluorine analysis is not feasible.

Two other relative dating techniques, *biostratigraphy* and *paleomagnetism*, have also proved quite useful in calibrating the ages of early hominid sites. Biostratigraphy is a relative technique based on fairly regular changes seen in the dentition and other anatomical structures in such groups as pigs, rodents, and baboons. Dating of sites is based on the presence of certain fossil species that also occur elsewhere in deposits whose dates have been determined. This technique has proved helpful in cross-correlating the ages of various sites in south, central, and east Africa. A final type of relative dating, paleomagnetism, is based on the shifting nature of the earth's geomagnetic pole. Although now oriented northward, the geomagnetic pole is known to have shifted several times in the past and at times was oriented to the south. By examining magnetically charged particles encased in rock, geologists can determine the orientation of these ancient "compasses." One cannot derive a date in years from this particular technique, but it is used to double-check other techniques.

In all these relative dating techniques, the age of geological layers or objects within them is impossible to calibrate. To determine age as precisely as possible,

Stratigraphy Sequential layering of deposits.

Stratum (*pl.*, strata) Geological layer.

scientists have developed a variety of chronometric techniques, many based on the phenomenon of radioactive decay. The theory is quite simple: Certain radioactive isotopes of elements are unstable, disintegrate, and form an isotopic variant of another element. Since the rate of disintegration follows a predictable mathematical pattern, the radioactive material serves as an accurate geological clock. By measuring the amount of disintegration in a particular sample, scientists have devised techniques for dating the immense age of the earth (and moon rocks) as well as material only a few hundred years old. Several techniques have been employed for a number of years and are now quite well known.

An important chronometric technique used in paleoanthropological research involves potassium-40 (^{40}K), which has a half-life of 1.25 billion years and produces argon-40 (^{40}Ar). That is, half the ^{40}K isotope changes to ^{40}Ar in 1.25 billion years. In another 1.25 billion years, half the remaining ^{40}K would be converted (i.e., only one-quarter of the original amount would still be present). Known as the K/Ar, or potassium-argon, method, this procedure has been extensively used in dating materials in the 5–1 m.y.a. range, especially in East Africa. Organic material, such as bone, cannot be measured, but the rock matrix in which the fossilized bone is found can be.

Strata that provide the best samples for K/Ar dating are those that have been heated to an extremely high temperature, such as that generated by volcanic activity. Heating drives off previously accumulated argon gas, thus "resetting" the clock to zero. As the material cools and solidifies, potassium (^{40}K) continues to break down to ^{40}Ar, but now the gas is physically trapped inside the cooling material. To date the geological material, it is reheated, and the escaping gas is then measured. Potassium-argon dating has been used to date very old events—such as the age of the earth—as well as those less than 2,000 years old.

Another well-known chronometric technique popular with archaeologists involves carbon-14 (^{14}C), with a half-life of 5,730 years. This method has been used to date material as recent as a few hundred years old and can be extended as far back as 75,000 years, although the probability of error rises rapidly after 40,000 years. The physical basis of this technique is also *radiometric*; that is, it is tied to the measurement of radioactive decay of an isotope (^{14}C) into another, more stable form. Radiocarbon dating has proved especially relevant for calibrating the latter stages of human evolution, including the Neandertals and the appearance of modern *Homo sapiens* (see Chapter 11).

Other methods have also proved useful in dating early hominid sites. For example, *fission-track dating* is a chronometric technique that works on the basis of the regular fissioning of uranium atoms. When certain types of crystalline rocks are observed microscopically, the "tracks" left by the fission events can be counted and an approximate age is thus calibrated. (Other techniques applicable to dating the later stages of human evolution are discussed briefly in Chapter 11; see Table 11–1.)

Many of the techniques just discussed are used together to provide *independent* checks for dating important early hominid sites. Each technique has a degree of error, and only by *cross-correlating* the results can paleoanthropologists feel confident regarding chronological placement of the fossil and archaeological remains they discover. This point is of the utmost importance, for a firm chronology forms the basis for making sound evolutionary interpretations (as discussed later in the chapter).

Early Hominids from Africa

Over the last 80 years, a tremendous number of hominid fossils have been discovered in Africa. The first finds came from South Africa, but by the 1970s, East Africa (particularly along the Rift Valley in Ethiopia, Kenya, and Tanzania) had taken preeminence. This shift in the focus and significance of discovery came about as a result of many factors. The geological circumstances found in East Africa produce a clearer stratigraphic picture and better association of hominids with archaeological artifacts, and equally important, these materials are much more easily datable (using chronometric methods). Moreover, generally fossils are easier to find in East Africa, although it is never easy anywhere to find hominid fossils! Erosion from wind, rain, and gravity expose fossils on the ground surface, where they can simply be picked up—assuming, of course, one knows exactly *where* to look. In South Africa, by contrast, the fossils are embedded in rock matrix, making precise archaeological recovery extraordinarily difficult. Nevertheless, excavations have continued at several South African sites. From this ongoing work, some new and highly productive locales have been explored, and as of this writing, perhaps the most intact early hominid skeleton ever discovered is being excavated at Sterkfontein Cave, just outside Johannesburg.

The saga of new and more intriguing African hominid discoveries is not yet completed—indeed, not even slowed. Just in 2002, perhaps the most remarkable discovery in the last 75 years was announced. What made this discovery (from Chad) so surprising was (1) its location (in central Africa, *not* in either South or East Africa), (2) its age (estimated at close to 7 m.y.a., making it by far the earliest hominid found anywhere), and (3) its physical appearnace (quite unexpected and unlike anything discovered previously; more on this presently).

See Virtual Lab 8, section I, for a discussion of the fossil evidence for the earliest hominids.

Thus, if we accept the latest discoveries and provision dating as accurate, hominid origins go back in Africa approximately 7 million years. Hominids, as far as current evidence indicates, stayed in Africa for the next 5 million years, first emigrating to other Old World locales 2 m.y.a. Thus, it appears that for the first 70 percent of hominid history, our family was restricted to Africa.

Earliest Traces

The distinction of being designated "the earliest hominid" is one that draws worldwide media coverage, but it is a notoriously fickle title. When this textbook was first published in 1992, the earliest hominid was dated at between 3 and 4 m.y.a. By the third edition (1998), based on some Ethiopian fossils, this had been pushed back to 4.4 m.y.a. By 2000 (based on Kenyan material), the date was further extended to close to 6 m.y.a. And in 2002, the startling find from Chad has suggested that the current bearer of the "earliest" title is 7 million years old.

This brief history is not intended to force unsuspecting students to memorize exactly what was found when. Our point is to illustrate how rapidly discoveries have taken place; in just the last 10 years, the known span of hominid existence has almost doubled!

CENTRAL AFRICA   The most stunning of these new finds is also the oldest. The fossil, a nearly complete cranium, was discovered in 2001 at a site called Toros-Menalla in northern Chad (Brunet et al., 2002). Provisional dating using faunal correlation (biostratigraphy; see p. 189) suggests a date nearly 7 m.y.a. (Vignaud et al., 2002). Surprisingly, the very early suggested age of this fossil places it at almost 1 million years earlier than *any* of the other proposed early hominids (and close to 3 million years earlier than the oldest well-established hominid discoveries).

The morphology of the fossil is unusual, with a combination of characteristics unlike that found in other early hominids. The braincase is small, estimated at no larger than a modern chimpanzee's (preliminary estimate in the range of 320 to 380 cm^3), but it is massively built, with huge browridges in front, a crest on top, and large muscle attachments in the rear (fig. 8–6). Yet, combined with these apelike features is a smallish vertical face containing front teeth very unlike an ape's. In fact, the lower face, being more tucked in under the brain vault (and not protruding, as in most other early hominids), is more of a *derived* feature more commonly expressed in much later hominids (especially members of genus *Homo*). Moreover, unlike the dentition seen in apes (and some early hominids), the upper canine is reduced and is worn down from the tip (rather than shearing along its side against the first lower premolar).

In recognition of this unique combination of characteristics, the lead researcher, Michael Brunet (of the University of Poiters, in France), has placed the Toros-Menalla remains into a new genus and species of hominid, *Sahelanthropus tchadensis* (Sahel being the region of the southern Sahara in North Africa).

These new finds from Chad have forced an immediate and significant reassessment of early hominid evolution. Two cautionary comments, however, are in order. First, the dating is only approximate, based, as it is, on biostratigraphic correlation with sites in Kenya (1,500 miles to the east). The faunal sequences, nevertheless, seem to be clearly bracketed by two very well-dated sequences in Kenya. Second, and perhaps more serious, is the hominid status of the Chad fossil. Given the facial structure and dentition, it is difficult to see how *Sahelanthropus* could be anything but a hominid. However, some researchers (Wolpoff et al., 2002) have raised questions regarding the evolutionary interpretation of *Sahelanthropus*, suggesting that this fossil may represent an ape rather than a hominid. As we have previously said, the best-defining anatomical characteristics of hominids relate to bipedal locomotion. Unfortunately, no **postcranial** elements have been recovered from Chad—at least not yet. Consequently, we do not yet know the locomotor behavior of *Sahelanthropus*— and this raises even more fundamental questions: What if further finds show this form not to be bipedal? Should we still consider it a hominid? What, then, are the defining characteristics of our family?

EAST AFRICA   Two areas in East Africa, one in the Tugen Hills area near Lake Baringo in central Kenya and the other from the Middle Awash area of northeastern Ethiopia, have also quite recently yielded very early hominid remains. The earlier of these finds (dated provisionally by radiometric methods to about 6 m.y.a.) come from four localities in the Tugen Hills and include mostly dental remains, but also some quite complete lower limb bones (the latter interpreted as clearly indicating bipedal locomotion) (Pickford and Senut, 2001; Senut et al., 2001). Following preliminary analysis of the fossils, the primary researchers

figure 8–6   A nearly complete cranium of *Sahelanthropus* from Chad, dating to 7 m.y.a.

Postcranial   (*post*, meaning "after") In a quadruped, referring to that portion of the body behind the head; in a biped, referring to all parts of the body *beneath* the head (i.e., from the neck down).

TABLE 8-2	In Summary: Key Very Early Fossil Hominid Discoveries (prior to 4 m.y.a.)			
	Site	Date (m.y.a.)	Taxonomic Designation	Fossil Sample
East Africa	Middle Awash (Ethiopia; five localities)	5.8–5.2	Ardipithecus	11 specimens; minimum 5 individuals, including teeth, 1 jaw fragment, and a few limb bones (including a complete toe bone)
	Aramis (Ethiopia)	4.4	Ardipithecus ramidus	Up to 56 individuals; some quite complete, including many postcranial elements
	Tugen Hills	~6.0	Orrorin tugenensis	13 specimens; minimum 5 individuals, including teeth, jaw fragments, and quite complete limb bones
Central Africa	Toros-Menalla	~7.0	Sahelanthropus tchadenis	Nearly complete cranium, 2 lower jaw fragments, 3 isolated teeth

(Brigitte Senut and Martin Pickford) have suggested placing these early hominids in a separate genus—*Orrorin*.

The last group of fossil hominids thought to date to the late Miocene come from five localities in the Middle Awash in the Afar Triangle of Ethiopia (Table 8–2). Radiometric dating places the age of these fossils in the very late Miocene, 5.8–5.2 m.y.a. The fossil remains themselves are very fragmentary. Some of the dental remains resemble some later fossils from the Middle Awash (discussed shortly), and Yohannes Hailie-Selassie, the researcher who first found and described these earlier materials, has provisionally assigned them to the genus *Ardipithecus* (see Table 8–2). In addition, some postcranial elements have been preserved, most informatively a toe bone, a phalanx from the middle of the foot (see Appendix A, fig. A–8). From clues in this bone, Hailie-Selassie concludes that this primate was a well-adapted biped (once again, the best-supporting evidence of hominid status).

From later in the geological record in the Middle Awash region, along the banks of the Awash River, a very large and significant assemblage of fossil hominids has been discovered at the **Aramis** site. Radiometric calibration firmly dates this site at about 4.4 m.y.a.

Aramis (air´-ah-miss)

Fossil remains from Aramis were excavated between 1992 and 1995 and include up to 50 different individuals (Wolpoff, 1999). This crucial and quite large fossil assortment includes several dental specimens as well as an upper arm bone (humerus) and some fragmentary cranial remains. Most exciting of all, in 1995, 40 percent of a skeleton was discovered; there are also reports of other partial skeletons from Aramis. However, in all cases, the bones are encased in limestone matrix, thus requiring a long and tedious process to remove the fossils intact from the cementlike material surrounding them. In fact, as of this writing, the Aramis remains (including the skeletons) have not yet been fully described. Nevertheless, details from initial reports are highly suggestive that these remains are, in fact, very early hominids.

First of all, in an Aramis partial cranium, the *foramen magnum* is positioned farther forward in the base of the skull than is the case in quadrupeds (fig. 8–7). Second, features of the humerus also differ from those seen in quadrupeds, indicating that the Aramis humerus did not function in locomotion to support weight. From these two features, the provisional interpretation by Tim White, of the University of California, Berkeley, and his colleagues was that the Aramis

(a)

(b)

figure 8–7 Position of the fora-men magnum in (a) a human and (b) a chimpanzee. Note the more forward position in the human cranium.

Australopithecus An early hominid genus, known from the Plio-Pleistocene of Africa, characterized by bipedal locomotion, a relatively small brain, and large back teeth.

individuals were *bipedal*. Moreover, initial interpretation of the partial skeleton (while not yet fully cleaned and reported) also suggests obligate bipedalism (Wolpoff, 1999).

Nevertheless, these were clearly quite primitive hominids, displaying an array of characteristics quite distinct from other members of our family. These primitive characteristics include flattening of the cranial base and relatively thin enamel caps on the molar teeth. From measurements of the humerus head, Wolpoff (1999) estimates a body weight of 42 kg (93 pounds); if this humerus comes from a male individual, this weight estimate is very similar to that hypothesized for other Plio-Pleistocene hominids (see Table 8–6).

Thus, current conclusions (which will be either unambiguously confirmed or falsified as the skeleton is fully cleaned and studied) interpret the Aramis remains as among the earliest hominids yet known. These individuals, while very primitive hominids, were apparently bipedal, although not necessarily in the same way that later hominids were.

Tim White and colleagues have argued (White et al., 1995) that the fossil hominids from Aramis are so primitive and so different from other early hominids that they should be assigned to a new genus (and, necessarily, a new species as well): *Ardipithecus ramidus*. Most especially, the thin enamel caps on the molars are in dramatic contrast to all other confirmed early hominids, who show quite thick enamel. These other early hominid forms (all somewhat later than *Ardipithecus*) are placed in the genus **Australopithecus**. Moreover, White and his associates have further suggested that, as the earliest and most primitive hominid yet discovered, *Ardipithecus* may possibly be the root species for all later hominids. This view does not take into account the recently discovered Tugen Hills finds, which are provisionally assigned to the new genus *Orrorin*. However, this interpretation does encompass the earlier remains from the Middle Awash—which, for the moment, are also included within *Ardipithecus*.

Another intriguing aspect of all these late Miocene/early Pliocene locales (i.e., Tugen Hills, early Middle Awash sites, and Aramis) relates to the ancient environments associated with the suggested earliest of hominids. Rather than the more open grassland savanna habitats so characteristic of most later hominid sites, the environments at these early locales is more heavily forested.* Perhaps we are seeing at Aramis and these other ancient sites the very beginnings of hominid divergence, very soon after the division from the African apes!

Australopithecus *from East Africa*

The best-known, most widely distributed, and most diverse of the early African hominids are placed in the genus *Australopithecus*. Moreover, these hominids have an established time range of over 3 million years, stretching back as early as 4.2 m.y.a. and not becoming extinct until apparently close to 1 m.y.a.—making them the longest-enduring hominid yet documented. In addition, these hominids have been found in all the major geographical areas of Africa that

---

*The environmental context at Toros-Menalla is not yet clearly understood, as there is a mixing of indicators, ranging from forest to more open savanna.

have, to date, produced early hominid finds, namely south, central (Chad), and east Africa. From all these areas combined, there appears to have been considerable complexity in terms of evolutionary diversity; in fact, as many as eight species are recognized by many (but not all) authorities (see Appendix B for a complete listing and more discussion of early hominid fossil finds).

Before discussing this pivotal group of early hominids, we should make one further point. Many researchers prefer to divide what we are including in one genus (*Australopithecus*) into two different genera (*Australopithecus* and **Paranthropus**). As we will discuss later in this chapter (p. 211), there is a good evolutionary justification to split these diverse hominids into two genera. However, for simplicity sake (and following close to 50 years of general consensus), we will group all these forms together in the single genus *Australopithecus*. In any case, all these hominids share many features in common:

1. They are all clearly bipedal (although not necessarily identical to *Homo* in this regard).
2. They all have relatively small brains (i.e., at least compared to *Homo*).
3. They all have large teeth, particularly the back teeth, with thick to very thick enamel on the molars.

In short, then, all these species of *Australopithecus* are relatively small-brained, big-toothed bipeds.

The earliest finds of *Australopithecus* have been located at two sites in northern Kenya, dating from about 4.2–3.9 m.y.a. Like many of the other finds discussed in this chapter, these hominids were discovered quite recently (mostly in the mid-1990s). Among the fossils of these earliest **australopithecines** thus far discovered, a few postcranial pieces clearly indicate that locomotion was *bipedal*. There are, however, a few primitive features in the dentition, including a large canine and a **sectorial** lower first premolar (fig. 8–8).

Since these particular fossils have initially been interpreted as more primitive than all the later members of the genus, Meave Leakey and associates have provisionally assigned them to a separate species of *Australopithecus* (see Appendix B). Further study and (with some luck) additional more complete remains will help decide whether such a distinction is warranted.

Slightly later and much more complete remains of *Australopithecus* have come from the sites of Hadar (in Ethiopia) and Laetoli (in Tanzania). Much of this material has been known for some time (since the mid-1970s), and the fossils have been very well studied; indeed, in certain instances, they are quite famous. For example, the Lucy skeleton was discovered at Hadar in 1974, and the Laetoli footprints were first found in 1978.

Literally thousands of footprints have been found at Laetoli, representing more than 20 different kinds of animals (Pliocene elephants, horses, pigs, giraffes, antelopes, hyenas, and an abundance of hares). Several hominid footprints have also been found, including a trail more than 75 feet long made by at least two—and perhaps three—individuals (Leakey and Hay, 1979) (fig. 8–9). Such discoveries of well-preserved hominid footprints are extremely important in furthering our understanding of human evolution. For the first time, we can make *definite* statements regarding the locomotor pattern and stature of early hominids. Analyses of these Pliocene footprints suggest a stature of about 4 feet 9 inches for the larger individual and 4 feet 1 inch for the smaller individual.

Paranthropus (par´-an-throw´-puss) A genus of early hominid characterized by very large back teeth and jaws. Frequently, this genus is combined into *Australopithecus*.

Australopithecines (os-tra-loh-pith´-e-seens) The colloquial name for members of the genus *Australopithecus*. The term was first used as a subfamily designation, but is now mostly used informally.

Sectorial Adapted for cutting or shearing; among primates, refers to the compressed (side-to-side) first lower premolar, which functions as a shearing surface with the upper canine.

Sectorial lower first premolar

Lynn Kilgore

figure 8–8 Left lateral view of the teeth of a male patas monkey. Note how the large upper canine shears against the elongated surface of the sectorial lower first premolar.

figure 8–9 Hominid footprint from Laetoli, Tanzania. Note the deep impression of the heel and the large toe (arrow) in line (adducted) with the other toes.

Courtesy Peter Jones

Studies of these impression patterns clearly show that the mode of locomotion of these hominids was bipedal (Day and Wickens, 1980). As we have emphasized, the development of bipedal locomotion is the most important defining characteristic of early hominid evolution. Some researchers, however, have concluded that these early hominids were not bipedal in quite the same way that modern humans are. From detailed comparisons with modern humans, estimates of stride length, cadence, and speed of walking have been ascertained, indicating that the Laetoli hominids moved in a slow-moving ("strolling") fashion with a rather short stride (Chateris et al., 1981).

One extraordinary discovery at Hadar is the Lucy skeleton (fig. 8–10), found by Don Johanson eroding out of a hillside. This fossil is scientifically designated as Afar Locality (AL) 288-1, but is usually just called Lucy (after the Beatles song "Lucy in the Sky with Diamonds"). Representing almost 40 percent of a skeleton, this is one of the three most complete individuals from anywhere in the world for the entire period before about 100,000 years ago.*

Because the Laetoli area was covered periodically by ashfalls from nearby volcanic eruptions, accurate dating is possible and has provided dates of 3.7–3.5 m.y.a. Dating from the Hadar region has not proved as straightforward; however, more complete dating calibration, using a variety of techniques (see p. 188), has determined a range of 3.9–3.0 m.y.a. for the hominid discoveries from this area (see Table 8–4).

Robert Jurmain

figure 8–10 "Lucy," a partial hominid skeleton, discovered at Hadar in 1974. This individual is assigned to Australopithecus afarensis. (photograph of cast)

Australopithecus afarensis from Laetoli and Hadar

Several hundred specimens, representing a minimum of 60 individuals (and perhaps as many as 100), have been removed from Laetoli and Hadar. At present, these materials represent the largest *well-studied* collection of early hominids and

---

*The others are a specimen from Sterkfontein, in South Africa (see p. 205), and a *H. erectus* skeleton from west of Lake Turkana, Kenya (see p. 232). Also note that the crushed and embedded skeleton from Aramis may be nearly as complete as Lucy.

as such are among the most significant of the hominids discussed in this chapter. Moreover, it has been suggested that fragmentary specimens from other locales in East Africa are remains of the same species as that found at Laetoli and Hadar. Most scholars refer to this species as *Australopithecus afarensis.*

Without question, *A. afarensis* is more primitive than any of the other later australopithecine fossils from South or East Africa (discussed subsequently). By "primitive" we mean that *A. afarensis* is less evolved in any particular direction than are later occurring hominid species. That is, *A. afarensis* shares more primitive features with other early homin*oids* and with living pongids than do later hominids, who display more derived characteristics.

For example, the teeth of *A. afarensis* are quite primitive. The canines are often large, pointed teeth. Moreover, the lower first premolar is semisectorial (i.e., it provides a shearing surface for the upper canine), and the tooth rows are parallel, even converging somewhat toward the back of the mouth (fig. 8–11).

The cranial portions that are preserved also display several primitive hominoid characteristics, including a crest in the back as well as several primitive features of the cranial base. Cranial capacity estimates for *A. afarensis* show a mixed pattern when compared to later hominids. A provisional estimate for the one partially complete cranium—apparently a large individual—gives a figure of 500 cm^3, but another, even more fragmentary cranium is apparently quite a bit smaller and has been estimated at about 375 cm^3 (Holloway, 1983). Thus, for some individuals (males?), *A. afarensis* is well within the range of other australopithecine species (Table 8–3), but others (females?) may have a significantly smaller cranial capacity. However, a detailed depiction of cranial size for *A. afarensis* is not possible at this time; this part of the skeleton is unfortunately too poorly represented. One thing is clear: *A. afarensis* had a small brain, probably averaging for the whole species not much over 420 cm^3.

On the other hand, a large assortment of postcranial pieces has been found at Hadar. Initial impressions suggest that relative to lower limbs, the upper limbs are longer than in modern humans (also a primitive hominoid condition). (This statement does not mean that the arms of *A. afarensis* were longer than the

figure 8–11 Jaw of *Australopithecus afarensis.* Maxilla, AL 200-1a, from Hadar, Ethiopia. (Note the parallel tooth rows and large canines.) (photograph of cast)

See Virtual Lab 8, section I, for a discussion of *Australopithecus afarensis.*

TABLE 8-3	Estimated Cranial Capacities in Early Hominids with Comparable Data for Modern Great Apes and Humans	
	Cranial Capacity	
Hominid	**Range (cm³)**	**Average(s) (cm³)**
Early Hominids		
Sahelanthropus		~350
Ardipithecus	Not presently known	Not presently known
Australopithecus afarensis		420
Later australopithecines		410–530
Early members of genus *Homo*		631
Contemporary Hominoids		
Human	1150–1750	1330
Chimpanzee	285–500	395
Gorilla	340–752	506
Orangutan	276–540	411
Bonobo	–	350

See Virtual Lab 10, section II, for a discussion of the evolution of hominid brain size.

legs.) In addition, the wrist, hand, and foot bones show several differences from modern humans (Susman et al., 1985). From such excellent postcranial evidence, stature can now be confidently estimated: *A. afarensis* was a short hominid. From her partial skeleton, Lucy is estimated to be only 3½ to 4 feet tall. However, Lucy—as demonstrated by her pelvis—was probably a female, and at Hadar and Laetoli, there is evidence of larger individuals as well. The most economical hypothesis explaining this variation is that *A. afarensis* was quite sexually dimorphic: The larger individuals are male and the smaller ones, such as Lucy, are female. Estimates of male stature can be approximated from the larger footprints at Laetoli, inferring a height of not quite 5 feet. If we accept this interpretation, *A. afarensis* was a very sexually dimorphic form indeed. In fact, for overall body size, this species may have been as dimorphic as *any* living primate (i.e., as much as gorillas, orangutans, or baboons).

In a majority of dental and cranial features, *A. afarensis* is clearly more primitive than later hominids. In fact, from the neck up, *A. afarensis* is so primitive that without any evidence from the limbs, one would be hard-pressed to call it a hominid at all (although the back teeth are large and heavily enameled, unlike pongids, and the position of the foramen magnum indicates an upright posture).

What, then, makes *A. afarensis* a hominid? The answer is revealed by its manner of locomotion. From the abundant limb bones recovered from Hadar and those beautiful footprints from Laetoli, we know unequivocally that *A. afarensis* walked bipedally when on the ground. (At present, we do not have nearly such good evidence concerning locomotion for *any* of the earlier hominid finds.) Whether Lucy and her contemporaries still spent considerable time in the trees and just how efficiently they walked have become topics of some controversy. Most researchers, however, agree that *A. afarensis* was an efficient habitual biped while on the ground. These hominids were also clearly *obligate* bipeds, which would have hampered their climbing abilities but would not necessarily have precluded arboreal behavior altogether. As one physical anthropologist has surmised: "One could imagine these diminutive early hominids making maximum use of *both* terrestrial and arboreal resources in spite of their commitment to exclusive bipedalism when on the ground. The contention of a mixed arboreal and terrestrial behavioral repertoire would make adaptive sense of the Hadar australopithecine forelimb, hand, and foot morphology without contradicting the evidence of the pelvis" (Wolpoff, 1983b, p. 451).

A Contemporaneous Non-Australopithecine Find?

The pace of hominid discoveries in East Africa has dramatically intensified in recent years, and many of these new discoveries have revealed a different combination of anatomical features from those recognized in remains discovered previously. Among the most distinctive and intriguing of these newer finds is a cranium unearthed in 1999 on the west side of Lake Turkana in northern Kenya (Leakey et al., 2001).

Dated to 3.5 m.y.a., this fossil hominid is thus contemporaneous with *Australopithecus afarensis*. Yet, it shows a quite distinctive combination of facial and dental features (most especially, a flat lower face and fairly small molar teeth). In these respects, this newly discovered Kenyan hominid is different from *A. afarensis*, and, in fact, from *all* known australopithecines. Because the skull has been severely distorted, cranial capacity is difficult to establish clearly. However, the best estimates suggest that the cranial capacity is similar to that of *Australopithecus* (i.e., in the range of 400–500 cm³).

Because of its unusual anatomical features, Meave Leakey and her colleagues have proposed an entirely new hominid genus for this cranium. Whether this designation will be substantiated by further, more detailed analysis remains to be seen. At minimum, this and all the other discoveries from recent years are forcing a major reassessment of the early stages of hominid evolution (see Appendix B).

Later East African Australopithecine Finds

An assortment of fossil hominids, including many specimens of later members of the genus *Australopithecus*, has been recovered from geological contexts with dates after 3 m.y.a. at several localities in East Africa. Up to 10 different such sites are now known (in the time range of 3–1 m.y.a.), but here we will concentrate on the three most significant ones: East Lake Turkana, West Lake Turkana (both in northern Kenya), and Olduvai Gorge (in northern Tanzania) (see Table 8–4 on p. 201).

KOOBI FORA (EAST LAKE TURKANA)   Under the direction of Richard Leakey and, for several years, the late Glynn Isaac, research in this vast arid area in northern Kenya has yielded the richest assemblage of Plio-Pleistocene hominids from the African continent. Current archaeological fieldwork is under the supervision of Offer Bar Yosef, of Harvard University. The current total exceeds 150 hominid specimens, probably representing at least 100 individuals and hominid fossils are dated at about 1.8 m.y.a. Among this fine sample are several complete skulls, many jaws, and an assortment of postcranial bones. Moreover, next to Olduvai Gorge (discussed shortly), sites on the east side of Lake **Turkana** have produced the most information concerning the behavior of early hominids.

WEST TURKANA   Across the lake from the fossil beds discussed above are other deposits that have yielded very exciting discoveries. In 1984, on the west side of Lake Turkana, a nearly complete skeleton of a 1.6-million-year-old *Homo erectus* adolescent was found (see Chapter 9), and the following year, a well-preserved 2.4-million-year-old skull was also found. This latter find—"the black skull"— is a most important discovery and has caused a major reevaluation of Plio-Pleistocene hominid evolution (fig. 8–12).

OLDUVAI GORGE   Located in the Serengeti Plain of northern Tanzania, **Olduvai** is a steep-sided valley resembling a miniature version of the Grand Canyon (fig. 8–13). (Indeed, the geological processes that formed the gorge are similar to what happened in the formation of the Grand Canyon.) Following millions of years of accumulation of several hundred feet of geological strata, faulting occurred about 70,000 years ago to the east of Olduvai. As a result, a gradient was established, and a rapidly flowing river proceeded to cut the gorge.

Olduvai today is thus a deep ravine cut into the almost mile-high grassland plateau of East Africa, and it extends more than 25 miles in total length—potentially including hundreds of early hominid localities. Climatically, the semiarid pattern with scrub vegetation observable today is thought to approximate conditions over most of the last 2 million years.

Turkana (tur-kahn´-ah)

figure 8–12 The "black skull," WT 17000, discovered at West Lake Turkana in 1985. This specimen is provisionally assigned to *Australopithecus aethiopicus*. It is called the "black skull" owing to the dark color from the fossilization (mineralization) process.

Olduvai (ohl´-doo-vye)

figure 8–13 View of the main gorge at Olduvai. Note the clear sequence of geological beds. The discontinuity to the right is a major fault line.

Robert Jurmain

Since the 1930s, when they first worked there, Olduvai came to be identified with Louis and Mary Leakey, two of the key founders of modern paleoanthropology. Louis, thanks to *National Geographic* and television, became more famous than any other paleoanthropologist of his generation. Although occupied with lecture tours, Leakey continued to make periodic trips to Olduvai up until his death in 1972. Mary Leakey, for over 40 years, was responsible for directing archaeological excavations at Olduvai (and later, Laetoli) and was instrumental in many of the most exciting discoveries. She retired from active fieldwork in 1983 and continued her writing and research until her death in 1996.

The greatest contribution that Olduvai has made to paleoanthropological research is the establishment of an extremely well-documented and correlated *sequence* of geological, paleontological, archaeological, and hominid remains over the last 2 million years. At the very foundation of all paleoanthropological research is a well-established geological picture, and at Olduvai, owing to four decades of work, this picture is understood in minute detail. Paleontological evidence of fossilized animal bones also has been retrieved in great abundance. More than 150 species of extinct animals have been recognized, and careful analysis of these remains has yielded voluminous information concerning the ecological conditions of early hominid habitats.

The archaeological sequence at Olduvai is also extremely well documented. Due to Mary Leakey's meticulous excavations and analyses, a more complete picture of the behavior of early hominids has emerged from Olduvai than from any other locality.

Finally, fossilized remains of several hominids have been found at Olduvai, ranging in time from the earliest occupation levels (circa 1.85 m.y.a.) to fairly recent *Homo sapiens*. Of the more than 40 individuals represented, many are quite fragmentary, but a few (including four skulls and a nearly complete foot) are excellently preserved (see Table 8–4). While the center of hominid discoveries has now shifted to other areas of East Africa, it was the initial discovery by Mary Leakey in 1959 of the "Zinj" (a robust australopithecine) cranium that focused the world's attention on this remarkably rich area. This famous discov-

TABLE 8-4	In Summary: Key East African *Australopithecus* and Early *Homo* Discoveries	
Site	**Dates (m.y.a.)**	**Fossil Sample**
Olduvai (N. Tanzania)	1.85–1.0	48 specimens; australopithecines; early *Homo*
Turkana (N. Kenya; eastern side of Lake Turkana)	1.9–1.3	More than 150 specimens; many australopithecines; several early *Homo*
(West side of Lake Turkana	3.5–1.6	2 nearly complete crania; 3 jaw fragments, isolated teeth; 1 nearly complete skeleton (*H. erectus*)
Hadar (N.E. Ethiopia)	3.9–3.0	Minimum of 40 individuals (maximum of 65); early australopithecines (*A. afarensis*)
Laetoli (N. Tanzania)	3.7–3.5	24 hominids; early australopithecines (*A. afarensis*); also, well-preserved footprints

ery provides an excellent example of how financial ramifications directly result from well-publicized hominid discoveries. Prior to 1959, the Leakeys had worked sporadically at Olduvai for almost three decades on a financial shoestring. During this time, they made marvelous paleontological and archaeological discoveries, but there was little support for much-needed large-scale excavation. However, following the discovery of Zinj, the National Geographic Society funded the research, and within the next year, more earth was moved than in the previous 30 years. Ongoing work at Olduvai has yielded yet further hominid finds, with a partial skeleton being discovered by researchers from the Institute of Human Origins in 1987.

Early Homo

In addition to the robust australopithecine remains in East Africa, there is another largely contemporaneous hominid that is quite distinctive. In fact, as best documented by fossil discoveries from Olduvai and Koobi Fora, these materials have been assigned to the genus *Homo*—and thus are different from all species assigned to *Australopithecus*.

The earliest appearance of genus *Homo* in East Africa may be as ancient as that of the robust australopithecines. (As we have discussed, the black skull from West Turkana has been dated to approximately 2.5 m.y.a.) Discoveries in the 1990s from central Kenya and from the Hadar area of Ethiopia suggest early *Homo* was present in East Africa by 2.4–2.3 m.y.a.

The presence of a **Plio-Pleistocene** hominid with a significantly larger brain than seen in *Australopithecus* was first suggested by Louis Leakey in the early 1960s on the basis of fragmentary remains found at Olduvai Gorge. Leakey and his colleagues gave a new species designation to these fossil remains, naming them ***Homo habilis***.

The *Homo habilis* material at Olduvai ranges in time from 1.85 m.y.a. for the earliest to about 1.6 m.y.a. for the latest. Due to the fragmentary nature of the fossil remains, interpretations have been difficult and much disputed. The most

See Virtual Lab 10 for a discussion of the evolution of the genus *Homo*.

Plio-Pleistocene Pertaining to the Pliocene and first half of the Pleistocene, a time range of 5–1 m.y.a. For this time period, many early fossil hominids have been found in Africa.

Homo habilis (hab´-ih-liss) A species of early *Homo*, well known from East Africa but perhaps also found in other regions.

(a)

(b)

figure 8–14 A nearly complete early *Homo* cranium from East Lake Turkana (ER 1470), one of the most important single fossil hominid discoveries from East Africa. (a) Frontal view (b) Lateral view.

immediately obvious feature distinguishing the *H. habilis* material from the australopithecines is cranial size. For all the measurable *H. habilis* skulls, the estimated average cranial capacity is 631 cm^3, compared to 520 cm^3 for all measurable robust australopithecines and 442 cm^3 for the less robust species (McHenry, 1988) (see Table 8–3). *Homo habilis*, therefore, shows an increase in cranial size of about 20 percent over the larger of the australopithecines and an even greater increase over some of the smaller-brained forms (from South Africa, discussed shortly). In their initial description of *H. habilis*, Leakey and his associates also pointed to differences from australopithecines in cranial shape and in tooth proportions (larger front teeth relative to back teeth and narrower premolars).

The naming of this fossil material as *Homo habilis* ("handy man") was meaningful from two perspectives. First of all, Leakey argued that members of this group were the early Olduvai toolmakers. Second, and most significantly, by calling this group *Homo*, Leakey was arguing for at least *two separate branches* of hominid evolution in the Plio-Pleistocene. Clearly, only one could be on the main branch eventually leading to *Homo sapiens*. By labeling this new group *Homo* rather than *Australopithecus*, Leakey was guessing that he had found our ancestors.

Because the initial evidence was so fragmentary, most paleoanthropologists were reluctant to accept *H. habilis* as a valid taxon distinct from *all* australopithecines. Later discoveries, especially from Lake Turkana, of better-preserved fossil material have shed further light on early *Homo* in the Plio-Pleistocene. The most important of this additional material is a nearly complete cranium discovered at Koobi Fora (fig. 8–14). With a cranial capacity of 775 cm^3, this individual is well outside the known range for australopithecines and actually overlaps the lower boundary for *Homo erectus*. In addition, the shape of the skull vault is in many respects unlike that of australopithecines. However, the face is still quite robust (Walker, 1976), and the fragments of tooth crowns that are preserved indicate that the back teeth in this individual were quite large. Dating of the Koobi Fora early *Homo* material places it contemporaneous with the Olduvai remains—that is, about 1.8–1.6 m.y.a.

On the basis of evidence from Olduvai and Koobi Fora, we can reasonably postulate that one or more species of early *Homo* were present in East Africa probably by 2.4 m.y.a., developing in parallel with at least one line of australopithecines. These two hominid lines lived contemporaneously for a minimum of 1 million years, after which the australopithecine lineage apparently disappeared forever. At the same time, probably the early *Homo* line was evolving into a later form, *Homo erectus*, which in turn developed into *H. sapiens*.

South African Hominids

Earliest Discoveries

The first quarter of the twentieth century saw the discipline of paleoanthropology in its scientific infancy. Informed opinions considered the likely origins of the human family to be in Asia, where fossil forms of a primitive kind of *Homo* had been found in Indonesia in the 1890s. Europe was also considered a center of hominid evolution, for spectacular discoveries there of archaic *Homo sapiens* (including the famous Neandertals) and millions of stone tools had come to light, particularly in the early 1900s.

Few scholars would have given much credence to Darwin's prediction:

> In each region of the world the living mammals are closely related to the extinct species of the same region. It is, therefore, probable that Africa was formally inhabited by extinct apes closely allied to the gorilla and chimpanzee, and as these two species are now man's nearest allies, it is somewhat more probable that our early progenitors lived on the African continent than elsewhere. (Darwin, *The Descent of Man*, 1871)

figure 8–15 Raymond Dart, shown working in his laboratory.

Moreover, it would be many more decades before the East African discoveries would come to light. It was in such an atmosphere of preconceived biases that the discoveries of a young Australian-born anatomist were to jolt the foundations of the scientific community in the 1920s. Raymond Dart (fig. 8–15) arrived in South Africa in 1923 at the age of 30 to take up a teaching position in Johannesburg. Fresh from his evolution-oriented training in England, Dart had developed a keen interest in human evolution. Consequently, he was well prepared when startling new evidence began to appear at his very doorstep.

The first clue came in 1924, when Dart received a shipment of fossils from the commercial limeworks quarry at Taung (200 miles southwest of Johannesburg). He immediately recognized something that was quite unusual, a natural **endocast** of a higher primate. The endocast fit into another limestone block containing the fossilized front portion of the skull, face, and lower jaw (fig. 8–16). However, these were difficult to see clearly, for the bone was hardened into a cemented limestone matrix. Dart patiently chiseled away for weeks, later describing the task:

Endocast A solid impression of the inside of the skull, often preserving details relating to the size and surface features of the brain.

> No diamond cutter ever worked more lovingly or with such care on a precious jewel—nor, I am sure, with such inadequate tools. But on the seventy-third day, December 23, the rock parted. I could view the face from the front, although the right side was still imbedded. . . . What emerged was a baby's face, an infant with a full set of milk teeth and its permanent molars just in the process of erupting. I doubt if there was any parent prouder of his offspring than I was of my Taung baby on that Christmas. (Dart, 1959, p. 10)

As indicated by the formation and eruption of the teeth, the Taung child was probably about three to four years old. Interestingly, the rate of development of this and many other Plio-Pleistocene hominids was more like that of apes than of modern *Homo* (Bromage and Dean, 1985). Dart's initial impression that this form was a hominoid was confirmed when he could observe the face and teeth more clearly. However, as it turned out, it took considerably more effort before the teeth could be seen completely, since Dart worked for four years to separate the upper and lower jaws.

figure 8–16 The Taung child, discovered in 1924. The endocast is in back, with the fossilized bone mandible and face in front.

But Dart was convinced long before he had an unimpeded view of the dentition that this discovery was a remarkable one, an early hominoid from South Africa. The question was, What kind of hominoid? Dart realized that it was extremely improbable that this specimen could have been a forest ape, for South Africa has had a relatively dry climate for millions of years.

If not an ape, then what was it? Features of the skull and teeth of this small child held clues that Dart seized on almost immediately. The *foramen magnum* at the base of the skull (see fig. 8–7) was farther forward in the Taung skull than in modern great apes, though not as much as in modern humans. From this fact Dart concluded that the head was balanced *above* the spine, indicating erect posture. In addition, the forehead did not recede as much as in apes, the milk canines were exceedingly small, and the newly erupted permanent molars were very large, broad teeth. In all these respects, the Taung fossil was more akin to hominids than to apes. There was, however, a disturbing feature that was to confuse many scientists for several years: The brain was quite small. More recent studies have estimated the Taung child's brain size at approximately 405 cm^3 (which translates to a full adult estimate of 440 cm^3), not very large (for a hominid) when compared to modern great apes (see Table 8–3).

The estimated cranial capacity of the Taung fossil falls within the range of modern great apes, and gorillas actually average about 10 percent greater. It must, however, be remembered that gorillas are very large animals, whereas the Taung specimen derives from a population where adults may have averaged less than 80 pounds. Since brain size is partially correlated with body size, comparing such differently sized animals is unjustified. A more meaningful comparison would be with the bonobo (*Pan paniscus*), whose body weight is comparable. Bonobos have adult cranial capacities averaging 356 cm^3 for males and 329 cm^3 for females, and thus the Taung child, versus a *comparably sized* ape, displays a 25 percent increase in cranial capacity.

Despite the relatively small size of the brain, Dart saw that the Taung fossil was no ape. Realizing the immense importance of his findings, Dart promptly reported them in the British scientific weekly *Nature* on February 7, 1925—a bold venture, since Dart, only 32, was presumptuously proposing an entirely new view of human evolution. The small-brained Taung child was christened by Dart ***Australopithecus africanus*** (southern ape of Africa), which he saw as a kind of halfway "missing link" between modern apes and humans. This concept of a single "missing link" was a fallacious one, but Dart correctly emphasized the hominid-like features of the fossil.

Not all scientists were ready for such a theory from such an "unlikely" place. Hence, Dart's report was received with indifference, disbelief, and even caustic scorn. Dart realized that more complete remains were needed. The skeptical world would not accept the evidence of one partial immature individual, no matter how suggestive the clues. Most scientists in the 1920s regarded this little Taung child as an interesting aberrant form of ape. Clearly, more fossil evidence was needed, particularly adult crania (since these would show more diagnostic features). Not an experienced fossil hunter himself, Dart sought further assistance in the search for more australopithecines.

Further Discoveries of South African Hominids

Soon after publication of his controversial theories, Dart found a strong ally in Robert Broom (fig. 8–17). From two of Dart's students, Broom learned of another commercial limeworks site, called **Sterkfontein,** not far from Johannesburg (and now, counting the more recent discoveries, the most prolific of South African sites; Table 8–5). Here, as at Taung, the quarrying involved blasting out large sections with dynamite, leaving piles of debris that often con-

Australopithecus africanus
(os-tral-oh-pith´-e-kus af-ri-kan´-us)

figure 8–17 Robert Broom.

Sterkfontein (sterk´-fon-tane)

TABLE 8-5	In Summary: Key South African Pliocene and Early Pleistocene Hominid Discoveries		
Site	Dates (m.y.a.)	Taxonomic Designation	Fossil Sample
Swartkrans	1.8–1.0	*Australopithecus robustus* (also called *Paranthropus*); early *Homo*	About 200 specimens; best sample of South African robust australopithecines
Drimolen	2.0–1.5	*Australopithecus (Paranthropus) robustus*	79 specimens, including most complete australopithecine cranium from anywhere
Taung	3.0–2.0??	*Australopithecus africanus*	1 individual; first early hominid found in Africa
Sterkfontein	3.3–2.6	*Australopithecus africanus;* early *Homo?; Homo erectus* (also called *Homo ergaster*)	More than 700 specimens (the most prolific early hominid site in South Africa—and perhaps in all of Africa); many teeth; several well-preserved crania; 4 partial skeletons

tained fossilized remains. Accordingly, Broom asked the quarry manager to keep his eyes open for fossils, and when Broom returned to the site in August 1936, the manager asked, "Is this what you are looking for?" Indeed it was, for Broom held in his hand the endocast of an adult australopithecine—exactly what he had set out to find! Looking further over the scattered debris, Broom was able to find most of the rest of the skull of the same individual.

Such remarkable success, just a few months after beginning his search, was not the end of Broom's luck, for his magical touch was to continue unabated for several more years. In the 1930s and 1940s, Broom discovered two other hominid sites, including **Swartkrans,** the second most productive of all South African Plio-Pleistocene locales (it has since yielded hundreds of fossils). Numerous extremely important discoveries came from these additional sites, discoveries that would eventually swing the tide of intellectual thought to the views that Dart expressed back in 1925.

Since the 1970s, more systematic exploration of the South African hominid sites has continued, and numerous important discoveries have been made. The most spectacular new find was made in 1997 at Sterkfontein, where the remains of a virtually complete australopithecine skeleton were found by Ron Clarke and his associates from the University of Witwatersrand (fig. 8–18). Most of the remains are still embedded in the surrounding limestone matrix and may require years for removal, cleaning, and reconstruction (Clarke, 1998).

As we will discuss in more detail shortly, dating of all the South African Plio-Pleistocene sites has proved most difficult; estimates for the Sterkfontein australopithecine skeleton are between 3.6 and 2.5 m.y.a. Even before the remains have been fully excavated, this is still recognized as an unusual and highly significant find. Because such complete individuals are so rare in the hominid fossil record, this discovery has tremendous potential to shed more light on the precise nature of early hominid locomotion. For example, will the rest of the skeleton confirm what foot bones of the same individual have implied regarding arboreal climbing in this bipedal hominid (see p. 198)? Moreover, relative proportion of brain size to body size, better estimates of overall body size, relative proportions of the limbs, and much more can be more accurately assessed from such a completely preserved skeleton.

Swartkrans (swart´-kranz)

Robert Jurmain

figure 8–18 Australopithecine skeleton embedded in limestone matrix at Sterkfontein. Much of the skeleton still is not visible. Clearly seen are the cranium (with articulated mandible) and part of an upper limb.

Transvaal Museum, South Africa

figure 8–19 A gracile australopithecine cranium from Sterkfontein (Sts 5). Discovered in 1947, this specimen is the best-preserved gracile skull yet found in South Africa.

Review of Hominids from South Africa

The Plio-Pleistocene hominid discoveries from South Africa are most significant. First, they were the initial hominid discoveries in Africa and helped point the way to later finds in East Africa. Second, morphology of the South African hominids shows broad similarities to the forms in East Africa, but with several distinctive features, which argues for separation at least at the species level. Finally, there is a large assemblage of hominid fossils from South Africa, and exciting discoveries are still being made (fig. 8–19).

Further discoveries are also coming from entirely new sites. In the 1990s, the site known as Drimolen was found in South Africa, very near to Sterkfontein and Swartkrans (Keyser, 2000). While only provisionally published thus far, we do know that close to 80 specimens have been recovered—including the most complete *Australopithecus* cranium found anywhere in Africa.

A truly remarkable collection of early hominids, the remains from South Africa, coming from nine different caves, exceed 1,000 (counting all isolated teeth as separate items), and the number of individuals is now more than 200 (see Table 8–5). From an evolutionary point of view, the most meaningful remains are those of the pelvis, which now include portions of nine ossa coxae (see p. 183). Remains of the pelvis are so important because, better than any other area of the body, this structure displays the unique requirements of a bipedal animal (as in modern humans *and* in our hominid forebears).

"ROBUST" AUSTRALOPITHECINES   In addition to the discoveries in East Africa, there are also numerous finds of robust australopithecines in South Africa. Like their East African cousins, the South African robust forms also have small cranial capacities. (The only measurable specimen equals 530 cm^3; the Drimolen cranium is smaller and might come from a female, but no cranial measurements have as yet been published.) They also possess large broad faces and very large premolars and molars (although not as massive as in East Africa). Owing to the differences in dental proportions, as well as important differences in facial architecture (Rak, 1983), most researchers now agree that there is a species-level difference between the later East African robust variety and the South African group.

Despite these differences, all members of the robust lineage appear to be specialized for a diet made up of hard food items, such as seeds and nuts. For many years, paleoanthropologists (e.g., Robinson, 1972) had speculated that robust australopithecines concentrated their diet on heavier vegetable foods than those seen in the diet of other early hominids. More recent research that included examining microscopic polishes and scratches on the teeth (Kay and Grine, 1988) has confirmed this view.

"GRACILE" AUSTRALOPITHECINES   Another variety of australopithecine (also small-brained, but not as large-toothed as the robust varieties) is known from Africa. However, while the robust lineage is represented in both East and South Africa, this other (gracile) australopithecine form is known only from the southern part of the continent. First named *A. africanus* by Dart for the single individual at Taung, this australopithecine is also found at other sites, especially Sterkfontein (figs. 8–19 and 8–20).

Traditionally, it had been thought that there was a significant variation in body size between the gracile and robust forms. But as mentioned earlier and

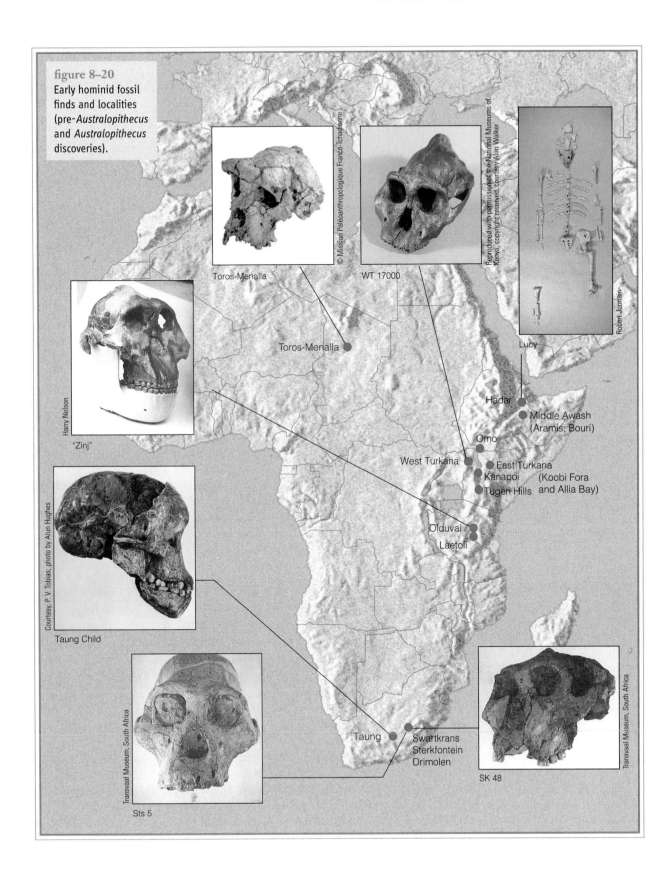

figure 8–20
Early hominid fossil finds and localities (pre-*Australopithecus* and *Australopithecus* discoveries).

Toros-Menalla

© Mission Paléoanthropologique Franco-Tchadienne

WT 17000

Reproduced with permission of the National Museums of Kenya, copyright reserved, courtesy Alan Walker

Robert Jurmain

Lucy

Harry Nelson

"Zinj"

Courtesy, P. V. Tobias; photo by Alun Hughes

Taung Child

Toros-Menalla

Hadar
Middle Awash (Aramis; Bouri)
Omo
West Turkana
East Turkana
Kanapoi   (Koobi Fora
Tugen Hills   and Allia Bay)
Olduvai
Laetoli

Taung
Swartkrans
Sterkfontein
Drimolen

Transvaal Museum, South Africa

Sts 5

Transvaal Museum, South Africa

SK 48

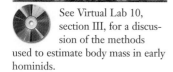

See Virtual Lab 10, section III, for a discussion of the methods used to estimate body mass in early hominids.

TABLE 8-6	Estimated Body Weights and Stature in Plio-Pleistocene Hominids			
	Body Weight		Stature	
	Male	Female	Male	Female
A. afarensis	45 kg (99 lb)	29 kg (64 lb)	151 cm (59 in.)	105 cm (41 in.)
A. africanus	41 kg (90 lb)	30 kg (65 lb)	138 cm (54 in.)	115 cm (45 in.)
South African "robust"	40 kg (88 lb)	32 kg (70 lb)	132 cm (52 in.)	110 cm (43 in.)
East African "robust"	49 kg (108 lb)	34 kg (75 lb)	137 cm (54 in.)	124 cm (49 in.)
H. habilis	52 kg (114 lb)	32 kg (70 lb)	157 cm (62 in.)	125 cm (49 in.)

Source: After McHenry, 1992.

shown in Table 8–6, there is not much difference in body size among the australopithecines. In fact, most of the differences between the robust and gracile forms are found in the face and dentition.

The facial structure of the gracile australopithecines is more lightly built and somewhat dish-shaped compared to the more vertical configuration seen in robust specimens. But the most distinctive difference observed between gracile and robust australopithecines is in the dentition. Compared to modern humans, they both have relatively large teeth, which are, however, definitely hominid in pattern. In fact, more emphasis is on the typical back-tooth grinding complex among these early forms than is seen in modern humans; therefore, if anything, australopithecines are "hyperhominid" in their dentition. (In other words, they are dentally more *derived* than are modern humans.) Robust forms emphasize this trend to an extreme degree, showing deep jaws and much-enlarged back teeth, particularly the molars, leaving little room in the front of the mouth for the anterior teeth (incisors and canines). These differences in the relative proportions of the teeth and jaws best define a gracile, as compared to a robust, australopithecine (fig. 8–21). In fact, most of the differences in skull shape we have discussed can be directly attributed to contrasting jaw function in the two forms. Both the sagittal crest and broad vertical face of the robust form are related to the muscles and biomechanical requirements of the heavy back-tooth chewing adaptation seen in this animal.

EARLY *HOMO* IN SOUTH AFRICA   As in East Africa, early members of the genus *Homo* have also been found in South Africa, apparently living contemporaneously with australopithecines. At both Sterkfontein and Swartkrans, and perhaps Drimolen as well, fragmentary remains have been recognized as most likely belonging to *Homo*. In fact, Ron Clarke (1985) has shown that the key fossil of early *Homo* from Sterkfontein (Stw 53) is nearly identical to the OH 24 *Homo habilis* cranium from Olduvai.

However, a problem with both OH 24 and Stw 53 is that while most experts agree that they belong to the genus *Homo*, there is considerable disagreement as to whether they should be included in the species *habilis*. The relationships of the Plio-Pleistocene fossil hominids to one another and the difficulties of such genus and species interpretation will be discussed in the following sections. A time line for the Plio-Pleistocene hominids discussed in the text is shown in figure 8–22.

figure 8–21 Morphology and variation of robust australopithecines. (Note both the typical features and the range of variation as shown in different specimens.)

Sagittal crest

Postorbital constriction

ER 406 (Koobi Fora) Superior view

WT 17000 (West Turkana)

Small incisor and canine teeth

Broad cheekbones (zygomatics)

OH 5 ("Zinj;" Olduvai)

SK 48 (Swartkrans)

Large backwardly extending zygomatic arch

Very large molar teeth

ER 732 (Koobi Fora)

ER 729 (Koobi Fora)

Note: The size and proportions of this specimen differ from ER 406 and OH 5 (above), and this individual has been suggested as a female A. boisei.

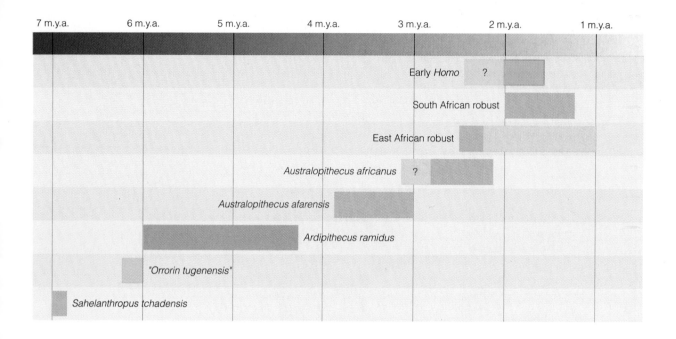

figure 8–22 Time line of early hominids. Note that most dates are approximations. Question marks indicate those estimates that are most tentative.

Interpretations: What Does It All Mean?

By this time, it may seem that anthropologists are obsessed with finding small scraps buried in the ground and then assigning them confusing numbers and taxonomic labels impossible to remember. We must realize that the collection of all the basic fossil data is the foundation of human evolutionary research. Without fossils, our speculations would be completely hollow. Several large, ongoing paleoanthropological projects are now collecting additional data in an attempt to answer some of the more perplexing questions about our evolutionary history.

The numbering of specimens, which may at times seem somewhat confusing, is an attempt to keep the designations neutral and to make reference to each individual fossil as clear as possible. The formal naming of finds as *Australopithecus, Homo habilis,* or *Homo erectus* should come much later, since it involves a lengthy series of complex interpretations. Assigning generic and specific names to fossil finds is more than just a convenience; when we attach a particular label, such as *A. africanus,* to a particular fossil, we should be fully aware of the biological implications of such an interpretation.

From the time that fossil sites are first located to the eventual interpretation of hominid evolutionary events, several steps are necessary. Ideally, they should follow a logical order, for if interpretations are made too hastily, they confuse important issues for many years. Here is a reasonable sequence:

1. Selecting and surveying sites
2. Excavating sites and recovering fossil hominids
3. Designating individual finds with specimen numbers for clear reference
4. Cleaning, preparing, studying, and describing fossils

5. Comparing with other fossil material—in chronological framework if possible
6. Comparing fossil variation with known ranges of variation in closely related groups of living primates and analyzing ancestral and derived characteristics
7. Assigning taxonomic names to fossil material

The task of interpretation is still not complete, for what we really want to know in the long run is what happened to the populations represented by the fossil remains. Indeed, in looking at the fossil hominid record, we are looking for our ancestors. In the process of eventually determining those populations that are our most likely antecedents, we may conclude that some hominids are on evolutionary side branches. If this conclusion is accurate, those hominids necessarily must have become extinct. It is both interesting and relevant to us as hominids to try to find out what influenced some earlier members of our family to continue evolving while others died out.

Continuing Uncertainties—Taxonomic Issues

As previously discussed, paleoanthropologists are concerned with making biological interpretations of variation found in the hominid fossil record. Most especially, researchers endeavor to assign extinct forms to particular genera and species. We saw that for the diverse array of Miocene hominoids, the evolutionary picture is exceptionally complex. As new finds accumulate, there is continued uncertainty even as to family assignment, to say nothing of genus and species!

For the very end of the Miocene and for the Plio-Pleistocene, the situation is considerably clearer. First, there is a larger fossil sample from a more restricted geographical area (south, central, and east Africa) and from a more concentrated time period (spanning about 6 million years, from 7 to 1 m.y.a.). Second, more complete specimens exist (e.g., Lucy), and we thus have good evidence for most parts of the body. Accordingly, there is considerable consensus on several basic aspects of evolutionary development during the Plio-Pleistocene. For materials prior to 4 m.y.a., not all scholars are as yet convinced of clear hominid status. However, for fossils dating later than 4 m.y.a., researchers agree unanimously that these forms are hominids (members of the family Hominidae). And as support for this point, all these forms are seen as habitual, well-adapted bipeds, committed at least in part to a terrestrial niche. Moreover, researchers generally agree as to genus-level assignments for most of the forms, although *Sahelanthropus, Orrorin,* and *Ardipithecus* have all been so recently named as to not yet be fully evaluated and accepted (there is also some disagreement regarding how to group the robust australopithecines).

As for species-level designations, little consensus can be found. Indeed, as new fossils have been discovered, the picture seems to muddy further. Once again, we are faced with a complex evolutionary process. In attempts to deal with it, we impose varying degrees of simplicity. In so doing, we hope that the evolutionary processes will become clearer—not just for introductory students, but for professional paleoanthropologists and textbook authors as well! Nevertheless, evolution is not a simple process, and disputes and disagreements are bound to arise, especially in making such fine-tuned interpretations as species-level designations.

It may prove impossible to work out clear patterns of relationships among the early hominids. Despite our best attempts, the number and complexity of hominid groups (more technically called *taxa*), which seem to increase monthly, may frustrate all attempts at simplification.

One particularly difficult obstacle is the varied combination of anatomical characteristics, seen especially in the earliest suggested members of the hominid family. For example, *Sahelanthropus* has a very primitive-looking braincase (especially in the back) combined with a fairly advanced hominid-looking face and canine teeth. Similarly, *Orrorin* combines what some claim are very chimpanzee-looking teeth with a highly efficient bipedal gait. Lastly, *Ardipithecus* combines some aspects of primitive-looking teeth with other components of a suggested bipedal gait. Moreover, from preliminary conclusions by some researchers familiar with the *Ardipithecus* finds, the manner of locomotion is thought to have been very different from any other hominid (suggesting it might have been a very derived hominid and thus an unlikely ancestor of later forms).

Fueled by all these admittedly confusing combinations of characteristics is the suspicion by some researchers (e.g., Bernard Wood, 2002) that roughly similar characteristics (like some form of bipedality or reduction of the canine teeth) could have evolved more than once—that is, separately in different lineages of hominids (or possibly even in other hominoids closely related to hominids). This evolutionary process results from what we have called *homoplasy* (see p. 157). If, indeed, this inherently messy evolutionary factor was widespread among our late Miocene and Pliocene relatives, it may prove almost impossible to discern which forms are related to others and which ones are more closely related to us. Worse yet, it may prove extremely tricky even to be able to identify some of these forms as hominids at all.

Putting It All Together

Despite all the difficulties, paleoanthropologists still want to understand the broad patterns of early hominid evolution. The interpretation of our paleontological past in terms of which fossils are related to other fossils and how they might be related to modern humans is usually shown diagrammatically in the form of a **phylogeny.** Such a diagram is a family tree of fossil evolution. (Note that strict practitioners of cladistics prefer to use cladograms; see pp. 158–159.) This kind of interpretation is the eventual goal of evolutionary studies, but it is the final goal, only after adequate data are available to understand what is going on.

Phylogeny A schematic representation showing ancestor-descendant relationships, usually in a chronological framework.

Another, more basic way to handle these data is to divide the fossil material into subsets. This avoids (for the moment) what are still problematic phylogenetic relationships. Accordingly, for the Plio-Pleistocene hominid material from Africa, we can divide the data into three broad groupings:

Set I. Pre-*Australopithecus*/basal hominids (7.0–4.4 m.y.a.)   The earliest (and most primitive) collection of remains that have been classified as hominids are those from Toros-Menalla, the Tugen Hills, and the Middle Awash, the latter area also including the site of Aramis. These fossils have, for the moment, been assigned to three separate (and newly proposed) genera: *Sahelanthropus*, *Orrorin*, and *Ardipithecus* and are hence each provisionally interpreted as being generically distinct from all the other early hominid forms (listed in sets II and

III). Analysis thus far indicates that at least for the later Aramis fossils, these forms were likely bipedal, but with a primitive dentition. Brain size of *A. ramidus* is not yet known, but was almost certainly quite small.

Set II. *Australopithecus*

Subset A. Early primitive forms (4.2–3.0 m.y.a.) This grouping comprises one well-known species, *A. afarensis*, especially well documented at Laetoli and Hadar. Slightly earlier, closely related forms (perhaps representing a distinct second species) come from two other sites and are provisionally called "*Australopithecus anamensis*." Best known from analysis of the *A. afarensis* material, the hominids in this set are characterized by a small brain, large teeth (front and back), and a bipedal gait (probably still allowing for considerable climbing).

Subset B. Later, more derived *Australopithecus* (2.5–1.4 m.y.a.; possibly as early as 3.5 m.y.a.) This group is composed of numerous species. (Most experts recognize at least three; some subdivide this material into five or more species.) Remains have come from several sites in both South and East Africa. All of these forms have very large back teeth and do not show appreciable brain enlargement (i.e., encephalization) compared to *A. afarensis*.

Set III. Early *Homo* (2.4–1.8 m.y.a.) The best-known specimens are from East Africa (East Turkana and Olduvai), but early remains of *Homo* have also been found in South Africa (Swartkrans and possibly Sterkfontein and Drimolen). This group is composed of possibly just one, but probably more than one, species. Early *Homo* is characterized (compared to *Australopithecus*) by greater encephalization, altered cranial shape, and smaller (especially molars) and narrower (especially premolars) teeth.

Although hominid fossil evidence has accumulated in great abundance, the fact that so much of the material has been discovered so recently makes any firm judgments concerning the route of human evolution premature. However, paleoanthropologists are certainly not deterred from making their "best guesses," and diverse hypotheses have abounded in recent years. The vast majority of the hundreds of recently discovered fossils from Africa is still in the descriptive and early analytical stages. At this time, the construction of phylogenies of human evolution is analogous to building a house with only a partial blueprint. We are not even sure how many rooms there are! Until the existing fossil evidence has been adequately studied, to say nothing about possible new finds, speculative hypotheses must be viewed with a critical eye.

Summary

 n figure 8–23, we present a simplified scheme showing tentative relationships among the early African fossil hominids discussed in this chapter. Question marks indicate those relationships that are most tentative, particularly obvious for all the earliest material (the pre-*Australopithecus* fossils, dated prior to 4 m.y.a.). Indeed, at present, with all this material so recently discovered and seemingly displaying highly complex patterns of hominid evolution, it is unwise to make anything but the most general of hypotheses.

figure 8–23 A very tentative phylogenetic reconstruction of early hominid evolution.

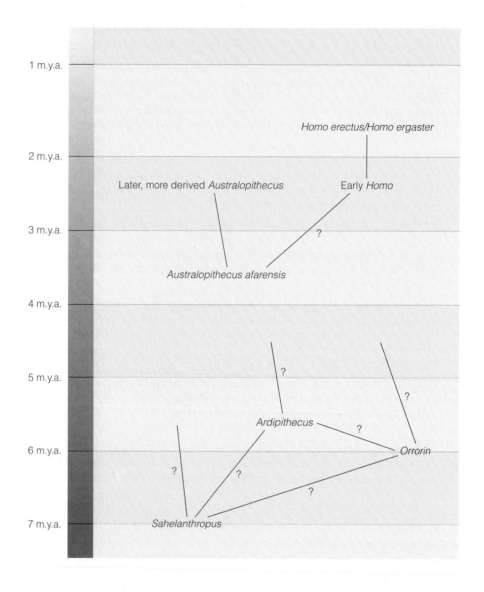

The picture after 4 m.y.a. is somewhat clearer. It appears, for the moment, that *Australopithecus afarensis* still can be viewed as a good potential common ancestor of most (if not all) later hominids. The relationships among the later, more derived australopithecines are not as clear, nor is it certain which of the earlier Pliocene fossils is most closely related to *Homo*. As a further study aid, Table 8–7 presents the early hominid materials we consider the most significant. For those keen to pursue a more detailed evaluation of the early hominids, see Appendix B.

Science is a journey of discovery, seeking to find as many documented facts as possible. Science is also a search for clarity. The last few years of paleoanthropological research have emmensely enriched our record of facts. The search for clarity continues. No doubt, more discoveries are in the offing. We certainly live in interesting times.

TABLE 8-7	Chronological Summary of Most Significant Hominid Fossils Discussed in this Chapter			
Epoch	**Site**	**Dates (m.y.a.)**	**Taxonomic Designation**	**Comments**
Plio-Pleistocene	East Turkana (Koobi Fora) and Olduvai	1.8–1.0	Derived *Australopithecus* and early *Homo*	Highly derived *Australopithecus* and first relatively complete fossils of early *Homo*
	Taung and Sterkfontein	3.3–2.0?	*Australopithecus africanus*	Best-known early hominid from South Africa; many well-preserved fossils
	Hadar and Laetoli	3.7–3.0	*Australopithecus afarensis*	Earliest well-documented group of early hominids; potentially ancestral to later *Australopithecus* and early *Homo*
	Aramis	4.4	*Ardipithecus ramidus*	Earliest large sample of hominid fossils; not yet well described; likely shows very unusual mosaic of characteristics (some highly derived)
Miocene	Toros-Menalla	~7.0	*Sahelanthropus*	Earliest proposed hominid fossils; unusual mosaic of characteristics

Questions for Review

1. (a) Why is postcranial evidence (particularly the lower limb) so crucial in showing the australopithecines (or other early forms) as definite hominids? (b) What particular aspects of the australopithecine pelvis and lower limb are hominid-like?
2. In what ways are the remains of *Sahelanthropus* and *Ardipithecus* primitive? How do we know that these forms are hominids? How sure are we?
3. Why are some Plio-Pleistocene hominids from East Africa called "early *Homo*" (or *H. habilis*)? What does this imply for the evolutionary relationships of the australopithecines?
4. Why is the dating control better in East Africa than in South Africa?
5. Discuss the first thing you would do if you found an early hominid fossil and were responsible for its formal description and publication. What would you include in your publication?
6. Discuss two current disputes regarding taxonomic issues concerning early hominids. Try to give support for alternative positions.
7. Why would one use the taxonomic term *Paranthropus* in contrast to *Australopithecus?*
8. What is a phylogeny? Construct one for early hominids (7.0–1 m.y.a.). Make sure you can describe what conclusions your scheme makes. Also, try to defend it.
9. What are the most recently discovered of the earliest hominid materials, and how are they, for the moment, incorporated into a phylogenetic scheme? How secure do you think this interpretation is?

Suggested Further Readings

Agnew, Neville and Martha Demas. 1998. "Preserving the Laetoli Footprints." *Scientific American* 279(3): 44–57.

Conroy, Glenn C. 1997. *Reconstructing Human Origins. A Modern Synthesis.* New York: Norton.

Corruccini, Robert S., and Russel L. Ciochon (eds.). 1994. *Integrative Paths to the Past: Paleoanthropology Advances in Honor of F. Clark Howell.* Englewood Cliffs, NJ: Prentice Hall.

Delson, Eric (ed.). 1985. *Ancestors: The Hard Evidence.* New York: Liss.

Grine, Fred (ed.). 1988. *Evolutionary History of the Robust Australopithecines.* New York: Aldine de Gruyter.

Rak, Yoel. 1983. *The Australopithecine Face.* New York: Academic Press.

Tattersall, Ian. 2000. "Once We Were Not Alone." *Scientific American* 282(1): 56–62.

Wolpoff, Milford H. 1999. *Paleoanthropology.* 2nd ed. Boston: McGraw-Hill.

Multimedia Resources

 Companion Web Site

Anthropology Online: The Wadsworth Anthropology Resource Center
Visit **http://anthropology.wadsworth.com** and click on the Companion Web Site for Jurmain/Kilgore/Trevathan/Nelson's *Essentials of Physical Anthropology,* Fifth Edition, to access a wide range of enrichment material to aid in your study of anthropology. Among the useful options for each chapter's self-study are learning objectives, flashcards, Internet exercises, Web links, InfoTrac College Edition exercises, and practice quizzes that can be scored and emailed to your instructor.

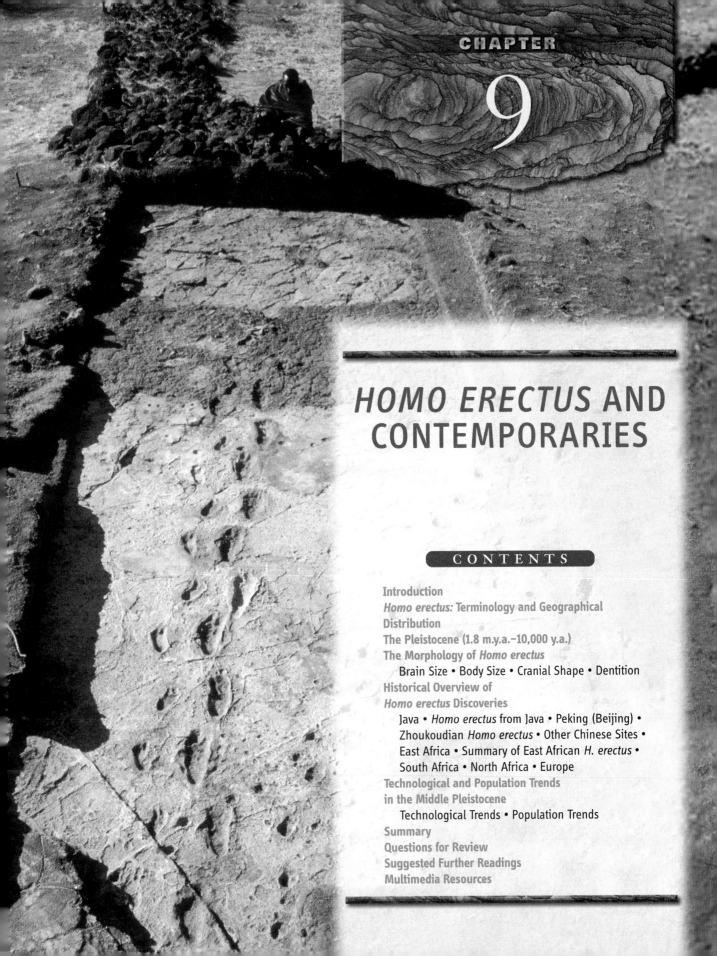

HOMO ERECTUS AND CONTEMPORARIES

CONTENTS

See the following sections of the CD-ROM for topics covered in this chapter: Virtual Lab 10.

Introduction

In Chapter 8, we traced the earliest evidence of hominid evolution by reviewing the abundant fossil material from Africa that documents the origins of *Australopithecus*, *Homo*, and earlier forms, dating from the late Miocene and extending up through the Pliocene and early Pleistocene. In this chapter, we take up what might be called the next stage of hominid evolution, the appearance and dispersal of *Homo erectus* (see fig. 9–2).

Homo erectus was a widely distributed species and was in fact the first hominid (for which we have definite evidence) to have expanded into vast new regions of the Old World (although it now appears that the first hominid migrants to leave Africa were perhaps a form of early *Homo* or, alternatively, an early, primitive, form of *Homo erectus*). Moreover, as a species, *H. erectus* existed over an exceptionally long time, spanning well over 1 million years. If one judges species success by longevity, *H. erectus* appears to be the most successful hominid that has ever existed. How can we explain the remarkable success of this species?

In this chapter, we discuss many of the physical changes that characterized *H. erectus*, especially as compared to what came before (early *Homo*) and after (*Homo sapiens*). Certainly, some of the physical alterations, such as increased brain size, larger body size, and dental modifications, help account for the success of *H. erectus*. But that is not the whole story. As we have emphasized, hominid evolution has long been characterized by a biocultural interaction. Thus, it is only through explaining the behavioral capacities of *Homo erectus* (in concert with morphological change) that we can understand the success of this hominid species. For this reason, we also highlight some of the abundant archaeological evidence and related biocultural reconstructions that have so long occupied and fascinated paleoanthropologists.

Homo erectus: *Terminology and Geographical Distribution*

The discoveries of fossils now referred to as *H. erectus* go back to the nineteenth century. Later in this chapter, we will discuss in some detail the historical background of these earliest discoveries in Java and the somewhat later discoveries in China. From this work, as well as presumably related finds in Europe and North Africa, a variety of taxonomic names were suggested. The most significant of these earlier terms were *Pithecanthropus* (for the Javanese remains) and *Sinanthropus* (for the fossils from northern China).

It is important to realize that taxonomic *splitting* (which this terminology reflects) was quite common in the early years of paleoanthropology. Only after World War II and with the incorporation of the Modern Synthesis into paleontology (see p. 76) did more systematic biological thinking come to the fore. Most of the fossils previously given these varied names are today placed within the species *Homo erectus*.

Discoveries in the last few decades have established *well-dated* finds of *H. erectus* in East Africa from geological contexts chronometrically dated as old as 1.8 m.y.a. In addition, new dates first published in 1994 by geologists from the Berkeley Geochronology Laboratory (Swisher et al., 1994) have suggested that two localities in Java are as old as those in East Africa (with dates of 1.8 and 1.6 m.y.a.). These early dates have come as somewhat of a surprise to many paleoanthropologists, but as you will see, there is now growing evidence for an early dispersal of hominids outside of Africa—that is, one *well before* 1 m.y.a.

See Virtual Lab 10 for an interactive map showing the distribution of *Homo erectus.*

Current interpretations thus view the first hominid dispersal out of Africa as occurring between 1.5 and 2 m.y.a. A likely route would have taken these hominids through southwestern Asia, and there are some intriguing hints from a site in Israel that this route was indeed exploited quite early on. The most conclusive evidence from Israel is archaeological, including a number of stone tools dated (by paleomagnetism and faunal correlation) to 1.4–1.3 m.y.a. In addition, there are some fragmentary hominid remains, including cranial pieces and two teeth. Unfortunately, the association of these hominid remains with the tools at a date prior to 1 m.y.a. is uncertain. Consequently, there is not yet *definitive* fossil evidence of *H. erectus* (or a close relative) from southwest Asia. Nevertheless, these archaeological discoveries are highly suggestive and fit with the overall emerging pattern of an early hominid dispersal from Africa.

More than likely, these first continental migrants were members of *H. erectus* or a group closely related to *H. erectus* (although an earlier dispersal of an even more primitive member of genus *Homo* cannot be ruled out). The most significant early finds of hominids in Europe (indeed perhaps the earliest finds anywhere outside of Africa) come from the Dmanisi site in the Republic of Georgia (fig. 9–1). Dating to more than 1.7 m.y.a., these fossils (including three recently discovered crania) are in some ways similar to their African cousins and together might represent a species that is closely related to but different from *Homo erectus* (see p. 234 for further discussion). Another recent find pushing back the antiquity of hominids in western Europe has come from the 500,000-year-old Boxgrove site in southern England, where a hominid tibia (shinbone) was unearthed in 1994. And still another recent find (1994), from the Ceprano site in central Italy, may be the best evidence yet of *H. erectus* in Europe (Ascenzi et al., 1996). Provisional dating of a partial cranium from this important site suggests a date greater than 700,000 years ago. The primary researchers, as well as Rightmire (1998), conclude that cranial morphology places this specimen quite close to *H. erectus.*

Courtesy, Professor Günter Bräuer

figure 9–1 Dmanisi mandible.

Finally, some other fossil remains from Spain, also discovered in 1994 and announced in 1995, may well be the oldest hominids yet found in western Europe (see fig. 9–2 for locations of these hominid sites). From the Gran Dolina site in the highly productive Atapuerca region of northern Spain, where numerous, somewhat more recent hominid fossils have also been discovered (discussed in Chapter 10), several fragments of at least four individuals have been found (Carbonell et al., 1995). The dating, based on paleomagnetic determinations (see p. 189), places the Gran Dolina hominids at approximately 780,000 y.a.* (Parés and Pérez-González, 1995). If this dating is further corroborated, these early Spanish finds would be *at least* 250,000 years older than any other hominid yet discovered in western Europe. Because all the 36 pieces thus far identified are quite fragmentary, the taxonomic assignment of these fossils still remains problematic. Initial analysis, however, suggests that most of the European fossils are *not H. erectus.* Whether any of these early European hominids, except perhaps for the Ceprano cranium, belong within the species *Homo erectus* thus still remains to be determined.

---

*y.a. stands for "years ago."

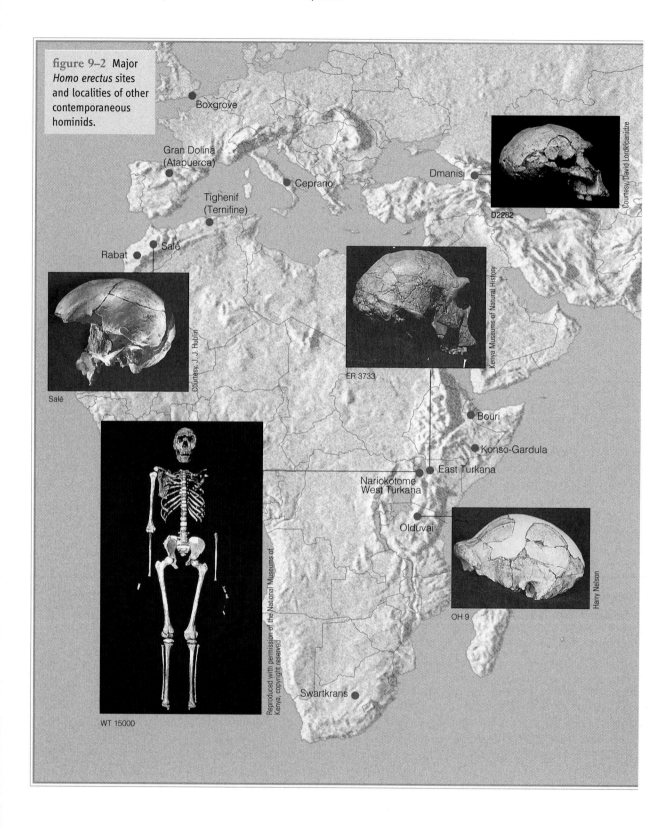

figure 9–2 Major *Homo erectus* sites and localities of other contemporaneous hominids.

Boxgrove

Gran Dolina (Atapuerca)

Ceprano

Dmanisi

D2282

Courtesy David Lordkipanidze

Tighenif (Ternifine)

Salé

Rabat

ER 3733

Kenya Museums of Natural History

Salé

Courtesy, J. J. Hublin

Bouri

Konso-Gardula

East Turkana

Nariokotome West Turkana

Olduvai

OH 9

Harry Nelson

WT 15000

Swartkrans

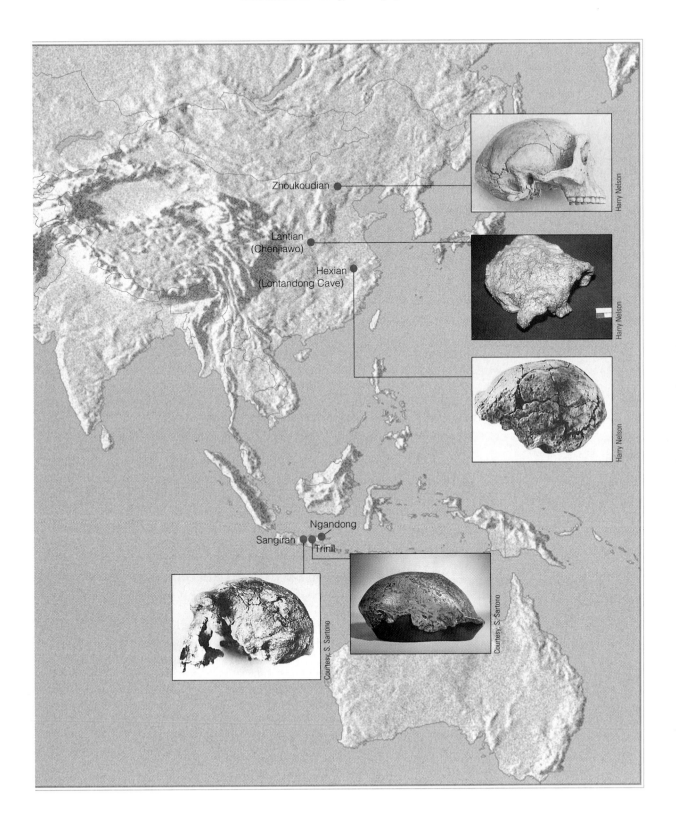

The dispersal of *Homo erectus* was influenced by climate, topography, water boundaries, and access to food and other resources. Paleoenvironmental reconstructions are thus of crucial importance in understanding the expansion of *H. erectus* to so many parts of the Old World. The long temporal span of *H. erectus* begins very early in the **Pleistocene** and extends to fairly late in that geological epoch. To comprehend the world of *Homo erectus*, we must understand how environments shifted during the Pleistocene.

Pleistocene The epoch of the Cenozoic from 1.8 m.y.a. until 10,000 y.a. Frequently referred to as the Ice Age, this epoch is associated with continental glaciations in northern latitudes.

The Pleistocene (1.8 m.y.a.–10,000 y.a.)

During much of the Pleistocene (also known as the Age of Glaciers or Ice Age), large areas of the Northern Hemisphere were covered with enormous masses of ice, which advanced and retreated as the temperature fell and rose. An early classification of glacial (and interglacial) Europe divided the Pleistocene into four major glacial periods. However, climatic conditions varied in different areas of Europe, and distinctive glacial periods are also now known for the North Sea, England, and eastern Europe, not to mention Asia and North America. New dating techniques have revealed a much more complex account of glacial advance and retreat, and the many oscillations of cold and warm temperatures during the Pleistocene affected both plants and animals.

The Pleistocene, which lasted more than 1.75 million years, was a significant period in hominid evolutionary history and encompassed the appearance and disappearance of *Homo erectus*. By the end of the Pleistocene, modern humans had already appeared, dependence on culture had dramatically increased, and domestication of plants and animals—one of the great cultural revolutions of human history—was either about to commence or had already begun. Given this background on the time span in which *H. erectus* lived, let us examine more closely this predecessor of *H. sapiens*.

The Morphology of Homo erectus

Brain Size

Homo erectus differs in several respects from both early *Homo* and *Homo sapiens*. The most obvious feature is cranial size (which, of course, is closely related to brain size). Early *Homo* had cranial capacities ranging from as small as 500 cm^3 to as large as 800 cm^3. *H. erectus*, on the other hand, shows considerable brain enlargement, with a cranial capacity of 600* to 1,250 cm^3 (with a mean of approximately 900 cm^3). However, in making such comparisons, we must bear in mind two key questions: What is the comparative sample, and what were the overall body sizes of the species being compared?

---

*This small lower range for *H. erectus* cranial capacity comes from the new evidence from Dmanisi, which might represent an early, primitive, form of *H. erectus* (or early *Homo*).

In relation to the first question, you should recall that many scholars are now convinced that there was more than one species of early *Homo* in East Africa around 2 m.y.a. If so, only one of these could have been ancestral to *H. erectus*. (Indeed, it is possible that neither species gave rise to *H. erectus* and that perhaps we have yet to find direct evidence of the ancestral species.) Taking a more optimistic view that at least one of these fossil groups is a likely ancestor of later hominids, the question still remains—which one? If we choose the smaller-bodied sample of early *Homo* as our presumed ancestral group, then *H. erectus* shows as much as a 40 percent increase in cranial capacity. However, if the comparative sample is the larger-bodied group of early *Homo* (as exemplified by skull 1470, from East Turkana), then *H. erectus* shows a 25 percent increase in cranial capacity.

As we previously discussed, brain size is closely tied to overall body size. We have made a point of the increase in *H. erectus* brain size; however, it must be realized that *H. erectus* was also considerably larger overall than earlier members of the genus *Homo*. In fact, when *H. erectus* is compared with the larger-bodied early *Homo* sample, *relative* brain size is about the same (Walker, 1991). Furthermore, when considering the relative brain size of *H. erectus* in comparison with *H. sapiens*, it is seen that *H. erectus* was considerably less encephalized than later members of the genus *Homo*.

Body Size

As we have just mentioned, *H. erectus* was larger than earlier hominids, as was conclusively shown by the discovery of a nearly complete skeleton in 1984 from **Nariokotome** (on the west side of Lake Turkana in Kenya). From this specimen (and from less complete individuals at other sites), some *Homo erectus* adults are estimated to have weighed well over 100 pounds, with an average adult stature of about 5 feet 6 inches (McHenry, 1992; Ruff and Walker, 1993; Walker and Leakey, 1993). Another point to keep in mind is that *Homo erectus* was quite sexually dimorphic—at least as indicated by the East African specimens. Thus, for male adults, weight and stature in some individuals may have been considerably greater than the average figures just mentioned. In fact, it is estimated that if the Nariokotome boy had survived, he would have attained an adult stature of over 6 feet (Walker, 1993).

Associated with the large stature (and explaining the significant increase in body weight) is also a dramatic increase in robusticity. In fact, this characteristic of very heavy body build was to dominate hominid evolution not just during *H. erectus* times, but through the long transitional era of archaic *Homo sapiens* as well. Only with the appearance of anatomically modern *H. sapiens* do we see a more gracile skeletal structure, which is still characteristic of most modern populations.

Cranial Shape

The cranium of *Homo erectus* displays a highly distinctive shape, partly as a result of increased brain size, but probably more correlated with significant body size (robusticity). The ramifications of this heavily built cranium are reflected in thick cranial bone (most notably in Asian specimens) and large browridges (supraorbital tori) in the front of the skull and a projecting **nuchal torus** at the rear (fig. 9–3).

See Virtual Lab 10, section III, for an interactive exercise covering the estimation of body mass from a fossil femur.

Nariokotome (nar´-ee-oh-ko´-tow-may)

Nuchal torus (nuke´-ul) (nuchal, meaning "neck") A projection of bone in the back of the cranium where neck muscles attach, used to hold up the head. The nuchal torus is a distinctive feature of *H. erectus*.

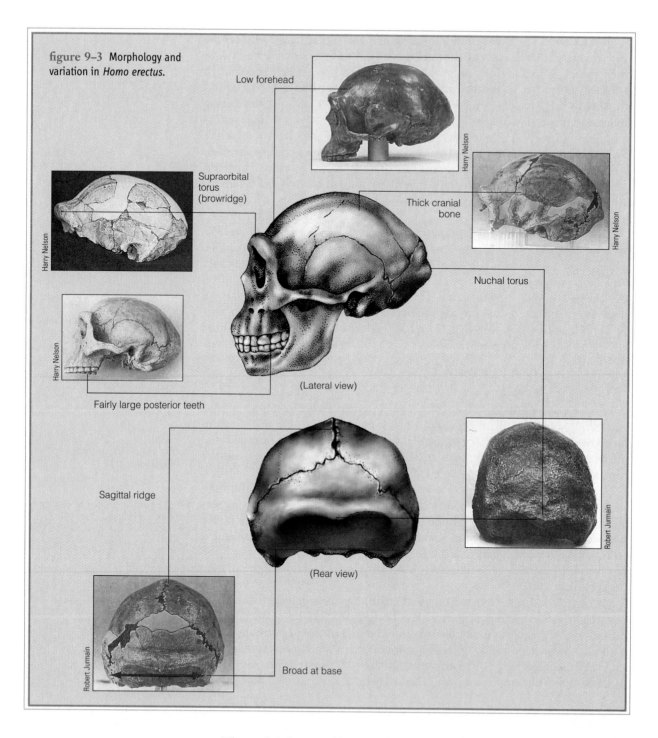

figure 9–3 Morphology and variation in *Homo erectus*.

Low forehead

Supraorbital torus (browridge)

Thick cranial bone

Nuchal torus

Fairly large posterior teeth

(Lateral view)

Sagittal ridge

(Rear view)

Broad at base

Harry Nelson

Harry Nelson

Harry Nelson

Harry Nelson

Robert Jurmain

Robert Jurmain

The vault is long and low, receding back from the large browridges with little forehead development. Moreover, the cranium is wider at the base compared with earlier *or* later species of genus *Homo*. The maximum breadth is below the ear opening, giving a pentagonal contour to the cranium (when viewed from behind). In contrast, both early *Homo* crania and *H. sapiens* crania have more vertical sides, and the maximum width is *above* the ear openings.

Dentition

The dentition of *Homo erectus* is much like that of *Homo sapiens*, but the earlier species exhibits somewhat larger teeth. However, compared with early *Homo*, *H. erectus* does show some dental reduction.

Another interesting feature of the dentition of some *H. erectus* specimens is seen in the incisor teeth. On the back (lingual) surfaces, the teeth are scooped out in appearance, forming a surface reminiscent of a shovel. Accordingly, such teeth are referred to as "shovel-shaped" incisors, and they are also found in several modern human populations (fig. 9–4). It has been suggested that teeth shaped in this manner are an adaptation in hunter-gatherers for processing foods, a contention not yet proved (or really even framed in a testable manner). One thing does seem likely: Shovel-shaped incisors are probably an ancestral feature of the species *H. erectus*, as the phenomenon has been found not just in the Chinese specimens, but also in the early individual from Nariokotome.

figure 9–4 Shovel-shaped incisors, shown here in a modern *Homo sapiens* individual.

Robert Jurmain

Historical Overview of Homo erectus *Discoveries*

In our discussion of early hominids, we traced the evolutionary developments in *chronological* order, that is, discussing the oldest specimens first. Here we take a different approach and discuss the finds in the order in which they were discovered. We believe that this approach is useful, as the discoveries cover a broad range of time—indeed, almost the entire history of paleoanthropology. Given this relatively long history of scientific discovery, the later finds were assessed in the light of earlier ones (and thus can still be best understood within a historical context).

Java

Dutch anatomist Eugene Dubois (1858–1940) (fig. 9–5) was the first scientist to deliberately design a research plan that would take him from his anatomy lab to where fossil bones might be buried. Up until this time, embryology and comparative anatomy were considered the proper methods of studying humans and their ancestry, and the research was done in the laboratory. Dubois changed all this.

The publication of Darwin's *Origin of Species* in 1859, had ushered in a period of intellectual excitement. This stimulating intellectual climate surrounded the youthful Eugene Dubois, who left Holland for Sumatra in 1887 to search for, as he phrased it, "the missing link."

In October 1891, along the Solo River, near the town of Trinil, the field crew unearthed a skullcap that was to become internationally famous. The following year, a human femur was recovered about 15 yards upstream in what Dubois claimed was the same level as the skullcap. Dubois assumed that the skullcap (with a cranial capacity of slightly over 900 cm³) and the femur belonged to the same individual.

After studying these discoveries for a few years, Dubois startled the world in 1894 with a paper provocatively titled "*Pithecanthropus erectus*, A Manlike Species of Transitional Anthropoid from Java." Dubois' views were harshly criticized; yet after the original fossils were examined by other scholars, his views were taken more seriously. Eventually, there was general acceptance

figure 9–5 Eugene Dubois, discoverer of the first *H. erectus* fossil to be found.

The New York Academy of Medicine Library

that Dubois was correct in identifying the skull as representing a previously undescribed species; that his estimates of cranial capacity were reasonably accurate; that *Pithecanthropus erectus*, or *H. erectus* as we call it today, is the ancestor of *H. sapiens*; and that bipedalism preceded enlargement of the brain.

By 1930, the controversy had faded, especially in the light of important new discoveries near Peking (Beijing), China, in the late 1920s (discussed shortly). Similarities between the Beijing skulls and Dubois' *Pithecanthropus* were obvious, and scientists pointed out that the Java form was not an "apeman," as Dubois contended, but rather was closely related to modern *Homo sapiens*.

One might expect that Dubois would welcome the finds from China and the support they provided for the human status of *Pithecanthropus*, but Dubois would have none of it. He refused to recognize any connection between Beijing and Java and described the Beijing fossils as "a degenerate Neanderthaler" (von Koenigswald, 1956, p. 55). He also refused to accept the classification of "Pithecanthropus" in the same species with later finds from Java.

Homo erectus from Java

Six sites in eastern Java have yielded all the *H. erectus* fossil remains found to date on that island. The dating of these fossils has been hampered by the complex nature of Javanese geology. It has been generally accepted that most of the fossils belong in the Middle Pleistocene and are less than 800,000 years old. However, as we noted earlier, new dating estimates have suggested one find (from Modjokerto) to be close to 1.8 million years old and another fossil from the main site of Sangiran to be approximately 1.6 million years old.

At Sangiran, where the remains of at least five individuals have been excavated, the cranial capacities of the fossils range from 813 cm^3 to 1,059 cm^3. Another site called Ngandong has also been fruitful, yielding the remains of 12 crania (fig. 9–6). The dating here is also confusing, but the Upper Pleistocene has been suggested, which may explain the larger cranial measurements of the Ngandong individuals as well as features that are more modern than those found on other Javanese crania. Recently published dates for the Ngandong site are very recent, remarkably so, in fact. Using two specialized dating techniques (discussed in Chapter 11; see p. 282), Swisher and colleagues from the Berkeley Geochronology Laboratory have determined from animal bones found at the site (and presumably associated with the hominids) a date ranging from about 50,000 years ago to as recently as 25,000 years ago (Swisher et al., 1996). If these dates are further confirmed, it would show a *very* late survival of *Homo erectus* in Java, long after these hominids had disappeared elsewhere. They would thus be contemporary with *Homo sapiens*—which, by this time, had expanded widely in the Old World (see Chapter 10).

We cannot say much about the *H. erectus* way of life in Java. Very few artifacts have been found, and those have come mainly from river terraces, not from primary sites: "On Java there is still not a single site where artifacts can be associated with *H. erectus*" (Bartstra, 1982, p. 319).

Peking (Beijing)

The story of Peking *H. erectus* is another saga filled with excitement, hard work, luck, and misfortune. Europeans had known for a long time that "dragon bones," used by the Chinese as medicine and aphrodisiacs, were actually ancient

Courtesy, S. Sartono

figure 9–6 Rear view of a Ngandong skull. Note that the cranial walls slope downward and outward (or upward and inward), with the widest breadth low on the cranium, giving it a pentagonal form.

mammal bones. Scientists eventually located one of the sources of these dragon bones at the remarkable site of **Zhoukoudian.** Serious excavations were begun in the 1920s, under the direction of a young Chinese geologist, Pei Wenshong. In 1929, a fossil skull was discovered, and Pei brought the specimen to anatomist Davidson Black (fig 9–7). Because the fossil was embedded in hard limestone, it took Black four months of hard, steady work to free it from its tough matrix. The result was worth the labor. The skull, that of a juvenile, was thick, low, and relatively small, but in Black's mind there was no doubt it belonged to an early hominid. The response to this discovery, quite unlike that which greeted Dubois almost 40 years earlier, was immediate and enthusiastically favorable.

Franz Weidenreich (fig. 9–8), a distinguished anatomist well known for his work on European fossil hominids, succeeded Black. After Japan invaded China in 1933, Weidenreich decided to move the fossils from Beijing to prevent them from falling into the hands of the Japanese. Weidenreich left China in 1941, taking excellent prepared casts, photographs, and drawings of the fossil material with him. After he left, the bones were packed, and arrangements were made for the U.S. Marine Corps in Beijing to take them to the United States. The bones never reached the United States, and they have never been found. To this day, no one knows what happened to them, and their location remains a mystery.

Zhoukoudian *Homo erectus*

The fossil remains of *H. erectus* discovered by the earlier work in the 1920s and 1930s as well as some more recent excavations (fig. 9–9) constitutes by far the largest collection of *H. erectus* material found anywhere. Included in this excellent sample are 14 skullcaps (fig. 9–10), other cranial pieces, and more than 100 isolated teeth, but only a scattering of postcranial elements (Jia and Huang, 1990). Various interpretations to account for this unusual pattern of preservation have been offered—ranging from ritualistic treatment or cannibalism by

Zhoukoudian (zhoh´-koh-dee´-en)

figure 9–7 Davidson Black, responsible for the first study of the Zhoukoudian fossils.

figure 9–8 Franz Weidenreich.

figure 9–10 *H. erectus* (cast of specimen from Zhoukoudian). From this view, the supraorbital torus, low vault of the skull, and nuchal torus can clearly be seen.

figure 9–9 Zhoukoudian Cave. The grid on the wall was drawn for purposes of excavation. The entrance to the cave can be seen near the grid.

See Virtual Lab 10, section I, for a 3-D animation of a Zhoukoudian cranium.

the hominids themselves to the more mundane suggestion that the *H. erectus* remains are simply the leftovers of the meals of giant hyenas (discussed shortly).

Nevertheless, the hominid remains belong to upward of 40 male and female adults and children and constitute a considerable amount of evidence. With the meticulous work by Weidenreich, the Zhoukoudian fossils have led to a good overall picture of the eastern *H. erectus* of China. Peking *H. erectus*, like that from Java, possesses typical *H. erectus* features, including the supraorbital torus in front and the nuchal torus behind; also, the skull is keeled by a sagittal ridge, the face protrudes, the incisors are shoveled, and, like the Javanese forms, the skull shows the greatest breadth near the bottom.

CULTURAL REMAINS   More than 100,000 artifacts have been recovered from this vast site that was occupied intermittently for almost 250,000 years. According to the Chinese (Wu and Lin, 1983, p.86), Zhoukoudian "is one of the sites with the longest history of habitation by man or his ancestors." The occupation of the site has been divided into three cultural stages:

Earliest Stage (460,000–420,000 y.a.)*   The tools are large, close to a pound in weight, and made of soft stone, such as sandstone.

Middle Stage (370,000–350,000 y.a.)   Tools become smaller and lighter (under a pound), and these smaller tools comprise approximately two-thirds of the sample.

Final Stage (300,000–230,000 y.a.)   Tools are still small, and the tool materials are of better quality. The coarse quartz of the earlier periods is replaced by a finer quartz, sandstone tools have almost disappeared, and flint tools increase in frequency by as much as 30 percent.

As you can see, the early tools are crude and shapeless but become more refined over time. Common tools at the site are choppers and chopping tools, but retouched flakes were fashioned into scrapers, points, burins, and awls (fig. 9–11).

The way of life at Zhoukoudian has traditionally been described as that of hunter-gatherers who killed deer and horses as well as other animals and gathered fruits, berries, and ostrich eggs. Fragments of charred ostrich eggshells, the

figure 9–11 Chinese tools from Middle Pleistocene sites. (Adapted from Wu and Olsen, 1985.)

Quartzite chopper

Flint point

Flint awl

Graver, or burin

---

*These dates should be considered tentative until more precise chronometric techniques are available.

abundant deposits of hackberry seeds unearthed in the cave, and the flourishing plant growth surrounding the cave all suggest that meat was supplemented by the gathering of herbs, wild fruits, tubers, and eggs. Layers of what has long been thought to be ash in the cave, over 18 feet deep at one point, suggest to some researchers the use of fire by *H. erectus;* however, whether Beijing hominids could actually make fire is unknown. Wu and Lin (1983, p. 94) state that "Peking Man was a cave dweller, a fire user, a deer hunter, a seed gatherer and a maker of specialized tools," but several questions about Zhoukoudian *H. erectus* remain unanswered.

Did *H. erectus* at Zhoukoudian use language? If by language we mean articulate speech, it is unlikely. Nevertheless, some scholars believe that speech originated early in hominid evolution; others argue that speech did not originate until up to 200,000 years later in the Upper Paleolithic, with the origin of anatomically modern humans (see Chapter 11). We agree with Dean Falk when she writes, "Unfortunately, what it is going to take to *settle* the debate about when language originated in hominids is a time machine. Until one becomes available, we can only speculate about this fascinating and important question" (1989, p. 141).

Did these hominids wear clothes? Almost surely clothing of some type, probably in the form of animal skins, was worn. Winters in Beijing are harsh today and appear to have been bitter during the Middle Pleistocene as well. Moreover, awls were found at Zhoukoudian, and one of the probable bone tools may be a needle.

What was the life span of *H. erectus* at Zhoukoudian? Apparently, not very long, and infant and childhood mortality was probably very high. Studies of the fossil remains reveal that almost 40 percent of the bones belong to individuals under the age of 14, and only 2.6 percent are estimated to be in the 50- to 60-year age-group (Jia, 1975).

This picture of Zhoukoudian life has been challenged by several researchers. Lewis Binford and colleagues (Binford and Ho, 1985; Binford and Stone, 1986a, 1986b) reject the description of Beijing *H. erectus* as hunters and argue that the evidence clearly points to them as scavengers.

Using techniques of taphonomy (discussed in Chapter 8), Noel Boaz and colleagues have even questioned whether the *H. erectus* remains at Zhoukoudian represent evidence of hominid habitation of the cave. By carefully comparing the types of bones as well as the damage to the bones found at Zhoukoudian with that seen in contemporary carnivore dens, Boaz and Ciochon (2001) have suggested that much of the materials in the cave likely accumulated through the activities of a giant extinct hyena. Indeed, they hypothesize that most of the *H. erectus* remains, too, are the food refuse of hyenic meals!

Boaz and his associates do recognize that the tools in the cave and possibly cut marks on some of the animal bones do provide evidence of hominid activities at Zhoukoudian. They also recognize that more detailed analysis is required to test their hypotheses and to "determine the nature and scope" of the *H. erectus* presence at Zhoukoudian.

Probably the most intriguing archaeological aspect of the presumed hominid behavior at Zhoukoudian has been the long-held assumption that *H. erectus* deliberately utilized fire inside the cave. The technological control of fire was one of the major cultural breakthroughs of all prehistory. By providing warmth, a means of cooking, an aid to further modify tools, and so forth, controlled fire would have been a giant technological innovation. While some potential early African sites have been suggested as giving evidence of hominid control of fire, it has long been concluded that the first *definite* evidence of hominid fire use comes from Zhoukoudian.

Now, new evidence has radically altered this assumption. Much more detailed excavations at Zhoukoudian were carried out in 1996 and 1997 by biologist Steve Weiner and colleagues. These researchers also carefully analyzed the soil samples they collected for distinctive chemical signatures (which would show whether fire had occurred in the cave) (Weiner et al., 1998). Weiner and his colleagues found that only rarely was any burnt bone found associated with tools, and in most cases the burning appeared to have taken place *after* fossilization (i.e., the bones were not cooked). Moreover, the "ash" layers mentioned earlier are not ash at all, but rather naturally accumulated organic sediment. This last conclusion was derived from chemical testing showing no sign whatsoever of wood burning inside the cave. Finally, the "hearths" that have figured so prominently in archaeological reconstructions of the fire control at this site are apparently not hearths at all. They simply are round depressions formed in the past by water collecting when the cave was more open to the elements.

Indeed, another provisional interpretation of the cave's geology suggests that the cave did not open in the manner of habitation sites, but had access only through a vertical shaft, leading archaeologist Alison Brooks to remark, "It wouldn't have been a shelter, it would have been a trap" (quoted in Wuethrich, 1998).

These serious doubts regarding control of fire, coupled with the suggestive evidence of bone accumulation by carnivores, have led anthropologists Noel Boaz and Russell Ciochon to conclude, "Zhoukoudian cave was neither hearth nor home" (Boaz and Ciochon, 2001).

Other Chinese Sites

More work has been done at Zhoukoudian than at any other Chinese site. Nevertheless, there are other hominid sites worth noting. Three of the more important sites, besides Zhoukoudian, include two sites in Lantian County (often simply referred to as Lantian) and another site in Hexian County (usually referred to as the Hexian find).

At Chenjiawo, in Lantian, an almost complete mandible containing several teeth was found in 1963. It is quite similar to those from Zhoukoudian but has been provisionally dated at about 650,000 y.a. If the dating is correct, this specimen would be older than the Beijing material. The following year, a partial cranium was discovered at Gongwangling, not far from Chenjiawo. Provisionally dated to as much as 1.15 m.y.a. (Etler and Tianyuan, 1994), the Gongwangling specimen may be the oldest Chinese *Homo erectus* fossil yet known.

Perhaps the most significant find was the 1980 Hexian discovery, where remains of several individuals were recovered. One of the specimens is a well-preserved cranium (with a cranial capacity of about 1,025 cm³) lacking much of its base. Dated roughly at 250,000 y.a., it is not surprising that this Hexian cranium displays several advanced features. The cranial constriction, for example, is not as pronounced as in earlier forms, and certain temporal and occipital characteristics are "best compared with the later forms of *H. erectus* at Zhoukoudian" (Wu and Dong, 1985, p. 87).

(a)

(b)

figure 9–12 (a) EV 9002 (Yunxian, China). The skull is in better shape than its companion, and its lateral view clearly displays features characteristic of *H. erectus:* flattened vault, receding forehead (frontal bone), angulated occiput, and supraorbital torus. (b) EV 9001 (Yunxian). Unfortunately, the skull was crushed, but it preserves some lateral facial structures absent in EV 9002.

In 1993, Li Tianyuan and Dennis Etler reported that two relatively complete skulls were discovered in 1989 at a hominid site in Yunxian County. The date given for the site is 350,000 y.a., which, if correct, would make these the most complete crania of this great antiquity in China (fig. 9–12).

The Yunxian crania are both large and robust, considerably exceeding in size those from Zhoukoudian. In general, the Yunxian individuals fit within *Homo erectus,* but in the facial region especially they also show some differences. Unfortunately, both skulls are still covered with a hard calcareous matrix, and critics argue that until the skulls are cleaned and the crushed parts properly put together, it is too early to make accurate assessments. In any case, these Yunxian crania will ultimately provide considerable data to help clarify hominid evolution in China and perhaps elsewhere in the Old World as well.

The Asian crania from both Java and China are mainly Middle Pleistocene fossils and share many similar features, which may be explained by *H. erectus* migration from Java to China about 800,000 years ago. African *H. erectus* forms are generally older than most Asian forms and are not as similar to them as Asian forms (i.e., from Java and China) are to each other.

East Africa

OLDUVAI Back in 1960, Louis Leakey unearthed a fossil skull at Olduvai (OH 9) that he identified as *H. erectus.* Skull OH 9 from Upper Bed II is dated at 1.4 m.y.a. and preserves a massive cranium but is faceless except for a bit of nose below the supraorbital torus. Estimated at 1,067 cm^3, the cranial capacity of OH 9 is the largest of all the African *Homo erectus* specimens. The browridge is huge, the largest known for any hominid in both thickness and projection, but the vault walls are thin. This latter characteristic of fairly thin cranial vault bones is seen in most East African *H. erectus* specimens, and in this respect, they differ from Asian *H. erectus* (in which cranial vaults are thick).

EAST TURKANA Some 400 miles north of Olduvai Gorge, on the northern boundary of Kenya, is Lake Turkana. Explored by Richard Leakey and colleagues since 1969, the eastern shore of the lake has been a virtual gold mine for australopithecine, early *Homo,* and *H. erectus* fossil remains.

The most significant *H. erectus* discovery from East Turkana is a nearly complete skull (fig. 9–13) dated at 1.8 m.y.a. (i.e., as early as the earliest *H. erectus* from Java). The cranial capacity is estimated at 848 cm^3, at the lower end of the

See Virtual Lab 10, section I, for a 3-D animation of East African *Homo erectus* specimens.

figure 9–13 ER 3733, the most complete East Turkana *H. erectus* cranium.

range for *H. erectus*, but this is not surprising considering its early date. The cranium generally resembles Asian *H. erectus* in many features (but with some important differences, discussed shortly).

Not many tools have been found at *H. erectus* sites in East Turkana. Oldowan types of flakes, cobbles, and core tools have been found, and the introduction of **Acheulian** tools about 1.4 m.y.a. replaced the Oldowan tradition.

WEST TURKANA*   In August 1984, Kamoya Kimeu, a member of Richard Leakey's team, added to his reputation as an outstanding fossil hunter when he discovered a small piece of skull near the base camp on the west side of Lake Turkana. Leakey and his colleague, Alan Walker of Pennsylvania State University, excavated the site known as Nariokotome in 1984 and again in 1985.

The dig was a resounding success. The workers unearthed the most complete *H. erectus* skeleton yet found (fig. 9–14). Known properly as WT 15000, the all but complete skeleton includes facial bones and most of the postcranial bones, a rare finding indeed for *H. erectus*, since these elements are scarce at other *H. erectus* sites.

Another remarkable feature of the find is its age. Its dating is based on the chronometric dates of the geological formation in which the site is located and is set at about 1.6 million years. The skeleton is that of a boy about 12 years of age and 5 feet 3 inches tall. Had he grown to maturity, his height, it is estimated, would have been more than 6 feet, taller than *H. erectus* was heretofore thought to have been. The postcranial bones appear to be quite similar, though not identical, to those of modern humans. The cranial capacity of WT 15000 is estimated at 880 cm³; brain growth was nearly complete, and it is estimated that the boy's adult cranial capacity would have been approximately 909 cm³ (Begun and Walker, 1993).

BOURI   Two sites from Ethiopia have yielded *H. erectus* fossils, the most significant coming from the Bouri locale in the Middle Awash region (the same area from which numerous remains of earlier hominids have come; see Chapter 8 and Appendix B). The recent discovery of a mostly complete cranium from Bouri is important because this individual (dated at approximately 1 m.y.a.) is more like Asian *H. erectus* than are most of the earlier East African remains we have discussed (Asfaw et al., 2002). Consequently, the suggestion by several researchers that East African fossils from the Lower-Middle Pleistocene are a different species from (Asian) *Homo erectus* is not supported by the morphology of the Bouri cranium (or, for that matter, by OH 9 either).

Summary of East African *H. erectus*

The *Homo erectus* remains from East Africa show several differences from the fossil samples from Java and China. Some African specimens (particularly exemplified by ER 3733, presumably a female, and WT 15000, presumably a male) are not as strongly buttressed in the cranium (by supraorbital or nuchal tori) and do not have such thick cranial bones as seen in Asian representatives of *H. erectus*.

Acheulian (ash´-oo-lay-en) Pertaining to a stone tool industry of the Lower and Middle Pleistocene characterized by a large proportion of bifacial tools (flaked on both sides). Acheulian tool kits are very common in Africa, Southwest Asia, and western Europe, but are less common elsewhere. (Also spelled "Acheulean.")

Reproduced with permission of the Kenya Museums of Natural History

figure 9–14 WT 15000 from Nariokotome, Kenya: the most complete *H. erectus* specimen yet found.

---

*WT is the symbol for West Turkana, that is, the west side of Lake Turkana. The east side is designated by ER—East Rudolf. Rudolf was the former name of the lake.

These differences, as well as others observed in the postcranial skeleton, have so impressed some researchers that they in fact argue for a *separate* species status for the African *H. erectus* remains (as distinct from the Asian samples).* Bernard Wood, the leading proponent of this view, has suggested that the name *Homo ergaster* be used for the African remains; *H. erectus* would then be reserved solely for the Asian material (Wood, 1991). In addition, the very early dates now postulated for the dispersal of *H. erectus* into Asia (Java) would argue for a more than 1-million-year separate history for Asian and African populations.

Nevertheless, this species division has not been fully accepted, and the current consensus (reflected in this text) is to continue to refer to all these hominids as *Homo erectus* (Kramer, 1993; Conroy, 1997; Rightmire, 1998; Asfaw et al., 2002). As with some earlier hominids, we accordingly will have to accommodate a considerable degree of intraspecific variation within this species. Wood has concluded, regarding variation within such a broadly defined *H. erectus* species, "It is a species which manifestly embraces an unusually wide degree of variation in both the cranium and postcranial skeleton" (Wood, 1992a, p. 329).

South Africa

A mandible was found among fossil remains collected at Swartkrans in South Africa in the 1940s and 1950s. This specimen, SK 15, was originally assigned to "*Telanthropus capensis,*" but is now placed within the genus *Homo* (there is, however, disagreement about its species designation). Rightmire (1990) suggests that it may be linked with *Homo erectus*, but others are not certain. If it is *H. erectus*, it would demonstrate that *H. erectus* inhabited South Africa as well as the other regions documented by other more complete fossil finds.

North Africa

With evidence from China and Java, it appears clear that *H. erectus* populations, with superior tools and weapons and presumably greater intelligence than their predecessors, had vastly expanded their habitat beyond that of early hominids. The earliest evidence for *H. erectus*, 1.8–1.6 m.y.a., comes from East Africa and Java and about 1 million years later in China. Early dispersal of *H. erectus* to Europe (prior to 1 m.y.a.) may also have occurred. It is not surprising, therefore, that *H. erectus* migrations would have taken them to northwest Africa as well.

North African remains, consisting almost entirely of mandibles (or mandible fragments) and a partial parietal bone, have been found at Ternifine (now Tighenif), Algeria, and in Morocco, at Sidi Abderrahman and Thomas Quarries. The three Ternifine mandibles and the parietal fragment are quite robust and have been dated to about 700,000 y.a. The Moroccan material is not as robust as Ternifine and may be a bit younger, at 500,000 years. In addition, an interesting cranium was found in a quarry north of Salé, in Morocco. The walls of the skull vault are thick, and several other features resemble those of *H. erectus*. Some features suggest that the Salé fossil is *H. sapiens*, but a date of 400,000 y.a. and an estimated cranial capacity of about 900 cm^3 throw doubt on that interpretation.

•Note, however, that other East African specimens from Olduvai, and especially from Bouri, are more like Asian fossils.

Europe

Recent discoveries in Europe are dramatically pushing back the time frame for earliest hominid occupation of this portion of the Old World. For several decades, it had been assumed that hominids did not reach Europe until late in the Middle Pleistocene (presumably after 400,000 y.a.) and were already identifiable as a form very similar to *Homo sapiens*. It was thus concluded that *H. erectus* (and contemporaries) never expanded there. As the new discoveries are evaluated, such assumptions are being questioned. The most exciting finds have come in just the last few years from Dmanisi in the Republic of Georgia.

Beginning in the early 1990s, a few pieces were found, but the most informative specimens are three well-preserved crania, the most recently discovered (in 2001) being almost complete (fig. 9–15). These remains are important because they are the best-preserved hominids of this antiquity found anywhere *outside* of Africa. Moreover, they show a mixed pattern of characteristics, some quite unexpected (Vekua et al., 2002).

In some respects the Dmanisi crania are similar to *H. erectus* (e.g., the long, low vault, wide base, and thickening along the sagittal midline; see especially fig. 9–15b and compare with fig. 9–4). In other characteristics, however, the Dmanisi individuals are different from other hominid finds outside of Africa. In particular, the most complete specimen (specimen 2700; see fig. 9–15c) has a less robust and thinner browridge, a projecting lower face, and a large upper canine. Thus, at least from the front, this skull is more reminiscent of the smaller early *Homo* specimens from East Africa than of *Homo erectus*. Moreover, cranial capacity in this individual is very small (estimated at only 600 cm³, well within the range of early *Homo*). In fact, all three Dmanisi crania show small cranial capacities (the other two estimated at 650 and 780 cm³).

A number of stone tools have also been recovered at Dmanisi. The tools are similar to early African implements and are quite different from the ostensibly more advanced technology of the Acheulian (the latter broadly associated with *H. erectus* in much of the Old World).

From these recent, somewhat startling revelations from Dmanisi several questions can be raised:

1. Was *Homo erectus* the first hominid to leave Africa—or was it an earlier form of *Homo?*
2. Did hominids require a large brain and sophisticated stone tool culture to disperse out of Africa?

figure 9–15 Dmanisi crania discovered in 1999 and 2001 and dated to 1.8–1.7 m.y.a. (a) Specimen 2282. (b) Specimen 2280. (c) Specimen 2700.

(a)

Courtesy, David Lordkipanidze

(b)

Courtesy, David Lordkipanidze

(c)

Courtesy, David Lordkipanidze

3. Was the large, robust body build of *H. erectus* a necessary adaptation for the initial occupation of Eurasia?

4. Did, in fact, *H. erectus* evolve primarily in Eurasia and then migrate *back* to Africa?

Of course, the Dmanisi discoveries are very new, so any conclusions we draw must be seen as highly tentative. Nevertheless, the recent evidence raises important and exciting possibilities. In regard to question 1, it now seems likely that the first transcontinental hominid migrants were a form of early *Homo* (similar to the smaller East African species, *Homo habilis*; see p. 201). At best, and as exemplified at Dmanisi, the first hominids to leave Africa were a very early form of *H. erectus*, much more primitive than any of the other specimens from Africa, Asia, or Europe previously discussed.

As for question 2, certainly the smaller individuals from Dmanisi did not have a large brain (by *H. erectus* standards), nor did they have an advanced stone tool culture (possessing instead tools very similar to the earliest ones from East and South Africa).

Thus far, no postcranial remains have been found at Dmanisi, so we do not know as yet the body structure of the earliest hominids to leave Africa. It is possible, however, that the overall body proportions (as with the face of the smallest Dmanisi cranium) resemble *Homo habilis* more than they do *H. erectus*. Thus, these first pioneers to leave Africa may have been, in the words of Phillip Rightmire (of the University of Binghamton and a coauthor of the first article announcing the 2001 Dmanisi discovery), "little people." That is, they may have been very different from the big-bodied, long-legged, full-blown *H. erectus* body plan.

And lastly, where did the full-blown *H. erectus* morphology first evolve? For decades it has been widely assumed that *H. erectus* evolved first in Africa and then emigrated to elsewhere in the Old World. But now, the teasing possibility exists that *H. erectus* evolved primarily in Eurasia, and only after attaining its fully characteristic morphology did it migrate back into Africa (as perhaps the Bouri cranium, dated to 1 m.y.a., suggests?).

The fossil remains from elsewhere in Europe *all* appear to be at least 1 million years later than Dmanisi, and they reflect a somewhat confusing evolutionary picture. For example, the skull from Ceprano (Italy) is the most definite *H. erectus* fossil from Europe (meaning *H. erectus* in the strict sense—to include Asian forms, but not those from Africa or Dmanisi). Yet, at a roughly contemporary time to Ceprano, the early material from Atapuerca (Spain) is different, and Spanish researchers have provisionally assigned these hominids to still another species of *Homo* (a view that has not been widely accepted). We should note that much of this early Pleistocene European fossil material is fragmentary, and all of it has been only recently found. Thus, all current interpretations are, for the moment, both tentative and controversial.

After about 400,000 y.a., the European fossil hominid record becomes increasingly abundant. Nevertheless, interpretations relating to the proper taxonomic assessment of many of these remains have been debated, in some cases for decades. In recent years, several of these somewhat later (i.e., Middle Pleistocene) specimens have been placed within a grouping of early *Homo sapiens* referred to as "archaic *Homo sapiens*." Needless to say, not everyone agrees. These enigmatic archaic *H. sapiens* specimens are discussed in Chapter 11. A time line for the *H. erectus* discoveries discussed in this chapter as well as other finds of more uncertain status is shown in figure 9–16.

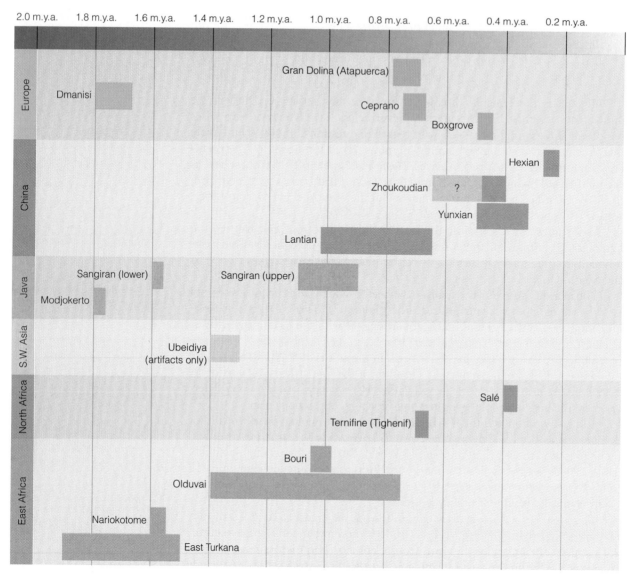

Note: Most dates are only imprecise estimates. However, the dates from East African sites are chronometrically determined and are thus much more secure. In addition, the early dates from Java are also radiometric and are gaining wide acceptance, although some researchers (e.g., Wolpoff, 1999) suggest that they are not secure and may be later than shown.

figure 9–16 Time line for *Homo erectus* discoveries and other contemporary hominids. Note that most dates are approximations.

Technological and Population Trends in the Middle Pleistocene

Technological Trends

Many researchers have noted the remarkable stasis of the physical and cultural characteristics of *Homo erectus* populations, which seemed to change so little in the more than 1.5 million years of their existence. There is, however, dispute on this point. Some scholars (Rightmire, 1981) see almost no detectable changes in cranial dimensions over more than 1 million years of *H. erectus* evolution.*

Other paleoanthropologists (e.g., Wolpoff, 1984), who use different methodologies to date and subdivide their samples, draw a different conclusion, seeing some significant long-term morphological trends. Accepting a moderate position, we can postulate that there were some changes: The brain of later *H. erectus* was somewhat larger, the nose more protrusive, and the body not as robust as in earlier forms. Moreover, there were modifications in stone tool technology.

Expansion of the brain presumably enabled *H. erectus* to develop a more sophisticated tool kit than seen among earlier hominids. The important change in this kit was a core worked on both sides, called a *biface* (known widely as a hand axe or cleaver; fig 9–17). The biface had a flatter core than the roundish earlier Oldowan pebble tool. And, probably even more important, this *core* tool was obviously a target design, that is, the main goal of the toolmaker. This greater focus and increased control enabled the stoneknapper to produce sharper, straighter edges, resulting in a more efficient implement. This Acheulian stone tool became standardized as the basic *H. erectus* all-purpose tool (with only minor modification) for more than a million years. It served to cut, scrape, pound, dig, and more—a most useful tool that has been found in Africa, parts of Asia, and later in western Europe. It should also be noted that Acheulian tool kits also included several types of small tools (fig. 9–18).

For many years, it was thought that a cultural "divide" separated the Old World—with Acheulian technology found *only* in Africa, southwest Asia, and western Europe, but not elsewhere (i.e., absent in eastern Europe and most of Asia). However, newly reported excavations from more than 20 sites in southern China have forced reevaluation of this hypothesis (Yamei et al., 2000). As noted, the most distinctive tools of the Acheulian are bifaces, and they are the very tools thought lacking throughout most of the Pleistocene in eastern Europe and most of Asia. The new archaeological assemblages from southern China are securely dated at abut 800,000 y.a. and contain numerous bifaces, very similar to contemporaneous Acheulian bifaces from Africa (see figs. 9–17 and 9–19b). It now appears likely that cultural traditions relating to stone tool technology were largely equivalent over the *full* geographical range of *H. erectus* and contemporaries.

While geographical distinctions are not so obvious, temporal changes in tool technology are evident. In early days, toolmakers employed a stone hammer (simply an ovoid-shaped stone about the size of an egg or a bit larger) to remove flakes from the core, thus leaving deep scars. Later, they used other materials, such as wood and bone. They learned to use these new materials as soft hammers, which gave them more control over flaking, thus leaving shallow scars, sharper edges, and a more symmetrical form. Toward the end of the Acheulian industry, toolmakers blocked out a core with stone hammers and then switched to wood or bone for defining the edges. This technique produced more elegant-appearing and pear-shaped implements.

Evidence of butchering is widespread at *H. erectus* sites, and in the past, such evidence has been cited in arguments for consistent hunting. For example, at the Olorgesailie site in Kenya (fig. 9–19), dated at approximately 800,000 y.a., thousands of Acheulian hand axes have been recovered in association with remains of large animals, including giant baboons (now extinct). However, the assumption

Courtesy, The Museum of Primitive Art and Culture, Peace Dale, RI, photo by William Turnbaugh

figure 9–17 Acheulian biface ("hand axe"), a basic tool of the Acheulian tradition.

(a)   (b)

(c)   (d)

figure 9–18 Small tools of the Acheulian industry. (a) Side scraper. (b) Point. (c) End scraper. (d) Burin.

---

*This conclusion does not include the Dmanisi remains, but refers to "full-blown" *H. erectus* specimens.

(a)

(b)

figure 9–19 (a) A Middle Pleistocene butchering site at Olorgesailie, Kenya, excavated by Louis and Mary Leakey, who had the catwalk built for observers. (b) A close-up of the Acheulian tools, mainly hand axes, found at the site.

of consistent hunting has been challenged, especially by archaeologists who argue that the evidence does not prove the hunting hypothesis. Instead, they suggest that *H. erectus* was primarily a scavenger, a hypothesis that also has not yet been proved conclusively. We thus discuss *H. erectus* as a potential hunter *and* scavenger. It is crucial to remember, too, that *gathering* of wild plant foods was also practiced by *H. erectus* groups. Indeed, probably a majority of the calories they consumed came from such gathering activities.

Moreover, as we have seen, the mere *presence* of animal bones at archaeological sites does not prove that hominids were killing animals or even necessarily exploiting meat. Indeed, as was the case in the earlier South African sites (discussed in Chapter 8), the hominid remains themselves may have been the meal refuse of large carnivores! Thus, in making interpretations of early hominid sites, we must consider a variety of alternatives. As Stanford University archaeologist Richard Klein has concluded regarding Middle Pleistocene sites, the interpretations are far from clear: "In sum, the available data do not allow us to isolate the relative roles of humans, carnivores, and factors such as starvation, accidents, and stream action in creating bone assemblages. . . . Certainly, as presently understood, the sites do not tell us how successful or effective *Homo erectus* was at obtaining meat" (1989, p. 221).

Population Trends

H erectus is the first hominid for which we have definite evidence of *wide* geographical dispersion (i.e., across more than one continent). Descendants of early *Homo* ancestors in Africa, the earliest migrants into Eurasia were still similar in many ways to their early *Homo* forebears (although they may be seen as a primitive form of *H. erectus*). Once established in Eurasia, and once attaining the full physical and cultural capacities of *H. erectus*, populations dispersed far and wide in the Old World—far beyond the relatively narrow ranges of earlier hominids.

The life of hunter-scavengers (and still, no doubt, *primarily* gatherers) was nomadic, and the woodland and savanna that covered the southern tier of Asia would have been an excellent environment for *H. erectus*, as it was similar to the econiche of their African ancestors. As the population grew, small groups budded off and moved on to find their own resource areas. This process, repeated again and again, led *H. erectus* east, crossing to Java, arriving there, it seems, as early as the most ancient known sites in East Africa itself.

Once in Java, it had been assumed that *H. erectus* would have found it impossible to venture farther south or east, since during the Pleistocene, deep water channels presumably separated Java completely from more southerly islands and Australia. However, recent reinterpretation (and firmer chronometric dates) of stone tools found on the island of Flores, 375 miles east of Java, has prompted some paleoanthropologists to reconsider this assumption (Gibbons, 1998). With a suggested date of 750,000 y.a. for these tools, it raises a most unexpected possibility: Could ancient *H. erectus* at this *very* early period construct oceangoing vessels (rafts?) that could navigate over deep, fast-moving waters?

While initial dating of the Flores stone materials appears reasonably good, the conclusion that the finds *prove* such seemingly advanced capabilities for *H. erectus* is not yet generally accepted. A number of troublesome issues remain to be resolved, the first being whether the lithic materials from Flores are *deliberate* tools or are simply naturally fractured rock. This latter possibility would argue against *H. erectus* (or any other hominid) having expanded south or east beyond Java at such an early date. Of course, the most unambiguous evidence would be fossil discoveries of *H. erectus* itself.

When we look back at the evolution of *H. erectus*, we realize how significant this early human's achievements were. It was *H. erectus* who increased in body size with more efficient bipedalism; who embraced culture wholeheartedly as a strategy of adaptation; whose brain was reshaped and increased in size to within *H. sapiens* range; who became a more efficient scavenger and likely hunter with greater dependence on meat; and who apparently established more permanent bases. In short, it was *H. erectus*, committed to a cultural way of life, who transformed hominid evolution to human evolution; or as Foley states, "The appearance and expansion of *H. erectus* represented a major change in adaptive strategy that influenced the subsequent process and pattern of human evolution" (1991, p. 425).

Summary

 *H*omo erectus remains are found in geological contexts dating from about 1.8 million to about 200,000 years ago (and perhaps much later), a period of more than 1.5 million years. The first finds were made by Dubois in Java, and later discoveries came from China and Africa. Differences from early *Homo* are notable in *H. erectus'* larger brain, taller stature, robust build, and changes in facial structure and cranial buttressing.

The long period of *H. erectus'* existence was marked by a remarkably uniform technology over space and time. Nevertheless, compared to earlier hominids, *H. erectus* and contemporaries introduced more sophisticated tools and probably ate novel and/or differently processed foods, using these new tools and at later sites perhaps fire as well. They were also able to move into different environments and successfully adapt to new conditions.

TABLE 9-1		Most Significant Hominid Fossils Discussed in this Chapter		
	Site	**Dates (y.a.)**	**Taxonomic Designation**	**Comments**
Asia	Java (6 locales)	1,8000,000– 25,000	*Homo erectus*	First *H. erectus* discovery; most finds in disturbed river terrace contexts
	China (6 locales; most significant is Zhoukoudian)	400,000+– 200,000?	*Homo erectus*	Up to 40 individuals at Zhoukoudian; also, many artifacts; Zhoukoudian, however, probably not primary living site
Europe	Ceprano	700,000?	*Homo erectus*	One individual; well-preserved cranium; Similar to Asian *H. erectus*
	Gran Dolina (Atapuerca, Spain)	780,000?	Quite likely not *H. erectus;* referred to by discoverers as "*Homo antecessor,*" but this designation not yet generally accepted	Remains quite incomplete; possibly oldest W. European fossil hominid discovery
	Dmanisi (Republic of Georgia)	1,800,000– 1,700,000	*Homo erectus/Homo ergaster* (very primitive example–or could be classified as early *Homo*)	3 well-preserved crania plus partial mandible; among the oldest *H. erectus* found anywhere
Africa	Bouri (Ethiopia)	1,000,000	*Homo erectus*	Well-preserved cranium plus postcranial bones; morphology quite similar to Asian *H. erectus*
	Nariokotome (West Turkana, Kenya)	1,600,000	*Homo erectus,* also frequently referred to as *Homo ergaster*	Nearly complete adolescent skeleton, probably of a male; shows some differences from Asian *H. erectus*
	East Turkana (Kenya)	1,800,000	*Homo erectus,* also frequently referred to as *Homo ergaster*	Well-preserved cranium plus several other postcranial remains likely coming from same group; cranium likely of female; shows several differences from Asian *H. erectus*

It is generally assumed that some *H. erectus* populations evolved to *H. sapiens,* since many fossils, such as Ngandong (and others discussed in Chapter 10), display both *H. erectus* and *H. sapiens* features. There remain questions about *H. erectus* behavior (e.g., did they hunt?) and about evolution to *H. sapiens* (was it gradual or rapid, and which *H. erectus* populations contributed genes to *H. sapiens?*). The search for answers continues.

Table 9–1 presents a brief summary of the most significant fossil finds discussed in this chapter.

Questions for Review

1. Describe the Pleistocene in terms of (a) relationship to glacial sequences and (b) the dating of fossil hominids.
2. Describe *Homo erectus.* How is *H. erectus* anatomically different from early *Homo?* From *H. sapiens?*
3. In what areas of the world have *Homo erectus* fossils been found?

4. In comparing *H. erectus* with earlier hominids, why is it important to specify which comparative sample is being used?

5. What was the intellectual climate in Europe in the latter half of the nineteenth century, especially concerning human evolution?

6. Why do you think there was so much opposition to Dubois' interpretation of the hominid fossils he found in Java?

7. Why do you think Zhoukoudian *H. erectus* was enthusiastically accepted, whereas the Javanese fossils were not?

8. Describe the way of life of *H. erectus* at Zhoukoudian as depicted by earlier researchers. What disagreements have been voiced about this conjecture?

9. *H. erectus* has been called the first human. Why?

10. What is the *H. erectus* evidence from Africa, and what questions of human evolution does the evidence raise?

11. *H. erectus* migrated to various points in Africa and vast distances to eastern Asia and elsewhere. What does this tell you about the species?

12. What kinds of stone tools have been found at *H. erectus* sites?

Suggested Further Readings

Day, Michael. 1986. *Guide to Fossil Man*. Chicago: University of Chicago Press.

Gore, Rick. 2002. "The First Pioneer? A New Find Shakes the Human Family Tree." *National Geographic* 202 (August), Front Supplement (not paginated).

Lewin, Roger. 1998. *Principles of Human Evolution: A Core Textbook*. New York: Blackwell Science.

Rightmire, G. P. 1990. *The Evolution of* Homo erectus. New York: Cambridge University Press.

Shapiro, Harry L. 1980. *Peking Man*. New York: Simon & Schuster.

Walker, Alan, and Richard Leakey (eds). 1993. *The Nariokotome* Homo erectus *Skeleton*. Cambridge, MA: Harvard University Press.

Wolpoff, Milford. 1984. "Evolution in *Homo erectus:* The Question of Stasis." *Paleobiology* 10: 389–406.

Multimedia Resources

 Companion Web Site

Anthropology Online: The Wadsworth Anthropology Resource Center
Visit **http://anthropology.wadsworth.com** and click on the Companion Web Site for Jurmain/Kilgore/Trevathan/Nelson's *Essentials of Physical Anthropology,* Fifth Edition, to access a wide range of enrichment material to aid in your study of anthropology. Among the useful options for each chapter's self-study are learning objectives, flashcards, Internet exercises, Web links, InfoTrac College Edition exercises, and practice quizzes that can be scored and emailed to your instructor.

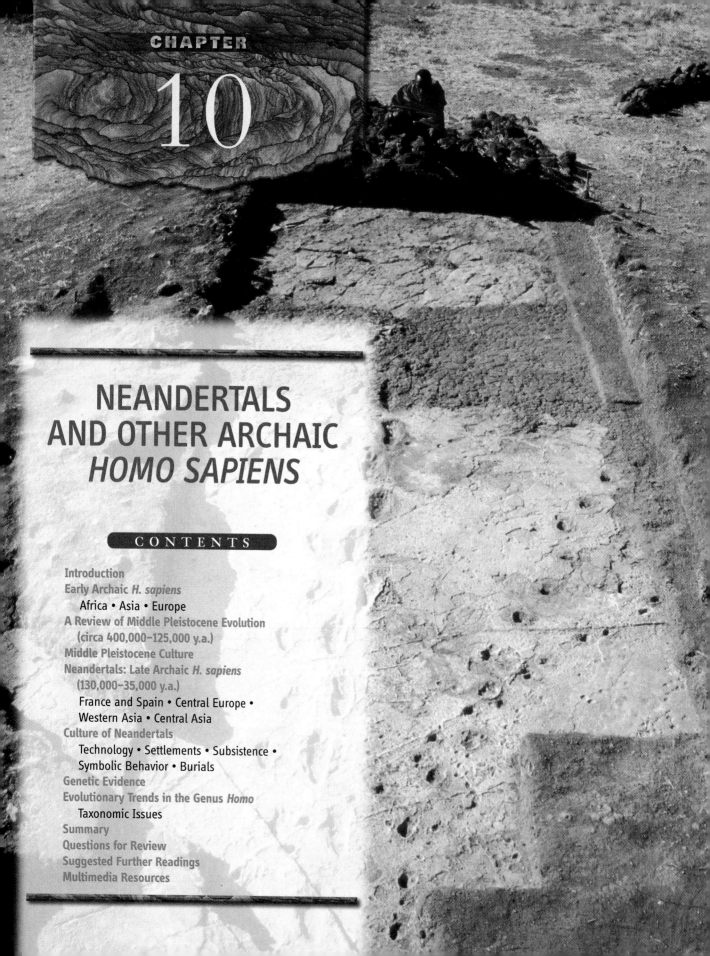

NEANDERTALS AND OTHER ARCHAIC *HOMO SAPIENS*

CONTENTS

Introduction

See the following sections of the CD-ROM for topics covered in this chapter: Virtual Lab 10, section I, and Virtual Lab 11.

I n the previous chapter, we saw that *Homo erectus* (or a close relative) first evolved in Africa and eventually spread to several other areas of the Old World. While there is some debate concerning the number of species present during the time from 1.8 m.y.a. until about 400,000 y.a., there is general recognition that all these hominids are at a stage (what is called a "grade") that comes prior to that of *Homo sapiens*.

What, then, of the next grade of human evolution, that which occurs after 400,000 y.a.? During this time period, we have considerable evidence of the emergence of *Homo sapiens*, with fossil material coming from several areas of the Old World. In the next chapter, we will discuss the origins and dispersal of modern *Homo sapiens*. However, the appearance of hominids essentially identical to ourselves (anatomically and, presumably, behaviorally as well) did not occur instantaneously.

Between 400,000 and 100,000 y.a., coming from widely scattered sites in Africa, Asia, and Europe, fossil evidence indicates that our species emerged as the result of a long and intermittent evolutionary process. In many respects, the hominids during this time period are *transitional* forms, retaining some characteristics of their immediate precursors (*Homo erectus*) as well as displaying some traits similar to their later descendants (modern *Homo sapiens*).

Paleoanthropologists do not entirely agree what name (or names) to use for this varied group of transitional Middle Pleistocene hominids, but often refer to them as **archaic *Homo sapiens***. By contrast, hominids essentially identical to us are referred to as **anatomically modern *Homo sapiens***.

In this chapter, we will discuss the geographical localities, anatomy, and behavior of archaic *Homo sapiens* and will divide these hominids into two chronological groups: early archaic *Homo sapiens* and late archaic *Homo sapiens* (including especially the Neandertals).

Archaic *Homo sapiens* Earlier forms of *Homo sapiens* (including Neandertals) from the Old World that differ from *H. erectus* but lack the full set of characteristics diagnostic of modern *H. sapiens*.

Anatomically modern *Homo sapiens* All modern humans and some fossil forms, perhaps dating as early as 200,000 y.a.; defined by a set of derived characteristics, including cranial architecture and lack of skeletal robusticity; usually classified at the subspecies level as *Homo sapiens sapiens*.

Early Archaic H. sapiens

Many early archaic forms show morphological changes compared with *H. erectus*. These derived changes are reflected in brain expansion; increased parietal breadth (the basal portion of the skull is no longer the widest area, and therefore, the shape of the skull as seen from the rear is no longer pentagonal); some decrease in the size of the molars; and general decrease in cranial and postcranial robusticity.

A difficulty of major significance concerns exactly how to classify all this Middle Pleistocene hominid material. Here we take a conservative taxonomic approach and classify *all* of the specimens as archaic forms within the species *Homo sapiens*. However, a growing number of paleoanthropologists (e.g., Stringer, 1995; Larick and Ciochon, 1996; Rightmire, 1998) disagree with this interpretation and prefer to classify most, if not all, of the individuals into other species of the genus *Homo*. In this view, some of the earlier archaic forms could be ancestral to modern humans, but the later ones most likely would not be. As in other debates of this nature discussed in previous chapters, the essential issue concerns interpretation of intra- as compared to interspecific variation. We will return to this crucial topic at the end of this chapter.

A further complication in understanding archaic *H. sapiens* is that there is considerable variation both within and between samples of these hominids. Moreover, they are geographically very widely dispersed. In fact, archaic *H. sapiens* fossils have been found on the three continents of Africa, Asia, and Europe. In Europe, the well-known Neandertals are included in this category. (Neandertals are not found anywhere *except* Europe and western Asia.)

Africa

figure 10–1 Broken Hill (Kabwe). Note the very heavy supraorbital torus.

Harry Nelson

In Africa, archaic *H. sapiens* fossils have been found at several sites (figs. 10–1 and 10–2). One of the best known is Broken Hill (Kabwe). At this site in Zambia, a complete cranium, together with other cranial and postcranial elements belonging to several individuals, was discovered.

In this and other African early archaic specimens, a mixture of older and more recent traits can be seen. The skull's massive supraorbital torus (one of the largest of any hominid), low vault, and prominent occipital torus recall those of *H. erectus*. On the other hand, the occipital region is less angulated, the cranial vault bones are thinner, and the cranial base is essentially modern. Dating estimates of Broken Hill and most of the other early archaic *H. sapiens* specimens from Africa have ranged throughout the Middle and Upper Pleistocene, but recent estimates have given dates for most of the localities in the range of 150,000–125,000 y.a.

A total of eight other archaic *H. sapiens* crania from South and East Africa also show a combination of *H. erectus* and *H. sapiens* characteristics, and they are all mentioned in the literature as being similar to Broken Hill. The most important of these African finds come from the sites of Florisbad and Elandsfontein in South Africa, Laetoli in Tanzania, and Bodo in Ethiopia (see fig. 10–2). The general similarities in all these African archaic *H. sapiens* fossils may signify a fairly close genetic relationship of hominids from East and South Africa. It is also possible—although it seems most unlikely—that several populations were evolving in a somewhat similar way from *H. erectus* to a more *H. sapiens*-looking morphology.

We should point out that the evolutionary path of these hominids did not take a Neandertal turn. It seems that there were no Neandertals in Africa—nor were there any in the Far East (Table 10–1).

Asia

CHINA   Like their counterparts in Europe and Africa, Chinese archaic *H. sapiens** specimens also display both earlier and later characteristics. Chinese paleoanthropologists suggest that archaic *H. sapiens* traits, such as a sagittal ridge (see p. 224) and flattened nasal bones, are shared with *H. erectus*, especially those specimens from Zhoukoudian. They also point out that some of these features can be found in modern *H. sapiens* in China today, indicating substantial genetic continuity. That is, some Chinese researchers have argued that anatomically modern Chinese

---

*Chinese anthropologists prefer the term "early *Homo sapiens*" instead of "archaic *H. sapiens*."

TABLE 10-1	In Summary: Key Archaic *Homo sapiens* Discoveries (Outside of Europe)		
Site	**Dates (y.a.)***	**Human Remains**	**Comments**
Africa			
Bodo (Ethiopia)	Middle Pleistocene (600,000?)	Incomplete skull, part of braincase	Resembles Broken Hill; first evidence of scalping
Broken Hill (Kabwe) (Zambia)	Late Middle Pleistocene; (130,000 or older)	Nearly complete cranium, cranial fragments of second individual, miscellaneous postcranial bones	Massive browridge, low vault, prominent occipital torus; cranial capacity within range of modern *H. sapiens*
China			
Dali	Late Middle Pleistocene (230,000–180,000)	Nearly complete skull	Robust supraorbital ridge, low vault, retreating forehead, canine fossa
Jinniushan	Late Middle Pleistocene (200,000)	Partial skeleton, including a cranium	Thin cranial bones

*Also see figure 10–3.

did not evolve from *H. sapiens* in either Europe or Africa, evolving instead specifically in China from a separate *H. erectus* lineage.

Whether such regional evolution occurred in many areas of the world or, alternatively, whether anatomically modern migrants from Africa displaced local populations is the subject of a major ongoing debate in paleoanthropology. This important controversy will be the central focus of the next chapter.

Dali, the most complete skull of the late Middle or early Upper Pleistocene fossils in China, displays *H. erectus* and *H. sapiens* traits, but it is clearly classified as early *H. sapiens* (despite its relatively small cranial capacity of 1,120 cm^3). Several other Chinese specimens also reflect both earlier and later traits and are placed in the same category as Dali. In addition, the more recently discovered (1984) partial skeleton from Jinniushan, in northeast China, has been given a provisional date of 200,000 y.a. (Tiemel et al., 1994). The cranial capacity is fairly large (approximately 1,260 cm^3), and the walls of the braincase are thin—both modern features and quite unexpected in an individual this ancient (if the dating estimate does indeed hold up).

INDIA   In 1982, a partial skull was discovered in the Narmada Valley, in central India. Associated with this fossil were various hand axes, cleavers, flakes, and choppers. This Narmada specimen has been dated as Middle Pleistocene with a probable cranial capacity within the range of 1,155 to 1,421 cm^3. K. A. R. Kennedy (1991), who made a more recent study of the fossil, suggests that Narmada should be viewed as an early example of *H. sapiens*.

Europe

Various attempts have been made to organize European archaic *H. sapiens* of the Middle and early Upper Pleistocene in the time range of 400,000–150,000 y.a. (fig. 10–3). Because in many cases definite dates or adequate remains (or both) are lacking, it is difficult to be certain which fossils belong where in the evolutionary sequence. As already noted, what we find in Europe are fossils, such as those in Africa and China, whose features resemble both *H. erectus* and

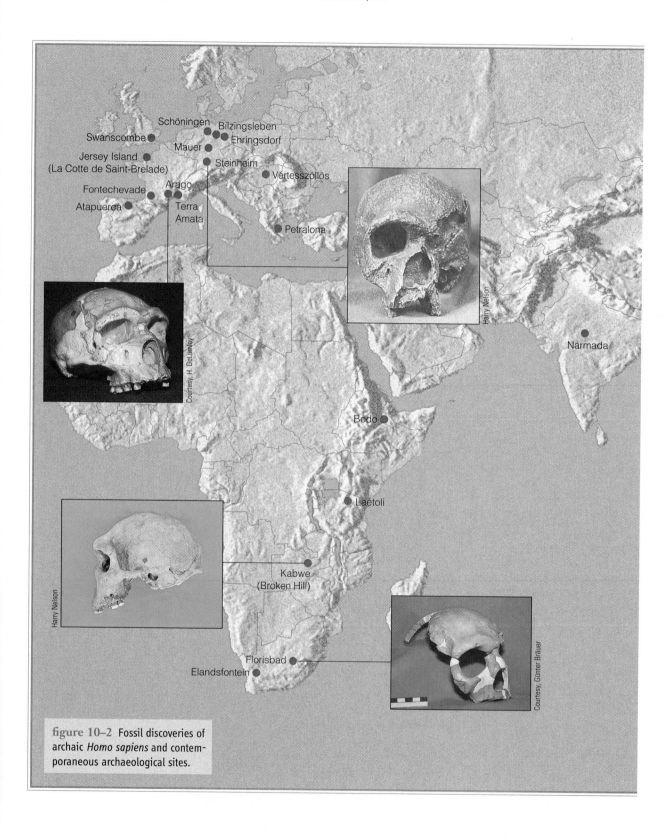

figure 10–2 Fossil discoveries of archaic *Homo sapiens* and contemporaneous archaeological sites.

Courtesy, Xinzhi Wu

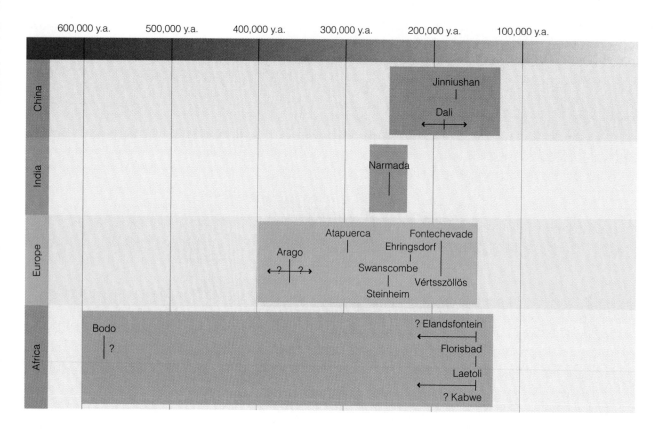

figure 10–3 Time line of early archaic *Homo sapiens*. Note that most dates are approximations. Question marks indicate those estimates that are most tentative.

H. sapiens. You should further note that the earliest fossil finds from western Europe (including those from Boxgrove in England and Atapuerca in Spain, discussed in Chapter 9) already show some of these transitional features.

The earliest archaic *H. sapiens* representatives from Europe show some resemblance to *H. erectus* in the robusticity of the mandible, thick cranial bones, pronounced occipital torus, heavy supraorbital torus, receding frontal bone, greatest parietal breadth near the base of the skull, and large teeth. (They, of course, also have one or more *H. sapiens* characteristics.) Examples of these early archaic forms from Europe include fossils from Steinheim, Swanscombe, and Vértesszöllös (see fig. 10–2). Later European archaic representatives also possess some *H. erectus* characteristics, but they also have one or more of the following traits: larger cranial capacity, more rounded occipital area, parietal expansion, and reduced tooth size (Table 10–2).

The later group, essentially from the latter half of the Middle Pleistocene, overlaps to some extent with the earlier group. From an evolutionary point of view, this later group may have evolved from the earlier one, and since many of these individuals display traits unique to Neandertals, they may in turn have given rise to the Neandertals. Examples of this somewhat later European transitional group include specimens from Fontechevade (France) and Ehringsdorf (Germany), as well as recent discoveries from Atapuerca, in northern Spain, in the same region as the recently discovered more ancient remains discussed in Chapter 9. This last site (called Sima de los Huesos), dated to approximately 300,000 y.a., has yielded the largest sample yet of archaic *H. sapiens* from anywhere in the world and includes the remains of at least 32 individuals (among

TABLE 10-2	In Summary: Key Early Archaic *Homo sapiens* in Europe		
Site	**Dates (y.a.)***	**Human Remains**	**Comments**
Arago (Tautavel) (France)	400,000–300,000; date uncertain	Face; parietal perhaps from same person; many cranial fragments; up to 23 individuals represented	Thick supraorbital torus, pronounced alveolar prognathism; parietal resembles Swanscombe
Atapuerca (Sima de los Huesos, northern Spain)	320,000–190,000, probably 300,000	Minimum of 32 individuals, including some nearly complete crania	Several resemblances to Neandertals; oldest evidence of deliberate disposal of dead; largest sample of archaic *H. sapiens* at any site
Steinheim (Germany)	Mindel-Riss Interglacial– 300,000–250,000; date uncertain	Nearly complete skull, lacking mandible	Pronounced supraorbital torus, frontal low, occipital rounded
Swanscombe (England)	Mindel-Riss Interglacial– 300,000–250,000; date uncertain	Occipital and parietals	Bones thick like *H. erectus*; occipital resembles Neandertal

*Also see figure 10–3.

which are several excellently preserved crania) (Arsuaga et al., 1993, 1997; Kunzig, 1997). Excavations continue at this remarkable site, where bones have somehow accumulated within a deep chamber inside a cave. There are also large numbers of carnivore remains (bear, fox), but these fossils are generally in separate locations from where the hominids were found. From initial descriptions, the hominid morphology has been interpreted as showing several indications of an early Neandertal-like pattern (arching browridges, projecting midface, and other features) (Rightmire, 1998).

A Review of Middle Pleistocene Evolution (circa 400,000–125,000 y.a.)

Like the *erectus/sapiens* mix in Africa and China, the fossils from Europe also exhibit a mosaic of traits from both species (fig. 10–4). However, it is important to note that the fossils from each continent differ; that is, the mosaic Chinese forms are not the same as those from Africa or Europe. Some European fossils, assumed to be earlier, are more robust and possess more similarities to *H. erectus* than to modern *H. sapiens*. The later Middle Pleistocene European fossils appear to be more Neandertal-like, but the uncertainty of dates prevents a clear scenario of the Middle Pleistocene evolutionary sequence.

The physical differences from *H. erectus* are not extraordinary. Bones remain thick, the supraorbital torus is prominent, and vault height shows little increase. There is, however, a definite increase in brain size and a change in the shape of the skull from pentagonal to globular as seen from the rear. There is also a trend, especially with the later Middle Pleistocene forms, toward less occipital angulation. It is interesting to note that in Europe, the changes move toward a Neandertal *H. sapiens* pattern, but in Africa and Asia, toward modern *H. sapiens*.

(a)

(b)

figure 10–4 Cast of an archaic *Homo sapiens* skull from Germany (Steinheim). (a) Frontal view showing damaged skull. (b) Basal view showing how the foramen magnum was enlarged, apparently for removal of the brain, perhaps for dietary or ritualistic purposes.

Middle Pleistocene Culture

The Acheulian technology of *H. erectus* carried over into the Middle Pleistocene with relatively little change until near the end of the period, when it became slightly more sophisticated. Bone, a very useful tool material, apparently went practically unused by archaic *H. sapiens*. Stone flake tools similar to those of the earlier era persisted, perhaps in greater variety. Archaic *H. sapiens* in Africa and Europe invented a method—the Levallois technique (fig. 10–5)—for controlling flake size and shape. Requiring several coordinated steps, this was no mean feat and suggests to many scholars increased cognitive abilities in late archaic *H. sapiens* compared to earlier archaic forms.

Interpretation of the distribution of artifacts during the later Middle Pleistocene has generated considerable discussion among archaeologists. We have noted (in Chapter 10) that there is a general geographical distribution characteristic of the Lower Pleistocene, with bifaces (mostly hand axes) found quite often at sites in Africa, but only rarely at sites in most of Asia, and not at all among the rich assemblage at Zhoukoudian. Moreover, where hand axes proliferate, the stone tool industry is referred to as Acheulian, while at localities without hand axes, various other terms are used (e.g., "chopper/chopping tool"—a misnomer, since most of the tools are actually flakes).

Acheulian assemblages have been found at many African sites as well as numerous European ones (e.g., Swanscombe in England and Arago in France). Nevertheless, the broad geographical distribution of what we call Acheulian should not blind us to the considerable intraregional diversity in stone tool industries. For example, while a variety of European sites do show a typical Acheulian complex, rich in bifacial hand axes and cleavers, other contemporaneous ones—for example, Bilzingsleben in Germany and Vértesszöllös in Hungary—do not. At these latter two sites, a variety of small retouched flake tools and flaked pebbles of various sizes were found, but no hand axes.

It thus appears that different stone tool industries coexisted in some areas for long periods. Various explanations (Villa, 1983) have been offered to account for this apparent diversity: (1) The tool industries were produced by different peoples (i.e., different cultures, perhaps hominids that also differed biologically); (2) the tool industries represent different types of activities carried out at separate locales; (3) the presence (or absence) of specific tool types—bifaces—represents the availability (or unavailability) of appropriate local stone resources.

Archaic *H. sapiens* populations continued to live both in caves and in open-air sites, but may have increased their use of caves. Did archaic *H. sapiens* control fire? Klein (1989, p. 255) suggests that these hominids did. He writes that there was a "concentration of burnt bones in depressions 50–60 cm across at Vértesszöllös" and that "fossil hearths have also been identified at Bilzingsleben and in several French caves that were probably occupied by early *H. sapiens*." Chinese archaeologists insist that many Middle Pleistocene sites in China contain evidence of human-controlled fire. However, not everyone is convinced.

That archaic *H. sapiens* built temporary structures is revealed by concentrations of bones, stones, and artifacts at several sites. Here, they manufactured artifacts and exploited the area for food. The stones may have been used to support the sides of a shelter.

In the Lazaret Cave in the city of Nice, in southern France, a shelter about 36 feet by 11 feet was built against the cave wall, and skins probably were hung over a framework of poles as walls for the shelter. The base was supported by rocks and large bones, and inside the shelter were two hearths. The hearth charcoal suggests that the hominid occupants used slow-burning oak and boxwood, which produced easy-to-rekindle embers. Very little stone waste was found inside the shelter, suggesting that they manufactured tools outside, perhaps because there was more light.

Archaeological evidence clearly alludes to the utilization of many different food sources, such as fruits, vegetables, seeds, nuts, and bird eggs, each in its own season. Marine life was also exploited. From Lazaret and Orgnac (southern France) comes evidence of freshwater fishing for trout, perch, and carp. The most detailed reconstruction of Middle Pleistocene life in Europe, however, comes from evidence at Terra Amata, on the southern coast of France (de Lumley and de Lumley, 1973; Villa, 1983). From this site has come fascinating evidence relating to short-term, seasonal visits by archaic *H. sapiens* groups, who built flimsy shelters, gathered plants, exploited marine resources, and possibly hunted medium-sized and large mammals.

The hunting capabilities of these early members of *H. sapiens*, as for earlier hominids, remain open to dispute. What seems clear is that the evidence does not yet unambiguously establish widely practiced advanced abilities. In earlier

Nodule

The nodule is chipped on the perimeter.

Flakes are radially removed from top surface.

A final blow at one end removes a large flake.

figure 10–5 The Levallois technique.

professional discussions (as well as in earlier editions of our texts), archaeological evidence from Terra Amata (in France) and Torralba and Ambrona (in Spain) was used to argue for significantly advanced hunting skills for archaic *H. sapiens* in Europe. However, reconstruction of these sites by Richard Klein and others has now cast doubt on those prior conclusions. Once again, we see that application of scientific rigor (which is simply good critical thinking) makes us question assumptions. And in so doing, we frequently must conclude that other less dramatic (and less romantic) explanations fit the evidence as well as or better than those based on initial imaginative scenarios.

A possible exception to the current, much more conservative view of the hunting skills of archaic *H. sapiens* comes from an archaeological site excavated on the Channel Island of Jersey off the west coast of France (see fig. 10–2). In a cave site called La Cotte de Saint-Brelade, many skeletal remains of large mammals (mammoth and woolly rhinoceros) were found in association with stone flakes. Unlike the remains from the sites mentioned earlier, the animals sampled at La Cotte de Saint-Brelade represent primarily subadults and adults in prime age (*not* what one would expect in naturally occurring accumulations). Moreover, the preserved elements also exhibit the kind of damage that further suggests hominid activities. Directly killing such large animals may not have been within the capabilities of the hominids (archaic *H. sapiens*?) who occupied this site. Thus, K. Scott, who led the excavations, has suggested that these early hominids may have driven their prey off a nearby cliff, bringing certain prized parts back to the cave for further butchering (Scott, 1980).

Another recent and exceptional find is also challenging assumptions regarding hunting capabilities of archaic *H. sapiens* in Europe. From the site of Schöningen in Germany, three remarkably well-preserved wooden spears were discovered in 1995 (Thieme, 1997). As we have noted before, fragile organic remains (such as wood) can rarely be preserved more than a few hundred years; yet these beautifully crafted implements are provisionally dated to 400,000–380,000 y.a.! Beyond this surprisingly ancient date, the spears are intriguing on a variety of other counts. Firstly, they are all large (about 6 feet long), very finely made, selected from hard spruce wood, and expertly balanced. Each spear would have required considerable planning, time, and skill to manufacture. Further, the weapons were most likely used as throwing spears, presumably to hunt large animals. Of interest in this context, bones of numerous horses were also recovered at Schöningen. Archaeologist Hartmut Thieme has thus concluded that "the spears strongly suggest that systematic hunting, involving foresight, planning and the use of appropriate technology, was part of the behavioural repertoire of pre-modern hominids" (1997, p. 807). Therefore, as with the remains from La Cotte de Saint-Brelade, these extraordinary spears from Schöningen make a strong case for advanced hunting skills practiced by at least some archaic *Homo sapiens* populations.

As documented by the fossil hominid remains as well as artifactual evidence from archaeological sites, the long period of transitional hominids in Europe was to continue well into the Upper Pleistocene (after 125,000 y.a.). However, the evolution of archaic *H. sapiens* was to take a unique turn with the appearance and expansion of the Neandertals.

Neandertals: Late Archaic H. sapiens *(130,000–35,000 y.a.)*

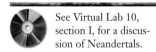

See Virtual Lab 10, section I, for a discussion of Neandertals.

Since their discovery more than a century ago, the Neandertals have haunted the best-laid theories of paleoanthropologists. They fit into the general scheme of human evolution, and yet they are misfits. Classified as *H. sapiens*, they are like us and yet different. It is not an easy task to put them in their place.*

While Neandertal fossil remains have been found at dates approaching 130,000 y.a., in the following discussion of Neandertals, we refer to those populations that lived especially during the last glaciation, which began about 75,000 y.a. and ended about 10,000 y.a. (fig. 10–6). We should also note that the evolutionary roots of Neandertals apparently reach quite far back in western Europe, as evidenced by the 300,000 y.a. remains from Sima de los Huesos, Atapuerca, in northern Spain. The majority of fossils have been found in Europe, where they have been most studied, and our description of Neandertals is based primarily on those specimens from western Europe, who are usually called *classic* Neandertals. Not all Neandertals—including others from eastern Europe and western Asia and those from the interglacial that preceded the last glacial—entirely conform to our description of the classic morphology. They tend to be less robust, perhaps because the climate in which they lived was not as cold as western Europe during the last glaciation.

One striking feature of Neandertals is brain size, which in these hominids actually was larger than that of *H. sapiens* today. The average for contemporary *H. sapiens* is between 1,300 and 1,400 cm^3, while for Neandertals it was 1,520 cm^3. The larger size may be associated with the metabolic efficiency of a larger brain in cold weather. The Inuit (Eskimo) brain also averages larger than that of other modern human populations (about the size of the Neandertal brain). It should also be pointed out that the larger brain size in both archaic and contemporary *Homo sapiens* in populations adapted to *cold* climates is partially correlated with larger body size, which has also evolved among these groups (see Chapter 12).

The classic Neandertal cranium is large, long, low, and bulging at the sides. Viewed from the side, the posterior portion of the occipital bone is somewhat bun-shaped, but the marked occipital angle typical of many *H. erectus* crania is absent. The forehead rises more vertically than that of *H. erectus*, and the browridges arch over the orbits instead of forming a straight bar (fig. 10–7).

Compared with anatomically modern humans, the Neandertal face stands out. It projects almost as if it were pulled forward. This feature can be seen when the distance of the nose and teeth from the eye orbits is compared with that of modern *H. sapiens*. Postcranially, Neandertals were very robust, barrel-chested, and powerfully muscled. This robust skeletal structure, in fact, dominates hominid evolution from *H. erectus* through archaic *H. sapiens*.

***Homo sapiens neanderthalensis* is the subspecific designation for Neandertals, although not all paleoanthropologists agree with this terminology. (The subspecies for anatomically modern *H. sapiens* is designated as *Homo sapiens sapiens*.)

Thal, meaning "valley," is the old spelling and is kept in the species designation (the "h" was always silent and not pronounced). The modern spelling is *tal* and is now used this way in Germany; we shall adhere to contemporary usage in the text with the spelling *Neandertal*.

figure 10–6 Correlation of Pleistocene subdivisions with archaeological industries and hominids. Note that the geological divisions are separate and different from the archaeological stages (e.g., Upper Pleistocene is *not* synonymous with Upper Paleolithic).

		GLACIAL	PALEOLITHIC	CULTURAL PERIODS (Archaeological Industries)	HOMINIDAE
UPPER PLEISTOCENE	10,000 — 20,000 — 30,000 — 40,000 — 50,000 — 75,000 — 100,000 —	Last glacial period / Last interglacial period	Upper Paleolithic / Middle Paleolithic	20,000 — Magdalenian / 25,000 — Solutrean / Gravettian / Aurignacian/ Perigordian / Chatelperronian / Mousterian	NEANDERTALS / MODERN SAPIENS
MIDDLE PLEISTOCENE	125,000 — 700,000 —	Earlier glacial periods	Lower Paleolithic	Acheulian	ARCHAIC H. SAPIENS / HOMO ERECTUS
LOWER PLEISTOCENE	1,800,000 —			Oldowan	AUSTRALO-PITHECUS / EARLY HOMO

Nevertheless, the Neandertals appear particularly robust, with shorter limbs than seen in most modern *H. sapiens* populations. Both the facial anatomy and robust postcranial structure of Neandertals have been interpreted by Erik Trinkaus (of Washington University in St. Louis) to reflect adaptation to rigorous living in a cold climate.

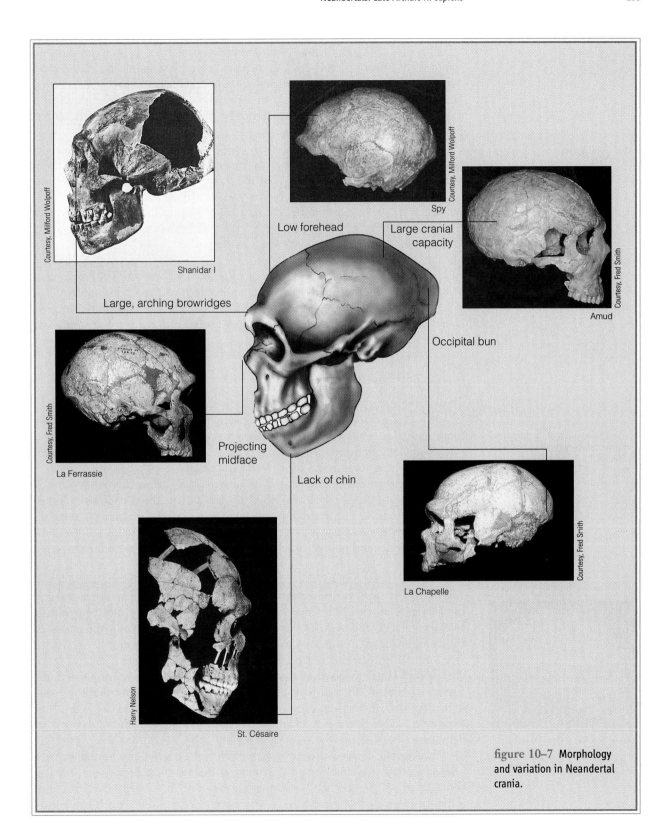

Low forehead

Large cranial capacity

Large, arching browridges

Occipital bun

Projecting midface

Lack of chin

Courtesy, Milford Wolpoff

Shanidar I

Courtesy, Milford Wolpoff

Spy

Courtesy, Fred Smith

Amud

Courtesy, Fred Smith

La Ferrassie

Harry Nelson

St. Césaire

Courtesy, Fred Smith

La Chapelle

figure 10–7 Morphology and variation in Neandertal crania.

For about 100,000 years, Neandertals lived in Europe and western Asia (see fig. 10–13 on pp. 260–261), and their coming and going has raised more questions and controversies than perhaps any other hominid group. As noted, Neandertal forebears date back to the later archaic *H. sapiens*. But these were transitional forms, and it is not until the last interglacial that Neandertals were fully recognizable.

Neandertal takes its name from the Neander Valley, near Düsseldorf, Germany. In 1856, workmen quarrying limestone caves in the valley came across some fossilized bones. The owner of the quarry believed them to be bear and gave them to a natural science teacher, who realized that they were not the remains of a cave bear, but rather the remains of an ancient human. Exactly what the bones represented became a *cause célèbre* for many years, and the fate of "Neandertal Man," as the bones were named, hung in the balance until later finds provided more evidence.

What swung the balance in favor of accepting the Neander Valley specimen as a genuine hominid fossil were other nineteenth-century finds similar to it. What is more important, the additional fossil remains brought home the realization that a form of human different from nineteenth-century Europeans had in fact once existed.

France and Spain

One of the most important Neandertal discoveries was made in 1908 at La Chapelle-aux-Saints in southwestern France. A nearly complete skeleton was found buried in a shallow grave in a **flexed** position, with several fragments of nonhuman long bones placed over the head, and over them, a bison leg. Around the body were flint tools and broken animal bones.

Flexed The position of the body in a bent orientation, with the arms and legs drawn up to the chest.

The skeleton was turned over for study to a well-known French paleontologist, Marcellin Boule, who published his analysis in three copious volumes. Boule depicted the La Chapelle Neandertal as a brutish, bent-kneed, not fully erect biped. As a result of this exaggerated interpretation, some scholars, and certainly the general public, concluded that all Neandertals were highly primitive creatures.

Why did Boule draw these conclusions from the La Chapelle skeleton? Apparently, he misconstrued Neandertal posture owing to the presence of spinal osteoarthritis in this older male. In addition, and probably more important, Boule and his contemporaries found it difficult to accept fully as a human ancestor an individual who appeared to depart from the modern pattern.

The skull of this male, who was possibly at least 40 years of age when he died, is very large, with a cranial capacity of 1,620 cm³. As is typical for western European "classic" forms, the vault is low and long, the supraorbital ridges are immense, with the typical Neandertal arched shape, the forehead is low and retreating, and the face is long and projecting. The back of the skull is protuberant and bun-shaped (figs. 10–7 and 10–8).

figure 10–8 La Chapelle-aux-Saints. Note the occipital bun, projecting face, and low vault.

Courtesy, Fred Smith

La Chapelle, however, is not a typical Neandertal, but an unusually robust male that "evidently represents an extreme in the Neandertal range of variation" (Brace et al., 1979, p. 117). Unfortunately, this skeleton, which Boule claimed did not even walk completely erect, was widely accepted as "Mr. Neandertal." But not all Neandertal materials express the suite of "classic Neandertal" traits to the degree seen in La Chapelle.

Another Neandertal site excavated recently in southern France has revealed further fascinating details relating to Neandertal behavior. From the 100,000- to 120,000-year-old Moula-Guercy cave site, Alban Defleur, Tim White, and colleagues have analyzed 78 broken hominid fragments representing probably six individuals (Defleur et al., 1999). The intriguing aspect of these remains concerns *how* they were broken. Detailed analysis of cut marks, pits, scars, and other features clearly suggests that the Neandertal individuals were *processed*—that is, they "were defleshed and disarticulated. After this, the marrow cavity was exposed by a hammer-on-anvil technique" (Defleur et al., 1999, p. 131). Moreover, the non-human bones at this site, especially the deer remains, were processed in an identical fashion. In other words, the Moula-Guercy Neandertals provide the best-documented evidence thus far of Neandertal *cannibalism*.

Some of the most recent of the western European Neandertals come from St. Césaire in southwestern France and are dated at about 35,000 y.a. (fig. 10–9). The bones were recovered from a bed including discarded chipped blades, hand axes, and other stone tools of an **Upper Paleolithic** tool industry associated with Neandertals. Another site, Zafarraya Cave in southern Spain, may provide yet a more recent time range for Neandertal occupation in Europe. During the 1980s and 1990s, a few pieces of hominid individuals were found at Zafarraya that have been interpreted as Neandertal in morphology. What is most interesting, however, is the *date* suggested for the site. French archaeologist Jean-Jacques Hublin, who has excavated the site, asserts that the date is close to 29,000 y.a.—a full 6,000 years later than St. Césaire.

Another site, also recently redated, is apparently about the same age as Zafarraya but is located in central Europe. Recent recalibration by radiocarbon dating has indicated that the later Neandertal levels at Vindija, in Croatia (discussed shortly), are about 28,000 to 29,000 years old (Smith et al., 1999). If one of these dates is further confirmed, then either Zafarraya or Vindija would gain the distinction of having the most recent Neandertals thus far discovered.

Yet a more recent site in Portugal has recently been interpreted as showing hybridization between Neandertals and modern *Homo sapiens*. (We will discuss this intriguing suggestion in more detail in Chapter 11.)

The St. Césaire, Zafarraya, and Vindija sites are fascinating for several reasons. Anatomically modern humans were living in central and western Europe by about 35,000 y.a. or a bit earlier. Therefore, it is possible that Neandertals and modern *H. sapiens* were living in close proximity for several thousand years (fig. 10–10). How did these two groups interact? Evidence from a number of French sites (Harrold, 1989) indicates that Neandertals borrowed technological methods and tools (such as blades) from the anatomically modern populations and thereby modified their own tools, creating a new industry, the **Chatelperronian**. However, such an example of cultural diffusion does not specify *how* the diffusion took place. Did the Neandertals become assimilated into modern populations? Did the two groups interbreed? It would also be interesting to know more precisely how long the coexistence of Neandertals and modern *H. sapiens* lasted.* No one knows the answers to these questions, but it

figure 10–9 St. Césaire, among the "last" Neandertals.

Harry Nelson

Upper Paleolithic A cultural period usually associated with early modern humans (but also associated with Neandertals) and distinguished by technological innovation in various stone tool industries. Best known from western Europe, similar industries are also known from central and eastern Europe and Africa.

Chatelperronian Pertaining to an Upper Paleolithic tool industry found in France and Spain, containing blade tools and associated with Neandertals.

---

*For a fictionalized account of the meeting between Neandertals and anatomically modern humans, see Bjorn Kurten's *Dance of the Tiger: A Novel of the Ice Age*. Another novel on the subject is Jean M. Auel's *Clan of the Cave Bear*. Several movies and a Discovery Channel production have also been made on this theme.

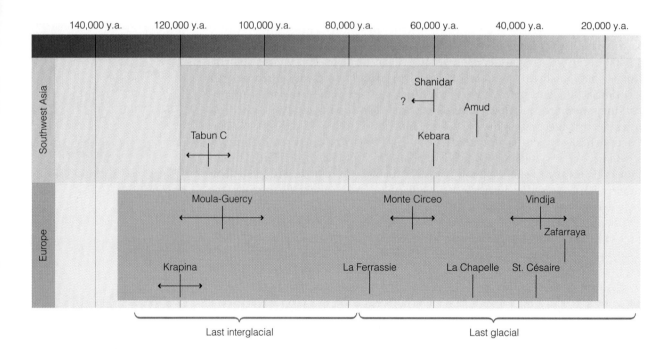

| | 140,000 y.a. | 120,000 y.a. | 100,000 y.a. | 80,000 y.a. | 60,000 y.a. | 40,000 y.a. | 20,000 y.a. |

Southwest Asia

Shanidar
? ←┬
        Amud
Tabun C   Kebara
←┼→

Europe

Moula-Guercy   Monte Circeo   Vindija
←┼→   ←┼→   ←┼→
                                  Zafarraya

Krapina   La Ferrassie   La Chapelle   St. Césaire
←┼→

Last interglacial   Last glacial

figure 10–10 Time line for Neandertal (*Homo sapiens neanderthalensis*) fossil discoveries.

(a)

(b)

figure 10–11 Krapina C.
(a) Lateral view showing characteristic Neandertal traits.
(b) Three-quarters view.

has been suggested that an average annual difference of 2 percent mortality between the two populations (i.e., modern *H. sapiens* individuals lived longer than Neandertals) would have resulted in the extinction of the Neandertals in approximately 1,000 years (Zubrow, 1989).

It should be noted that not all paleoanthropologists agree with the notion of the coexistence of Neandertals and Upper Paleolithic modern humans. For example, in a recent paper, David Frayer of the University of Kansas states, "There is still *no human fossil evidence* which supports the coexistence of Neanderthal and Upper Paleolithic forms in Europe" (emphasis added) (1992, p. 9). That is, despite the indications of cultural diffusion noted here, no European site has yet produced directly associated remains of *both* types of humans.

Central Europe

There are quite a few other European classic Neandertals, including significant finds in central Europe. At Krapina, Croatia, an abundance of bones (1,000 fragments representing up to 70 individuals) and 1,000 stone tools or flakes have been recovered (Trinkaus and Shipman, 1992). Krapina is an old site, perhaps the earliest showing the full "classic" Neandertal morphology, dating back to the last interglacial (estimated at 130,000–110,000 y.a.). Moreover, despite the relatively early date, the characteristic Neandertal features of the Krapina specimens (although less robust) are similar to the western European finds (fig. 10–11). Krapina is also important as an intentional burial site, one of the oldest on record.

Another interesting site in central Europe is Vindija, about 30 miles from Krapina. The site is an excellent source of faunal, cultural, and hominid materials stratified in *sequence* throughout much of the Upper Pleistocene. Neandertal fossils consisting of some 35 specimens are dated between about 42,000 and 28,000 y.a. (the latter date would be among the most recent of all Neandertal discoveries). Even though some of their features approach the morphology of early modern south-central European *H. sapiens*, the overall pattern is definitely Neandertal. However, these modified Neandertal features, such as smaller browridges and slight chin development, may also be seen as an evolutionary trend toward modern *H. sapiens*.

Fred Smith, of Northern Illinois University, takes the view that variation in Vindija cranial features points to a trend continuing on to the later anatomically modern specimens found in the upper levels of the cave. Does Vindija support the proposition that the origin of *H. sapiens* could have occurred here in central Europe? Smith does not insist on this interpretation and suggests that anatomically modern *Homo sapiens* could have come from elsewhere. But he does believe that there is at least some morphological and genetic continuity between the samples found in the lower and upper levels of the cave.

Western Asia

ISRAEL   In addition to European Neandertals, there are numerous important discoveries from southwest Asia. Several specimens from Israel display some modern features and are less robust than the classic Neandertals of Europe, but again the overall pattern is Neandertal. The best known of these discoveries is from Tabun (Mugharet-et-Tabun, "Cave of the Oven") at Mt. Carmel, a short drive south from Haifa (fig. 10–12). Tabun, excavated in the early 1930s, yielded a female skeleton, recently dated by thermoluminescence (TL) at about 120,000–110,000 y.a. If this dating proves accurate, it places the Tabun find as clearly contemporary with early modern *H. sapiens* found in nearby caves. (TL dating is discussed on p. 282.)

A more recent Neandertal burial, a male discovered in 1983, comes from Kebara, a neighboring cave of Tabun at Mt. Carmel. Although the skeleton is incomplete—the cranium and much of the lower limbs are missing—the pelvis,

figure 10–12 Excavation of the Tabun Cave, Mt. Carmel, Israel.

Harry Nelson

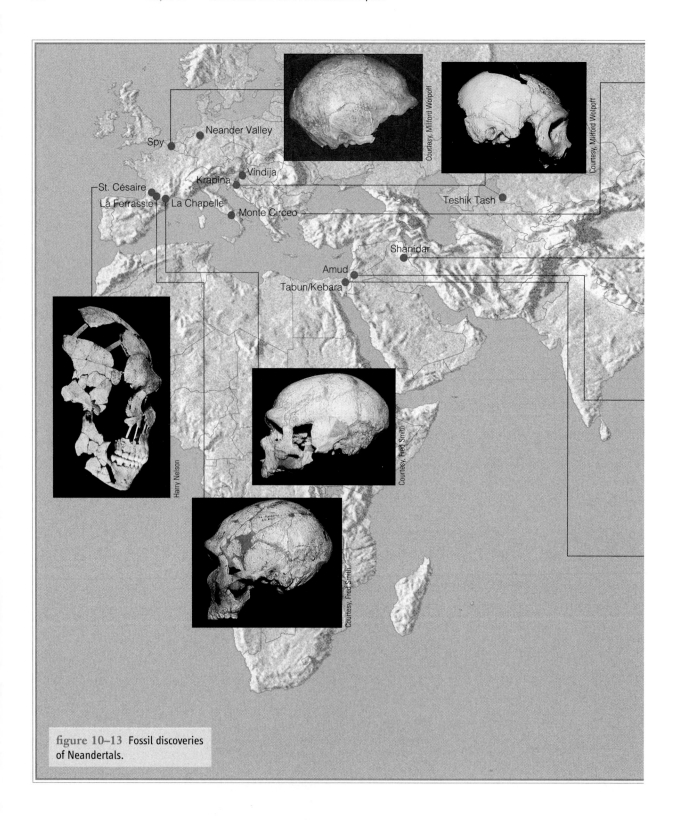

figure 10–13 Fossil discoveries of Neandertals.

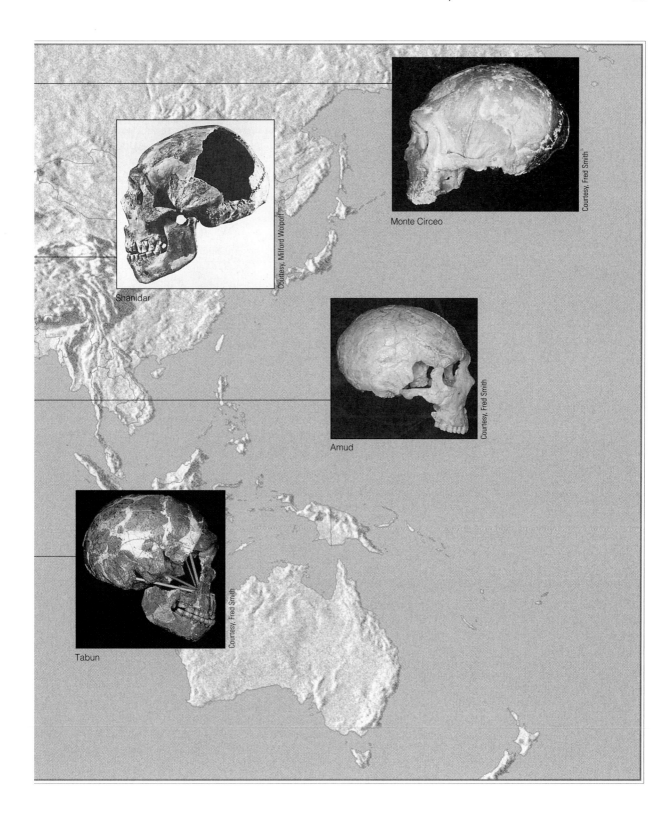

Shanidar
Courtesy, Milford Wolpoff

Monte Circeo
Courtesy, Fred Smith

Amud
Courtesy, Fred Smith

Tabun
Courtesy, Fred Smith

dated to 60,000 y.a., is the most complete Neandertal pelvis so far recovered. Also recovered at Kebara is a hyoid bone, the first from a Neandertal, and this find is especially important from the point of view of reconstructing language capabilities.*

IRAQ   A most remarkable site is Shanidar, in the Zagros Mountains of northeastern Iraq, where partial skeletons of nine individuals—males and females, seven adults and two infants—were found, four of them deliberately buried (Table 10–3). One of the more interesting individuals is Shanidar 1, a male who lived to be approximately 30 to 45 years old, a considerable age for a prehistoric human (fig. 10–14). His stature is estimated at 5 feet 7 inches, while his cranial capacity is 1,600 cm³. This individual shows several fascinating features:

> There had been a crushing blow to the left side of the head, fracturing the eye socket, displacing the left eye, and probably causing blindness on that side. He also sustained a massive blow to the right side of the body that so badly damaged the right arm that it became withered and useless; the bones of the shoulder blade, collar bone, and upper arm are much smaller and thinner than those on the left. The right lower arm and hand are missing, probably not because of poor preservation . . . but because they either atrophied and dropped off or because they were amputated. (Trinkaus and Shipman, 1992, p. 340)

In addition to these injuries, there was damage to the lower right leg (including a healed fracture of a foot bone). The right knee and left leg show signs of pathological involvement, and these changes to the limbs and foot may have left this man with a limping gait.

Courtesy, Milford Wolpoff

figure 10–14 Shanidar 1. Does he represent Neandertal compassion for the disabled?

TABLE 10-3	In Summary: Key Neandertal Fossil Discoveries		
Site	**Dates (y.a.)**	**Human Remains**	**Comments**
Vindija (Croatia)	42,000–28,000	35 specimens; almost entirely cranial fragments	Among the latest Neandertals; best evidence from southeastern Europe of later Neandertals (possibly "transitional")
La Chapelle (France)	50,000	Nearly complete adult male skeleton	Most famous Neandertal discovery; originally misinterpreted
Shanidar (Iraq)	70,000–60,000	9 individuals (partial skeletons)	Some individuals with severe trauma and other skeletal pathologies
Tabun (Israel)	110,000	2 (perhaps 3) individuals, including almost complete skeleton of adult female	Among the oldest Neandertal discoveries
Krapina (Croatia)	125,000–120,000	Up to 40 individuals, but very fragmentary	Perhaps earliest "classic" Neandertals; evidence of human bone processing

*The Kebara hyoid is identical to that of modern humans, suggesting that Neandertals did not differ from *H. sapiens sapiens* in this key element.

How such a person could perform normal obligations and customs is diffi-cult to imagine. However, both Ralph Solecki, who supervised the work at Shanidar Cave, and Erik Trinkaus, who has carefully studied the Shanidar remains, believe that to survive, he must have been helped by others: "A one-armed, partially blind, crippled man could have made no pretense of hunting or gathering his own food. That he survived for years after his trauma was a tes-tament to Neandertal compassion and humanity" (Trinkaus and Shipman, 1992, p. 341).*

Central Asia

UZBEKISTAN About 1,600 miles east of Shanidar in Uzbekistan, in a cave at Teshik-Tash, is the easternmost Neandertal discovery. The skeleton is that of a nine-year-old boy who appears to have been deliberately buried. It was reported that he was surrounded by five pairs of wild goat horns, suggesting a burial rit-ual or perhaps a religious cult, but owing to inadequate published documenta-tion of the excavation, this interpretation has been seriously questioned. The Teshik-Tash individual, like some specimens from Croatia and southwest Asia, also shows a mixture of Neandertal traits (heavy browridges and occipital bun) and modern traits (high vault and definite signs of a chin).

As noted, the Teshik-Tash site represents the easternmost location presently established for Neandertals. Thus, based on current evidence, it is clear that the geographical distribution of the Neandertals extended from France eastward to central Asia, a distance of about 4,000 miles.

Culture of Neandertals

Neandertals, who lived in the cultural period known as the Middle Paleolithic, are usually associated with the **Mousterian** industry (although the Mousterian industry is not always associated with Neandertals). In the early part of the last glacial period, Mousterian culture extended across Europe and North Africa into the former Soviet Union, Israel, Iran, and as far east as Uzbekistan and per-haps even China. Moreover, in Africa, the contemporaneous Middle Stone Age industry is broadly similar to the Mousterian.

Technology

Neandertals improved on previous prepared-core techniques (i.e., the Levallois) by inventing a new variation. They trimmed a flint nodule around the edges to form a disk-shaped core. Each time they struck the edge, they produced a flake, continuing this way until the core became too small and was discarded. Thus, the Neandertals were able to obtain more flakes per core than their predeces-sors. They then trimmed (retouched) the flakes into various forms, such as scrapers, points, and knives (fig.10–15).

Mousterian Pertaining to the stone tool industry associated with Neandertals and some modern *H. sapiens* groups; also called Middle Paleolithic. This industry is characterized by a larger proportion of flake tools than is found in Acheulian tool kits.

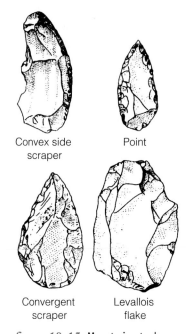

Convex side scraper   Point

Convergent scraper   Levallois flake

figure 10–15 Mousterian tools. (After Bordes.)

*K. A. Dettwyler (1991) asserts that Shanidar 1 could have survived without assistance and that there is no solid evidence that compassion explains this individual's survival.

Neandertal craftspeople elaborated and diversified traditional methods, and there is some indication of development in the specialization of tools used in skin and meat preparation, hunting, woodworking, and hafting. There is, however, still nearly a complete absence of bone tools, in strong contrast to the succeeding cultural period, the Upper Paleolithic. Nevertheless, Neandertals advanced their technology, which tended to be similar in basic tool types over considerable geographical distances, far beyond that of *H. erectus*. It is quite possible that their modifications in technology helped provide a basis for the remarkable changes of the Upper Paleolithic (discussed in the next chapter).

Settlements

People of the Mousterian culture lived in a variety of open sites, caves, and rock shelters. Living in the open on the cold tundra suggests the building of structures, and there is some evidence of such structures (although the last glaciation must have destroyed many open sites). At the site of Moldova, in the Ukraine (now an independent state and neighbor of Russia), archaeologists found traces of an oval ring of mammoth bones enclosing an area of about 26 by 16 feet and which may have been used to weigh down the skin walls of a temporary hut or tent. Inside the ring are traces of a number of hearths, hundreds of tools, thousands of waste flakes, and many bone fragments, quite possibly derived from animals brought back for consumption.

Evidence of life in caves is abundant. Windbreaks of poles and skin were probably erected at the cave mouth for protection against severe weather. Fire was in general use by this time and was no doubt used for cooking, warmth, light, and keeping predators at bay.

How large were Neandertal settlements, and were they permanent or temporary? These questions are not yet answered, but Binford (1981) suggests that the settlements were used repeatedly for short-term occupation.

Subsistence

Neandertals were successful hunters, as the abundant remains of animal bones at their sites demonstrate. But while it is clear that Neandertals could hunt large mammals, they may not have been as efficient at this task as were Upper Paleolithic hunters. Inferring from his detailed work in the Middle East, Harvard anthropologist Ofer Bar-Yosef (1994) has concluded that only after the beginning of the Upper Paleolithic was the spear-thrower, or atlatl (see p. 290), invented. Moreover, shortly thereafter, the bow and arrow may have greatly facilitated efficiency (and safety) in hunting large mammals. Lacking such long-distance weaponry, and thus mostly limited to close-proximity spears, Neandertals may have been more prone to serious injury—a hypothesis recently given some intriguing support by paleoanthropologists Thomas Berger and Erik Trinkaus. Berger and Trinkaus (1995) analyzed the pattern of trauma (particularly fractures) in Neandertals and compared it with that seen in contemporary human samples. Interestingly, the pattern in Neandertals—especially the relatively high proportion of head and neck injuries—matched most closely to that seen in contemporary rodeo performers. Berger and Trinkaus thus conclude, "The similarity to the rodeo distribution suggests frequent close encounters

See Virtual Lab 11 for a discussion of dietary reconstruction.

with large ungulates unkindly disposed to the humans involved" (Berger and Trinkaus, 1995, p. 841).

Meat was, of course, not the only component of Neandertal diet. Evidence (from Shanidar, for example) indicates that Neandertals gathered as well, consuming berries, nuts, and other plants.

It is assumed that in the bitter cold of the last glacial period, Neandertals wore clothing, and they probably had developed methods of curing skins. But since there is no evidence of sewing equipment, the clothing was probably of simple design, perhaps something like a poncho.

We know much more of European Middle Paleolithic culture than of any prior period, as it has been studied longer by more scholars. In recent years, however, Africa has been a target not only of physical anthropologists (as we have seen copiously documented in earlier chapters), but also of archaeologists, who have added considerably to our knowledge of African Pleistocene hominid history. In many instances, the technology and assumed cultural adaptations in Africa were similar to those in Europe and southwest Asia. We will see in the next chapter that the African technological achievements also kept pace with (or even preceded) those in western Europe.

Symbolic Behavior

There are a variety of hypotheses concerning the speech capacities of Neandertals. Many of these views are highly contradictory, with some scholars arguing that Neandertals were incapable of human speech. Nevertheless, the prevailing consensus has been that Neandertals were capable of articulate speech, even perhaps fully competent in the range of sounds produced by modern humans. Some fascinating new genetic evidence may again require reassessment of just when fully human language first emerged (Enard et al., 2002). In humans today, mutations in a single gene (locus) are known to produce serious language impairments. From an evolutionary perspective, what is perhaps most significant concerns the greater variability of the alleles at this locus in modern humans as compared to any other primate. An intriguing hypothesis explaining this increased variation postulates intensified selection acting on human populations, perhaps quite recently—and thus potentially after the evolutionary divergence of the Neandertals.

However, even if we were to conclude that Neandertals *could* speak, that does not necessarily prove that they had the same language capabilities of modern *Homo sapiens*. A major contemporary focus among paleoanthropologists is the apparently sudden expansion of modern *H. sapiens* (discussed in Chapter 11) and various explanations for the success of this group. Moreover, at the same time we are explaining how and why *H. sapiens sapiens* expanded its geographical range, we are left with the further problem of explaining what happened to the Neandertals. In making these types of interpretations, a growing number of paleoanthropologists suggest that *behavioral* differences are the key. Further corroboration of a recent evolutionary shift resulting from mutation of a crucial gene influencing language will bolster this view.

Upper Paleolithic *H. sapiens* is hypothesized to have possessed some significant behavioral advantages that Neandertals (and other archaic *H. sapiens*) lacked. Was it some kind of new and expanded ability to symbolize, communicate, organize social activities, elaborate technology, obtain a wider range of food resources, or care for the sick or injured, or was it some other factor? Were there, compared with *H. sapiens sapiens*, neurological differences that limited the Neandertals and thus contributed to their demise?

The direct anatomical evidence derived from Neandertal fossils is not especially helpful in specifically answering these questions. Ralph Holloway (1985) has maintained that Neandertal brains (at least as far as the fossil evidence suggests) do not differ significantly from that of modern *H. sapiens*. Moreover, Neandertal vocal tracts and other morphological features, compared with our own, do not appear seriously to have limited them.

Most of the reservations about advanced cognitive abilities in Neandertals have come from archaeological data. Interpretation of Neandertal sites, when compared with succeeding Upper Paleolithic sites (especially as documented in western Europe), have led to several intriguing contrasts, as shown in Table 10–4.

On the basis of this type of behavioral and anatomical evidence, Neandertals in recent years have increasingly been viewed as an evolutionary dead end. Whether their disappearance and ultimate replacement by anatomically modern Upper Paleolithic peoples (with their presumably "superior" culture) was solely the result of cultural differences or was also influenced by biological variation cannot at present be determined.

TABLE 10-4 Cultural Contrasts* Between Neandertals and Upper Paleolithic *Homo sapiens sapiens*

Neandertals	Upper Paleolithic *H. sapiens sapiens*
Tool Technology	
Numerous flake tools; few, however, apparently for highly specialized functions; use of bone, antler, or ivory very rare; relatively few tools with more than one or two parts	Many more varieties of stone tools; many apparently for specialized functions; frequent use of bone, antler, and ivory; many more tools comprised of two or more component parts
Hunting Efficiency and Weapons	
No long-distance hunting weapons; close-proximity weapons used (thus, more likelihood of injury)	Use of spear-thrower and bow and arrow; wider range of social contacts, perhaps permitting larger, more organized hunting parties (including game drives)
Stone Material Transport	
Stone materials transported only short distances—just "a few kilometers" (Klein, 1989)	Stone tool raw materials transported over much longer distances, implying wider social networks and perhaps trade
Art	
Artwork uncommon; usually small; probably mostly of a personal nature; some items perhaps misinterpreted as "art"; others may be intrusive from overlying Upper Paleolithic contexts; cave art absent	Artwork much more common, including transportable objects as well as elaborate cave art; well executed, using a variety of materials and techniques; stylistic sophistication
Burial	
Deliberate burial at several sites; graves unelaborated; graves frequently lack artifacts	Burials much more complex, frequently including both tools and remains of animals

*The contrasts are more apparent in some areas (particularly western Europe) than others (eastern Europe, Near East). Elsewhere (Africa, eastern Asia), where there were no Neandertals, the cultural situation is quite different. Moreover, even in western Europe, the cultural transformations were not necessarily abrupt, but may have developed more gradually from Mousterian to Upper Paleolithic times. For example, Straus (1995) argues that many of the Upper Paleolithic features were not consistently manifested until after 20,000 y.a.

Burials

It has been known for some time that Neandertals deliberately buried their dead. Indeed, the spectacular discoveries at La Chapelle, Shanidar, and elsewhere were the direct results of ancient burial, thus facilitating much more complete preservation. Such deliberate burial treatment extends back at least 90,000 years at Tabun. Moreover, some form of consistent "disposal" of the dead (but not necessarily below-ground burial) is evidenced at Atapuerca, Spain, where at least 32 individuals comprising more than 700 fossilized elements were found in a cave at the end of a deep vertical shaft. From the nature of the site and the accumulation of hominid remains, Spanish researchers are convinced that the site demonstrates some form of human activity involving deliberate disposal of the dead (Arsuaga et al., 1997).

The provisional 300,000-year-old age for Atapuerca suggests that Neandertals (more precisely, their immediate precursors) were, by the Middle Pleistocene, handling their dead in special ways, a behavior thought previously to have emerged only much later (in the Upper Pleistocene). And, apparently as far as current data indicate, this practice is seen in western European contexts well before it appears in Africa or in eastern Asia. For example, in the archaic *H. sapiens* sites at Laetoli, Kabwe, and Florisbad (discussed earlier), deliberate disposal of the dead is not documented. Nor is it seen in African early modern sites (e.g., Klasies River Mouth, dated at 120,000–100,000 y.a.; see p. 280).

Nevertheless, in later contexts (after 35,000 y.a.) in Europe, where anatomically modern *H. sapiens* (*H. sapiens sapiens*) remains are found in clear burial contexts, their treatment is considerably more complex than is seen in Neandertal burials. In these later (Upper Paleolithic) sites, grave goods, including bone and stone tools as well as animal bones, are found more consistently and in greater concentrations. Because many Neandertal sites were excavated in the nineteenth or early twentieth century, before the development of more rigorous archaeological methods, there are questions regarding numerous purported burials. Nevertheless, the evidence seems quite clear that deliberate burial was practiced at La Chapelle, La Ferrassie (eight graves), Tabun, Amud, Kebara, Shanidar, and Teshik-Tash (as well as at several other localities, especially in France). Moreover, in many instances, the *position* of the body was deliberately modified and placed in the grave in a flexed posture (see p. 256). Such a flexed position has been found in 16 of the 20 best-documented Neandertal burial contexts (Klein, 1989).

Finally, the placement of supposed grave goods in burials, including stone tools, animal bones (such as cave bear), and even arrangements of flowers, together with stone slabs on top of the burials, have all been postulated as further evidence of Neandertal symbolic behavior. However, in many instances, again due to poor excavation documentation, these assertions are questionable. Placement of stone tools, for example, is occasionally seen, but apparently was not done consistently. In those 33 Neandertal burials for which adequate data exist, only 14 show definite association of stone tools and/or animal bones with the deceased (Klein, 1989). It is not until the next cultural period, the Upper Paleolithic, that we see a major behavioral shift, as demonstrated in more elaborate burials and development of art.

See Virtual Lab 10, section I, for a discussion of the implications of DNA analysis of Neandertals.

Genetic Evidence

As a result of the revolutionary advances in molecular biology (discussed in Chapter 3), fascinating new avenues of research have become possible in the study of earlier hominids. The extraction, amplification, and sequencing of ancient DNA from contexts spanning the last 10,000 years or so are now becoming fairly commonplace (e.g., the analysis of DNA from the 5,000-year-old "Iceman" found in the Italian Alps).

Finding usable DNA in yet more ancient remains is much more difficult because the material has become more mineralized, obliterating organic components, including (usually) the DNA. Nevertheless, in the past few years, very exciting results have been announced relating to DNA found in three different Neandertal fossils. The first of these comes from the original Neander Valley specimen, and analysis was completed in 1997 (Krings et al., 1997); the other two come from Mezmaiskaya Cave in Russia (Ovchinnikov et al., 2000) and from Vindija in Croatia (Krings et al., 2000). In all cases, the individuals are by far the oldest hominid remains from which DNA has been recovered. The Neander Valley fossil is estimated at 70,000 years old, the Vindija remains are 42,000 y.a., and the Mezmaiskaya material is dated at 29,000 y.a. (*Note:* This places the latter among the most recent of all Neandertal discoveries.)

The technique used in the study of Neandertal fossils involved the extraction of mitochondrial DNA (mtDNA), amplification by PCR (see p. 60), and nucleotide sequencing of portions of the molecule. Results from the three specimens show that they are genetically more different from contemporary *Homo sapiens* populations than these latter populations are from each other (about three times as much). Extrapolating from these comparative data, Krings and colleagues (1997) have hypothesized that the Neandertal lineage separated from that of modern *H. sapiens* ancestors between 690,000 and 550,000 y.a.

The intriguing hypothesis, however, has not been fully confirmed and is most certainly not accepted by all paleoanthropologists. It is still not clear how rapidly mtDNA evolves, nor is it obvious how genetically different we should *expect* ancient hominids to be compared to us. (In other words, at present, we cannot rule out evolutionary relationships on the basis of available genetic evidence.) Nevertheless, such data probably offer the best hope of ultimately untangling the place of Neandertals in human evolution—and perhaps even of understanding something of their fate.

Evolutionary Trends in the Genus Homo

To understand the evolution of the various forms of *Homo sapiens* discussed in this chapter, it is useful to briefly review general trends of evolution in the genus *Homo* over the last 2 million years. In doing so, we see that at least three major *transitions* have taken place. Paleoanthropologists are keenly interested in interpreting the nature of these transitions, as they inform us directly regarding human origins. In addition, such investigations contribute to a broader understanding of the mechanics of the evolutionary process—at both the micro- and macroevolutionary levels.

The first transition of note was from early *Homo* to *Homo erectus*. This transition was apparently fairly restricted geographically (to Africa and perhaps parts of Eurasia) and appears to have been quite rapid (lasting 200,000 years at most, perhaps considerably less). It is important to recall that such a transition by no means implies that all early *Homo* groups actually evolved into *H. erectus*. In fact, many paleoanthropologists (part of a growing consensus) suggest that there was more than one species of early *Homo*. Clearly, only one could be ancestral to *H. erectus*. Even more to the point, only *some* populations of this one species would have been part of the genetic transformation (speciation) that produced *Homo erectus*.

The second transition is more complex and is the main topic of this chapter. It is the gradual change in populations of *H. erectus* grading into early *H. sapiens* forms—what we have termed archaic *H. sapiens*. This transition was not geographically restricted, as there is evidence of archaic *H. sapiens* widespread in the Old World (in East and South Africa, in China, India, and Java, and in Europe). Moreover, the transition appears not to have been rapid, but rather quite slow and uneven in pace from area to area. The complexity of this evolutionary transition creates ambiguities for our interpretations and resulting classifications.

For example, in Chapter 9, we included the Ngandong (Solo) material from Java within *Homo erectus*. However, there are several derived features in many of these specimens that suggest, alternatively, that they could be assigned to *Homo sapiens*. The dating (just recently indicating a date of only 29,000 y.a.) would argue that if this is a *H. erectus* group, it is a *very* late remnant, probably isolated *H. erectus* population surviving in southern Asia long after archaic *H. sapiens* populations were expanding elsewhere. Whatever the interpretation of Ngandong—either as a late *H. erectus* or as a quite primitive (i.e., not particularly derived) archaic *H. sapiens*—the conclusion is actually quite arbitrary (after all, the evolutionary process is continuous). We, by the nature of our classifications, have to draw the line *somewhere*.

Another important ramification of such considerations relates to understanding the nature of the *erectus/sapiens* transition itself. In Java, the transition (with late-persisting *H. erectus* genetic components) appears to have been slower than, for example, in southern Africa or in Europe. Nowhere, however, does this transition appear to have been as rapid as that which originally produced *H. erectus*. Why should this be so? To answer this question, we must consider basic evolutionary mechanisms (discussed in Chapter 4). First, the environments certainly differed from one region of the Old World to another during the time period 350,000–100,000 y.a. And recall that by the beginning of this time period, *H. erectus* populations had been long established in eastern and southern Asia, in North and East Africa, and in Europe. Clearly, we would not expect the same environmental conditions in northeast China as we would in Indonesia. Accordingly, natural selection could well have played a *differential* role, influencing the frequencies of alternative alleles in different populations in a pattern similar (but more intensive) to that seen in environmental adaptations of contemporary populations (see Chapter 12).

Second, many of these populations (in Java, southernmost Africa, and glacial Europe) could have been isolated and thus probably quite small. Genetic drift, therefore, also would have played a role in influencing the pace of evolutionary change. Third, advance or retreat of barriers, such as water boundaries or glacial ice sheets, would dramatically have affected migration routes.

Thus, it should hardly come as a surprise that some populations of *H. erectus* evolved at different rates and in slightly different directions from others. Some limited migration almost certainly occurred among the various populations. With sufficient gene flow, the spread of those few genetic modifications that distinguish earliest *H. sapiens* eventually did become incorporated into widely separated populations. This, however, was a long, slow, inherently uneven process.

What, then, of the third transition within the genus *Homo*? This is the transition from archaic *H. sapiens* to anatomically modern *H. sapiens*—and it was considerably *faster* than the transition we have just discussed. How quickly anatomically modern forms evolved and exactly *where* this happened is a subject of much contemporary debate—and is the main topic of the next chapter.

Taxonomic Issues

As we discussed in Chapter 9 (and briefly at the beginning of this chapter), there is considerable debate regarding how to classify much of the *Homo* fossil material prior to 35,000 years ago. Our view, followed throughout the discussions in Chapters 8 through 10, proposes a minimum number of species and thus interprets the evolutionary processes influencing the genus *Homo* in a fairly straightforward manner.

See the Glossary of Virtual Lab 10 for alternative phylogenies of the genus *Homo*.

However, this interpretation might well be *too* simplistic, and certainly, many paleoanthropologists now suggest much more diversity and complexity in the evolution of our genus. Accordingly, several new species of *Homo* have been proposed. In this text, we have classified the *Homo* fossil materials into three recognized species: *H. habilis*, *H. erectus*, and *H. sapiens*. We further noted that *H. habilis* might well be only one of two species of what we collectively called "early *Homo*." Moreover, in this chapter we made a clear distinction between archaic forms of *H. sapiens* and anatomically modern forms (*H. sapiens sapiens*). A diagrammatic phylogeny representing this interpretation is shown in figure 10–16.

figure 10–16 Phylogeny showing evolution of genus *Homo*, as discussed in the text. Only very modest species diversity is implied. (Contrast with figure 10–17.)

At the other end of the spectrum are views expressed by a number of researchers who subdivide the *Homo* material into a variety of species. In fact, at every major stage of the evolution of *Homo* over the last 2 million years, some professional opinion has argued seriously for more than one species. First, as noted in Chapter 8 (p. 213), early *Homo* is now frequently subdivided into two different species (usually named *H. habilis* and *H. rudolfensis*). Second, as briefly discussed in Chapter 9, what is usually called *H. erectus* is also partitioned into two species (*H. erectus* and *H. ergaster*, the latter referring primarily to African specimens but also including the material from Dmanisi).* And third (and most relevant to the present discussion), various forms of archaic *H. sapiens* have been assigned by other paleoanthropologists to two or three additional species of *Homo* (some researchers think even more species might be represented).

The major issues relating to these interpretations (and consequent classifications) of what we have termed "archaic *Homo sapiens*" are as follows:

1. The classification of individual fossils into "archaic *Homo sapiens*" is viewed by many as imprecise, since this is an ill-defined evolutionary group (and one quite geographically widespread). At minimum, many researchers have urged a more precise anatomical definition of exactly what "archaic *Homo sapiens*" means.

2. Several early archaic specimens are interpreted by paleoanthropologists as showing derived features different from *Homo sapiens*. These fossils come from Africa and Europe (e.g., Kabwe, Mauer) and are now often classified as *Homo heidelbergensis*.

3. Neandertals are also viewed by numerous researchers as representing a distinct species, what is called *Homo neanderthalensis*. In prior discussions, we have interpreted the variation as representing intraspecific differences; this alternative view argues for a greater degree of interspecific variability (with the inference that fertile interbreeding between Neandertals and *H. sapiens* would not have been possible).

Figure 10–17 shows a phylogeny incorporating these more complex, multiple-species interpretations and suggesting possible evolutionary relationships. For an introductory course, it is less important to memorize all the species names than to recognize what such interpretations imply about the evolutionary process—and what these differing views suggest about our origins.

Summary

D uring the Middle Pleistocene, significant changes occurred in *H. erectus* morphology. The changes, especially in cranial traits, led scientists to assign a new species designation to these forms (*Homo sapiens*). Because they exhibited a mosaic of *H. erectus* and *H. sapiens* characteristics, the name archaic *H. sapiens* is used to indicate that they were forms transitional

---

*The most recent discovery from Dmanisi (see p. 234) has thrown all those interpretations into disarray. There appears to be extreme intraspecific variation, as seen in the Dmanisi crania.

figure 10–17 Phylogeny showing multiple species of genus *Homo* with considerable species diversity represented.

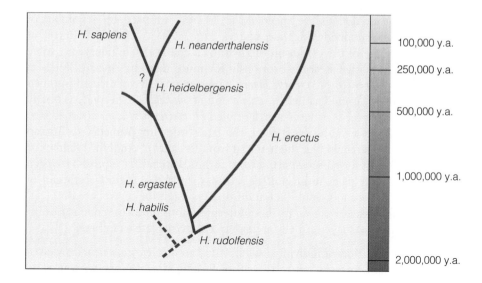

between *H. erectus* and anatomically modern humans. Some archaic *H. sapiens* populations possessed more derived modern traits than others, and these populations are sometimes referred to as later archaic *H. sapiens* or early *H. sapiens sapiens*. It has been suggested that some later European archaic forms were directly ancestral to Neandertals.

In addition to morphological changes among archaic forms, there were cultural developments as well. Archaic *H. sapiens* invented new kinds of tools and toolmaking techniques, exploited new foods, built more complex shelters, probably controlled fire, and may have used some form of speech.

In western Europe, archaic *H. sapiens* developed into a unique form—classic Neandertals—who apparently migrated from Europe to the Near East and then even further into Asia. Neandertals were physically robust and muscular, different from both early archaic forms and modern *H. sapiens*. Their culture was more complex than earlier archaic cultures, and it appears that in Europe and the Near East, they lived in areas also inhabited by modern *H. sapiens*. Whether modern forms in these areas evolved directly from Neandertals or migrated from Africa (or the Near East) and ultimately replaced Neandertals is one of the important issues currently being debated by paleoanthropologists.

Finally, we would emphasize that Neandertals and all humans on earth today belong to the same species, *H. sapiens*. There are physical differences between these forms, of course, and for that reason Neandertals are assigned to the subspecies *H. sapiens neanderthalensis* and anatomically modern forms to the subspecies *H. sapiens sapiens*.

We should point out that this assignment of a *separate* subspecies for the Neandertals emphasizes some notable degrees of variation; that is, Neandertals are viewed as more different from *any* modern group of *H. sapiens* than these groups differ from one another. Some scholars would even more dramatically emphasize this variation and thus assign Neandertals to a separate species from *Homo sapiens*. In this view, Neandertals would be placed in the separate species *Homo neanderthalensis*. Likewise, many paleoanthropologists would also subdivide what we call "early archaic *H. sapiens*" into another species. The behavioral

TABLE 10-5	Most Significant Archaic *Homo sapiens* Discoveries Discussed in this Chapter		
Site	Dates (y.a.)	Taxonomic Designation	Comments
La Chapelle	50,000	Neandertal (*Homo sapiens neanderthalensis, Homo neanderthalensis*)	Historically most important site in France in description of Neandertal morphology
Tabun	110,000	Neandertal (*Homo sapiens neanderthalensis, Homo neanderthalensis*)	Important early Neandertal site; shows clear presence of Neandertals in Near East
Atapuerca	320,000–190,000	Archaic *Homo sapiens* (*Homo sapiens neanderthalensis?*)	Large sample; earliest evidence in Europe of Neandertal morphology; evidence of disposal of the dead
Steinheim	300,000–250,000?	Archaic *Homo sapiens* (also referred to as: *Homo heidelbergensis*)	Transitional-looking fossil (between *H. erectus* and *H. sapiens*)
Swanscombe	300,000–250,000?	Archaic *Homo sapiens* (also referred to as: *Homo heidelbergensis*)	Transitional-looking fossil (between *H. erectus* and *H. sapiens*)
Jinniushan	200,000?	Archaic *Homo sapiens* (early *Homo sapiens*, as termed by the Chinese)	Possibly oldest example of *H. sapiens* in China

differences between Neandertals and anatomically modern *H. sapiens*, as interpreted from the archaeological record, are also discussed. These differences are emphasized by those scholars who view Neandertals as an evolutionary dead end.

As a further study aid, the most significant hominid fossil discoveries discussed in this chapter are presented in Table 10–5.

Questions for Review

1. In what respect does *H. sapiens* (broadly defined) contrast with *H. erectus*?
2. What is meant by "archaic" *H. sapiens*?
3. How does archaic *H. sapiens* contrast with anatomically modern *H. sapiens*?
4. In what areas of the world have archaic *H. sapiens* specimens been discovered? Compare and contrast the finds from two separate areas.
5. What do we mean when we say that archaic *H. sapiens* specimens are transitional?
6. Why have Neandertals been depicted (by the popular press and others) as being primitive? Do you agree with this interpretation? Why or why not?
7. In what general areas of the world have Neandertal fossil remains been discovered?
8. What evidence suggests that Neandertals deliberately buried their dead? What interpretations do such treatment of the dead suggest to you?
9. What physical characteristics distinguish the Neandertals from anatomically modern *Homo sapiens*?
10. What behavioral characteristics distinguish Neandertal culture from that of the Upper Paleolithic?

11. What two major transitions within the genus *Homo* have been discussed in this chapter and in Chapter 11? Compare these transitions for geographical distribution as well as for aspects of evolutionary pace.

12. Discuss why some paleoanthropologists subdivide the archaic *H. sapiens* material into more than one species. What does this interpretation imply biologically?

Suggested Further Readings

Mellars, Paul. 1995. *The Neanderthal Legacy. An Archaeological Perspective from Western Europe*. Princeton, NJ: Princeton University Press.

Shreeve, James. 1995. *The Neandertal Enigma*. New York: Morrow.

Stiner, Mary C. 1995. *Honor Among Thieves. A Zooarchaeological Study of Neandertal Ecology*. Princeton, NJ: Princeton University Press.

Stringer, Christopher, and Clive Gamble. 1993. *In Search of the Neanderthals*. New York: Thames and Hudson.

Trinkaus, Erik, and Pat Shipman. 1993. *The Neandertals: Changing the Image of Mankind*. New York: Knopf.

Multimedia Resources

 Companion Web Site

Anthropology Online: The Wadsworth Anthropology Resource Center Visit **http://anthropology.wadsworth.com** and click on the Companion Web Site for Jurmain/Kilgore/Trevathan/Nelson's *Essentials of Physical Anthropology*, Fifth Edition, to access a wide range of enrichment material to aid in your study of anthropology. Among the useful options for each chapter's self-study are learning objectives, flashcards, Internet exercises, Web links, InfoTrac College Edition exercises, and practice quizzes that can be scored and emailed to your instructor.

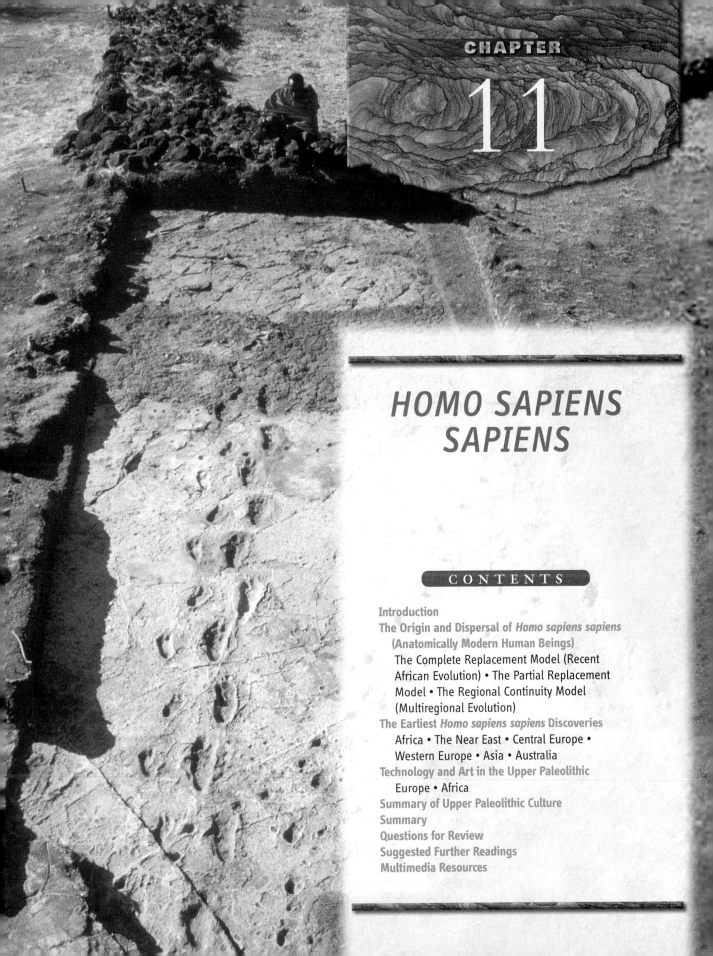

HOMO SAPIENS SAPIENS

CONTENTS

See the following sections of the CD-ROM for topics covered in this chapter: Virtual Lab 11, section IV and Virtual Lab 12, sections I and II.

Introduction

I n this chapter, we discuss anatomically modern humans, taxonomically known as *Homo sapiens sapiens*. As we discussed in Chapter 10, in some areas evolutionary developments produced early archaic *H. sapiens* populations exhibiting a mosaic of *H. erectus* and *H. sapiens* traits. In some regions, the trend emphasizing *H. sapiens* characteristics continued, and possibly as early as 200,000 y.a., transitional forms (between early archaic and anatomically modern forms) appeared in Africa. Given the nature of the evidence and ongoing ambiguities in dating, it is not possible to say exactly when anatomically modern *H. sapiens* first appeared. However, the transition and certainly the wide dispersal of *H. sapiens sapiens* in the Old World appear to have been relatively rapid evolutionary events. Thus, we can ask several basic questions:

1. *When* (approximately) did *H. sapiens sapiens* first appear?
2. *Where* did the transition take place? Did it occur in just one region or in several?
3. *What* was the pace of evolutionary change? How quickly did the transition occur?
4. *How* did the dispersal of *H. sapiens sapiens* to other areas of the Old World (outside that of origin) take place?

These questions concerning the origins and early dispersal of *Homo sapiens sapiens* continue to fuel much controversy among paleoanthropologists. And it is no wonder, for members of early *Homo sapiens sapiens* are our *direct* kin and are thus closely related to all contemporary humans. They were much like us skeletally, genetically, and (most likely) behaviorally as well. In fact, it is the various hypotheses relating to the behavioral capacities of our most immediate predecessors that have most fired the imagination of scientists and laypeople alike. In every major respect, these are the first hominids that we can confidently refer to as "fully human."

In this chapter, we will also discuss archaeological evidence from the Upper Paleolithic (see p. 289). This evidence will allow us to better understand technological and social developments during the period when modern humans arose and quickly came to dominate the planet.

The evolutionary story of *Homo sapiens sapiens* is really a biological autobiography of us all. It is a story that still has many unanswered questions; but several theories have been proposed that seek to organize the diverse information that is presently available.

The Origin and Dispersal of Homo sapiens sapiens *(Anatomically Modern Human Beings)*

There are two major theories that attempt to organize and explain modern human origins: the complete replacement model and the regional continuity model. These two views are quite distinct and in some ways diametrically opposed to each other. Moreover, the popular press has further contributed to a wide and incorrect perception of irreconcilable argument on these points by "opposing" scientists. Indeed, there is a third theory, which we call the partial replacement model, that is a compromise hypothesis incorporating some aspects of the two major theories. Because so much of our contemporary view of modern human origins is driven by the debates linked to these differing theories, let us begin by briefly reviewing each. We will then turn to the fossil evidence itself to see what it can contribute to resolving the questions we have posed.

The Complete Replacement Model (Recent African Evolution)

The complete replacement model, developed by British paleoanthropologists Christopher Stringer and Peter Andrews (1988), is based on the origin of modern humans in Africa and later replacement of populations in Europe and Asia (fig. 11–1). In brief, this theory proposes that anatomically modern populations arose in Africa within the last 200,000 years, then migrated from Africa, completely *replacing* populations in Europe and Asia. This model does not take into account any transition from archaic *H. sapiens* to modern *H. sapiens* anywhere in the world except Africa. A critical deduction of the Stringer and Andrews theory postulates the appearance of anatomically modern humans as a biological speciation event. Thus, in this view there could be no admixture of migrating African modern *H. sapiens* with local populations because the African modern humans were a *biologically* different species. In a taxonomic context, all of the archaic *H. sapiens* populations outside Africa would, in this view, be classified as belonging to different species of *Homo* (e.g., the Neandertals would be classified as *H. neanderthalensis*; see p. 271 for further discussion). While this speciation explanation fits nicely with, and in fact helps explain, *complete* replacement, Stringer has more recently stated that he is not dogmatic regarding this issue. Thus, he suggests that there may have been potential for interbreeding, but he argues that very little apparently took place.

 See Virtual Lab 12, section II, for a discussion of the Complete Replacement Model.

A crucial source of supporting evidence for the African origin hypothesis (and complete replacement elsewhere) has come from genetic data obtained from living peoples. Underlying this approach is the assumption that genetic patterning seen in contemporary populations will provide clues to relationships and origins of ancient *Homo sapiens*. However, as with numerous prior attempts to evaluate such patterning from more traditional data on human polymorphisms (e.g., ABO, HLA—see Chapter 12), the obstacles are enormous.

A recent innovation uses genetic sequencing data derived directly from DNA. The most promising application has come not from the DNA within the nucleus, but from DNA found in the cytoplasm—that is, mitochondrial DNA (mtDNA; see Chapter 3). You may recall that mitochondria are organelles found in the cell, but outside the nucleus. They contain a set of DNA, dissimilar from nuclear DNA, inherited only through the mother. Thus, mtDNA does not undergo the genetic recombination that occurs in nuclear DNA during meiosis.

Using mtDNA gathered from a number of different populations, scientists at the University of California, Berkeley, constructed "trees" (something like a family tree) that, they claimed, demonstrated that the entire population of the world today descended from a single African lineage. However, the methodology of these molecular biologists has been faulted. Using the same mtDNA material, other scientists constructed many trees that differed from those of the Berkeley group, and some of them are *without African roots* (i.e., the same data can be used statistically to show that *H. sapiens* arose in Asia, *not* in Africa).

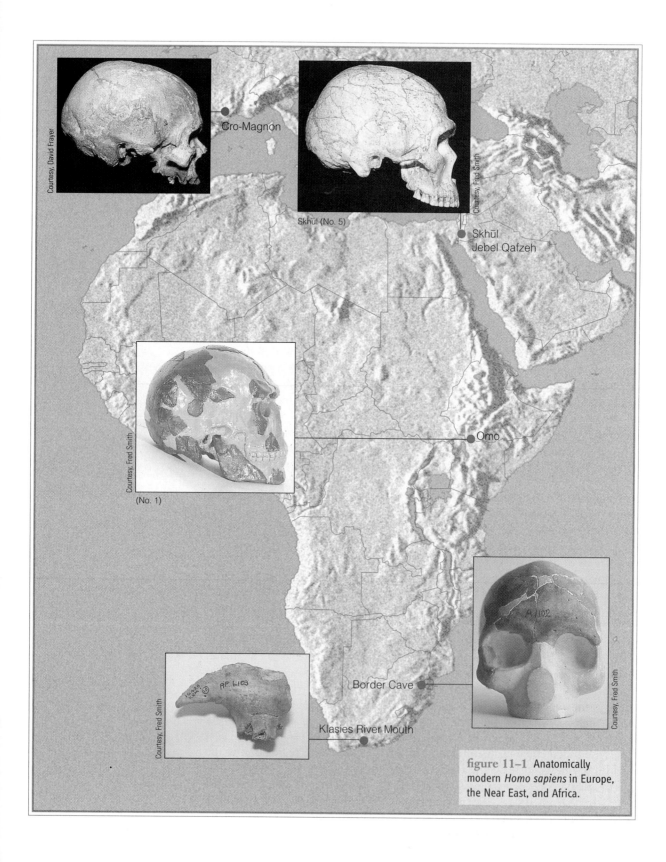

Courtesy, David Frayer

Cro-Magnon

Courtesy, Fred Smith

Skhūl (No. 5)

Skhūl
Jebel Qafzeh

Courtesy, Fred Smith

(No. 1)

Omo

Courtesy, Fred Smith

Border Cave

Courtesy, Fred Smith

Klasies River Mouth

figure 11–1 Anatomically modern *Homo sapiens* in Europe, the Near East, and Africa.

This question of the applicability of the mtDNA evidence continues to generate considerable disagreement. Paleoanthropologist Robert Corruccini of Southern Illinois University has been unimpressed with the entire approach, stating that "critical shortcomings of molecular population genetic assumptions and of analysis . . . render any mtDNA conclusions virtually useless to ruminations about human evolution" (Corruccini, 1994, p. 698). Likewise, Glenn Conroy (1997) has critiqued many of the oversimplifications inherent in the genetic data and consequent interpretations. However, molecular anthropologist Mark Stoneking of the Max Planck Institute (and one of the founders of this approach) remains much more confident in the general reliability of the mtDNA results, especially as they show a much greater diversity among contemporary African groups as compared to other world populations. Stoneking thus concludes: "Because non-African populations that predate the mtDNA ancestor apparently did not contribute mtDNAs to contemporary human populations, it follows that the spread of modern populations was accomplished with little or no admixture with resident non-African populations. If it were otherwise, there should be evidence of much more divergent mtDNA types in contemporary human populations" (Stoneking, 1993, pp. 66–67).

Recently, some further genetic data have helped bolster some of the main tenets of the complete replacement model. A team of Yale, Harvard, and University of Chicago researchers (Dorit et al., 1995) has investigated variation in the Y chromosome, finding *much* less variation in humans than in other primates. And another group of Yale researchers (Tishkoff et al., 1996), looking at DNA sequences on chromosome 12, again found much more variation among contemporary Africans than is seen in all the remainder of the world combined. Finally, the recent reports of the distinctive nature of Neandertal mtDNA (see p. 268) also argue that substantial replacement took place. Nevertheless, some geneticists find the results unconvincing (e.g., Templeton, 1996), and many paleoanthropologists (agreeing with the views expressed by Corruccini and Conroy) are extremely skeptical of the main conclusions derived from the genetic data.

The Partial Replacement Model

The partial replacement model also begins with African early archaic *H. sapiens*. Later, also in Africa, some of these archaic populations evolved into the first anatomically modern *H. sapiens*. This theory, proposed by Günter Bräuer of the University of Hamburg, postulates the earliest dates for African modern *Homo sapiens* at over 100,000 y.a. Bräuer sees the initial dispersal of *H. sapiens sapiens* out of South Africa as significantly influenced by shifting environmental conditions and thus as a gradual process. Moving into Eurasia, modern humans hybridized, probably to a limited degree, with resident archaic groups and eventually replaced them. The disappearance of archaic humans was therefore due to both hybridization and replacement and was a gradual and complex process. This model includes components of regional continuity, hybridization, and replacement, with the emphasis on replacement.

The Regional Continuity Model (Multiregional Evolution)

The regional continuity model is most closely associated with paleoanthropologist Milford Wolpoff of the University of Michigan and his associates (Thorne

See Virtual Lab 12, section II, for an animation of the Regional Continuity Model.

and Wolpoff, 1992; Wolpoff et al., 1994). These researchers suggest that local populations (not all, of course) in Europe, Asia, and Africa continued their indigenous evolutionary development from archaic *H. sapiens* to anatomically modern humans. A question immediately arises: How is it possible for different local populations around the globe to evolve with such similar morphology? In other words, how could anatomically modern humans arise separately in different continents and end up physically (and genetically) so similar? The multiregional model explains this phenomenon by (1) denying that the earliest modern *H. sapiens* populations originated *exclusively* in Africa and challenging the notion of complete replacement and (2) asserting that some gene flow (migration) between archaic populations was extremely likely, in which case modern humans cannot be considered a species separate from archaic forms.

Through gene flow and natural selection, according to the multiregional hypothesis, local populations would *not* have evolved totally independently from one another, and such mixing would have "prevented speciation between the regional lineages and thus maintained human beings as a *single*, although obviously *polytypic* [see p. 304], species throughout the Pleistocene" (Smith et al., 1989).

The Earliest Homo sapiens sapiens *Discoveries*

Current evidence strongly indicates that the earliest modern *H. sapiens* fossils come from Africa, but not everyone agrees on the dates or precisely which specimens are the modern forms and which are the archaic forms. With this cautionary note, we continue our discussion, but there undoubtedly will be corrections as more evidence is gathered.

Africa

In Africa, several early fossil finds have been interpreted as fully anatomically modern forms (see fig. 11–1). These specimens come from the Klasies River Mouth on the south coast (which could be the earliest find), Border Cave slightly to the north, and Omo Kibish 1 in southern Ethiopia. With the use of relatively new techniques, all three sites have been dated to about 120,000–80,000 y.a. The original geological context at Border Cave is uncertain, and the fossils may be younger than at the other two sites (see Table 11–1 and fig. 11–5). Some paleoanthropologists consider these fossils the earliest known anatomically modern humans. Problems with dating, context, and differing interpretations of the evidence have led other paleoanthropologists to question whether the *earliest* modern forms (fig. 11–2) really did evolve in Africa. Other modern *H. sapiens* individuals, possibly older than these Africans, have been found in the Near East.

The Near East

In Israel, early modern *H. sapiens* fossils (the remains of at least 10 individuals) were found in the Skhūl Cave at Mt. Carmel (figs. 11–3 and 11–4a), very near the Neandertal site of Tabun. Also from Israel, the Qafzeh Cave has yielded the

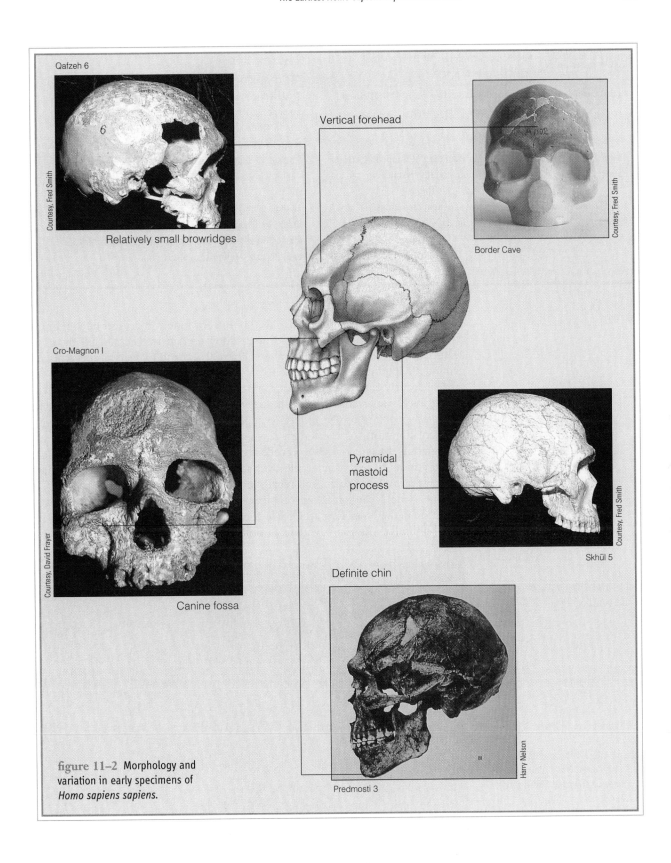

Qafzeh 6

Courtesy, Fred Smith

Relatively small browridges

Vertical forehead

Border Cave

Courtesy, Fred Smith

Cro-Magnon I

Courtesy, David Frayer

Canine fossa

Pyramidal mastoid process

Skhūl 5

Courtesy, Fred Smith

Definite chin

Predmosti 3

Harry Nelson

figure 11–2 Morphology and variation in early specimens of *Homo sapiens sapiens*.

TABLE 11-1   Additional Techniques for Dating Middle and Upper Pleistocene Sites

Technique	Physical Basis	Examples of Use
Uranium series dating	Radioactive decay of short-lived uranium isotopes	To date limestone formations (e.g., stalagmites) and ancient ostrich eggshells; to estimate age of Jinniushan site in China and Ngandong site in Java, both corroborated by ESR dates
Thermoluminescence (TL) dating	Accumulation of trapped electrons within certain crystals released during heating	To date ancient flint tools (either deliberately or accidentally heated); to provide key dates for the Qafzeh site
Electron spin resonance (ESR) dating	Measurement (counting) of accumulated trapped electrons	To date dental enamel; to corroborate dating of Qafzeh, Skhūl, and Tabun sites in Israel, Ngandong site in Java, Klasies River Mouth and Border Cave in South Africa, and the Lake Mungo site in Australia

Source: Cook et al., 1984; Aiken et al., 1993.

remains of at least 20 individuals (fig. 11–4b). Although their overall configuration is definitely modern, some specimens show certain archaic (i.e., Neandertal) features. Skhūl has been dated to about 115,000 y.a., and Qafzeh has been placed around 100,000 y.a. (Bar-Yosef, 1993, 1994) (fig. 11–5 on p. 284).

Such early dates for modern specimens pose some problems for those advocating local replacement (the multiregional model). How early do archaic *H. sapiens* populations (Neandertals) appear in the Near East? A recent chronometric calibration for the Tabun Cave suggests a date as early as 120,000 y.a. Neandertals thus may *slightly* precede modern forms in the Near East, but there would appear to be considerable overlap in the timing of occupation by these different *H. sapiens* forms. And recall, the modern site at Mt. Carmel (Skhūl) is very near the Neandertal site (Tabun). Clearly, the dynamics of *Homo sapiens* evolution in the Near East are highly complex, and no simple model may explain later hominid evolution adequately (Table 11–2).

figure 11–3 Mt. Carmel, studded with caves, was home to *H. sapiens sapiens* at Skhūl (and to Neandertals at Tabun and Kebara).

Courtesy, David Frayer

(a)   (b)

Central Europe

Central Europe has been a source of many fossil finds, including numerous fairly early anatomically modern *H. sapiens*. At several sites, it appears that some fossils display both Neandertal and modern features, which supports the regional continuity hypothesis (from Neandertal to modern). Some genetic continuity from earlier (Neandertal) to later (modern *Homo sapiens*) populations was perhaps the case at Vindija in Croatia, where typical Neandertals were found in earlier contexts (see p. 258).

Smith (1984) offers another example of local continuity from Mladeč, in the Czech Republic. Among the earlier European modern *H. sapiens* fossils, dated to about 33,000 y.a., the Mladeč crania display a great deal of variation, probably in part due to sexual dimorphism. Although each of the crania (except for one of the females) displays a prominent supraorbital torus, it is reduced from the typical Neandertal pattern. Even though there is some suggestion of continuity from Neandertals to modern humans, Smith is certain that, given certain

figure 11–4 (a) Skhūl 5. (b) Qafzeh 6. These specimens from Israel are thought to be representatives of early modern *Homo sapiens*. The vault height, forehead, and lack of prognathism are modern traits.

TABLE 11-2	In Summary: Key Early Modern *Homo sapiens* Discoveries from Africa and the Near East		
Site	**Dates (y.a.)**	**Human Remains**	**Comments**
Qafzeh (Israel)	110,000	Minimum of 20 individuals	Large sample; variability in expression of modern traits
Skhūl (Israel)	115,000	Minimum of 10 individuals	Earliest good evidence of modern *H. sapiens* outside of Africa
Omo-Kibish (Ethiopia)	120,000–80,000?	Cranium and postcranial remains	Second individual shows fewer modern traits
Klasies River Mouth (South Africa)	120,000?	Several individuals; highly fragmentary	Perhaps earliest modern *H. sapiens* in Africa

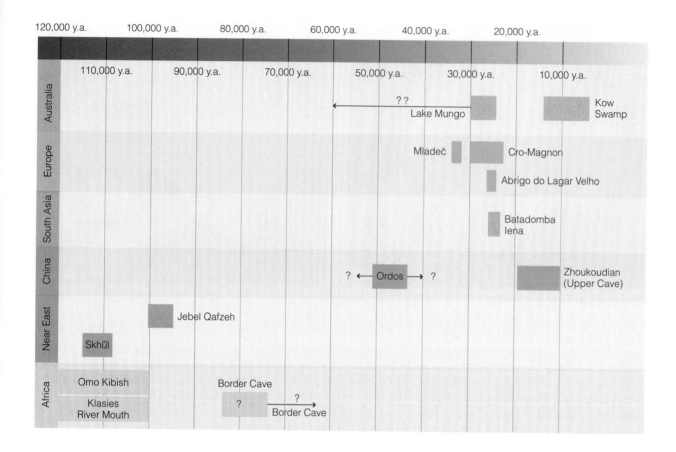

figure 11–5 Time line of *Homo sapiens sapiens* discoveries. Note that most dates are approximations. Question marks indicate those estimates that are most tentative.

anatomical features, the Mladeč remains are best classified as *H. sapiens sapiens*. Reduced midfacial projection, a higher forehead, and postcranial elements "are clearly modern *H. sapiens* in morphology and not specifically Neandertal-like in a single feature" (Smith, 1984, p. 174).

Western Europe

This area of the world and its fossils have received the greatest attention for several reasons, one of which is probably serendipity. Over the last century and a half, many of the scholars interested in this kind of research happened to live in western Europe, and the southern region of France happened to be a fossil treasure trove. Also, early on, discovering and learning about human ancestors caught the curiosity and pride of the local population.

Because of this scholarly interest beginning back in the nineteenth century, a great deal of data accumulated, with little reliable comparative information available from elsewhere in the world. Consequently, theories of human evolution were based almost exclusively on the western European material. It has only been in recent years, with growing evidence from other areas of the world and with the application of new dating techniques, that recent human evolutionary dynamics have been seriously considered on a worldwide basis.

There are many anatomically modern human fossils from western Europe going back 40,000 years or more, but by far the best-known sample of western European *H. sapiens* is from the **Cro-Magnon** site. A total of eight individuals were discovered in 1868 in a rock shelter in the village of Les Eyzies, in the Dordogne region of southern France (Gambier, 1989).

Associated with an **Aurignacian** tool assemblage, an Upper Paleolithic industry, the Cro-Magnon materials, dated at 30,000 y.a., represent the earliest of France's anatomically modern humans. The so-called "Old Man" (Cro-Magnon I) became the archetype for what was once termed the Cro-Magnon, or Upper Paleolithic, "race" of Europe (fig.11–6). Actually, of course, there is no such category, and Cro-Magnon I is not typical of Upper Paleolithic western Europeans and not even all that similar to the other two male skulls found at the site.

Considered together, the male crania reflect a mixture of modern and archaic traits. Cro-Magnon I is the most gracile of the three; the supraorbital tori of the other two males, for example, are more robust. The most modern-looking is the female cranium, the appearance of which may be a function of sexual dimorphism.

The question of whether continuous local evolution produced anatomically modern groups directly from Neandertals in some regions of Eurasia is far from settled. From central Europe, some variation indicates a combination of both Neandertal and modern characteristics and may suggest gene flow between the two different *H. sapiens* groups. However, tracing such relatively minor genetic changes—considering the ever-present problems of dating, lack of fossils, and fragmented fossil finds—has proved extremely difficult.

However, a newly discovered child's skeleton from Portugal has provided some of the best evidence yet of possible hybridization between Neandertals and anatomically modern *H. sapiens*. This important new hominid discovery from the Abrigo do Lagar Velho site was excavated in late 1998 and is dated to 24,500 y.a. (i.e., at least 5,000 years *later* than the last clearly Neandertal find).

Cro-Magnon (crow man´yon)

Aurignacian Pertaining to an Upper Paleolithic stone tool industry in Europe beginning at about 40,000 y.a.

 See Virtual Lab 12, section I, for a discussion of the transformation of physical characteristics that accompanied the evolution of modern *Homo sapiens*.

figure 11–6 Cro-Magnon I (France). In this specimen, modern traits are quite clear. (a) Lateral view. (b) Frontal view.

(a)

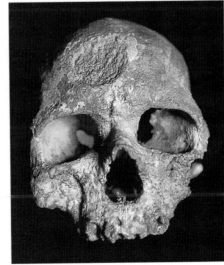

(b)

Courtesy, David Frayer

Courtesy, David Frayer

Associated with an Upper Paleolithic industry (see p. 289) and interred with red ocher and pierced shell is a fairly complete skeleton of a four-year-old child (Duarte et al., 1999). Cidália Duarte, Erik Trinkaus, and colleagues, who have studied the remains, found a highly mixed set of anatomical features. Many characteristics (of the teeth, lower jaw, and pelvis) were like those seen in anatomically modern humans. Yet, several other features (lack of chin, limb proportions, muscle insertions) were more similar to Neandertals. The authors thus conclude, "The presence of such admixture suggests the hypothesis of variable admixture between early modern humans dispersing into Europe and local Neandertal populations" (Duarte et al., 1999, p. 7608). These researchers thus argue that this new evidence provides strong support for the partial replacement model while seriously weakening the complete replacement model. However, the evidence from one child's skeleton—while intriguing—is certainly not going to convince everyone!

Asia

There are six early anatomically modern human localities in China, the most significant of which are Upper Cave at Zhoukoudian and Ordos in Mongolia. The fossils from these sites are all fully modern, and most are considered to be of quite late Upper Pleistocene age. Upper Cave at Zhoukoudian has been dated to between 18,000 and 10,000 y.a. The Ordos find may be the oldest anatomically modern material from China, perhaps dating to 50,000 y.a. or more (Etler, personal communication) (see fig. 11–5).

In addition, the Jinniushan skeleton discussed in Chapter 10 (see p. 245) has been suggested by some researchers (Tiemel et al., 1994) as hinting at modern features in China as early as 200,000 y.a. If this date (as early as that proposed for direct antecedents of modern *H. sapiens* in Africa) should prove accurate, it would cast doubt on the complete replacement model. Indeed, quite opposed to the complete replacement model and more in support of regional continuity, many Chinese paleoanthropologists see a continuous evolution from Chinese *H. erectus* to archaic *H. sapiens* to anatomically modern humans. This view is supported by Wolpoff, who mentions that materials from Upper Cave at Zhoukoudian "have a number of features that are characteristically regional" and that these features are definitely not African (1989, p. 83).*

In addition to the well-known finds from China, anatomically modern remains have also been discovered in southern Asia. At Batadomba Iena, in southern Sri Lanka, modern *Homo sapiens* finds have been dated to 25,500 y.a. (Kennedy and Deraniyagala, 1989).

Australia

During glacial times, the Indonesian islands were joined to the Asian mainland, but Australia was not. It is likely that by 50,000 y.a., Sahul—the area including New Guinea and Australia—was inhabited by modern humans. Bamboo rafts

---

*Wolpoff's statement supports his regional continuity hypothesis. His reference to Africa is a criticism of the complete replacement hypothesis.

may have been the means of crossing the sea between islands, which would not have been a simple exercise. Just where the future Australians came from is unknown, but Borneo, Java, and New Guinea have all been suggested.

Human occupation of Australia appears to have occurred quite early, with some archaeological sites dating to 55,000 y.a. Dating of the earliest Australian human remains (which are all modern *H. sapiens*), however, is controversial. The earliest finds thus far discovered have come from Lake Mungo in southeastern Australia. In agreement with archaeological context and radiocarbon dates, the hominids from this site have been dated at approximately 30,000–25,000 y.a. Newly determined age estimates, using ESR and uranium series dating (see Table 11–1) have dramatically extended the suggested time depth to about 60,000 y.a. (Thorne et al., 1999). The lack of correlation of these more ancient age estimates with other data, however, has provoked serious concerns among some researchers (Gillespie and Roberts, 2000).

Equally intriguing as these proposed early dates for the first Australians are recent reports of mitochondrial DNA sequences derived from the fossil remains from Lake Mungo (Adcock et al., 2001). While the primary researchers are confident that these samples are authentically ancient, the possibility of contamination cannot be entirely ruled out. Indeed, other researchers remain unconvinced that the mtDNA from Lake Mungo is ancient at all (Cooper et al., 2001). Obviously, given the controversies, we will need further corroboration for both the dating and DNA findings before passing judgment.

Unlike the more gracile early Australian forms from Lake Mungo are the Kow Swamp people, who are thought to have lived between about 14,000 and 9,000 years ago (figs. 11–7 and 11–8). The presence of certain archaic traits, such as receding foreheads, heavy supraorbital tori, and thick bones, are difficult to explain, since these features contrast with the postcranial anatomy, which matches that of recent native Australians (Table 11–3).

Courtesy, Milford Wolpoff

figure 11–7 Kow Swamp (Australia). Note the considerable robusticity in this relatively late Australian *Homo sapiens sapiens* cranium.

TABLE 11-3	In Summary: Key Early Modern *Homo sapiens* Discoveries from Europe, Asia, and Australia		
Site	**Dates (y.a.)**	**Human Remains**	**Comments**
Abrigo do Lagar Velho (Portugal)	24,500	Four-year-old child's skeleton	Shows mixture of traits; provisionally interpreted as evidence of hybridization
Cro-Magnon (France)	30,000	8 individuals	Most famous site of early modern *H. sapiens*; some variability in expression of modern traits
Ordos (Mongolia, China)	50,000	1 individual	Perhaps earliest evidence of *H. sapiens* in Asia
Kow Swamp (Australia)	14,000–9,000	Large sample (more than 40 individuals), including adults, juveniles, and infants	Very robust individuals
Lake Mungo (Australia)	?60,000–30,000	3 individuals, one a cremation	Early date is controversial; recent extraction and analysis of DNA (also controversial)

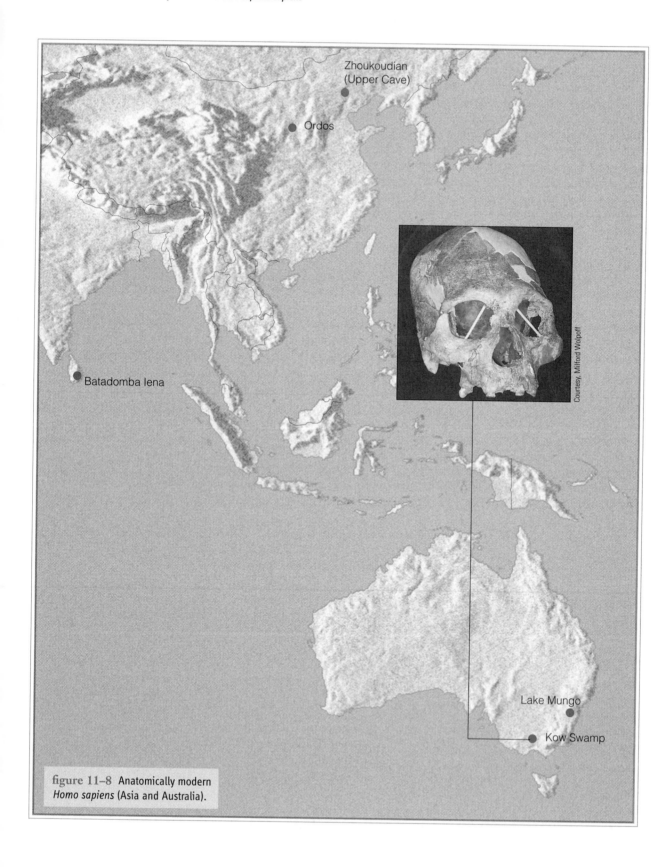

figure 11–8 Anatomically modern *Homo sapiens* (Asia and Australia).

Technology and Art in the Upper Paleolithic

Europe

The cultural period known as the Upper Paleolithic began in western Europe approximately 40,000 years ago (fig. 11–9). Upper Paleolithic cultures are usually divided into five different industries based on stone tool technologies: (1) Chatelperronian, (2) Aurignacian, (3) Gravettian, (4) Solutrean, and (5) Magdalenian. Major environmental shifts were also apparent during this period. During the last glacial period, at about 30,000 y.a., a warming trend lasting several thousand years partially melted the glacial ice. The result was that much of Eurasia was covered by tundra and steppe, a vast area of treeless country dotted with lakes and marshes. In many areas in the north, permafrost prevented the growth of trees but permitted the growth, in the short summers, of flowering plants, mosses, and other kinds of vegetation. This vegetation served as an enormous pasture for herbivorous animals, large and small, and carnivorous animals fed off the herbivores. It was a hunter's paradise, with millions of animals dispersed across expanses of tundra and grassland, from Spain through Europe and into the Russian steppes.

Large herds of reindeer roamed the tundra and steppes along with mammoths, bison, horses, and a host of smaller animals that served as a bountiful source of food. In addition, humans exploited fish and fowl systematically for the first time, especially along the southern tier of Europe. It was a time of relative affluence, and ultimately Upper Paleolithic people spread out over Europe, living in caves and open-air camps and building large shelters. Large dwellings with storage pits have been excavated in the former Soviet Union, with archaeological evidence of social status distinctions (Soffer, 1985). During this period, either western Europe or perhaps portions of Africa achieved the highest population density in human history up to that time.

In Eurasia, cultural innovations allowed humans for the first time to occupy easternmost Europe and northern Asia. In these areas, even during glacial warming stages, winters would have been long and harsh. Human groups were able to tolerate these environments probably because of better constructed structures as well as warmer, better fitting *sewn* clothing. The evidence for wide use of such tailored clothing comes from many sites and includes pointed stone tools such as awls and (by at least 19,000 y.a.) bone needles as well. Especially noteworthy is the clear evidence of the residues of clothing (including what has been interpreted as a cap, a shirt, a jacket, trousers, and moccasins) in graves at the 22,000-year-old Sungir site, located not far from Moscow (Klein, 1989).

Humans and other animals in the midlatitudes of Eurasia had to cope with shifts in climatic conditions, some of which were quite rapid. For example, at 20,000 y.a. another climatic "pulse" caused the weather to become noticeably colder in Europe and Asia as the continental glaciations reached their maximum extent for this entire glacial period (called the Würm in Eurasia). Meanwhile, the southern continents, too, experienced widespread climatic effects. Notably, in Africa around 20,000 y.a. it became significantly wetter, thus permitting reoccupation of areas in the north and south that had previously been abandoned.

figure 11–9 Cultural periods of the European Upper Paleolithic and their approximate beginning dates.

GLACIAL	UPPER PALEOLITHIC (beginnings)	CULTURAL PERIODS
W Ü R M	17,000 –	Magdalenian
	21,000 –	Solutrean
	27,000 –	Gravettian
	40,000 –	Aurignacian Chatelperronian
Middle Paleolithic		Mousterian

(a)   (b)

figure 11-10 (a) Burin. A very common Upper Paleolithic tool. (b) Solutrean blade. This is the best-known work of the Solutrean tradition. Solutrean stonework is considered the most highly developed of any Upper Paleolithic industry.

Magdalenian Pertaining to the final phase of the Upper Paleolithic stone tool industry in Europe.

Burins Small, chisel-like tools (with a pointed end) thought to have been used to engrave bone, antler, ivory, or wood.

As a variety of organisms attempted to adapt to these changing conditions, *Homo sapiens* had a major advantage: the elaboration of an increasingly sophisticated technology (and probably other components of culture as well). Indeed, probably one of the greatest challenges facing numerous late Pleistocene mammals was the ever more dangerously equipped humans—a trend that has continued to modern times.

The Upper Paleolithic was an age of technological innovation and can be compared to the past few hundred years in our recent history of amazing technological change after centuries of relative inertia. Anatomically modern humans of the Upper Paleolithic not only invented new and specialized tools (fig. 11–10), but, as we have seen, also greatly increased the use of (and probably experimented with) new materials, such as bone, ivory, and antler.

Solutrean tools are good examples of Upper Paleolithic skill and perhaps aesthetic appreciation as well (fig. 11–10b). In this lithic (stone) tradition, stoneknapping developed to the finest degree ever known. Using specialized flaking techniques, the artist/technicians made beautiful parallel-flaked lance heads, expertly flaked on both surfaces, with such delicate points that they can be considered works of art that quite possibly never served, or were intended to serve, a utilitarian purpose.

The last stage of the Upper Paleolithic, known as the **Magdalenian**, saw even more advances in technology. The spear-thrower (fig. 11–11), a wooden or bone hooked rod (called an *atlatl*), acted to extend the hunter's arm, thus enhancing the force and distance of a spear throw. For catching salmon and other fish, the barbed harpoon is a clever example of the craftsperson's skill. There is also evidence that the bow and arrow may have been used for the first time during this period. The introduction of the punch technique (fig. 11–12) provided an abundance of standardized stone blades that could be fashioned into **burins** (see fig. 11–10a) for working wood, bone, and antler; borers for drilling holes in skins, bones, and shells; and knives with serrated or notched edges for scraping wooden shafts into a variety of tools.

The elaboration of many more specialized tools by Upper Paleolithic peoples probably made more resources available to them and may also have had an impact on the biology of these populations. C. Loring Brace of the University of Michigan has suggested that with more efficient tools used for food processing, anatomically modern *H. sapiens* would not have required the large front teeth (incisors) seen in earlier populations. With relaxed selection pressures (no longer favoring large anterior teeth), incorporation of random mutations would through time lead to reduction of dental size and accompanying facial features. In particular, the lower face became less prognathic (as compared to archaic specimens) and thus produced the concavity of the cheekbones called a *canine fossa* (see fig. 11–2). Moreover, as the dental-bearing portion of the lower jaw

figure 11-11 Spear-thrower (atlatl). Note the carving.

(a) A large core is selected and the top portion is removed by use of a hammerstone.

(b) The objective is to create a flat surface called a striking platform.

Striking platform

(c) Next, the core is struck by use of a hammer and punch (made of bone or antler) to remove the long narrow flakes (called blades).

(d) Or the blades can be removed by pressure flaking.

(e) The result is the production of highly consistent sharp blades, which can be used, as is, as knives; or they can be further modified (retouched) to make a variety of other tools (such as burins, scrapers, and awls).

regressed, the buttressing below would have become modified into a *chin*, that distinctive feature seen in anatomically modern *H. sapiens*.

In addition to their reputation as hunters, western Europeans of the Upper Paleolithic are even better known for their symbolic representation, what has commonly been called "art." Certainly, in the famous caves of France and Spain (discussed shortly), we easily relate to an aesthetic property of the images—one that *may* have been intended by the people who created them. But here we cannot be certain. Our own cultural perspectives create labels (and categories) such as "art," which in itself *assumes* aesthetic intent. While such a cultural orientation is obviously a recognizable part of Western culture, many other contemporary peoples would not relate to this concept within their own cultural context. Furthermore, prehistoric peoples during the Upper Paleolithic did not necessarily create their symbols as true artistic representations. Rather, these representations may have served a variety of quite utilitarian and/or social functions—as do contemporary highway signs or logos on a company's letterhead. Would we call these symbols art?

Given these uncertainties, archaeologist Margaret Conkey of the University of California, Berkeley, refers to Upper Paleolithic cave paintings, sculptures, engravings, and so forth, as "visual and material imagery" (Conkey, 1987, p. 423). We will continue to use the term *art* to describe many of these prehistoric representations, but you should recognize that we do so mainly as a cultural convention—and perhaps a limiting one.

Moreover, the time depth for these prehistoric forms of symbolic imagery is quite long, encompassing the entire Upper Paleolithic (from at least 35,000 to 10,000 y.a.). Over this time span there is considerable variability in style, medium, content, and no doubt meaning as well. In addition, there is an

figure 11–12 **The punch blade technique.**

See Virtual Lab 11, section IV, for a discussion of blade manufacture.

figure 11–13 Magdalenian bone artifact. Note the realistic animal engraving on this object, the precise function of which is unknown.

extremely wide geographical distribution of symbolic images, best known from many parts of Europe, but now also well documented from Siberia, North Africa, South Africa, and Australia. Given the 25,000-year time depth of what we call "Paleolithic art" and its nearly worldwide distribution, there is indeed marked variability in expression.

In addition to cave art, there are numerous examples of small sculptures excavated from sites in western, central, and eastern Europe. Beyond these quite well-known figurines, there are numerous other examples of what is frequently termed "portable art," including elaborate engravings on tools and tool handles (fig. 11–13). Such symbolism can be found in many parts of Europe and was already well established early in the Aurignacian (by 33,000 y.a.). Innovations in symbolic representations also benefited from, and probably further stimulated, technological advances. New methods of mixing pigments and applying them were important in rendering painted or drawn images. Bone and ivory carving and engraving were made easier with the use of special stone tools (see fig. 11–10). At two sites in the Czech Republic, Dolni Vestonice and Predmosti (both dated at 27,000 y.a.), small animal figures were fashioned from fired clay— the first documented use of ceramic technology anywhere (and preceding later pottery invention by more than 15,000 years!).

Female figurines, popularly known as "Venuses," were sculpted not only in western Europe, but in central and eastern Europe and Siberia as well. Some of these figures were realistically carved, and the faces appear to be modeled after actual women (fig. 11–14). Other figurines may seem grotesque, with sexual characteristics exaggerated, perhaps for fertility or other ritual purposes (fig. 11–15).

It is, however, during the final phases of the Upper Paleolithic, particularly during the Magdalenian, that European prehistoric art reached its climax. Cave

figure 11–14 Venus of Brassempouy. Upper Paleolithic artists were capable of portraying human realism (shown here) as well as symbolism (depicted in fig. 11–15). (a) Frontal view. (b) Lateral view.

(a)   (b)

art is now known from more than 150 separate sites, the vast majority from southwestern France and northern Spain. Apparently, in other areas the rendering of such images did not take place in deep caves. Peoples in central Europe, China, Africa, and elsewhere certainly may have painted or carved representations on rockfaces in the open, but these images long since would have eroded. Thus, it is fortuitous that the people of at least one of the many sophisticated cultures of the Upper Paleolithic chose to journey belowground to create their artwork, preserving it not just for their immediate descendants, but for us as well.

In Lascaux Cave of southern France, immense wild bulls dominate what is called the Great Hall of Bulls, and horses, deer, and other animals adorn the walls in black, red, and yellow, drawn with remarkable skill. In addition to the famous cave of Lascaux, there is equally exemplary art from Altamira Cave in Spain. Indeed, discovered in 1879, Altamira was the first example of advanced cave art recorded in Europe. Filling the walls and ceiling of the cave are superb portrayals of bison in red and black, the "artist" taking advantage of bulges to give a sense of relief to the paintings. The cave is a treasure of beautiful art whose meaning has never been satisfactorily explained. It could have been religious or magical, a form of visual communication, or art for the sake of beauty.

Yet another spectacular example of cave art from western Europe was discovered in late 1994. On December 24, a team of three French cave explorers chanced upon a fabulous discovery in the valley of the Ardèche at Combe d'Arc (fig. 11–16). Inside the cave, called the Grotte Chauvet after one of its discoverers, preserved unseen for perhaps 30,000 years are many hundreds of images, including stylized dots, stenciled human handprints, and, most dramatically, hundreds of animal representations. Included are depictions of such typical Paleolithic subjects as bison, horse, ibex, auroch, deer, and mammoth. But quite surprisingly, there are also numerous images of animals rarely portrayed elsewhere—such as rhino, lion, and bear (fig. 11–17). Three animals seen at Grotte Chauvet—a panther, a hyena, and an owl—have never before been documented at cave sites. The artwork, at least after provisional study, seems to consistently repeat several stylistic conventions, causing French researchers to suggest that the images all may have been produced by the same artist. Provisional dating has placed the paintings during the Aurignacian (perhaps more than 30,000 y.a.), and thus Grotte Chauvet may be considerably earlier than the Magdalenian sites of Lascaux and Altamira. The cave was found as Paleolithic peoples had left it, and the initial discoverers, as well as archaeologists, have been careful not to disturb the remains. Among the archaeological traces already noted are dozens of footprints on the cave floor, produced by bears as well as by humans. We do not know yet how far the cave extends or what crucial artifactual remains lie along the floor.

A familiar motif seen at Grotte Chauvet and elsewhere is the representation of human hands, usually in the form of outlines. Apparently, the technique used was to liquefy the pigment and blow it onto a hand held flat against the cave wall. At one site in France, at least 159 such hand outlines were found (Leroi-Gourhan, 1986). Another stylistic innovation was the partial sculpting of a rock face—in what is called bas-relief (a technique used much later, for example, by the ancient Greeks at the Parthenon). Attaining depths of up to 6 inches, some of the Paleolithic sculptures are quite dramatic and were attempted on a fairly

figure 11–15 Venus of Willendorf, Austria. (*Note:* This figure is among the most exaggerated and should be compared with fig. 11–14.)

Jim Cartier/Photo Researchers

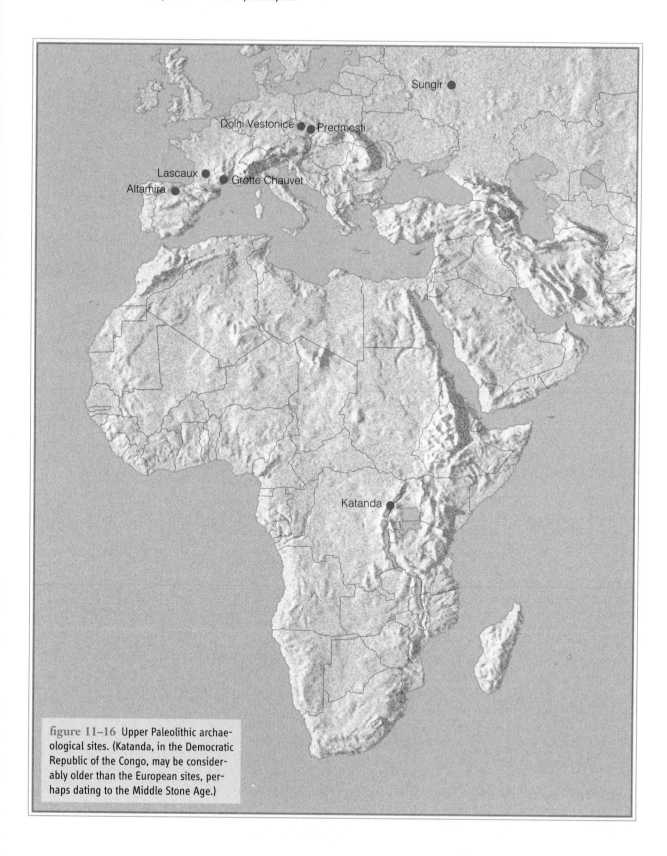

figure 11–16 Upper Paleolithic archaeological sites. (Katanda, in the Democratic
Republic of the Congo, may be considerably older than the European sites, perhaps dating to the Middle Stone Age.)

Jean Clottes/Document elaborated with the support of the French Ministry of Culture and Communication, Regional Direction for Cultural Affairs, Rhône-Alpes, Regional Department of Archaeology.

(a)

Jean-Marie Chauvet/Document elaborated with the support of the French Ministry of Culture and Communication, Regional Direction for Cultural Affairs, Rhône-Alpes, Regional Department of Archaeology.

(b)

figure 11–17 Cave art from Grotte Chauvet, France. (a) Bear. (b) Aurochs and rhinoceros.

grand scale. In one rock shelter in southwest France, several animals (including mountain goats, bison, reindeer, and horses) and one human figure are depicted in bas-relief. Interestingly, these representations were carved in an area also used as a living site—quite distinct from the special-purpose contexts in the deep cave locations. These bas-reliefs were executed throughout the Magdalenian, always in areas immediately adjacent to those of human habitation.

Strikingly, subject matter seems to differ by location and type of art motif. In portable art, common themes are horses and reindeer as well as stylized human figures; rarely are bison represented. However, in cave contexts, bison and horses are frequently seen, but almost never do we see reindeer (although in Europe, reindeer were probably the most common meat source). Cave artists were thought heretofore to have depicted carnivores only rarely, but the new finds at Grotte Chauvet give us a further perspective on the richness *and* diversity of Paleolithic art.

Ever since ancient art was discovered, attempts have been made to interpret the sculptures, paintings, and other graphic material found in caves or on rocks and tools at open-air archaeological sites. One of the early explanations of Upper Paleolithic art emphasized the relationship of paintings to hunting. Hunting rituals were viewed as a kind of imitative magic that would increase prey animal populations or help hunters successfully find and kill their quarry. As new hypotheses were published, their applicability and deficiencies were discussed. When many of these new hypotheses faded, others were expounded, and the cycle of new hypotheses followed by critiques continued.

Among these hypotheses, the association of ritual and magic is still considered viable because of the importance of hunting in the Upper Paleolithic. Nevertheless, other ideas about these graphics have been widely discussed, including the viewing of Upper Paleolithic art from a male/female perspective and the consideration of a prevalent dots-and-lines motif as a notational system associated with language, writing, or a calendar (Marshack, 1972). Other perspectives and ongoing questions include why certain areas of caves were used for painting, but not other, similar areas; why certain animals were painted, but not others; why males were painted singly or in groups, but women only in groups; why males were painted near animals, but women never were; and why groups of animals were painted in the most acoustically resonant areas. (Were rituals perhaps performed in areas of the cave with the best acoustic properties?) It should be noted that given the time depth, different contexts, and variable styles of symbolic representations, no *single* explanation regarding their meaning is likely to prove adequate. As one expert has concluded, "It is clear that there can no longer be a single 'meaning' to account for the thousands of images, media, contexts, and uses of what we lump under the term 'paleolithic art'" (Conkey, 1987, p. 414).

A recent explanation for the florescence of cave art in certain areas has been suggested by archaeologists Clive Gamble (1991) and Lawrence Straus (1993), who point to the severe climatic conditions during the maximum (coldest interval) of the last glacial, around 20,000–18,000 y.a. It was during this period in southwestern France and northern Spain that most of the cave art was created. Straus notes that wherever there are clusters of living sites, there are cave art sanctuaries and residential sites with abundant mobile art objects. The caves could have been meeting places for local bands of people and locations for group activities. Bands could share hunting techniques and knowledge, and paintings and engravings served as "encoded information" that could be passed on across generations. Such information, Straus argues, would have been crucial for dealing with the severe conditions of the last glacial period.

Africa

Early accomplishments in rock art, perhaps as early as in Europe, are seen in southern Africa (Namibia), where a site containing such art is dated between 28,000 and 19,000 y.a. In addition, evidence of portable personal adornment is seen as early as 38,000 y.a. in the form of beads fashioned from ostrich eggshells.

In terms of stone tool technology, microliths (thumbnail-sized stone flakes hafted to make knives, saws, etc.) and blades characterize Late Stone Age* African industries. There was also considerable use of bone and antler in central Africa, perhaps some of it quite early. Recent excavations in the Katanda area of the eastern portion of the Democratic Republic of the Congo have shown remarkable development of bone craftwork. In fact, preliminary reports by Alison Brooks of George Washington University and John Yellen of the National Science Foundation have demonstrated that these technological achievements rival those of the more renowned European Upper Paleolithic (Yellen et al., 1995).

The most important artifacts discovered at Katanda are a dozen intricately made bone tools excavated from three sites along the Semiliki River (not far from Lake Rutanzige—formerly, Lake Edward) (see fig. 11–16). These tools, made from the ribs or long bone splinters of large mammals, apparently were first ground to flatten and sharpen them, and then some were precisely pressure-flaked to produce a row of barbs. In form these tools are similar to what have been called "harpoons" from the later Upper Paleolithic of Europe (Magdalenian, circa 15,000 y.a.). Their function in Africa, as well, is thought to have been for spearing fish, which archaeological remains indicate were quite large (catfish weighing up to 150 pounds!). In addition, a few carved bone rings with no barbs were also discovered, but their intended function (if indeed they were meant to have a utilitarian function at all) remains elusive.

The dating of the Katanda sites is crucial for drawing useful comparisons with the European Upper Paleolithic. However, the bone used for the tools retained no measurable nitrogen and thus proved unsuitable for radiocarbon dating (perhaps it was too old and beyond the range of this technique). As a result, the other techniques now used for this time range—thermoluminescence, electron spin resonance, and uranium series dating (see Table 11–1)—were all applied. The results proved consistent, indicating dates between 180,000 and 75,000 y.a.[†]

However, there remain some difficulties in establishing the clear association of the bone implements with the materials that have supplied the chronometric age estimates. Indeed, Richard Klein, a coauthor of one of the initial reports (Brooks et al., 1995), does not accept the suggested great antiquity for these finds and believes they may be much younger. Nevertheless, if the early age estimates should hold up, we once again will look *first* to Africa as the crucial source area for human origins—not just for biological aspects, but for cultural aspects as well.

*The Late Stone Age in Africa is equivalent to the Upper Paleolithic in Eurasia.

†If these dates prove accurate, Katanda would actually be earlier than Late Stone Age (and thus be considered Middle Stone Age).

Summary of Upper Paleolithic Culture

As we look back at the Upper Paleolithic, we can see it as the culmination of 2 million years of cultural development. Change proceeded incredibly slowly for most of the Pleistocene, but as cultural traditions and materials accumulated and the brain (and, we assume, intelligence) expanded and reorganized, the rate of change quickened.

Cultural evolution continued with the appearance of early archaic *H. sapiens* and moved a bit faster with later archaic *H. sapiens*. Neandertals in Eurasia and their contemporaries elsewhere added deliberate burials, technological innovations, and much more.

Building on existing cultures, late Pleistocene populations attained sophisticated cultural and material heights in a seemingly short (by previous standards) burst of exciting activity. In Europe and central Africa particularly, there seem to have been dramatic cultural innovations that saw big game hunting, potent new weapons (including harpoons, spear-throwers, and possibly the bow and arrow), body ornaments, needles, "tailored" clothing, and burials with elaborate grave goods (the latter perhaps indicating some sort of status hierarchy).

This dynamic age was doomed, or so it appears, by the climatic changes of about 10,000 y.a. As the temperature slowly rose and the glaciers retreated, animal and plant species were seriously impacted, and humans were thus affected as well. As traditional prey animals were depleted or disappeared altogether, other means of obtaining food were sought.

Grinding hard seeds or roots became important, and as familiarity with plant propagation increased, domestication of plants and animals developed. Dependence on domestication became critical, and with it came permanent settlements, new technology, and more complex social organization. The continuing story of human evolution and the ways we study contemporary population diversity will be the topics of the remainder of this text.

Summary

he date and location of the origin of anatomically modern human beings have been the subjects of a fierce debate for the past decade, and the end is not in sight. One hypothesis (complete replacement) claims that anatomically modern forms first evolved in Africa more than 100,000 y.a. and then, migrating out of Africa, completely replaced archaic *H. sapiens* in the rest of the world. Another school (regional continuity) takes a diametrically different view and maintains that in various geographical regions of the world, local groups of archaic *H. sapiens* evolved directly to anatomically modern humans. A third hypothesis (partial replacement) takes a somewhat middle position, suggesting an African origin but also accepting some later hybridization outside of Africa.

The Upper Paleolithic was an age of extraordinary innovation and achievement in technology and art. Many new and complex tools were introduced, and

TABLE 11-4	Most Significant Modern *Homo sapiens* Discoveries Discussed in this Chapter		
Site	Dates (y.a.)	Human Remains	Comments
Abrigo do Lagar Velho (Portugal)	24,500	Four-year-old child's skeleton	Possible evidence of hybridization between Neandertals and modern *H. sapiens*
Cro-Magnon (France)	30,000	8 individuals	Famous site of early modern *H. sapiens*, but there are dozens of other sites in Europe and elsewhere
Qafzeh (Israel)	110,000	Minimum of 20 individuals	Quite early site; shows considerable variation
Skhūl (Israel)	115,000	Minimum of 10 individuals	Earliest well-dated modern *H. sapiens* outside of Africa (and nearly contemporaneous with earliest African finds); also perhaps contemporaneous with neighboring Tabun Neandertal site
Lake Mungo (Australia)	?60,000–30,000	3 individuals	Early dating estimate is surprising; if confirmed, would be earlier than established evidence in Europe or Asia

their production indicates fine skill in working wood, bone, and antler. Cave art in France and Spain displays the masterful ability of Upper Paleolithic painters, and beautiful sculptures have been found at many European sites. Sophisticated symbolic representations have also been found in Africa and elsewhere. Upper Paleolithic *Homo sapiens* displayed amazing development in a relatively short period of time. The culture produced during this period led the way to still newer and more complex cultural techniques and methods.

As a further study aid, the most significant fossil discoveries discussed in this chapter are presented in Table 11–4.

Questions for Review

1. What characteristics define anatomically modern *H. sapiens*?
2. How do the characteristics of modern *H. sapiens* compare with those of archaic *H. sapiens*?
3. What are the three major theories that seek to explain the origin and dispersal of *Homo sapiens sapiens*? Compare and critically discuss these three views.
4. How have data from mitochondrial DNA been used to support an African origin of *H. sapiens sapiens*? What other genetic data have recently been analyzed, and how do they accord with the mtDNA results?

5. Discuss (and compare) the early evidence of anatomically modern humans from two different regions.
6. It is said that the Upper Paleolithic was a time of technological innovation. Support this statement with specific evidence, and compare the Upper Paleolithic with cultural data from earlier in the Pleistocene.
7. From which regions has cave art, dating to the Upper Pleistocene, been discovered? Particularly for the cave art of Europe, what explanations of its meaning have been proposed?

Suggested Further Readings

Aitken, M. J., C. B. Stringer, and P. A. Mellars (eds.). 1993. *The Origin of Modern Humans and the Impact of Chronometric Dating*. Princeton, NJ: Princeton University Press.

Klein, Richard. 1999. *The Human Career: Human Biological and Cultural Origins*. 2nd ed. Chicago: University of Chicago Press.

Klein, Richard (with Blake Edgar). 2002. *The Dawn of Human Culture*. New York: John Wiley & Sons.

Nitecki, Matthew H., and Doris V. Nitecki (eds.). 1994. *Origins of Anatomically Modern Humans*. New York: Plenum.

Smith, Fred, and Frank Spencer (eds.). 1984. *The Origin of Modern Humans*. New York: Liss.

Wolpoff, Milford. 1999. *Paleoanthropology*. 2nd ed. New York: McGraw-Hill.

Multimedia Resources

 Companion Web Site

Anthropology Online: The Wadsworth Anthropology Resource Center Visit **http://anthropology.wadsworth.com** and click on the Companion Web Site for Jurmain/Kilgore/Trevathan/Nelson's *Essentials of Physical Anthropology*, Fifth Edition, to access a wide range of enrichment material to aid in your study of anthropology. Among the useful options for each chapter's self-study are learning objectives, flashcards, Internet exercises, Web links, InfoTrac College Edition exercises, and practice quizzes that can be scored and emailed to your instructor.

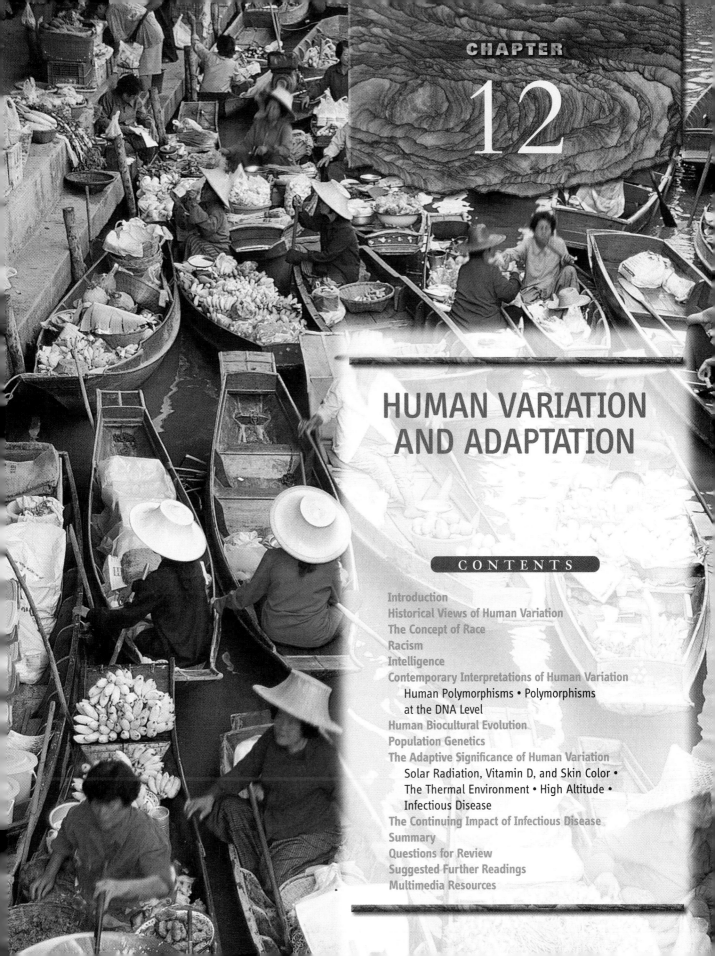

CHAPTER

12

HUMAN VARIATION AND ADAPTATION

CONTENTS

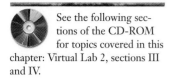

See the following sections of the CD-ROM for topics covered in this chapter: Virtual Lab 2, sections III and IV.

Introduction

I n Chapters 3 and 4, we saw how physical characteristics are influenced by the DNA in our cells. Furthermore, we discussed how individuals inherit genes from parents and how variations in genes (alleles) can produce different expressions of traits. In Chapter 4, we also focused on how the basic principles of inheritance relate to evolutionary change.

In this chapter, we turn once again to topics directly related to genetics—namely, biological diversity in humans and how humans adapt physically to environmental challenges. Following a discussion of historical attempts at explaining human phenotypic diversity and racial classification, we examine contemporary methods of interpreting diversity. In recent years, several new techniques have emerged that permit direct examination of the DNA molecule, revealing differences between individuals even at the level of single nucleotides. But even as discoveries of different levels of diversity emerge, geneticists have also revealed that our species is remarkably uniform genetically, particularly when compared to other species.

Later in the chapter, we consider human phenotypic variation within the context of adaptation to specific environmental contexts. Hence, we examine how populations and individuals differ in their adaptive response to such factors as ultraviolet radiation, heat, cold, and high altitude. Finally, we consider the significant role of infectious disease in human evolution and adaptation.

Historical Views of Human Variation

The first step toward understanding natural phenomena is the ordering of variation into categories that can then be named, discussed, and perhaps studied. Historically, when different groups of people came into contact with one another, they offered explanations for the physical differences they saw. Because skin color was so noticeable, it was one of the more frequently explained traits, and most systems of racial classification were based on it.

As early as 1350 B.C., the ancient Egyptians had classified humans on the basis of skin color: red for Egyptian, yellow for people to the east, white for those to the north, and black for Africans south of the Sahara (Gossett, 1963, p. 4). In the sixteenth century, after the discovery of the New World, Europe embarked on a period of intense exploration and colonization in both the New and Old Worlds. Resulting from this contact was an increased awareness of human diversity.

Throughout the eighteenth and nineteenth centuries, European and American scientists concentrated primarily on describing and classifying the biological variation in humans as well as in nonhuman species. The first scientific attempt to describe the newly discovered variation between human populations was Linnaeus' taxonomic classification, which placed humans into four separate categories (Linnaeus, 1758). Linnaeus assigned behavioral and intellectual qualities to each group, with the least complimentary descriptions going to black Africans. This ranking was typical of the period and reflected the almost universal European view that Europeans were superior to all other peoples.

Johann Friedrich Blumenbach (1752–1840), a German anatomist, classified humans into five races. Although Blumenbach's categories came to be described simply as white, yellow, red, black, and brown, he also used criteria other than skin color. Moreover, Blumenbach emphasized that racial categories based on skin color were arbitrary and that many traits, including skin color, were not discrete phenomena. Blumenbach pointed out that to attempt to classify all humans using such a system would be to omit completely all those who did not neatly fall into a specific category. Furthermore, it was recognized by Blumenbach and others that traits such as skin color showed overlapping expression between groups.

In 1842, Anders Retzius, a Swedish anatomist, developed the *cephalic index* as a method of describing the shape of the head. The cephalic index, derived by dividing maximum head breadth by maximum length and multiplying by 100, gives the ratio of head breadth to length. (It is important to note that the cephalic index does not measure head size.) The cephalic index is still used to assess head shape, but, in the nineteenth century, it was viewed as a scientific technique that could be used to categorize groups of people. Furthermore, because people could be neatly categorized by a single number, it provided an extremely efficient method for describing variation. Individuals with an index of less than 75 had long, narrow heads and were termed **dolichocephalic**. **Brachycephalic** individuals, with broad heads, had an index of over 80; and those whose indices were between 75 and 80 were *mesocephalic*.

Dolichocephalic Having a long, narrow head in which the width measures less than 75 percent of the length.

Brachycephalic Having a broad head in which the width measures more than 80 percent of the length.

Northern Europeans tended to be dolichocephalic, while southern Europeans were brachycephalic. Not surprisingly, these results led to heated and nationalistic debate over whether one group was superior to another. Furthermore, when it was shown that northern Europeans shared their tendency to long, narrow heads with several African populations, the cephalic index ceased to be considered a reliable indicator of race.

By the mid-nineteenth century, populations were ranked essentially on a scale based on skin color (along with size and shape of the head), with Africans at the bottom. Moreover, Europeans themselves were ranked so that northern, light-skinned populations were considered superior to their southern, somewhat darker-skinned neighbors.

The fact that non-Europeans were viewed as "uncivilized" implied an inferiority of character and intellect. This view was based in a concept now termed **biological determinism**, which in part holds that there is an association between physical characteristics and such attributes as intelligence, morals, values, abilities, and even social and economic differences between groups. In other words, cultural variations are *inherited* in the same manner as biological variations. It follows, then, that there are inherent behavioral and cognitive differences between groups, and therefore, some groups are *by nature* superior to others. Following this logic, it is a simple matter to justify the persecution and even enslavement of other peoples simply because their appearance differs from what is familiar.

Biological determinism The concept that various attributes and behaviors (e.g., intelligence, values, morals) are governed by biological (genetic) factors; the inaccurate association of various behavioral attributes with certain biological traits, such as skin color.

After 1850, biological determinism was a constant theme underlying common thinking as well as scientific research in Europe and the United States. Deterministic (and what we today would call racist) views were held to some extent by most people, including such notable figures as Thomas Jefferson, Georges Cuvier, Benjamin Franklin, Charles Lyell, Abraham Lincoln, Charles Darwin, and Oliver Wendell Holmes. Commenting on this usually deemphasized characteristic of notable historical figures, the late evolutionary biologist

Stephen J. Gould (1981, p. 32) emphasized that "all American culture heroes embraced racial attitudes that would embarrass public-school mythmakers."

Francis Galton (1822–1911), a cousin of Charles Darwin, shared an increasingly common fear among nineteenth-century Europeans that "civilized society" was being weakened by the failure of natural selection to completely eliminate unfit and inferior members (Greene, 1981, p. 107). Galton wrote and lectured on the necessity of "race improvement" and suggested governmental regulation of marriage and family size, an approach he called **eugenics**. Although eugenics had its share of critics, its popularity flourished throughout the 1930s, but nowhere was it more attractive than in Germany, where the viewpoint took a disastrous turn. The false idea of pure races was increasingly extolled as a means of reestablishing a strong and prosperous state. Eugenics was seen as scientific justification for purging Germany of its "unfit," and many of Germany's scientists continued to support the policies of racial purity and eugenics during the Nazi period (Proctor, 1988, p. 143), when they served as justification for condemning millions of people to death.

But at the same time, many scientists were turning away from racial typologies and classification in favor of a more evolutionary approach. No doubt for some, this shift in direction was motivated by their growing concerns over the goals of the eugenics movement. Probably more important, however, was the synthesis of genetics and Darwin's theories of natural selection during the 1930s. As discussed in Chapter 4, this breakthrough influenced all the biological sciences, and some physical anthropologists began to apply evolutionary principles to the study of human variation.

Eugenics The philosophy of "race improvement" through the forced sterilization of members of some groups and encouraged reproduction among others; an overly simplified, often racist, view that is now discredited.

The Concept of Race

All contemporary humans are members of the same **polytypic** species, *Homo sapiens*. A polytypic species is one composed of local populations that differ from one another with regard to the expression of one or more traits. Moreover, *within* local populations there is a great deal of phenotypic and genotypic variation between individuals. Many species are polytypic.

In discussions of human variation, people have traditionally clumped together various attributes such as skin color, shape of the face, shape of the nose, hair color, hair form (curly, straight), and eye color. People possessing particular *combinations* of these and other traits have been placed together into categories associated with specific geographical localities. Such categories are called *races*.

We all think we know what we mean by the word *race*, but in reality, the term has had a number of meanings since it gained common usage in English in the 1500s. It has been used synonymously with *species*, as in "the human race". Since the 1600s, race has also referred to various culturally defined groups, and this meaning still enjoys popular usage. For example, one hears expressions such as "the English race" or "the Japanese race," where the reference is actually to nationality. Another often-heard phrase is "the Jewish race," when the speaker is really talking about a particular ethnic and religious identity.

Polytypic Referring to species composed of populations that differ with regard to the expression of one or more traits.

Thus, while *race* is usually a term with biological connotations, it is also one with enormous social significance. Moreover, there is still a widespread perception that there is an association between certain physical traits (skin color, in particular) and various culturally patterned behavioral attributes (such as attitudes toward women, value placed on education, occupational preferences, and morality). Therefore, in many cultural contexts, a person's social identity is strongly influenced by the manner in which he or she expresses those physical traits traditionally used to define "racial groups." Characteristics such as skin color are highly visible, and they facilitate an immediate and superficial designation of individuals into socially defined categories. However, so-called racial traits are not the only phenotypic expressions that contribute to social identity. Sex and age are also critically important. But aside from these two variables, an individual's biological and/or *ethnic* background is still inevitably a factor that influences how he or she is initially perceived and judged by others.

References to national origin (e.g., African, Asian) as substitutes for racial labels has become more common in recent years, both within and outside anthropology. Within anthropology, the term *ethnicity* was proposed in the early 1950s as a means of avoiding the more emotionally charged term *race*. Strictly speaking, *ethnicity* refers to cultural factors, but the fact that the words *ethnicity* and *race* are used interchangeably reflects the social importance of phenotypic expression and demonstrates once again how phenotype is associated with culturally defined variables.

In its most common biological usage, race refers to geographically patterned phenotypic variation within a species. By the seventeenth century, naturalists had begun to describe races in plants and nonhuman animals, because they recognized that when populations of a species occupied different regions, they sometimes differed from one another in the expression of one or more traits. But even today, there are no established criteria by which races of plants and animals are to be assessed.

Prior to World War II, most studies of human variation focused on visible phenotypic variation between large, geographically defined populations, and these studies were largely descriptive. Since that time, the emphasis has shifted to the examination of differences in allele frequencies (see Chapter 4) within and between populations as well as the adaptive significance of phenotypic and genotypic variation. Hence the application of evolutionary principles to the study of modern human variation has replaced the superficial nineteenth-century view of race *based solely on observed phenotype*. Additionally, the genetic emphasis dispelled previously held misconceptions that races were fixed biological units that did not change over time and that were composed of individuals who all conformed to a particular *type*.

Clearly, there are phenotypic differences between humans, and some of these differences roughly correspond to particular geographical locations, a fact that raises certain questions. Is there any adaptive significance attached to observed phenotypic variation? What is the degree of underlying genetic variation that influences it? Is genetic drift a factor? These questions place considerations of human variation within a contemporary evolutionary framework.

Although, in part, physical anthropology has its roots in attempts to explain human diversity, anthropologists have never been in complete agreement on the topic of race, although no contemporary scholar subscribes to pre–Modern Synthesis concepts of races (human and nonhuman) as fixed biological entities. Many who continue to use broad racial categories do not view them as particularly important, especially from a genetic perspective, because the amount of genetic variation accounted for by differences *between* groups is greatly exceeded by the variation that exists *within* groups (see p. 162). But given these considerations, there are those who see variation in outwardly expressed phenotype, particularly because of its potential adaptive value, as worthy of investigation and explanation within the framework of evolutionary principles (Brues, 1991).

Forensic anthropologists in particular find the phenotypic criteria associated with race to have practical applications because they are frequently called on by law enforcement agencies to assist in the identification of human skeletal remains. Inasmuch as unidentified human remains are often those of crime victims, identification must be as accurate as possible. The most important variables in such identification are the individual's sex, age, stature, and "racial" or "ethnic" background. Using metric and nonmetric criteria, forensic anthropologists employ a number of techniques for establishing broad population affinity, and they are generally able to do so with about 80 percent accuracy.

On the other side of the issue, there are numerous physical anthropologists who argue that race is a meaningless concept when applied to humans. Race is an outdated creation of the human mind that attempts to simplify biological complexity by organizing it into categories. Thus, human races are a product of the human tendency to superimpose order on complex natural phenomena. While classification may have been an acceptable approach some 150 years ago, it is viewed as no longer valid given the current state of genetic and evolutionary science.

Objections to racial taxonomies have also been raised because classification schemes are *typological* in nature, meaning that categories are discrete and based on stereotypes or ideals that comprise a specific set of traits. Thus, in general, typologies are inherently misleading, because there are always many individuals in any grouping who do not conform to all aspects of a particular type.

In any "racial" group, there will be individuals who fall into the normal range of variation for another group with regard to one or several characteristics. For example, two people of different ancestry might vary with regard to skin color, but they could share any number of other traits, such as height, shape of head, hair color, eye color, or ABO blood type. In fact, they could easily share more similarities with each other than they do with many members of their own populations.

Moreover, as we have stressed, because the characteristics that have traditionally been used to define races are polygenic, they exhibit a continuous range of expression. It thus becomes difficult, if not impossible, to draw discrete boundaries between races with regard to many traits. This limitation becomes clear if you ask yourself, "At what point is hair color no longer dark brown, but medium brown; or no longer light brown, but blond?"

The scientific controversy over race will diminish as we increase our understanding of the genetic diversity (and uniformity) of our species. Given the rapid changes in genome studies and the fact that very few genes contribute to outward expressions of phenotype, dividing the human species into racial categories is not a biologically meaningful way to look at human variation. But in spite of all the scientific discussion that has ensued, among the general public, variations on the theme of race will continue (at least for a while) to be the most common view of human biological and cultural variation. Given this fact, it falls to anthropologists and biologists to continue to explore the issue so that, to the best of our abilities, accurate information regarding human variation is available for anyone who seeks informed explanations of complex phenomena.

Racism

Racism is based on the previously mentioned, false belief that such factors as intellect and various cultural attributes are inherited along with physical characteristics. Such beliefs also commonly rest on the assumption that one's own group is superior to other groups.

Because we have already alluded to certain aspects of racism, such as the eugenics movement and persecution of people based on racial or ethnic misconceptions, we will not belabor the point here. However, it is important to point out that racism is hardly a thing of the past, nor is it restricted to European and American whites. Racism is a cultural, not a biological, phenomenon, and it is found worldwide.

Ultimately, racism is one of the more dangerous aspects of human behavior. We continue to see manifestations of racism in the United States and elsewhere. The rioting that occurred in Los Angeles in 1992, after the acquittal of white police officers accused of beating an African American suspect named Rodney King, was a clear example of the tensions among the diverse populations of large urban centers. Sadly, the twentieth century provided numerous examples of ethnic/racial conflict, and the twenty-first century has begun by following its example. But it is important to point out that virtually all these conflicts were due to cultural, not biological, differences between the participants. The unspeakable genocidal events of the Holocaust during World War II, in Cambodia in the 1970s, and in Rwanda in 1994; the tragedies of Bosnia, Croatia, and Kosovo; and the devastating terrorist attacks on the United States on September 11, 2001, all bespeak the outcomes of intolerance of groups we call "others," however we define the term.

We end this brief discussion of racism with an excerpt from an article, "The Study of Race," by Sherwood Washburn, a well-known physical anthropologist at the University of California, Berkeley. Although written some years ago, the statement is as fresh and applicable today as it was when it was written:

> Races are products of the past. They are relics of times and conditions which have long ceased to exist.
>
> Racism is equally a relic supported by no phase of modern science. We may not know how to interpret the form of the Mongoloid face, or why Rh is of high incidence in Africa, but we do know the benefits of education and of economic progress. We . . . know that the roots of happiness lie in the biology of the whole species and that the potential of the species can only be realized in a culture, in a social system. It is knowledge and the social system which give life or take it away, and in so doing change the gene frequencies and continue the million-year-old interaction of culture and biology. Human biology finds its realization in a culturally determined way of life, and the infinite variety of genetic combinations can only express themselves efficiently in a free and open society. (Washburn, 1963, p. 531)

Intelligence

As we have shown, belief in the relationship between race and specific behavioral attributes is popular even today, but evidence is lacking that personality or any other behavioral trait differs genetically *between* human groups. Most scientists would agree with this last statement, but one question that has produced controversy both inside scientific circles and among laypeople is whether population affinity and **intelligence** are associated.

Both genetic and environmental factors contribute to intelligence, although it is not yet possible to measure accurately the percentage each contributes. What can be said is that IQ scores and intelligence are *not* the same thing. IQ scores can change during a person's lifetime, and average IQ scores of different populations overlap. Such differences in average IQ scores that do exist between groups are difficult to interpret, given the problems inherent in the design of the IQ tests. Moreover, complex cognitive abilities, however measured, are influenced by multiple loci and are thus polygenic.

Innate factors set limits and define potentials for behavior and cognitive ability in any species. In humans, the limits are broad and the potentials are not fully known. Individual abilities result from complex interactions between genetic and environmental factors. One product of this interaction is learning, and the ability to learn is influenced by genetic and other biological components. Undeniably, there are differences between individuals regarding these biological components. However, elucidating what proportion of the variation in test scores is due to biological factors probably is not possible. Moreover, innate differences in abilities reflect individual variation *within* populations, not inherent differences *between* groups. Comparing populations on the basis of IQ test results is a misuse of testing procedures, and there is no convincing evidence *whatsoever* that populations vary with regard to cognitive abilities, regardless of the assertions in some popular books. Unfortunately, despite the lack of evidence of mental inferiority of some populations and mental superiority of others, and despite the questionable validity of intelligence tests, racist attitudes toward intelligence continue to flourish.

Intelligence Mental capacity; ability to learn, reason, or comprehend and interpret information, facts, relationships, meanings, etc.; the capacity to solve problems, whether through the application of previously acquired knowledge or through insight.

Contemporary Interpretations of Human Variation

Human Polymorphisms

As you know, traits such as the ABO blood groups and the various genetic conditions presented in Chapter 4 are Mendelian traits because they can be linked to the action of single, identified loci. Consequently, these simple genetic mechanisms are much more easily studied than are the polygenic characteristics usually associated with traditional racial studies (e.g, skin color, hair form, and shape of face) because the loci that govern these complex traits have not been identified. But new technologies are emerging that will, in the near future, permit the detailed analysis of loci associated with polygenic traits.

Of greatest use in contemporary studies of human variation are traits that differ in expression among various populations and between individuals. Such characteristics with different phenotypic expressions are called **polymorphisms.**

Polymorphisms Characteristics that are governed by a genetic locus with more than one allele. Polymorphic traits have more than one expression. ABO blood type is an example of a Mendelian polymorphic trait. Eye color is a polygenic example.

A genetic trait is *polymorphic* if the locus that governs it has two or more alleles. (Refer back to p. 71 for a discussion of the ABO blood group system governed by three alleles at one locus.)

Clearly, understanding polymorphisms requires evolutionary explanations, and geneticists use polymorphisms as a principal tool to understand evolutionary processes in modern populations. Moreover, by using these polymorphisms to compare allele frequencies between different populations, we can begin to reconstruct the evolutionary events that link human populations with one another.

By the 1960s, the study of *clinal distributions* of individual polymorphisms had become a popular alternative to the racial approach to human diversity. A **cline** is a gradual change in the frequency of a trait or allele in populations dispersed over geographical space. In humans, the various expressions of polymorphic traits exhibit a more or less continuous distribution from one region to another. Most of the traits that have been shown to have a clinal distribution are Mendelian traits. The distribution of the *A* and *B* alleles in the Old World provides a good example of a clinal distribution (fig. 12–1). Clinal distributions are generally thought to reflect microevolutionary influences of natural selection and/or gene flow. Consequently, interpretations of clinal distributions are framed in evolutionary terms.

The ABO system is interesting from an anthropological perspective because the frequencies of the *A*, *B*, and *O* alleles vary tremendously among humans. In most groups, *A* and *B* are only rarely found in frequencies greater than 50 percent, and usually, frequencies for these two alleles are considerably lower. Most human groups, however, are polymorphic for all three alleles. Occasionally, as in native South American Indians, frequencies of the *O* allele reach 100 percent,

Cline A gradual change in the frequency of genotypes and phenotypes from one geographical region to another.

figure 12–1 Distribution of the *B* allele in the indigenous populations of the world. (After Mourant et al., 1976.)

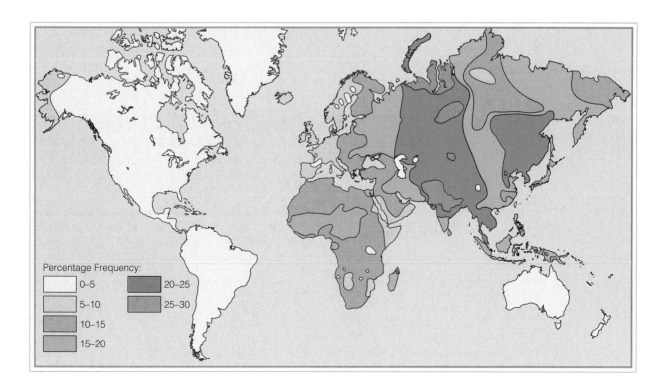

Percentage Frequency:

- 0–5
- 5–10
- 10–15
- 15–20
- 20–25
- 25–30

and this allele is said to be "fixed" in these populations. (you could say that in these groups, the ABO blood system is not a polymorphic trait.) Indeed, in most indigenous New World populations, the frequency of *O* is at least 80 percent. Uncommonly high frequencies of *O* are also found in northern Australia, and some islands off the Australian coast show frequencies exceeding 90 percent. In these populations, the high frequencies of the *O* allele are probably due to genetic drift (founder effect), although the influence of natural selection cannot be entirely ruled out.

Examining single traits can be informative regarding potential influences of natural selection or gene flow. This approach, however, is limited when we try to sort out population relationships, since the study of single traits, by themselves, can yield confusing interpretations regarding likely population relationships. A more meaningful approach is to study several traits simultaneously.

An excellent and early example of this approach to human diversity was undertaken by Harvard population geneticist R. D. Lewontin (1972). Lewontin calculated population differences in allele frequency for 17 polymorphic characteristics. In his analysis, he divided his sample into seven geographical areas, and he included several equally weighted population samples within each region (Table 12–1). He then calculated how much of the total genetic variability within our species could be accounted for by these population subdivisions, and the results were surprising. Only 6.3 percent of the total genetic variation was explained by differences between major population groups (Lewontin's seven geographical units). In other words, close to 94 percent of human genetic diversity occurs *within* these groups. The larger population subdivisions within the geographical clusters (e.g., within the category Caucasians, Arabs, Basques, Welsh) account for another 8.3 percent. Thus, geographical and local "races" together account for just 15 percent of all human genetic variation, leaving the remaining 85 percent unaccounted for. Hence, the vast majority of genetic differences among human beings is explained in terms of differences from one village to another, one family to another, and, to a significant degree, one person to another, even within the same family.

Our visual perceptions tell us that human races exist. But the visible traits most frequently used to make racial distinctions (skin color, hair form, nose shape, etc.) do not provide an accurate picture of the actual pattern of *genetic variation*. Simple polymorphic traits provide a more objective basis for accurate biological comparisons of human groups. Indeed, Lewontin concluded his analysis with a ringing condemnation of traditional studies: "Human racial classification is of no social value and is positively destructive of social and human

TABLE 12-1	Population Groupings Used by Lewontin in Population Genetics Study (1972)
Geographical Group	Examples of Populations Included
Caucasians	Arabs, Armenians, Tristan da Cunhans
Black Africans	Bantu, San, U.S. blacks
Asians	Ainu, Chinese, Turks
South Asians	Andamanese, Tamils
Amerinds	Aleuts, Navaho, Yanomama
Oceanians	Easter Islanders, Micronesians
Australians	All treated as a single group

relations. Since such racial classification is now seen to be of virtually no genetic or taxonomic significance either, no justification can be offered for its continuance" (Lewontin, 1972, p. 397).

Polymorphisms at the DNA Level

Mitochondrial DNA (mtDNA) (see p. 46) can be used to make comparisons between individuals and between populations. Ongoing work is establishing that some mtDNA regions are more variable than others but that for the *total* mtDNA genome, variation within *Homo sapiens* is less pronounced than in other species (e.g., chimpanzees). The possible evolutionary reasons for this surprising finding might relate to a quite recent origin of modern *Homo sapiens* from a restricted ancestral population base, thus producing a founder effect. The evolutionary ramifications of such a process on the dispersal of modern humans were discussed in Chapter 11.

As with mtDNA analysis, continuing research of the *Human Genome Project* has facilitated the direct study of the DNA contained within human chromosomes that is, nuclear DNA. Thus, considerable insight has been gained regarding human variation *directly at the DNA level*. By using enzymes to cut the DNA of different individuals and comparing the results, researchers have observed great variation in the number and length of the DNA fragments at numerous DNA sites.

In addition, new molecular technologies have uncovered a host of other regions of DNA variability. Scattered throughout the human genome are hundreds of sites where DNA segments are repeated—in some cases, just a few times, in other cases, many hundreds of times. These areas of nucleotide repetitions are called *microsatellites*, and they are extraordinarily variable from person to person. In fact, everyone is unique for their particular arrangement, and using current analytical approaches, the individual pattern produces a distinctive "DNA fingerprint." When using techniques to amplify tiny amounts of DNA (e.g., from a drop of blood, a hair, or a semen stain), millions of copies of the DNA molecule can be produced and then analyzed (see p. 60). As a result, forensic identification of individual human remains at sites of mass disasters (such as the World Trade Center) or from traces left by suspects at crime scenes can be done with great accuracy.

Finally, researchers are beginning to expand their approach and map patterns of variation at individual nucleotide sites. Of course, it has been recognized for some time that changes of individual DNA bases can occur within functional loci, producing what are called "point mutations." The sickle-cell allele at the hemoglobin beta locus is the best-known example of such a mutation in humans.

What has only been recently appreciated, however, is that such single nucleotide alterations also frequently occur in *noncoding* portions of DNA, and these sites, together with those in coding regions of DNA, are all referred to as *single nucleotide polymorphisms (SNPs)*. Already, more than a million such sites have been recognized dispersed throughout the human genome (96 percent of which are in noncoding DNA), and these single nucleotide polymorphisms are extraordinarily variable (the International SNP Map Working Group, 2001). Thus, at the beginning of the twenty-first century, geneticists have gained access to a vast biological "library," documenting the population patterning and genetic history of our species.

Population geneticists Geneticists who study the frequencies of alleles, genotypes, and phenotypes in populations.

Population geneticists are just beginning to take advantage of these new opportunities. While traditional polymorphic traits, such as ABO, are still being investigated, more and more attention is being directed at the remarkably variable DNA polymorphisms. For example, mitochondrial and nuclear DNA analyses of microsatellites have provided new insights into genetic patterning in India, both between and within major population groups (Raychoudhury et al., 2001; Reddy et al., 2001). In the New World, recent work has compared the mitochondrial DNA patterning between prehistoric groups (from which ancient DNA was extracted, amplified, and sequenced) and contemporary Native Americans (O'Roruke et al., 2000).

Another fruitful area of recent research holds great promise for future advances. Our specific genetic knowledge of polygenic traits has been woefully inadequate. However, by identifying specific loci at the DNA level (or using these highly variable regions as "markers" for ever-smaller areas of specific chromosomes), geneticists will soon be able to isolate particular gene variants contributing to skin color, stature, hypertension, and a host of other previously enigmatic human phenotypic traits.

As you can see, the recently developed tools now used by geneticists permit the study of human genetic variation at a level never before conceived. Such research will have a profound influence on our changing views of human diversity in the coming years. Moreover, through the use of these new techniques, the broader history of *Homo sapiens* is coming under closer genetic scrutiny. As we discussed in Chapter 11, analysis of mitochondrial DNA has provided insight into the origins and dispersal of anatomically modern humans. Further investigations, using both mitochondrial and nuclear DNA, will yield more fine-tuned data to help resolve this still-controversial period of our evolutionary history (Mitchell et al., 1999; Harpending and Rogers, 2001).

Human Biocultural Evolution

We have defined culture as the human strategy of adaptation. Human beings live in cultural environments that are continually modified by human activity; thus, evolutionary processes are understandable only within this *cultural* context. You will recall that natural selection pressures operate within specific environmental settings. For humans and many of our hominid ancestors, this means an environment dominated by culture. For example, the sickle-cell allele has not always been an important genetic factor in human populations. Before the development of agriculture, humans rarely, if ever, lived close to mosquito-breeding areas. With the spread in Africa of **slash-and-burn agriculture**, perhaps in just the last 2,000 years, penetration and clearing of tropical rain forests occurred. As a result of this deforestation, open, stagnant pools provided prime mosquito-breeding areas in close proximity to human settlements. New DNA analyses have further confirmed such a recent origin and spread of the sickle-cell allele in West Africa. A recent study of a population from Senegal has estimated the origin of the Hb^S mutation in this group at between 1,250 and 2,100 y.a. (Currat et al., 2002).

Thus, quite recently, malaria, for the first time, struck human populations with its full impact, and as a selective force it was powerful indeed. No doubt, humans attempted to adjust culturally to these circumstances, and numerous

Slash-and-burn agriculture A traditional land-clearing practice whereby trees and vegetation are cut and burned. In many areas, fields are abandoned after a few years and clearing occurs elsewhere.

biological adaptations also probably came into play. The sickle-cell trait is one of these biological adaptations. However, there is a definite cost involved with such an adaptation. Carriers have increased resistance to malaria and presumably higher reproductive success, but some of their offspring may be lost through the genetic disease sickle-cell anemia. So there is a counterbalancing of selective forces with an advantage for carriers *only* in malarial environments. The genetic patterns of recessive traits such as sickle-cell anemia are discussed in Chapter 4.

Following World War II, extensive DDT spraying by the World Health Organization began systematically to control mosquito-breeding areas in the tropics. Forty years of DDT spraying killed many mosquitoes, but natural selection, acting on these insect populations, produced several DDT-resistant strains (fig. 12–2). Accordingly, malaria is again on the rise, with several hundred thousand new cases reported annually in India, Africa, and Central America.

A genetic trait (such as sickle-cell trait) that provides a reproductive advantage to the heterozygote in certain environments is a clear example of natural selection in action among human populations. The precise evolutionary mechanism in the sickle-cell example is termed a **balanced polymorphism.** A polymorphism, as we have defined it, is a trait with more than one allele at a locus in a population. So when an allele like that for sickle-cell is found in a population in frequencies approaching 10 percent, the trait is clearly polymorphic. The sickle-cell allele has a higher frequency than can be accounted for by mutation *alone* and thus demands a fuller evolutionary explanation. In this case, the additional mechanism is natural selection.

This brings us back to the other part of the term *balanced polymorphism.* By "balanced," we are referring to the interaction of selective pressures operating in a malarial environment. Some individuals (mainly homozygous normals) will be removed by the infectious disease malaria and some (homozygous recessives) will die of the inherited disease sickle-cell anemia. Those with the highest reproductive success are the heterozygous carriers. But what alleles do they carry? Clearly, they are passing *both* the normal allele and the sickle-cell allele to offspring, thus maintaining both alleles at fairly high frequencies. Since one allele in this population will not significantly increase in frequency over the other allele, this situation will reach a balance and persist, at least as long as malaria continues to be a selective factor.

Another example of human biocultural evolution concerns the ability to digest milk. In all human populations, infants and young children can digest milk, an obvious necessity for any young mammal. One ingredient of milk is the sugar *lactose,* which is broken down by humans and other mammals by the enzyme *lactase.* In most mammals, including humans, the gene coding for lactase production "switches off" by adolescence. If too much milk is then ingested, it ferments in the large intestine, leading to diarrhea and severe gastrointestinal upset. Among many African and Asian populations—a majority of humankind today—most adults are intolerant of milk (Table 12–2).

Recent evidence has suggested a simple dominant mode of inheritance for **lactose intolerance.** The environment also plays a role in expression of the trait—that is, whether a person will be lactose-intolerant—since intestinal bacteria can somewhat buffer the adverse effects. Because these bacteria will increase with previous exposure, some tolerance can be acquired, even in individuals who genetically have become lactase-deficient.

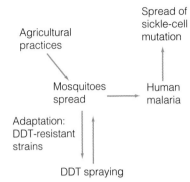

figure 12–2 Evolutionary interactions affecting the frequency of the sickle-cell allele.

Balanced polymorphism The maintenance of two or more alleles in a population due to the selective advantage of the heterozygote.

TABLE 12-2

Frequencies of Lactose Intolerance

Population Group	Percent
U.S. whites	2–19
Finnish	18
Swiss	12
Swedish	4
U.S. blacks	70–77
Ibos	99
Bantu	90
Fulani	22
Thais	99
Asian Americans	95–100
Native Americans	85

Source: Lerner and Libby, 1976, p. 327.

Lactose intolerance The inability to digest fresh milk products, caused by the discontinued production of *lactase,* the enzyme that breaks down lactose, or milk sugar.

Why do we see variation in lactose tolerance among human populations? Throughout most of hominid evolution, milk was unavailable after weaning. Perhaps, in such circumstances, continued action of an unnecessary enzyme might inhibit digestion of other foods. Therefore, there *may* be a selective advantage for the gene coding for lactase production to switch off. The question can then be asked, Why can some adults (the majority in some populations) tolerate milk? The distribution of lactose-tolerant populations is very interesting, revealing the probable influence of cultural factors on this trait.

European groups, who are generally lactose-tolerant, are partially descended from groups of the Middle East. Often economically dependent on pastoralism, these groups raised cows and/or goats and no doubt drank considerable quantities of milk. In such a cultural environment, strong selection pressures would act to shift allele frequencies in the direction of more lactose tolerance. Modern European descendants of these populations apparently retain this ancient ability.

Even more informative is the distribution of lactose tolerance in Africa. For example, groups such as the Fulani and Tutsi, who have been pastoralists probably for thousands of years, have much higher rates of lactose tolerance than nonpastoralists.

As we have seen, the geographical distribution of lactose tolerance is related to a history of cultural dependence on fresh milk products. There are, however, some populations that rely on dairying but are not characterized by high rates of lactose tolerance. It has been suggested that such populations traditionally have consumed their milk produce as cheese and other derivatives in which the lactose has been broken down by bacterial action (Durham, 1981).

The interaction of human cultural environments and changes in lactose tolerance among human populations is another example of biocultural evolution. In the last few thousand years, cultural factors have initiated specific evolutionary changes in human groups. Such cultural factors have probably influenced the course of human evolution for at least 3 million years, and today they are of paramount importance.

Population Genetics

As we defined it in Chapter 4, a *population* is a group of interbreeding individuals. More precisely, a population is the group within which one is most likely to find a mate. As such, a population is marked by a degree of genetic relatedness and shares a common **gene pool.**

In theory, this is a straightforward concept. In every generation, the genes (alleles) are mixed by recombination and rejoined through mating. What emerges in the next generation is a direct product of the genes going into the pool, which in turn is a product of who is mating with whom.

In practice, however, describing human populations is difficult. The largest population of *Homo sapiens* that could be described is the entire species. All members of a species are *potentially* capable of interbreeding, but are incapable of fertile breeding with members of other species. Our species is thus a *genetically* closed system. The problem arises not in describing who potentially can interbreed, but in isolating exactly the pattern of those individuals who are doing so.

Gene pool The total complement of genes shared by reproductive members of a population.

Factors that determine mate choice are geographical, ecological, and social. If individuals are isolated on a remote island in the middle of the Pacific, there is not much chance of their finding a mate outside the immediate vicinity. Such **breeding isolates** are fairly easily defined and are a favorite target of microevolutionary studies. Geography plays a dominant role in producing these isolates by rather strictly determining the range of available mates. But even within these limits, cultural rules can easily play a deciding role by prescribing who is most appropriate among those who are potentially available.

Human population segments within the species are defined as groups with relative degrees of **endogamy** (marrying/mating within the group). These are, however, not totally closed systems. Gene flow often occurs between groups, and individuals may choose mates from distant localities. With the modern advent of rapid transportation, greatly accelerated rates of **exogamy** (marrying/mating outside the group) have emerged.

Most humans today are not so clearly defined as members of particular populations as they would be if they belonged to a breeding isolate. Inhabitants of large cities may appear to be members of a single population, but within the city, social, ethnic, and religious boundaries crosscut in a complex fashion to form smaller population segments. In addition to being members of these highly open local population groupings, we are simultaneously members of overlapping gradations of larger populations—the immediate geographical region (a metropolitan area or perhaps a state), a section of the country, a nation, and ultimately, the entire species.

Once specific human populations have been identified, the next step is to ascertain what evolutionary forces, if any, are operating on this group. To determine whether evolution is taking place at a given locus, we measure allele frequencies for specific traits and compare these observed frequencies with a set predicted by a mathematical model: the **Hardy-Weinberg equilibrium** equation. The approach used by physical anthropologists to measure evolution using this model is called **population genetics.** Just how the equation is used is illustrated in Appendix C. The Hardy-Weinberg formula provides a tool to establish whether allele frequencies in a human population are indeed changing. In Chapter 4, we discussed several factors that act to change allele frequencies, including

1. New variation (i.e., *mutation*)
2. Redistributed variation (i.e., *gene flow* or *genetic drift*)
3. Selection of "advantageous" allele combinations that promote reproductive success (i.e., *natural selection*)

Note that factors 1 and 2 contitute the first stage of the evolutionary process, as first emphasized by the Modern Synthesis, while factor 3 is the second stage.

Breeding isolates Populations that are clearly isolated geographically and/or socially from other breeding groups.

Endogamy Mating with individuals from the same group.

Exogamy Mating pattern whereby individuals obtain mates from groups other than their own.

Hardy-Weinberg theory of genetic equilibrium The mathematical relationship expressing—under ideal conditions—the predicted distribution of alleles in populations; the central theorem of population genetics.

Population genetics A mathematical and statistical approach used to measure and explain evolutionary change in contemporary populations.

The Adaptive Significance of Human Variation

Today, biological anthropologists view human variation as the result of such evolutionary factors as genetic drift, founder effect, gene flow, and adaptations to environmental conditions, both past and present. Cultural adaptations have also played an important role in the evolution of *Homo sapiens*, and although in this discussion we are primarily concerned with biological issues, we must still consider the influence of cultural practices on human adaptive response.

All organisms must maintain the normal functions of internal organs, tissues, and cells in order to survive, and this task must be accomplished within the context of an ever-changing environment. Even during the course of a single, seemingly uneventful day, there are numerous fluctuations in temperature, wind, solar radiation, humidity, and so on. Physical activity also places **stress** on physiological mechanisms. The body must accommodate all these changes by compensating in some manner to maintain internal constancy, or **homeostasis**, and all life forms have evolved physiological mechanisms that, within limits, achieve this goal.

Physiological response to environmental change is, to some degree, influenced by genetic factors. We have already defined adaptation as a functional response to environmental conditions in populations and individuals. In a narrower sense, adaptation refers to *long-term* evolutionary (i.e., genetic) changes that characterize all individuals within a population or species.

Examples of long-term adaptations in *Homo sapiens* include some physiological responses to heat (sweating) and deeply pigmented skin in tropical regions. Such characteristics are the results of evolutionary change in species or populations, and they do not vary as the result of short-term environmental change. For example, the ability to sweat is not lost in people who spend their entire lives in predominantly cool areas. Likewise, individuals born with deeply pigmented skin will not become pale, even if never exposed to intense sunlight.

Short-term physiological response to environmental change, which occurs in all people, is called **acclimatization**. Tanning, which occurs in all people, is a form of acclimatization. Another example is the very rapid increase in hemoglobin production that occurs when lowland natives travel to higher elevations. This increase provides the body with more oxygen in an environment where oxygen is less available. In both these examples, the physiological change is temporary. Tans fade once exposure to sunlight is reduced; and hemoglobin production drops to original levels following a return to lower altitudes.

In the following discussion, we present some examples of how humans respond to environmental challenges. Some of these examples illustrate adaptations that characterize the entire species. Others illustrate adaptations seen in only some populations. And still others illustrate the process of acclimatization.

Solar Radiation, Vitamin D, and Skin Color

Skin color is often cited as an example of adaptation and natural selection in human populations. In general, skin color in populations, prior to European contact, follows a particular geographical distribution, especially in the Old World. Figure 12–3 illustrates that populations with the greatest amount of pigmentation are found in the tropics, while lighter skin color is associated with more northern latitudes, particularly the inhabitants of northwestern Europe.

Skin color is mostly influenced by the pigment *melanin*, a granular substance produced by specialized cells (*melanocytes*) found in the epidermis. All humans appear to have approximately the same number of melanocytes. It is the amount of melanin and the size of the melanin granules that vary.

Melanin has the capacity to absorb potentially dangerous ultraviolet (UV) rays present (although not visible) in sunlight. Therefore, melanin provides pro-

Stress In a physiological context, any factor that acts to disrupt homeostasis; more precisely, the body's response to any factor that threatens its ability to maintain homeostasis.

Homeostasis A condition of balance or stability within a biological system, maintained by the interaction of physiological mechanisms that compensate for changes (both external and internal).

Acclimatization Physiological response to changes in the environment that occurs during an individual's lifetime. Such responses may be short-term. The capacity for acclimatization may typify an entire population or species. This capacity is under genetic influence and thus is subject to evolutionary factors such as natural selection.

See Virtual Lab 2, section IV, for an exercise on the adaptive significance of skin color.

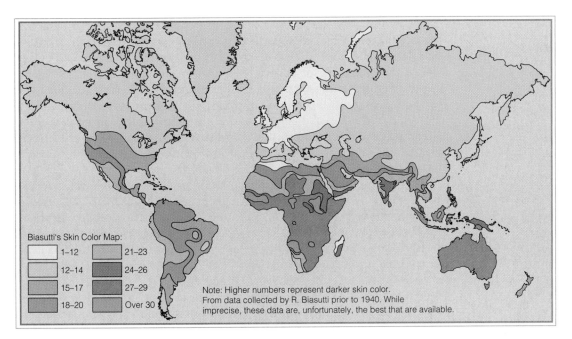

Biasutti's Skin Color Map:

1–12	21–23
12–14	24–26
15–17	27–29
18–20	Over 30

Note: Higher numbers represent darker skin color. From data collected by R. Biasutti prior to 1940. While imprecise, these data are, unfortunately, the best that are available.

tection from overexposure to ultraviolet radiation, which can cause genetic mutations in skin cells. These mutations may ultimately lead to skin cancer, which, if left untreated, can eventually spread to other organs and result in death.

As already mentioned, exposure to sunlight triggers a protective mechanism in the form of tanning, which results from temporarily increased melanin production (acclimatization). This protective response occurs in all humans except albinos, who carry a genetic mutation that prevents their melanocytes from producing melanin (fig. 12–4). Moreover, tanning is limited in many fair-complexioned people of northern European descent who do produce small amounts of melanin but have a reduced capacity for temporary increases in melanin production.

Natural selection appears to have favored dark skin in areas nearest the equator, where the sun's rays are most direct and thus where exposure to UV light is most intense. However, as hominids migrated out of Africa into Europe and Asia, selective pressures changed. Not only were these populations moving away from the tropics, where ultraviolet rays were most direct, but they were also moving into areas where it was cold and cloudy during winter. Bear in mind, too, that physiological adaptations were not sufficient to meet the demands of living in colder climates. Therefore, we must assume that these populations had adopted certain cultural practices, such as wearing animal skins or other types of clothing. Although clothing would have added necessary warmth, it also would have effectively blocked exposure to sunlight. Consequently, the advantages provided by deeply pigmented skin in the tropics were no longer important, and selection for melanin production may have been relaxed (Brace and Montagu, 1977).

However, relaxed selection favoring dark skin may not be adequate to explain the very depigmented skin seen especially in some northern Europeans. Perhaps another factor, the need for adequate amounts of vitamin D, was also critical. The theory concerning the possible role of vitamin D, known as the *vitamin D hypothesis*, offers the following explanation.

figure 12–3 Geographical distribution of skin color among the indigenous populations of the world. (After Biasutti, 1959.)

figure 12–4 An African albino.

Norman Lightfoot/PhotoResearchers

Vitamin D is produced in the body partly as a result of the interaction between ultraviolet radiation and a substance similar to cholesterol. It is also available in some foods, including liver, fish oils, egg yolk, butter, and cream. Vitamin D is necessary for normal bone growth and mineralization, and some exposure to ultraviolet radiation is therefore essential. Insufficient amounts of vitamin D during childhood result in *rickets*, which often leads to bowing of the long bones of the legs and deformation of the pelvis. Pelvic deformities are of particular concern for women, for they can lead to a narrowing of the birth canal, which, in the absence of surgical intervention, frequently results in the death of both mother and infant during childbirth.

This example illustrates the potential for rickets as a significant selective factor favoring less pigmented skin in regions where climate and other factors operate to reduce exposure to UV radiation. It is obvious how reduced exposure to sunlight due to climate and increased use of clothing could have been detrimental to dark-skinned individuals in more northern latitudes. In these individuals, melanin would have blocked absorption of the already reduced amounts of available ultraviolet radiation required for vitamin D synthesis. Therefore, selection pressures would have shifted over time to favor individuals with lighter skin. There is substantial evidence, both historically and in contemporary populations, to support this theory.

During the latter decades of the nineteenth century in the United States, African American inhabitants of northern cities suffered a higher incidence of rickets than whites. Northern blacks were also more commonly affected than blacks living in the South, where exposure to sunlight is greater. (The supplementation of milk with vitamin D was initiated to alleviate this problem.) Another example is seen in Britain, where darker-skinned East Indians and Pakistanis show a higher incidence of rickets than people with lighter skin (Molnar, 1983).

Jablonski (Jablonski, 1992; Jablonski and Chaplin, 2000) offers an additional explanation for the distribution of skin color, one that focuses on the role of UV radiation in the degradation of folate. Folate is a B vitamin that is not stored in the body and must be replenished through dietary sources. Folate deficiencies in pregnant women are associated with numerous complications, including maternal death, and in children they can lead to growth retardation and other serious conditions. Folate also plays a crucial role in **neural tube** development very early in embryonic development, and in this context, deficiencies can lead to defects that include various expressions of **spina bifida**. The consequences of severe neural tube defects can include pain, infection, paralysis, and even death. It goes without saying that neural tube defects can dramatically reduce the reproductive success of affected individuals.

A number of studies have shown that UV radiation rapidly depletes folate serum levels both in laboratory experiments and in light-skinned individuals. These findings have implications for pregnant women and children and also for the evolution of dark skin in hominids. Jablonski and Chaplin propose that the earliest hominids may have had light body skin covered with dark hair, as is seen in chimpanzees and gorillas. (Both have darker skin on exposed body parts). But as loss of body hair in hominids occurred, dark skin evolved rather quickly as a protective response to the damaging effects of UV radiation on folate.

Perhaps more social importance has been attached to variation in skin color than to any other single human biological trait. But aside from its probable

Neural tube In early embryonic development, the anatomical structure that develops to form the brain and spinal cord.

Spina bifida A condition in which the arch of one or several vertebrae fails to fuse and form a protective barrier around the spinal cord.

adaptive significance relative to UV radiation, skin color is no more important physiologically than many other biological characteristics. Still, from an evolutionary perspective, skin color provides a good example of how the forces of natural selection have produced geographically patterned variation as the consequence of two conflicting selective forces: the need for protection from overexposure to UV radiation, on the one hand, and the need for adequate UV exposure for vitamin D synthesis on the other.

The Thermal Environment

Mammals and birds have evolved complex mechanisms to maintain a constant internal body temperature. While reptiles must rely on exposure to external heat sources to raise body temperature and energy levels, mammals and birds possess physiological mechanisms that, within certain limits, increase or reduce the loss of body heat. The optimum internal body temperature for normal cellular functions is species-specific, and for humans it is approximately 98.6°F.

Homo sapiens is found in a wide variety of habitats, with thermal environments ranging from exceedingly hot (in excess of 120°F) to bitter cold (less than –60°F). In such extremes, particularly cold, human life would not be possible without cultural innovations. But even accounting for the artificial environments in which we live, such external conditions place the human body under enormous stress.

RESPONSE TO HEAT All available evidence suggests that the earliest hominids evolved in the warm-to-hot savannas of East Africa. The fact that humans cope better with heat than they do with cold is testimony to the long-term adaptations to heat that evolved in our ancestors.

In humans, as well as certain other species, such as horses, sweat glands are distributed throughout the skin. This wide distribution of sweat glands makes possible the loss of heat at the body surface through evaporative cooling, a mechanism that has evolved to the greatest degree in humans.

The capacity to dissipate heat by sweating is seen in all humans to an almost equal degree, with the average number of sweat glands per individual (approximately 1.6 million) being fairly constant. However, there is variation in that persons not generally exposed to hot conditions do experience a period of acclimatization that initially involves significantly increased perspiration rates (Frisancho, 1993). An additional factor that enhances the cooling effects of sweating is increased exposure of the skin through reduced amounts of body hair. We do not know when in our evolutionary history loss of body hair began, but it represents a species-wide adaptation.

Heat reduction through evaporation can be expensive, and indeed dangerous, in terms of water and sodium loss. Up to 3 liters of water can be lost by a human engaged in heavy work in high heat. The importance of this fact can be appreciated if you consider that the loss of 1 liter of water is approximately equivalent to losing 1.5 percent of total body weight, and loss of 10 percent of body weight can be life threatening.

Another mechanism for radiating body heat is **vasodilation**, whereby capillaries near the skin's surface widen to permit increased blood flow to the skin. The visible effect of vasodilation is flushing, or increased redness of the skin, particularly of the face, accompanied by warmth. But the physiological effect is

Vasodilation Expansion of blood vessels, permitting increased blood flow to the skin. Vasodilation permits warming of the skin and also facilitates radiation of warmth as a means of cooling. Vasodilation is an involuntary response to warm temperatures, various drugs, and even emotional states (blushing).

to permit heat, carried by the blood from the interior of the body, to be emitted from the skin's surface to the surrounding air. (Some drugs, including alcohol, also produce vasodilation, which accounts for the increased redness and warmth of the face in some people.)

Body size and proportions are also important in regulating body temperature. Indeed, there seems to be a general relationship between climate and body size and shape in birds and mammals. In general, within a species, body size (weight) increases as distance from the equator increases. In humans, this relationship holds up fairly well, but there are numerous exceptions.

Two rules that pertain to the relationship between body size, body proportions, and climate are *Bergmann's rule* and *Allen's rule*.

1. *Bergmann's rule (concerns the relationship of body mass or volume to surface area)*: In mammalian species, body size tends to be greater in populations that live in colder climates. This is because as mass increases, the relative amount of surface area decreases proportionately. Because heat is lost at the surface, it follows that increased mass allows for greater heat retention and reduced heat loss.

2. *Allen's rule (concerns shape of the body, especially appendages)*: In colder climates, shorter appendages, with increased mass-to-surface ratios, are adaptive because they are more effective at preventing heat loss. Conversely, longer appendages, with increased surface area relative to mass, are more adaptive in warmer climates because they promote heat loss.

According to these rules, the most suitable body shape in hot climates is linear with long arms and legs. In a cold climate, a more suitable body type is stocky with shorter limbs. Considerable data gathered from several human populations generally conform to these principles. In colder climates, body mass tends, on average, to be greater and characterized by a larger trunk relative to arms and legs (Roberts, 1973). People living in the Arctic tend to be short and stocky, while many sub-Saharan Africans, especially East African pastoralists, are tall and linear (fig. 12–5). But there is much human variability regarding body proportions, and not all populations conform so readily to Bergmann's and Allen's rules.

RESPONSE TO COLD   Human physiological responses to cold combine factors that increase heat retention with those that enhance heat production. Of the two, heat retention is more efficient because it requires less energy. This is an important point because energy is derived from dietary sources. Unless food resources are abundant, and in winter they frequently are not, any factor that conserves energy can have adaptive value.

Short-term responses to cold include increased metabolic rate and shivering, both of which generate body heat, at least for a short time. **Vasoconstriction**, another short-term response, restricts heat loss and conserves energy. In addition, humans possess a subcutaneous (beneath the skin) fat layer that provides an insulative layer throughout the body. Behavioral modifications include increased activity, wearing warmer clothing, increased food consumption, and assuming a curled-up position.

Increases in metabolic rate (the rate at which cells break up nutrients into their components) release energy in the form of heat. Shivering also generates muscle heat, as does voluntary exercise. But these methods of heat production

Vasoconstriction Narrowing of blood vessels, reducing blood flow to the skin. Vasoconstriction is an involuntary response to cold and reduces heat loss at the skin's surface.

(a)   (b)

Renee Lynn/Photo Researchers

George Holton/Photo Researchers

figure 12–5 (a) This African woman has the linear proportions characteristic of many inhabitants of sub-Saharan Africa. (b) By comparison, the Inuit woman is short and stocky. These two individuals serve as good examples of Bergmann's and Allen's rules.

are expensive because they require an increased intake of nutrients to provide energy. (Perhaps this explains why we tend to have a heartier appetite during the winter and why we also tend to increase our intake of fats and carbohydrates, the very sources of energy our bodies require.)

In general, people exposed to chronic cold (meaning much or most of the year) maintain higher metabolic rates than those living in warmer climates. The Inuit (Eskimo) people living in the Arctic maintain metabolic rates between 13 and 45 percent higher than observed in non-Inuit control subjects (Frisancho, 1993). Moreover, the highest metabolic rates are seen in inland Inuit, who are exposed to even greater cold stress than coastal populations. Traditionally, the Inuit had the highest animal protein and fat diet of any human population in the world. Such a diet, necessitated by the available resource base, served to maintain the high metabolic rates required by exposure to chronic cold.

Vasoconstriction restricts capillary blood flow to the surface of the skin, thus reducing heat loss at the body surface. Because retaining body heat is more economical than creating it, vasoconstriction is very efficient, provided temperatures do not drop below freezing. However, if temperatures do fall below freezing, continued vasoconstriction can allow the skin temperature to decline to the point of frostbite or worse.

Long-term responses to cold vary among human groups. For example, in the past, desert-dwelling native Australian populations were subjected to wide temperature fluctuations from day to night. As they wore no clothing and did not build shelters, their only protection from temperatures that hovered only a few degrees above freezing was provided by sleeping fires. They experienced continuous vasoconstriction throughout the night, and this permitted a degree of skin cooling most people would find extremely uncomfortable. But there was no threat of frostbite, and continued vasoconstriction helped to prevent excessive internal heat loss.

By contrast, the Inuit experience intermittent periods of vasoconstriction and vasodilation. This compromise provides periodic warmth to the skin that helps prevent frostbite in below-freezing temperatures. At the same time, because vasodilation is intermittent, energy loss is restricted, with more heat retained at the body's core.

The preceding examples illustrate but two of the many ways in which human populations vary with regard to adaptation to cold. Although all humans respond to cold stress in much the same manner, there is variation in how adaptation and acclimatization are manifested.

High Altitude

Today, perhaps as many as 25 million people live at altitudes above 10,000 feet. In Tibet, permanent settlements exist above 15,000 feet, and in the Andes, they can be found as high as 17,000 feet (fig. 12–6).

At such altitudes, multiple factors produce stress on the human body. These include **hypoxia** (reduced available oxygen), more intense solar radiation, cold, low humidity, wind (which amplifies cold stress), a reduced nutritional base, and rough terrain. Of these, hypoxia exerts the greatest amount of stress on human physiological systems, especially the heart, lungs, and brain.

Hypoxia results from reduced barometric pressure. It is not that there is less oxygen in the atmosphere at high altitudes; rather, it is less concentrated. Therefore, to obtain the same amount of oxygen at 9,000 feet as at sea level, people must make certain physiological alterations aimed at increasing the body's ability to transport and utilize efficiently the oxygen that is available.

People who reside at higher elevations, especially recent immigrants, display a number of manifestations of their hypoxic environment. Reproduction, in particular, is affected through increased rates of infant mortality, mis-

Hypoxia Lack of oxygen. Hypoxia can refer to reduced amounts of available oxygen in the atmosphere (due to lowered barometric pressure) or to insufficient amounts of oxygen in the body.

figure 12–6 (a) La Paz, Bolivia, at just over 12,000 feet above sea level, is home to more than 1 million people. (b) A household in northern Tibet, situated at an elevation of over 15,000 feet above sea level.

Courtesy, William Pratt

(a)

Courtesy, L.G. Moore

(b)

carriage, and prematurity. Low birth weight is also more common and is attributed to decreased fetal growth due to impaired maternal-fetal transport of oxygen (Moore and Regensteiner, 1983). But there is also some evidence to suggest that low birth weight may actually have some adaptive value in high-altitude natives.

Compared to populations at lower elevations, lifelong residents of high altitude display slowed growth and maturation. Other differences include larger chest size, associated, in turn, with greater lung volume and a larger heart.

Compared to high-altitude natives, nonnatives exhibit some differences in acclimatization and adaptation to hypoxia. Frisancho (1993) calls these different responses adult acclimatization and developmental acclimatization. *Adult acclimatization* occurs upon exposure to high altitude in people born at low elevation. The responses may be short-term modifications, depending on duration of stay, but they begin within hours of the altitude change. These changes include an increase in respiration rate, heart rate, and production of red blood cells. (Red blood cells contain hemoglobin, the protein responsible for transporting oxygen to organs and tissues.)

Developmental acclimatization occurs in high-altitude natives whose adaptations are acquired during growth and development. (Note that this type of acclimatization is present only in people who grow up in high-altitude areas, not in those who moved there as adults.) In addition to greater lung capacity, people born at high altitudes are more efficient than migrants at diffusing oxygen from the blood to bodily tissues. Hence, they do not rely as heavily on increased red cell formation as do newcomers. Developmental acclimatization serves as a good example of physiological plasticity by illustrating how, within the limits set by genetic factors, development can be influenced by environment.

There is evidence that some populations have adapted to high altitudes. Indigenous peoples of Tibet who have inhabited regions higher than 12,000 feet for around 25,000 years may have made genetic (i.e., evolutionary) accommodations to hypoxia. Altitude does not appear to affect reproduction in these people to the degree it does in other populations. Infants have birth weights as high as those of lowland Tibetan groups and higher than those of recent (20 to 30 years) Chinese immigrants. This fact may be the result of alterations in maternal blood flow to the uterus during pregnancy (Moore et al., 1994).

Another line of evidence concerns the utilization of glucose (blood sugar). Glucose is critical in that it is the only source of energy used by the brain, and it is also utilized, although not exclusively, by the heart. Both highland Tibetans and the Quechua (inhabitants of high-altitude regions of the Peruvian Andes) burn glucose in a way that permits more efficient use of oxygen. This implies the presence of genetic mutations in the mitochondrial DNA that directs how cells use glucose. It also implies that natural selection has acted to increase the frequency of these advantageous mutations in these groups.

There is no certain evidence that Tibetans and Quechua have made evolutionary changes to accommodate high-altitude hypoxia. Moreover, the genetic mechanisms that underlie these populations' unique abilities have not been identified. The data are intriguing, however, and they strongly suggest that selection has operated to produce evolutionary change in these two groups. If further study supports these findings, we will have an excellent example of evolution in action producing long-term adaptation at the population level.

Infectious Disease

Infection, as opposed to other disease categories, such as degenerative or genetic disease, is a category that includes those pathological conditions caused by microorganisms (viruses, bacteria, or fungi). Throughout the course of human evolution, infectious disease has exerted enormous selective pressures on populations and thus has influenced the frequency of certain alleles that affect the immune response. But as important as infectious disease has been as an agent of natural selection in human populations, its role in this regard is not very well documented.

Malaria provides perhaps the best-documented example of the evolutionary role of disease. Earlier you saw how malaria has operated in some African and Mediterranean populations to alter allele frequencies at the locus governing hemoglobin formation. In spite of extensive long-term eradication programs, malaria still poses a serious threat to human health. Indeed, the World Health Organization estimates the number of people currently infected with malaria to be between 300 and 500 million worldwide. This number is increasing, too, as drug-resistant strains of the disease-causing microorganism become more common (Olliaro et al., 1995).

Another example of the selective role of infectious disease is indirectly provided by AIDS (acquired immune deficiency syndrome). In the United States, the first cases of AIDS were reported in 1981. Since that time, perhaps as many as 1.5 million have been infected by HIV (human immunodeficiency virus), the agent that causes AIDS. As of December 2003, around 500,000 people had died in the United States, but worldwide, there were 23 million deaths and another 42 million were infected.

HIV is transmitted from person to person through the exchange of bodily fluids, usually blood or semen. It is not spread through casual contact. Within six months of infection, most persons test positive for anti-HIV antibodies, meaning that their immune system has recognized the presence of foreign antigens and has responded by producing antibodies. However, serious HIV-related symptoms may not appear in infected people for years, and in the United States, the average "latency period" is over 11 years.

Like all viruses, HIV must invade certain types of cells and alter the functions of those cells to produce more virus particles in a process that eventually leads to cell destruction. (The manner in which HIV accomplishes this task is different from that of many other viruses.) HIV can attack various types of cells, but it especially targets so-called T4 helper cells, which are major components of the immune system. As HIV infection spreads and T4 cells are destroyed, the patient's immune system begins to fail. Consequently, he or she begins to exhibit symptoms caused by various **pathogens** that are commonly present but usually kept in check by a normal immune response. When an HIV-infected person's T cell count drops to a level that indicates immune suppression, and when symptoms of "opportunistic" infections appear, the patient is said to have AIDS.

By the early 1990s, scientists were aware of a number of patients who had been HIV positive for 10 to 15 years but continued to show few if any symptoms. Awareness of these patients led researchers to suspect that some individuals possess a natural immunity or resistance to HIV infection. This was

See Virtual Lab 2, section III, for a discussion of the human adaptive response to malaria.

Pathogens Substances or microorganisms, such as bacteria, fungi, or viruses, that cause disease.

shown to be true in late 1996 with the publication of two different studies (Dean et al., 1996; Samson et al., 1996) that demonstrated a mechanism for resistance to HIV.

These two reports describe a genetic mutation that concerns a major protein "receptor site" on the surface of certain immune cells, including T4 cells. (Receptor sites are protein molecules that enable HIV and other viruses to invade cells.) In this particular situation, the mutant allele results in a malfunctioning receptor site, and current evidence now strongly suggests that individuals who are homozygous for this allele may be completely resistant to many types of HIV infection. In heterozygotes, infection may still occur, but the course of HIV disease is markedly slowed.

Interestingly, and for unknown reasons, the mutant allele occurs mainly in people of European descent, among whom its frequency is about 10 percent. Samson and colleagues (1996) reported that in the Japanese and West African samples they studied, the mutation was absent, but Dean and colleagues (1996) reported an allele frequency of about 2 percent among African Americans. These researchers speculate that the presence of the allele in African Americans may be entirely due to genetic admixture (gene flow) with European Americans. Moreover, they suggest that this polymorphism exists in Europeans as a result of selective pressures favoring an allele that originally occurred as a rare mutation. But it is critical to note that the original selective agent was *not* HIV. Instead, it was some other, as yet unidentified pathogen that requires the same receptor site as HIV. Researchers may be close to identifying which pathogen, or group of pathogens, it was. In December 1999, a group of scientists reported that the myxoma poxvirus, which is related to the virus that causes smallpox, can use the same receptor site as does HIV. These authors (Lalani et al., 1999) suggest that the agent that selected for the altered form of the receptor site may have been smallpox. While this conclusion has not yet been proved or even really investigated, it offers an exciting avenue of research with the possibility of revealing how a mutation that has been favored by selection because it provides protection against one disease can increase resistance to another malady (AIDS) as well.

Examples such as sickle-cell anemia and AIDS are continually revealing new insights into the complex interactions between disease organisms and their host populations. These insights in turn provide a growing basis for understanding the many variations between individuals and populations that have arisen as adaptive responses to infectious disease.

Smallpox, once a deadly viral disease, may provide a good example of how exposure to infectious agents can produce polymorphisms in host populations. During the eighteenth century, smallpox is estimated to have accounted for 10 to 15 percent of all deaths in parts of Europe. However, by 1977, through massive vaccination programs, the World Health Organization declared the smallpox virus to be extinct. But because viral samples were still maintained in the United States and Russia, there are now fears that smallpox could be used as an agent for biological warfare.

Smallpox had a higher incidence in persons with either blood type A or AB than in type O individuals, a fact that has been explained by the presence of an antigen on the smallpox virus that is similar to the A antigen. It follows that when some type A individuals were exposed to smallpox, their immune systems failed to recognize the virus as foreign and thus did not mount an adequate immune response. Consequently, in regions where smallpox was common in the past, it could have altered allele frequencies at the ABO locus by selecting against the *A* allele.

The best-known epidemic in history was that of the Black Death (bubonic plague) in the mid-fourteenth century. Bubonic plague is caused by a bacterium and is transmitted from rodents to humans by fleas. In just a few years, this deadly disease had spread (following trade routes and facilitated by rodent-infested ship cargoes) from the Caspian Sea throughout the Mediterranean area to northern Europe. During the initial exposure to this disease, as many as one-third of the inhabitants of Europe died.

A lesser-known but even more devastating example was the influenza **pandemic** that broke out in 1918 at the end of World War I. This was actually one of a series of influenza outbreaks, but it has remained notable for its still unexplained virulence and the fact that it accounted for the deaths of over 21 million people worldwide.

While we have no clear-cut evidence of a selective role for bubonic plague or influenza, this does not mean that one does not exist. The tremendous mortality that these diseases (and others) are capable of producing certainly increases the likelihood that they influenced the development of human adaptive responses in ways we have not yet discovered.

The effects of infectious disease on humans are mediated culturally as well as biologically. Innumerable cultural factors, such as architectural styles, subsistence techniques, exposure to domesticated animals, and even religious practices, all affect how infectious disease develops and persists within and between populations.

Until about 10,000 to 12,000 years ago, all humans lived in small nomadic hunting and gathering groups. As these groups rarely remained in one location more than a few days at a time, they had minimal contact with refuse heaps that housed disease **vectors**. But with the domestication of plants and animals, people became more sedentary and began living in small villages. Gradually, villages became towns, and towns, in turn, developed into densely crowded, unsanitary cities.

As long as humans lived in small bands, there was little opportunity for infectious disease to have much of an impact on large numbers of people. Even if an entire local group or band were wiped out, the effect on the overall population in a given area would have been negligible. Moreover, for a disease to become **endemic** in a population, sufficient numbers of people must be present. Therefore, small bands of hunter-gatherers were not faced with continuous exposure to endemic disease.

But with the advent of settled living and association with domesticated animals, opportunities for disease increased. As sedentary life permitted larger group size, it became possible for some diseases to become permanently established in some populations. Moreover, exposure to domestic animals, such as cattle, provided an opportune environment for the spread of such maladies as tuberculosis. The crowded, unsanitary conditions that characterized parts of all cities until the late nineteenth century and that persist in much of the world today further added to the disease burden borne by human inhabitants.

Pandemic An extensive outbreak of disease affecting large numbers of people over a wide area; potentially, a worldwide phenomenon.

Vectors Agents that transmit disease from one carrier to another. Mosquitoes are vectors for malaria, just as fleas are vectors for bubonic plague.

Endemic Continuously present in a population.

The Continuing Impact of Infectious Disease

Until the twentieth century, infectious disease was the number one cause of death in all human populations. Even today, in many developing countries, as much as half the mortality is due to infectious disease, compared to about 10 percent in the United States. In the United States and other developed nations, with improved living conditions and sanitation and especially with the widespread use of antibiotics beginning in the late 1940s, infectious disease gave way to heart disease and cancer as the leading causes of death.

Optimistic predictions held that infectious disease would be a thing of the past in developed countries and, with the introduction of antibiotics and improved living standards, in developing nations as well. But by the mid-1980s, such predictions were increasingly seen to be wrong, partly because of HIV/AIDS. Between 1980 and 1992, the number of deaths in the United States in which infectious disease was the underlying cause rose from 41 to 65 per 100,000, an increase of 58 percent (Pinner et al., 1996). During that same period, there was a 25 percent increase in infectious disease mortality among people aged 65 and older, from 271 to 338 per 100,000. And deaths due to respiratory tract infections rose from 25 to 30 deaths per 100,000.

Increase in the prevalence of infectious disease is perhaps partly due to the overuse of antibiotics. It is estimated that half of all antibiotics prescribed in the United States are used to treat viral conditions, such as colds and flu. Because antibiotics are completely ineffective against viruses, such therapy not only is useless, but may also have dangerous long-term consequences. There is a growing concern in the biomedical community over the effects of antibiotic and pesticide use, practices that have flourished since the 1950s. Antibiotics have exerted selective pressures on bacterial species that have, over time, developed antibiotic-resistant strains (an excellent example of natural selection). Consequently, the past few years have seen the *reemergence* of many bacterial diseases, including influenza, pneumonia, tuberculosis, and cholera, in forms that are less responsive to treatment.

Tuberculosis is now listed as the world's leading killer of adults by the World Health Organization (Colwell, 1996). In fact, the number of tuberculosis cases has risen 28 percent since the mid-1980s worldwide, with an estimated 10 million infected in the United States alone. Although not all infected persons develop active disease, an estimated 30 million are believed to have died from TB in the 1990s worldwide. One very troubling aspect of the increase in tuberculosis infection is that newly developed strains of *Mycobacterium tuberculosis*, the bacterium that causes TB, are resistant to antibiotics and other treatments.

Cholera, a dangerous and often fatal gastrointestinal disease caused by *Vibrio cholerae*, a bacterium found in sewage-contaminated water, has periodically occurred in epidemic proportions throughout history, including outbreaks in the nineteenth century in New York, Philadelphia, and London. Currently, cholera claims about 100,000 lives annually in Asia alone, and an antibiotic-resistant strain, first identified in India in 1992, is spreading throughout Southeast Asia. Recent cholera outbreaks throughout much of South America, India, Bangladesh, China, and parts of Southeast Asia have been partly attributed to rising ocean temperatures, lack of sanitation, and overcrowding.

Various treatments for nonbacterial conditions have also become ineffective. One such example is the appearance of chloroquin-resistant malaria, which has rendered chloroquin (the traditional preventive medication) virtually useless in some parts of Africa. And many insect species have developed resistance to commonly used pesticides.

In addition to threats posed by resistant strains of pathogens, there are other factors that may contribute to the emergence (or reemergence) of infectious disease. Scientists are becoming increasingly concerned over the potential for global warming to expand the geographical range of numerous tropical disease vectors, such as mosquitoes. And the destruction of natural environments not only contributes to global warming, but also has the potential of allowing disease vectors formerly restricted to local areas to spread to new habitats.

One other factor associated with the rapid spread of disease and directly related to technological change is the mixing of people at an unprecedented rate. Indeed, an estimated 1 million people per day cross national borders by air (Lederberg, 1996)! In addition, new road construction and wider availability of motor-driven vehicles allow more people (armies, refugees, truck drivers, etc.) to travel farther and faster than ever before.

Fundamental to all these factors is human population size (see p. 367), which, as it continues to soar, causes more environmental disturbance and, through additional human activity, adds further to global warming. Moreover, in developing countries, where as much as 50 percent of mortality is due to infectious disease, overcrowding and unsanitary conditions increasingly contribute to increased rates of communicable illness. One could scarcely conceive of a better set of circumstances for the appearance and spread of communicable disease, and it remains to be seen if scientific innovation and medical technology are able to meet the challenge.

It is still not clear what the long-term consequences of twentieth-century antibiotic therapy, environmental change, and human population growth will be on disease patterns. But there are many scientists who fear that we may not be able to develop new antibiotics and treatments fast enough to keep pace with the appearance of potentially deadly new bacteria and other pathogens. Thus, we have radically altered the course of evolution in some microbial species, just as they have altered our own evolutionary course in the past and clearly continue to do so in the present.

Summary

n this chapter, we investigated some of the ways in which humans differ from one another, both within and between populations. We first explored how this variation was approached in the past, in terms of racial typologies. We then discussed contemporary approaches that describe simple genetic polymorphisms for which allele frequencies may be calculated, and we emphasized new techniques in which genetic data are obtained from direct analyses of mitochondrial and nuclear DNA. Moreover, we reviewed the theoretical basis of the population genetics approach, the subdiscipline of physical anthropology that seeks to measure genetic diversity among humans. Data on polymorphic traits can be used to understand aspects of human microevolution. For humans, of course, culture also plays a crucial evolutionary role, and the sickle-cell trait and lactose intolerance are thus discussed from a biocultural perspective.

The chapter also considered how populations vary with regard to physiological adaptations to a number of environmental conditions, including solar radiation, heat, cold, and high altitude. We also focused on how infectious disease influences evolutionary processes, and we particularly emphasized AID/HIV and the dynamic relationship between pathogens and human hosts.

The topic of human variation is very complicated, and the biological and cultural factors that have contributed to that variation and that continue to influence it are manifold. But from an explicitly evolutionary perspective, it is through the investigation of changes in allele frequencies in response to environmental conditions that we will continue to elucidate the diverse adaptive potential that characterizes our species.

Questions for Review

1. What is a polytypic species?
2. What is a biological definition of race?
3. What is biological determinism?
4. What was the eugenics movement, and what were its goals?
5. How is a population defined? Discuss why, in human groups, defining particular populations can be very difficult.
6. What kinds of variations have been discovered at the DNA level? Why is knowledge of such variation important (i.e., what are some of the uses of analysis of such variability)?
7. How has the sickle-cell allele come to be common in some parts of the world? Why is it thought to be a good example of natural selection?
8. What biocultural interactions have occurred that help explain the distribution of lactose intolerance?
9. What is homeostasis?
10. Under what conditions might light skin color be adaptive? Under what conditions might dark skin color be adaptive?
11. What physiological adjustments do humans show in coping with cold stress?
12. What physiological adjustments do humans show in coping with heat stress?
13. What do body size and shape have to do with adaptation to climate?
14. What are two effects of exposure to high altitude?
15. How has infectious disease influenced human evolution?
16. How has susceptibility to HIV been shown to vary between populations? What genetic and biological factors have led to this variation?
17. Discuss current culturally mediated factors that may contribute to the spread of infectious disease. Provide examples.

Suggested Further Readings

Cavalli-Sforza, L. L., 2000. *Genes, People, and Languages*. New York: North Point Press.

Cavalli-Sforza, L. L., P. Mendoza, and A. Piazza. 1994. *The History and Geography of Human Genes*. Princeton: Princeton University Press.

Discover. 1994. Special Issue: The Science of Race. 15 (November).

Gould, Stephen Jay. 1981. *The Mismeasure of Man*. New York: Norton.

Jacoby, R., and N. Glauberman (eds). 1995. *The Bell Curve Debate*. New York: Times Books.

Journal of the American Medical Association. 1996. Entire issue. 275 (January 17). (Numerous articles pertaining to climate change and reemergence of infectious diseases.)

Leffell, David J., and Douglas E. Brash. 1996. "Sunlight and Skin Cancer." *Scientific American* 275(1): 52–59.

Nesse, Randolph M., and George C. Williams. 1998. "Evolution and the Origins of Disease." *Scientific American* 279(5): 86–93.

O'Brien, Stephen J., and Michael Dean. 1997. "In Search of AIDS-Resistance Genes." *Scientific American* 277(3): 44–51.

Olson, Steve. 2002. *Mapping Human History: Discovering the Past Through Our Genes*. Boston: Houghton Mifflin.

Ramenofsky, Ann F. 1992. "Death by Disease." *Archaeology* 45(2): 47–49.

Relethford, John H. 2001. *Genetics and the Search for Modern Human Origins*. New York: Wiley-Liss.

Multimedia Resources

 Companion Web Site

Anthropology Online: The Wadsworth Anthropology Resource Center
Visit **http://anthropology.wadsworth.com** and click on the Companion Web Site for Jurmain/Kilgore/Trevathan/Nelson's *Essentials of Physical Anthropology*, Fifth Edition, to access a wide range of enrichment material to aid in your study of anthropology. Among the useful options for each chapter's self-study are learning objectives, flashcards, Internet exercises, Web links, InfoTrac College Edition exercises, and practice quizzes that can be scored and emailed to your instructor.

Paleopathology:
Diseases and Injuries of Bone

In Chapter 12, we discussed micro-evolutionary processes acting on contemporary humans. An important component of such studies relates to an understanding of the role of *disease* as it has influenced adaptations in *Homo sapiens*. Indeed, in the last few thousand years especially, infectious disease has likely been the single most important selective influence on recent human populations.

Some of the most significant biocultural adaptive shifts occurred with the development of agriculture. We have noted in Chapter 12 some of the biocultural dynamics that influenced the spread of the sickle-cell allele over the last 2,000 years.

In the study of human disease, how do we obtain some time depth, thus extending our perspective back from strictly contemporary contexts? The primary source of information relating to the relative recent history of disease (i.e., over the last few thousand years) comes from skeletons. Archaeological skeletal material provides evidence about a variety of pathological conditions, making it possible to expand our knowledge both *through time* and *across space* to include a wide array of different human populations. In this way, physical anthropologists and archaeologists working together maximize the clear advantages of an anthropological perspective.

The branch of physical anthropology that studies injury and disease in earlier populations is called *paleopathology*. Within this subdiscipline, anthropologists, often working with medical specialists, contribute to our knowledge of the history and geographical distribution of human diseases such as rheumatoid arthritis, tuberculosis, and syphilis. In addition, patterns of disease and trauma in specific groups can further illuminate how these peoples were affected by various environmental and cultural factors.

In most cases, paleopathologists work exclusively with dry, skeletonized specimens. Occasionally, however, under unusual circumstances, soft tissues—such as skin, hair, cartilage, or even internal organs—may also be preserved. For example, artificial mummification was practiced in ancient Egypt and Chile, and natural mummification may also occur in extremely dry climates (such as in the American Southwest and parts of North Africa).

figure 1 Naturally mummified tissue on a cranium from Nubia (part of the modern country of the Sudan; c. A.D. 700–1400).

Lynn Kilgore

In addition, in permanently wet environments such as bogs, where bacterial action is forestalled, soft tissues can endure. For example, there are the famous bog bodies discovered in Denmark and England. In such circumstances, preservation may be quite extraordinary.

One major category of pathological process that leaves its mark on bone is trauma. Injuries in ancient human populations may be manifested in the skeleton as fractures (which frequently are well healed), dislocations, or wounds (e.g., from projectile points).

figure 2 Fracture of a right femur (thigh bone) seen from the rear. (The normal left femur is shown for comparison.) Such an injury is extremely severe, even life threatening, but in this individual the bone healed remarkably well.

figure 3 Embedded piece of obsidian projectile point in a lumbar vertebra from a central California male, 25 to 40 years old. The portion being held was found with the burial and may have been retained during life in soft tissue (muscle?). The injury shows some healing.

figure 4 Unfused portion along the midline of a sacrum from a central California male, 16 to 18 years old. This condition, called "spina bifida occulta," is a fairly common, genetically influenced, asymptomatic condition.

Other categories of skeletal abnormality include those that are *congenital* (present at birth) and *hereditary* (genetically determined). Rarely in skeletal collections are severe hereditary maladies (such as dwarfism) clearly diagnostic. More commonly, modifications are subtle and probably asymptomatic (i.e., not producing symptoms).

Tumors are another category of bone pathology, and, very rarely, malignant, life-threatening conditions can reliably be diagnosed from skeletal remains. (Usually, conditions such as lung or colon cancer kill the person *before* the skeleton becomes involved.)

A very common condition seen in all skeletal populations is degenerative

figure 5 Numerous lesions of the cranium (such erosive lesions were also found in other bones), probably the result of a disseminated (metastasized) cancer, possibly originating from the breast, shown here in an Inuit female.

figure 6 Bony lipping around the margins of two lumbar vertebrae (see arrows).

Paleopathology: *Diseases and Injuries of Bone*
(continued)

arthritis. Bone changes are most visible around the margins of vertebral body surfaces or are either peripheral to the margins or on the articular surfaces of appendicular joints (such as the knee).

In common conditions such as arthritis (seen in all human groups), the most informative approach is to compare *frequencies* of involvement in different populations. Such an approach is called *paleoepidemiology* and is best controlled when the study samples are partitioned by sex and age (the latter is especially important in age-related diseases, such as arthritis).

Because infectious disease has been such an important selective factor in human evolution and adaptation, it is an important disease

figure 7 Extreme degenerative arthritis of a knee joint in an adult female from Nubia.

figure 9 Extreme reaction in a cranium from an Alaskan Inuit (Eskimo), diagnostic of syphilis (although other possibilities must be considered).

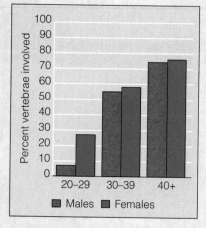

figure 8 Bar graph showing incidence of vertebral body arthritis (osteophytosis) controlling for age and sex. The frequencies shown here are for a medieval Nubian population, and such information can be compared with data from other groups.

category for paleopathological inquiry. Unfortunately, many infectious processes do not leave evidence in bone, because affected individuals either recover or die before bone tissue becomes involved. But some conditions, such as syphilis or tuberculosis, occasionally produce bone reaction. Interpretation of such processes in skeletons from varied geographical and chronological contexts provides some of the best biological data regarding the history of significant human diseases.

In recent years, the techniques of DNA fingerprinting have been added to the arsenal of tools used in the identification of infectious disease in archaeological populations. Perhaps the most successful of these

figure 10 Probable case of tuberculosis, as seen in the thoracic vertebrae of an individual from Pueblo Bonito, New Mexico. As the disease progresses, one or more vertebrae can collapse (see arrow), producing a severe forward angulation of the spine.

figure 11 Dr. Arthur Aufderheide (right) and Dr. Wilmar Salo (left) examine DNA fingerprints obtained by PCR. From this analysis these researchers were the first to obtain such clear molecular evidence of tuberculosis in the pre-Columbian New World.

investigations to date has been the recovery of a segment of DNA that is unique to *Mycobacterium tuberculosis*, the bacterium that causes tuberculosis, from a 1,000-year-old mummy from Peru. This discovery, which would have been impossible without the use of PCR amplification techniques, has provided the most definitive evidence to date for the existence of tuberculosis in the New World prior to European contact.

Probably the most common conditions seen in ancient human groups are those that affect the teeth. In some groups, abrasive diets (and perhaps use of the teeth as tools) resulted in severe wear throughout the dentition.

Other types of dental lesions include caries (popularly called "cavities"), abscesses, loss of teeth (with resorbed sockets and loss of bone in the jaws), and improperly erupted teeth.

Courtesy, Art Aufderheide

figure 12 Lung tissue from which *Mycobacterium tuberculosis* DNA samples were taken.

Robert Jurmain

figure 13 Severe dental wear in the upper jaw (maxilla) of a central California male, 301 years old. There is almost no enamel left on most of the teeth.

Robert Jurmain

figure 14 Severe abscess in the maxilla of a California Indian male, 31 to 40 years old. Despite the degree of bone reaction, such lesions can be asymptomatic.

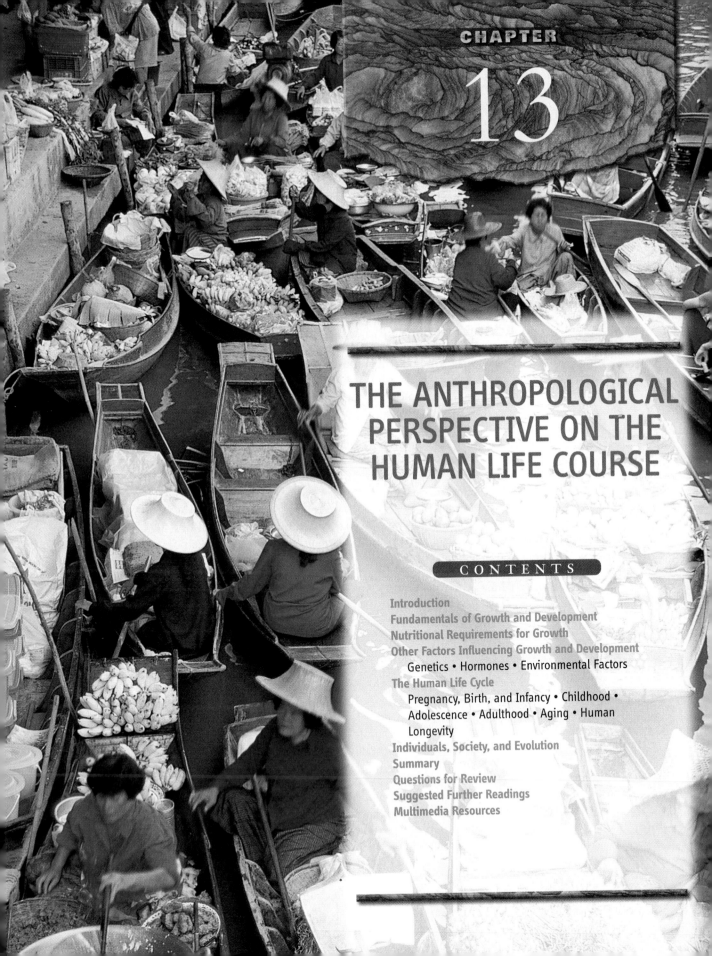

CHAPTER

13

THE ANTHROPOLOGICAL PERSPECTIVE ON THE HUMAN LIFE COURSE

Introduction

hroughout this book, we have emphasized the importance of the anthropological perspective for understanding human beings through time and space. As defined in the first chapter, anthropology is the study of humankind. Unlike most other fields that have humans as their focus, the anthropological approach to humankind draws on and integrates research about people from all parts of the earth and from both past and contemporary cultures. An anthropological perspective on the life course will serve as a way of further illustrating the breadth of this approach.

Because this is a physical anthropology text, we have placed primary emphasis on human biological evolution and adaptation. We have learned that our biology is the result of millions of years of evolutionary history: 225 million years of mammalian evolution, 65 million years of primate evolution, 5 million years of hominid evolution, 2–2.5 million years of evolution of the genus *Homo*. But are we just another mammal, just another primate? In some ways, of course, we are like other mammals and other primates. But as emphasized throughout the text, modern human beings are the result of *biocultural evolution*. In other words, human biology and behavior today have been shaped by the biological and cultural forces that operated on our ancestors. In fact, it would be fruitless to attempt an understanding of modern human biology and diversity without considering that humans have evolved in the context of culture. It would be like trying to understand the biology of fish without considering that they live in water.

A good place to explore the interaction of biology and culture is the human life course. If we consider how a human develops from an embryo into an adult and examine the forces that operate on that process, then we will have a better perspective of how both biology and culture influence our own lives. Throughout this book, we have focused on the primate order (Chapters 5 and 6), the evolution of the family Hominidae (Chapters 8 through 11), and populations of modern *Homo sapiens* (Chapters 11 and 12). We continue the focus on modern humans in this chapter, but our interest shifts to the life course to understand how past and present evolutionary and cultural forces operate on our own lives. Another name for this chapter might be "Anthropology of the Individual."

There is, of course, much variation in the extent to which cultural factors interact with genetically based biological characteristics; these variable interactions influence how characteristics are expressed in individuals. Some genetically based characteristics will be exhibited no matter what the cultural context of growth and development happen to be. If a person inherits two alleles for albinism, for example (see Chapter 4), he or she will be deficient in production of the pigment melanin, resulting in lightly colored skin, hair, and eyes. This phenotype will emerge regardless of the cultural environment in which the person lives.

Other characteristics, such as intelligence, body shape, and growth will reflect the interaction of environment and genes. We know, for example, that each of us is born with a genetic makeup that influences the maximum stature we can achieve in adulthood. But to reach that maximum stature, we must be properly nourished during our growing years and avoid many childhood diseases and other stresses that inhibit growth. What factors determine whether we are well fed and receive good medical care? In the United States, socioeconomic status is probably the primary determinant of nutrition and health. Thus, socioeconomic status is an example of a cultural factor that affects growth.

Fundamentals of Growth and Development

The terms *growth* and *development* are often used interchangeably, but they actually refer to different processes. **Growth** refers to an increase in mass or number of cells, whereas **development** refers to the differentiation of cells into different types of tissues and their subsequent maturation. Increase in cell number is referred to as *hyperplasia*, and increase in cell size, or mass, is called *hypertrophy*. Some cells are manufactured only once and are usually not replaced if damaged (e.g., some nerve and muscle cells); some cells are continuously dying and being replaced (skin and red blood cells); and some can be regenerated if damaged (cells in the liver, kidneys, and most glands). (See Chapter 3 for discussions of cell division.)

In humans, growth begins at conception and continues until the late teens or early 20s. Typically, well-nourished humans grow fairly rapidly during the first two trimesters (6 months) of fetal development, but growth slows during the third trimester. After birth, the rate of development increases and remains fairly rapid for about four years, at which time it decreases again to a relatively slow, steady level that is maintained until puberty. At puberty, there is once again a very pronounced increase in growth. During this so-called **adolescent growth spurt,** Western teenagers typically grow 9 to 10 cm per year. Subsequent to the adolescent growth spurt, the rate of development declines again and remains slower until adult stature is achieved by the late teens (fig. 13–1).

Growth curves for boys and girls are significantly different, with the adolescent growth spurt occurring approximately two years earlier in girls than in boys. At birth, there is slight **sexual dimorphism** in many body measures (e.g., height, weight, head circumference, and body fat), but the major divergence in these characteristics does not occur until puberty.

The head is a relatively large part of the body at birth. The continued growth of the brain after birth occurs at a rate far greater than that of any other part of the body, with the exception of the eyeball. At birth, the human brain is about 25 percent of its adult size. By 6 months of age, the brain has doubled in

Growth Increase in mass or number of cells.

Development Differentiation of cells into different types of tissues and their maturation.

Adolescent growth spurt The period during adolescence in which well-nourished teens typically increase in stature at greater rates than at other points in the life cycle.

Sexual dimorphism Differences in physical characteristics between males and females of the same species. For example, humans are slightly sexually dimorphic for body size, with males being taller, on average, than females of the same population.

figure 13–1 Distance and velocity curves of growth in height for a healthy American girl. (a) The distance curve shows the height attained in a given year. (b) The velocity curve plots the amount gained in a given year.

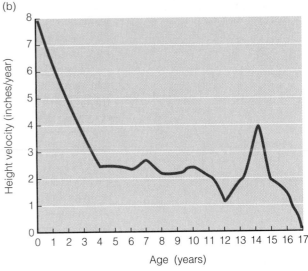

size, reaching 50 percent of adult size. It reaches 75 percent of adult size at age 2½ years, 90 percent at age 5 years, and 95 percent by age 10 years. There is only a very small spurt at adolescence, making the brain an exception to the growth curves characteristic of most other parts of the body. As we will see later in this chapter, this pattern of brain growth, including the relatively small amount of growth before birth, is unusual among primates and other mammals. By contrast, the typical picture for most mammalian species is that at least 50 percent of adult brain size has been attained prior to birth. For humans, however, the narrow pelvis necessary for walking bipedally provides limits on the size of the fetal head that can be delivered through it (Rosenberg and Trevathan, 2001). That limitation, in addition to the value of having most brain growth occur in the more stimulating environment outside the womb, has resulted in human infants being born with far less of their total adult brain size than most other mammals. (As we saw in Chapter 9, this pattern of delayed maturation was probably already established in hominid evolution by 1.5 m.y.a.)

Nutritional Requirements for Growth

Nutrition has an impact on human growth at every stage of the life cycle. During pregnancy, for example, a woman's diet can have a profound effect on the development of her fetus and the eventual health of the child. Moreover, the effects are transgenerational, because a woman's own supply of eggs is developed while she herself is *in utero* (see Chapter 3). Thus, if a woman is malnourished during pregnancy, the eggs that develop in her female fetus may be damaged in a way that will impact the health of her future grandchildren.

Nutrients needed for growth, development, and body maintenance include proteins, carbohydrates, lipids (fats), vitamins, and minerals. The specific amount that we need of each of these nutrients coevolved with the types of foods that were available to human ancestors throughout our evolutionary history. For example, the specific pattern of amino acids required in human nutrition (the **essential amino acids**) reflects an ancestral diet high in animal protein. Unfortunately for modern humans, these coevolved nutritional requirements are often incompatible with the foods that are available and typically consumed today. To understand this mismatch of our nutritional needs and contemporary diets, we need to examine the impact of agriculture on human evolutionary history.

The preagricultural diet, while perhaps high in animal protein, was low in fats, particularly saturated fats. The diet was also high in complex carbohydrates (including fiber), low in salt, and high in calcium. We do not need to be reminded that the contemporary diet that typifies many industrialized societies has the opposite configuration of the one just described. It is high in saturated fats and salt and low in complex carbohydrates, fiber, and calcium (Table 13–1). There is very good evidence that many of today's diseases in industrialized countries are related to the lack of fit between our diet today and the one with which we evolved (Eaton, Shostak, and Konner, 1988).

Many of our biological and behavioral characteristics evolved because in the past they contributed to adaptation; but today these same characteristics may be maladaptive. An example is our ability to store fat. This capability was an advantage in the past, when food availability often alternated between abundance

Essential amino acids The 9 (of 22) amino acids that must be obtained from the food we eat because they are not synthesized in the body in sufficient amounts.

TABLE 13-1	Preagricultural, Contemporary American, and Recently Recommended Dietary Composition		
	Preagricultural Diet	Contemporary Diet	Recent Recommendations
Total dietary energy (%)			
Protein	33	12	12
Carbohydrate	46	46	58
Fat	21	42	30
Alcohol	~0	(7–10)	–
P:S ratio*	1.41	0.44	1
Cholesterol (mg)	520	300–500	300
Fiber (g)	100–150	19.7	30–60
Sodium (mg)	690	2,300–6,900	1,000–3,300
Calcium (mg)	1,500–2,000	740	800–1,500
Ascorbic acid (mg)	440	90	60

*Polyunsaturated: saturated fat ratio.
Source: © 1988 by S. Boyd Eaton, M.D., Marjorie Shostack and Melvin Konner, M.D., Ph.D. Reprinted by permission of HarperCollins Publishers, Inc.

and scarcity. Those who could store fat during the times of abundance could draw on those stores during times of scarcity and remain healthy, resist disease, and, for women, maintain the ability to reproduce. Today, people with adequate economic resources spend much of their lives with a relative abundance of foods. Considering the number of disorders associated with obesity, the formerly positive ability to store extra fat has now turned into a liability. Our "feast or famine" biology is now incompatible with the constant feast many of us indulge in today.

Perhaps no disorder is as clearly linked with dietary and lifestyle behaviors as the form of diabetes mellitus that typically has its onset in later life, referred to variously as Type II diabetes or NIDDM (non–insulin dependent diabetes mellitus). In 1900, diabetes ranked twenty-seventh among the leading causes of death in the United States; today it ranks seventh. Moreover, the threat to world health from this disease is growing, with projections of an increase in incidence between 2000 and 2010 of 57 percent in Asia, 50 percent in Africa, 44 percent in South America, and 23 percent in North America (Zimmet, Alberti, and Shaw, 2001). Part of this projected increase will be due to decreases in other causes of death (e.g., infectious diseases), but much of it has to do with lifestyle and dietary changes associated with modernization and globalization, especially the decrease in levels of daily activity and increase in dietary intake of fats and refined carbohydrates.

It is clear that both deficiencies and excesses of nutrients can cause health problems and interfere with childhood growth. Certainly, many people in all parts of the world, both industrialized and developing, suffer from inadequate supplies of food of any quality. We read daily of thousands dying from starvation due to drought, warfare, or political instability. The blame must be placed not only on the narrowed food base that resulted from the emergence of agriculture, but also on the increase in human population that occurred when people began to settle in permanent villages and have more children. Today, the crush of billions of humans almost completely dependent on cereal grains means that millions face undernutrition, malnutrition, and even starvation. (See Chapter 14 for a further discussion of world population growth and related problems.)

In summary, our nutritional adaptations were shaped in an environment that included times of scarcity alternating with times of abundance. The variety of foods consumed was so great that nutritional deficiency diseases were rare. Small amounts of animal foods were probably an important part of the diet in many parts of the world. In northern latitudes, subsequent to approximately 1 million years ago, meat was an important part of the diet, but because such meat was low in fats, the negative effects of high meat intake that we see today did not occur. Our diet today is often incompatible with the adaptations that evolved in the millions of years preceding the development of agriculture. The consequences of that incompatibility include both starvation and obesity.

Other Factors Influencing Growth and Development

Genetics

Genetic factors set the underlying limitations and potentialities for growth and development, but the life experience and environment of the organism determine how the body grows within those parameters. How do we assess the relative contributions of genes and the environment in their effects on growth? Much of our information comes from studies of monozygotic and dizygotic twins. Monozygotic ("identical") twins come from the union of a single sperm and ovum and share 100 percent of their genes. Dizygotic ("fraternal") twins come from separate ova and sperm and share only 50 percent of their genes, just as any other siblings from the same parents. If monozygotic twins with identical genes but different growth environments are exactly the same in stature at various ages (i.e., show perfect correlation or *concordance* for stature), then we can conclude that genes are the primary, if not the only, determinants of stature. Most studies of twins reveal that under normal circumstances, stature is "highly correlated" for monozygotic twins, leading to the conclusion that stature is under fairly strong genetic control (Table 13–2). Weight, on the other hand, seems to be more strongly influenced by diet, environment, and individual experiences than by genes.

TABLE 13-2	Correlation Coefficients for Height Between Monozygotic (MZ) and Dizygotic (DZ) Twin Pairs from Birth to Age 8			
			DZ	
Age	Total *N*	MZ	Same Sex	Different Sex
Birth	629	0.62	0.79	0.67
3 months	764	0.78	0.72	0.65
6 months	819	0.80	0.67	0.62
12 months	827	0.86	0.66	0.58
24 months	687	0.89	0.54	0.61
3 years	699	0.93	0.56	0.60
5 years	606	0.94	0.51	.068
8 years	444	0.94	0.49	0.65
Source: From Wilson, 1979, after Bogin, 1988, p. 163.				

Hormones

One of the primary ways in which genes have an effect on growth and development is through their effects on hormones. Hormones are substances produced in one cell that have an effect on another cell (see p. 48). Most hormones are produced by *endocrine* glands; they are transported in the bloodstream, and almost all have an effect on growth. The hypothalamus (located at the base of the forebrain) can be considered the relay station, control center, or central clearinghouse for most hormonal action. This control center receives messages from the brain and other glands and sends out messages that stimulate hormonal action. Most of the hormonal messages transmitted from the hypothalamus result in the inhibition or release of other hormones.

Two hormones that are important in growth include growth hormone and insulin. Growth hormone, secreted by the anterior pituitary, promotes growth and has an effect on just about every cell in the body. Tumors and other disorders can result in excessive or insufficient amounts of growth hormone secretion, which in turn can result in gigantism or dwarfism. One group of people who have notably short stature are African Efe pygmies. Recent research suggests that altered levels of growth hormone and its controlling factors interact with nutritional factors and infectious diseases to produce the relatively short adult stature of these people (Shea and Bailey, 1996), providing another example of the interaction of biological and cultural forces.

Environmental Factors

Environmental factors, such as altitude and climate, have effects on growth and development. Perhaps the primary influence of such external factors comes from their effects on nutrition, but there is evidence of independent effects as well. For example, as noted in Chapter 12, infant birth weight is lower at high altitude, and this is so even when such factors as nutrition, smoking, and socioeconomic status are taken into consideration. In the United States, the percentage of low-birth-rate (LBW) infants (those weighing less than 2,500 g, or 5.7 pounds) is about 6.5 percent at sea level, rising to 10.4 percent at 5,000 feet and almost 24 percent above 10,000 feet. In a Bolivian study, the mean birth weight was 3,415 g (7.8 pounds) at low elevations and 3,133 g (7.1 pounds) at high elevations (Haas et al., 1980). Most studies of children have found that those at high elevations are shorter and lighter than those at low elevations.

In general, populations in cold climates tend to be heavier and have longer trunks and shorter extremities than populations in tropical areas. This reflects Bergmann's and Allen's rules, discussed in Chapter 12. Exposure to sunlight also appears to have an effect on growth, most likely through its effects on vitamin D production. Children tend to grow more rapidly in times of high sunlight concentration (i.e., in the summer in temperate regions and in the dry season in monsoonal tropical regions). Vitamin D, necessary for skeletal growth, requires sunlight for its synthesis (see p. 316–317).

Among the most significant environmental factors having an effect on growth and development is infectious disease, such as malaria, influenza, cholera, and tuberculosis (see pp. 324–328). These diseases have their greatest impact during childhood and can delay growth, particularly when coupled with malnutrition. In fact, the effects of infectious disease and malnutrition are said to be *synergistic;* that is, each worsens the effect of the other so that in combination their effects are potentially more damaging than either is acting alone. Unfortunately, they often occur together because chronic malnutrition lowers resistance to disease organisms that are present in the environment.

The Human Life Cycle

As noted in earlier chapters, primatologists and other physical anthropologists view primate and human growth and development from an evolutionary perspective, with an interest in how natural selection has operated on the life cycle from conception to death, a perspective known as *life history theory*. Why, for example, do humans have longer periods of infancy and childhood compared with other primates? What accounts for differences seen in the life cycles of such closely related species as humans and chimpanzees? Life history research seeks to answer such questions.

Not all animals have clearly demarcated phases in their lives; moreover, among mammals, humans have more such phases than do other species (fig. 13–2). Protozoa, among the simplest of animals, have only one phase; many invertebrates have two: larval and adult. Almost all mammals have at least three phases: prenatal, infancy, and adulthood. Most primates have four phases: prenatal, infancy, juvenile (usually called childhood in humans), and adult. Monkeys, apes, and humans add a phase between the juvenile phase and adulthood that is referred to as the subadult period (adolescence, or teenage, in humans). Finally, for humans there is the addition of a sixth phase in women, the postreproductive years following menopause. One could argue that during the course of primate evolution, more recently evolved forms have longer life spans and more divisions of the life span into phases, or stages.

Most of these life cycle stages are well marked by biological transitions. The prenatal phase begins with conception and ends with birth; infancy is the period of nursing; childhood, or the juvenile phase, is the period from weaning to sexual maturity (puberty in humans); adolescence is the period from puberty to the end of growth; adulthood is marked by the birth of the first child and/or the com-

figure 13–2 Life cycle stages for various animal species.

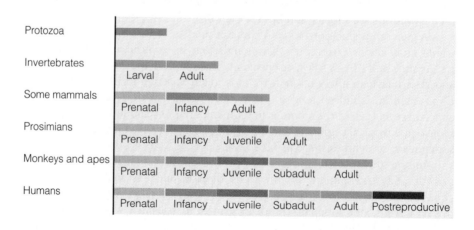

pletion of growth; and menopause is recognized as having occurred one full year after the last menstrual cycle. These biological markers are similar among higher primates, but for humans, there is an added complexity: They occur in cultural contexts that define and characterize them. Puberty, for example, has very different meanings in different cultures. A girl's first menstruation (**menarche**) is often marked with ritual and celebration, and a change in social status typically occurs with this biological transition. Likewise, **menopause** is often associated with a rise in status for women in non-Western societies, whereas it is commonly seen as a negative transition for women in many Western societies. As we shall see, collective and individual attitudes toward these life cycle transitions have an effect on growth, development, and health.

Menarche The first menstruation in girls, usually occurring in the early to mid-teens.

Menopause The end of menstruation in human women, usually occurring at around age 50.

Pregnancy, Birth, and Infancy

The biological aspects of conception and gestation can be discussed in a fairly straightforward way, drawing information from what is known about reproductive biology at the present time: A sperm fertilizes an egg; the resulting zygote travels through a uterine (fallopian) tube to become implanted in the uterine lining; and the embryo develops until it is mature enough to survive outside the womb, at which time birth occurs. But this is clearly not all there is to human pregnancy and birth. Female biology may be similar the world over, but cultural rules and practices are the primary determinants of who will get pregnant, as well as when, where, how, and by whom.

Once pregnancy has occurred, there is much variation in how a woman should behave, what she should eat, where she should and should not go, and how she should interact with other people. Almost every culture known, including our own, imposes dietary restrictions on pregnant women. Many of these appear to serve an important biological function, particularly that of keeping the woman from ingesting toxins that would be dangerous for the fetus. (Alcohol is a good example of a potential toxin whose consumption in pregnancy is discouraged in the United States.) The food aversions to coffee, alcohol, and other bitter substances that many women experience during pregnancy may be evolved adaptations to protect the embryo from toxins. The nausea of early pregnancy may also function to limit the intake of foods potentially harmful to the embryo at a critical stage of development (Profet, 1988; Williams and Nesse 1991).

Birth is an event that is celebrated with ritual in almost every culture studied. In fact, the relatively little fanfare associated with childbirth in the United States is unusual by world standards. Because risk of death for both mother and child is so great at birth, it is not surprising that it is surrounded with ritual significance. Perhaps because of the high risk of death, we tend to think that birth is far more difficult in humans than it is in other mammals. But since almost all primate infants have large heads relative to body size, birth is challenging to many primates (fig. 13–3).

An undeveloped brain seems necessary for birth to occur through a narrow pelvis, but it may also be advantageous for other reasons. For a species as dependent on learning as we are for survival, it may be adaptive for most of our brain growth to take place in the presence of environmental stimuli rather than in the relatively unstimulating uterus. This may be particularly true for a species dependent on language. The language centers of the brain develop in the first three years figure 13–3 The relation between the average diameter of the birth canal of adult females and average head length and breadth of newborns of the same species. (After Jolly, 1985.)

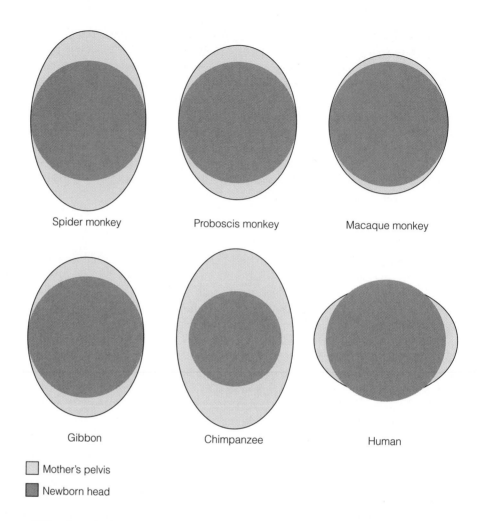

Spider monkey   Proboscis monkey   Macaque monkey

Gibbon   Chimpanzee   Human

☐ Mother's pelvis

■ Newborn head

of life, when the brain is undergoing its rapid expansion; these three years are considered a critical period for the development of language in the human child.

Infancy is defined as the period during which nursing takes place, typically lasting about four years in humans. When we consider how unusual it is for a mother to nurse her child for even a year in the United States or Canada, this figure may surprise us. But considering that four or five years of nursing is the norm for chimpanzees, gorillas, and orangutans and for women in foraging societies, most anthropologists conclude that four years was the norm for most humans in the evolutionary past (Eaton, Shostak, and Konner, 1988). Other lines of evidence confirm this pattern, including the lack of other foods that infants could consume until the origin of agriculture and the domestication of milk-producing animals. In fact, if the mother died during childbirth in pre-agricultural populations, it is very likely that the child died also, unless there was another woman available who could nurse the child. Jane Goodall has noted that this is also true for chimpanzees: Infants who are orphaned before they are weaned do not usually survive. Even those orphaned after weaning are still emotionally dependent on their mothers and exhibit clinical signs of depression for a few months or years after the mother's death, assuming they survive the trauma (Goodall, 1986).

Human milk, like that of other primates, is extremely low in fats and protein. Such a low nutrient content is typical for species in which mothers are seldom or never separated from their infants and nurse in short, frequent bouts. Not coincidentally, prolonged, frequent nursing suppresses ovulation in marginally nourished women (Konner and Worthman, 1980); this behavior helps to maintain a four-year birth interval, during which infants have no nutritional competition from siblings. Thus, nursing served as a natural birth control mechanism in the evolutionary past, as it does in some populations today.

Breast milk also provides important antibodies that contribute to infant survival. Throughout the world, breast-fed infants have far greater survival rates than those who are not breast-fed or who are weaned too early. The only exception is in societies where scientifically developed milk substitutes are readily available and appropriately used. The importance of adequate nutrients during this period of rapid brain growth cannot be overestimated. Thus, it is not surprising that there are many cultural practices designed to ensure successful nursing.

Childhood

Humans have unusually long childhoods, reflecting the importance of learning for our species. *Childhood* is that time between weaning and puberty when the brain is completing its growth and the acquisition of technical and social skills is taking place. For most other mammals, once weaning has occurred, getting food is left to individual effort. Humans may be unique in the practice of providing food for children or juveniles (Lancaster and Lancaster, 1983). Such sustained care requires much extra effort by parents, but the survival rate of offspring is a great deal higher than in other primates (Table 13–3). During childhood, the roles of fathers and older siblings become very significant. While mothers are highly involved with caring for new infants, the socialization and child care of other children often fall to other family or community members. Clearly, family environment, stress, and other biosocial factors have a major impact on children's health (Flinn, 1999).

TABLE 13-3	Providing for Juveniles	
	Percent of Those Who Survive	
	Weaning	**Adolescence**
Lion	28	15
Baboon	45	33
Macaque	42	13
Chimpanzee	48	38
Provisioned macaques	82	58
Human Populations		
!Kung[*]	80	58
Yanomamo [†]	73	50
Paleoindian [††]	86	50

[*]   A hunting and gathering population of southern Africa.
[†]   Horticultural population of South America.
[††] Preagricultural people of the Americas.

Source: Adapted from Lancaster and Lancaster, 1983.

Adolescence

A number of biological events mark the transition to adolescence for both males and females. These include increase in body size, change in body shape, and the development of testes and penes in boys, and breasts in girls. Hormonal changes are the driving forces behind all these physical alterations, especially increased testosterone production in boys and increased estrogen production in girls. As already noted, menarche (the first menstruation) is a clear sign of puberty in girls and is usually the marker of this transition in cultures where the event is ritually celebrated.

A number of factors affect the onset of puberty in humans, including genetics, gestational experience, nutrition, disease, activity levels, and stress. In humans and other primates, females reach sexual maturity before males do. An illustration of the effect of diet and other lifestyle factors on puberty is seen in the trend toward a lower age of menarche that has been noted in human populations in the last hundred years and the tendency for girls who are very active and thin to mature later than those who are heavier and less active. Socioeconomic factors are also implicated in this trend: In less developed nations, girls from higher social classes tend to mature earlier than girls from lower social classes. In general, physical development has accelerated in the past several decades along with worldwide improvements in public health and nutrition (Worthman, 1999).

Adolescence is the time between puberty and the completion of physical growth or the social recognition of adulthood. This social recognition may result from marriage, bearing a child, or a particular accomplishment. In nonhuman primates, the equivalent stage is defined in males as the time from which they are capable of fertilization to the time when physical growth is complete. At this point, they have male-specific features and size and are recognized as adults by other members of the social group. Females begin to engage in sexual behavior, exhibiting signs of sexual receptivity before they are capable of bearing young. These early cycles are usually not ovulatory and define the period of adolescence for them. Adulthood comes with the first pregnancy.

Adulthood

Pregnancy and child care occupy much of a woman's adult life in most cultures, as they likely did throughout hominid evolution. For most women, the years from menarche to menopause are marked by monthly menstruation, except when they are pregnant or nursing. A normal menstrual cycle has two phases: the follicular phase, in which the egg is preparing for ovulation, marked by high estrogen production; and the luteal phase, during which the uterus is preparing for implantation, marked by high progesterone production. If the egg is not fertilized, progesterone production drops off and menstruation, the shedding of the uterine lining, occurs. A woman who never becomes pregnant may have as many as 400 cycles between menarche and menopause. Because reliable contraceptives were unavailable in the past, this high number of menstrual cycles is probably a relatively recent phenomenon. It has been suggested, in fact, that highly frequent menstrual cycling may be implicated in several cancers of the female reproductive organs, especially of the breast, uterus, and ovaries (Eaton et al., 1994). During the course of human evolution, females may have had as few as 60 menstrual cycles in their entire lives, unless they were sterile or not sexually active.

At the social level, adulthood for women in the majority of world cultures means, in addition to caring for children, participation in economic activities. Adulthood for men typically includes activities related to subsistence, religion, politics, and family. Women may be equally or less involved in these activities, depending on the culture.

During adulthood, the status of an individual may change as new skills are acquired or new achievements made. Where such records are kept, status may be defined by chronological age, as seen in the common pattern of retirement at age 65 or 70 in the United States.

For women, menopause, or the end of menstruation, is a sign of entry into a new phase of the life cycle. Estrogen and progesterone production begin to decline toward the end of the reproductive years until ovulation (and thus menstruation) ceases altogether. This occurs at approximately age 50 in all parts of the world. Throughout human evolution, the majority of females (and males) did not survive to age 50; thus, few women lived much past menopause. But today, this event occurs when women have as much as one-third of their active and healthy lives ahead of them. As already noted, such a long postreproductive period is not found in other primates. Female chimpanzees and monkeys experience decreased fertility in their later years, but most continue to have monthly cycles until their deaths. Occasional reports of menopause in apes and monkeys have been noted, but it is far from a routine and expected event.

Why do human females have such a long period during which they can no longer reproduce? One theory relates to parenting. Because it takes about 12 to 15 years before a child becomes independent, it has been argued that females are biologically "programmed" to live 12 to 15 years beyond the birth of their last child (Mayer, 1982). This hypothesis assumes that the maximum human life span for preagricultural humans was about 65 years, a figure that corresponds to what is known for contemporary hunter-gatherers and for prehistoric populations. Another theory that has been gaining attention is known as the "grandmother hypothesis." This proposes that women who lived several years beyond the independence of their last children would be freed to provide food and other resources to their children and grandchildren. Because these practices would likely increase the survival of grandchildren, productive postmenopausal years would be favored by natural selection (Hawkes et al., 1997). A third theory regarding menopause suggests that it was not itself favored by natural selection; rather it is an artifact of the extension of the human life span that has occurred in the last several centuries.

Aging

Postreproductive years are physiologically somewhat well defined for women, but "old age" is a very ambiguous concept. In the United States, we tend to associate old age with physical ailments and decreased activity. Thus, a person who is vigorous and active at age 70 might not be regarded as "old," whereas another who is frail and debilitated at age 55 may be considered old.

One reason we are concerned with this definition is that old age is generally regarded negatively and is typically unwelcome in the United States, a culture noted for its emphasis on youth. This attitude is quite different from that of many other societies, where old age brings with it wealth, higher status, and new freedoms, particularly for women. This is because high status is often correlated with knowledge, experience, and wisdom, which are themselves associated with greater age in most societies. Such has been the case throughout most of history, but today, in technologically developed countries, knowledge is changing so rapidly that the old may no longer control the most relevant knowledge.

By and large, people today are living longer than they did in the past because, in part, they are not dying from infectious diseases. Currently, the top five killers in the United States, for example, are heart disease, cancer, stroke, accidents, and chronic obstructive lung disease. Together these account for 75 percent of deaths (Eaton, Shostak, and Konner, 1988). All these conditions are considered "diseases of civilization" in that most can be accounted for by conditions in the modern environment that were not present in the past. Examples include cigarette smoke, air and water pollution, alcohol, automobiles, high-fat diets, and environmental carcinogens. It should be noted, however, that the high incidence of these diseases is also a result of people living to older ages because of factors such as improved hygiene, regular medical care, and new medical technologies.

Human Longevity

Relative to most other animals, humans have a long life span (Table 13–4). The maximum life span potential, estimated to be about 120 years, has probably not changed in the last several thousand years, although life expectancy at birth (the average length of life) has increased significantly in the last 100 years, probably owing to the decreased influence of infectious diseases, which typically take their toll on the young (Crews and Harper, 1998).

To some extent, aging is something we do throughout our entire lives. But we usually think of aging as **senescence,** the process of physiological decline in all systems of the body that occurs toward the end of the life course. Actually, throughout adulthood, there is a gradual decline in our cells' abilities to synthesize proteins, in immune system function, in muscle mass (with a corresponding increase in fat mass) and strength, and in bone mineral density (Lamberts, van den Beld, and van der Lely, 1997). This decline is associated with an increase in risk for the chronic degenerative diseases that are usually listed as the causes of death in industrialized nations.

As you know, most causes of death that have their effects after the reproductive years will not necessarily be subjected to the forces of natural selection. One explanation for why we age and are affected by chronic degenerative diseases like atherosclerosis, cancers, and hypertension is that genes that enhance reproductive success in earlier years (and thus were favored by natural selection) may have detrimental effects in later years. These are referred to as **pleiotropic genes,** meaning that they have multiple effects at different times in the life span or under different conditions (Williams, 1957). For example, genes that enhance the function of the immune system in the early years may also damage tissue so that cancer susceptibility increases in later life (Nesse and Williams, 1994). Alternatively, cancer-protecting genes may override genes for organ and tissue renewal in later life.

Pleiotropy may help us understand evolutionary reasons for aging, but what are the causes of senescence in the individual? Much attention has been focused

TABLE 13-4

Maximum Life Spans for Selected Species

Organism	Approximate Maximum Life Span (in years)
Bristlecone pine	5,000
Tortoise	170
Rockfish	140
Human	120
Blue whale	80
Indian elephant	70
Gorilla	39
Domestic dog	34
Rabbit	13
Rat	5

Source: Stini, 1991.

Senescence The process of physiological decline in body function that occurs with aging.

Pleiotropic genes Genes that have more than one effect; genes that have different effects at different times in the life cycle.

recently on free radicals, highly reactive molecules that can damage cells. Protection against these by-products of normal metabolism is provided by antioxidants such as vitamins A, C, and E and by a number of enzymes (Kirkwood, 1997). Ultimately, damage to DNA can occur, which in turn contributes to the senescence of cells, the immune system, and other functional systems of the body. Additionally, there is evidence that programmed cell death is also a part of the normal processes of development that can obviously contribute to senescence.

Another hypothesis for senescence is known as the "telomere hypothesis." In this view, the DNA sequence at the end of each chromosome, known as the telomere, is shortened each time a cell divides. Cells that have divided many times throughout the life course have short telomeres, eventually reaching the point at which they can no longer divide and are unable to maintain healthy tissues and organs. Telomere length changes have also been implicated in cancers. In the laboratory, the enzyme telomerase can lengthen telomeres, making the cell young again. For this reason, the gene for telomerase has been called the "immortalizing gene." Although this research is not likely to lead to a lengthening of the life span, it may contribute to better health throughout an individual's lifetime.

Far more important than genes in the aging process, however, are lifestyle factors, such as smoking, physical activity, diet, and medical care. Interestingly, there is evidence that caloric restriction may actually contribute to longer life spans (Kirkwood, 2002). Life expectancy at birth varies considerably from country to country and among socioeconomic classes within a country. Throughout the world, women have higher life expectancies than men.

A Japanese girl born in 2001, for example, can expect to live to age 84, a boy to age 78. Girls and boys born in that same year in the United States have life expectancies of 80 and 73, respectively. In contrast to these children in industrialized nations, girls and boys in Mali have life expectancies of only 48 and 46, respectively. Many African nations have seen life expectancy drop below 40 owing to deaths from AIDS. For example, before the AIDS epidemic, Zimbabweans had a life expectancy of 65 years; today life expectancy in Zimbabwe is 39.

Individuals, Society, and Evolution

Throughout this chapter we have discussed ways in which evolutionary history, genes, and the environment affect the human life course from infancy until death. Humans are social animals, however, and we now turn our attention to the ways in which natural selection has acted upon the behaviors of humans imbedded in social contexts. Examining human social behavior in an evolutionary framework is known as *behavioral ecology*, which we discussed in Chapter 6 in the context of primate behavior. Of course, humans are primates, and many biological anthropologists are interested in the extent to which evolution can explain contemporary human behaviors. Behavioral ecologists suggest that humans, like other animals, behave in ways that increase their fitness, or reproductive success. This includes behaviors affecting mating and parenting success. Finding mates and taking care of offspring require time and energy, and as we know all too well, both of these commodities exist in finite amounts. Thus, reproductive efforts require trade-offs in time, energy, and resources invested in mating and parenting. When we read about these concepts as they pertain to monkeys and apes, most of us probably do not find much with which to disagree. But to suggest that evolutionary processes have an impact on human behavior today raises a lot of issues, some of which are not so easily resolved.

For example, this view argues that natural selection is not limited to physical and physiological responses, but has had an effect on the way humans think—in other words, on human cognition, perception, and memory. The argument goes something like this: The ability to remember a dangerous event that may have resulted in loss of life would be favorably selected if it prevented a person from being caught in a similar situation. The ability to distinguish a wildebeest (food) from a lion (danger) would be selectively favored. Likewise, economic behaviors involved in the allocation of resources to increase survival and reproductive success would be favored.

The study of how natural selection has influenced how humans and other primates think is often called *evolutionary psychology*. Among the topics explored by evolutionary psychologists are mate attraction, sexuality, aggression, and violence. As you might guess, all of these are hot topics, and there is no end in sight to the controversy that surrounds them.

Aggression and violence, particularly on the part of males, is the subject of a number of books and papers in evolutionary psychology. Wrangham and Peterson (1996), for example, contrast the behaviors of our two closest living relatives, the chimpanzees and the bonobos. Most striking is that chimpanzee society seems to be based on male-male competition and aggression leading occasionally to violence both within and between troops, whereas bonobo society is described as a female-dominated community based on cooperation and peaceful interaction (fig. 13–4). To Wrangham and Peterson, these two behavior patterns represent the extremes of human societies and also show potentials for both violence and peace that may be rooted in human evolutionary history.

figure 13–4 (a) These chimpanzees exhibit an aggressive reaction when confronted by others. (b) The bonobos show more relaxed expressions.

(a)   (b)

On the other hand, they clearly acknowledge the role of culture and society in fostering aggression and violence in males. Mirroring some of the discussions of terrorism today, chimpanzee communities with abundant resources have far fewer incidents of violence than communities with limited resources; in general, bonobos live in areas of relative resource abundance. But whatever their roots, it appears to many observers that war, genocide, rape, rioting, and terrorism are unwelcome legacies of human evolutionary history. Unfortunately, because of recent events linked to terrorists, these arguments resonate more profoundly and convincingly than they did when the last edition of this textbook was written. Perhaps by the next edition, the pendulum of thinking about world events will have swung toward the idea that peaceful cooperation is more fundamental to human behavior.

To suggest that some of our behaviors reflect our evolutionary history is not to say that there are genes for such behaviors. No matter how you cut it, behavior is an extremely complex phenomenon, and its expression depends on a combination of myriad genes, environmental context, and individual experience. There is really no way of predicting how an individual mother or father will allocate resources in the task of child rearing, but behavioral ecologists argue that patterns can be seen when populations (or even the entire species) are examined for allocation of parenting resources.

Despite its limitations and challenges, examining human behavior as a product of evolution not only helps explain and understand some aspects of our lives, but also allows predictions that can be examined and tested through field observations, demographic studies, and other methods. We can take an example from the human life cycle to illustrate this. As already noted, the basic argument underlying behavioral ecology is that natural selection will favor individual actions and choices that increase reproductive success. If that is the case, it would make sense for human females to breed as early in their life cycle as possible and for as long as possible and to have children spaced very closely together. Let us examine each of these assumptions more closely.

The onset of menarche in girls is affected by several factors, including genetic patterns (girls tend to become mature at about the same age as their mothers), nutrition, stress, and disease. It also appears that a certain amount of body fat is necessary for menarche and the maintenance of ovulation (Frisch, 1988). Both diet and activity levels affect the accumulation of body fat. As noted, there is a tendency for girls who are very active and thin to mature later than those who are heavier and less active. High activity and low body fat also characterize many ballet dancers and marathon runners, who often cease to menstruate during periods of intense training. Since pregnancy and nursing require an increase in caloric consumption, body fat may serve as a signal to the body that there is enough caloric reserve to support a pregnancy. When the levels of body fat fall too low, ovulation may cease temporarily to prevent initiation of a pregnancy that is likely to fail.

If early maturity results in higher numbers of surviving offspring, then it is predicted that natural selection would favor those members of a population who mature earlier. Until the advent of settled living, it is likely that females became pregnant as soon as they were biologically able to do so. This would be advantageous in view of the fact that individual life expectancy would have been low. Paleodemographic studies indicate a mortality rate of at least 50 percent in subadults in preindustrial populations; and of the half that survived to adulthood, most did not survive to age 50. Given the reality of short life spans combined with the long period of infant dependency, producing offspring as early as possible may have contributed to the reproductive success of females, particularly early hominid females. If we use chimpanzees as a model for this discussion, it is noteworthy that with one exception, no infant chimpanzee orphaned prior to the age of three has survived. Consequently, one could argue that a similar situation applied to early hominids, who, in addition to the numerous risk factors faced by chimpanzees, were subject to greater degrees of predation pressure. Hence, an early hominid female's chances of rearing even one offspring to the point it could survive without her were enhanced by giving birth as soon as she reached sexual maturity.

The high rates of adolescent pregnancy that typify so many cultures today reflect this ancient biological heritage. Today, however, there may be disadvantages to early maturity. If delayed maturity is associated with higher-quality care of the offspring (fig. 13–5), then offspring survival may improve, resulting in a net increase in fitness for those who mature a few years later. Unfortunately, all too frequently today in many parts of the world, young girls become reproductively mature long before they are socially mature. And if they are also sexually active, they may become pregnant before they have finished school or obtained the skills necessary for economic self-sufficiency. This means that the quality of care that they can provide their offspring will be compromised. It is known that the infant mortality rate in humans rises rapidly as mothers' age at first birth decreases (Stearns, 1992). In contemporary society, it is likely that those who delay reproducing until they are emotionally, socially, and economically mature will have more surviving offspring than those who begin their parenting careers before they themselves have matured. But if the young, maturing parents have sufficient help from their extended families, religious organizations, or government agencies, early childbearing may not compromise their fitness. Clearly, the road to reproductive success is more complicated than most theories of behavioral ecology suggest, although they serve as useful models on which to base predictions about behavior. Scientific models are often simplistic, but this is necessary to test hypotheses about behavior.

figure 13–5 Human infants require extensive parental care, especially in the first few years of life.

SW Productions/Getty Images

Summary

This chapter has reviewed the fundamental concepts of growth and development and how those processes occur within the contexts of both biology and culture. Diet has an important effect on growth, and human nutritional requirements themselves result from biocultural evolution. The preagricultural human diet was reviewed, with the suggestion that many of our contemporary ills may result from incompatibilities between our evolved nutritional requirements and the foods that are currently consumed. In particular, the preagricultural diet was probably high in complex carbohydrates and fiber and low in fat and sodium. Diets for many contemporary people are low in complex carbohydrates and fiber and high in fat and sodium. This type of diet has been implicated in many current health problems.

The human life cycle can be divided into six phases: prenatal, infancy, juvenile, subadult, adult, and postreproductive. Each is fairly well defined by biological markers. Pregnancy lasts about nine months in humans, and infants are born with only about 25 percent of their adult brain size. This means that human infants are helpless at birth and therefore dependent on their parents for a long time. Birth is somewhat more challenging for humans than for other mammals because of the very close correspondence between maternal pelvic size (narrow because of bipedalism) and fetal head size (large, even though the brain is relatively undeveloped). Infancy is the period of nursing, approximately four years for most humans and apes. The unusually long period of childhood in humans is important as the time in which social and technological skills are acquired. Sexual maturation is apparent at puberty, but full adult status is not achieved until growth has been completed and childbearing capabilities are reached. The last phase of the human life cycle, the postreproductive period, is marked in women by menopause, the cessation of menstruation and ovulation.

For humans in society, legacies from evolutionary history include thought processes and behaviors that reflect natural selection operating on individuals to increase reproductive success, or fitness. A review of behavioral ecology summarizes the ways in which genes, environment, and culture have interacted to produce complex adaptations to equally complex challenges. Critical review of hypotheses for such human behaviors as aggression, violence, nurturance, and reproduction reveals the complexity of this interrelationship.

Questions for Review

1. What is meant by the analogy "Water is to fish as culture is to humans"?
2. What is sexual dimorphism? List some examples in humans.
3. Briefly describe human brain growth.
4. What are essential amino acids? Develop a scenario for how our requirements for these amino acids might have evolved.
5. What were the characteristics of the preagricultural human diet? What are the major differences today?
6. Why is nursing important for infant health? What is the proposed relationship between nursing and ovulation?
7. What is the proposed significance of providing food for children beyond the age of weaning?
8. What biological changes occur in males and females at puberty? What role do lifestyle factors appear to play in determining the onset of puberty in girls?
9. How have attitudes toward the elderly changed in modern, high-tech cultures?
10. Why are humans living longer today than they did in the past?
11. What are some of the proposed explanations for why we age?
12. Provide examples for how natural selection might act on human behaviors such as parenting and aggression.

Suggested Further Readings

Bogin, Barry. 1988. *Patterns of Human Growth*. Cambridge, England: Cambridge University Press.

Cohen, Mark Nathan. 1989. *Health and the Rise of Civilization*. New Haven: Yale University Press.

Diamond, Jared. 1992. *The Third Chimpanzee: The Evolution and Future of the Human Animal*. New York: Harper Collins.

Eaton, S. Boyd, Marjorie Shostak, and Melvin Konner. 1988. *The Paleolithic Prescription*. New York: Harper & Row.

Ellison, Peter T. 2001. *On Fertile Ground: A Natural History of Human Reproduction*. Cambridge, MA: Harvard University Press.

Potts, M., and R. Short. 1999. *Ever Since Adam and Eve: The Evolution of Human Sexuality*. Cambridge, England: Cambridge University Press.

Stewart-Macadam, Patricia, and Katherine A. Dettwyler. 1995. *Breastfeeding: Biocultural Perspectives*. Hawthorne, NY: Aldine de Gruyter.

Trevathan, Wenda R. 1987. *Human Birth: An Evolutionary Perspective*. Hawthorne, NY: Aldine de Gruyter.

Wrangham, Richard, and Dale Peterson. 1996. *Demonic Males: Apes and the Origins of Human Violence*. Boston: Houghton Mifflin.

Multimedia Resources

 Companion Web Site

Anthropology Online: The Wadsworth Anthropology Resource Center Visit **http://anthropology.wadsworth.com** and click on the Companion Web Site for Jurmain/Kilgore/Trevathan/Nelson's *Essentials of Physical Anthropology*, Fifth Edition, to access a wide range of enrichment material to aid in your study of anthropology. Among the useful options for each chapter's self-study are learning objectives, flashcards, Internet exercises, Web links, InfoTrac College Edition exercises, and practice quizzes that can be scored and emailed to your instructor.

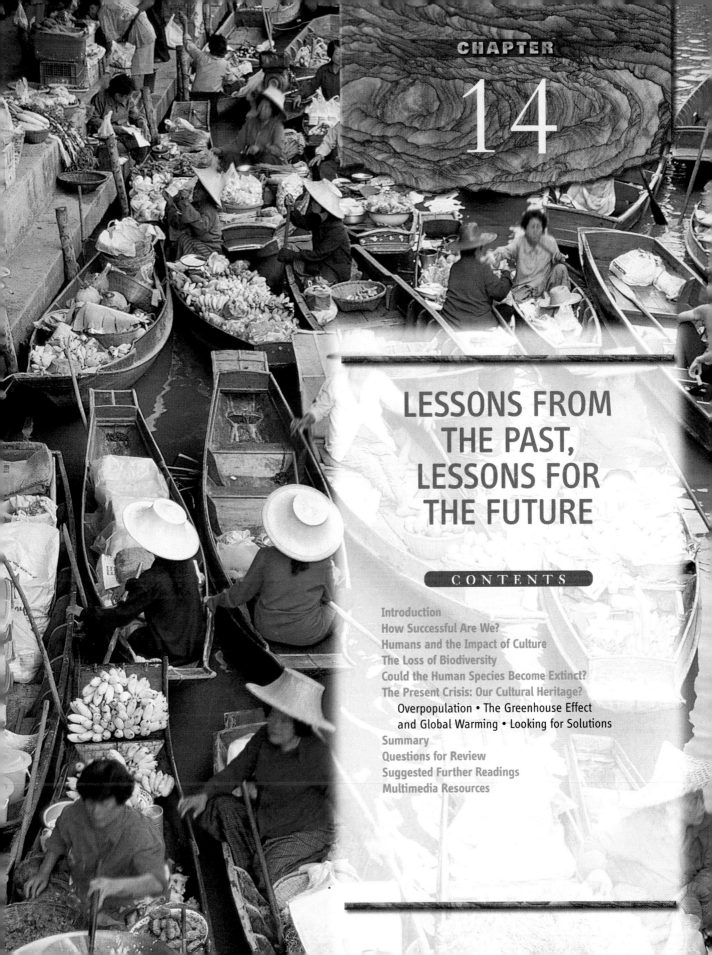

LESSONS FROM THE PAST, LESSONS FOR THE FUTURE

CONTENTS

Introduction

omo sapiens is but one of approximately 1.4 million living species thus far known to science. All of these organisms, including bacteria and plants, ultimately are the contemporary result of the same basic evolutionary processes, and all share the same DNA material. But more than any other life form, humans, through cultural innovation and ever-expanding numbers, have come to dominate the planet.

The preceding chapters have traced the evolutionary history of *Homo sapiens*. In our discussion of such topics as evolution and adaptation, we have emphasized the importance of culture in the development of our species. Such investigations of human evolution and the interplay between biology and culture can provide useful information about why humans behave the way they do. Moreover, they help us understand how a medium-sized bipedal primate came to occupy a position of dominance over many other forms of life on earth.

In this chapter, we briefly discuss some of the challenges that face humanity today, challenges that have emerged as a result of our own doing. In this discussion, we emphasize our place in nature and focus on how, since the domestication of plants and animals, we have altered the face of our planet, while at the same time shaping the destiny of thousands of species, including ourselves.

Although anthropology texts do not usually dwell on the topics included here, we feel that it is important to consider them, however brief and simplified our treatment must be. We are living during a critical period in the earth's history. Indeed, the future of much of life as we know it will be decided forever in the next few decades. It is crucial that we, as individuals, cities, and nations, make wise decisions, and to do this we must be well informed. The importance of acquiring knowledge cannot be overstated, for our decisions will be irrevocable.

It is valid to ask such questions as, What is the future of *Homo sapiens*? Will we continue to thrive? What kind of world will our descendants inherit? What is the future of the millions of other species? Perhaps we, as anthropologists, are in a position to address these and many other questions of immediate concern. The study of human biological and cultural evolution, coupled with an examination of the results of early human activities, can provide some insights from the past that may help illuminate the future. At the very least, we can provide students with an anthropological perspective on the serious problems that face us today.

How Successful Are We?

As we have emphasized, humans are animals and, more specifically, primates. Like all life forms on earth, our very existence is based in the molecule DNA. As all living forms share this same genetic foundation, it is highly probable that all life has evolved from a common ancestor and that human beings are part of a continuum made up of biologically related species.

Yet, we humans tend to view ourselves as separate from all other life forms, and we have come to regard our species as the masters of the planet. In Western cultures, this view has been reinforced by the conventionally held Old

Testament assertion that humans shall have *dominion* over the nonhuman animals. The teachings of Islam and certain other religions and philosophies can also be interpreted in a similar manner. (The Old Testament, in Genesis, actually presents two separate versions; the second conveys a quite different meaning: that humans are to have "stewardship" over other animals.) Moreover, there is the prevailing view that nature represents an array of resources that exists primarily to be exploited for the betterment of humankind. This view is as widely held today, unfortunately, as ever before. More than merely being anthropocentric, such a perspective reveals a misplaced, unjustified arrogance.

By most standards, *Homo sapiens* is a successful species. There are currently more than 6 billion human beings living on this planet. Each one of these 6,000,000,000 individuals comprises upwards of 20 trillion cells. Nevertheless, we and all other multicellular organisms contribute but a small fraction of all the cells on the planet—the vast majority of which are bacteria. Thus, if we see life ultimately as a competition among reproducing organisms, bacteria are the winners, hands down.

Bacteria, then, could be viewed as the dominant life form on earth. However, even when only considering multicellular animals, there are additional lessons in evolutionary humility. As mammals, we are members of a group that includes about 4,000 species—a group of animals that has been on the decline over the last several million years. Looking even more specifically, as primates, we see ourselves belonging to a grouping that today numbers not even 200 species (and is also probably declining since its peak several million years ago). Compare these species numbers with those estimated for insects. Over 750,000 insect species have been identified, and estimates are as high as 30 million (Wilson, 1992)! Number of species (as an indicator of biological diversity) is as good a barometer of evolutionary success as any other. By this standard, humans (and our close relatives) could hardly be seen as the most successful of species.

Evolutionary success can also be gauged by species longevity. As we have seen, fossil evidence indicates that *Homo sapiens* has been on the scene for at least 200,000 years and perhaps as long as 400,000 years. Such time spans, seen through the perspective of a human lifetime, may seem enormous. But consider this: Our immediate predecessor, *Homo erectus*, had a species longevity of about 1.5 million years. In other words, we as a species would need to exist another million years simply to match *Homo erectus*! If such considerations as these are not humbling enough, remember that some sharks and turtles have thrived basically unchanged structurally for 400 million years (although many of these species are now seriously threatened).

Humans and the Impact of Culture

As you have learned, because humans increasingly came to use culture as a means of adapting to the natural environment, physical anthropologists view culture as an adaptive strategy. Stone tools, temporary shelters, animal products (including animal skin clothing), and the use of fire all permitted earlier populations to expand from the tropics and exploit resources in regions previously unavailable to them. In fact, it was culture that enabled humans to become increasingly successful as time passed.

For most of human history, technology remained simple, and the rate of culture change was slow. Indeed, humans enjoyed what could be termed a "comfortable" relationship with this unique adaptive strategy. However, as technologies became more complex, and especially when humans began to adopt an agricultural lifestyle, their relationship with culture became more complicated and, over time, less and less comfortable.

From the archaeological record, it appears that around 15,000 years ago, influenced in part by climate change and the extinction of many large-bodied prey species, some human groups began to settle down, abandoning their nomadic lives. Moreover, by about 10,000 years ago (and probably earlier), some peoples had learned that by keeping domestic animals and growing crops, they had more abundant and reliable food supplies. The domestication of plants and animals is seen as one of the most significant events in human history, one that was to have far-reaching consequences for the entire planet.

Keeping domesticated plants and animals requires a settled way of life, and increased sedentism, combined with more reliable food sources, led to increased population growth. Viewed from the perspective of twenty-first-century humans living in industrialized societies, it might seem that adopting a settled lifestyle would lead to better health and nutrition. Yet, scientists believe that health and nutrition among hunter-gatherers was, in fact, quite good compared to that of humans living in early settlements, for, as you learned in Chapter 12, with settled lifestyle comes increased exposure to infectious disease. Thus, it can justifiably be said that increased exposure to infectious disease was one of the earliest alterations in the harmonious relationship between humans and cultural innovation. Furthermore, as you read in Chapter 12, infectious disease has been and continues to be a powerful selective force acting upon human populations.

Early agriculturalists, for whom we have only crude population estimates, probably numbered a few million worldwide. At this level, population density was still quite low, but human activity was already beginning to have an impact on the natural environment. In truth, it would be erroneous to assume that human activities have only recently come to have environmental consequences. Indeed, human impact on local environments increased dramatically as soon as people began to live in permanent settlements. (Furthermore, people themselves suffered harmful results of this shift in subsistence strategies.) Consequently, many of the earth's features we think of as natural actually came about as the result of human activities. For example, prior to the **Neolithic**, when people began to live in permanent settlements, much of Britain and continental Europe was blanketed with forests and woodlands. The moorlands and, to some extent, the peat bogs that have provided evocative settings for so many English novels are the result of deforestation that commenced over 5,000 years ago (fig. 14–1). In Britain, local woodland clearing by hunter-gatherers began during the late **Mesolithic**, and it accelerated around 5,000 years ago with the adoption of farming. Late Bronze Age peoples (c. 4,000–3,500 y.a.) continued the process on an even larger scale, so that by 2,500 years ago, many of England's forests were disappearing (Bell and Walker, 1992). Today, the majority of European woodlands exist as discontinuous patches—the result of processes that continued until fairly recent times but that originated with prehistoric farmers.

Unfortunately, humans began to exploit, and increasingly depend on, nonrenewable resources. Forests can be viewed as renewable resources, provided

Neolithic The period during which humans began to domesticate plants and animals. The Neolithic is also associated with increased sedentism. Dates for the Neolithic vary from region to region, depending on when domestication occurred.

Mesolithic The period preceding the Neolithic, during which humans increasingly exploited smaller animals (including fish), increased the variety of tools they used, and became somewhat less nomadic.

they are given the opportunity for regrowth. However, in many areas, forest clearing was virtually complete and was inevitably followed by soil erosion, frequent overgrazing, and overcultivation, which led to further soil erosion (fig. 14–2). Therefore, in those areas, trees became a nonrenewable resource, perhaps the first resource to have this distinction.

It would not be in error to state that since the advent of settled life, and to some extent prior to it, humans have virtually waged war on trees. Early European explorers and settlers recorded extensive burning of woodlands and forests by indigenous groups of hunter-gatherers in North America and Australia, practiced presumably to clear undergrowth and drive animals from cover. The effect of such burning was not inconsequential, and as people began to live in agricultural communities and later in towns and cities, the impact on forests became devastating. In fact, as shown in fig. 14–3, only about one-fifth of the earth's original forests remain intact today, and much of the clearing occurred centuries and even millennia ago.

There are many reasons for cutting forests, and the earliest of these were to clear the land for cultivation and grazing and to provide firewood and lumber for construction. As small communities grew into towns and cities, wood came to be used for shipbuilding, fortifications, and even the construction of temples and palaces. In short, the human experience over the last 10,000 to 15,000 years would not have been possible without the exploitation of woodlands and forests.

figure 14–1 The moorland in the foreground is the result of woodland clearing some 2,000 years ago in southwest England.

figure 14–2 Deforestation and erosion in Madagascar.

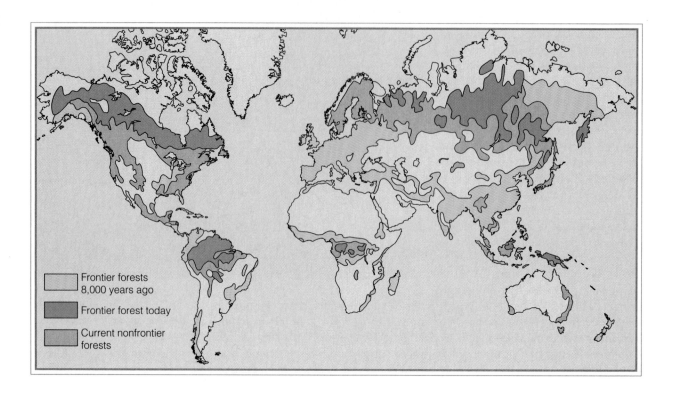

Frontier forests
8,000 years ago

Frontier forest today

Current nonfrontier
forests

figure 14–3 Map of deforestation.

One of the earliest documented examples of humankind's appetite for lumber is the cutting of the famous cedars of Lebanon. Over 3,000 years ago, the eastern Mediterranean (modern-day Israel, Jordan, Lebanon, and Syria), southern Turkey, and Mesopotamia (in present-day Iraq) had become major sources of valuable cedar, fir, cypress, and other woods. But by far the most highly prized wood was Lebanese cedar, which was cut and shipped throughout the eastern Mediterranean, where it was used in the construction of buildings and ships (fig. 14–4). The Old Testament tells us that King Solomon's temple was made of cedar from Lebanon, and numerous other texts, written over several centuries, document the extensive use and desirability of this precious wood. Not surprisingly, the deforestation of the mountains of Lebanon was eventually so complete that what "forest" remains today is but small patches and stands of trees.

Just to prove the old adage, "The more things change, the more they stay the same," it is informative to note that classical scholars (most notably Plato and Aristotle) bemoaned the effects of deforestation and other forms of environmental degradation in Greece and other areas of the Mediterranean basin. They warned that the cutting of forests and overuse of land led to soil erosion, disrupted water supplies, agricultural decline, and even climate change. Their views, expressed some 2,400 years ago, are verified by combined archaeological and geological data that show sequences of soil accumulation followed by intense human occupation, then soil erosion, and finally, abandonment of archaeological sites throughout Greece. Furthermore, this sequence of episodes dates to around 5,000 years ago. But, given the relatively small size of human populations, even by the time of the ancient Greeks and Romans, the human impact on ecosystems mostly remained a localized, not global, phenomenon.

Nevertheless, these impacts were in some cases significant. The barren (but enchanting) landscape of Greece and much of what is now desert in the Middle East and the Sahara Desert in Africa are the direct legacy of overgrazing (mostly by goats) and subsequent erosion over the last few thousand years.

Destruction of natural resources in the past has also had severe consequences for people living today. The 1990 typhoon and severe flooding that killed over 100,000 people in Bangladesh were partly due to previous deforestation of regions in the Himalayas of northern India. There is also evidence that continued erosion and flooding in China are partly the result of deforestation that occurred in the past. Lastly, many scientists have long speculated that the collapse of the Maya civilization of southern Mexico around 1,000 years ago was at least partly due to overcultivation of land and depletion of nutrient-poor tropical soils.

figure 14-4 This eighth-century B.C. Assyrian panel depicts the transport of cedar logs from Lebanon to Assyria.

Archaeologists can provide many examples of what humans have done wrong in the past. But just as importantly, they are also able to provide us with positive examples from earlier cultures, innovative techniques that, for all our modern wisdom, we still have yet to match. For example, in the Andean highlands of South America, soil is very poor and subject to erosion. Agricultural peoples living in the region today (in Bolivia and Peru), even with considerable input from modern technology, still can barely scrape together a meager existence. Yet, such unrelenting poverty was not always the case in this part of the world. Five hundred years ago, the Inka ancestors of these peoples reaped enormous wealth from this same land and built from it one of the largest, best-organized empires in the world. How did they do it?

Archaeologist Clark Erickson sought an answer. By examining Inka agricultural fields, terracing, and irrigation, he was able to extrapolate the ancient techniques and duplicate many of the same methods. This was no mere academic exercise, however, for the next step was to teach these methods to the modern farmers. As a result, crop yields have vastly improved, with less environmental damage, with less use of fertilizer, and at less cost than before!

The Loss of Biodiversity

Although the term *biodiversity* is currently a popular one, many people do not really understand what it means. Biodiversity is the totality of all living things, from bacteria and fungi to trees and humans. The term refers not only to species, but to individuals and the various genetic combinations they represent, as well as to entire ecosystems. The fact that we are currently losing biodiversity is indisputable. What we are not certain of is the exact rate of loss or what its impact will be.

The geological record indicates that in the past 570 million years, there have been at least 15 mass extinctions, two of which altered all of the earth's ecosystems (Ward, 1994). The first of these major extinction events took place some 250 million years ago and resulted from climatic change subsequent to the joining of all the earth's landmasses into one supercontinent.

The second event occurred around 65 million years ago and ended 150 million years of evolutionary processes that, among other things, had produced the dinosaurs. This mass extinction is believed by many researchers to have resulted from climatic changes following the impact of an asteroid.

A third major extinction event, perhaps of the same magnitude, is occurring now, and according to some scientists, it may have begun in the late Pleistocene or early **Holocene** (Ward, 1994). Unlike all other mass extinctions, the current one has not been caused by continental drift, climate change (so far), or collisions with asteroids. Rather, these recent and ongoing extinctions are due to the activities of a single species—*Homo sapiens*.

Many scientists, in fact, believe that several large mammalian species were pushed toward extinction by overhunting by earlier human populations, particularly near the end of the Pleistocene, some 10,000 years ago. In North America, at least 57 mammalian species became extinct, including the mammoth, mastodon, giant ground sloth, saber-toothed cat, several large rodents, and numerous ungulates (hooved mammals) or grazing animals (Lewin, 1986; Simmons, 1989). There is no dispute that climate change (warming) was a crucial factor in these extinctions, but hunting and other human activities may also have been important. Although there is some dispute as to when humans first entered North America from Asia, it is certain that they were firmly established by at least 12,000 years ago (and probably much earlier).

We have no direct evidence that early American big game hunters contributed to extinctions; but we do have evidence of what can happen to indigenous species when new areas are colonized by humans for the first time. Within just a few centuries of human occupation of New Zealand, the moa, a large flightless bird, was exterminated. Madagascar serves as a similar example. In the last thousand years, after the arrival of permanent human settlement, 14 species of lemurs, in addition to other mammalian and bird species, have become extinct (Jolly, 1985; Napier and Napier, 1985). One such species was *Megaladapis*, a lemur that weighed an estimated 300 pounds (Fleagle, 1999)! Lastly, scientists have debated for years whether the extinction of all large-bodied animals (some 60 species) in Australia during the late Pleistocene was due to human hunting and other activities or to climate change. Recently, Miller and colleagues (1999), using four different techniques, were able to date the rapid extinction of a large flightless bird, *Genyornis newtoni*, to about 50,000 years ago, a date that roughly coincides with the arrival of humans in Australia. This study suggests that the simultaneous extinction of this species in a number of localities occurred during a period of relative climatic stability and therefore is best explained as a consequence of human activities, especially the widespread burning of large areas and subsequent changes in vegetation. Previous studies have suggested that the incidence of fires increased substantially in Australia after the arrival of humans, and ethnographic reports indicate that the practice was common among indigenous Australians.

Hunter-gatherers, for whom we have some ethnographic evidence, differed in their views regarding conservation of prey species. Some groups believed that overhunting would anger deities. Others (some Great Basin Indians, for

Holocene The most recent epoch of the Cenozoic. Following the Pleistocene, it is estimated to have begun 10,000 years ago.

example) killed large numbers only every several years, allowing populations of game species, such as antelope, time to replenish. Still others avoided killing pregnant females or were conscientious about using all parts of the body to avoid waste. Nevertheless, there were some groups, such as the Hadza of the Pacific Northwest Coast, who appear not to have been especially concerned with conservation.

Moreover, hunting techniques were frequently incompatible with conservation. Prior to domestication of the horse (or its availability in the New World), the only effective way to hunt large herd animals was to organize game drives. In some cases, fire was used to drive stampeding animals into blind canyons or human-made "corrals." Other times, bison were driven over cliffs or into *arroyos* (narrow, deep gullies). Unfortunately, this practice often led to unavoidable waste, as more animals might be killed than could be utilized (even though it was common practice to store dried meats for future use). Moreover, there might be so many animals that it was impossible to retrieve those at the bottom of the pile.

The Olsen-Chubbuck site in eastern Colorado is a bison kill site where, in one hunt some 10,000 years ago, 190 bison (*Bison occidentalis*) were driven into an arroyo. (This species, approximately 25 percent larger than the familiar *Bison bison*, is believed to have become extinct approximately 7,000 years ago.) Of the 190 animals killed, 170 (90 percent) were partially or completely butchered (Wheat, 1972). The 20 complete skeletons of those left unbutchered were found at the bottom of the arroyo, where they would have been virtually inaccessible.

The evidence at Olsen-Chubbuck suggests a certain degree of overkill. In addition to the 20 untouched animals, many of those that were partially butchered appear to have remained mostly intact. As the Olsen-Chubbuck scenario was played out thousands of times over the course of many centuries, it is likely that such game drives contributed to the demise of at least some of the large-bodied prey species of the New World.

Since the end of the Pleistocene, human activities have continued to take their toll on nonhuman species. Today, however, species are disappearing at an unprecedented rate. Hunting, which occurs for a number of reasons other than acquisition of food, continues to be a factor. Competition with introduced nonnative species, such as pigs, goats, and rats, has also contributed to the problem. But in most cases, the most important single cause of extinction is habitat reduction.

Habitat reduction is a direct result of the burgeoning human population and the resulting need for building materials, grazing and agricultural land, and living areas. We are all aware of the risk to such visible species as the elephant, panda, rhinoceros, tiger, and mountain gorilla, to name a few. These risks are real, and within your lifetime some of these will certainly become extinct, at least in the wild. But the greatest threat to biodiversity is to the countless unknown species that live in the world's rain forests (fig. 14–5).

It is estimated that over half of all plants and animals on earth live in rain forests. By 1989, these habitats had been reduced to a little less than half their original size—that is, down to about 3 million square miles. The annual net loss between 1980 and 1995 was almost 67,000 square miles. As Harvard biologist E. O. Wilson puts it: "The loss is equal to the area of a football field every second. Put another way, in 1989 the surviving rain forests occupied an area about that of the continuous forty-eight states of the United States, and they were being reduced by an amount equivalent to the size of Florida every year" (Wilson, 1992, p. 275). By the year 2022, half the world's remaining rain forests figure 14–5 Stumps of recently felled forest trees are still visible in this newly cleared field in Rwanda. The haze is wood smoke from household fires.

will be gone if destruction continues at its present rate. This will result in a loss of between 10 and 22 percent of all rain forest species, or 5 to 10 percent of all plant and animal species on earth (Wilson, 1992).

Should we care about the loss of biodiversity? If so, why? In fact, most people do not show much concern. Moreover, reasons as to why we should care are usually stated in terms of the benefits (known and unknown) that humans may derive from rain forest species. An example of such a benefit is the chemical taxol (derived from the Pacific yew tree), which may be an effective treatment for ovarian and breast cancer.

It is undeniable that humans stand to benefit from continued research into potentially useful rain forest products. However, such anthropocentric reasons are not the sole justification for preserving the earth's biodiversity. Each species that is lost is the product of millions of years of evolution, and each fills a specific econiche. Quite simply, the destruction of so much of the planet's biota is within our power. But ethically, we must ask ourselves, is it within our rights?

Could the Human Species Become Extinct?

An obvious answer to this question is yes. After all, eventually (in a few billion years) there will be no sun, and ultimately no earth, so all life here will cease to exist. Of course, science fiction writers have long envisioned wide-ranging colonization of the galaxy by interstellar voyagers from earth. Perhaps such a circumstance will come about. Certainly, on this planet, we are the only species with the ability to envision our possible fate, and we alone have the capacity to do something about it.

However, it is only through such cultural and technological means that we as a species have a chance to endure. There are no biological guarantees. Most species that have existed on this planet have long since died out. Such could be the expected fate for all living forms.

Evolution, as commonly rendered in nature programs on television and in popular books, presents a misleading picture. We often are told that *species* are adapting to survive. But an understanding of evolutionary processes shows such statements to be nonsense. Life forms, through the central process of natural selection, compete as *individuals*. Their success in such competition is measured solely by their individual abilities to reproduce. Life forms, in following this biological imperative, may indeed prove to be individually successful but at the same time may be contributing to a situation highly detrimental to the species. For example, it is through such maximization of individual reproductive success that overpopulation occurs. Severe overexploitation of resources, a population "crash," and even complete extinction may ensue. But the individual organism obviously cannot foresee such a calamity and will, accordingly, act to maximize its own success—regardless of the ultimate effects on the species.

Humans, as we will discuss shortly, are in the midst of an explosive population increase. An increase of this magnitude is by no means unique, although it is probably unprecedented in such a large animal (and in one so environmentally "hungry"). Another biological lesson shows that we are but part of an integrated ecological system. As we expand so rapidly (and appear so successful in the short term), we cannot predict the potential negative effects of this very "success" for the long term.

It is clear, then, that all life forms *can* become extinct, even hominids. Robust australopithecines are sometimes depicted as overly specialized, rather dimwitted vegetarians. Yet, they were highly successful hominids in their own right and may have had significant cognitive and cultural capacities. One thing we know for certain: They endured for at least 1.5 million years; in the end, however, they vanished. As hominids, we can learn from such evolutionary history—if we choose to. To ignore the past might well condemn us to repeat it.

The Present Crisis: Our Cultural Heritage?

It would be difficult to escape the media attention given today to environmental problems. At some level, everyone is aware that problems exist. Unfortunately, it seems that few are aware of how serious the situation is, and even fewer still are prepared to do anything about it.

Overpopulation

If we had to point to one single challenge facing humanity, a problem to which virtually all others are tied, it would have to be population growth. We currently are trapped in a destructive cycle of our own making. Human population size has skyrocketed as we have increased our ability to produce food surpluses. As population size increases, more and more land is converted to crops, pasture, and construction, providing more opportunities for yet more people. Additionally, through the medical advances of the twentieth century, we have reduced mortality at both ends of the life cycle. Thus, fewer people die in childhood, and having survived to adulthood, they live longer than ever before. Although these medical advances are unquestionably beneficial to individuals (who has not benefited from medical technology?), it is also clear that there are significant detrimental consequences to the species and to the planet.

Population size, if left unchecked, increases exponentially, that is, as a function of some percent, like compound interest in a bank account. Currently, human population increases worldwide at an annual rate of about 1.8 percent. Although this figure may not seem too startling at first, it deserves some examination. In addition, it is useful to discuss doubling time, or the amount of time it takes for a population to double in size.

Scientists estimate that around 10,000 years ago, only about 5 million people inhabited the earth (not even half as many as live in Los Angeles County today). By A.D. 1650, there were perhaps 500 million, and by 1800, 1 billion. In other words, between 10,000 years ago and A.D. 1650 (a period of 9,650 years), population size doubled seven and a half times. On average, then, the doubling time between 10,000 years ago and 1650 was about 1,287 years. But from 1650 to 1800 it doubled again, which means that doubling time had been reduced to 150 years (Ehrlich and Ehrlich, 1990). And in the 37 years between 1950 and 1987, world population doubled from 2 billion to 4 billion. It is interesting to note that people born in the early 1950s were the first *ever* to see human population double during their lifetime.

Dates and associated population estimates up to the present are as follows: mid-1800s, 1 billion; 1930s, 2 billion; mid-1960s, 3 billion; mid-1980s, 4 billion; present, 6 billion (fig. 14–6). To state this problem in terms we can appreciate, we add 1 billion people to the world's population approximately every 11 years. That comes out to 90 to 95 million every year and roughly a quarter of a million every day!

figure 14–6 Line graph depicting exponential growth of human population. Note that for almost all of the last 5,000 years, the number of humans increased very slowly. It was not until 1650 that population size was even half a billion (500 million). The rapid increase to 1 billion by about 1850 is, in part, attributable to the Industrial Revolution. Population increase occurs as a function of some percent (in some developing countries, the annual rate is over 3 percent). With advances in food production and medical technologies, humans are now undergoing a population explosion, as this graph illustrates.

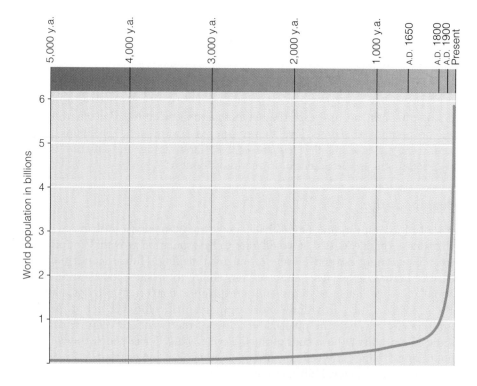

The rate of growth is not equally distributed among all nations. Although the world's rate of increase has ranged from 1.7 to 2.1 percent since the 1950s (Ehrlich and Ehrlich, 1990), it is the developing countries that share most of the burden (not to be interpreted as blame). During the 1980s, the population of Kenya grew at a rate of a little over 4 percent per year, while India added a million per month, and 36,000 babies were born every day in Latin America.

Fortunately, by the end of the twentieth century, rates of human population growth began to decline. The average number of children per female *worldwide* had dropped from 4.3 in 1960 to 2.6 in 2000. Moreover, by 2000, the replacement rate of 2.1 children per female (i.e., the number of births, accounting for early infant mortality, required for population size to increase) had been achieved in all western European countries, Thailand, and the nonimmigrant population of the United States (Wilson, 2000). It must also be mentioned that for the first time in history, the population of South Africa is now declining, but this fact is due primarily to the high incidence of HIV/AIDS (approximately 30 percent of adults are infected).

The decrease in family size worldwide is attributable to several factors, including the shift to a global economy, the migration of rural populations to urban centers with concomitant shifts in employment from agriculture to manufacturing and service sectors, and, at least in some countries, the increasing empowerment of women that has meant better education, increased opportunities in the workplace, and access to family planning.

The most recent United Nations International Conference on Population and Development set as its goal the development of a plan to contain the world's population to about 7.3 billion by the year 2015 and to prevent future growth. Otherwise, by the year 2050, human numbers could approach 10 billion. The United Nations plan emphasizes women's education, health, and rights throughout the world, but has met with stiff resistance from religious groups opposed to abortion and contraception.

The United Nations goal is an admirable but ambitious one, and achieving it will be a formidable task. Although the average number of live births per woman has declined, it will still be next to impossible to prevent huge population increases in the next century. Bear in mind that *approximately half of all people currently living in the developing world are less than 15 years old.* These young people have not yet reproduced, but they will.

You might logically ask, Can we not make technological changes sufficient to feed all these people? Certainly this and similar questions are being asked more frequently today than in the past. There surely are methods that would more efficiently utilize agricultural lands already available. Clearly, there are better ways to distribute the food surpluses already produced (in the United States in particular). But can we continue forever to make technological changes sufficient to feed ever-growing numbers of humans? Is there enough land to support an endless demand for housing, crop cultivation, and grazing? Is there enough water? We probably can develop technologies to meet our species' increasing needs for a while. But can we do so and still meet the requirements of thousands of undomesticated species? The answer for the immediate future is: probably not. For the long term, without major changes in human population growth, the answer is: certainly not.

The Greenhouse Effect and Global Warming

With increases in numbers comes greater consumption of nonrenewable resources. At the same time, activities involved in the production of goods and services produce waste and pollution, all of which leads to further environmental degradation.

Consider for a moment the fact that much of the energy used for human activities is derived from the burning of fossil fuels such as oil and coal (nonrenewable resources). The burning of fossil fuels increases the amount of carbon dioxide emitted into the atmosphere, and this, in turn, traps heat. Increased production of carbon dioxide and other "greenhouse gases," such as methane and chlorofluorocarbons (CFCs), is of growing concern to many in the scientific community who anticipate potentially dramatic climate change in the form of global warming. Deforestation, both in the tropics and North America, also has the potential to contribute to global warming, for we are reducing the number of trees available to absorb carbon dioxide. Moreover, in the tropics, trees are burned as land is cleared, a practice that releases carbon dioxide contained within vegetation into the atmosphere. In fact, an estimated 20 percent of all carbon dioxide emissions are accounted for by the burning of the Amazon rain forest alone (Ehrlich and Ehrlich, 1990). As a sobering note, Friends of the Earth, an environmental organization, estimated that between 50,000 and 80,000 fires were burning in the forests of Brazil at any given time during October 1991. And in Indonesia, an estimated 370,000 to 740,000 acres of forest were burned in 1997 alone (European Union GIS/Remote Sensing Expert Group, 1997). Most of these fires were caused by land-clearing activities in a region already suffering from severe drought. Because these fires also destroyed peat deposits (layers of ancient, decayed vegetation that serve as storehouses of carbon), an estimated 810 million to 2.6 billion metric tons (2,240 pounds) of carbon were released into the atmosphere. This amounts to between 13 to 40 percent of the world's annual carbon emissions from the burning of fossil fuels (Page et al., 2002).

The scientific community is now in almost complete agreement that we are seeing the effects of global warming. But while there is no doubt that greenhouse gases are building up in the atmosphere, there are still uncertainties as to the extent of the role played by human agricultural and industrial activities. (We should comment here that most of this uncertainty comes from politicians and others who do not wish to assume the political and financial costs associated with the enormous changes to business and industrial practices that would be necessary just to mitigate the effects and pace of climate change.) Uncertainty also surrounds the issue of the myriad ways climate change will be manifested. What is certain is that since records began being kept in 1860, the 1990s were the hottest decade, followed closely by the 1980s. The year 2002 has the distinction of being the warmest year on record, with 1998 running a close second. It is also accepted that the surface temperature of the earth has increased 0.3–0.6°C (0.54–1.1°F). The need for concern cannot be overstated. An increase in the mean annual temperature worldwide of even 0.5–1°C (1–2°F) could result in some melting of the polar caps with subsequent flooding of coastal areas.

Global warming is the result of the interactions of many factors, and the consequences of these interactions are not possible to predict with accuracy. But the consensus among scientists from many disciplines is that in general we can anticipate dramatic fluctuations in weather patterns with alterations in precipitation levels. The results of changing temperatures and rainfall include loss of agricultural lands due to desertification in some regions and flooding in others; increased human hunger and undernutrition; extinction of numerous plant and animal species; and altered patterns of infectious disease. Regarding the latter, health officials are particularly concerned about the spread of mosquito-borne diseases such as malaria, dengue fever, and yellow fever as warmer temperatures increase the geographical range of those species that serve as vectors for these potentially fatal conditions. And, in addition to altering the geographical distribution of insect and vertebrate disease vectors, changing climate conditions can also increase the range and reproductive rates of the very microbes that cause infectious disease.

Looking for Solutions

The massive problems facing our planet reflect an adaptive strategy gone awry. Indeed, it would seem that we no longer enjoy a harmonious relationship with culture. Instead, culture has become the environment in which we live, and every day that environment becomes increasingly hostile. All we need do is examine the very air we breathe to realize that we have overstepped our limits (fig. 14–7).

figure 14–7 Air pollution, increasingly a factor in human respiratory disease, is caused by human activities.

What can be done? Are the problems we have created amenable to human solution? Perhaps, but any objective assessment of the future offers little optimism. The declining quality of the air, depletion of the ozone layer, the greenhouse effect, reduced amounts of arable land, and the accumulation of refuse already seem catastrophic problems in a world of 6 billion people. How well does the world *now* cope with feeding, housing, and educating its inhabitants? What quality of life do the majority of the world's people enjoy right now? What kind of world have we wrought for the other organisms that share our planet as many are steadily isolated into fragments of what were once large habitats? If these concerns are not currently overwhelming enough, what kind of world will we see in 30 years, when the world's population numbers perhaps 8 billion?

In recent years, environmental concerns have been more widely discussed. Some world leaders now frequently pay lip service to preserving the environment. All this is well and good, but the real test of any policy will be the willingness of the world's population to sacrifice *now* for rewards that will not become apparent for perhaps several decades.

If there is any real chance of reversing current trends, *everyone* will have to sacrifice. In the developing world, family planning must universally be adopted to halt population expansion. Most cultures are so constructed, however, as to make such behavioral change very difficult. And sacrifice on the part of the developing world alone would not be adequate to stem the tide. It is entirely too convenient for someone from North America to point at residents of Bangladesh and demand that they control their rate of reproduction (it runs two to three times that of the United States). But consider this: The average American uses an estimated 400 times the resources consumed by a resident of Bangladesh (Ehrlich and Ehrlich, 1990)! The United States *alone* produces 25 to 30 percent of all carbon dioxide emissions into the atmosphere. Clearly, much of the responsibility for current problems rests squarely on the shoulders of the industrialized West.

In addition to population containment, the developed nations (most especially, the United States) must get along with far fewer resources. To accomplish any meaningful reduction in our wasteful habits, major behavioral changes and personal sacrifice will be required. For example, private automobile transportation (especially with only one passenger) and large, single-family dwellings are luxuries we enjoy, but they are luxuries the planet can ill afford. In addition, the dogs, cats, horses, and other pets we so prize are enormously costly in terms of resources. Must we then give up our pets as well? We could also ask, Wouldn't it be less costly to reduce our dietary intake of meat and grow grain to feed people directly?

Who is prepared to make the sacrifices that are required? Whence will the leadership come? The planet already faces serious problems, and there is little time left for indecision. Either we, as members of the species *Homo sapiens*, find the courage to make dramatic personal sacrifices, or we are doomed to suffer the consequences of our own folly.

Summary

tudies of human evolution have much to contribute to our understanding of how we, as a single species, came to exert such control over the destiny of our planet. It is a truly phenomenal story of how a small apelike creature walking on two feet across the African savanna challenged nature by learning to make stone tools. From these humble beginnings came large-brained humans who, instead of stone tools, have telecommunications satellites, computers, and nuclear arsenals at their fingertips. The human story is indeed unique and wonderful. Our two feet have carried us not only across the plains of Africa, but onto the polar caps, the ocean floor, and even across the surface of the moon! Surely, if we can accomplish so much in so short a time, we can act responsibly to preserve our home and the wondrous creatures who share it with us.

Questions for Review

1. How is human culture related to environmental degradation and overpopulation?
2. How are loss of biodiversity, environmental degradation, and human population growth related?
3. What is the current estimate of human population worldwide?
4. Are humans the most successful of all species? Why? How is success defined?
5. As early as the Mesolithic and Neolithic, human activities began to alter the landscape. Give two examples.
6. Human activities may have influenced extinction in the past as well as today. Give two examples.
7. Why do we say that culture, as an adaptive strategy, has gone awry?

Suggested Further Readings

Bell, Martin, and Michael J. C. Walker. 1992. *Late Quaternary Environmental Change*. New York: Wiley.

Fagan, Brian. 2000. *The Little Ice Age*. New York: Basic Books.

Gore, Al. 1992. *Earth in the Balance*. Boston: Houghton Mifflin.

Karl, Thomas R., Neville Nicholls, and Jonathan Gregory. 1997. "The Coming Climate." *Scientific American* 276(5): 78–83.

Monastersky, Richard. 1996. "Health in the Hot Zone." *Science News* 149(14): 218–219.

Runnels, Curtis N. 1995. "Environmental Degradation in Ancient Greece." *Scientific American* 272(3): 96–99.

Ward, Peter. 1994. *The End of Evolution*. New York: Bantam Books.

Wilson, Edward O. 1992. *The Diversity of Life*. Cambridge, MA: Harvard University Press.

——— 2002. *The Future of Life*. New York: Knopf.

World Resources. 1996–97. *A Guide to the Global Environment*. A joint publication by The World Resources Institute, the United Nations Environment Programme, the United Nations Development Programme, and the World Bank.

Multimedia Resources

 Companion Web Site

Anthropology Online: The Wadsworth Anthropology Resource Center Visit **http://anthropology.wadsworth.com** and click on the Companion Web Site for Jurmain/Kilgore/Trevathan/Nelson's *Essentials of Physical Anthropology*, Fifth Edition, to access a wide range of enrichment material to aid in your study of anthropology. Among the useful options for each chapter's self-study are learning objectives, flashcards, Internet exercises, Web links, InfoTrac College Edition exercises, and practice quizzes that can be scored and emailed to your instructor.

Atlas of Primate Skeletal Anatomy

Parietal

Temporal
Zygomatic
Occipital

Cervical vertebrae (7)

Lumbar vertebrae (5)

Ilium

Sacrum

Pubis

Ischium

Femur

Patella

Tibia

Fibula

Tarsals (7)
Metatarsals (5)
Phalanges (14)

Frontal

Maxilla
Mandible

Clavicle

Scapula

Sternum

Ribs

Thoracic vertebrae (12)

Humerus

Ulna

Radius

Carpals (8)

Metacarpals (5)

Phalanges (14)

figure A-1 Human Skeleton
(*Homo sapiens*)–bipedal hominid.

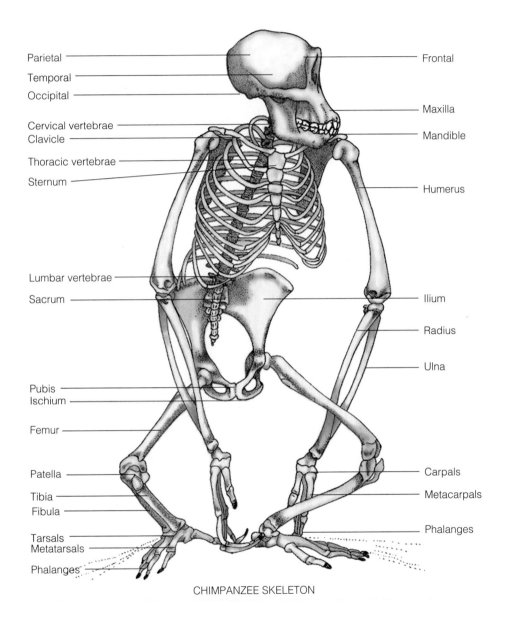

Parietal

Temporal

Occipital

Cervical vertebrae

Clavicle

Thoracic vertebrae

Sternum

Lumbar vertebrae

Sacrum

Pubis

Ischium

Femur

Patella

Tibia

Fibula

Tarsals

Metatarsals

Phalanges

Frontal

Maxilla

Mandible

Humerus

Ilium

Radius

Ulna

Carpals

Metacarpals

Phalanges

CHIMPANZEE SKELETON

figure A-2 Chimpanzee skelton (*Pan troglodytes*)–knuckle-walking pongid.

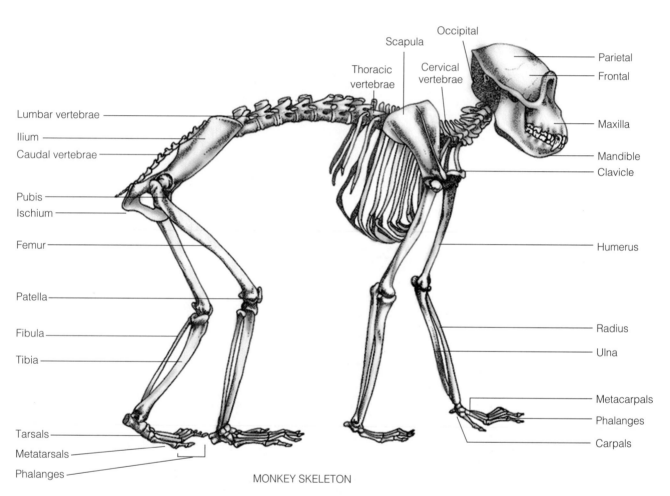

Occipital

Scapula

Thoracic
vertebrae

Cervical
vertebrae

Parietal

Frontal

Lumbar vertebrae

Ilium

Caudal vertebrae

Maxilla

Mandible

Clavicle

Pubis

Ischium

Femur

Humerus

Patella

Fibula

Tibia

Radius

Ulna

Metacarpals

Phalanges

Carpals

Tarsals

Metatarsals

Phalanges

MONKEY SKELETON

figure A–3 Monkey skeleton (rhesus macaque; *Macaca mulatta*)–a typical quadrupedal primate.

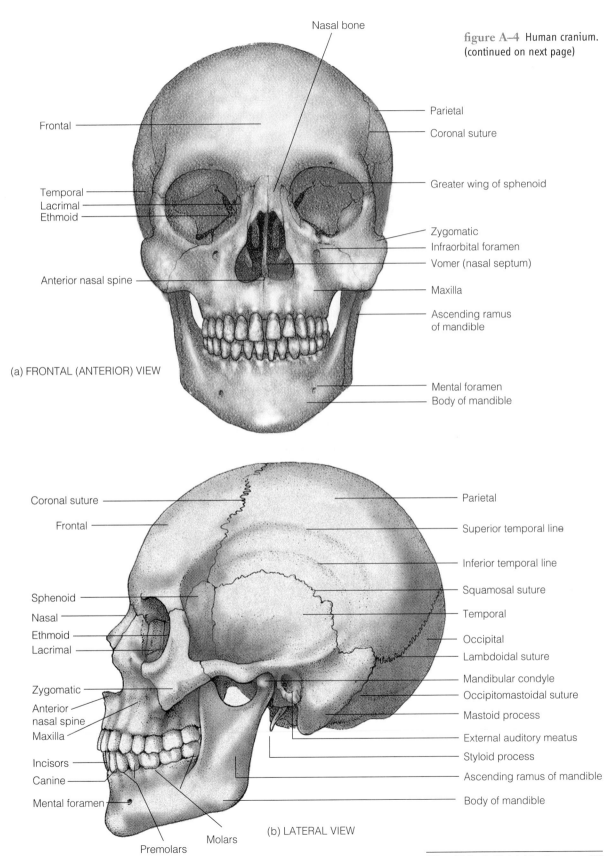

Nasal bone

figure A–4 Human cranium.
(continued on next page)

Parietal

Coronal suture

Frontal

Greater wing of sphenoid

Temporal
Lacrimal
Ethmoid

Zygomatic
Infraorbital foramen
Vomer (nasal septum)

Anterior nasal spine

Maxilla

Ascending ramus
of mandible

(a) FRONTAL (ANTERIOR) VIEW

Mental foramen
Body of mandible

Coronal suture

Parietal

Frontal

Superior temporal line

Inferior temporal line

Sphenoid

Squamosal suture

Nasal

Temporal

Ethmoid

Occipital

Lacrimal

Lambdoidal suture

Zygomatic

Mandibular condyle

Anterior
nasal spine

Occipitomastoidal suture

Maxilla

Mastoid process

Incisors

External auditory meatus

Canine

Styloid process

Ascending ramus of mandible

Mental foramen

Body of mandible

Premolars

Molars

(b) LATERAL VIEW

Incisors

Canine

Premolars

Maxilla

Molars

Zygomatic arch

Vomer

Foramen spinosum

Styloid process

External auditory meatus

Jugular foramen

Hypoglossal canal

Mastoid foramen

Inferior nuchal line

Superior nuchal line

External occipital protuberance

Zygomatic bone

Zygomatic process of maxilla

Palatine bone

Zygomatic process of temporal

Sphenoid

Pterygoid process

Mandibular fossa

Carotid canal

Stylomastoid foramen

Foramen magnum

Occipital condyle

Parietal

Occipital

(c) BASILAR VIEW

Frontal

Bregma

Inferior temporal line

Superior temporal line

Coronal suture

Parietal

Sagittal suture

Lambdoidal suture

Occipital

(d) SUPERIOR VIEW

Sagittal suture

Lambda

Occipital

Mastoid process

Parietal

Lambdoidal suture

Nuchal line

(e) REAR VIEW

figure A–4 Human cranium.
(continued)

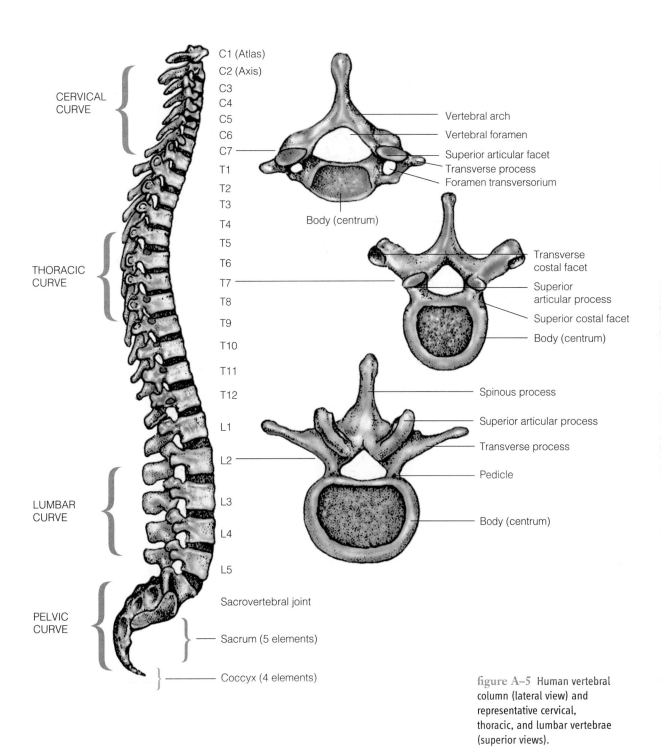

CERVICAL CURVE

C1 (Atlas)
C2 (Axis)
C3
C4
C5
C6
C7

Vertebral arch
Vertebral foramen
Superior articular facet
Transverse process
Foramen transversorium

Body (centrum)

T1
T2
T3
T4

THORACIC CURVE

T5
T6
T7
T8
T9
T10
T11
T12

Transverse costal facet
Superior articular process
Superior costal facet
Body (centrum)

L1

Spinous process
Superior articular process
Transverse process
Pedicle

LUMBAR CURVE

L2
L3
L4
L5

Body (centrum)

PELVIC CURVE

Sacrovertebral joint
Sacrum (5 elements)
Coccyx (4 elements)

figure A–5 Human vertebral column (lateral view) and representative cervical, thoracic, and lumbar vertebrae (superior views).

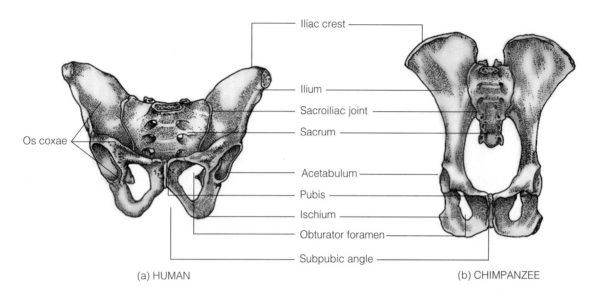

(a) HUMAN   (b) CHIMPANZEE

Figure A–6 Pelvic girdles.

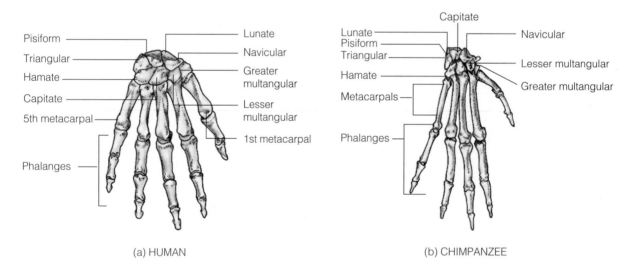

(a) HUMAN   (b) CHIMPANZEE

figure A–7 Hand anatomy.

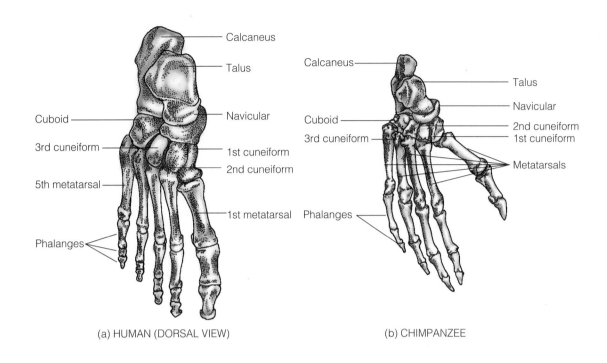

(a) HUMAN (DORSAL VIEW)

Calcaneus

Talus

Navicular

Cuboid

3rd cuneiform

5th metatarsal

1st cuneiform

2nd cuneiform

1st metatarsal

Phalanges

(b) CHIMPANZEE

Calcaneus

Talus

Navicular

Cuboid

3rd cuneiform

2nd cuneiform

1st cuneiform

Metatarsals

Phalanges

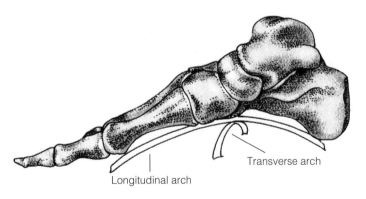

(c) HUMAN (MEDIAL VIEW)

Longitudinal arch

Transverse arch

figure A–8 Foot (pedal) anatomy.

Summary of Early Hominid Fossil Finds from Africa

Sahelanthropus

Taxonomic designation:
Sahelanthropus tchadensis
Year of first discovery: 2001
Dating: ~7 m.y.a.
Fossil material: Nearly complete cranium, 2 jaw fragments, 3 isolated teeth

Location of finds: Toros Menalla, Chad, central Africa

Ardipithecus

Taxonomic designation:
Ardipithecus ramidus
Year of first discovery: 1992
Dating: Earlier sites, 5.8–5.6 m.y.a.; Aramis, 4.4 m.y.a.
Fossil material: Earlier materials: 1 jaw fragment, 4 isolated teeth, postcranial remains (foot phalanx, 2 hand phalanges, 2 humerus fragments, ulna). Later sample (Aramis) represented by many fossils, including up to 50 individuals (many postcranial elements, including at least 1 partial skeleton). Considerable fossil material retrieved from Aramis but not yet published; no reasonably complete cranial remains yet published.

Location of finds: Middle Awash region, including Aramis (as well as earlier localities), Ethiopia, East Africa

Orrorin

Taxonomic designation:
Orrorin tugenensis
Year of first discovery: 2000
Dating: ~6 m.y.a.
Fossil material: 2 jaw fragments, 6 isolated teeth, postcranial remains (femoral pieces, partial humerus, hand phalanx). No reasonably complete cranial remains yet discovered.

Location of finds: Lukeino Formation, Tugen Hills, Baringo District, Kenya, East Africa

Australopithecus anamensis

Taxonomic designation:
Australopithecus anamensis
Year of first discovery: 1965 (but not recognized as separate species at that time); more remains found in 1994 and 1995.
Dating: 4.2–3.9 m.y.a.
Fossil material: Total of 22 specimens, including cranial fragments, jaw fragments, and postcranial pieces (humerus, tibia, radius). No reasonably complete cranial remains yet discovered.

Location of finds: Kanapoi, Allia Bay, Kenya, East Africa

Australopithecus afarensis

Taxonomic designation:
Australopithecus afarensis
Year of first discovery: 1973
Dating: 3.7–3.0 m.y.a.
Fossil material: Large sample, with up to 65 individuals represented: 1 partial cranium, numerous cranial pieces and jaws, many teeth, numerous postcranial remains, including partial skeleton. Fossil finds from Laetoli also include dozens of fossilized footprints.

Location of finds: Laetoli (Tanzania), Hadar (Ethiopia), also likely found at East Turkana (Kenya) and Omo (Ethiopia), East Africa

Kenyanthropus

Taxonomic designation:
Kenyanthropus platyops
Year of first discovery: 1999
Dating: 3.5 m.y.a.
Fossil material: Partial cranium, temporal fragment, partial maxilla, 2 partial mandibles

Location of finds: Lomekwi, West Lake Turkana, Kenya, East Africa

Australopithecus garhi

Taxonomic designation:
Australopithecus garhi
Year of first discovery: 1997
Dating: 2.5 m.y.a.
Fossil material: Partial cranium, numerous limb bones

Location of finds: Bouri, Middle Awash, Ethiopia, East Africa

Australopithecus aethiopicus

Taxonomic designation:
Australopithecus aethiopicus
(also called *Parantropus aethiopicus*)
Year of first discovery: 1985
Dating: 2.4 m.y.a.
Fossil material: Nearly complete cranium

Location of finds: West Lake Turkana, Kenya

Australopithecus boisei

Taxonomic designation:
Australopithecus boisei (also called *Paranthropus boisei*)
Year of first discovery: 1959
Dating: 2.4–1.2 m.y.a.
Fossil material: 2 nearly complete crania, several partial crania, many jaw fragments, dozens of teeth. Postcrania less represented, but parts of several long bones recovered.

Location of finds: Olduvai Gorge and Peninj (Tanzania), East Lake Turkana (Koobi Fora), Chesowanja (Kenya), Omo (Ethiopia)

Australopithecus africanus

Taxonomic designation:
Australopithecus africanus
Year of first discovery: 1924
Dating: ~3.3–1.0 m.y.a.
Fossil material: 1 mostly complete cranium, several partial crania, dozens of jaws/partial jaws, hundreds of teeth, 4 partial skeletons representing significant parts of the postcranium

Location of finds: Taung, Sterkfontein, Makapansgat, Gladysvale (all from South Africa)

Australopithecus robustus

Taxonomic designation:
Australopithecus robustus (also called *Paranthropus robustus*)
Year of first discovery: 1938
Dating: ~2–1 m.y.a.
Fossil material: 1 complete cranium, several partial crania, many jaw fragments, hundreds of teeth, numerous postcranial elements

Location of finds: Kromdraai, Swartkrans, Drimolen, Cooper's Cave, possibly Gondolin (all from South Africa)

Early *Homo*

Taxonomic designation:
Homo habilis

Year of first discovery:
1959/1960

Dating: 2.4–1.8 m.y.a.

Fossil material: 2 partial crania, other cranial pieces, jaw fragments, several limb bones, partial hand, partial foot, partial skeleton

Early *Homo*

Taxonomic designation:
Homo rudolfensis

Year of first discovery: 1972

Dating: ~1.8 m.y.a.

Fossil material: 4 partial crania, 1 mostly complete mandible, other jaw pieces, numerous teeth, a few postcranial elements (none directly associated with crania)

Location of finds: Olduvai Gorge (Tanzania), Lake Baringo (Kenya), Omo (Ethiopia), Sterkfontein (?) (South Africa)

Location of finds: East Lake Turkana (Koobi Fora), Kenya, East Africa

APPENDIX C
Population Genetics

As noted in Chapter 12, the basic approach in population genetics makes use of a mathematical model called the Hardy-Weinberg equilibrium equation. The Hardy-Weinberg theory of genetic equilibrium postulates a set of conditions in a population where *no* evolution occurs. In other words, none of the forces of evolution are acting, and all genes have an equal chance of recombining in each generation (i.e., there is random mating of individuals). More precisely, the hypothetical conditions that such a population would be *assumed* to meet are as follows:

1. The population is infinitely large. This condition eliminates the possibility of random genetic drift or changes in allele frequencies due to chance.
2. There is no mutation. Thus, no new alleles are being added by molecular changes in gametes.
3. There is no gene flow. There is no exchange of genes with other populations that can alter allele frequencies.
4. Natural selection is not operating. Specific alleles confer no advantage over others that might influence reproductive success.
5. Mating is random. There are no factors that influence who mates with whom. Thus, any female is assumed to have an equal chance of mating with any male.

If all these conditions are satisfied, allele frequencies will not change from one generation to the next (i.e., no evolution will take place), and a permanent equilibrium will be maintained as long as these conditions prevail. An evolutionary "barometer" is thus provided that may be used as a standard against which actual circumstances are compared. Similar to the way a typical barometer is standardized under known temperature and altitude conditions, the Hardy-Weinberg equilibrium is standardized under known evolutionary conditions.

Note that the idealized conditions that define the Hardy-Weinberg equilibrium are just that: an idealized, *hypothetical* state. In the real world, no actual population would fully meet any of these conditions. But do not be confused by this distinction. By explicitly defining the genetic distribution that would be *expected* if *no* evolutionary change were occurring (i.e., in equilibrium), we can compare the *observed* genetic distribution obtained from actual human populations. The evolutionary barometer is thus evaluated through comparison of these observed allele and genotype frequencies with those expected in the pre-defined equilibrium situation.

If the observed frequencies differ from those of the expected model, then we can say that evolution is taking place at the locus in question. The alternative, of course, is that the observed and expected frequencies do not differ sufficiently to state unambiguously that evolution is occurring at a locus in a population. Indeed, frequently this is the result that is obtained, and in such cases, population geneticists are unable to delineate evolutionary changes at the particular locus under study. Put another way, geneticists are unable to reject what statisticians call the *null hypothesis* (where "null" means nothing, a statistical condition of randomness).

The simplest situation applicable to a microevolutionary study is a genetic trait that follows a simple Mendelian pattern and has only two alleles (*A, a*). As you recall from earlier discussions, there are then only three possible genotypes: *AA, Aa, aa*. Proportions of these genotypes (*AA:Aa:aa*) are a function of the *allele frequencies* themselves (percentage of *A* and percentage of *a*). To provide uniformity for all genetic loci, a standard notation is employed to refer to these frequencies:

> Frequency of dominant allele (*A*) = *p*
> Frequency of recessive allele (*a*) = *q*

Since in this case there are only two alleles, their combined total frequency must represent all possibilities. In other words, the sum of their separate frequencies must be 1:

$$p \quad + \quad q \quad = \quad 1$$

| (frequency of *A* alleles) | (frequency of *a* alleles) | (100% of alleles at that locus) |

To ascertain the expected proportions of genotypes, we compute the chances of the alleles combining with one another into all possible combinations. Remember, they all have an equal chance of combining, and no new alleles are being added.

These probabilities are a direct function of the frequency of the two alleles. The chances of all possible combinations occurring randomly can be simply shown as

$$\begin{array}{r} p \ + \ q \\ \times \ p \ + \ q \\ \hline pq \ + \ q^2 \\ p^2 \ + \ pq \\ \hline p^2 \ + \ 2pq \ + \ q^2 \end{array}$$

Mathematically, this is known as a binomial expansion and can also be shown as

$$(p + q)(p + q) = p^2 + 2pq + q^2$$

What we have just calculated is simply:

Allele Combination	Genotype Produced	Expected Proportion in Population
Chances of *A* combining with *A*	*AA*	$p \times p = p^2$
Chances of *A* combining with *a*;	*Aa*	$p \times q$
a combining with *A*	*aA*	$p \times q$ $= 2\,pq$
Chances of *a* combining with *a*	*aa*	$q \times q = q^2$

Thus, p^2 is the frequency of the *AA* genotype, *2pq* is the frequency of the *Aa* genotype, and q^2 is the frequency of the *aa* genotype, where *p* is the frequency of the dominant allele and *q* is the frequency of the recessive allele in a population.

Calculating Allele Frequencies: An Example

How geneticists use the Hardy-Weinberg formula is best demonstrated through an example. Let us assume that a population contains 200 individuals, and we will use the MN blood group locus as the gene to be measured. This gene produces a blood group antigen—similar to ABO—located on red blood cells. Because the *M* and *N* alleles are codominant, we can ascertain everyone's phenotype by taking blood samples and observing reactions with specially prepared antisera. From the phenotypes, we can then directly calculate the *observed* allele frequencies. So let us proceed.

All 200 individuals are tested, and the results are shown in Table C–1. Although the match between observed and expected frequencies is not perfect, it is close enough statistically to satisfy equilibrium conditions. Since our population is not a large one, sampling may easily account for the small observed deviations. Our population is therefore probably in equilibrium (i.e., at this locus, it is not evolving). At the minimum, what we can say scientifically is that we cannot reject the *null hypothesis*.

TABLE C–1 Calculating Allele Frequencies in a Hypothetical Population

Observed Data

Genotype	Number of individuals*	Percent	Number of Alleles M	N
MM	80	40%	160	0
MN	80	40%	80	80
NN	40	20%	0	80
Totals	200	100%	240 +	160 = 400
		Proportion:	.6 +	.4 = 1

*Each individual has two alleles. Thus, a person who is *MM* contributes two *M* alleles to the total gene pool. A person who is *MN* contributes one *M* and one *N*. Two hundred individuals, then, have 400 alleles for the *MN* locus.

Observed Allele Frequencies

$M = .6(p)$

$N = .4(q)$ ($p + q$ should equal 1, and they do)

Expected Frequencies

What are the predicted genotypic proportions if genetic equilibrium (no evolution) applies to our population? We simply apply the Hardy-Weinberg formula:
$p^2 + 2pq + q^2$.

p^2	=	(.6)(.6)	=	.36
$2pq$	=	2(.6)(.4) = 2(.24)	=	.48
q^2	=	(.4)(.4)	=	.16
Total				1.00

There are only three possible genotypes (*MM:MN:NN*), so the total of the relative proportions should equal 1; as you can see, they do.

Comparing Frequencies

How do the expected frequencies compare with the observed frequencies in our population?

	Expected Frequency	Expected Number of Individuals	Observed Frequency	Actual Number of Individuals with Each Genotype
MM	.36	72	.40	80
MN	.48	96	.40	80
NN	.16	32	.20	40

APPENDIX D
Sexing and Aging the Skeleton

The field of physical anthropology that is directly concerned with the analysis of skeletal remains is called *osteology*. Using an osteological perspective allows researchers to study skeletons of both human and nonhuman primates to understand the ways in which hominids are similar to, and distinct from, other primates. Moreover, paleoanthropologists also use many of the same techniques to analyze the remains of fossil hominids (which mostly consist of teeth and bones). In more recent contexts, encompassing the last few thousand years, skeletal remains of *Homo sapiens* have been investigated by osteologists to learn about the size, nutritional status, and diseases present in prior human populations.

Two very important questions that osteologists ask when analyzing a skeleton are the sex and age of the individual. Such basic demographic variables as sex and age are crucial in any comprehensive osteological analysis, especially of human remains.

Sexing the Skeleton

During infancy and childhood, male and female skeletons do not differ much. Consequently, osteologists usually cannot determine the sex of a skeleton of someone who died before 13 to 15 years of age. However, during development, *sexual dimorphism* is increasingly manifested in the skeleton, making sex determination feasible in adult remains, provided enough of the skeleton is present.

The differences between male and female skeletons are most clearly expressed in the pelvis (*pl.*, pelves), and this variation is due to the requirements of childbirth in females. In particular, during hominid evolution, the dual influences of bipedal locomotion and relatively large-brained newborns placed adaptive constraints on pelvic anatomy. As a result, in females the pelvis is generally broader and more splayed out than in males. The most useful criteria for sex determination are listed in Table D–1 and illustrated in Figure D–1. While these criteria, taken together, are good indicators of sex, you should be aware that none, taken in isolation, is accurate in all cases. Moreover, this is not a complete listing of all traits used in sexing skeletons, although it does include those most commonly used.

There are also sex differences in cranial dimensions, most especially relating to facial proportions. However, these differences are not as consistent as those in the pelvis. Therefore, it is important to recognize patterns of cranial

TABLE D-1	Differences Between the Male and Female Pelvis	
Pelvic Characteristic	Female	Male
General	Muscle attachments less robust; overall appearance sometimes less massive	Muscle attachments more robust; overall appearance sometimes more massive
Subpubic angle	Wider (more than 90°)	Narrower (less than 90°)
Greater sciatic notch	Wider—more open (more than 68°)	Narrower—more closed (less than 68°)
Ischiopubic ramus (medial view)	Thinner	Thicker
Ventral arc (elevated ridge on ventral surface of pubis)	Frequently present	Absent
Sacrum	Wider and straighter	Narrower and more curved

figure D–1 Male and female pelves compared.

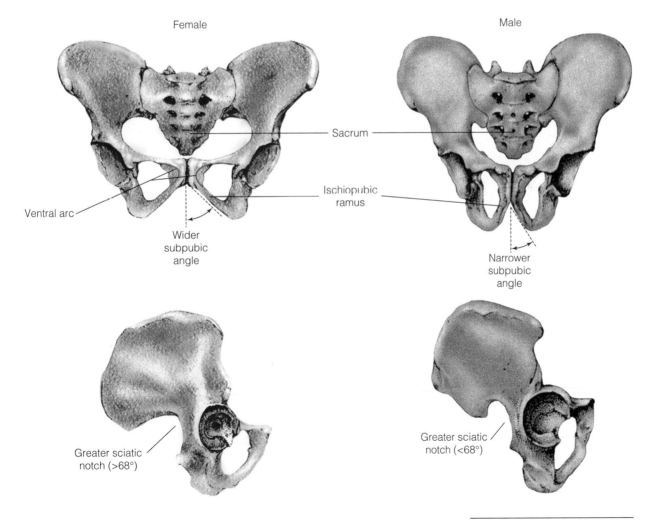

Female

Male

Sacrum

Ischiopubic ramus

Ventral arc

Wider subpubic angle

Narrower subpubic angle

Greater sciatic notch (>68°)

Greater sciatic notch (<68°)

TABLE D-2	Cranial Variation Between Males and Females	
Cranial Feature	Females	Males
Points of muscle attachment (e.g., mastoid process)	Less pronounced	Larger, more pronounced
Supraorbital torus (browridge)	Less pronounced or absent	More pronounced
Supraorbital rim (upper margin of eye orbit)	Sharper	More rounded
Palate	More shallow	Deeper

variation as they are expressed in different populations. The cranial features most commonly used for sex determination are listed in Table D–2 (see also fig. D–2). These differences reflect the fact that in males, the skeleton is larger than in females. The bones are denser, and areas of muscle attachment are frequently more robust. However, such differences are not consistently expressed across various populations, and knowledge of relevant population variation is thus important in drawing reasonable determinations of sex.

Determining Age

During growth, the skeleton and dentition undergo developmental changes that occur within known age ranges. Thus, estimating age in individuals who were younger than 20 when they died is based primarily on the presence of deciduous (baby) and permanent teeth, the appearance of ossification centers of bones, and the fusion of the ends of long bones to bone shafts.

figure D–2 Cranium and mandible.

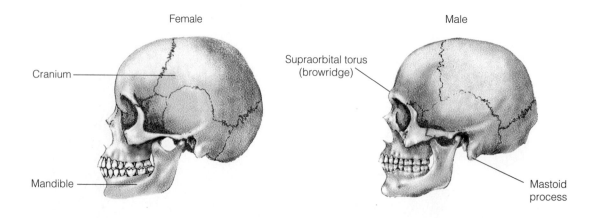

Dental Eruption

Age estimation based on dental eruption is useful in individuals up to approximately 15 years of age. The third molar (wisdom tooth) erupts after this time, but the age of eruption of this tooth (if it forms at all) is highly variable. Thus, the third molar is not a very reliable indicator of age except that its presence indicates that the individual was at least a young adult (fig. D–3).

Bone Growth

The size of long bones, the development of secondary ossification centers (epiphyses), and the degree of fusion of epiphyses to bone shafts are just as important as dental eruption. Postcranial bones are preceded by a cartilage model that is gradually replaced by bone, both in the diaphyses (shafts) and the secondary centers (the ends of the bones, or epiphyses). In children and adolescents, bones continue to grow until the epiphyses fuse to the diaphyses. Because this fusion occurs within different age ranges in different bones, the age of an individual can be estimated by determining which epiphyses have fused and which have not (fig. D–4). The characteristic undulating appearance of the unfused surfaces helps differentiate immature elements from the broken end of a mature bone.

figure D–3 Dental development.

Gumline

(a) Birth: The crowns for all the deciduous teeth (shown in color) are present; no roots, however, have yet formed.

First permanent molar crown

(b) 2 years: All deciduous teeth (shown in color) are erupted; the first permanent molar and permanent incisors have crowns (unerupted) formed, but no roots.

Third molar

(c) 12 years: All permanent teeth are erupted except the third molar (wisdom tooth).

Head fuses to shaft:
males aged 16 to 18,
females aged 15 to 17

Greater tubercle fuses
to head at 2 to 4 years

Proximal
epiphysis

Diaphysis

(a) Birth

(b) 5 years

(c) 10 years

(d) 15 years

(e) 16+ years

Trochlea fuses to lower shaft:
males aged 14 to 16,
females aged 13 to 15

Medial epicondyle fuses:
males aged 16 to 18,
females aged 15 to 17

figure D–4 Skeletal age: epi-physeal union in the humerus. Some regions of the humerus exhibit some of the earliest fusion centers in the body, while others are among the latest to complete fusion (not until late adolescence).

Other Skeletal Changes

Once a person has reached physiological maturity (by the early 20s), determinations of age become more difficult and less precise. Several techniques are used, and these are based on the occurrence of progressive, regular changes in the face of the pubic symphysis (the most common technique), in the sternal ends of the ribs, and in the auricular surface of the ilium (where the ilium articulates with the sacrum). Other indicators are closure of the cranial sutures and cellular changes that are determined by microscopic examination of cross sections of long bones. Degenerative changes, such as arthritis, osteoporosis, and wear of dental enamel, can also aid in the determination of relative age (older versus younger), but they provide imprecise estimates. In fact, it is very difficult to age accurately the skeletons of adults. For example, the presence of severe tooth wear would imply that the individual was not young, but enamel attrition varies between populations and depends on many factors, including diet. Moreover, the appearance of many degenerative changes is influenced by disease, trauma, and the biological makeup of individuals. Thus, at present, osteologists must be content to use broad age ranges when estimating age at death in mature skeletons.

PUBIC SYMPHYSEAL FACE   The face of the pubic symphysis in young individuals is characterized by a billowing surface (with ridges and furrows) such as that seen on the surface of an epiphysis (fig. D–5). The symphyseal face undergoes regular age-related changes from the age of about 18 onward.

The first aging technique based on alterations of the pubic symphysis was developed by T. W. Todd (1920, 1921), utilizing dissection room cadavers. McKern and Stewart (1957) developed a technique by analyzing a sample of American males killed in the Korean War. Both of the samples from which these systems were derived, however, have limitations. The dissection room sample used by Todd contained some individuals of uncertain age, and the Korean War sample was predominantly made up of young white males, with few being older than 35.

More recently, a system has been developed by Katz and Suchey (1986) based on an autopsy sample of 739 males for whom documentation of age was provided by death certificates. This sample has proved more representative of the general population than the earlier samples. Because this technique is derived from data collected from a large sample of people of known age at death, it is currently the most accurate method available for estimating age in adult human skeletal remains.

figure D–5 Skeletal age: remodeling of the pubic symphysis. This area of the pelvis shows systematic changes progressively throughout adult life. Two of these stages are shown in (b) and (c).

Pubic symphysis

(a) Position of the pubic symphysis.

(b) Age 21. The face of the symphysis shows the typical "billowed" appearance of a young joint; no rim present.

(c) Age mid-50s. The face is mostly flat, with a distinct rim formed around most of the periphery.

Glossary

Acclimatization Physiological response to changes in the environment that occurs during an individual's lifetime. Such responses may be short-term. The capacity for acclimatization may typify an entire population or species. This capacity is under genetic influence and thus is subject to evolutionary factors such as natural selection.

Acheulian (ash´-oo-lay-en) Pertaining to a stone tool industry of the Lower and Middle Pleistocene characterized by a large proportion of bifacial tools (flaked on both sides). Acheulian tool kits are very common in Africa, Southwest Asia, and western Europe, but are less common elsewhere. (Also spelled "Acheulean.")

Adaptation Functional response of organisms or populations to the environment. Adaptation results from evolutionary change, specifically as a result of natural selection.

Adaptive niche The entire way of life of an organism: where it lives, what it eats, how it gets food, how it avoids predators, etc.

Adaptive radiation The relatively rapid expansion and diversification of life forms into new ecological niches.

Adolescent growth spurt The period during adolescence in which well-nourished teens typically increase in stature at greater rates than at other points in the life cycle.

Affiliative Pertaining to amicable associations between individuals. Affiliative behaviors, such as grooming, reinforce social bonds and promote group cohesion.

Allele frequency In a population, the percentage of all the alleles at a locus accounted for by one specific allele.

Alleles Alternate forms of a gene. Alleles occur at the same locus on homologous chromosomes and thus govern the same trait. However, because they are different, their action may result in different expressions of that trait. The term is often used synonymously with *genes*.

Altruism Any behavior or act that benefits another individual but poses some potential risk or cost to oneself.

Amino acids Small molecules that are the components of proteins.

Analogies Similarities between organisms based strictly on common function, with no assumed common evolutionary descent.

Anatomically modern *Homo sapiens* All modern humans and some fossil forms, perhaps dating as early as 200,000 y.a.; defined by a set of derived characteristics, including cranial architecture and lack of skeletal robusticity; usually classified at the subspecies level as *Homo sapiens sapiens*.

Ancestral (primitive) Referring to characters inherited by a group of organisms from a remote ancestor and thus not diagnostic of groups (lineages) branching subsequent to the time the character first appeared.

Anthropocentric Viewing nonhuman phenomena in terms of human experience and capabilities; emphasizing the importance of humans over everything else.

Anthropoids Members of a suborder of Primates, the *Anthropoidea* (pronounced "ann-throw-poid´-ee-uh"). Traditionally, the suborder includes monkeys, apes, and humans.

Anthropology The field of inquiry that studies human culture and evolutionary aspects of human biology; includes cultural anthropology, archaeology, linguistics, and physical (or biological) anthropology.

Anthropometry Measurement of human body parts. When osteologists measure skeletal elements, the term *osteometry* is often used.

Antigens Large molecules found on the surface of cells. Several different loci governing antigens on red and white blood cells are known. (Foreign antigens provoke an immune response in individuals.)

Arboreal Tree-living; adapted to life in the trees.

Arboreal hypothesis The traditional view that primate characteristics can be explained as a consequence of primate diversification into arboreal habitats.

Archaic *Homo sapiens* Earlier forms of *Homo sapiens* (including Neandertals) from the Old World that differ from *H. erectus* but lack the full set of characteristics diagnostic of modern *H. sapiens*.

Artifacts Objects or materials made or modified for use by hominids. The earliest artifacts tend to be tools made of stone or, occasionally, bone.

Aurignacian Pertaining to an Upper Paleolithic stone tool industry in Europe beginning at about 40,000 y.a.

Australopithecines (os-tra-loh-pith´-e-seens) The colloquial name for members of the genus *Australopithecus*. The term was first used as a subfamily designation, but is now mostly used informally.

Australopithecus An early hominid genus, known from the Plio-Pleistocene of Africa, characterized by bipedal locomotion, a relatively small brain, and large back teeth.

Autonomic Pertaining to physiological responses not under voluntary control. An example in chimpanzees would be the erection of body hair during excitement. An example in humans is blushing. Both convey information regarding emotional states, but neither is a deliberate behavior, and communication is not intended.

Autosomes All chromosomes except the sex chromosomes.

Balanced polymorphism The maintenance of two or more alleles in a population due to the selective advantage of the heterozygote.

Behavioral ecology The study of the evolution of behavior, emphasizing the role of ecological factors as agents of natural selection. Behaviors and behavioral patterns have been selected for because they increase reproductive fitness in individuals (i.e., they are adaptive) in specific ecological contexts.

Binocular vision Vision characterized by overlapping visual fields provided by forward-facing eyes; essential to depth perception.

Binomial nomenclature (*binomial*, meaning "two names") In taxonomy, the convention established by Carolus Linnaeus whereby genus and species names are used to refer to species. For example, *Homo sapiens* refers to human beings.

Biocultural Pertaining to the concept that biology makes culture possible and that culture influences biology.

Biocultural evolution The mutual, interactive evolution of human biology and culture; the concept that biology makes culture possible and that developing culture further influences the direction of biological evolution; a basic concept in understanding the unique components of human evolution.

Biological continuum The fact that organisms are related through common ancestry and that behaviors and traits seen in one species are also seen in others to varying degrees. (When expressions of a phenomenon continuously grade into one another so that there are no discrete categories, they are said to exist on a continuum. Color is one such phenomenon.)

Biological determinism The concept that various attributes and behaviors (e.g., intelligence, values, morals) are governed by biological (genetic) factors; the inaccurate association of various behavioral attributes with certain biological traits, such as skin color.

Biological species concept A depiction of species as groups of individuals capable of fertile interbreeding but reproductively isolated from other such groups.

Bipedal locomotion Walking on two feet. Walking habitually on two legs is the single most distinctive feature of the hominids.

Bipedally On two feet. Walking habitually on two legs is the single most distinctive feature of the family Hominidae.

Brachiation A form of locomotion in which the body is suspended beneath the hands and support is alternated from one forelimb to the other; arm swinging.

Brachycephalic Having a broad head in which the width measures more than 80 percent of the length.

Breeding isolates Populations that are clearly isolated geographically and/or socially from other breeding groups.

Burins Small, chisel-like tools (with a pointed end) thought to have been used to engrave bone, antler, ivory, or wood.

Catastrophism The view that the earth's geological landscape is the result of violent cataclysmic events. This view was promoted by Cuvier, especially in opposition to Lamarck.

Centromere The constricted portion of a chromosome. After replication, the two strands of a double-stranded chromosome are joined at the centromere.

Cercopithecines (serk oh-pith´-eh-seens) The subfamily of Old World monkeys that includes baboons, macaques, and guenons.

Chatelperronian Pertaining to an Upper Paleolithic tool industry found in France and Spain, containing blade tools and associated with Neandertals.

Chordata The phylum of the animal kingdom that includes vertebrates.

Chromosomes Discrete structures composed of DNA and protein found only in the nuclei of cells. Chromosomes are visible only under magnification during certain stages of cell division.

Chronometric (*chronos*, meaning "time," and *metric*, meaning "measure") Referring to a dating technique that gives an estimate in actual number of years.

Cladistics An approach to classification that seeks to make rigorous evolutionary interpretations based solely on analysis of certain types of homologous characters (those considered derived characters).

Cladogram A chart showing evolutionary relationships as determined by cladistic analysis. It is based solely on interpretation of shared derived characters. No time component is indicated, and ancestor-descendant relationships are *not* implied.

Classification In biology, the ordering of organisms into categories, such as orders, families, and genera, to show evolutionary relationships.

Cline A gradual change in the frequency of genotypes and phenotypes from one geographical region to another.

Clone An organism that is genetically identical to another organism. The term may also be used to refer to genetically identical DNA segments and molecules.

Codominance The expression of two alleles in heterozygotes. Because neither allele is dominant or recessive, both influence the phenotype.

Codons The triplets of messenger RNA bases that correspond to specific amino acids during protein synthesis.

Colobines (kole´-uh-beans) The subfamily of Old World monkeys that includes the African colobus monkeys and Asian langurs.

Communication Any act that conveys information, in the form of a message, to another individual. Frequently, the result of communication is a change in the behavior of the recipient. Communication may not be deliberate but may be the result of involuntary processes or a secondary consequence of an intentional action.

Complementary Referring to the fact that DNA bases form base pairs in a precise manner. For example, adenine can bond only to thymine. Thus, these two bases are said to be *complementary* because one requires the other to form a complete DNA base pair.

Continental drift The movement of continents on sliding plates of the earth's surface. As a result, the positions of large landmasses have shifted dramatically during the earth's history.

Continuum A set of relationships in which all components fall along a single integrated spectrum. All life reflects a single biological continuum.

Core area The portion of a home range containing the highest concentration of resources.

Crepuscular Active during the evening or dawn.

Culture All aspects of human adaptation, including technology, traditions, language, religion, marriage patterns, and social roles. Culture is a set of learned behaviors that is transmitted from one generation to the next by nonbiological means.

Cusps The elevated portions (bumps) on the chewing surfaces of premolar and molar teeth.

Cytoplasm The portion of the cell contained within the cell membrane, excluding the nucleus. The cytoplasm consists of a semifluid material and contains numerous structures involved with cell function.

Data (*sing.*, datum) Facts from which conclusions can be drawn; scientific information.

Deoxyribonucleic acid (DNA) The double-stranded molecule that contains the genetic code. DNA is a main component of chromosomes.

Derived (modified) Referring to characters that are modified from the ancestral condition and thus *are* diagnostic of particular evolutionary lineages.

Development Differentiation of cells into different types of tissues and their maturation.

Displays Sequences of repetitious behaviors that serve to communicate emotional states. Nonhuman primate displays are most frequently associated with reproductive or agonistic behavior.

Diurnal Active during the day.

Dolichocephalic Having a long, narrow head in which the width measures less than 75 percent of the length.

Dominance hierarchies Systems of social organization wherein individuals within a group are ranked relative to one another. Higher-ranking individuals have greater access to preferred food items and mating partners than lower-ranking individuals. Dominance hierarchies have sometimes been referred to as "pecking orders."

Dominant Describing a trait governed by an allele that can be expressed in the presence of another, different allele (i.e., in heterozygotes). Dominant alleles prevent the expression of recessive alleles in heterozygotes. (This is the definition of *complete* dominance.)

Ecological Pertaining to the relationship between organisms and all aspects of their environment (temperature, predators, other animals, vegetation, availability of food and water, types of food, etc.).

Ecological niches The positions of species within their physical and biological environments, together making up the *ecosystem*. A species' ecological niche is defined by such components as diet, terrain, vegetation, type of predators, relationships with other species, and activity patterns, and each niche is unique to a given species.

Empirical Relying on experiment or observation; from the Latin *empiricus*, meaning "experienced."

Endemic Continuously present in a population.

Endocast A solid impression of the inside of the skull, often preserving details relating to the size and surface features of the brain.

Endogamy Mating with individuals from the same group.

Endothermic (*endo*, meaning "within" or "internal") Able to maintain internal body temperature through the production of energy by means of metabolic processes within cells; characteristic of mammals, birds, and perhaps some dinosaurs.

Enzymes Specialized proteins that initiate and direct chemical reactions in the body.

Epochs Categories of the geological time scale; subdivisions of periods. In the Cenozoic, epochs include the Paleocene, Eocene, Oligocene, Miocene, and Pliocene (from the Tertiary) and the Pleistocene and Holocene (from the Quaternary).

Essential amino acids The 9 (of 22) amino acids that must be obtained from the food we eat because they are not synthesized in the body in sufficient amounts.

Estrus (ess´-truss) Period of sexual receptivity in female mammals (except humans), correlated with ovulation. When used as an adjective, the word is spelled "estrous."

Ethnocentric Viewing other cultures from the inherently biased perspective of one's own culture. Ethnocentrism often results in cultures being seen as inferior to one's own.

Ethnographies Detailed descriptive studies of human societies. In cultural anthropology, an ethnography is traditionally the study of a non-Western society.

Eugenics The philosophy of "race improvement" through the forced sterilization of members of some groups and encouraged reproduction among others; an overly simplified, often racist, view that is now discredited.

Evolution A change in the genetic structure of a population. The term is also frequently used to refer to the appearance of a new species.

Evolutionary systematics A traditional approach to classification (and evolutionary interpretation) in which presumed ancestors and descendants are traced in time by analysis of homologous characters.

Exogamy Mating pattern whereby individuals obtain mates from groups other than their own.

Faunal Referring to animal remains; in archaeology, specifically refers to the fossil remains of animals.

Fitness Pertaining to natural selection, a measure of relative reproductive success of individuals. Fitness can be measured by an individual's genetic contribution to the next generation compared to that of other individuals.

Fixity of species The notion that species, once created, can never change; an idea diametrically opposed to theories of biological evolution.

Flexed The position of the body in a bent orientation, with the arms and legs drawn up to the chest.

Forensic anthropology An applied anthropological approach dealing with legal matters. Physical anthropologists work with coroners and others in the identification and analysis of human remains.

Founder effect A type of genetic drift in which allele frequencies are altered in small populations that are taken from, or are remnants of, larger populations.

Frugivorous (fru-give´-or-us) Having a diet composed primarily of fruit.

Gametes Reproductive cells (eggs and sperm in animals) developed from precursor cells in ovaries and testes.

Gene A sequence of DNA bases that specifies the order of amino acids in an entire protein or, in some cases, a portion of a protein. A gene may be made up of hundreds or thousands of DNA bases.

Gene flow Exchange of genes between populations.

Gene pool The total complement of genes shared by the reproductive members of a population.

Genetic drift Evolutionary changes—that is, changes in allele frequencies—produced by random factors. Genetic drift is a result of small population size.

Genetics The study of gene structure and action and the patterns of inheritance of traits from parent to offspring. Genetic mechanisms are the underlying foundation for evolutionary change.

Genome The entire genetic makeup of an individual or species. In humans, it is estimated that each individual possesses approximately 3 billion DNA nucleotides.

Genotype The genetic makeup of an individual. Genotype can refer to an organism's entire genetic makeup or to the alleles at a particular locus.

Genus A group of closely related species

Geological time scale The organization of earth history into eras, periods, and epochs; commonly used by geologists and paleoanthropologists.

Grooming Picking through fur to remove dirt, parasites, and other materials that may be present. Social grooming is common among primates and reinforces social relationships.

Growth Increase in mass or number of cells.

Habitual bipedalism Bipedal locomotion on the ground is the form of locomotion shown by hominids most of the time.

Hardy-Weinberg theory of genetic equilibrium The mathematical relationship expressing—under ideal conditions—the predicted distribution of alleles in populations; the central theorem of population genetics.

Hemoglobin A protein molecule that occurs in red blood cells and binds to oxygen molecules.

Heterodont Having different kinds of teeth; characteristic of mammals, whose teeth consist of incisors, canines, premolars, and molars.

Heterozygous Having different alleles at the same locus on members of a pair of homologous chromosomes.

Holocene The most recent epoch of the Cenozoic. Following the Pleistocene, it is estimated to have begun 10,000 years ago.

Home range The entire area exploited by an animal or group of animals.

Homeostasis A condition of balance or stability within a biological system, maintained by the interaction of physiological mechanisms that compensate for changes (both external and internal).

Hominidae The taxonomic family to which humans belong; also includes other, now extinct, bipedal relatives.

Hominids Colloquial term for members of the family Hominidae, which includes all bipedal hominoids back to the divergence from African great apes.

Hominoidea The formal designation for the superfamily of anthropoids that includes apes and humans.

Homo habilis (hab´-ih-liss) A species of early *Homo*, well known from East Africa but perhaps also found in other regions.

Homologies Similarities between organisms based on descent from a common ancestor.

Homologous Referring to members of chromosome pairs. Homologous chromosomes carry genes that govern the same traits. During meiosis, homologous chromosomes pair and exchange segments of DNA. They are alike with regard to size and also position of the centromere.

Homoplasy (*homo*, meaning "same," and *plasy*, meaning "growth") The separate evolutionary development of similar characteristics in different groups of organisms.

Homozygous Having the same allele at the same locus on both members of a pair of chromosomes.

Hormones Substances (usually proteins) that are produced by specialized cells and that travel to other parts of the body, where they influence chemical reactions and regulate various cellular functions.

Human Genome Project An international effort aimed at sequencing and mapping the entire human genome.

Hybrids Offspring of mixed ancestry; heterozygotes.

Hypothesis (*pl.*, hypotheses) A provisional explanation of a phenomenon. Hypotheses require verification.

Hypoxia Lack of oxygen. Hypoxia can refer to reduced amounts of available oxygen in the atmosphere (due to lowered barometric pressure) or to insufficient amounts of oxygen in the body.

Intelligence Mental capacity; ability to learn, reason, or comprehend and interpret information, facts, relationships, meanings, etc.; the capacity to solve problems, whether through the application of previously acquired knowledge or through insight.

Interspecific Between species; refers to variation beyond that seen within the same species to include additional aspects seen between two different species.

Intraspecific Within species; refers to variation seen within the same species.

Ischial callosities Patches of tough, hard skin on the buttocks of Old World monkeys and chimpanzees.

K-selected Pertaining to an adaptive strategy whereby individuals produce relatively few offspring, in whom they invest increased parental care. Although only a few infants are born, chances of survival are increased for each individual because of parental investments in time and energy. Examples of nonprimate K-selected species are birds and canids (e.g., wolves, coyotes, and dogs).

Lactose intolerance The inability to digest fresh milk products, caused by the discontinued production of *lactase*, the enzyme that breaks down lactose, or milk sugar.

Large-bodied hominoids Those hominoids including the great apes (orangutans, chimpanzees, gorillas) and hominids, as well as all ancestral forms back to the time of divergence from small-bodied hominoids (i.e., the gibbon lineage).

Locus (*pl.*, loci) (lo´-kus, lo-sigh´) The position on a chromosome where a given gene occurs. The term is sometimes used interchangeably with *gene*, but this usage is technically incorrect.

Macaques (muh-kaks´) Group of Old World monkeys comprising several species, including rhesus monkeys.

Macroevolution Changes produced only after many generations, such as the appearance of a new species.

Magdalenian Pertaining to the final phase of the Upper Paleolithic stone tool industry in Europe.

Mammalia The technical term for the formal grouping (class) of mammals.

Material culture The physical manifestations of human activities; includes tools, art, and structures. As the most durable aspects of culture, material remains make up the majority of archaeological evidence of past societies.

Meiosis Cell division in specialized cells in ovaries and testes. Meiosis involves two divisions and results in four daughter cells, each containing only half the original number of chromosomes. These cells can develop into gametes.

Menarche The first menstruation in girls, usually occurring in the early to mid-teens.

Mendelian traits Characteristics that are influenced by alleles at only one genetic locus. Examples include many blood types, such as ABO. Many genetic disorders, including sickle-cell anemia and Tay-Sachs disease, are also Mendelian traits.

Menopause The end of menstruation in human women, usually occurring at around age 50.

Mesolithic The period preceding the Neolithic, during which humans increasingly exploited smaller animals (including fish), increased the variety of tools they used, and became somewhat less nomadic.

Messenger RNA (mRNA) A form of RNA that is assembled on a sequence of DNA bases. It carries the DNA code to the ribosome during protein synthesis.

Metazoa Multicellular animals; a major division of the animal kingdom.

Microevolution Small changes occurring within species, such as a change in allele frequencies.

Midline An anatomical term referring to a hypothetical line that divides the body into right and left halves.

Mitochondria (*sing.*, mitochondrion) Structures contained within the cytoplasm of eukaryotic cells that convert energy, derived from nutrients, into a form that is used by the cell.

Mitochondrial DNA (mtDNA) DNA found in the mitochondria that is inherited only from the mother.

Mitosis Simple cell division; the process by which somatic cells divide to produce two identical daughter cells.

Molecules Structures made up of two or more atoms. Molecules can combine with other molecules to form more complex structures.

Morphology The form (shape, size) of anatomical structures; can also refer to the entire organism.

Mosaic evolution A pattern of evolution in which the rate of evolution in one functional system varies from that in other systems. For example, in hominid evolution, the dental system, locomotor system, and neurological system (especially the brain) all evolved at markedly different rates.

Mousterian Pertaining to the stone tool industry associated with Neandertals and some modern *H. sapiens* groups; also called Middle Paleolithic. This industry is characterized by a larger proportion of flake tools than is found in Acheulian tool kits.

Mutation A change in DNA. Technically, mutation refers to changes in DNA bases (specifically called point mutations); also refers to changes in chromosome number and/or structure.

Multidisciplinary Pertaining to research that involves mutual contributions and cooperation of several different experts from various scientific fields (i.e., disciplines).

Natural selection The mechanism of evolutionary change first articulated by Charles Darwin; refers to genetic change or changes in the frequencies of certain traits in populations due to differential reproductive success between individuals.

Neolithic The period during which humans began to domesticate plants and animals. The Neolithic is also associated with increased sedentism. Dates for the Neolithic vary from region to region, depending on when domestication occurred.

Neural tube In early embryonic development, the anatomical structure that develops to form the brain and spinal cord.

Nocturnal Active during the night.

Nondisjunction The failure of homologous chromosomes or chromosome strands to separate during cell division.

Nuchal torus (nuke´-ul) (nuchal, meaning "neck") A projection of bone in the back of the cranium where neck muscles attach, used to hold up the head. The nuchal torus is a distinctive feature of *H. erectus*.

Nucleotides Basic units of the DNA molecule, composed of a sugar, a phosphate, and one of four DNA bases.

Nucleus A structure (organelle) found in all eukaryotic cells. The nucleus contains chromosomes (nuclear DNA).

Obligate bipedalism Since major anatomical changes in the spine, pelvis, and the lower limb are required for bipedal locomotion, once hominids adapted to this mode of locomotion, it made other forms of locomotion on the ground impossible. (In other words, bipedalism became the *only* form of hominid terrestrial locomotion.)

Omnivorous Having a diet consisting of many food types (i.e., plant materials, meat, and insects).

Osteology The study of skeletal material. Human osteology focuses on the interpretation of the skeletal remains of past groups. Some of the same techniques are used in paleo-anthropology to study early hominids.

Paleoanthropology The interdisciplinary approach to the study of earlier hominids—their chronology, physical structure, archaeological remains, habitats, etc.

Paleopathology The branch of osteology that studies the evidence of disease and injury in human skeletal (or, occasionally, mummified) remains.

Paleospecies Species defined from fossil evidence, often covering a long time span.

Pandemic An extensive outbreak of disease affecting large numbers of people over a wide area; potentially, a worldwide phenomenon.

Paranthropus (par´-an-throw´-puss) A genus of early hominid characterized by very large back teeth and jaws. Frequently, this genus is combined into *Australopithecus*.

Pathogens Substances or microorganisms, such as bacteria, fungi, or viruses, that cause disease.

Phenotypes The observable or detectable physical characteristics of an organism; the detectable expressions of genotypes.

Phenotypic ratio The proportion of one phenotype to other phenotypes in a group of organisms. For example, Mendel observed that there were approximately three tall plants for every short plant in the F_2 generation. This is expressed as a phenotypic ratio of 3:1.

Phylogenetic tree A chart showing evolutionary relationships as determined by phylogenetic systematics. It contains a time component and implies ancestor-descendant relationships.

Phylogeny A schematic representation showing ancestor-descendant relationships, usually in a chronological framework.

Plasticity The capacity to change. In a physiological context, the ability of systems or organisms to make alterations in order to respond to differing conditions.

Pleiotropic genes Genes that have more than one effect; genes that have different effects at different times in the life cycle.

Pleistocene The epoch of the Cenozoic from 1.8 m.y.a. until 10,000 y.a. Frequently referred to as the Ice Age, this epoch is associated with continental glaciations in northern latitudes.

Plio-Pleistocene Pertaining to the Pliocene and first half of the Pleistocene, a time range of 5–1 m.y.a. For this time period, many early fossil hominids have been found in Africa.

Polyandry A mating system wherein a female continuously associates with more than one male (usually two or three) with whom she mates. Among nonhuman primates, this pattern is seen only in marmosets and tamarins.

Polygenic Referring to traits that are influenced by genes at two or more loci. Examples of such traits are stature, skin color, and eye color. Many polygenic traits are also influenced by environmental factors.

Polymerase chain reaction (PCR) A method of producing thousands of copies of a DNA segment using the enzyme DNA polymerase.

Polymorphisms Characteristics that are governed by a genetic locus with more than one allele. Polymorphic traits have more than one expression. ABO blood type is an example of a Mendelian polymorphic trait. Eye color is a polygenic example.

Polytypic Referring to species composed of populations that differ with regard to the expression of one or more traits.

Population Within a species, a community of individuals where mates are usually found.

Population geneticists Geneticists who study the frequencies of alleles, genotypes, and phenotypes in populations.

Population genetics A mathematical and statistical approach used to measure and explain evolutionary change in contemporary populations.

Postcranial (*post*, meaning "after") In a quadruped, referring to that portion of the body behind the head; in a biped, referring to all parts of the body *beneath* the head (i.e., from the neck down).

Prehensility The ability to grasp objects, as by the hands and/or feet of primates.

Primate A member of the order of mammals Primates (pronounced "pry-may´-tees"), which includes prosimians, monkeys, apes, and humans.

Primatologists Scientists who study the evolution, anatomy, and behavior of nonhuman primates. Those who study behavior in noncaptive animals are usually trained as physical anthropologists.

Primatology The study of the biology and behavior of nonhuman primates (prosimians, monkeys, and apes).

Primitive Referring to a trait or combination of traits present in an ancestral form.

Principle of independent assortment The distribution of one pair of alleles into gametes does not influence the distribution of another pair. The genes controlling different traits are inherited independently of one another.

Principle of segregation Genes (alleles) occur in pairs (because chromosomes occur in pairs). During gamete production, the members of each gene pair separate, so that each gamete contains one member of each pair. During fertilization, the full number of chromosomes is restored, and members of gene or allele pairs are reunited.

Prosimians Members of a suborder of Primates, the *Prosimii* (pronounced "pro-sim´-ee-eye"). Traditionally, the suborder includes lemurs, lorises, and tarsiers.

Protein synthesis The assembly of chains of amino acids into functional protein molecules. The process is directed by DNA.

Proteins Three-dimensional molecules that serve a wide variety of functions through their ability to bind to other molecules.

Protohominids The earliest members of the hominid lineage, as yet only barely represented in the fossil record. Thus, their structure and, especially, behavior are reconstructed hypothetically.

Punctuated equilibrium The concept that evolutionary change proceeds through long periods of stasis punctuated by rapid periods of change.

Quadrupedal Using all four limbs to support the body during locomotion; the basic mammalian (and primate) form of locomotion.

Quantitatively In a manner involving measurements of quantity and including such properties as size, number, and capacity. When data are quantified, they are expressed numerically and are capable of being tested statistically.

r-selected Pertaining to an adaptive strategy that emphasizes relatively large numbers of offspring and reduced parental care (compared to K-selected species). (*K-selection* and *r-selection* are relative terms; e.g., mice are r-selected compared to primates but K-selected compared to many fish species.)

Recessive Describing a trait that is not expressed in heterozygotes; also refers to the allele that governs the trait. For a recessive allele to be expressed, there must be two copies of the allele (i.e., the individual must be homozygous).

Recombinant DNA technology A process in which genes from the cell of one species are transferred to somatic cells or gametes of another species.

Recombination The exchange of DNA between homologous chromosomes during meiosis; also called "crossing over."

Replicate To duplicate. The DNA molecule is able to make copies of itself.

Reproductive strategies The complex of behavioral patterns that contributes to individual reproductive success. The behaviors need not be deliberate, and they often vary considerably between males and females.

Reproductive success The number of offspring an individual produces and rears to reproductive age; an individual's genetic contribution to the next generation, as compared to the contributions of other individuals.

Rhinarium (rine-air´-ee-um) The moist, hairless pad at the end of the nose seen in most mammalian species. The rhinarium enhances an animal's ability to smell.

Ribonucleic acid (RNA) A single-stranded molecule, similar in structure to DNA. The three forms of RNA are essential to protein synthesis.

Ribosomes Structures composed of a specialized form of RNA and protein. Ribosomes are found in the cell's cytoplasm and are essential to the manufacture of proteins.

Science A body of knowledge gained through observation and experimentation; from the Latin *scientia*, meaning "knowledge."

Scientific method A research method whereby a problem is identified, a hypothesis (or hypothetical explanation) is stated, and that hypothesis is tested through the collection and analysis of data. If the hypothesis is verified, it becomes a theory.

Scientific testing The precise repetition of an experiment or expansion of observed data to provide verification; the procedure by which hypotheses and theories are verified, modified, or discarded.

Sectorial Adapted for cutting or shearing; among primates, refers to the compressed (side-to-side) first lower premolar, which functions as a shearing surface with the upper canine.

Selective pressures Forces in the environment that influence reproductive success in individuals. In the example of the peppered moth, birds applied the selective pressure.

Senescence The process of physiological decline in body function that occurs with aging.

Sex chromosomes In mammals, the X and Y chromosomes.

Sexual dimorphism Differences in physical characteristics between males and females of the same species. For example, humans are slightly sexually dimorphic for body size, with males being taller, on average, than females of the same population.

Sexual selection A type of natural selection that operates on only one sex within a species. It is the result of competition for mates, and it can lead to sexual dimorphism with regard to one or more traits.

Shared derived Relating to specific character states shared in common between two forms and considered the most useful for making evolutionary interpretations.

Sites Locations of discoveries. In paleontology and archaeology, a site may refer to a region where a number of discoveries have been made.

Slash-and-burn agriculture A traditional land-clearing practice whereby trees and vegetation are cut and burned. In many areas, fields are abandoned after a few years and clearing occurs elsewhere.

Social structure The composition, size, and sex ratio of a group of animals. Social structures, in part, are the result of natural selection in specific habitats, and they function to guide individual interactions and social relationships.

Sociobiology The study of the relationship between natural selection and behavior. Unlike the approach of behavioral ecology, sociobiological theory does not strongly emphasize ecological factors.

Socioecology The study of animals and all aspects of their habitats that attempts to identify relationships between components of the environment and behavior.

Somatic cells Basically, all the cells in the body except those involved with reproduction.

Specialized Evolved for a particular function; usually refers to a specific trait (e.g., incisor teeth), but may also refer to the entire way of life of an organism.

Speciation The process whereby a new species evolves from a prior species. Speciation is the most basic process in macroevolution.

Species A group of organisms that can interbreed to produce fertile offspring. Members of one species are reproductively isolated from members of all other species (i.e., they cannot mate with them to produce fertile offspring).

Spina bifida A condition in which the arch of one or several vertebrae fails to fuse and form a protective barrier around the spinal cord.

Stereoscopic vision The condition whereby visual images are, to varying degrees, superimposed on one another. This provides for depth perception, or the perception of the external environment in three dimensions. Stereoscopic vision is partly a function of structures in the brain.

Stratigraphy Sequential layering of deposits.

Stratum (*pl.*, strata) Geological layer.

Stress In a physiological context, any factor that acts to disrupt homeostasis; more precisely, the body's response to any factor that threatens its ability to maintain homeostasis.

Taxonomy The branch of science concerned with the rules of classifying organisms on the basis of evolutionary relationships.

Territories Areas that will be aggressively protected against intrusion, particularly by other members of the same species.

Theory A broad statement of scientific relationships or underlying principles that has been at least partially verified.

Transfer RNA (tRNA) The type of RNA that binds to specific amino acids and transports them to the ribosome during protein synthesis.

Transmutation The change of one species to another. The term *evolution* did not assume its current meaning until the late nineteenth century.

Uniformitarianism The theory that the earth's features are the result of long-term processes that continue to operate in the present as they did in the past. Elaborated on by Lyell, this theory opposed catastrophism and provided for immense geological time.

Upper Paleolithic A cultural period usually associated with early modern humans (but also associated with Neandertals) and distinguished by technological innovation in various stone tool industries. Best known from western Europe, similar industries are also known from central and eastern Europe and Africa.

Variation (genetic) Inherited differences between individuals; the basis of all evolutionary change.

Vasoconstriction Narrowing of blood vessels, reducing blood flow to the skin. Vasoconstriction is an involuntary response to cold and reduces heat loss at the skin's surface.

Vasodilation Expansion of blood vessels, permitting increased blood flow to the skin. Vasodilation permits warming of the skin and also facilitates radiation of warmth as a means of cooling. Vasodilation is an involuntary response to warm temperatures, various drugs, and even emotional states (blushing).

Vectors Agents that transmit disease from one carrier to another. Mosquitoes are vectors for malaria, just as fleas are vectors for bubonic plague.

Vertebrates Animals with bony backbones; includes fishes, amphibians, reptiles, birds, and mammals.

World view General cultural orientation or perspective shared by members of a society.

Zygote A cell formed by the union of an egg and a sperm cell. It contains the full complement of chromosomes (in humans, 46) and has the potential of developing into an entire organism.

Bibliography

Adcock, Gregory J., Elizabeth S. Snow, Dennis Simon, et al.
  2001 "Mitochondrial DNA Sequences in Ancient Australians: Implications for Modern Human Origins." *Proceedings of the National Academy of Sciences,* **98**:537–542.
Aitken, M. J., C. B. Stringer, and P. A. Mellars (eds.)
  1993 *The Origin of Modern Humans and the Impact of Chronometric Dating.* Princeton, NJ: Princeton University Press.
Alexander, R.D.
  1974 "The Evolution of Social Behavior." *Ann. Rev. Ecol. Syst.,* **5**:325–383.
Arsuaga, Juan-Luis, et al.
  1993 "Three New Human Skulls from the Sima de los Huesos Middle Pleistocene Site in Sierra de Atapuerca, Spain." *Nature,* **362**:534–537.
Arsuaga, J. L., I. Martinez, A. Garcia, et al.
  1997 "Sima de los Huesos (Sierra de Atapuerca, Spain). The Site." *Journal of Human Evolution,* **33**:109–127.
Ascenzi, A., I. Bidditu, P. F. Cassoli, et al.
  1996 "A Calvarium of Late *Homo erectus* from Ceprano, Italy." *Journal of Human Evolution,* **31**:409–423.
Asfaw, Berhane, Tim White, Owen Lovejoy, et al.
  1999 "*Australopithecus garhi*: A New Species of Early Hominid from Ethiopia." *Science,* **284**:629–635.

Badrian, Alison and Noel Badrian
  1984 "Social Organization of *Pan paniscus* in the Lomako Forest, Zaire." *In: The Pygmy Chimpanzee,* Randall L. Susman (ed.), New York: Plenum Press, pp. 325–346.
Badrian, Noel and Richard K. Malenky
  1984 "Feeding Ecology of *Pan paniscus* in the Lomako Forest, Zaire." *In: The Pygmy Chimpanzee,* Randall L. Susman (ed.), New York: Plenum Press, pp. 275–299.
Bartlett, Thad. Q., Robert W. Sussman, and James M. Cheverud
  1993 "Infant Killing in Primates: A Review of Observed Cases with Specific References to the Sexual Selection Hypothesis." *American Anthropologist,* **95**(4):958–990.
Bartstra, Gert-Jan
  1982 "*Homo erectus erectus*: The Search for Artifacts." *Current Anthropology,* **23**(3):318–320.

Bar-Yosef, O.
  1993 "The Role of Western Asia in Modern Human Origins." *In:* M. J. Aitken, et al. (eds.), q.v., pp. 132–147.

———
  1994 "The Contributions of Southwest Asia to the Study of the Origin of Modern Humans." *In: Origins of Anatomically Modern Humans,* M.H. Nitecki and D. V. Nitecki (eds.), New York: Plenum Press, pp. 23–66.
Bearder, Simon K.
  1987 "Lorises, Bushbabies & Tarsiers: Diverse Societies in Solitary Foragers." *In:* Smuts, et al., q.v., pp. 11–24.
Begun, D. and A. Walker
  1993 "The Endocast." *In:* A. Walker and R. E. Leakey (eds), q.v., pp. 326–358.
Bell, Martin and Michael J. C. Walker
  1992 *Late Quaternary Environmental Change.* New York: John Wiley and Sons.
Ben Shaul, D. M.
  1962 "The Composition of the Milk of Wild Animals." *International Zoo Yearbook,* **4**:333–342.
Berger, Thomas and Erik Trinkaus
  1995 "Patterns of Trauma Among the Neandertals." *Journal of Archaeological Science,* **22**:841–852.
Binford, Lewis R.
  1981 *Bones. Ancient Men and Modern Myths.* New York: Academic Press.
Binford, Lewis R. and Chuan Kun Ho
  1985 "Taphonomy at a Distance: Zhoukoudian, 'The Cave Home of Beijing Man'?" *Current Anthropology,* **26**:413–442.
Binford, Lewis R. and Nancy M. Stone
  1986a "The Chinese Paleolithic: An Outsider's View." *AnthroQuest,* Fall 1986(1):14–20.

———
  1986b "Zhoukoudian: A Closer Look." *Current Anthropology,* **27**(5):453–475.
Boaz, N. T. and Russell L. Ciochon
  2001 "The Scavenging of *Homo erectus pekinensis*." *Natural History,* **110**(2):46–51.

Boesch, Christophe and H. Boesch
1989   "Hunting Behavior of Wild Chimpanzees in the Tai National Park." *American Journal of Physical Anthropology*, **78**:547–573.

——— 1990   "Tool Use and Tool Making in Wild Chimpanzees." *Folia Primatologica*, **54**:86–99.

Bogin, Barry
1988   *Patterns of Human Growth*. Cambridge: Cambridge University Press.

Brace, C. L. and Ashley Montagu
1977   *Human Evolution* (2nd Ed.). New York: Macmillan.

Brace, C. Loring, H. Nelson, and N. Korn
1979   *Atlas of Human Evolution* (2nd Ed.). New York: Holt, Rinehart & Winston.

Bromage, Timothy G. and Christopher Dean
1985   "Re-evaluation of the Age at Death of Immature Fossil Hominids." *Nature*, **317**:525–527.

Brooks, Alison, et al.
1995   "Dating and Context of Three Middle Stone Age Sites with Bone Points in the Upper Semliki Valley, Zaire." *Science*, **268**:548–553.

Brown, T. M. and K. D. Rose
1987   "Patterns of Dental Evolution in Early Eocene Anaptomorphine Primates Comomyidael from the Bighorn Basin, Wyoming." *Journal of Paleontology*, **61**:1–62.

Brunet, Michel, et al.
1995   "The First Australopithecine 2,500 Kilometers West of the Rift Valley (Chad)." *Nature*, **378**:273–274.

Carbonell, E., et al.
1995   "Lower Pleistocene Hominids and Artifacts from Atapuerca-TDG (Spain)." *Science*, **269**:826–830.

Carrol, Robert L.
1988   *Vertebrate Paleontology and Evolution*. New York: W. H. Freeman and Co.

Cartmill, Matt
1972   "Arboreal Adaptations and the Origin of the Order Primates." *In: The Functional and Evolutionary Biology of Primates*, R. H. Tuttle (ed.), Chicago: Aldine-Atherton, pp. 97–122.

——— 1992   "New Views on Primate Origins." *Evolutionary Anthropology*, **1**:105–111.

Cavalli-Sforza, L. L., A. Piazza, P. Menozzi, and J. Mountain
1988   "Reconstruction of Human Evolution: Bringing Together Genetic, Archaeological, and Linguistic Data." *Proceedings of the National Academy of Sciences*, **85**:6002–6006.

Charteris, J., J. C. Wali, and J. W. Nottrodt
1981   "Functional Reconstruction of Gait from Pliocene Hominid Footprints at Laetoli, Northern Tanzania." *Nature*, **290**:496–498.

Ciochon, Russell L. and Robert S. Corruccini (eds.)
1983   *New Interpretations of Ape and Human Ancestry*. New York: Plenum Press.

Clarke, R. J.
1985   "*Australopithecus* and Early *Homo* in Southern Africa." *In: Ancestors: The Hard Evidence*, E. Delson (ed.), New York: Alan R. Liss, pp. 171–177.

Clarke, Ronald J. and Phillip V. Tobias
1995   "Sterkfontein Member 2 Foot Bones of the Oldest South African Hominid." *Science*, **269**:521–524.

Cleveland, J. and C. T. Snowdon
1982   "The Complex Vocal Repertoire of the Adult Cotton-top Tamarin (*Saguinus oedipus oedipus*)." *Zeitschrift Tierpsychologie*, **58**:231–270.

Colwell, Rita R.
1996   "Global Climate and Infectious Disease: The Cholera Paradigm." *Science*, **274**(5295):2025–2031.

Conkey, M.
1987   "New Approaches in the Search for Meaning? A Review of the Research in 'Paleolithic Art.'" *Journal of Field Archaeology*, **14**:413–430.

Conroy, Glenn C.
1997   *Reconstructing Human Origins. A Modern Synthesis*. New York: Norton.

Conroy, G. C., M. Pickford, B. Senut, J. van Couvering, and P. Mein
1992   "*Otavipithecus namibiensis*, First Miocene Hominoid from Southern Africa." *Nature*, **356**:144–148.

Cook, J., C. B. Stringer, A. Currant, H. P. Schwarcz, and A. G. Wintle
1982   "A Review of the Chronology of the European Middle Pleistocene Record." *Yearbook of Physical Anthropology*, **25**:19–65.

Cooper, Alan, Andrew Rambaut, Vincent Macaulay, et al.
2001   "Human Origins and Ancient DNA." Letter to *Science*, **282**:1655–1656.

Corruccini, Robert S.
1994   "Reaganomics and the Fate of the Progressive Neandertals." *In: R. Corruccini and R. Ciochon (eds.), q.v., pp. 697–708.

Crews, D. E. and G. J. Harper
1998   "Ageing as Part of the Developmental Process." *In: The Cambridge Encyclopedia of Human Growth and Development*, S. J. Ulijaszek, et al. (eds.), Cambridge: Cambridge University Press, pp. 425–427.

Cummings, Michael
2000   *Human Heredity. Principles and Issues* (5th Ed.). St. Paul: Wadsworth/West Publishing Co.

Current, M., G. Trabuchet, D. Rees, et al.
2002   "Molecular Analysis of the Beta-Globin Gene Cluster in the Niokholo Mandenka Population Reveals a Recent Origin of the Beta S Senegal Mutation." *American Journal of Human Genetics*, **70**:207–223.

Curtin, R. and P. Dolhinow
1978   "Primate Social Behavior in a Changing World." *American Scientist*, **66**:468–475.

Dart, Raymond
1959   *Adventures with the Missing Link*. New York: Harper & Brothers.

Darwin, Charles
   1859   *On the Origin of Species*. A Facsimile of the First
          Edition, Cambridge, MA: Harvard University
          Press (1964).

   ───
   1871   *The Descent of Man and Selection in Relation to Sex*.
          Republished, 1981, Princeton: Princeton University
          Press.
Darwin, Francis (ed.)
   1950   *The Life and Letters of Charles Darwin*. New York:
          Henry Schuman.
Day, M. H. and E. H. Wickens
   1980   "Laetoli Pliocene Hominid Footprints and
          Bipedalism." *Nature*, **286**:385–387.
Dean, M., M. Carring, C. Winkler, et al.
   1996   "Genetic Restriction of HIV-1 Infection and
          Progression to AIDS by a Deletion Allele of the
          CKR5 Structural Gene." *Science*, **273**:1856–1862.
Defleur, A, T. White, P. Valensi, et al.
   1999   "Neanderthal Cannibalism at Moula-Guercy,
          Ardèche, France." *Science*, **286**:128–131.
de Lumley, Henry and M. de Lumley
   1973   "Pre-Neanderthal Human Remains from Arago Cave
          in Southeastern France." *Yearbook of Physical
          Anthropology*, **16**:162–168.
Dene, H. T., M. Goodman, and W. Prychodko
   1976   "Immunodiffusion Evidence on the Phylogeny of the
          Primates." *In: Molecular Anthropology*, M. Goodman,
          R. E. Tashian, and J. H. Tashian (eds.), New York:
          Plenum Press, pp. 171–195.
deReuter, J. R.
   1986   "The Influence of Group Size on Predator Scanning
          and Foraging Behavior of Wedge-Capped Capuchin
          Monkeys (*Cebus olivaceus*)." *Behaviour*, **98**:240–258.
Desmond, Adrian and James Moore
   1991   *Darwin*. New York: Warner Books.
Dettwyler, K. A.
   1991   "Can Paleopathology Provide Evidence for
          Compassion?" *American Journal of Physical
          Anthropology*, **84**:375–384.
de Waal, Frans
   1982   *Chimpanzee Politics*. London: Jonathan Cape.

   ───
   1989   *Peacemaking among Primates*. Cambridge: Harvard
          University Press.

   ───
   1999   "Cultural Primatology Comes of Age." *Nature*,
          399:635–636.
Doran, D. M. and A. McNeilage
   1998   "Gorilla Ecology and Behavior." *Evolutionary
          Anthropology*, **6**(4):120–131.
Dorit, R. L., H. Akashi, and W. Gilbert
   1995   "Absence of Polymorphism at the Zfy Locus on the
          Human Y Chromosome." *Science*, **268**:1183–1185.

Duarte, C., J. Mauricio, P. B. Pettitt, et al.
   1999   "The Early Upper Paleolithic Human Skeleton from
          the Abrigo do Lagar Velho (Portugal) and Modern
          Human Emergence in Iberia." *Proceedings of the
          National Academy of Sciences*, **96**:7604–7609.
Durham, William
   1981   Paper presented to the Annual Meeting of
          the American Anthropological Association,
          Washington, D.C., Dec. 1980. Reported in *Science*,
          211:40.

Eaton, S. Boyd, Marjorie Shostak, and Melvin Konner
   1988   *The Paleolithic Prescription*. New York: Harper
          and Row.
Ehrlich, Paul R. and Anne H. Ehrlich
   1990   *The Population Explosion*. New York: Simon &
          Schuster.
Erickson, Clark
   1998   "Applied Archaeology and Rural Development:
          Archaeology's Potential Contribution to the Future."
          In: M. Whiteford and S. Whiteford (eds.), *Crossing
          Currents: Continuity and Change in Latin America*.
          Upper Saddle, NJ: Prentice-Hall, pp. 34–45.
Etler, Dennis A. and Li-Tianyuan
   1994   "New Archaic Human Fossil Discoveries in China
          and Their Bearing on Hominid Species Definition
          During the Middle Pleistocene." *In*: R. Corruccini
          and R. Ciochon (eds.), q.v., pp. 639–675.

Falk, Dean
   1983   "The Taung Endocast: A Reply to Holloway."
          American Journal of Physical Anthropology, **60**:479–489.

   ───
   1989   "Comments." *Current Anthropology*, **30**:141.
Fedigan, Linda M.
   1983   "Dominance and Reproductive Success in Primates."
          Yearbook of Physical Anthropology, **26**:91–129.
Fleagle, John
   1988/ *Primate Adaptation and Evolution*. New York:
   1999   Academic Press. (2nd Ed.), 1999.

   ───
   1994   "Anthropoid Origins." *In*: R. S. Corruccini and
          R. L. Ciochon (eds.), q.v., pp. 17–35.
Flinn, Mark V.
   1999   "Family Environment, Stress, and Health During
          Childhood." *In*: Panter-Brick, C. and C. M.
          Worthman (eds.), *Hormones, Health, and Behavior:
          A Socio-ecological and Lifespan Perspective*. Cambridge:
          Cambridge University Press, pp. 105–138.
Foley, R. A.
   1991   "How Many Species of Hominid Should There Be?"
          Journal of Human Evolution, **30**: 413–427.
Fossey, Dian
   1983   *Gorillas in the Mist*. Boston: Houghton Mifflin.

Fouts, Roger S., D. H. Fouts, and T. T. van Cantfort
  1989 "The Infant Loulis Learns Signs from Cross-Fostered Chimpanzees." *In:* R. A. Gardner, et al., q.v., pp. 280–292.

Frayer, David
  1992 "Evolution at the European Edge: Neanderthal and Upper Paleolithic Relationships." *Préhistoire Européenne*, 2:9–69.

Frazer, K. L., X. Chen, D. A. Hinds, et al.
  2003 "Genomic DNA Insertions and Deletions Occur Frequently Between Humans and Nonhuman Primates." *Genome Research*, 3:341–346.

Frisancho, A. Roberto
  1978 "Nutritional Influences on Human Growth and Maturation." *Yearbook of Physical Anthropology*, 21:174–191.

————
  1993 *Human Adaptation and Accommodation.* Ann Arbor: University of Michigan Press.

Frisch, Rose E.
  1988 "Fatness and Fertility." *Scientific American*, 258:88–95.

Gabrunia, Leo, Abesalom Vekua, David Lordkipanidze, et al.
  2000 "Earliest Pleistocene Hominid Cranial Remains from Dmanisi, Republic of Georgia: Taxonomy, Geological Setting, and Age." *Science*, 288:1019–1025.

Gambier, Dominique
  1989 "Fossil Hominids from the Early Upper Palaeolithic (Aurignacian) of France." *In:* P. Mellars and C. Stringer (eds.), q.v., pp. 194–211.

Gamble, C.
  1991 "The Social Context for European Palaeolithic Art." *Proceedings of the Prehistoric Society*, 57:3–15.

Gardner, R. Allen, B. T. Gardner, and T. T. van Cantfort (eds.)
  1989 *Teaching Sign Language to Chimpanzees.* Albany: State University of New York Press.

Garner, K. J. and O. A. Ryder
  1996 "Mitochondrial DNA Diversity in Gorillas." *Molecular Phylogenetics and Evolution*, 6:39–48.

Gebo, Daniel L., Marian Dagosto, K. Christopher Beard, and Tao Qi
  2000 "The Smallest Primates." *Journal of Human Evolution*, 38:585–594.

Gee, Henry
  1996 "Box of Bones 'Clinches' Identity of Piltdown Palaeontology Hoaxer." *Nature*, 381:261–262.

Gibbons, Anne
  1998 "Ancient Tools Suggest *Homo erectus* was a Seafarer." Research News, *Science*, 279:1635–1637.

Gillespie, B. and R. G. Roberts
  2000 "On the Reliability of Age Estimate for Human Remains at Lake Mungo." *Journal of Human Evolution*, 38:727–732.

Gingerich, Phillip D.
  1985 "Species in the Fossil Record: Concepts, Trends, and Transitions." *Paleobiology*, 11:27–41.

Goodall, Jane
  1986 *The Chimpanzees of Gombe.* Cambridge: Harvard University Press.

Gossett, Thomas F.
  1963 *Race, the History of an Idea in America.* Dallas: Southern Methodist University Press.

Gould, Stephen Jay
  1981 *The Mismeasures of Man.* New York: W. W. Norton.

————
  1985 "Darwin at Sea—and the Virtues of Port." *In:* Stephen Jay Gould, *The Flamingo's Smile. Reflections in Natural History.* New York: W. W. Norton, pp. 347–359.

————
  1987 *Time's Arrow, Time's Cycle.* Cambridge: Harvard University Press.

Gould, S. J. and N. Eldredge
  1977 "Punctuated Equilibria: The Tempo and Mode of Evolution Reconsidered." *Paleobiology*, 3:115–151.

Gould, S. J. and R. Lewontin
  1979 "The Spandrels of San Marco and the Panglossian Paradigm: A Critique of the Adaptionist Programme." *Proceedings of the Royal Society of London*, 205:581–598.

Grant, P. R.
  1986 *Ecology and Evolution of Darwin's Finches.* Princeton: Princeton University Press.

Groves, Colin P.
  2001a *Primate Taxonomy.* Washington, DC: Smithsonian Institution Press.

————
  2001b "Why Taxonomic Stability Is a Bad Idea, or Why Are There So Few Species of Primates (or Are There?)." *Evolutionary Anthropology*, 10(6):191–197.

Gursky, Sharon
  2002 "The Behavioral Ecology of the Spectral Tarsier, *Tarsius spectrum*." *Evolutionary Anthropology*, 11(6):226–234.

Haas, J. D., E. A. Frongillo, Jr., C. D. Stepick, et al.
  1980 "Altitude, Ethnic and Sex Difference in Birth Weight and Length in Bolivia." *Human Biology*, 52:459–477.

Haile-Selassie, Yohannes
  2001 "Late Miocene Hominids from the Middle Awash, Ethiopia." *Nature*, 412:178–181.

Harlow, Harry F. and Margaret K. Harlow
  1961 "A Study of Animal Affection." *Natural History*, 70:48–55.

Harrold, Francis R.
  1989 "Mousterian, Chatelperronian and Early Aurignacian in Western Europe: Continuity or Discontinuity." *In: The Human Revolution*, P. Mellars and C. Stringer (eds.), Princeton, NJ: Princeton University Press, pp. 212–231.

Heyer, E.
  1999 "One Founder/One Gene Hypothesis in a New Expanding Population: Saguenay (Quebec, Canada)." *Human Biology*, 71:99–109.

Holloway, Ralph L.
1983   "Cerebral Brain Endocast Pattern of *Australopithecus afarensis* Hominid." *Nature*, **303**:420–422.

Hrdy, Sarah Blaffer
1977   *The Langurs of Abu*. Cambridge, MA.: Harvard University Press.

———
1999   *Mother Nature: A History of Mothers, Infants, and Natural Selection*. New York: Pantheon Books.

Hrdy, Sarah Blaffer, Charles Janson, and Carel van Schaik
1995   "Infanticide: Let's Not Throw Out the Baby with the Bath Water." *Evolutionary Anthropology*, **3**(5):151–154.

The International SNP Map Working Group
2001   "A Map of Human Genome Sequence Variation Containing 1.42 Million Single Nucleotide Polymorphisms." *Nature*, **409**:928–933.

Isbell, L. A.
1994   "Predation on Primates: Ecological Patterns and Evolutionary Consequences." *Evolutionary Anthropology*, **3**(2):61–71.

Isbell, L. A. and T. P. Young
1993   "Social and Ecological Influences on Activity Budgets of Vervet Monkeys and Their Implications for Group Living." *Behavioral Ecology and Sociobiology*, **32**:377–385.

Izawa, K. and A. Mizuno
1977   "Palm-Fruit Cracking Behaviour of Wild Black-Capped Capuchin (*Cebus apella*)." *Primates*, **18**:773–793.

Jablonski, Nina G. and George Chaplin
2000   "The Evolution of Skin Coloration." *Journal of Human Evolution*, **39**:57–106.

Jerison, H. J.
1973   *Evolution of the Brain and Behavior*. New York: Academic Press.

Jia, Lan-po
1975   *The Cave Home of Peking Man*. Peking: Foreign Language Press.

Jia, L. and Huang Weiwen
1990   *The Story of Peking Man*. New York: Oxford University Press.

Johanson, Donald and Maitland Edey
1981   *Lucy: The Beginnings of Humankind*. New York: Simon & Schuster.

Johanson, D. C. and T. D. White
1979   "A Systematic Assessment of Early African Hominids." *Science*, **202**:321–330.

Jolly, Alison
1985   *The Evolution of Primate Behavior* (2nd Ed.). New York: Macmillan.

Kano, T.
1992   *The Last Ape. Pygmy Chimpanzee Behavior and Ecology*. Stanford: Stanford University Press.

Kay, R., M. Cartmill, and M. Balow
1998   "The Hypoglossal Canal and the Origins of Human Vocal Behavior" (abstract). *American Journal of Physical Anthropology, Supplement*, **26**:137.

Kelley, R. I., D. Robinson, E. G. Puffenberger, et. al.
2002   "Amish Lethal Microcephaly: A New Metabolic Disorder with Severe Congenital Microcephaly and 2-Ketoglutaric Aciduria." *American Journal of Medical Genetics*, **112**(4):318–326.

Kennedy, K. A. R.
1991   "Is the Narmada Hominid an Indian *Homo erectus?*" *American Journal of Physical Anthropology*, **86**:475–496.

Keyser, André W.
2000   "New Finds in South Africa." *National Geographic*, (May):76–83.

King, Barbara J.
1994   *The Information Continuum*. Santa Fe: School of American Research.

Kirkwood, T. B. L.
1997   "The Origins of Human Ageing." *Philosophical Transactions of the Royal Society of London B.*, **352**:1765–1772.

———
2002   "Evolution of Ageing." *Mechanisms of Ageing and Development*, **123**:737–745.

Klein, R. G.
1989/   *The Human Career. Human Biological and*
1999   *Cultural Origins*. Chicago: University of Chicago Press. (2nd Ed.), 1999.

Konner, Melvin and Carol Worthman
1980   "Nursing Frequency, Gonadal Function, and Birth Spacing among !Kung Hunter-Gatherers." *Science*, **207**:788–791.

Kramer, Andrew
1993   "Human Taxonomic Diversity in the Pleistocene: Does *Homo erectus* Represent Multiple Hominid Species?" *American Journal of Physical Anthropology*, **91**:161–171.

Krings, Matthias, Cristen Capelli, Frank Tscentscher, et al.
2000   "A View of Neandertal Genetic Diversity." *Nature Genetics*, **26**:144–146.

Krings, Matthias, Anne Stone, Ralf W. Schmitz, et al.
1997   "Neandertal DNA Sequences and the origin of Modern Humans." *Cell*, **90**:19–30.

Kunzig, Robert
1997   "Atapuerca. The Face of an Ancestral Child." *Discover*, **18**:88–101.

Lack, David
1966   *Population Studies of Birds*. Oxford: Clarendon.

Lalani, A. S., J. Masters, W. Zeng, et al.
1999   "Use of Chemokine Receptors by Poxviruses." *Science*, **286**:1968–71.

Lamberts, S. W. J., A. W. van den Beld, and A. J. van der Lely
1997   "The Endocrinology of Aging." *Science*, **278**:419–424.

Lancaster, J. B. and C. S. Lancaster
1983   "Prenatal Investment: The Hominid Adaptation." *In:*
Ortner, D. J. (ed.), *How Humans Adapt: A Biocultural
Odyssey.* Washington DC: Smithsonian Institution
Press.

Larick, Roy and Russell L. Ciochon
1996   "The African Emergence and Early Asian Dispersals
of the Genus *Homo.*" *American Scientist*, **84**:538–551.

Leakey, M. D. and R. L. Hay
1979   "Pliocene Footprints in Laetolil Beds at Laetoli,
Northern Tanzania." *Nature*, **278**:317–323.

Leakey, Meave G., et al.
1995   "New Four-Million-Year-Old Hominid Species from
Kanapoi and Allia Bay, Kenya." *Nature*, **376**:565–571.

Lederberg, Joshua
1996   "Infection Emergent." *Journal of the American Medical
Association*, **275**(3):243–245.

Leroi-Gourhan, André
1986   "The Hands of Gargas." *October* **37**:18–34.

Lewin, Roger
1986   "Damage to Tropical Forests, or Why Were There So
Many Kinds of Animals?" *Science*, **234**:149–150.

Lewontin, R. C.
1972   "The Apportionment of Human Diversity." *In:
Evolutionary Biology* (Vol. 6), T. Dobzhansky, et al.
(eds.), New York: Plenum, pp. 381–398.

Linnaeus, C.
1758   *Systema Naturae.*

MacKinnon, J. and K. MacKinnon
1980   "The Behavior of Wild Spectral Tarsiers."
International Journal of Primatology, **1**:361–379.

Makalowski, W.
2000   "Genomic Scrap Yard: How Genomes Utilize All
That Junk." *Gene*, **259**(1–2):61–67.

Marshack, A.
1972   *The Roots of Civilization.* New York: McGraw-Hill
Publishing Co.

Mayer, Peter
1982   "Evolutionary Advantages of Menopause." *Human
Ecology*, **10**:477–494.

Mayr, Ernst
1970   *Population, Species, and Evolution.* Cambridge: Harvard
University Press.

McConkey, Edwin H. and Ajit Varki
2000   "A Primate Genome Project Deserves High Priority."
Letters. *Science*, **289**:1295.

McGrew, W. C.
1992   *Chimpanzee Material Culture. Implications for Human
Evolution.* Cambridge: Cambridge University Press.

———
1998   "Culture in Nonhuman Primates?" *Annual Review of
Anthropology*, **27**:301–328.

McHenry, Henry
1988   "New Estimates of Body Weight in Early Hominids
and Their Significance to Encephalization and
Megadontia in 'Robust' Australopithecines." *In:* F. E.
Grine (ed.), q.v., pp. 133–148.

McKusick, V. A. (with S. E. Antonarakis, et al.)
1998   *Mendelian Inheritance in Man.* (12th Ed.). Baltimore:
Johns Hopkins University Press.

McRae, M.
1997   "Road Kill in Cameroon." *Natural History*,
106(1):36–46.

Mitchell, R. J., S. Howlett, N. G. White, et al.
1999   "Deletion Polymorphism in the Human COL1AZ
Gene: Genetic Evidence of a Non-African Population
Whose Descendants Spread to All Continents."
Human Biology, **71**:901–914.

Mittermeir, R. A. and D. Cheney
1987   "Conservation of Primates in Their Habitats."
In: B. B. Smuts, et al., q.v., pp. 477–496.

Molnar, Stephen
1983   *Human Variation. Races, Types, and Ethnic Groups*
(2nd Ed.). Englewood Cliffs: Prentice-Hall.

Moore, Lorna G. and Judith G. Regensteiner
1983   "Adaptation to High Altitude." *Annual Reviews of
Anthropology*, **12**:285–304.

Moore, Lorna G., et al.
1994   "Genetic Adaptation to High Altitude." *In:* Stephen
C. Wood and Robert C. Roach (eds.), *Sports and
Exercise Medicine.* New York: Marcel Dekker, Inc.,
pp. 225–262.

Napier, John
1967   "The Antiquity of Human Walking." *Scientific
American*, **216**:56–66.

Napier, J. R. and P. H. Napier
1967   *A Handbook of Living Primates.* New York: Academic
Press.

———
1985   *The Natural History of the Primates.* London: British
Museum (Natural History).

Neese, R. M. and G. C. Williams
1994   *Why We Get Sick.* New York: Times Books.

Nishida, T., M. Hiraiwa-Hasegawa, T. Hasegawa, and
Y. Takahata
1985   "Group Extinction and Female Transfer in Wild
Chimpanzees in the Mahale National Park,
Tanzania." *Zeitschrift Tierpsychologie*, **67**:284–301.

Nishida, T., H. Takasaki, and Y. Takahata
1990   "Demography and Reproductive Profiles." *In: The
Chimpanzees of the Mahale Mountains*, T. Nishida (ed.),
Tokyo: University of Tokyo Press, pp. 63–97.

Nowak, Ronald M.
1999   *Walker's Primates of the World.* Baltimore: Johns
Hopkins University Press.

Oates, John F., Michael Abedi-Lartey, W. Scott McGraw, et al.
 2000 "Extinction of a West African Red Colobus Monkey." *Conservation Biology*, **14**(5):1526–1532.

O'Brien, S. J., et al.
 2002 "The Promise of Comparative Genomics in Mammals." *Science*, 286(5439):458–481.

Olliaro, Piero
 1996 "Malaria, the Submerged Disease." *Journal of the American Medical Association*, **275**(3):230–233.

O'Rourke, D. H., M. G. Hayes, and S. W. Carlyle
 2002 "Spatial and Temporal Stability of mtDNA Haplogroup Frequencies in Native North America." *Human Biology*, **72**:15–34.

Ovchinnikov, Igor V., Anders Gotherstrom, Galina P. Romanova, et al.
 2000 "Molecular Analysis of Neanderthal DNA from the Northern Caucasus." *Nature*, **404**:490–493.

Page, Susan E., et al.
 2002 "The Amount of Carbon Released from Peat and Forest Fires in Indonesia During 1997." *Nature*, **420**:61–65.

Palumbi, Stephen R.
 2001 *The Evolution Explosion: How Humans Cause Rapid Evolutionary Change*. New York: W. W. Norton

Parés, Josef M. and Alfredo Pérez-González
 1995 "Paleomagnetic Age for Hominid Fossils at Atapuerca Archaeological Site, Spain." *Science*, **269**:830–832.

Pennisi, Elizabeth
 2001 "The Human Genome." *Science*, **291**:1177–1180.

Peres, C. A.
 1990 "Effects of Hunting on Western Amazonian Primate Communities." *Biological Conservation* **54**:47–59.

Phillips, K. A.
 1998 "Tool Use in Wild Capuchin Monkeys." *American Journal of Primatology*, **46**(3):259–261.

Pickford, Martin and Brigitte Senut
 2001 "The Geological and Faunal Context of Late Miocene Hominid Remains from Lukeino, Kenya." *C. R. Acad. Sci. Paris, Sciences de la Terre et des Planètes*, **332**:145–152.

Pinner, Robert W., Steven M. Teutsch, Lone Simonson, et al.
 1996 "Trends in Infectious Diseases Mortality in the United States." *Journal of the American Medical Association*, **275**(3):189–193.

Potts, Richard
 1991 "Why the Oldowan? Plio-Pleistocene Toolmaking and the Transport of Resources." *Journal of Anthropological Research*, **47**:153–176.

———
 1993 "Archeological Interpretations of Early Hominid Behavior and Ecology." *In*: D. T. Rasmussen (ed.), q.v., pp. 49–74.

Proctor, Robert
 1988 "From Anthropologie to Rassenkunde." *In*: *Bones, Bodies, Behavior. History of Anthropology* (Vol. 5), W. Stocking, Jr. (ed.), Madison: University of Wisconsin Press, pp. 138–179.

Profet, M.
 1988 "The Evolution of Pregnancy Sickness as a Protection to the Embryo Against Pleistocene Teratogens." *Evolutionary Theory*, **8**:177–190.

Pulliam, H. R. and T. Caraco
 1984 "Living in Groups: Is There an Optimal Size?" *In*: *Behavioral Ecology: An Evolutionary Approach* (2nd Ed.), J. R. Krebs and N. B. Davies (eds.), Sunderland, Mass.: Sinauer Associates.

Rak, Y.
 1983 *The Australopithecine Face*. New York: Academic Press.

Rasmussen, D. T. (ed.)
 1993 *The Origin and Evolution of Humans and Humanness*. Boston: Jones and Bartlett.

Reddy, B. Mohan, Guangyun Sun, Javier Rodriguez Luis, et al.
 2001 "Genomic Diversity of Thirteen Short Tandem Repeat Loci in a Substructured Caste Population, Golla, of Southern Andhra Pradesh, India." *Human Biology*, **73**:175–190.

Relethford, John H. and Henry C. Harpending
 1994 "Craniometric Variation, Genetic Theory, and Modern Human Origins." *American Journal of Physical Anthropology*, **95**:249–270.

Richard, A. F. and S. R. Schulman
 1982 "Sociobiology: Primate Field Studies." *Annual Reviews of Anthropology*, **11**:231–255.

Ridley, Mark
 1993 *Evolution*. Boston: Blackwell Scientific Publications.

Rightmire, G. P.
 1981 "Patterns in the Evolution of *Homo erectus*." *Paleobiology*, **7**:241–246.

———
 1990 *The Evolution of* Homo erectus. New York: Cambridge University Press.

———
 1998 "Human Evolution in the Middle Pleistocene: The Role of *Homo heidelbergensis*." *Evolutionary Anthropology*, **6**:218–227.

Roberts, D. F.
 1973 *Climate and Human Variability*. An Addison-Wesley Module in Anthropology, No. 34. Reading, MA: Addison-Wesley.

Robinson, J. T.
 1972 *Early Hominid Posture and Locomotion*. Chicago: University of Chicago Press.

Rose, M. D.
 1991 "Species Recognition in Eocene Primates." *American Journal of Physical Anthropology*, Supplement 12, p. 153.

Rosenberg, K. and Wenda Trevathan
 2001 "The Evolution of Human Birth." *Scientific American*, **285**:72–77.

Rosenberg, M. J., R. Agarwala, G. Bouffard, et al.
2002   "Mutant Deoxynucleotide Carrier Is Associated with Congenital Microcephaly." *Nature Genetics,* **32**(1):175–179.

Roychoudhury, S., S. Roy, A. Basu, et al.
2001   "Genomic Structures and Population Histories of Linguistically Distinct Tribal Groups of India." *Human Genetics,* **109**:339–350.

Rudran, R.
1973   "Adult Male Replacement in One-Male Troops of Purple-Faced Langurs (*Presbytis senex senex*) and its Effect on Population Structure." *Folia Primatologica,* **19**:166–192.

Rumbaugh, D. M.
1977   *Language Learning by a Chimpanzee: The Lana Project.* New York: Academic Press.

Ruvolo, M., D. Pan, S. Zehr, T. Goldberg, et al.
1994   "Gene Trees and Hominoid Phylogeny." *Proceedings of the National Academy of Sciences,* **91**:8900–8904.

Samson, M., F. Libert, B. J. Doranz, et al.
1996   "Resistance to HIV-1 Infection in Caucasian Individuals Bearing Mutant Alleles of the CCR-5 Chemokine Receptor Gene." *Nature* **382**(22):722–725.

Savage-Rumbaugh, S.
1986   *Ape Language: From Conditioned Responses to Symbols.* New York: Columbia University Press.

Savage-Rumbaugh, S. and R. Lewin
1994   *Kanzi. The Ape at the Brink of the Human Mind.* New York: John Wiley and Sons.

Savage-Rumbaugh, S., K. McDonald, R. A. Sevic, W. D. Hopkins, and E. Rupert
1986   "Spontaneous Symbol Acquisition and Communicative Use by Pygmy Chimpanzees (*Pan paniscus*)." *Journal of Experimental Psychology: General,* **115**(3):211–235.

Schaller, George B.
1963   *The Mountain Gorilla.* Chicago: University of Chicago Press.

Scott, K.
1980   "Two Hunting Episodes of Middle Paleolithic Age at La Cotte Sainte-Brelade, Jersey (Channel Islands)." *World Archaeology,* **12**:137–152.

Scriver, Charles R.
2001   "Human Genetics: Lessons from Quebec Populations." *Annual Review of Genomics and Human Genetics,* **2**:69–101.

Semaw, S., P. Renne, W. K. Harris, et al.
1997   "2.5-million-year-old Stone Tools from Gona, Ethiopia." *Nature,* **385**:333–336.

Senut, Brigitte, Martin Pickford, Dominique Grommercy, et al.
2001   First Hominid from the Miocene (Lukeino Formation, Kenya). *C. R. Acad. Sci. Paris, Sciences de la Terre et des Planètes,* **332**:137–144.

Seyfarth, Robert M.
1987   "Vocal Communication and Its Relation to Language." *In:* Smuts, et al., *Primate Societies.* Chicago: University of Chicago Press, pp. 440–451.

Seyfarth, Robert M., Dorothy L. Cheney, and Peter Marler
1980a "Monkey Responses to Three Different Alarm Calls." *Science,* **210**:801–803.

———
1980b "Vervet Monkey Alarm Calls." *Animal Behavior,* **28**:1070–1094.

Shea, Brian T. and Robert C. Baily
1996   "Allometry and Adaptation of Body Proportions and Stature in African Pygmies." *American Journal of Physical Anthropology,* **100**:311–340.

Sibley, Charles and Jon E. Ahlquist
1984   "The Phylogeny of the Hominoid Primates as Indicated by DNA-DNA Hybridization." *Journal of Molecular Evolution,* **20**:2–15.

Simmons, J. G.
1989   *Changing the Face of the Earth.* Oxford: Basil Blackwell Ltd.

Simons, E. L.
1972   *Primate Evolution.* New York: Macmillan.

Smith, Fred H.
1984   "Fossil Hominids from the Upper Pleistocene of Central Europe and the Origin of Modern Europeans." *In:* F. H. Smith and F. Spencer (eds.), *The Origins of Modern Humans.* New York: Alan R. Liss, pp. 187–209.

Smith, Fred H., A. B. Falsetti, and S. M. Donnelly
1989   "Modern Human Origins." *Yearbook of Physical Anthropology,* **32**:35–68.

Smith, Fred H., Erik Trinkaus, Paul B. Pettitt, et al.
1999   "Direct Radiocarbon Dates for Vindija G_1 and Velika Pécina Late Pleistocene Hominid Remains." *Proceedings of the National Academy of Sciences,* **96**:12281–12286.

Smuts, B., et al. (eds.)
1987   *Primate Societies.* Chicago: University of Chicago Press.

Soffer, Olga
1985   *The Upper Paleolithic of the Central Russian Plain.* New York: Academic Press.

Stanford, C. B., J. Wallis, H. Matama, and J. Goodall
1994   "Patterns of Predation by Chimpanzees on Red Colobus Monkeys in Gombe National Park." *American Journal of Physical Anthropology,* **94**(2):213–228.

Steklis, Horst D.
1985   "Primate Communication, Comparative Neurology, and the Origin of Language Re-examined." *Journal of Human Evolution,* **14**:157–173.

Stelzner, J. and K. Strier
1981   "Hyena Predation on an Adult Male Baboon." *Mammalia,* **45**:106–107.

Stoneking, Mark
1993   "DNA and Recent Human Evolution." *Evolutionary Anthropology,* **2**:60–73.

Straus, Lawrence Guy
  1993 "Southwestern Europe at the Last Glacial Maximum."
        Current Anthropology, **32**:189–199.
Strier, Karen B.
  2002 *Primate Behavioral Ecology.* (2nd Ed.). Boston: Allyn
        and Bacon.
Stringer, C. B.
  1995 "The Evolution and Distribution of Later Pleistocene
        Human Populations." *In:* E. Vrba, et al. (eds.), q.v.,
        pp. 524–531.
Stringer, C. B. and P. Andrews
  1988 "Genetic and Fossil Evidence for the Origin of
        Modern Humans." *Science*, **239**:1263–1268.
Struhsaker, T. T.
  1967 "Auditory Communication among Vervet Monkeys
        (*Cercopithecus aethiops*)." *In: Social Communication
        Among Primates*, S. A. Altmann (ed.), Chicago:
        University of Chicago Press.

  1975 *The Red Colobus Monkey.* Chicago: University of
        Chicago Press.
Struhsaker, Thomas T. and Lysa Leland
  1979 "Socioecology of Five Sympatric Monkey Species
        in the Kibale Forest, Uganda." *Advances in the Study
        of Behavior*, Vol. 9, New York: Academic Press,
        pp. 159–229.

  1987 "Colobines: Infanticide by Adult Males." *In:* B. Smuts,
        et al. (eds.), q.v., pp. 83–97.
Sugiyama, Y. and J. Koman
  1979 "Tool-using and -making Behavior in Wild
        Chimpanzees at Bossou, Guinea." *Primates*,
        20:513–524.
Sumner, D. R., M. E. Morbeck, and J. Lobick
  1989 "Age-Related Bone Loss in Female Gombe
        Chimpanzees." *American Journal of Physical
        Anthropology*, **72**:259.
Susman, Randall L. (ed.)
  1984 *The Pygmy Chimpanzee. Evolutionary Biology and
        Behavior.* New York: Plenum.
Susman, Randall L., Jack T. Stern, and William L. Jungers
  1985 "Locomotor Adaptations in the Hadar Hominids." *In:
        Ancestors: The Hard Evidence*, E. Delson (ed.), New
        York: Alan R. Liss, pp. 184–192.
Sussman, Robert W.
  1991 "Primate Origins and the Evolution of Angiosperms."
        American Journal of Primatology, **23**:209–223.
Sussman, Robert W., James M. Cheverud, and Thad Q. Bartlett
  1995 Infant Killing as an Evolutionary Strategy: Reality or
        Myth?" *Evolutionary Anthropology*, **3**(5):149–151.
Swisher, C. C. III, G. H. Curtis, T. Jacob, et al.
  1994 "Age of the Earliest Known Hominids in Java,
        Indonesia." *Science*, **263**:1118–1121.
Swisher, C. C., W. J. Rink, S. C. Anton, et al.
  1996 "Latest *Homo erectus* of Java: Potential
        Contemporaneity with *Homo sapiens* in Southwest
        Java." *Science*, **274**:1870–1874.

Szalay, Frederick S. and Eric Delson
  1979 *Evolutionary History of the Primates.* New York:
        Academic Press.

Templeton, Alan R.
  1996 "Gene Lineages and Human Evolution." *Science*,
        272:1363–1364.
Tenaza, R. and R. Tilson
  1977 "Evolution of Long-Distance Alarm Calls in Kloss'
        Gibbon." *Nature*, **268**:233–235.
Thieme, Hartmut
  1997 "Lower Palaeolithic Hunting Spears from Germany."
        Nature, **385**:807–810.
Thorne, A., R. Grün, G. Mortimer, et al.
  1999 "Australia's Oldest Human Remains: Age of the Lake
        Mungo 3 Skeleton." *Journal of Human Evolution*,
        36:591–612.
Thorne, A. G. and M. H. Wolpoff
  1992 "The Multiregional Evolution of Humans." *Scientific
        American*, **266**:76–83.
Tiemel, Chen, Yang Quan, and Wu En
  1994 "Antiquity of *Homo sapiens* in China." *Nature*,
        368:55–56.
Tishkoft, S. A., E. Dietzsch, W. Speed, et al.
  1996 "Global Patterns of Linkage Disequilibrium at the
        CD4 Locus and Modern Human Origins." *Science*,
        271:1380–1387.
Tobias, Phillip
  1971 *The Brain in Hominid Evolution.* New York: Columbia
        University Press.

  1983 "Recent Advances in the Evolution of the Hominids
        with Especial Reference to Brain and Speech."
        Pontifical Academy of Sciences, *Scrita Varia*,
        50:85–140.
Trinkaus, Erik and Pat Shipman
  1992 *The Neandertals.* New York: Alfred A. Knopf.

Villa, Paola
  1983 *Terra Amata and the Middle Pleistocene Archaeological
        Record of Southern France.* University of California
        Publications in Anthropology, Vol. 13. Berkeley:
        University of California Press.
Visalberghi, E.
  1990 "Tool Use in Cebus." *Folia Primatologica*, **54**:146–154.
Von Koenigswald, G. H. R.
  1956 *Meeting Prehistoric Man.* New York: Harper &
        Brothers.

Walker, A.
  1976 "Remains Attributable to *Australopithecus* from East
        Rudolf." *In: Earliest Man and Environments in the Lake
        Rudolf Basin*, Y. Coppens, et al. (eds.), Chicago:
        University of Chicago Press, pp. 484–489.

1991   "The Origin of the Genus *Homo*." *In:* S. Osawa and T. Honjo (eds.), *Evolution of Life.* Tokyo: Springer-Verlag, pp. 379–389.

1993   "The Origin of the Genus *Homo*." *In:* D. T. Rasmussen (ed.), *The Origin and Evolution of Humans and Humanness.* Boston: Jones and Bartlett, pp. 29–47.

Walker, Alan and R. E. Leakey
1993   *The Nariokotome* Homo erectus *Skeleton.* Cambridge: Harvard University Press.

Walsh, P. D., K. A. Abernathy, M. Bermejo, et al.
2003   "Catastrophic Ape Decline in Western Equatorial Africa." *Nature,* **422:**611–614.

Ward, Peter
1994   *The End of Evolution.* New York: Bantam.

Waterston, R. H., K. Lindblad-Toh, E. Birney, et al. (Mouse Genome Sequencing Consortium)
2002   Initial Sequencing and Comparative Analysis of the Mouse Genome. *Nature,* **421:**520–562.

Watson, J. B. and F. H. C. Crick
1953a   "Genetical Implications of the Structure of the Deoxyribonucleic Acid." *Nature,* **171:**964–967.

1953b   "A Structure for Deoxyribonucleic Acid." *Nature,* **171:**737–738.

Weiner, J. S.
1955   *The Piltdown Forgery.* London: Oxford University Press.

Weiner, Steve, Qinqi Xu, Paul Goldberg, Jinyi Liu, and Ofer Bar-Yosef
1998   "Evidence for the Use of Fire at Zhoukoudian, China. *Science,* **281:**251–253.

Wheat, Joe Ben
1972   "The Olsen-Chubbuck Site; A Paleo-Indian Bison Kill." *American Antiquity,* **37:**1–180.

White, Tim D., Gen Suwa, and Berhane Asfaw
1994   "*Australopithecus ramidus,* a New Species of Early Hominid from Aramis, Ethiopia." *Nature,* **371:**306–312.

1995   Corrigendum (White, et al., 1994). *Nature,* **375:**88.

Whiten, A., J. Goodall, W. C. McGrew, et al.
1999   "Cultures in Chimpanzees." *Nature,* **399:**682–685.

Williams, G. C.
1957   "Pleiotopy, Natural Selection, and the Evolution of Senescence." *Evolution,* **11:**398–411.

Williams, George C. and Randolph M. Nesse
1991   "The Dawn of Darwinian Medicine." *The Quarterly Review of Biology,* **66:**1–22.

Wilmut, I., A. E. Schnieke, et al.
1997   "Viable Offspring Derived from Fetal and Adult Mammalian Cells." *Nature,* **385:**810–813.

Wilson, E. O.
1992   *The Diversity of Life,* Cambridge, MA: The Belknap Press of Harvard University Press.

2002   *The Future of Life.* New York: Alfred A. Knopf.

Wolpoff, Milford H.
1984   "Evolution in *Homo erectus:* The Question of Stasis." *Paleobiology,* **10:**389–406.

1989   "Multiregional Evolution: The Fossil Alternative to Eden." *In:* P. Mellars and C. Stringer, (eds.) q.v., pp. 62–108.

1999   *Paleoanthropology.* (2nd Ed.). New York: McGraw-Hill.

Wolpoff, M., et al.
1994   "Multiregional Evolutions: A World-Wide Source for Modern Human Populations." *In:* M. H. Nitecki and D. V. Nitecki (eds.), q.v., pp. 175–199.

Wood, Bernard
1991   *Koobi Fora Research Project IV: Hominid Cranial Remains from Koobi Fora.* Oxford: Clarendon Press.

1992   "Origin and Evolution of the Genus *Homo*." *Nature,* **355:**783–790.

Worthman, Carol
1999   "Evolutionary Perspectives on the Onset of Puberty." *In:* Trevethan, W. R., E. O. Smith, and J. J. McKenna (eds.), *Evolutionary Medicine.* New York: Oxford University Press.

Wrangham, R. W.
1990   "An Ecological Model of Female-Bonded Primate Groups." *Behaviour,* **75:**262–300.

Wrangham, Richard and Dale Peterson
1996   *Demonic Males: Apes and the Origins of Human Violence.* New York: Houghton Mifflin.

Wu, Rukang and Xingren Dong
1985   "*Homo erectus* in China." *In: Palaeoanthropology and Palaeolithic Archaeology in the People's Republic of China,* R. Wu and J. W. Olsen (eds.), New York: Academic Press, pp. 79–89.

Wu, Rukang and S. Lin
1983   "Peking Man." *Scientific American,* **248:**(6)86–94.

Wuehrich, Bernice
1998   "Geological Analysis Damps Ancient Chinese Fires." *Science,* **28:**165–166.

Yamei, Hon, Richard Potts, Yaun Baoyin, et al.
2000   "Mid-Pleistocene Acheulean-like Stone Technology of the Bose Basin, South China." *Science,* **287:**1622–1626.

Yellen, John E., et al.
1995   "A Middle Stone Age Worked Bone Industry from Katanda, Upper Semliki Valley, Zaire." *Science,* **268:**553–556.

Zimmet, P., K. G. M. M. Alberti, and Jonathan Shaw
2001   "Global and Societal Implications of the Diabetes Epidemic." *Nature,* **414:**782–787.

Zubrow, Ezra
1989   "The Demographic Modeling of Neanderthal Extinction." *In:* P. Mellars and C. Stringer (eds.), q.v., pp. 212–231.

Credits

This page constitutes an extension of the copyright page. We have made every effort to trace the ownership of all copyrighted material and to secure permission from copyright holders. In the event of any question arising as to the use of any material, we will be pleased to make the necessary corrections in future printings. Thanks are due to the following authors, publishers, and agents for permission to use the material indicated.

1, chapter opener (red blood cells), Andrew Syred/Getty Images; 2, Fig. 1–1, Courtesy, Peter Jones; 3, Fig. 1–2, © Bettmann/CORBIS; 5, Fig. 1–3a, Lynn Kilgore; 5, Fig. 1–3b, Lynn Kilgore; 5, Fig. 1–3c, Lynn Kilgore; 5, Fig. 1–3d, Robert Jurmain; 10, Fig. 1–4, © Kenneth Garrett/NGS Image Collection; 11, Fig. 1–5, Lynn Kilgore; Fig. 1–6, Courtesy, Judith Regensteiner; 12, Fig. 1–7, Courtesy, Bonnie Pedersen/Arlene Kruse; 13, Fig. 1–8, Lynn Kilgore; Fig. 1–9, Courtesy, Lorna Pierce/Judy Suchey; 18, Fig. 1, Robert Jurmain; Fig. 2, Robert Jurmain; 19, Fig. 3, Robert Jurmain; Fig. 4, Robert Jurmain; 20, Fig. 5, © Bettmann/CORBIS; Fig. 6, Courtesy, Margaret Maples; 21, Fig. 7, Robert Jurmain; Fig. 8, Robert Jurmain; 22, Fig. 9, Courtesy, L. G. Moore; Fig. 10, Courtesy, L. G. Moore; Fig. 11, Courtesy, Kathleen Galvin; 26, Fig. 2–1, Courtesy, Dept. of Library Services, American Museum of Natural History; 27, Fig. 2–2, Courtesy, Dept. of Library Services, American Museum of Natural History; Fig. 2–3, © Bettmann/CORBIS; 28, Fig. 2–4, © Bettmann/CORBIS; 29, Fig. 2–6, Courtesy, Dept. of Library Services, American Museum of Natural History; 30, Fig. 2–7, Courtesy, Dept. of Library Services, American Museum of Natural History; Fig. 2–8, Courtesy, Dept. of Library Services, American Museum of Natural History; 31, Fig. 2–9, Courtesy, Dept. of Library Services, American Museum of Natural History; 33, Fig. 2–12, (wolf) John Giustina/Getty Images, (all other dogs) Lynn Kilgore; 34, Fig. 2–13, Courtesy, Dept. of Library Services, American Museum of Natural History; 36, Fig. 2–14a, Michael Tweedie/Photo Researchers; Fig. 2–14b, Breck P. Kent/

Animals Animals; 54, Fig. 3–6, Biophoto Associates/Science Source/Photo Researchers; 65, Fig. 4–1, Courtesy, Dept. of Library Services, American Museum of Natural History; 74, Fig. 4–5a, Corbis; Fig. 4–5b, Lynn Kilgore; Fig. 4–5c, Corbis; Fig. 4–5d, Lynn Kilgore; Fig. 4–5e, Lynn Kilgore; Fig. 4–5f, Lynn Kilgore; 88, chapter opener (Chinese Golden monkeys), Tim Davis/Corbis; 93, Fig. 5–3, Lynn Kilgore; 96, Fig. 5–5a, Raymond Mendez/Animals Animals; Fig. 5–5b, Robert L. Lubeck/Animals Animals; Fig. 5–5c, Marc van Roosmalen/Conservation International; Fig. 5–4d, © Zoological Society of San Diego, photo by Ron Garrison; Fig. 5–5e, Andrew Young/Conservation International; Fig. 5–5f, © Jay Dickman/CORBIS; Fig. 5–5g, © Kevin Schafer/CORBIS; Fig. 5–5h, R. A. Mittermeier/Conservation International; 97, Fig. 5–4i, Courtesy, Bonnie Pedersen/Arlene Kruse; Fig. 5–4j, Courtesy, Jean De Rousseau; Fig. 5–4k, Lynn Kilgore; 5–4l, Robert Jurmain; Fig. 5–4m, Courtesy, San Francisco Zoo; Fig. 5–4n, David Haring, Duke University Primate Zoo; Fig. 5–4o, © Tom McHugh/Photo Researchers, Inc.; Fig. 5–4p, Joe MacDonald/Animals Animals; Fig. 5–5q, Courtesy, Fred Jacobs; Fig. 5–4r, Robert Jurmain; Fig. 5–4s, Courtesy, Bonnie Pedersen/Arlene Kruse; Fig. 5–4t, Courtesy, Arlene Kruse/Bonnie Pedersen; Fig. 5–4u, Lynn Kilgore; 98, Fig. 5–5a–d, Redrawn by Stephen Nash from original art in Fleagle, John G., *Primate Adaptation and Evolution*, 1988, Elsevier Science. Reprinted by permission of publisher and Stephen Nash.; 103, Fig. 5–11, Courtesy, Fred Jacobs; Fig. 5–12, Courtesy, Fred Jacobs; Fig. 5–13, Courtesy, San Francisco Zoo; Fig. 5–14, Courtesy, Bonnie Pedersen/Arlene Kruse; 104, Fig. 5–15, David Haring, Duke University Primate Zoo; 105, Fig. 5–17a, Andrew Young/Conservation International; Fig. 5–17b, R. A. Mittermeier/Conservation International; Fig. 5–17c, Marc van Roosmalen/Conservation International; Fig. 5–17d, © Jay Dickman/CORBIS; Fig. 5–17e, © Kevin Schafer/CORBIS; 106, Fig. 5–18, © Zoological Society of San Diego, photo by Ron Garrison; Fig. 5–19, Raymond Mendez/

Animals Animals; Fig. 5–21, Robert L. Lubeck/Animals Animals; 107, Fig. 5–23, Robert Jurmain; 108, Fig. 5–24a, Courtesy, Bonnie Pedersen/Arlene Kruse; Fig. 5–24b, Courtesy, Bonnie Pedersen/Arlene Kruse; Fig. 5–25, Robert Jurmain; 109, Fig. 5–27, Lynn Kilgore; 110, Fig. 5–28, Robert Jurmain, photo by Jill Matsumoto/Jim Anderson; 111, Fig. 5–30a, Lynn Kilgore; Fig. 5–30b, Lynn Kilgore; Fig. 5–31a, Lynn Kilgore; Fig. 5–32b, Lynn Kilgore; 112, Fig. 5–32a, Robert Jurmain, photo by Jill Matsumoto/Jim Anderson; Fig. 5–32b, Robert Jurmain, photo by Jill Matsumoto/Jim Anderson; 113, Fig. 5–33, Courtesy, Ellen Ingmanson; 117, Fig. 5–34, Courtesy, J. Oates; 120, Fig. 1, Courtesy, The Jane Goodall Institute, photographed by Penelope Breeze; Fig. 2, Courtesy, Bonnie Pedersen/Arlene Kruse; Fig. 3, Peter Weit/© Bettmann/CORBIS; Fig. 4, Robert Jurmain; 122, Fig. 5, Robert Jurmain; Fig. 6, Courtesy, Ann Rademacher; 123, Fig. 7, Lynn Kilgore; 124, Fig. 8, Courtesy, The Jane Goodall Institute; Fig. 9, Courtesy, Julie Bittnoff; 125, Fig. 10, From Harrison, C. et al., 1983. Cytogen. Cell Genet 35:21–27. S. Karger, A. G. Basel; 126, Fig. 11, Jim Moore/Anthro Photo; Fig. 12, Jim Moore/Anthro Photo; 130, Fig. 6–1, Joe MacDonald/Animals Animals; 132, Fig. 6–2, Lynn Kilgore; 134, Fig. 6–3, Lynn Kilgore; Fig. 6–4, Lynn Kilgore; 135, Fig. 6–5, Adapted with permission of the publishers from *The Chimpanzees of Gombe* by Jane Goodall, Cambridge, Mass.: Harvard University Press, © 1986 by the President and Fellows of Harvard College.; 136, Fig. 6–6, Lynn Kilgore; 137, Fig. 6–7a, Robert Jurmain; Fig. 6–7b, Courtesy, Meredith Small; Fig. 6–8c, Lynn Kilgore; Fig. 6–8d, Courtesy, Arlene Kruse/Bonnie Pedersen; 139, Fig. 6–8, Lynn Kilgore; 142, Fig. 6–9a, Courtesy, David Haring, Duke University Primate Center; Fig. 6–9b, Courtesy, Arlene Kruse/Bonnie Pedersen; Fig. 6–9c, Robert Jurmain; Fig. 6–9d, © Tom McHugh/Photo Researchers, Inc.; Fig. 6–9e, Robert Jurmain; Fig. 6–10, Harlow Primate Laboratory, University of Wisconsin; Fig. 6–11a, Courtesy, Jane Goodall Institute; Fig. 6–11b, Courtesy, Carol Lofton/Distinctive Images; 147, Fig. 6–12,

Index

Page numbers in *italics* indicate figures or illustrations. Page numbers in **bold** indicate definitions.

diabetes, Type II, 341
diet
    in humans, 340–342, *341*
    in primates, 94–95
differential net reproductive success, 37–38
discrete traits, 69
disease. *See* infectious disease
displays, 135, *135*
diurnal, **91**
divergent large toe, 184, *185*
dizygotic twins, 342
Dmanisi site, 219, *219*, 234–235, *234*, *240*
DNA (deoxyribonucleic acid), **46**, *49*
    fingerprint, 311
    fingerprinting, 335–336, *335*
    hybridization, 101
    mitochondrial. *See* mitochondrial DNA (mtDNA)
    noncoding portions of, 311
    nuclear, 46
    replication of, 48, *49*
    sequencing, 101, 268
    structure of, 47–48, *47*
    to determine evolution of modern humans, 277, 279
dolichocephalic, **303**
Dolly (cloned sheep), 61
domestication, of plants and animals, 360
dominance, in primates, 132–133
dominance hierarchies, **132**
dominance, principle of, **66**
dominant traits, **65**–68
double helix, 47, *49*
Down syndrome, 60
Drimolen site, *10*, *205*, 206, 208, 213
Duarte, Cidália, 286
Dubois, Eugene, 225–226, *225*

E

East Turkana, *H. erectus* finds, 231–232, *231*, *240*
ecological, **129**
ecological niches, **164**, 165
ecological species concept, *161*
ecology, behavioral, 129–130
economic anthropology, 7
ectothermic, 167
Egypt, 170, *170*
Elandsfontein site, 244
electron spin resonance (ESR) dating, *282*, 287
empirical, **14**
end scraper, *237*
endemic, **326**
endocast, **203**
endocrine glands, 343
endogamy, **315**
endothermic, **167**
environmental issues, 367
    greenhouse effect and global warming, 370–371
    overpopulation, 367–369, *368*
    solutions, 371–372

enzymes, **48**
Eocene epoch, 169
epochs, *164*, **166**
ER 406 (Koobi Fora), *209*
ER 729 (Koobi Fora), *209*
ER 732 (Koobi Fora), *209*
ER 1470 (East Turkana), *202*
ER 3733 (East Turkana), *220*, *231*, *232*
Erickson, Clark, 363
Essay on the Principle of Population, An (Malthus), 30, 33
essential amino acids, **340**
estrous swelling, in chimpanzees, *139*
estrus, **108**
ethnicity, 305
    See also race
ethnocentric, **15**
ethnographies, **7**
ethogram, 122
ethologies, **7**
eugenics, **304**
eukaryotic cell, *46*
Europe
    archaic *H. sapiens* finds in, 245, *246*, 248–249
    early *H. sapiens sapiens* in, 283–286
    H. erectus sites in, 234–235, *234*
EV 9001 (Yunxian site), *231*
EV 9002 (Yunxian site), *231*
evolution, **4**, **24**
    behavior and, 353
    biocultural, 6, 180, 312–314, 338
    branching, *160*
    as change in frequency of alleles in a population from
        one generation to the next, 76, 81–82, 84,
        309–310, 315
    complete replacement model, 277–279, *278*, 286
    definition of, **76**–77
    history of theory of, 24–25
        constraints on nineteenth-century evolutionary
            theory, 38–39
        path to natural selection, 26–34
        scientific revolution, 25–26
    mechanism of, *28*
    Modern Synthesis, 76, 176, 218
    modes of evolutionary change, 175
        gradualism v. punctuationalism, 175–176
    mosaic, **180**
    multiregional, 279–280
    opposition to theory of, 39–41
    organization levels, *85*
    partial replacement model, 279, 286
    significance of meiosis in, 59
    of vertebrates, 163–166, *165*
    See also population genetics
evolutionary psychology, 352–353
evolutionary systemics, **158**
exogamy, **315**
exons, 51, 53
extinctions, 364
eye contact, in primates, 134

radiometric dating, 190
rain forests, loss of, 365–366, 370
Ray, John, 26
recessive traits, **65**–68
recognition species concept, *161*
recombinant DNA technology, **60**–61
recombination, **59**, 81, *85*
reduction division, of cells, 57, *58*, 59
refugees, resettlement of, 7
regional continuity model for evolution of modern humans, 279–280, 283
regulatory genes, 52
relationships, among nonhuman primates, 138
relative dating, 188
replicate, **48**, 49
replication, 53, *56*, *58*
representational value of symbols, 148–149
reproductive patterns, 138–141
reproductive strategies, **140**–141
reproductive success, **35**, 133
reptiles
        brain of, *167*
        evolution of, 174
Retzius, Anders, 303
rhinarium, **102**
ribonucleic acid (RNA), **46**, 50–51
        See also messenger RNA (mRNA); transfer RNA (tRNA)
ribosomes, **46**, 50
rickets, 318
Rightmire, Phillip, 235
Russian royal family, 20
Rwanda, genocide in, 307

S
sagittal crest, 208, *209*
        in *H. erectus*, *224*
Sahelanthropus tchadensis, 192, *192*, *193*, 207, 210, 211, 212
        cranial capacity, *197*
Sahul area, 286–287
Salé site, *220*, 233
Salo, Dr. Wilmar, *335*
Sangrian site, *H. erectus* finds, 226
Savage-Rumbaugh, Sue, 145, 148–149
savanna baboons. *See* baboons
Schöningen site, 252
science, **14**
scientific method, **14**
        physical anthropology and, 14–15
scientific revolution, 25–26
scientific testing, of hypotheses, **14**–15
Scopes, John, 40
Scopes Monkey Trial, 40
Scott, K., 252
scrapers, *263*
second division, of cells, 57, *58*, 59
sectorial lower first premolar, **195**
sedentism, effects of, 360–361
segregation, principle of, 64–**66**

selective pressures, **35**, 36
semibrachiators, 99
semiquadrupedal posture, 111
senescence, **350**
senses, in primates, 91–92
sex chromosomes, **54**
sexual dimorphism, **108**, 110, 111, 162
        in *Australopithecus*, 198
        in *H. erectus*, 223
sexual dimorphism, **339**
sexual selection, **140**–141
Shanidar I skull, *255*, *262*
Shanidar site, *260–262*, *262*, *262*, 267
shared derived characteristics, **159**
Sherman (chimpanzee), 148–149
shovel-shaped incisors, 225, *225*
siamangs, 109–110
sickle-cell allele, 82, *83*, 84, 311, 312–313, *313*
sickle-cell anemia, *71*
side scraper, *237*
sifakas, 103, *103*
silverback, 112
Sima de los Huesos site. *See* Atapuerca site
Simons, Elwyn, 169
Sinanthropus, 218
single nucleotide polymorphisms, 311
sites, **187**
Sivapithecus, 173, *173*
SK 48 (Swartkrans), 207, *209*
skeletal abnormalities, 331–333
Skhūl 5, *278*, *279*, *281*, *283*
Skhūl Cave site, *278*, *280*, *281*, *282*, *282*, *283*, *299*
skin color
        as adaptation to solar radiation, 316–319
        classification by, 303
        folate and, 318
        geographical distribution of, *317*
slash-and-burn agriculture, **312**
smallpox, 325–326
smell, sense of, 91
Smith, Fred, 259
social behavior, in primates, 132–138
social structure, **128**
        in primates, 128
        of species, 130–131
sociobiology, **130**
socioecology, **130**
        of primates, 130
solar radiation, interaction with skin color and vitamin D, 316–319, 343
Solecki, Ralph, 263
Solutrean industry, *289*, *289*, *290*
somatic cells, **46**, 53
spear-thrower, 264, 290, *290*
specialized, **90**
specialized characteristics, 175
speciation, 4, *160*, **160**, 280

World Political Map

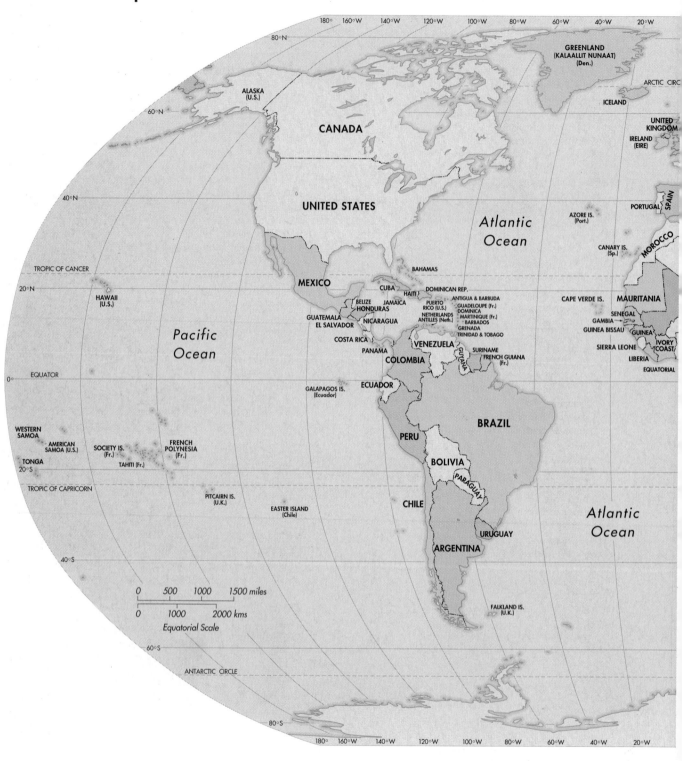

GREENLAND (KALAALLIT NUNAAT) (Den.)

ARCTIC CIRC

80°N

60°N

ALASKA (U.S.)

CANADA

ICELAND

UNITED KINGDOM

IRELAND (EIRE)

40°N

UNITED STATES

Atlantic Ocean

AZORE IS. (Port.)

PORTUGAL

SPAIN

TROPIC OF CANCER

CANARY IS. (Sp.)

MOROCCO

20°N

HAWAII (U.S.)

MEXICO

BAHAMAS

CUBA

HAITI

DOMINICAN REP.

CAPE VERDE IS.

MAURITANIA

BELIZE
HONDURAS

JAMAICA

PUERTO RICO (U.S.)

ANTIGUA & BARBUDA

GUADELOUPE (Fr.)
DOMINICA
MARTINIQUE (Fr.)

SENEGAL

GAMBIA

Pacific Ocean

GUATEMALA
EL SALVADOR

NICARAGUA

NETHERLANDS ANTILLES (Neth.)

BARBADOS

GUINEA BISSAU

GRENADA
TRINIDAD & TOBAGO

GUINEA

COSTA RICA

SIERRA LEONE

IVORY COAST

PANAMA

VENEZUELA

SURINAME

GUYANA

FRENCH GUIANA (Fr.)

LIBERIA

COLOMBIA

EQUATORIAL

GALAPAGOS IS. (Ecuador)

ECUADOR

EQUATOR 0°

BRAZIL

WESTERN SAMOA

PERU

AMERICAN SAMOA (U.S.)

SOCIETY IS. (Fr.)

FRENCH POLYNESIA (Fr.)

TONGA

TAHITI (Fr.)

BOLIVIA

20°S

PARAGUAY

TROPIC OF CAPRICORN

PITCAIRN IS. (U.K.)

EASTER ISLAND (Chile)

CHILE

Atlantic Ocean

URUGUAY

40°S

ARGENTINA

FALKLAND IS. (U.K.)

0	500	1000	1500 miles
0	1000		2000 kms

Equatorial Scale

60°S

ANTARCTIC CIRCLE

80°S

180° 160°W 140°W 120°W 100°W 80°W 60°W 40°W 20°W